Forgery

in

Christianity

A Documented Record of the
Foundations of the Christian Religion

Joseph Wheless

ISBN 1-56459-225-1

FOREWORD

THE DISEASE AND THE CURE

> "ALL TRUTH is safe, and nothing else is
> safe; and he who keeps back the truth, or
> withholds it from men, from motives of ex-
> pediency, is either a coward or a criminal, or
> both."
> MAX MÜLLER, *The Science of Religion*, p. 11.

> "The time has come for honest men to de-
> nounce false teachers and attack false gods."
> *Luther Burbank*

MAN IS A RELIGIOUS ANIMAL—is incurably religious," are com-
monplaces of clerical rhetoric. The priestly "Doctors of
Divinity" who unctuously utter these pious—and apocryphal
—platitudes—fathered by the wish,—urge the incurable state of
mind—the religious neurosis—of their patients in proof of the
divinely ordered nature of the malady, as patent of the necessity and
importance of their "sacred science" of soul-cure, and the divine
warrant for their continuance in perpetuity in their practice upon
otherwise damned humanity.

It is the ghostly Doctors themselves, however, who by their
quackeries have created the fiction of the disease, and who purposely
keep the patient opiated and on the crutches of Faith, in order to
"make their calling and election sure," and to perpetuate their thrall-
ing dominion over the mind and money of man. The first recorded
priestly ban—by threat and fear of death—was on Nature's own
Golden Specific for superstition and priestcraft,—the fruit of the
Tree of Knowledge: "Thou shalt not eat of it: for in the day that
thou eatest thereof thou shalt surely die." (Gen. ii, 17.) A warden
with a flaming sword was posted to guard the Tree: sword, and rack,
and stake, civil and political outlawry, social and business ostracism
and loss of living, odious *Odium Theologicum* and foul calumny, have

ever since been—so far as possible yet are the consecrated weapons of priestcraft to keep mankind ignorant and obedient to the priests. "No beast in nature is so implacable as an offended saint," is axiomatic of those who prate of loving their enemies. As *Jurgen* picturesquely says: "The largest lake in Hell is formed by the blood which the followers of the 'Prince of Peace' have shed in advancing his cause,"—and their selfish own,—as we shall abundantly see in the following pages.

FAITH IN A FATAL DECLINE

Howbeit, their pulpits and their press are lugubriously vocal with Jeremiads bewailing the ever-swelling tide of Unbelief in the land,— throughout Christendom. The Church statistics, notoriously padded after the Biblical model of the Censuses in the Wilderness, can claim at most some forty-odd millions of adherents—many of them by lip-service and non-paying (therefore negligible), and others many non-distinguished for piety or common honesty—out of the hundred and twenty-odd millions of our American population. The Reverend Rector of Trinity Church in New York City—(one of the wealthiest deadhand taxfree land monopolists in America)—thus bewails: "In America we are dealing with a country, the majority of whose inhabitants are pagans. . . . Only forty percent of the population acknowledges affiliation with any Church." (*N. Y. Times*, Mch. 15, 1930.) The ex-Secretary of the Home Missions Council of one of the great Churches bemoans: "There has been a tremendous revolution in the history of the Church. . . . The country church is waning and dying. . . . The revolution under our eyes *is found in the mode of thinking* of the whole country." (*N. Y. Times*, Jan. 8, 1930). An effective cause is found in the recent survey report of the Federal Council of Churches, to be in "the acceptance of a scientific view of life . . . general questioning of formerly revered authority . . . with absolute religious and ethical authority dethroned. . . . Women have made no comparable advance in participation in church affairs. . . . It can hardly be said that the church is an influential factor in the lives of the working classes." (*N. Y. Herald-Tribune*, Jan. 31, 1930.) A curious confession of likely cause and effect,—in the mental calibre of the credent—is stated by the Reverend publicity counsel of a national Church: "All sermons should be keyed to the mentality of a fifteen-year-old youth. . . . Half the people of the United States have the mentality of a fifteen-year-old youth. Most church-goers enjoyed the 'children's sermon' more than the one on religious philosophy. . . . The average man can carry only one idea at a time." (*Herald-Tribune*, Jan. 28, 1930.)—Verily, "Of such is the Kingdom of Heaven."

All Fools' Day seems to be a sort of New Year's for ecclesiastical statistics and general stock-taking of the faithful: annually at that time the very religious *Christian Herald* publishes its collect of figures on Church membership; the *Catholic Directory* emits its own; and the generality of Divines gives voice to holy Lamentations and pious warnings to the Church and to the ungodly. From this year's extensive crop a little sheaf is added, the matter being important to our purposes, and curiously instructive as depicting the accelerated downward tobogganing of the Faith. The Report of the *Christian Herald* discloses: "The total of communicants last year [1929] was 50,006,566," of which number it assigns a total of 18,051,680 to the *fourteen sects* of Catholic dis-Unity (*Herald-Tribune*, Apl. 26, 1930); though the figures of the *Catholic Directory* are 20,178,202. (*Ib.* Apl. 16, 1930). Under the alarming caption—"Warns Protestant Church it is Lagging," the Report of the Director of the Church Survey bemoans: "The Protestant Church in America is not keeping pace with the population. . . . American Protestantism increased from 7 in each 100 of the population in 1800 to 24 in each 100 of the population of 1900. During the past thirty years Protestantism has not increased its ratio of the population as much as one member more per hundred."—This is a very notable disclosure: that for a whole century the very vocal and intolerant Protestant population of this country has varied between 7% and 24% of the total population, and is today less than 25%:—yet this petty minority dingdongs that this is a "Christian country," and imposes its ludicrous medieval "Blue Laws" and tyrannous proscriptions—as will be noted—upon the great anti-clerical majority of the people. And further striking figures follow from the same source: "A study made in 1912—[*i.e.* before Woman Suffrage],—exclusively in cities, found two-thirds of the Protestant city membership consisted of

women. . . . There has been a steady proportionate decrease of interest in religion among women of the United States. . . . It was
also found [in this present Survey] that only 18 percent of the
country population is in Church membership, although it is customary to think of country people as highly religious.—[They, too, are
becoming more educated.] In New York City, the Church population
is reported equally divided among Protestants, Roman Catholics and
Jews. Only *about eight percent* of the population are members of the
Protestant churches,"—thus only some 24% of the people of New
York City among all three much-divided sects. (*N. Y. Times*, May
5, 1930.) In a recent abusive set of letters by three True Believers of
the same family name (one a Rev.), addressed to the Editor of a
Metropolitan paper for writing sanely about the Tabooed Subject
of Birth Control, this was denounced as an "insult to over 2,000,000"
Faithful in this City. (*Herald-Tribune*, Apl. 12, 1930.) But the
Faithful boast of their 444 churches in Greater New York: if each
had the exaggerated membership of 1,000,—let the reader do his own
figuring and note the result. And foreign immigration of the Faithful
has been sadly curtailed of late by law.

The true significance to the Church of the great slump in its membership—and hence revenues, is crudely "given away" by the Very
Rev. Episcopal Bishop of Long Island, lamenting like conditions in
his Diocese: "The growth of population during the last decade on
Long Island has been a challenge to the Church. . . . The Episcopal
Bishop of the diocese advocated [in a public address] a *drive* to
bring into the church the *wealthy residents* of Long Island."
(*Herald-Tribune*, May 6, 1930.) The Most Rev. Episcopal superior
of the last-lamenting has made a famous discovery, and with oracular
gravity which evokes a smile he assigns its cause: "There are no
great poets, painters, writers, nor musicians—[only great Manni-
kins of Bishops]—today, and the cause of this artistic deficiency
can be found in the moderns' total disregard for religion." (Episc.
Bishop of Manhattan: *Herald-Tribune*, Apl. 21, 1930.) And the
Highly Rev. Bishop of the National Capital thus portentously, and
truly, glooms: "There is an organized movement, world-wide in scope,
to unsettle Christian ideals and Christian institutions, both in Russia and elsewhere" (*Ib.* May 13, 1930) ;—which, judging by the age-

old gigantic failure of both—as herein we shall see,—is not so much
to be wondered.

So far as Russia is concerned—(and the fact and the reason for
it apply as well to every other "Christian" country),—the reason
is truly stated by the pious Editor of *Atlantis* in a Jeremiad of confession before the Institute of Citizenship just held in Atlanta: "For
a thousand years, *ever since* Russia became a Christian country, and
more especially in the last 200 years, when the Czar became the official head of the Church, the State religion in Russia was one of the
*means whereby the Russian people were oppressed, exploited and
kept in ignorance. . . .* The Russian people had a score to settle
with the Church after the revolution, and they took full advantage
of it" (*N. Y. Times*, Apl. 8, 1930), a like chance for which all Christendom is looking. The very religious Editor continues to confess:
"It is useless to deny that the Church, in most instances, has lost its
hold upon vast majorities of the people." (*Ibid.*) At the Christian
Herald Institute of Religion held this year at Buck Hill Falls, Pa.,
a perfect symposium of Jeremiads bewailed Faith on the Toboggan:
"Unless emphasis on elaborate creeds does not cease, we will deliver
ourselves into the hands of the Humanists for *the defeat which we
deserve.*" . . . "The Church is simply going to pieces in the small
towns of the Middle West. . . . The paganization of rural America
is going on so fast that if we wait for even the union of closely allied
denominations to be accomplished, it will mean ruination." . . .
"The greatest difficulty in effecting mergers of churches lies in *personalities and prejudices.*" (*Herald-Tribune*, May 15, 1930.) Thus today,
after nearly two thousand years of the "sweetness and light" of our
Divine Christian religion, "personalities and prejudices" among those
taught to love even their enemies persist and keep the Fold of Christ
divided into mutually-hating Flocks; precisely so that the olden
Pagan sneer at the early Christians is perfectly befitting their successors today: "There is no wild beast so ferocious as Christians who
differ concerning their faith." (Lecky, *Rationalism in Europe*, ii, 31.)

To conclude this review of pregnant figures and confessions, two
luminous revelations are in one day made of cause and effect. Says
the eminent Rev. President of the National Bible Institute: ". . . because the Bible has ceased to have authority either in the pulpit

or in the pew. Decline in church attendance and decrease in church membership are almost invariably traceable to unbelief in the divine inspiration and authority of the Bible,"—due to increasing knowledge of its true character, as herein revealed. (*Herald-Tribune*, May 26, 1930.) And the ghastly irony and joke of the whole huge bankruptcy of Faith is thus exposed by the egregious Pastor of a Brooklyn Baptist Flock, who images the Missionary "selling" the Faith to the benighted Heathen: " 'I have a religion here that will do you poor heathen a lot of good. Of course *it hasn't succeeded very well at home*, but we are sure it will do *you* a lot of good.' " (*Ibid.*) It's just like God told the Jews: You shan't sell the dead carcasses found by the way to the Chosen; "but thou shalt give it unto the stranger that is in thy gates, that he may eat it; or thou mayst sell it unto an alien"! (Deut. xiv, 21.) So the dead cats of Faith are flung out of the sanctuary as unfit for the Knowing, but are peddled to the ignorant heathen for whatever the refuse may bring of clerical revenue.

Like conditions exist in all priest-ridden lands. The Rt. Rev. Archbishop of Canterbury in his call for the decennial Lambeth Conference for 1930, at which over sixty of the Episcopal bishops of this country are to attend, sounds a fateful monition: "The *new knowledge of the Bible and still more of the universe in which we live* still confuses and bewilders the beliefs of many of our clergy and people. There are tendencies in the life of our Church which suggest the prevalence of forms of belief . . . which almost exclude belief in God the Father and God the Holy Spirit." (*Herald-Tribune*, Mch. 12, 1930.) Wails the Rev. Pyke to the annual Assembly of the National Council of Evangelical Churches of England: "A large part of England has lapsed into semi-heathenism; . . . our half-filled churches." (*Herald-Tribune*, Apl. 20, 1930.) Such creed-searchings and churchly lamentations over their moribund condition may be multiplied into volumes.

Some potent cure thus seems to be at work. This curative specific is simply increasing popular knowledge: "Know the truth and the truth shall make you free," is the Golden Recipe for the religious disorder. What Cicero said of the Pythian Oracles may as truly be applied to every form of priestcraft: "When men began to be less credulous, their power vanished."

FOREWORD

Day by day, as knowledge increaseth and spreads amongst the people in the pews as well as among the parsons, does it become more difficult and embarrassing for the pulpiteers to "put over" their tales of myth and magic to the hearers of the Word. Even the clergy are becoming awakened to the stinging truth aimed at priests and the priest-taught by Prof. Shotwell: "Where we can understand, it is a moral crime to cherish the un-understood," and are beginning to feel the humiliation of their false position. A noted clerical educator, Dr. Reinold Niebuhr, professor of Christian Ethics in that hotbed of every heresy, the Union Theological Seminary, in his textbook suggestively entitled *Leaves from the Notebook of a Tamed Cynic*, makes this confession of recognized Dishonesty in the mass of clerical teaching and preaching: "As a teacher your only interest is to discover the truth. As a *preacher you must conserve other interests besides the truth.* It is your business to deal circumspectly with the whole religious inheritance lest the virtues [?] which are involved in the older traditions perish through your iconoclasm. *That is a formidable task and a harrassing one; for* one can never be quite sure *where pedagogical caution* ends AND DISHONESTY BEGINS"! (Quoted by Alva Johnston in *N. Y. Herald-Tribune*, Mch. 8, 1930.)

The great Church Father, Bishop St. Augustine (of whom more hereafter), was wise to the psychology of—at least—Pagan religion —the mode of its incipience and the manner of its age-long persistence. The priests and the priest-taught, he tells, instilled the virus of superstition into their victims when "small and weak," when they knew not to resist or healthily to react against the contaminating inoculation; "then, afterwards, it was necessary that succeeding generations should *preserve the traditions of their ancestors, drinking in this superstition with their mother's milk.*" (Augustine, *City of God*, xxii, 6.) Thinks one that this cunning *modus operandi* is confined only to Pagan priestcrafts and superstitions?

If, instead of the saintly Doctors of Hebrao-Christian Divinity, injecting their saving "opiate of the people" into the cradled babes of Christ, it were the abhorred Doctors of Mohammedan or Mormon Divinity who got to the cradles first,—those infant souls would all but surely be lost to the Christ, and in their God's tender mercy, as assured by the sainted Augustine, would spend eternity crawling on

xiii

the candent floors of Hell, playing with the "worm that never dies":
hardly from the cradle to the grave could all the Christian purges
for Sin and pills for Sal[i]vation of Soul, later administered, serve for
effective catharsis of the venom of those Christianly-hated "superstitions, drunk in with their mother's milk."

This truth is strikingly stated in an eloquent period by Ingersoll,
and stunningly confirmed and confessed by the syndicated Prophet
of Protestantism below to be quoted. The former opens his classic
Why I Am an Agnostic, with these trenchant words:

"For the most part we inherit our opinions. We are the heirs of habits
and mental customs. Our beliefs, like the fashions of our garments, depend
on where we were born. We are moulded and fashioned by our surroundings. Environment is a sculptor—a painter.

"If we had been born in Constantinople, the most of us would have
said: 'There is no God but Allah, and Mohammed is his prophet.' If our
parents had lived on the banks of the Ganges, we would have been worshippers of Siva, longing for the heaven of Nirvana.

"As a rule, children love their parents, believe what they teach, and
take great pride in saying that the religion of mother is good enough
for them. . . .

"The Scotch are Calvinists because their fathers were. The Irish are
Catholics because their fathers were. The English are Episcopalians because their fathers were, and the Americans are divided into a hundred
sects because their fathers were. . . . Children are sometimes superior
to their parents, modify their ideas, change their customs, and arrive at
different conclusions." (*Works*, iv, .5–6; cf. *Is It God's Word?* 2nd. ed.
p. v.)

The truth thus uttered by the great Agnostic finds its confirmation curiously wrung from the lips of the Bellwether of would-be
"reconciliationists" of primitive Superstition and modern Science.
In a metropolitan newspaper carrying his syndicated "Daily Counsel" to the love-lorn and the misty-minded, a Virginia Believer puts
to him challengingly the question direct: "Do you mean to imply
that belief is largely a matter of environment, and if so, would *you*
not have been as firm a follower of Mahomet as you are of Christ if
you had been born of Mahometan parentage and brought up in that
faith?" For once there was no chance for Conmanian suppleness of
evasion, so the blunt and confusing truth is forced: Yes! "It is fairly

certain that had I been *cradled* in Mohametans [*sic*] I should now have been turning toward Mecca at the appointed hours"! (*N. Y. Herald-Tribune*, Oct. 29, 1929.) Thus the champion special pleader for the fast fading faith of Christ confesses away the divinely self-evident "truth" of his Christian faith, admits that it is the result not of independent thought and convincing proofs to his mind, but the inheritance of the cradle and the nursery,—that that towering intellect would today be bearing witness to the "revealed truth" of a false God and religion, if he had chanced to be "born that way"! Allah would to him—and to millions—be true and living God and Jehovah a crude barbarian myth, but for the accident of birth and teaching,—a reversal of the whole scheme of salvation! Thus the Cradle determines the Creed; it is the virus of the superstition-germ first injected which infects the credulity-center of the brain and colors too-oft through life the whole concept of "religious truth" in the mind of the patient.

The psychology of the priestly maxim—"*Disce primum quod credendum est*—Learn first what is to be believed," and the persistent virulence of the virus thus injected, is aptly signified by the Rev. Wenner, 83-year old Bellwether of Lutheranism in America, and for 61 years pastor of one of its oldest sheep-folds in New York City: "I do not think that time has produced many changes in the attitude of Lutheran worshippers,—because of the stable nature of the religious education we give the youth of our sect. From the *age of six onward* we instruct them in the tenets of our faith, and *they usually abide*." (*N. Y. Herald-Tribune*, Oct. 10, 1929.)

The predilect precept of the Doctors of every brand of Divinity forever is: "Catch 'em in the cradle, and get 'em inoculated before they know." In the bib and rattle period, the childish brain is a soft, clean surface, "soft as wax to be moulded into vice," as His Holiness says: helpless it receives and retains whatever is first impressed or imposed upon it: true religion or false, Christ or Crishna or Santa Claus, Holy Ghost or the ghosts of Afric superstition. "Give us a child until it is seven, and we've got it cinched for life," is the ghoulish axiom of all the Faiths: "Suffer little children to come unto me, for of such is the Kingdom of Heaven,"—as of the heathen Nirvana. How godly a work is it to sear the thoughtless child mind with the

brand of Faith; how infamous and damnable to offer to the "immature" and inept youth in college freedom from the stigma of credulity!
How crude and cruel for the Chinese to bind and cripple for life the
feet of their girl children; how fiendish the custom of sundry savage
tribes, ignorant of the "Light of the World," to clamp the infant
heads between boards so as to produce the hideous deformity of skull
so esthetically popular among them; but how pleasing to gods and
priests to fetter the child mind in the bonds of Faith, and so to dwarf
and deaden the mind's most precious faculty— Reason! "To suc-
ceed," eloquently said Ingersoll, "the theologians invade the cradle,
the nursery. In the brain of innocence they plant the seeds of superstition. They pollute the minds and imaginations of children. They
frighten the happy with threats of pain—they soothe the wretched
with gilded lies. . . . All of these comforting and reasonable things
are taught by the ministers in their pulpits—by teachers in Sunday
schools and by parents at home. The children are victims. They are
assaulted in the cradle—in their mother's arms. Then, the school-
master carries on the war against their natural sense, and all the
books they read are filled with the same impossible truths. The poor
children are helpless. The atmosphere they breathe is filled with lies
—lies that mingled with their blood." (*Works*, iv, 10). This unholy
cradle-robbing goes on with vehement zest. The Churches, the Federal Council of Churches, the Vicar of God and his adjutants, all
ply amain the arts of enslaving the babe in the cradle, the child in
the school. In the Encyclical of December 31, 1929, the right of the
Church to the child is proclaimed as above that of parents and State;
the secular public schools are damned, and the *prole* of the Faithful
are forbidden to attend and mingle with the "irreligious" State pupils:
"the frequenting of non-Catholic schools, namely, those which are
open to Catholic and non-Catholic alike, is forbidden to Catholic
children," as such a school is not "a fit place for Catholic students,"
who must be baited with "the supernatural." (*Current History*, Mch.
1930, p. 1091, *passim*.) Yet the banned and cursed Public Schools of
New York City, forbidden to the Faithful child, the ecclesiastical
City government fills with Faithful teachers for the purpose of "bootlegging" the forbidden supernaturalism into them; a work so widespread and active, that the Cardinal Archbishop of the City, address-

ing over 2000 of the Catholic Teachers Association, "praises their work of teaching faith in City Institutions." (*N. Y. Times*, Nov. 25, 1928.) And every rationalist effort to counteract such illegal propaganda and to free the schools from the pernicious influences of superstition, is denounced and opposed by the Bible bootleggers of every brand of Faith; and in the brave instance of Russia, a medieval orgy of prayer-assault on High Heaven is made, to counsel God what he ought to do to the Russians for their "godless" efforts to save the children of that Church-cursed land from the superstitions of priestcraft.

In an ironical letter to the English press, in which he "enters the lists against the British critics of Moscow's anti-clerical policy," George Bernard Shaw, writing under a transparent Russian pseudonym, says: "In Russia we take religious questions very seriously. We protect our children very carefully against proselytizers of our fantastic sects until they are old enough to make up their own minds. To us, it is inconceivable that a government would tolerate the inculcation upon helpless children of beliefs that will not stand the most strenuous scientific examination or in which the teachers themselves do not honestly believe. . . . We cannot understand why the so-called Articles of Religion, which have been described by one of the most learned and intellectually gifted of your churchmen as capable of being professed only by 'fools, bigots or liars,' are deliberately taught as divine truths in your schools. . . . Russia is setting an example of intellectual and moral integrity to the whole world, while England is filling its temples with traders, persecuting its clergy, and bringing up children to be scoffers to whom religion means nothing but hypocrisy and humbug." (*Herald-Tribune*, Apl. 7, 1930.)

Thus the Church enchains the Reason. The proudest boast today of the Church for its ex-Pagan Saint Augustine, is that: "as soon as a contradiction—[between his "philosophy" and his religious doctrines]—arises, he *never hesitates* to subordinate his philosophy to religion, *reason to faith*"! (*Cath. Encyc.* ii, 86.) So this great ex-Pagan Saint of the Church surrenders his reason to faith, and avers: "I would not believe the Gospels to be true, unless the authority of the Catholic Church constrained me"! (Augustine, *De Genesi.*)

Ingersoll, in one of his glowing, devastating periods of oratory, said: "Somebody ought to tell the truth about the Bible!" That I have already essayed quite comprehensively to do. In my recent work, *Is It God's Word?* (Alfred A. Knopf, Inc., New York, 1926, 2nd and 3rd Editions), I devote some five hundred pages to "An Exposition of the Fables and Mythology of the Bible and of the Impostures of Theology," as my thesis is defined in my sub-title. "A farrago of palpable nonsense," in the words of the Dean of American critics, is about all that remains of Holy Writ as the pretended "Word of God," as the result of that searching analysis.

That study was limited, in most part, to the sacred texts for the internal evidences, which themselves so abundantly afford, of their own falsity and primitive-minded fatuity. On the other phase of inquiry I there limited myself to the suggestive remark: "The gospels are all priestly forgeries over a century after their pretended dates" (p. 279; cf. p. 400), purposing then to complement the work by this sequel or companion volume, treating the frauds and forgeries of religion and the Church.

Taking up now more particularly the second phase of my subject, I here propose to treat of the inveterate forgeries, frauds, impostures, and mendacities of Priestcraft and its Theology. I shall be explicit and plain spoken, and unmistakably state my purpose and my proofs. For nearly two thousand years the priestcraft of Christendom, for purposes of domination by fear and greedy exploitation through imposture upon credulity, has consigned to earthly fire and sword, and to eternal damnation all who dared to dissent or to protest; the priestly word "miscreant," *misbeliever*, has become the synonym for everything foul and criminal in human nature. The day of reckoning and of repudiation is at hand; Priestcraft has here its destroying answer, in very plain and unafraid words.

This book is a grave indictment, impossible to be made or to be credited unless supported at every point by incontrovertible facts. These I promise to produce and array in due and devastating order.

THE INDICTMENT

I charge, and purpose to prove, from unimpeachable texts and historical records, and by authoritative clerical confessions, beyond the possibility of denial, evasion, or refutation:

FOREWORD

1. That the Bible, in its every Book, and in the strictest legal and moral sense, is a huge forgery.

2. That every Book of the New Testament is a forgery of the Christian Church; and every significant passage in those Books, on which the fabric of the Church and its principal Dogmas are founded, is a further and conscious later forgery, wrought with definite fraudulent intent.

3. Especially, and specifically, that the "famous Petrine text"—"Upon this Rock I will build my church"—the cornerstone of the gigantic fabric of imposture,—and the other, "Go, teach all nations,"—were never uttered by the Jew Jesus, but are palpable and easily-proven late Church forgeries.

4. That the Christian Church, from its inception in the first little Jewish-Christian religious societies until it reached the apex of its temporal glory and moral degradation, was a vast and tireless Forgery-mill.

5. That the Church was founded upon, and through the Dark Ages of Faith has battened on—(yet languishes decadently upon)—monumental and petty forgeries and pious frauds, possible only because of its own shameless mendacity and through the crass ignorance and superstition of the sodden masses of its deluded votaries, purposely kept in that base condition for purposes of ecclesiastical graft and aggrandizement through conscious and most unconscionable imposture.

6. That every conceivable form of religious lie, fraud and imposture has ever been the work of Priests; and through all the history of the Christian Church, as through all human history, has been—and, so far as they have not been shamed out of it by skeptical ridicule and exposure, yet is, the age-long stock in trade and sole means of existence of the priests and ministers of all the religions.

7. That the clerical mind, which "reasons in chains," is, from its vicious and vacuous "education," and the special selfish interests of the priestly class, incapable either of the perception or the utterance of truth, in matters where the interests of priestcraft are concerned.

As the Catholic-Protestant-Skeptic Bayle, of seventeenth century fame, said: "I am most truly a Protestant; for I protest indifferently against all systems and all sects" of religious imposture.

FOREWORD

My accusal, therefore, is not limited in purpose, scope or effect to any one Church or sect, but is aimed alike at all of the discordant factions of ancient Jewish and more modern Christian faith. For, as has been well said, "Faith is not knowledge, no more than that three is four, but eminently contained in it; so that he that knows, believes, and something more; but he that believes many times does not know—nay, if he doth barely and merely believe, he doth never know." The same critical cleric at another place said: "still less was it ever intended that men should so prostitute their reason, as to believe with infallible faith what they are unable to prove with infallible arguments." (Chillingworth, *Religion of Protestants*, pp. 66, 412.) With infallible facts I purpose to blast the false pretenses of Priest-forged Faith.

It is matter of fact, that for some 1500 years of this Era there was but one "True Church" of Christ; and that Church claims with conscious pride the origin and authorship of all the New Testament Books, out of its own Holy bosom, by its own canonized Saints. The New Testament Books are, therefore, distinctively Catholic documents. That Church, therefore,—if these its credentials and documents are forgeries,—as from its own records I shall prove—itself forged all the Books of the New Testament and all the documents of religious dogma and propaganda the forgery of which shall be proved in this book, and did itself perpetrate all the pious frauds herein revealed, and is their chief beneficiary. All the other Christian sects, however, are sprung or severed from the original One True Church;—"all other forms of the Christian religion . . . originated by secession from the True Church, . . . and their founders . . . were externally members of the Church." (*CE.* vii, 367.) All these Protestant sects, therefore, with full knowledge of the guilty facts and partakers in the frauds, found their claim to Divinity—and priestly emoluments—upon and through those tainted titles, and thus yet fully share the guilt as accomplices after the fact. The "Reformed" Sects, on breaking away from the old Monopoly of Forgery, appropriated the least clumsy and more plausible of the pious Counterfeit of Christianity, and for the centuries since have industriously and knowingly been engaged in passing the stolen counterfeit upon their own unsuspecting flocks; they are therefore equally guilty with the original Forgers of the Faith.

xx

FOREWORD

The proofs of my indictment are marvellously easy. They are to be found in amplest store of history and accredited ecclesiastic authorities, and in abounding incautious admissions made by the accredited spokesmen of the Accused: upon these I shall freely and fully draw for complete proofs of my every specification. These damning things of the Church, scattered through many clerical volumes and concealed in many archives, are not well known to the pious or preoccupied layman. My task is simply to bring together the documentary proofs and expose them before the astonished eyes of the modern reader; that is the prime merit of my work. To accomplish this purpose with unimpeachable certitude, I need and make no apology for the liberal use of quotation marks in presenting the ensuing startling array of accusations and confessions; to be followed by the plenary proofs.

As in the judicial process, I shall, before proceeding to the concrete proofs, define first the crime charged, and outline the scope of the evidence to be presented. I shall first make a *prima facie* justification of the charges, by citing a few generalities of confession of guilt, with corroborations by weighty supporting authorities, and thus create the proper "atmosphere" for the appreciation of the facts. Then shall come the shaming proofs in astounding detail.

FORGERY DEFINED

Forgery, in legal and moral sense, is the utterance or publication, with intent to deceive or defraud, or to gain some advantage, of a false document, put out by one person in the name of and as the genuine work of another, who did not execute it, or the subsequent alteration of a genuine document by one who did not execute the original. This species of falsification extends alike to all classes of writings, promissory notes, the coin or currency of the realm, to any legal or private document, or to a book. All are counterfeit or forged if not authentic and untampered.

A definition by a high ecclesiastical authority may appropriately be cited, as it thoroughly defines the chronic clerical crime. The *Catholic Encyclopedia* thus defines the crime:

FOREWORD

"Forgery (Lat. *falsum*) differs very slightly from fraud. It consists in the deliberate untruthfulness of an assertion, or in the deceitful presentation of an object, and is based on an intention to deceive and to injure while using the externals of honesty. Forgery is truly a falsehood and is a fraud, but it is something more. . . . A category consists in *making use of such forgery, and is equivalent to forgery proper.* . . . The Canonical legislation [dealt principally with] the production of absolutely false documents and the alteration of authentic . . . for the sake of certain advantages. . . .

"Canon law connects forgery and the use of forged documents, on the presumption that *he who would make use of such documents must be either the author or instigator of the forgery.* In canon law forgery consists not only in the fabrication or substitution of an entirely false document, but even by partial substitution, or by any alteration affecting the sense and bearing of an authentic document or any substantial point, such as names, dates, signature, seal, favour granted, by erasure, by scratching out or writing one word over another, and the like." (*Catholic Encyclopedia,* vi, 135, 136.)

Under every phase and phrase of this its own clerico-legal definition, the Church is guilty,—is most guilty.

A "beginning of miracles" of confession of ecclesiastical guilt of forgery of Church documents is made in the same above article by the *Encyclopedia,*—very many others will follow in due course from the same source:

"Substitution of false documents and tampering with genuine ones was quite a trade in the Middle Ages. Innocent III (1198) points out nine species of forgery [of ecclesiastical records] which had come under his notice." (*CE.* vi, 136.)

But such frauds of the Church were not confined to the Middle Ages; they begin even with the beginning of the Church and infest every period of its history for fifteen hundred years and defile nearly every document, both of "Scriptures" and of Church aggrandizement. As truly said by Collins, in his celebrated *Discourse of Free Thinking:*

"In short, *these frauds are very common in all books which are published by priests or priestly men.* . . . For it is certain they may plead the authority of the Fathers for Forgery, Corruption and mangling of Authors, with more reason than for any of their Articles of Faith." (p. 96.)

xxii

FOREWORD

Bishop Eusebius of Cæsarea, the great "Father of Church History" (324 A. D.) whom Niebuhr terms "a very dishonest writer,"—of which we shall see many notable instances,—says this: "But it is not our place to describe the sad misfortunes which finally came upon [the Christians], as we do not think it proper, moreover, to record their divisions and unnatural conduct to each other before the persecution —[by Diocletian, 305 A. D.]. Wherefore we have decided *to relate nothing concerning them except* things in which we can vindicate the Divine judgment. . . . But we shall introduce into this history in general *only those events* which may be useful first to ourselves and afterwards to posterity." (*Ecclesiastical History*, viii, 2; *N&PNF.* i, 323–324.)

Eusebius himself fraudulently "subscribed to the [Trinitarian] Creed formed by the Council of Nicæa, but making no secret, in the letter which he wrote to his own Church, of the *non-natural sense* in which he accepted it." (*Cath. Encyc.* v, 619.) As St. Jerome says, "Eusebius is the most open champion of the Arian heresy," which denies the Trinity. (Jerome, *Epist.* 84, 2; *N&PNF.* vi, 176.) Bishop Eusebius, as we shall see, was one of the most prolific forgers and liars of his age of the Church, and a great romancer; in his hair-raising histories of the holy Martyrs, he assures us "that on some occasions the bodies of the martyrs who had been devoured by wild beasts, upon the beasts being strangled, were found alive in their stomachs, even after having been fully digested"! (quoted, Gibbon, *History*, Ch. 37; Lardner, iv, p. 91; *Diegesis*, p. 272). To such an extent had the "pious frauds of the theologians been thus early systematized and raised to the dignity of a regular doctrine," that Bishop Eusebius, "in one of the most learned and elaborate works that antiquity has left us, the Thirty-second Chapter of the Twelfth Book of his *Evangelical Preparation*, bears for its title this scandalous proposition: 'How it may be.Lawful and Fitting to use Falsehood as a Medicine, and for the Benefit of those who Want to be Deceived' "—(quoting the Greek title; Gibbon, *Vindication*, p. 76).

St. John Chrysostom, the "Golden Mouthed," in his work *On the Priesthood*, has a curious panygeric on the clerical habit of telling lies: "Great is the force of deceit! provided it is not excited by a treacherous intention." (*Comm. on I Cor. ix, 19; Diegesis*, p. 309.) Chrysostom was one of the Greek Fathers of the Church, concerning whom Dr. (later Cardinal) Newman thus apologetically spoke: "The Greek Fathers thought that, when there was a *justa causa, an untruth need not be a lie.* . . . Now, as to the just cause, . . . the Greek Fathers make them such as these—self-defense, charity, *zeal for God's honour,* and the like." (Newman, *Apology for His Life,* Appendix G, p. 345–6.) He says nothing of his favorites, the Latin Fathers; but we shall hear them described, and amply see them at work lying in their zeal for God's honor, and to their own dishonor.

The Great Latin Father St. Jerome (c. 340–420), who made the celebrated Vulgate Version of the Bible, and wrote books of the most marvelous Saint-tales and martyr-yarns, thus describes the approved methods of Christian propaganda, of the Fathers, Greek and Latin alike, against the Pagans:

"To confute the opposer, now this argument is adduced and now that. One argues as one pleases, saying one thing while one means another. . . . Origen, Methodius, Eusebius, and Apollinaris write at great length against Celsus and Porphyry. Consider how subtle are the arguments, how insidious the engines with which they overthrow what the spirit of the devil has wrought. Sometimes, it is true, they are compelled *to say not what they think but what is needful.* . . .

"I say nothing of the Latin authors, of Tertullian, Cyprian, Minutius, Victorianus, Lactantius, Hilary, lest I should appear not so much to be defending myself as to be assailing others. I will only mention the APOSTLE PAUL. . . . He, then, if anyone, ought to be calumniated; we should speak thus to him: 'The proofs which you have used against the Jews and against other heretics bear a different meaning in their own contexts to that which they bear in your Epistles. We see passages taken captive by your pen and pressed into service to win you a victory, which in volumes from which they are taken have no controversial bearing at all . . . the line so often adopted by strong men in controversy—of *justifying the means by the result."* (Jerome, *Epist. to Pammachus,* xlviii, 13; *N&PNF.* vi, 72–73; See *post,* p. 230.)

Of Eusebius and the others he again says, that they "presume at the price of their soul to assert dogmatically whatever first comes into their head." (Jerome, *Epist.* li, 7; *id.* p. 88.) And again, of the incentive offered by the gullible ignorance of the Faithful, for the glib mendacities of the priests: "There is nothing so easy as by sheer volu-

bility to deceive a common crowd or an uneducated congregation."
(*Epist.* lii, 8; p. 93.) Father Jerome's own high regard for truth and
his zeal in propaganda of fables for edification of the ignorant ex-
pagan Christians is illustrated in numberless instances. He tells us of
the river Ganges in India, which "has its source in Paradise"; that in
India "are also mountains of gold, which however men cannot approach by reason of the griffins, dragons, and huge monsters which
haunt them; for such are the guardians which avarice needs for its
treasures." (*Epist.* cxxv, 6; *N&PNF.* vi, 245.) He reaches the climax
in his famous *Lives of sundry Saints.* He relates with all fervor the
marvelous experiences of the "blessed hermit Paulus," who was 113
years of age, and for sixty years had lived in a hole in the ground in
the remotest recesses of the desert; his nearest neighbor was St.
Anthony, who was only ninety and lived in another hole four days'
journey away. The existence and whereabouts of Paulus being revealed
to Anthony in a vision, he set out afoot to visit the holy Paulus. On
the way, "all at once he beholds a creature of mingled shape, half horse
half man, called by the poets Hippo-centaur," with whom he holds
friendly converse. Later "he sees a mannikin with hooked snout, horned
forehead, and extremities like goat's feet," this being one of the desert
tribe "whom the Gentiles worship under the names of Fauns, Satyrs,
and Incubi," and whose strange language Anthony was rejoiced to
find that he could understand, as they reasoned together about the
salvation of the Lord. "Let no one scruple to believe this incident,"
pleads Father Jerome; "its truth is supported by" one of these creatures that was captured and brought alive to Alexandria and sent
embalmed to the emperor at Antioch. Finally holy Anthony reached
the retreat of the blessed Paulus, and was welcomed. As they talked, a
raven flew down and laid a whole loaf of bread at their feet. "See," said
Paulus, "the Lord truly loving, truly merciful, has sent us a meal. For
the last sixty years I have always received half a loaf; but at your
coming the Lord has doubled his soldier's rations." During the visit
Paulus died; Anthony "saw Paulus in robes of snowy white ascending
on high among a band of angels, and the choirs of prophets and apostles." Anthony dragged the body out to bury it, but was without means
to dig a grave; as he was lamenting this unhappy circumstance, "behold, two lions from the recesses of the desert with manes flying on

their necks came rushing along; they came straight to the corpse of the blessed old man," fawned on it, roared in mourning, then with their paws dug a grave just wide and deep enough to hold the corpse; came over and licked the hands and feet of Anthony, and ambled away. (Jerome, *Life of Paulus the First Hermit, N&PNF.* vi, 299 *seq.*)

So gross and prevalent was the clerical habit of pious lies and pretenses "to the glory of God," that St. Augustine, about 395 A. D., wrote a reproving treatise to the Clergy, *De Mendacio* (On Lying), which he found necessary to supplement in 420 with another book, *Contra Mendacium* (Against Lying). This work, says Bishop Wordsworth, "is a protest against these 'pious frauds' which have brought discredit and damage on the cause of the Gospel, and have created prejudice against it, from the days of Augustine to our own times." (*A Church History*, iv, 93, 94.) While Augustine disapproves of downright lying even to trap heretics,—a practice seemingly much in vogue among the good Christians: "It is more pernicious for Catholics to lie that they may catch heretics, than for heretics to lie that they may not be found out by Catholics" (*Against Lying*, ch. 5; *N&PNF.* iii, 483); yet this Saint heartily approves and argues in support of the chronic clerical characteristics of *suppressio veri*, of suppression or concealment of the truth for the sake of Christian "edification," a device for the encouragement of credulity among the Faithful which has run riot through the centuries and flourishes today among the priests and the ignorant pious: "It is lawful, then, either to him that discourses, disputes, and preaches of things eternal, or to him that narrates or speaks of things temporal pertaining to *edification* of religion or piety, to *conceal* at fitting times *whatever seems fit to be concealed;* but to tell a lie is never lawful, therefore neither to conceal by telling a lie." (Augustine, *On Lying*, ch. 19; *N&PNF.* iii, 466.) The great Bishop did not, however, it seems, reck his own rede when it came to preaching unto edification, for in one of his own sermons he thus relates a very notable experience: "I was already Bishop of Hippo, when I went into Ethiopia with some servants of Christ there to preach the Gospel. In this country we saw many men and women *without heads*, who had two great eyes in their breasts; and in countries still more southly, we saw people who had but one eye in their foreheads." (Augustine, *Sermon 37;* quoted in Taylor, *Syn-*

xxvi

tagma, p. 52; *Diegesis,* p. 271; Doane, *Bible Myths,* p. 437.) To the mind's eye the wonderful spectacle is represented, as the great Saint preached the word of God to these acephalous Faithful: we see the whole congregation of devout and intelligent Christians, without heads, watching attentively without eyes, listening intently without ears, and understanding perfectly without brains, the spirited and spiritual harangue of the eloquent and veracious St. Augustine. And every hearer of the Sermon in which he told about it, believed in fulness of faith and infantile credulity every word of the noble Bishop of Hippo, giving thanks to God that the words of life and salvation had been by him carried to so remarkable a tribe of God's curious children.

Pope Gregory the Great (590–604), in one momentary lapse in his own arduous labors of propagating "lies to the glory of God," made the pious gesture, "God does not need our lies"; but His Church evidently did, for the pious work went lyingly on; a work given immense impetus by His Holiness Gregory himself, in his mendacious *Dialogues* and other papal output,—with little abatement unto this day.

A further admission of the inveteracy of ecclesiastical forgery and fraud may be cited from the *Catholic Encyclopedia.* Speaking deprecatingly of the "incredible liberty of discussion" which to the shock and scandal of the pious prelates "prevailed in Rome under the spell of the Renaissance,"—when men's minds were beginning to awaken from the intellectual and moral stupor of the Dark Ages of Faith, the Catholic thesaurus of archaic superstition and "Catholic Truth," admits:

"This toleration of evil [*sic; i. e.:*—the free discussion of Church doctrines and documents]—bore one good consequence: it allowed historical criticism to begin fair. There was need for a revision which is not yet complete, ranging over *all that has been handed down* from the Middle Ages under the style and title of the Fathers, the Councils, the Roman and other official archives. *In all these departments forgery and interpolations as well as ignorance* had wrought mischief on a great scale." (*CE.* xii, 768.)

To these preliminary confessions of the guilty Church may be added the corroborating testimony of several eminently accredited historical authorities.

FOREWORD

Middleton, in his epochal *Free Inquiry* into the lying habits and miracles of the Churchmen, says: "Many spurious books were forged in the earliest times of the Church, in the name of Christ and his apostles, which passed upon all the Fathers as genuine and divine through several successive ages." (Middleton, *Free Inquiry, Int. Disc.* p. xcii; London, 1749.)

The same author, whose book set England ringing with its exposures of the lies and fraudulent miracles of the Church, makes this acute and accurate summing up of his evidences:

"It will not appear strange to those who have given any attention to the history of mankind, which will always suggest this sad reflection: That the greatest zealots in religion, or the leaders of sects and parties, whatever purity or principles they pretend to, have seldom scrupled to make use of a commodious lie for the advancement of what they call the truth. And with regard to these very Fathers, there is not one of them, as an eminent writer of ecclesiastical history declares, who made any scruple in those ages of using the *hyperbolical style* to advance the honor of God and the salvation of men." (*Free Inq.* p. 83; citing Jo., *Hist. Eccles.* p. 681.)

Lecky, the distinguished author of the *History of European Morals*, devotes much research into what he describes as "the deliberate and apparently perfectly unscrupulous forgery of a whole literature, destined to further the propagation either of Christianity as a whole, or of some particular class of tenets." (Lecky, *Hist. of European Morals*, vol. i, p. 375.)

In his very notable *History of Rationalism*, speaking of that Christian "epoch when faith and facts did not cultivate an acquaintance," the same author, Lecky, thus describes the state of intellectual and moral obliquity into which the Church had forced even the ablest classes of society:

"During that gloomy period the only scholars in Europe were priests and monks, who conscientiously believed that no amount of falsehood was reprehensible which conduced to the edification of the people. . . . All their writings, and more especially their histories, became tissues of the wildest fables, so grotesque and at the same time so audacious, that they were the wonder of succeeding ages. And the very men who scattered these fictions broadcast over Christendom, taught at the same time that credulity

xxviii

was a virtue and skepticism a crime." (Lecky, *Hist. of Rationalism*, i, 396.)

In the same work last quoted, Lecky again, speaking of what he terms "the pious frauds of theologians," which, he shows were "systematized and raised to the dignity of a regular doctrine," says of the pious Fathers:

"The Fathers laid down as a distinct proposition that pious frauds were justifiable and even laudable, and if they had not laid this down they would nevertheless have practiced them as a necessary consequence of their doctrine of exclusive salvation. Immediately all ecclesiastical literature became tainted with a spirit of the most unblushing mendacity. Heathenism was to be combatted, and therefore prophecies of Christ by Orpheus and the Sibyls were forged, lying wonders were multiplied. . . . Heretics were to be convinced, and therefore interpolations of old writings or complete forgeries were habitually opposed to the forged Gospels. . . . The tendency . . . triumphed wherever the supreme importance of dogmas was held. Generation after generation it became more universal; it continued till the very sense of truth and the very love of truth seemed blotted out from the minds of men." (Lecky, *Rationalism in Europe*, i, 396–7.)

There is thus disclosed a very sharp and shaming contrast between the precept of the Lord Buddha: "Thou shalt not attempt, either by words or action, to lead others to believe that which is not true," and the confessed debasing principle of the Church, that the maintenance of its creed—(even by the methods of fraud, forgery and imposture above hinted and to be evidenced)—is superior to the principles of morality:

"To undo the creed is to undo the Church. The integrity of the rule of faith is more essential to the cohesion of a religious society than the strict practice of its moral precepts"! (*CE.* vii, 259).

With its consciousness of the shifty and shady practices of its "sacred" profession, the Christian priestcraft differs not from the Pagan in the sneer of Cicero: "*Cato mirari se aiebat, quod non rideret haruspex, cum haruspicem vidisset,*—Cato used to wonder how one of our priests can forbear laughing when he sees another." (Quoted *Opera*, Ed. Gron., p. 3806.) We shall see all too well that the Pagan estimate holds good for the Christian; that, as said by the "universal scholar" Grotius: "Ecclesiastical history consists of nothing but the wickedness of the governing clergy,—*Qui legit historiam Ecclesiasticam, quid legit nisi Episcoporum vicia?*" (*Epistolæ*, p. 7, col. 1).

The universality of the frauds and impostures of the Church, above barely hinted at, and the contaminating influence of such example, are by now sufficiently evident; they will be seen to taint and corrupt every phase of the Church and of the ecclesiastical propaganda of the Faith. As is well said by Middleton in commenting on these and like pious practices of the Holy Church: "And no man surely can doubt, but that those, who would either forge, or make use of forged books, would, in the same cause, and for the same ends, make use of forged miracles" (*A Free Inquiry, Introd. Discourse,* p. lxxxvii);—as well as of forged Gospels, Epistles, Creeds, Saint-tales—vast extensions of pious frauds of which we shall see a plethora of examples.

The proofs here to be arrayed for conviction are drawn from original sources, chiefly those inexhaustible mines of priestly perversions of fact and truth, the labored and ludicrous volumes of the "Fathers of the Church," and its most accredited modern American spokesman, the *Catholic Encyclopedia.* Hence it cannot be justly complained that this presentation of *facts* of Church history is unfair or untrue; all but *every fact* of secular and of Church history herein recounted to the shame and guilt of Holy Church is taken *verbatim* from the Church's own histories and historians. These clerical works of confession and confusion are for the most part three ponderous sets of volumes; they are readily accessible for verification of my recitals, and for further instances, in good libraries and bookshops; the libraries of the Union Theological Seminary and of Columbia University, in New York City, were the places of the finds here recorded. Cited so often, space will be saved for more valuable uses by citing by their initials,—which will become very familiar—my chief ecclesiastical authorities, towit:

The *Ante-Nicene Fathers*, cited as *ANF.;* A Collection of the extant Writings of all the Founders of Christianity down to the Council of Nicæa, or Nice, in 325 A. D. American Reprint, eight volumes. The Christian Literature Publishing Co., Buffalo, N. Y., 1885.

FOREWORD

The *Nicene and Post-Nicene Fathers*, cited as *N&PNF.*; First and Second Series; many volumes; same publishers.

The *Catholic Encyclopedia*, cited as *CE.*; fifteen volumes and index, published under the *Imprimatur* of Archbishop Farley; New York, Robert Appleton Co., 1907–9.

The *Encyclopedia Biblica*, cited as *EB.*, four volumes; Adam & Charles Black, London, 1899; American Reprint, The Macmillan Co., New York, 1914.

The clerical confessions of lies and frauds in the ponderous volumes of the *Catholic Encyclopedia* alone suffice, and to spare, to wreck the Church and to destroy utterly the Christian religion. We shall see.

RELIGIOUS LAWS OF OUTLAWRY

The land, the religious world, even today is ringing with the furious din of religious intolerance, bigotry and persecution; pestiferous Medieval laws are imposed to stop the voice of Science teaching truths which impugn the ignorant myths of Bible and Theology. Tennessee and several States of the Union have passed laws making criminal the teaching of scientific facts which contradict "the story of the divine creation of man as taught in the Bible," and like Hillbilly legislation is sought in all the States. The True Church lays down this amazing limitation on learning: "When a clearly defined dogma contradicts a scientific assertion, *the latter has to be revised*"! (*CE.* xiii, 607.) The civilized portion of the world has just been shocked at the potential judicial murder and outrage sanctioned by law in North Carolina, as likewise in a number of other States, making outlaws of honest persons who, as parties in interest or witnesses in actions civil and criminal, refuse to take the ridiculous and degrading Form of Oath "upon the Holy Evangelists of Almighty God, in token of his engagement to speak the truth, as he hopes to be saved in the way and method of salvation pointed out in that blessed volume; and in further token that, if he should swerve from the truth, he may be justly deprived of all the blessings of the Gospel, and be made liable to that vengeance which he has imprecated on his own head." (*Consol. Stat. N. C., 1919*, sec. 3189.)

Under this infamous statute, in the late so-called Gastonia, N. C.

murder trial, the wife of one of the defendants, who had testified that her husband was not present and had no part in the shooting, was challenged as a witness and impeached, her testimony discredited, and her husband convicted for want of her evidently candid testimony: but true or not, the principle of infamy is the same—a citizen on trial for his liberty was refused the benefit of evidence under this damnable statute, and he and his wife made outlaws—refused "the equal protection of the law"! In Maryland, later in the same year 1929, a chicken-thief, caught in the act of robbery by the owner, was discharged in court because the owner of the property, a Freethinker, was not permitted under the infamous similar statute of that godly State to give testimony in court against the criminal: the case would have been the same, if the life or liberty of the Infidel citizen had been at stake,—he was an outlaw denied the "equal protection of the law"! The benighted State of Arkansas—("Now laugh!")—declares infamously in its Constitution: "*No person who denies the being of a God shall hold any office in the civil government of this State, nor be competent to testify as a witness in any court*"! (*Const. Ark.*, Art. XIX, sec. 26.) Under this accursed act of outlawry, Charles Lee Smith, of New York City, a native of Arkansas, went to his home city of Little Rock in the Fall of 1928 to oppose the degrading proposition proposed as a law in a popular initiative election, forbidding the teaching of Evolution in the State-supported schools and universities; he made some remarks reflecting upon the personal integrity of the Almighty, as well as denying his existence; twice was he arrested, thrown into jail, convicted, and was denied the right to testify as a witness in his own behalf; he is today on bail to answer to the decision of the Supreme Court of that State, an outlaw, denied the "equal protection of the law" of the land! The hypocrisy and self-stultification imposed by such detestable laws, is finely illustrated: At the recent annual meeting of the American Law Institute, I denounced this Article to a leader of the Arkansas Bar, and appealed to him to "start something" to get rid of it. He shrugged his shoulders, smiled in sympathy, and said: "It is in the Constitution, and too difficult to get it out." Then, dropping into Spanish, so that others at the table might not understand, he added: "*Yo no creo nada,—y no digo nada*— I believe nothing—and I say nothing"! While these infamies are inflicted upon the citizens of this country by law imposed by a bigoted and ignorant minority of superstitious parsons and their docile dupes;—aye, even if imposed by an overwhelming majority, or by authentic decree of God himself,—the free and fearless defiers of Church and despisers of its Superstition will fight it on to the death, till every trace of these infamies is purged out of the statute books of these sovereign States! This is due and solemn notice and defiance to the intolerant religious oppressors and their deluded dupes.

Medieval laws against the fictitious crime of "Blasphemy" survive in a dozen American States, protecting by law the Christian superstition of the old Hebrew God. A model of them all is this infamous enactment of the Church-ridden Massachusetts: "Whoever wilfully blasphemes the holy name of God by denying, cursing or contumeliously reproaching God, his creation, government or final judging of the world, or by cursing or contumeliously reproaching Jesus Christ or the Holy Ghost—[the whole Divine Family],—or by cursing or contumeliously reproaching or exposing to contempt or ridicule, the holy word of God contained in the holy scriptures shall be punished by imprisonment in jail for not more than one year or by fine of not more than three hundred dollars, and may also be bound to good behavior." (*Gen. Laws Mass.*, 1921; Chap. 272, sec. 36.) Expressed contempt is held in lighter pecuniary estimation in the Yankee "Nutmeg State," the fine being only $100.00, plus the year in gaol. (*Gen. Stat. Conn.*, 1918, sec. 6395.) In both States, under these infamous laws, persons have been indicted, tried and convicted within the past two years! Throughout the Union are odious religious statutes, "Blue Laws" and Sunday Laws, penalizing innocuous diversions and activities of the people on days of religious Voodoo: Sunday, as we shall see, being a plagiarization from the religion of Mithras, and created a secular holiday—not a religious Holy Day—by law of the Pagan Constantine. Such laws sometimes prove troublesome to the pious Puritans themselves; an amusing instance of their boomerang effect being now chronicled to the annoyed and sneering world. Some "400" of the True Believers of the "Holy Name Society" of St. Peter's R. C. Church of New Brunswick, in the saintly State of New Jersey, including several City "Fathers" stuck their legs under the loaded tables of the local hostlery for a "Holy Communion Breakfast" the past Sun-

FOREWORD

day; as they began to eat they discovered to their pious dismay that there was no bread on the tables, although the reservation had long before been made, with particular stress on a special brand of rolls, made only in the godless town of Newark. Consternation reigned, with much confusion and hurried telephoning by the management. In the midst of it came a 'phone call from the driver of the roll-delivery truck, from the local Hoosgow: "I've been arrested for the violation of section 316 of the Laws of 1798, which prohibits the delivery of bread and rolls on the Sabbath and also forbids a man to kiss his wife on that day"! Some of the sachems called the chief of police and angrily demanded that this holy law be violated by delivering the blessed rolls; the driver was arraigned before the Recorder, who "released him with a warning," and he consummated the violation by delivering the forbidden rolls to the angry Holy Namers. (*Herald-Tribune*, May 14, 1930.)

Now, throughout the State, and in far off Ohio, at the instigation of the parsons, these pestiferous pious laws are being forced into enforcement, headlined—"Blue Law Net Busy in Jersey," and recorded: "Hundreds of names and addresses were in the possession of the police today because their owners played golf, tennis or radios, bought or sold gasoline, cigarettes or groceries, or operated trolley cars, busses or trains in this capital city (of Trenton) on the Sabbath," with much more of detail; and in the same column, a dispatch from Dover, Ohio, that the police used tear-gas bombs to dislodge the operator from the projection-box of a local "movie" theater, who, with the owner and four employees, was "arrested for violation of the Sunday closing law"! (*N. Y. Sun*, May 26, 1930.) And all this medieval absurdity of repressive penal legislation to enforce obsolete religious observance by disbelievers, in a land whose every constitution proclaims the complete separation of State and Church! But for the defiance of fearless heroes of Rationalism who have through the ages contended, and suffered martyrdom by rack and stake in defense of human liberty, rack and stake and fiendish torture would yet be the penalty, rather than fine and jail, for violators of the odious proscriptions of Church and Church-minded, Church-driven, politicians. To know fully the insidious and intensive efforts being made throughout our country by the dupes of priestcraft to undermine and destroy the

xxxiv

liberties and rights of free men in the interest of canting religious Pharisaism, bent on rule and ruin, every true friend of freedom and enemy of the Church, should read intently and keep ever at hand for an arsenal of defense, Maynard Shipley's stirring book, *The War on Modern Science; A Short History of the Fundamentalist Attacks on Evolution and Modernism*—(Knopf, 1929),—which to read doth "make the angry passions rise" in righteous wrath against these pious conspirators against American liberties and the innate rights of man. The Church, too, through the ages has been and yet nefariously is "in politics," seeking to dictate and dominate and impose its malign superstitions by law: witness the two last presidential campaigns, and the pernicious activities of the Methodist Board of Intolerance, Meddling and Public Nuisance, as now being revealed by the Lobbying Investigation Committee of the United States Senate, whereby it is shown seeking to suborn and subordinate all to its intolerant superstitious dominance. In most European countries the True Church maintains its blatant "Catholic Party" in the elections and in the parliaments; here its operations are via the "grape-vine route," but effective, as through the corrupt machinations of St. Tammany; while the Methodist Party and the Baptist Party, and their allies the Ku Klux Klan pursue the same evil ends through vocal frightening of cheap politicians and of large sections of the people and press. The very pious Editor of the *Christian Herald* has just published a book on "The Church in Politics," in which with cynical frankness he asserts its right and discloses its odious methods.

These odious things are all the work and blighting effects of the unholy *Odium Theologicum* of Priestcraft, poisoning men's minds with the rancors of obsolete superstitious beliefs.

Remove the cause, the cure is automatically and quickly effected. To contribute to the speedier consummation of this supreme boon is the motive and justification of this book. It gives to the unctuous quack "Doctors of Divinity" a copious dose out of their own nauseous Pharmacopæia of Priestly Mendacity. As its takes its deadly effect upon themselves, haply their "incurably religious" duped patients may begin to evidence hopeful symptoms of a wholesome, speedy and complete cure from their priest-made malady.

"Fraud," says Ingersoll, "is hateful to its victims." The compelling proofs of duplicious fraud of priestcraft and Church exposed in this book must convince even the most credulous and devout Believer, that the system of "revealed religion" which he "drew in with his mother's milk" and has in innocent ignorance suffered in his system ever since, is simply a veneered Paganism, unrevealed and untrue; is a huge scheme of priestly imposture to exploit the credulous and to live in power and wealth at his expense. Luther hit the bull's-eye of the System—before he established another to pass the same old counterfeit: The Church exists mostly for wealth and self-aggrandizement; to quit paying money to the priests would kill the whole scheme in a couple of years. This is the sovereign remedy. Let him that hath ears to hear, hear; and govern himself accordingly. Every awakened Believer must feel outraged in his dignity and self-respect, and in disgust must repudiate the Creed and its impostors.

When a notorious Criminal is arraigned at the bar of Justice and put to trial for deeds of crime and shame, it is his crimes, his criminal career and record, which are the subject of inquiry,—which are exposed and denounced—for conviction. No weight in attenuation is accorded to sundry sporadic instances—(if any)—between crimes or as cloaks for crime—of his canting piety and gestures of benevolence towards his victims, the dupes of his duplicity. Thus the Church and its Creed are here arraigned on their record of Crime,—"extenuating naught, naught setting down in malice";—simply exposing truly its own convicting record and confessions of its criminality, for condign judgment upon it.

Goliath of Gath was a very big Giant; but a small pebble, artfully slung, brought him to a sudden and violent collapse, a huge corpse. This TNT. bomb of a book, loaded with barbèd *facts*, is flung full *in facia ecclesiæ*—into the face of the Forgery-founded Church and all her discordant broods. The "gates of hell" will be exploded!

> But yesteryear the Church of God in might
> Has stood against the world; now *lies* she here,
> And none so poor to do her reverence!

JOSEPH WHELESS

New York City
780 Riverside Drive
June 1, 1930

CONTENTS

Foreword: vii

  I: PAGAN FRAUDS—CHRISTIAN PRECE-
       DENTS   3

 II: HEBREW HOLY FORGERIES   45

III: CHRISTIAN "SCRIPTURE" FORGERIES   91

 IV: THE SAINTLY "FATHERS" OF THE
      FAITH   123

  V: THE "GOSPEL" FORGERIES   172

 VI: THE CHURCH FORGERY MILL   238

VII: THE "TRIUMPH" OF CHRISTIANITY   295

   INDEX   *Follows page* 406

FORGERY IN CHRISTIANITY

"Being crafty, I caught you with guile" . . .
*"For if the truth of God hath more abounded
through my LIE unto his glory; why yet am
I also adjudged a sinner?"*

St. Paul.

*"What profit has not that fable of Christ
brought us!"*

Pope Leo X.

CHAPTER I

PAGAN FRAUDS—CHRISTIAN PRECEDENTS

"Neither in the confusion of paganism, nor in the defilement of heresy, nor yet in the blindness of Judaism, is religion to be sought, but among those *alone* who are called Catholic Christians." (St. Augustine, *De Vera Religione,* v.)

EVERY RELIGION, PRIESTCRAFT, and Sacred Book, other than the Roman Catholic Christian, is thus branded as false in fact and fraudulent in practice. The Jews, however, excluded by those who have expropriated their ancient faith, make the same imputations of falsity and fraud against the Christian religion, based on their own ancient sacred Scriptures, and founded, as the Christians claim, by a Jewish Incarnation of the Hebrew God,—which, say the Jews, is a horrid blasphemy; and they brand the Sacred Books of Christian origin as false and forged.

The Christians, all their hundreds of warring Sects, in their turn impute to the Jews the blasphemous repudiation and monstrous murder of the Son of the ancient Hebrew God, Yahveh; and with ample usury of blood and torture have visited that fabulous iniquity upon the hapless sons and daughters of Jewry unto half a hundred generations of "God's Chosen People."

But, of the countless Sects of Christians, one alone, *it* avers, is of the True Faith; all the others are false and beyond the hope of heaven: "Whoever will be saved, it is necessary above all else that he hold to the Catholic Faith,"—so reads the venerable forged Athanasian Creed. (*CE.* ii, 33, 34.) The Protestant Sects, however, though they all admit the same origin and accept in full fatuity of faith most of the same forged sacred writings for their rule of faith as the One True Church, yet apply the scornful epithet "Antichrist" to their venerable

Mother in Christ; freely dub a dozen of her canonical sacred Books of Jewish origin, and most of her thousands of canonized Saints, forgeries and frauds; and assert many of her most holy dogmas and sacraments to be blasphemous and degrading superstitions. The while their own scores of hostile factions mutually recriminate each the others as blind leaders of the blind and perverters of the sacred Truth.

It will serve a useful purpose to take a look behind all this dust-and-smoke screen of *"Odium Theologicum"* and make a brief survey of the origins of religious superstitions and priestcraft, and of the known and admitted falsities and frauds of Paganism, and some venerable other religious *Isms*. This will demonstrate that these same things are now part and parcel of Christianity. This induces the inquiry, Wherein the data of Christianity as a whole may haply differ from the admitted frauds of the false religions and priestcrafts of the Past. We shall learn whether and to what degree truth may be found in any of the confused and confusing Christian claims of Truth.

THE DAWN-MAN AND THE SHAMAN

"There is no origin for the idea of an after-life save the conclusion which the savage draws from the notion suggested by dreams."—*Herbert Spencer*.

Lo, the poor Indian, with his untutored mind, saw his god in clouds and heard him in the wind. Ages before him, the Dawn-man, the earliest Cave-man, saw his shadow in the sun, his reflection in the water, and crudely thought that he had a sort of shadowy double, which accompanied him and at times showed itself visible to him. At night, when the Dawn-man, gorged with raw and often putrid flesh, in a nightmare dream saw terrible monsters assailing him, or in more normal sleep wandered forth and visited distant scenes of his previous roamings, or saw, as in the flesh living and acting before his eyes, his dead father or friend, thus he got further immature notions of a double, "ka," or detachable spirit of man, dwelling within him, which could leave the body and return at will, or which survived the death of the body and lived on in spirit form, and could revisit the old habitation and hold converse with, do good or harm to, the frightened living. Thus came the belief in the existence and survival after death of this

4

double or spirit-ghost; thus the notion of the immortality of the soul, a primitive belief held by every people of antiquity, and surviving yet by inheritance among the priest-taught of modern times.

These strange phantoms of the night naturally worked further upon the fear-filled mind of the early child-men, terrified by the frightful vicissitudes of life, the violent deaths by wild animals, the storms and floods that killed and maimed them, the lightnings and thunders that terrified them. All these things were to them clearly the manifestations of the anger and revenge of the departed spirits, especially of the Old Man of the clan who had bossed it in life and had grudges against all who had not been sufficiently obedient to him. Awaking from these dread visions of the night, the frightened Dawn-man would relate the uncanny visitations to his fellows, who would have like ghostly dream-stuff to exchange; together they would wonder whether something could be done to propitiate or placate the wandering ghost-men and to win their favor for benefits to be had from their superior other-worldly status and powers.

It could not be long before some old and crafty member of the no-madic clan would hint that he had known the Old Man well during life, had been very friendly with him living and had a powerful influence with him; that he was wise to the ways and whims of ghosts or gods; and no doubt he could get in touch with his spirit and cajole him into reasonableness and favor. This suggestion meeting with awed acquiescence, it would quickly be followed by the forthright bold claim to super-ghostly powers, and by sundry weird mumblings and mystic rites and incantations the old faker would further awe the clan into credulous faith in the claim. The new spiritualist would pretend to get into communion with the Old Man's spirit, and to receive from him "revelations" of his will and commands for the obedience of the clan. Thus began spirit-worship or religion—the fancied relations between man and the spirits of the dead or gods. Here, too, we have the first shaman, medicine-man, magician, witch-doctor, or what-not; in a word, the first priest; and the priestly game was on. The pretended ghost-cajoler would naturally be held in dread awe and reverence by his credulous dupes, and would gain enormous respect and prestige; he could quit the drudgery of hunting and fishing for his precarious living, and let the awed and believing members of the clan keep him in food and idle ease: here the first social parasite. This is priestcraft —by whatever name and in whatever age and guise pursued.

A very modern instance comes to hand and is added for confirmation. Fortunately, or lamentably for Christian pretensions, there yet exist in the world races of very primitive descendants of Adam, who yet preserve their primeval forms of superstition and priestcraft, wherein may be seen their origins in yet active reality of operation. In no more remote a region of these our United States than the Diomede Islands of the Aleutian archipelago of Alaska, tribal superstition and primitive priestcraft may be seen in all their ridiculous crudity today. In the Report of the Stoll-McCracken Expedition of the American Museum of Natural History, 1928, primitive religious superstition and the power of the priest are graphically described; with simple change of form and ritual it is Religion through the Ages, the war-blessers and rain-makers in action to cajole and control the deity through his priests. As one reads the following extracts from the Report, let him see what differences he may discover, other than of technique, between the Diomeder and the Dupe of any other Cult. "For the Diomeder humbles himself before the imaginary forces of his spirit world, often disregarding the realities of life with typical primitive inconsistency. . . . The only powers really worthy of his respect are the supernatural ones. This is why the Eskimo medicine man, or angutkok, as he is called, holds a position of such influence. He is the middleman between the natural and supernatural world. The Diomeders have no real chiefs or any system of government. Each family is able to manage its own affairs. The common events of life take care of themselves. But whatever is unusual, whatever cannot be readily understood, engages the attention of every Diomeder. Such things as sickness and weather, good or bad luck and the complicated workings of nature fascinate him because they are utterly beyond his comprehension. Indeed, superstition is the basis of the angutkok's hold over his people. It is chiefly for his supposed alliance with the forces of the supernatural that he is venerated. . . . He is supposed to have marvellous powers over bodily ailments. . . . The power of conversation with the ancestral spirits is one of the angutkok's strongest holds upon his public. For the ancestral spirits are said to exert a tremendous influence over the lives of the natives. The Diomeder's

6

attitude toward them is more than one of wholesome respect. It is made up of a definite and deep-seated fear. This is because the spirits, if they choose, can send down either good luck or bad—and usually elect the latter. And clever must be the ruses whereby they may be tricked into benignity. For a departed soul, no matter how kindly has been its earthly owner, is a potential agent of misfortune and must be treated accordingly." (*New York Times Magazine*, Dec. 16, 1928, p. 9.) The methods of incantation, of placating the spirits and gods, the charms and amulets used for these conjurations, differ only in material from those in holy vogue today in some very Christian countries. Angutkok, shaman, medicine-man, exorciser, priest, Pennsylvania Witch-doctors, nature-fakers and superstition-mongers, parasites preying on ignorance and fear—the whole genealogy of dupe-craft, of priest-craft,—what difference in kind and craft is discernible between the one and the others of the god-placating, devil-chasing *Genus Shamanensis?* Bombarding the irate god with eggs, as with the Diomedes, or by the prayer of faith as with more up-to-date God-compellers, the cause is the same, and the effect is equally ineffective and desultory.

The *Catholic Encyclopedia*, describing the Doctors of Divinity as in vogue among sundry African tribes, well describes the entire confraternity in all religions: "Certain specialists, however, exist, known to us as sorcerers, witch-doctors, etc. who are familiar with the mysterious secrets of things, who make use of them on behalf of those interested, and hand them down to chosen disciples." (*CE.* i, 183.) One of the highest and most potent functions of all these primitive shamans and devil-doctors is the conjuring of the infinitude of devils which afflict the inner-works of the superstitious, and work havoc in weather, crops, herds, etc.; the practice and its ceremonial of incantation are very elaborate in some modern schemes: "This ceremony takes up over thirty pages of the Roman Ritual. It is, however, but rarely used—[in these more enlightened and skeptical days], and never without the express permission of the Bishop, for there is *room for no end of deception and hallucination* when it is a question of *dealing with the unseen powers*"! (*CE.* i, 142). Thus the System is yet in vogue; and its priestcraft has waxed very powerful and very wealthy. Artificial Fear and Credulity are its sole source and sustenance. As the Roman poet Lucretius said: "Fear was the first thing on earth to make gods."

Reinach, after a critique of many varied definitions of Religion, thus formulates his own—which a moment's reflection upon the infinite sacred *"Thou Shalt Not's"* of Faith will fully justify: "A sum of scruples (Taboos) which impede the free exercise of our faculties." (*Orpheus*, 1930 ed. p. 3.)

As primitive society progressed towards organization, the Headman of the clan or tribe would find advantage in a close and not disinterested association with the Shaman, whose intimations of good from the spirits or dreadful evil would assist powerfully in the subordination and control of maybe otherwise ambitious or unruly subjects: thus began the coöperation of ruler and priest for the subjection of the ruled. Later yet, as government and priestcraft developed, the ruler was also priest or the priest ruler, as in early Egypt and Assyria, and as in ancient theocratic Israel before the Kings and after the return from Captivity. So too, later, in Greece and Rome. In Egypt and under the Empire in Rome the King was God, in Egypt by divine descent, in Rome by apotheosis. Even Alexander of Macedon was a god by divine generation, as declared by the Pagan Oracle of Jupiter Ammon, to the great scandal of Alexander's mother Olympias, who was wont to complain, "I wish that Alexander would cease from incessantly embroiling me with the wife of Jupiter!" Thus priestcraft thrived and gained immense dominion over the superstitious minds of men, to say nothing of powers and prestige unlimited, privileges, immunities, wealth and aggrandizement beyond rivalry—in ancient Pagan times.

The temples of the ancient gods throughout Pagandom were marvels of sumptuous wealth and beauty, thanks to the lavish munificence of rulers and the offerings of the votaries of the respective false gods. The Temple of Diana at Ephesus, the Parthenon or Temple of the Virgin-goddess at Athens, were wonders of the ancient world. The greatest ruins of antiquity yet standing in splendid ruin or unearthed by the excavations of the archeologists, are the temples of the Pagan gods, testifying in their decayed grandeur to their pristine magnificence and wealth.

Through the priests and the fear of the gods the rulers ruled:

8

PAGAN FRAUDS—CHRISTIAN PRECEDENTS

"Thus saith our god" was the awful sanction of their commands and of their legal enactments. The Hebrews had no word for "religion"; their nearest approximation to the idea is the oft-repeated Bible phrase, "The fear of Yahveh [the Lord]." The ancient Code of Hammurabí, graven on the stela discovered by De Morgan in the ruins of Susa at the beginning of this century and now preserved in the Louvre at Paris, represents the King humbly receiving the Code of Laws from the great god Bel through the Sun-god Shamash; this for its greater sanction to obedience by the superstitious people, who knew no better than to believe the pious fraud of the priests and King. A thousand years more or less later, the Hebrew God Yahveh, along with many divine laws, delivered to Moses his Code of Commandments neatly scratched with his own finger on two stone slabs; of these, like the grave of Moses, no man knoweth the whereabouts unto this day. It was plain but pious fraud for Hammurabí to issue his laws under the name of his god. Common sense and common honesty make us disbelieve and condemn the Hammurabí fraud, and no one chides us for disbelieving it. Perforce we must believe the Moses-tale of identical import, or be dubbed atheists, reviled and ostracized, and be damned in the Christian Hell forever, to boot. Both fables of Divine enactment were invented for and served the same purpose—to dupe the credulous to believe and obey King and Priest. Is it honest?

This principle, involved in the pretense of divine sanctions, and effective through the coöperation of King and Priest for dominion over the ruled, was frankly recognized by many ancient writers, and even by some lauded as salutary for the ignorant. Critias, friend of Socrates, saw the State "with false reason covering truth," which by this device "quenched lawlessness with laws." Diodorus Siculus admitted it to be the duty of the State "to establish effective gods to do the work of police," and laid it down, that "It is to the interest of States to be deceived in religion." Livy admires the wisdom of Numa, who "introduced the fear of the gods as a most efficacious means of controlling an ignorant and barbarous populace." Polybius, the celebrated Greek historian, gives his philosophic admiration to the religious system of the Romans as an effective means of government of the populace:

"In my opinion their object is to use it as a check upon the common people. If it were possible to form a State wholly of philosophers, such a cus-

9

tom would perhaps be unnecessary. But seeing that every multitude is fickle and full of lawless desires, unreasoning anger and violent passions, the only recourse is to keep them in check by mysterious terrors and scenic effects of this sort. Wherefore, to my mind, the ancients were not acting without purpose or at random, when they brought in among the Vulgar those opinions about the gods and the belief in the punishments in Hades." (*Historiæ,* quoted by Glover, *The Conflict of Religions in the Early Roman Empire,* pp. 3–4.)

This pious notion of God and religion as the Big Policeman of the common herd, is not yet extinct. The Attorney General of England, in a celebrated State trial for the sale of a copy of Thomas Paine's *The Age of Reason,* urged to the jury the necessity "to prevent its circulation among the industrious poor"; for, he declaimed, "Of all human beings *they* stand most in need of the consolations of religion; . . . because no man can be expected to be faithful to the *authority of man* who revolts against the government of God"! (*Williams' Case,* 26 *Howard's State Trials,* p. 719; 1798–99.) But times and creeds change; this is the Twentieth century. The professional religionists of today, however, forever dingdong the old "Morality Lie," that without the God-given Ten Commandments and like divine laws, ministered by them and reënacted and enforced by the State—there can be no morality, no human virtues, no decent government. The "True Church" makes mighty boast of its "saving civilization" after the Fall of Rome by the industrious preachment—as we shall amply see —of pious lies and practice of most unholy frauds among the semi-pagan Christian peoples who rose—despite the Church—on the ruins of Rome,—

> " . . . Whilst human kind
> Throughout the lands lay miserably crushed
> Before all eyes beneath Religion—who
> Would show her head along the region skies,
> Glowering on mortals with her hideous face."
> (Lucretius, *De Rerum Natura,* I.)

PAGANISM AT THE CROSS-ROADS WITH CHRISTIANITY

At the time of the advent of "that newer form of Paganism later called Christianity," the Græco-Roman world seethed with religions in a great state of flux and re-formation. Wonder-workers, miracle-mongers, impostors in the guise of gods and Christs abounded. Simon Magus, Apollonius of Tyana, Apuleius, Alexander, Porphyry, Iamblichus,—performed prodigies of divine power and were hailed as genuine gods,—just as were Paul and Barnabas (Acts xiv, 11–12), and, later, Jesus the Christ. Of these Pagan and Jewish "Christs" two will be briefly noted, for their very important Christian contacts and analogies. But first, some analogies of Pagan priestly fakeries.

The petty frauds of the Pagan priests to dupe their credulous votaries would fill a large book; the ancient poets and philosophers, and modern histories of Gentilic religions, abound in instances. Simply for examples of a few of the more common frauds of the Pagan priests, outdone a thousand-fold by the Christian priests and Church, as—(out of the *Catholic Encyclopedia*) we shall see,—we may mention some well-known pious frauds of the Greeks and Romans prevalent around the beginning of the Christian era and forming the religious atmosphere of the times in which the new faith was born and propagated.

False prophecies and miracles and fraudulent relics were the chief reliance among the Pagans, as among the Christians, for stimulating the faith, or credulity, of the ignorant and superstitious masses. The images of the gods were believed to be endowed with supernatural power. Of some, the wounds could bleed; of others, the eyes could wink; of others, the heads could nod, the limbs could be raised; the statues of Minerva could brandish spears, those of Venus could weep; others could sweat; paintings there were which could blush. The Holy Crucifix of Boxley, in Kent, moved, lifted its head, moved its lips and eyes; it was broken up in London, and the springs exposed, and shown to the deriding public; but this relation is out of place,—this was a pious Christian, not Pagan, fake. One of the marvels of many centuries was the vocal statue of Memnon, whose divine voice was heard at the first dawn of day, "the sweet voice of Memnon" which greeted the sun, as sung by poets and attested by inscriptions on the statue made by noted visitors, who credited the assertion of the priests that the voice was that of the god Ammon; the secret was discovered by Wilkinson: a cavity in which a priest was concealed, who struck a stone at sunrise when the worshippers were assembled, thus giving out a melodious ringing sound. Very famous was the Palladium or statue of Minerva, thrown down from heaven by Zeus into Troy, and guarded sacredly in the citadel as protection of the city, which was believed to be impregnable so long as the statue was in the city; Ulysses and Diomede entered the city in disguise and stole out the sacred statue to the Greek camp; thence Æneas is said to have taken it to Italy, where it was preserved in the Temple of Vesta. Many cities of Greece and Rome claimed to have the genuine original. Another miraculous statue of like divine origin was that of "the great goddess, Diana" at Ephesus, which the Townclerk (in Acts xix, 35) declared that all men knew "fell down from Jupiter." Other holy relics galore were preserved and shown to the pious: The Ægis of Jove, forged by Vulcan and ornamented with the head of the Gorgon; the very tools with which the Trojan horse was made, at Metapontum; the sceptre of Pelops, at Chæronea; the spear of Achilles, at Pharselis; the sword of Memnon, at Nicomedia; the hide of the Chalcydonian boar, among the Tegeates; the stone bearing the authentic marks of the trident of Neptune, at Athens; the Cretans exhibited the tomb of Zeus, which earned for them their reputation as Liars. But Mohammedans show the tomb of Adam and Christians that of Peter! There were endless shrines and sanctuaries at which miracle-cures could be performed: oracular temples full of caverns, and secret passages,—that of the Cumæan Sibyl has recently been explored, and its fraudulent devices exposed. The gods themselves came down regularly and ate the fine feasts spread before their statues. In the apocryphal History of Bel and the Dragon, interpolated in the True Church's Book of Daniel (Chapter xiv), the Holy Ghost tells how this hero trapped the priests who stole at night through secret passages into the throne-room of the god and ate the good things furnished by the pious King and people. The gods came frequently to earth, too, and with the connivance of the priests kept amorous tryst in the temples with unsuspecting pious ladies, edifying instances of which are related by Herodotus and Josephus, among other chroniclers of the wiles of priestcraft.

Pagan prodigies of every conceivable kind were articles of popular credulity, affecting the commonalty as well as many of the highest category. The great Emperor Augustus, obedient to dreams, went begging money through the streets of Rome, and used to wear the skin of a seacalf to protect himself against lightning. Tiberius placed greater faith in the efficacy of laurel leaves; both remedies are highly praised by Pliny. Caligula would crawl under the bed in thunder storms; the augurs had listed eleven kinds of lightning with different significations. Comets and dreams portended the gravest crises. Cicero and Valerius Maximus cite numerous instances of dreams being verified by the event. Livy relates with perfect faith innumerable prodigies, though he acutely observed, that "the more prodigies are believed, the more they are announced." The Emperors made numerous enactments against sorcery, divination, and all kinds of magic; the "Christian" Emperor, Constantine, prohibited all forms of magic, but specially excepted and authorized "that which was intended to avert hail and lightning,"—one of the specialties of the Christian priests. Such puerilities of the prevalent superstitions might be multiplied to fill volumes. (See Case, *Experiences with the Supernatural*, etc.)

APOLLONIUS OF TYANA

Apollonius of Tyana was one of the most notable of these wonder-working Christs. So extremely moral and pure were his doctrines and his conduct, and so mighty the works he wrought, that the Pagans insisted that Apollonius was the actual personage whom the Christians called Jesus Christ. By all reports, implicitly credited, Apollonius had raised the dead, healed the sick, cast out devils, freed a young man from a lamia or vampire with whom he was enamored, prophesied, seen in one country events which were occurring in another, as from Ephesus the assassination of Domitian at Rome, and had filled the world with the fame of his miracles and of his sanctity, just as did Jesus Christ. Apollonius was born about the same time as Jesus of Nazareth; the legends of their lives and deeds were very similar; the former, at least, has been justly described as "among that least obnoxious class of impostors, who pretend to be divinely gifted, with a view to secure attention and obedience to precepts, which, delivered in the usual way, would be generally neglected." (Anthon, *Classical Dictionary*, p. 165: see generally, Lecky, *Hist. of European Morals*, i, 372, *passim;* any good Encyclopedia.) Recall the current histories of Mohammed, the Mormon Joseph Smith, Mother Eddy—Jesus Christ—for instances of analogous pretensions.

This customary pretense of wonder-workers is confirmed by the great Church Father Lactantius, in his *Divine Institutes*, dedicated to the "Christian" Emperor Constantine, in which he combated the Pagan imputation that Jesus was a magician, like Apollonius and Apuleius, whose wonder-workings he admits. Like all the Fathers, as we shall see, Lactantius, an ex-Pagan, had firm faith in magic, and believed all the magical wonders of the Pagan magicians as veritable miracles wrought by the divine power of demons or devils. He says that the Pagans "endeavored to overthrow his [Jesus'] wonderful deeds [by showing] that Apollonius performed equal or even greater deeds." But,"It is strange," he argues, "that he omitted to mention Apuleius, of whom many and wonderful things are accustomed to be related. . . . If Christ is a magician because He performed wonderful deeds, it is plain that Apollonius, who, according to your description, when Domitian wished to punish him, suddenly disappeared on his trial, was more skilful than He who was both arrested and crucified. . . . It was evident, therefore, that he [Apollonius] was both a man and a magician; and *for this reason he affected divinity under the title of a name belonging to another [Hercules], for in his own name he was unable to attain it*." (Lact. *Div. Inst.* Bk. V, ch. iii; *ANF.* vii, 138, 139.)

SIMON MAGUS

Most notorious and important, from the viewpoint of the rising Christianity, was the Samaritan impostor, Simon Magus, the "great power of God," vouched for by divine inspiration as having "used sorcery, and bewitched the people of Samaria," he having "of a long time bewitched them with sorceries," as the Holy Ghost of God ridiculously assures us in Acts viii. Not content with his own "great power of God," Simon, having seen some of the apostles at work bestowing the Holy Ghost on the peasants, offered money for the gift of like power to himself, but was curtly rebuked and refused by Peter. The especial importance of Simon Magus is his legendary Scriptural contact with the fisherman Peter, which developed, under the early Christian propensity for expansive mendacity, into a veritable literature of pious lies and prodigies associated with Simon and Peter, which was the chiefest if not sole basis, be it remembered, for the false pretense, later developed, as we shall duly see, of the "sojourn" of Peter at Rome as Bishop and Pope. As these legends of the Samaritan impostor are wholly Christian impostures, the *Catholic Encyclopedia* will be called upon for an account of the Patristic canards. "By his magic arts," says our exponent of "Catholic Truth," Simon was called Magus, or the Magician; the account just given from *Acts* is "the sole authoritative [?] report that we have about him"; and it confesses the chronic mendacity of the Fathers by the remark, "The statements of the [clerical] writers of the second century concerning him are largely legendary, and it is difficult or rather impossible to extract from them any historical fact the details of which are established with certainty." Let us remember this characterization of these same Fatherly writers, who, lying about Simon *and* Peter together, in Rome, yet tell unvarnished truth about Peter alone, or Peter and Paul together, in Rome.

I may remark, that serious argument is made, that Paul himself is maliciously intended by some of the Fathers under the name of Simon, the constant conflict between Paul and Peter being disguised under the accounts of the inveterate struggles of Simon and Peter. (See *Encyc. Bib.* vol. iv, Art. *Simon Magus.*) The childish and fabulous histories of the Fathers regarding Simon and Peter and Paul in Rome and their contests of magic powers, are thus related:

"St. Justin of Rome ('*First Apolog.*' xxvi, lvi; '*Dialog. c. Tryphonem,* cxx), describes Simon as a man who, at the instigation of demons, claimed to be a god. Justin says further that Simon came to Rome during the reign of the Emperor Claudius and by his magic arts won many followers so that these erected on an island in the Tiber a statue to him as a divinity with the inscription 'Simon the Holy God.' The statue, however, that Justin took for one dedicated to Simon was undoubtedly one to the old Sabine divinity Semo Sancus (797) . . . The later anti-heretical writers who report Simon's residence at Rome, take Justin and the apocryphal Acts of Peter as their authority, so that *their testimony is of no value.* [p. 793.] . . .

"Simon plays an important part in the 'Pseudo-Clementines.' He appears here as the chief antagonist of the Apostle Peter, by whom he is everywhere followed and opposed. The alleged magical arts of the magician and Peter's efforts against him are described in a way that is absolutely imaginary. The entire account lacks all historical basis [citing several

15

works]. . . . The apocryphal Acts of St. Peter give an entirely different account of Simon's conduct at Rome and of his death. In this work also great stress is laid upon the struggle between Simon and the Apostles Peter and Paul at Rome. By his magic arts Simon had also sought to win the Emperor Nero for himself, an attempt in which he had been thwarted by the apostles. As proof of the truth of his doctrines Simon offered to ascend into the heavens before the eyes of Nero and the Roman populace; by magic he did rise in the air in the Roman Forum, but the prayers of the Apostles Peter and Paul caused him to fall, so that he was severely injured and shortly afterwards died miserably. . . . This legend led later to the erection of a church dedicated to the apostles on the alleged spot of Simon's fall near the Via Sacra above the Forum. *The stones of the pavement on which the apostles knelt in prayer and which are said to contain the impression of their knees, are now in the wall of the Church of Santa Francesca Romana."* (*CE.* xiii, 797, 798.)

With respect to that statue erected in the Tiber to "Simon the Holy God," the account, above mentioned, does not do justice to Father Justin's invention; it is thus explicit: he says that Simon "performed feats of magic by demonic arts in Rome during the reign of Claudius, was held to be a god, and was honored by Senate and People with a statue in the middle of the Tiber, between the two bridges, bearing the inscription in Latin: '*Simoni, Deo sancto.* . . . To Simon the holy God.' The base of the pillar referred to was dug up on the island in the Tiber, at the place indicated by Justin, in 1574; the inscription, which was deciphered, runs: '*Semoni Sanco deo fidio sacrum . . . Sex. Pompeius . . . donum dedit.*' Thus the pillar was dedicated to the Sabine god Semo Sancus, and not by the Senate and People, but by the piety of a private individual." (*EB.* iv, 4538–9; cf. *CE.* xiii, 797–8.) The same authority, referring to the clerical fabrications above mentioned, says: "The Pseudo-Clementine Homilies and Recognitions contain yet another element of the very greatest importance. In them Simon displays features which are unquestionably derived from Paul, and plainly show him to be a caricature of that apostle drawn by an unfriendly hand." (*EB.* iv, 4540, with citations in proof.) Simon proclaimed as his doctrine—"asserting that none could possibly have salvation without being baptized in his name" (Tert., *Adv. Hæreses*, c. i; *ANF.* iii, 649); which group plagiarized the sentiment from the other, Christians, or Simoneans, I cannot verify.

16

SUPERSTITIONS AND REVELATIONS

The Pagans would appear almost to have been good Christians: they had their gods, (whom they fondly called Saviour and Messiah); the deaths and resurrections of gods; devils, angels, and spirits good, bad and indifferent; their heavens, hells and purgatories; they believed in immortality of the soul,—witness the Pyramids and the tombs of the Kings, as of Tut-ankh-Amen in Egypt, and of the Queen Shub-Ad, just unearthed in Ur of the Chaldees; their elaborate sacrifices, animal and human, even of their dear little children to appease their gods, as in Carthage and Canaan,—a chronic Hebrew practice. Virgin-births of demigods by the intervention of gods and human maids were common-places of Pagan faith, as were Virgin-mothers and god-child: the Christians imported theirs from Egypt—the Madonna statues of Isis and the Child Horus—of universal vogue at the beginning of this era of the Christ—may be seen in almost any first-class Museum, as the Metropolitan in New York and the University in Philadelphia. This popular Pagan device, the "Mother of God" and her God-baby-in-arms, was taken over as a Christian sop to the crowds of Pagans who were being enticed and forced into the Church; it was violently opposed by many of the more intelligent Churchmen: "Nestorius [Bishop of Constantinople about 404] had declared against the *new* and, as he asserted, *idolatrous* expression 'Mother of God' (Theotokos), thereby opposing the *sentiments and wishes of the humbler people*" (*CE.* iii, 101); and in protest Nestorius left the Catholic Church and founded one of the most wide-spread and powerful "heresies," which exists in the East to the present time. The Pagans had their holy mysteries and sacraments, baptisms of water and of blood, communions with the gods at their sacred altars, partaking of sacred meals to ingest the divine spirit and become godlike; they believed in the resurrection of the dead, and in final judgments meting rewards and punishments according to the deeds done in the flesh,—the Egyptian Book of the Dead, 3000 years B. C., giving priestly prescriptions for use before the judgment seat of Osiris, is found in almost every tomb of those able to pay for the hieroglyphic papyrus rolls. The Pagans had their holy days (from which the Christians plagiarized their Christ-

17

mas, Easter, Rogation Days, etc.); their monks, nuns, religious processions carrying images of idols (like those of saints today); incense, holy water, holy oil, chants, hymns, liturgies, confessions of sins to priests, forgiveness of sins by priests, revelations by gods to priests, prophecies, sacred writings of "holy bibles," Pontiffs, Holy Fathers, holy crafty priesthoods. All these sacrosanct things of Christian "Revealed Religion," were age-old pre-Christian Pagan myths and superstitions.

I puzzle myself to understand how there could be "divine revelations," to Jews and Christians, of things which for ages had been indentically ancient Pagan delusions and the inventions and common holy stock in trade of all Pagan priestcrafts. Indeed and in truth, there can be no divine revelation of miraculous "facts" and "heavenly dogmas" which for centuries had been, and in the early Christian ages were, the current mythology of credulous Pagandom. This I shall make exceeding clear.

CHRISTIAN "REVELATION" DEFINED AND DISPROVED

This paragraph is one of the most important in this book, and to it I invite specially serious attention and thought. It will disclose the substantial identity of Christianity with the most popular and widespread "Pagan" religion of the times, Mithraism, or the Persian Zoroastrian religion, the closest and all but successful rival of Christianity in the Roman world, and which might indeed have been successful, but that, soon after Constantine prostituted the Empire to the Church,—"with the triumph of Christianity Mithraism came to a sudden end. The laws of Theodosius signed its death warrant." (*CE.* x, 402.) That there may be no suspicion that the recital of these remarkable identities of Christian "revelation" with Pagan inventions is fanciful or exaggerated, the tale shall be told in the quoted words of the *Catholic Encyclopedia,* which naïvely makes so many extraordinary admissions without seeming to be aware of their fatal implications.

"The essence of Revelation lies in the fact that it is the direct speech of God to man," says the Holy Ghost speaking through the Vatican

Council (1870), thus confirming what I have above said, that "divine revelation" cannot be of Pagan myths already current and long known to everyone. The same Heavenly Instructor tells us what Revelation is: "Revelation may be defined as the communication of some truth by God to a rational creature through means which are beyond the ordinary course of nature. The truths thus revealed may be such as are otherwise inaccessible to the human mind—*mysteries*, which even when *revealed*, the intellect of man is incapable of fully penetrating. . . . The Decree 'Lamentabili' (3 July, 1907) declares that the dogmas which the Church proposes *as revealed* are '*truths which have come down to us from heaven*' and *not* 'an interpretation of religious facts *which the human mind has acquired* by its own strenuous efforts.' " (*Vatican Decrees*, 1870; *CE.* xiii, 1.) And, asserts *CE.*: "The existence of revelation is as reasonably established as any historical fact"! (*CE.* xiii, 607.) Isn't *CE.* funny!

Divine Revelation is thus of things not previously known and which the revelationless mind of man is incapable of acquiring or inventing by its own efforts. Divine Revelation rests thus upon the same principle as the Law of Patents and Copyright. A book published, that is made known and given to the world cannot be the subject of subsequent copyright even by its author. When an application for a patent is presented, the first act is to search the records to ascertain whether a similar art or article has ever previously been known and in use: if so, no patent can be obtained: the thing lacks novelty. So exactly with "revelation": if some impostor or deluded person (*e. g.* Mohammed or Joseph Smith) claims that he has received a personal—and therefore necessarily private—"revelation" from some god, the only way whereby he can get a valid patent of authenticity and credibility for his "revelation," is to prove that its subject-matter has never before been known and in credulous circulation; the moment that from the search of the records—of other, or comparative religions,—it is shown that the same proposition has been previously known and current, in use and practice among some other priestcraft and its votaries—the thing is no revelation: the claim is a fraud. Let us see how this indisputable rule works to the destruction and proof of fraudulency of the "divine revelations" of Christian credulity.

19

MITHRAISM—AND CHRISTIAN MYTH

The Religion of Zoroaster, known as Mithraism, is confessed by *CE.* to be a *divinely revealed Monotheism*, or worship of a One God, and having a divinely revealed Moral Code comparable to the Christian,—a sacred system claimed by Christians to be a monopoly of the Hebrew-Christian religion to the exclusion of all heathen systems. This notable confession reads: "The Avesta system may be best defined as MONOTHEISM, modified by a physical and moral dualism, with an ethical system based on a *Divinely revealed* moral code and human free will." (*CE.* ii, 156.) Though it quotes a Jesuit as saying: "Mithraism is the highest religious result to which human reason *unaided* by Revelation, can attain." (*Id.*) Revealed or invented, it is virtually identical with Christianity; but as the mythic Mithraic god could not "reveal" anything, the human reason which devised Mithraism was quite equal to the Christian God so far as devising mythology and ethics is an attribute of godhead.

Mithraism is one of the oldest religious systems on earth, as it dates from the dawn of history before the primitive Iranian race divided into the sections which became Persian and Indian, as this same religion is contained both in the Persian Avesta and Indian Vedas. Thus its "revealed" or invented Monotheism by ages outdates the "revelation" of Yahveh to Moses; and it is yet a living faith to some thousands of surviving Parsees: "The religious cult is [yet] scrupulously maintained as of old. The ancient traditional and nationally characteristic national virtues of truth and open-handed generosity flourish exceedingly in the small, but highly intelligent community" of Parsees in India. (*CE.* ii, 156.)

The religion of Mithra anciently dominated Persia and the vast regions of the Orient; it entered Europe following the conquests of Alexander the Great. When in 65–63 B. C. the conquering armies of Pompey were largely converted by its high precepts, they brought it with them into the Roman Empire. Mithraism spread with great rapidity throughout the Empire, and was adopted, patronized and protected by a number of the Emperors up to the time of Constantine; it was only overthrown by the proscriptive laws and sword of Constantine and Theodosius, who "signed its death warrant" at the behest of.

20

the triumphant and intolerant Christians, who absorbed virtually the entire system of Mithraism. But let *CE.* proceed with the story. The reader is asked to check mentally each of the uninspired details of Pagan invention with the "divinely revealed" *identities* of the Christian Faith.

"MITHRAISM"—PRE-CHRISTIAN CHRISTIANITY

"Mithraism is a pagan religion consisting mainly of the cult of the ancient Indo-Iranian Sun-God Mithra. It entered Europe from Asia Minor after Alexander's conquest, spread rapidly over the whole Roman Empire at the beginning of our era, reached its zenith during the third century, and vanished under the *repressive regulations* of Theodosius at the end of the fourth. [Of late it has been] brought into prominence mainly because of its supposed [?] *similarity to Christianity.*

"The origin of the cult of Mithra dates from the time that Hindus and Persians still formed one people, for the god Mithra occurs in the religion and sacred books of both races, *i. e.* in the Vedas and in the Avesta. . . . After the conquest of Babylon (538 B. c.) this Persian cult came into contact with Chaldean astrology and with the national worship of Marduk. For a time the two priesthoods of Mithra and Marduk coexisted in the capital and Mithraism borrowed much from this intercourse. . . . This religion, in which the Iranian element remained predominant, came, after Alexander's conquest, in touch with the Western world. When finally the Romans took possession of the Kingdom of Pergamum (in 133 B. c.), occupied Asia Minor, and stationed two legions of soldiers on the Euphrates, *the success of Mithraism was secured.* It spread rapidly from the Bosphorus to the Atlantic, from Illyria to Britain. Its foremost apostles were the legionaries; hence it spread first to the frontier stations of the Roman army.

"Mithraism was emphatically a soldier religion; Mithra, its hero, was especially a divinity of fidelity, manliness, and bravery; the stress it laid on good-fellowship and brotherliness, its exclusion of women, and the secret bond among its members have suggested the idea that Mithraism was Masonry among the Roman soldiery." Several of the Roman Emperors, down to Licinius, colleague of Constantine, built temples to Mithra, and issued coins with his symbols. "But with the triumph of Christianity [after Constantine] Mithraism came to a sudden end. The laws of Theodosius [proscribing it under penalty of death, to please the Christians] signed its death warrant. Though he was still worshipped a thousand years later by the Manichees. (p. 402). . . .

"*Ahura Mazda and Ahriman.*—This incarnate evil (Ahriman) rose with the army of darkness to attack and depose Oromasdes (Ahura Mazda).

21

They were however thrown back into hell, whence they escape, wander over the face of the earth and afflict man. . . . As evil spirits ever lie in wait for hapless man, he needs a friend and *saviour, who is Mithra.* . . . *Mithra is the Mediator between God and Man.* The Mithraists . . . battled on Mithra's side against all impurity, against all evil within and without. They believed in the immortality of the soul; sinners after death were dragged down to hell; the just passed through the seven spheres of the planets, leaving at each planet a part of their lower humanity until, as pure spirits, they stood before God. At the end of the world Mithra will descend to earth, . . . and will make all drink the beverage of immortality. He will thus have proved himself *Nabarses,* 'the never conquered.' . . .

"The *fathers* conducted the worship. The chief of the fathers, a sort of *pope, who always lived at Rome,* was called 'Pater Patratus' . . . The members below the grade of pater called one another 'brother,' and social distinctions were forgotten in Mithraic unity. . . . A *sacred meal* was celebrated of bread and haoma juice for which in the West wine was substituted. This meal was supposed to give the participants *supernatural virtue.* . . .

"Three times a day prayer was offered the sun towards east, south, or west according to the hour. SUNDAY was *kept holy* in honour of Mithra, and the sixteenth of each month was sacred to him as *Mediator.* The *25 December* was observed as *his birthday,* the Natalis Invictis, the rebirth of the winter-sun, unconquered by the rigours of the season." (pp. 403–404.) It may be noted that Sunday was made a Pagan holiday by edict of Constantine. In the fifth Tablet of the Babylonian (Chaldean) Epic of Creation, by the great God Marduk, we read, lines 17 and 18: "On the *seventh day* he appointed *a holy day,* And to cease from all work he commanded." (*Records of the Past,* vol. ix; quoted, Clarke, *Ten Great Religions,* ii, p. 383.)

To resume with *CE.*: "No proof of immorality or obscene practices has ever been established against Mithraism; and as far as can be ascertained, or rather conjectured, it had an elevating and invigorating effect on its followers. [So different from Christianity!] . . .

"*Relation to Christianity.*—A similarity between Mithra and Christ struck even early observers, such as Justin, Tertullian, and other Fathers, and in recent times has been urged to prove *that Christianity is but an adaptation of Mithraism,* or at least the outcome of the same religious ideas and aspirations. Some apparent [they are *very* apparent] similarities exist; but in a number of *details*—[it is substance that is identical]—it is quite as probable that Mithraism was the borrower from Christianity.—[But these essential identities are found in the Vedas and Avesta, of maybe two thousand years before Christianity; Zoroaster, who gave final form to the creed, lived some 600 years before the Christ!]—It is not unnatural to suppose that a religion which swept the whole world, should have been copied at least in some details by another religion which was quite popular during the third century—[and for nine, or twenty centuries before!] Similarity in words and names means nothing; it is the *sense* that matters. [To be sure; we proceed to see more of the sense—the essence—to be identical] . . .

"Mithra is called a *mediator;* and so is Christ . . . And so in similar instances. Mithraism had a *Eucharist,* but the idea of the sacred banquet is as old as the human race and existed at all ages and amongst all peoples.—[Not much "divine revelation" in this the greatest of Christian mysteries!].—Mithra *saved the world* by sacrificing a bull—[just as the Jews saved themselves]; Christ by sacrificing Himself. . . . Mithraism was all comprehensive and *tolerant* of every other cult; Christianity was essentially *exclusive, condemning every other religion in the world,* alone and unique in its majesty." (*CE.* x, 402–404.)

But this "unique majesty" was hidden away in the catacombs of Rome for quite three centuries; coming out, it condemned and persecuted to death every other religion because rivals for the rich perquisites of priestcraft and dominion.

The above striking analogies, or identities, between the ages-old Mithraism and the "newer Paganism called Christianity," compelling as they are of the certainty of "borrowing" by Christianity, are dwarfed by the evidences now to be presented in the confessions of *CE.,* that the Jews first, then the Christians, took over bodily from the Babylonians and the Persians, not only the entire celestial and infernal systems of those two closely related religions, but virtually that high ethic, or moral code—"the highest religious result to which human reason unaided by revelation, can attain,"—which Christians so loudly pretend is, by "divine revelation" of their God—theirs alone, while all other peoples "sat in darkness and in the shadow of death" without its saving light. Christianity looks with disdain on the Mithraic religion because it is a "dualism"; that is, the Evil Spirit was separately created apart from the Good God; while it is a fundamental tenet of the Christian Faith, that its God himself created the Christian Devil and all evil—and is therefore morally responsible for all his deviltry.

Speaking particularly of Angelology,—though the admission will be found to apply to all the other features to be noticed,—*CE.* shows

23

that all this is an importation into Judaism from the Persians and Babylonians: "That the Persian domination and the Babylonian Captivity exercised a large influence upon the Hebrew *conception*—[*not*, therefore, a revelation]—of the angels is acknowledged in the Talmud of Jerusalem (Rosh Haschanna, 56), where it is said that [even] *the names of the angels were introduced from Babylon*. . . . Stress has been laid upon the similarity of the 'seven who stand before God' and the seven Amesha-Spentas of the Zend-Avesta. . . . It is easy for the student to trace the influence of surrounding nations and of other religions in the Biblical account of angels" (*CE*. i, 481);—which seriously cripples the notion of divine revelation regarding these celestial messengers of God. Again it indicates the "connection between the angels of the Bible, and the 'great archangels' or 'Amesha-Spentas' of the Zend-Avesta"; also "we find an interesting parallel to the 'angel of the Lord' in Nebo, 'the minister of Merodach.' . . . The Babylonian *sukalli* corresponded to the spirit-messengers of the Bible; they declared their Lord's will and executed his behests." . . . "The belief in guardian angels . . . was also the belief of the Babylonians and Assyrians"; the origin of the Bible "cherubim" was the same, as also of guardian angels, "as their monuments testify, for a figure now in the British Museum might well serve for a modern representation." For detailed accounts, see the articles "Angels" and "Guardian Angels," in *CE*. And so of Demons and Demonology, and Demoniac possession: "In many ways one of the most remarkable demonologies is that presented in the Avesta"; Ahriman being their chief devil, or *Daeva;* "the original meaning of the word is 'shining one,' and it comes from a primitive Aryan root *div*, which is *likewise the source* of the Greek Zeus and the Latin Deus. But while these words, like the Sanskrit *deva*, retain the good meaning, *daeva* has come to mean 'an evil spirit.' There is at least a coincidence, *if no deeper* significance, in the fact that, while the word in its original sense was synonymous with 'Lucifer,' it has now come to mean much the same as *devil*" (*CE*. iv, 714–15, *pasism;* 764). Lucifer, in the Bible, having also been originally "a shining one" in Heaven, was cast out into Hell and is now the Devil.

With these preliminaries of identity between the invention of angels and devils of Mithraic Paganism and Hebrew-Christian "revelation," we will now let *CE.* confess further identities, both of "revelation" and of the "divinely revealed moral code,"—summarized from the Mithraic Zend-Avesta. We seem to be reading the Catechism or a tract on "Christian Evidences."

"The name of the Supreme God of the Avestic system is Ahura Mazda, which probably signifies the All-Wise Lord. . . . Ahura Mazda is a pure Spirit; his chief attributes are eternity, wisdom, truth, goodness, majesty, power. He is the creator of all good creatures—*not*, however, of Evil, of evil beings—[as is the Christian God]. He is the supreme Lawgiver, the Rewarder of moral good, and the Punisher of moral evil. He dwells in Eternal Light, . . . a kind of manifestation of His presence, like the Old Testament *Shekinah.* . . . We find frequent enumerations of the attributes of Ahura Mazda; thus these are said to be 'omniscience, all-sovereignty, all goodness.' Again He is styled 'Supreme Sovereign, Wise Creator, Supporter, Protector, Giver of good things, Virtuous in acts, Merciful, Pure Lawgiver, Lord of the Good Creations.' . . .

"Opposed to Ahura Mazda, or Ormuzd, is His rival, Anro Mainyus, (later Ahriman), the Evil Spirit. He is conceived as existing quite independently of Ahura Mazda, apparently from eternity, but destined to destruction at the end of time. Evil by nature and in every detail the exact opposite of Ahura Mazda, he is the creator of all evil, both moral and physical.—[But of the Christian God: "I Jehovah create evil"; *Isa.* xlv, 7]. . . .

"The specific name of Ahura Mazda in opposition to the Evil Spirit is Spento Mainyus, THE HOLY SPIRIT: and Ahura Mazda and Spento Mainyus are synonymous throughout the Avesta. [p. 154]. . . .

"Around Ahura Mazda is a whole hierarchy of spirits, corresponding very closely to our 'angels.' . . . Of the good spirits who surround Ahura, the most important are the Amesha Spentas ('Holy Immortals' or 'Holy Saints'), generally reckoned as six in number (but seven when Ahura Mazda is included). . . . Most of all Vohu Manah rises to a position of unique importance. . . . Vohu Manah is conceived as the 'SON OF THE CREATOR,' and *identified* with the Alexandrian LOGOS [of John i, 1]. Asha, also, is the Divine Law, Right, Sanctity (cf. Psalm 118), and occupies a most conspicuous place throughout the Avesta. . . . With him are associated in a trio [TRINITY], Rashnu (Right, Justice), and MITHRA.—[These Aryan names sound unfamiliar; but as *CE.* has assured, "names mean nothing; it is the sense that matters";—and here we have the whole Jewish-Christian hierarchies of Heaven and Hell a thousand years before Jewish-Christian "revelation" identities!] . . .

"Face to face with the hierarchy of celestial spirits is a diabolical one, that of the *daevas* (Pers. *div* or *dev*) and *druj's* of the Evil Spirit. They

fill exactly the places of the *devils* in Christian and Jewish theology. . . .
Perhaps the most frequently mentioned of all is Aeshma, the Demon of
Wrath or Violence, *whose name has come down to us* in the Asmodeus
(*Aeshmo daeva*) of the Book of Tobias [Tobit]. . . .

"In the midst of the secular warfare that has gone on from the beginning between the two hosts of Good and Evil stands Man. Man is the creature of the Good Spirit, but endowed with a free will and power of choice,
able to place himself on the side of Ahura Mazda or on that of Anro Mainyus. The former has given him, through His Prophet Zarathushtra (Zoroaster) *His Divine Revelation and law.* According as man obeys or disobeys
this Divine Law his future lot will be decided; *by it he will be judged at his
death.* The whole ethical system is built upon this great principle, *as in
the Christian theology*—["revelation"?]. Moral good, righteousness, sanc-
tity(asha) is according to the Divine will and decrees; Man by his *free
will* conforms to, or transgresses, these. The Evil Spirit and his innumerable hosts tempt Man to deny or transgress the Divine Law, *as he tempted
Zoroaster himself, promising him as a reward the sovereignty of the whole
world.*—[Exactly Jesus and the Devil.]—'No,' replied the Prophet, 'I will
not renounce it, even if body and soul and life should be severed!' (Vendi-
dad, xix, 25, 26).—["Thou shalt not tempt the Lord thy God, for it is
written,"—may sound more Godlike but maybe little more heroic.] . . .

"The moral teaching *is closely akin to our own.* Stress is constantly laid
on the necessity of goodness in thought, word, and deed.—["Through the
Three Steps, the good thought, the good word, and the good deed, I enter
Paradise."]—Note the emphatic recognition of sin in thought. Virtues and
vices are enumerated and estimated *much as in Christian ethics.* Special
value is attributed to the virtues of religion, truthfulness, purity, and generosity to the poor (p. 155). Heresy, untruthfulness, perjury, sexual sins,
violence, tyranny, are especially reprobated. . . .

"The soul of the just passes over the bridge into *a happy eternity, into
heaven,* the abode of Ahura and His blessed angels. The wicked soul falls
from the fatal bridge and is precipitated *into hell.* Of this abode of misery
a lively description occurs in the later Pahlavi 'Vision of Arda Viraf,'
whose visit to *the Inferno,* with realistic description of *the torments,*
vividly recalls that of Dante. . . .

"At the end of time, the approach of which is described in the Pahlavi
literature *in terms strikingly like those of our Apocalypse,* will come
Saoshyant (SAVIOUR) under whom will occur the *Resurrection of the
Dead,* the *General Judgment,* the *renewal of the whole world*—["a new
heaven and a new earth"]—*by a general conflagration* and terrible flood of
burning matter ["the heavens being on fire shall be dissolved, and the elements shall melt with fervent heat"]. This terrible flood will purify all
creatures; even the wicked will be purified from all stains, and even hell
will be cleansed and added to the 'new heavens and new earth.' Meanwhile
26

a mighty combat takes place between Soashyant [the "Saviour"] and his followers and the demon hosts of the Evil Spirit, who are utterly routed and destroyed forever. . . .

"The highest religious result to which human reason unaided by Revelation can attain"! (*CE.* ii, 154–156, *passim.*)

Thus "human reason unaided by revelation" had attained, ages before Moses, the Prophets, and Jesus Christ, a system of religious beliefs and a moral code in substantial identity with the "divine revelations" of God to Moses, the Prophets, and his Son Jesus Christ. At the time of the Advent of the Latter, and for three hundred years later, throughout the Roman Empire, that is, throughout the well-known world, this wonderful Pagan invention, with its "Pope" and Seat in Imperial Rome, and patronized by the Emperors, lived along side with and mightily rivalled the struggling Faith hid in the catacombs,— until its rival Christians got hold of the sword under Constantine, and "triumphed," its "death warrant was signed" in blood by the laws of the persecuting Christians. Did any God wondrously "reveal" to the Christians these holy Pagan dreams and myths? What a waste of while for a God to mysteriously "reveal" these "heathen deceits" thousands of years old, and that everybody in the world already knew!

BUDDHISM IN CHRISTIANITY

The account given by *CE.* of the Lord Buddha and of Buddhism, by the simple substitution of the names Christ—[the Saviour of Buddhism is Crishna, the "incarnation" of the supreme god Vishnu]— and Christianity, might well be mistaken for a homily on our own holy faith and its Founder—who would no more recognize present-day Christianity than would Buddha the crass superstition which is today tagged with his holy name. Says *CE.:*

"It is noteworthy that Buddha was a contemporary of two other famous religious philosophers, Pythagoras and Confucius. In the sacred books of later times Buddha is depicted as a character without a flaw, adorned with every grace of mind and heart. There may be some hesitation in taking the highly colored portrait of Buddhist tradition as an exact representation of the original, but Buddha may be credited with the qualities of a great and good man. . . . In all pagan antiquity no character has been depicted as so noble and attractive. . . .

27

"Buddha's order was composed only of those who renounced the world to live a life of contemplation *as monks and nuns.* . . . [In the time of King Asoka, 3rd century B. C.] Buddhism was in a most flourishing condition; it had become a formidable rival of the older religion [Brahmanism], while a tolerant and kindly spirit—[unknown to Christianity]—was displayed towards other forms of religion. . . . [By the seventh century A. D.—here it parallels Christianity again] an excessive devotion to statues and relics, the employment of magic arts to keep off evil spirits, and the observance of many gross superstitions, complete the picture of Buddhism, a sorry representation of what Buddha made known to men. . . . The vast majority of the adherents of Buddhism cling to forms of creed and worship that Buddha, if alive, would reprobate—[as would Christ in the case of Christianity]. Northern Buddhism became the very opposite of what Buddha taught to men, and in spreading to foreign lands *accommodated itself to the degrading superstitions of the people it sought to win*—[precisely as we shall see that Christianity did to inveigle the Pagans]. . . .

"Between Buddhism and Christianity there are a number of resemblances, at first sight striking. The Buddhist order of monks and nuns offers points of similarity with Christian monastic systems, particularly the mendicant orders. There are *moral aphorisms* ascribed to Buddha that are *not unlike* some of *the sayings of Christ.* Most of all, in the legendary life of Buddha . . . there are *many parallelisms,* some more, some less striking, *to the Gospel stories of Christ.* A few *third rate scholars* [contend that these are borrowings from Buddhism. Why not, as everything else is "borrowed" or filched?]. . . .

"One of its most attractive features . . . was *its practice of benevolence* towards the sick and needy. Between Buddhists and Brahmins there was a *commendable rivalry in maintaining dispensaries of food and medicine"* —long claimed as a holy monopoly of "Christian charity." (*CE.* iii, 28– 34, *passim.*)

As elsewhere recounted, the Holy Ghost made a curious mistake in inspiring the certification of sundry Saints, and the Lord Buddha was himself canonized by Holy Church, as St. Josaphat, and the "Life" of this holy Saint was highly edifying to the Faithful as well as effective in spreading the Christian truth: "During the Middle Ages the 'Life of Barlaam and Josaphat' had been translated into some twenty languages, English included, so that *in reality the story of Buddha became the vehicle of Christian truth* in many nations"! (*CE.* i, 713.)

It is now evident, and will further so appear, that there is no single novel feature nor "revealed truth" in all the Christian religion: our

28

Holy Faith is all a hodgepodge or pot pourri of the credulities of every superstition from Afric Voodooism to the latest one anywhere in holy vogue among the credulous. Even our "idea" of God with its superlatives of "revealed" high attributes is very primitive: "The *idea* of a Being higher than man, invisible, inaccessible, master of life and death, orderer of all things, seems to exist everywhere, among the Negritos, the Hottentots, the Bantu, the Nigritians, the Hamites; for everywhere this Being has a name. He is the 'Great,' the 'Ancient One,' the 'Heavenly One,' the 'Bright One,' the 'Master,' sometimes the 'Author' or 'Creator'. . . . Nowhere is He represented under any image, for He is incapable of representation." (*CE.* i, 183, 184.)

Cardinal Newman, commenting on Dean Milman's "History of the Jews," groups a number of these Paganisms in Christianity, and says that Milman arrays facts "admitted on all hands," to wit: "that the doctrine of the Logos is Platonic; that of the Incarnation Indian; that of a divine Kingdom Judaic; that of angels and demons (and a Mediator) Persian; that the connection of sin with the body is Gnostic; the idea of a new birth Chinese and Eleusinian; that of sacramental virtue Pythagorian; that of Trinity common to East and West; and that of the rites of baptism and sacrifice equally ubiquitous"! (Newman, *Essays, Critical and Historical*, 7th ed., p. 231; as summarized by the Rt. Hon. J. M. Robertson in *A History of Freethought in the XIXth Century*, p. 145–6. London, 1929.)

Such is our holy Christian "Faith which was once delivered unto the saints," which "superstition, drunk in with their mother's milk," yet persists with the ignorant and those who do not or will not know the truth.

That Christianity is indeed but a "new form of Paganism," and especially after it became the official or State religion, consciously and purposely, in furtherance of the Imperial policy of "One State, one Religion," perfected the amalgamation of the salient features of all the fluxing religions of the Empire so as to bring all Pagans within the one State-Church, is accredited by secular and Church history; and is quite ingenuously revealed by *CE.*, treating of the influence of Constantine on Christianity:

"Long before this, belief in the old polytheism had been shaken. The world was fully ripe for monotheism or its modified form, henotheism; but this monotheism offered itself in varied guises, under the forms of Oriental religions: in the worship of the Sun, in the veneration of Mithras, in Judaism, and in Christianity. Whoever wished to make a violent break with the past and his surroundings sought out some Oriental form of worship which did not demand from him too great a sacrifice. Some . . . believed that they could appropriate [the truth contained in Judaism and Christianity] without being obliged on that account to renounce the beauty of other worships. Such a man was the Emperor Alexander Severus (222–235); another so minded was Aurelian (270–275), whose opinions were confirmed by Christians like Paul of Samosata. Not only Gnostics and other heretics, but *Christians who considered themselves faithful, held in a measure to the worship of the Sun.* Leo the Great in his day (440–461) says that *it was the custom of many Christians to stand on the steps of the Church of St. Peter and pay homage to the Sun by obeisance and prayers.*

"When such conditions prevailed it is easy to understand that many of the emperors yielded to the delusion that they could *unite all their subjects* in the adoration of *the one Sun-god who combined in himself* the Father-God of the Christians and the much-worshipped Mithras; thus *the empire could be founded anew on the unity of religion.* It looks almost as though the last persecution of the Christians were directed more against all irreconcilables and extremists than against the great body of Christians. . . .

"It was especially in the West that the veneration of Mithras predominated—[after centuries of Christianity!]. Would it not be possible to gather all the different nationalities around his altars? Could not Sol Deus Invictus, to whom even Constantine dedicated his coins for a long time, or Sol Mithras Deus Invictus, venerated by Diocletian and Galerius, become the supreme god of the empire? Constantine . . . had not absolutely rejected the thought even after a miraculous event [!] had strongly influenced him in favour of the God of the Christians,—[who, however, worshipped the Sun!] . . .

"For a time it seemed as if *merely tolerance and equality* were to prevail. Constantine showed equal favour to both religions. As pontifex maximus he watched over the heathen worship and protected its rights. . . . In the dedication of Constantinople in 330 a ceremonial half pagan, half Christian was used. The chariot of the Sun-god was set in the market-place, and over its head was placed the Cross of Christ—[*not* the original, which his mother had not yet been reputed by the priests to have discovered—*i. e.* "invented,"—of which more anon], while the Kyrie Eleison was sung. Shortly before his death Constantine confirmed the *privileges of the priests* of the ancient gods. . . .

"In the same way religious freedom and tolerance could not continue as a form of equality; the age was not ready for such a conception: [with more of the like, p. 299;—which is untrue, as Constantine himself had proclaimed religious freedom in the Edict of Milan of 313, and we have just seen it admitted in Buddhism, and it prevailed at all times in the Roman Empire, until the "Christian Emperors" gave the Church the sword, as in Chapter VII exemplified]. . . . *Without realizing the full import of his actions,* Constantine granted the Church one privilege after another. As early as 313 the Church obtained immunity for its ecclesiastics, *including freedom from taxation.* . . . Constantine moreover *placed Sunday under the protection of the State*—[*as a Pagan holiday,* as cited. *post*]. It is true that *the believers in Mithras also observed Sunday as well as Christmas.* Consequently Constantine speaks *not* of the day of the Lord, but of the everlasting day of the Sun. . . .

"Of Constantine's sons the eldest, Constantine II, showed decided leanings to heathenism, and his coins bear many pagan emblems; the second and favourite son, Constantius, was a more pronounced Christian, but it was Arian—[anti-Divinity of Christ]—Christianity to which he adhered. Constantius was an unwavering opponent of paganism; he *closed all the temples and forbade sacrifices under pain of death.* His maxim was: *'Cesset superstitio; sacrificiorum aboleatur insania'*—('Let superstition cease; let the folly of sacrifices be abolished'). *Their successors had recourse to persecution against heretics and pagans.* Their laws (Cod. Theod. XVI, v; [*post, Chapter VII*]) had an unfavourable influence on the Middle Ages and *were the basis* of the *much-abused* [!] Inquisition." (*CE.* iv, 297–301, *passim.*)

Thus was the ultimate merger and total identity of Paganism with "the new Paganism called Christianity" finally established by law and by Imperial policy of "One State and One Religion," to which conformity was enforced by laws of confiscation and death; all the other religions of the Empire were fused by fire and sword into a bastard Christianity; and the mental and moral benightedness known as the Dark Ages of Faith fell as a pall over Christendom for a thousand years until the renaissance of Pagan culture and freedom of thought darkly dawned over the world, and has fearfully struggled into a brightening day, whose motto of Hope is again *"Cesset Superstitio"!* when Constantine's funest "League with Death and Covenant with Hell" of State and Church will soon in reality be a forgotten Scrap of Paper!

ALL DEVILISH IMITATIONS!

The pious Christian Fathers were themselves sorely puzzled and scandalized by these same things; their books are replete with naïve

31

attempts to explain the mystery of it,—which they attributed to the blasphemous wiles of the Devil,—that "the Devil had blasphemously imitated the Christian rites and doctrines";—"always seeing in pagan analogies the trickery of devils." (*CE.* xi, 393.) "It having reached the Devil's ears," says the devout Father Justin Martyr, "that the prophets had foretold the coming of Christ, the Son of God, he set the heathen Poets to bring forward a great many who should be called the sons of Jove. The Devil laying his scheme in this, to get men to imagine that the *true* history of Christ was of the same character as the prodigious fables related of the sons of Jove." (I *Apology,* ch. 54; *ANF.* i, 181–182.)

Not only the Fathers, but the Bible, Hebrew and Christian, recognized and affirmed the actuality and ever-living reality of the Pagan gods, though the late post-exilic writer of the 95th Psalm maliciously dubs them devils: "All the gods [Heb. *elohim*] of the nations are devils" (Heb. *elilim*—not much difference between them—in Hebrew; Ps. xcvi, 5); and this view the Christian forger of the Epistle under the name of Paul to the Corinthians confirms: "The things which the Gentiles sacrifice, they sacrifice to devils" (I Cor. x, 20). Though these malevolent flings at the venerable divinities of Pagandom are in direct violation of the Siniatic Law of God—"Thou shalt not revile the gods" (Ex. xxii, 28);—the Hebrew Yahveh being, according to divine revelation, simply one of many gods—"a God above all gods," even "God of gods and Lord of lords," who "judgeth among the [other] gods."

Fathers Justin, Tertullian, and many another, says the *CE.,* could only "see in all pagan law and ritual an immense pillage of Jewish traditions, and, in all the gods, Moses"; the error and folly of which notion, argues our authority, is demonstrated by reference to Middleton's *Letter from Rome,* in which he, with Calvin, "saw an exact conformity between popery and paganism." (*CE.* xii, 393.) Whether Middleton and Calvin were so far in error and folly in this opinion, our researches will reveal. Collins, too, in his *Discourse,* supports with good authorities the opinions of Middleton and Calvin. He cites Father Origen as "so far from disowning an agreement between [Pagan] Platonism and Christianity, that a great part of his book *Contra Celsum* consists in showing the conformity between them."

32

Likewise, he says, Amelius, a heathen Platonist, who flourished in the third century, upon reading the first verses of St. John the Evangelist, exclaimed: "*Per Jovem, barbarus iste cum nostro Platone sentit*—By Jove, this barbarian agrees with our Plato"; and he quotes the celebrated saying of Cardinal Palavicino—"*Senza Aristotele noi mancavamo di molti Articoli di Fede*—Without Aristotle we should be without many Articles of Faith." (Collins, *Discourse of Free Thinking*, p. 127.)

Not only did the Fathers and the Church admit with implicit faith the living reality of the gods of heathendom, their powers, oracles, miracles and other "analogies" to the Christian faith, they even made of such analogies their strongest apologies, or arguments, in defense of the truth of the Christian tenets. In his *Apologia* addressed to the Emperor Hadrian, Father Justin reasons from analogy thus:

"By declaring the Logos, the first-begotten of God, our Master, Jesus Christ, to be born of a Virgin, without any human mixture, we [Christians] say no more in this than what you [Pagans] say of those whom you style the Sons of Jove. For you need not be told what a parcel of sons the writers most in vogue among you assign to Jove. . . .

"As to the Son of God, called Jesus, should we allow him to be nothing more than man, yet the title of 'the Son of God' is very justifiable, upon the account of his wisdom, considering that you [Pagans] have your Mercury in worship under the title of The Word, a messenger of God. . . .

"As to his [Jesus] being born of a Virgin, you have your Perseus to balance that." (Justin, *Apologia*, I, ch. xxii; *ANF*. i, 170.)

The good Fathers carried their argument by analogy into proof of all sorts of holy Christian mysteries; the Pagan Oracles and miracles were undeniably valid and true, why not therefore their new Christian counterparts? "Without a single exception," says the historian of European Morals, "the Fathers maintained the reality of the Pagan miracles as fully as their own. The oracles had been ridiculed and rejected by numbers of the philosophers, but the Christians unanimously admitted their reality. They appealed to a long series of Oracles as predictions of their faith; not until 1696 was there a denial of their supernatural character, when a Dutch Anabaptist minister, Van Dale, in a remarkable book, *De Origine Progressu Idolatriae*, asserted in opposition to the unanimous voice of ecclesiastical authority, that they were simple impostures." (Lecky, *History of European Morals*, i, 374–375, *et seq.*; see pp. 378–381, *et seq.*) The Christian Fathers and their followers made themselves so ridiculous by their fatuous faith in the Sibyls that they were derisively called "Sibyllists" by the Pagans.

THE SIBYLLINE ORACLES

The most curious in all respects, and for our present purposes the most instructive of the ancient Pagan religious frauds, are the Sibylline Oracles, which, extensively reinforced by Jewish and Christian forgeries, were perhaps the most potent and popular "proofs" of the early Church for the divinity of Jesus Christ and the truth of the Christian religion; thus they deserve special notice here. All will remember, from their school histories of ancient Rome, the well-known legend of one of the Sibyls who came to King Tarquin the Second with nine volumes of Oracles, which she offered to sell to him for a very high price; being refused, she went away and burned three of the books, and returning offered the remaining six at the same price; again the King refused to buy, and she departed, burned three more of the books, and returned with the last three for which she demanded the original price. Astonished at this conduct and greatly impressed, the King consulted his augurs and was advised to secure the remaining treasures of prophecy before it was too late; he did so, and immediately the Seeress disappeared and was never seen again. The precious tomes were deposited with great care and jealously guarded in the Temple of Jupiter Capitolinus; a college of priests was instituted to have charge of them; and the divine Oracles were consulted with great solemnity only in times of the greatest crises of the State. The books were finally destroyed when the Capitol was burned during the wars of Sylla, but many others continued in existence.

The oracles were composed in Alexandrine verse, and claimed to be the work of inspired Pagan prophetesses called Sibyls; they enjoyed the greatest vogue and were believed with the most implicit faith by Pagans and Christians alike. There were a number of these Sibyls, and the number of the volumes of oracles is differently estimated as a dozen or more; those with which we are chiefly concerned are the Roman Cumæan and Greek Erythræan Sibyls and the Oracles going under their names. The inveterate bent of the priestly mind for forgery in furtherance of its holy mission of imposture, led to the prompt adoption and corruption of these Pagan frauds, for the propagation first of the Jewish, then of the Christian Faith. "Because of the vogue enjoyed by these heathen oracles," says the *Catholic Encyclopedia,* "and because of *the influence they had in shaping the religious views of the period,* the Hellenistic Jews in Alexandria, during the second century B. C. composed [*i. e.* forged] verses in the same form, and circulated them among the Pagans as a means of diffusing Judaistic doctrines and teaching. This custom was continued down into Christian times, and *was borrowed by some Christians,* so that in the second or third century, a *new class of Oracles emanating from Christian sources came into being.* Hence the Sibylline Oracles can be classed as Pagan, Jewish, or *Christian.* In many cases, however, the Christians merely revised or interpolated the Jewish documents, and thus we have two classes of Christian Oracles, those adopted from Jewish sources and those entirely written by Christians. . . . It seems clear, however, that the Christian Oracles and those revised from Jewish sources all emanated from the same circle [or band of Christian forgers] and *were intended to aid in the diffusion of Christianity.*

"The Sibyls are quoted frequently by the early Fathers and Christian writers, Justin, Athenagoras, Theophilus, Clement of Alexandria, etc. . . . They were known and used during the Middle Ages in both the East and the West. . . . They all purport to be the work of the Sibyls." (*CE.* v. xiii, p. 770.)

Most notable of these forged Christian addenda to the Pagan-Jewish forged Oracles, is found in Book VIII, a lengthy composite of Jewish and Christian fraud, consisting of some 500 hexameter verses. The first 216 verses, says the *CE.,* "are most likely the work of a second century Jew, while the latter part (verses 217–500), beginning with an acrostic on the symbolical Christian word *Ichthus* is undoubtedly Christian, and dates most probably from the third century." (*CE.* xiii, 770.) *Ichthus* is the Greek word for fish, and the fish was the fitting and universal symbol of the early Christians as typical of the "catch" of the Apostolic fishers of men. This cabalistic word *Ichthus,* worked into the professedly Pagan Oracle in the form of an acrostic, is composed of the initial letters of the popular name and title of the Son of the Christian God, in the Greek: "*Iesous Christos Theou Uios Soter*—Jesus Christ, Son of God, Saviour." This fish anagram was an ancient Pagan symbol of fecundity, of great vogue and veneration throughout Pagandom, and was adopted by Christendom for the double reason that the initials acrostically formed the name and title of its new deity, and that in the ancient science fish were supposed to be generated in the water without carnal copulation, and were thus peculiarly symbolic of the Virgin-born Christ. Says Tertullian: "We, little fishes, after the example of our *Ichthus,* are born in water." (*On Baptism,* ch. i; *ANF.* iii, 669.)

The Church historian, Bishop Eusebius, preserves the Acrostic, taken from the Erythræan Sibyl, but says: "Many people, though they allowed the Erythræan Sibyl to have been a prophetess, yet reject this Acrostic, suspecting it to have been forged by the Christians"; which suspicion the good Bishop refutes by an appeal to Cicero, who, he assures, had read and translated it into Latin. (Eusebius, *Oration on Const.,* chs. 18–19; I, 274–5.) Father St. Augustine quotes the verses and says: "The Erythræan Sibyl has indeed written some things clearly and manifestly relating to Christ. . . . There are some, who suspected all these prophecies which relate to Christ, and passed under the name of the Sibyl, to have been forged by the Christians." (Aug., *De Civ. Dei,* xviii, 23; *N&PNF.* ii, 372–3.) Father Clement of Alexandria attributes to the Sibyls the same inspiration as the Old Testament, and cites Peter and Paul as appealing to them for a prediction of the life and character of Jesus Christ, Peter and Paul speaking thus: "Take the Greek books in your hand, and look into the Sibyl. How clearly she speaks of one God, and of the things to come; then take Hystaspes also and read, and you will find the Son of God much more clearly and evidently described." (*Strom.* I, 6, p. 761, Ed. Oxon.; also Lact., *De ver. sap.,* I, 4, 15; *Free Inquiry,* p. 34.)

The importance of the Sibylline Oracles, speaking through countless "interpolations" forged by Christian pens, for not only the propagation of the faith among the Pagans, but as actual *proofs* of the truth of the fictitious *"facts"* of Christianity, cannot be over-estimated; this justifies the following extracts from the *Divine Institutes* of Lactantius. The greater part, I dare say, of the seven Books of that notable work, addressed to the "mighty Emperor Constantine," is devoted to arguments and proofs of Jesus Christ and the principal events of his recorded life and acts, drawn copiously from the heathen gods and the forged Oracles of the Sibyls. These *proofs*, to the minds of Father Lactantius and of all the Fathers, as to the Pagans generally, were "more strong than proofs of Holy Writ"; for, he says, "perhaps the sacred writings [in the Old Testament] speak falsely when they teach [such and so about Jesus]; . . . *the Sibyls before taught the same things in their verses.*" Citing scores of Sibylline "prophecies" forged by the Christians for the belief and persuasion of the Pagans, who were effectively "refuted by these testimonies" and *thus* "brought to Christ," some of them, says Lactantius, urge that these prophetic verses "were not by the Sibyls, but made up and composed by our own writers," as the fact is above confessed by *CE.;* but, not so, argues the great Apologist; "do not Cicero and other Pagan authors, dead long before Jesus, testify to the Sibyls?"—Yes, to the Sibyls and their utterances then extant; not to the later Christian forgeries in their names. Moreover, these Christian "interpolations" imputed to the Sibyls, exactly as the muddled, ambiguous, meaningless "prophecies" of the Old Testament writings, meant nothing and were not understood to mean anything, until Jesus Christ came along, and these Jewish and Pagan mummeries were seized upon by the avid forging Christians to make up and pad out the pretended life and wondrous acts of the Christ. Even a cursory examination and the marginal cross-references will demonstrate, that virtually every act imputed in the New Testament Gospels to the Nazarene, was cut to fit of some scrap of mummery or pretended "prophecy" of Hebrew Scriptures and Sibylline Oracles. Of numberless instances of the latter quoted in the *Divine Institutes*, a few typical ones only can be here cited, but they are illuminating of the Christ-tales.

In Book I, chapter vi is entitled, "Of Divine Testimonies, and of the Sibyls and their Predictions." Appealing for faith to Constantine, the chapter begins: "Now let us pass to divine testimonies"; and he cites and quotes, in numerous chapters, the Pagan gods Mercury, Hermes Trismegistus, Apollo, and other mythic deities and personages, all testifying to the One Christian God and to his Son Jesus. After infinite such appeals for proofs, we come to Book IV, a veritable arsenal of manufactured "divine testimonies"; and we pause to con with wonder chapter xv, "Of the Life and Miracles of Jesus, and Testimonies concerning Him." Jesus, after his baptism, says Lactantius, "began to perform the greatest miracles, not by magical powers, but by heavenly strength and power. . . . His powers were those which *Apollo called* wonderful. . . . And he performed all these things not by His hands, or the application of any remedy, but by His word and command, as the *Sibyl* had foretold: 'Doing all things by His word, and healing every disease.' "

Many chapters are replete with instances of the miracles of Jesus, alleged each of them to have been foretold by one or another of the Sibyls, and quoting the Christian-forged prophetic verses in proof. The Christ came to fulfill the Law; "and the Sibyl shows that it would come to pass that this law would be destroyed by the Son of God: 'But when all these things which I told you shall be accomplished, then all the law is fulfilled with respect to Him.' " (c. xvii.) Of a few others, and the arguments above sketched, I quote the text:

"What can be more wonderful, either in narration or in action? But the Sibyl had before foretold that it would take place, whose verses are related to this effect:

> 'With five loaves at the same time, and with two fishes,
> He shall satisfy five thousand men in the wilderness;
> And afterwards taking all the fragments that remain,
> He shall fill twelve baskets to the hope of many.'

"But perhaps the sacred writings speak falsely when they teach that there was such power in Him, that by His command He compelled the winds to obey Him, the seas to serve Him, diseases to depart, the dead to be submissive. Why should I say that the Sibyls before had taught the same things in their verses? one of whom, already mentioned, thus speaks:

> 'He shall still the winds by His word, and calm the sea
> As it rages, treading with feet of peace and in faith.'

"And again another which says:

'He shall walk on the waves, He shall release men from disease.   1
He shall raise the dead, and drive away many pains;
And from the bread of one wallet there shall be a satisfying [of men].'

"Some, *refuted by these testimonies*, are accustomed to have recourse to the assertion that these poems were not by the Sibyls, but made up and composed by our own writers. But he will assuredly not think this who has read Cicero [*De Natura Deorum*, ii], and Varro, and other ancient writers, who make mention of the Erythræan and the other Sibyls from whose books we bring forth these examples; and these authors died before the birth of Christ according to the flesh. But I do not doubt that these poems were in former times regarded as ravings, since no one understood them. For they announced some marvellous wonders, of which neither the manner, nor the time, nor the author was signified. Lastly the Erythræan Sibyl says that it would come to pass that she would be called mad and deceitful. But assuredly

'They will say that the Sibyl
Is mad, and deceitful: but when all things shall come to pass,
Then ye will remember me; and no one will any longer
Say that I, the prophetess of the great God, am mad.'

"Therefore they were neglected for many ages; but they received attention *after* the nativity and passion of Christ had revealed secret things. Thus it was also with the utterances of the prophets, which were read by the people of the Jews for fifteen hundred [!] years and more, but yet *were not understood* until after Christ had explained them by His word and by His works. For the prophets spoke of Him; nor could the things which they said have been in any way understood, *unless* they had been altogether fulfilled." (Lact., *Div. Inst.*, Bk. IV, chap. xv; *ANF.* vii, 115, 116.)

In view of these "divine testimonies" of Pagan Oracles forged by pious Christians in proof of their Christ, need one wonder that the like testimonies in the Gospels themselves may be under suspicion of like forgery? We shall have the proofs in their due order. Father Justin Martyr treats these Pagan books of Christian evidences, as prophetic Scriptures and divine, and speaking of their prohibition by the Roman Emperors, says: "By the contrivance of Demons it was made a capital crime to read them, in order to deter men from coming to a knowledge of what is good." (*Apologia*, I, ch. 77; *ANF.* i, 178.)

That heathens and even devils may be specially endued with the gift of prophecy by God for his glory, and God may make use of the Devil-in-Chief for this purpose, is expressly asserted by Pope Benedict XIV (*Heroic Virtue*, III, 144, 150). And "the Angelic Doctor," St. Thomas Aquinas, "in order to prove that the heathens were capable of prophecy, refers to the instance of the Sibyls, who make clear mention of the mysteries of the Trinity, of the Incarnation of the Word, of the Life, Passion, and Resurrection of Christ. It is true that the Sibylline poems now extant became in course of time interpolated; but as Benedict XIV (1740–1758) remarks, this does not hinder much of them, *especially what the early Fathers referred to*, from being *genuine and in no wise apocryphal*"! (*CE.* xii, 474.)

Thus the Holy Ghost of God, speaking through its official mouthpiece, its Vice-God on earth, infallibly guarded by the Spirit against the possibility of error, in the year 1742 of our Era of Christ, sings the Doxology of these admitted frauds of paganish and forging Christianity, and canonizes them as the God-inspired origin of the holiest mysteries of Christian revelation. The inference is inevitable, that Pagan Sibyls, Christian Church Fathers, and Vicars of God, are strongly characterized by Ignorance and Imposture.

A noted classical and critical authority, Anthon, contemplating the shifts of the new Christianity rising from the débâcle of Paganism, falls into a philosophical reflection, pertinent alike to the old and the new systems of priestcraft:

"When a religion has fallen and been succeeded by another, the more zealous advocates of the new belief sometimes find themselves in a curious state of embarrassment. So it is with regard to the heathen system and the Christian code. Among the numerous oracles given to the world in former days, some have chanced to find a remarkable accomplishment; and the pious but ill-judging Christian, unable to ascribe them to deities in whom man no longer believes, is driven to create for them a different origin. 'God,' says Rollin, 'in order to punish the blindness of the heathen, sometimes permits evil spirits to give responses conformable to the truth.' (Rollin, *Histoire Ancienne*, I, 387.) The only evil spirit which had an agency in the oracular responses of antiquity was *that spirit of crafty imposture which finds so congenial a home among an artful and cunning priesthood*." (Anthon, *Classical Dictionary*, 4th ed., p. 929; Art. *Oraculum*.)

40

PAGAN FRAUDS—CHRISTIAN PRECEDENTS

The historian of European Morals, in his amazing review of the infinite variety and number of superstitions, frauds, forgeries, false miracles and lying oracles of Pagandom, which were taken over almost *en masse* by the Christians, and implicitly and with childlike credulity accepted and believed, taught and preached by every Christian Father of the Church, by the infallible popes, and the millions of their ignorant and superstitious ex-Pagan lay dupes, makes this very pertinent and just remark apropos the value of their pious opinions, testimonies and "traditions" of the origins of the Christian faith:

"To suppose that men who held these opinions were capable, in the second and third centuries, of ascertaining with any degree of just confidence whether miracles had taken place in Judæa in the first century, is grossly absurd; nor would the conviction of their reality have made any great impression on their minds at a time when miracles were supposed to be so abundantly diffused." (Lecky, *Hist. Europ. Morals,* i, 375.)

The confession that the vast mass of Christian miracles were Pagan frauds and lies taken *en bloc* over into Christianity to make a good showing as against the Pagans and to dupe the superstitious new converts, is made by *CE.*, with the notable further admission that the only alteration made was that the Pagan gods were made over into Christian saints: "This transference was promoted by the numerous cases in which *Christian saints became the successors of local deities,* and Christian worship supplanted the ancient local worship. This explains the great number of similarities between gods and saints. For the often maintained metamorphosis of gods into saints no proof is to be found." This immense confession of Christian fraudulency and imposture, in conjuring fictitious Pagan gods—which according to Christian faith were all *actual devils,*—into canonized *Saints of God* and Holy Church, is several times repeated by *CE.*, of which this instance is before me: "It has indeed been said that the 'Saints are the successors to the Gods.' Instances have been cited . . . of *statues of pagan Gods baptized and transformed into Christian Saints*"! (*CE.* xv, 710; cf. *Is It God's Word?* 5, 7–9.) This truly wonderful psycho-religious miracle is thereupon wrought: The idolatrous Pagan who just before the "baptism" actually *worshipped* these "statues of the Pagan gods," immediately afterwards simply *venerated* or *adored* the same gods "baptized and transformed into Christian saints,"—fully comprehending the non-understandable hair-splitting theological distinction between pious "*dulia*" and idolatrous "*latria*," as defined by Holy Church and droned by *CE.* in its article on Idolatry. And vast hordes of utterly illiterate and stupid Faithful go into the True Churches every day, kneel before and pray to these same Pagan gods conjured into Christian saints—with countless other counterfeit near-divinities of their near-Idolatry—and appreciate the difference to a split-second of devotion and true Faith. 'Tis passing strange.

A very remarkable confession of purposeful fraud, with the mechanics of the fraud, and the vast extent of it in faking Pagan miracle-lies into Christian truth of the most driveling nonsense, reads:

"Manifold as the varieties of [miracle] legends now seem to be, there are fundamentally not so very many different notions utilized. The legend considers the saint as a kind of lord of the elements, who commands the water, rain, fire, mountain, and rock; he changes, enlarges, or diminishes objects; flies through the air; delivers from dungeons—(examples, *Peter, Paul*)—and gallows; takes part in battles, and even in martyrdom is invulnerable; animals, the wildest and the most timid, serve him (*e. g.,* the stories of the bear as a beast of burden; the ring in the fish; the frogs becoming silent, etc.); his birth is glorified by a miracle; a voice, or letters, from Heaven proclaim his identity—[all these score for Jesus the Christ]; bells ring of themselves; the heavenly ones enter into personal intercourse with him (betrothal of Mary); he speaks with the dead and beholds heaven, hell, and purgatory; forces the devil to release people from compacts; he is victorious over dragons; etc. Of all this the *authentic* [?] Christian narratives know nothing—[a confession that every saint-tale of Bible and Church is a lie].

"But whence does this world of fantastic concepts arise? A glance at *the pre-Christian religious narratives will dispel every doubt. All* these stories are anticipated by the Greek chroniclers, writers of myths, collectors of strange tales, neo-Platonism, and neo-Pythagorism. One need only refer to the '*Ellados Periegesis*' of Pausanius, or glance through the codices collected by Photius in his '*Bibliotheca,*' to recognize what great importance was attached to the *reports of miracles* in antiquity by both the educated and uneducated." . . .

Reversing only the order of the sentences, and *CE.* reversing the truth of the answer it gives to its own question, the confession of shame continues:

PAGAN FRAUDS—CHRISTIAN PRECEDENTS

"But how was the transference of [these miracle] legends to Christianity consummated? ... Hellenism had already recognized this [fraudulent] characteristic of the religious fable, and would thus have been obliged to free itself from it in the course of time, had not *the competition with Christianity* forced the champions of the ancient polytheism to seek again in the ancient fables incidents to set against the miraculous power of Christ. [!] In this way *popular illusions found their way from Hellenism to Christianity.*" (*CE*. ix, 129–30.)

And in 1900 years no priest, bishop, pope, depositaries and guardians of divine truth, has ever said a word to prevent or put end to this shameful prostitution of mind of their poor grovelling dupes, but to this day perpetuate them in it. Far from ending the shameful thing, many bishops and popes have won the title *Mendax Maximus* by peddling these Pagan lies as God's truth; as witness this one instance from the article we are quoting: "St. Augustine (*De Cura*, xii) and also [Pope] St. Gregory the Great (Dialogues, IV, xxxvi) —[the greatest book of Lies outside the Bible]—relate of a man, who died by an error of the Angel of Death and was again restored to life, the same story which is already given by Lucian in his 'Philopseudes.' " (*Ib.* p. 130.) Such, verily for shame, is "that new Paganism later called Christianity."

Mythology has well been called the Theology of dead religions. The world is a vast cemetery of deceased gods and teeming scrapheap of decayed and discarded priest-imposed religious beliefs— superstitions. All the dead gods and religions of Paganism, all the yet surviving but fast moribund deities and faiths of the XXth Century world, all—(except—the Jews and Christians say, their own),— *all* were admittedly the fraudulent handiwork of priests and professional god-and-myth makers. In a word, short and ugly, but true— every priest of every god and religion (saving, for the nonce, the Jewish-Christian ones)—was a conscious and unconscionable falsifier and impostor,—a common liar for his god. All plied their artful, unholy priestcraft in the name of gods, for power and pelf, those grafting Pagan priests. No Christian will, or truthfully can, deny this portentous fact. The verdict of lying guilt of Pagan Priestcraft is unanimous.

No one can now doubt that Lecky, after voluminous review of pre-

Christian frauds and impostures, spoke the precise historical truth: "Christianity floated into the Roman Empire on the wave of credulity that brought with it this long train of Oriental superstitions and legends." (*Hist. of European Morals*, i, 373–4.)

The mainstream of Oriental superstition and priestly imposture will now be seen to swell with the turgid flood of Hebrew fables and forgery, before pouring the mingled flood of myth and fraud into the pure tide of Christian Truth;—where, Presto! change! it is beheld transformed—"baptized"—into the "revealed mysteries" and "Catholic Truth" of God!

CHAPTER II

HEBREW HOLY FORGERIES

"Hinneh lash-sheqer asah et sheqer sepharim—Behold, the lying pen of the scribes hath wrought lies." Jeremiah, viii, 8.

SUNDRY HOLY HEBREW men of old, we are told on the authority of the name of the *pseudo*-first Jewish-Christian Pope, "spake as they were moved by the Holy Ghost" (2 Peter, i, 21). These literary movings of the Spirit were sometime reduced to writing in "Sacred Scriptures"; and again later Christian authority assures: "All scripture is given by inspiration of God" (2 Tim. iii, 16),—though this is a falsified rendition; the true reading is: "Every scripture suitable for edification is divinely inspired," as the original Greek text is quoted by Father Tertullian. (*ANF.* iv, 16.)

It is the popular supposition that the 66—(Catholic Bible 73)—"little books" which comprise the Bible as we know it, are the whole sum of Hebrew and Christian "sacred writings," which have claimed and have been accorded the sanction of Divine inspiration and "treated by the Church as canonical." The term "canonical" in ecclesiastical parlance means Books accepted as divinely inspired; books which "were definitely *canonized*, or adjudged to have a uniquely Divine or authoritative quality," as is the authorative definition. (*CE.* iii, 267.) "Canonicity depends on inspiration." (*EB.* i, 653.) The holy Hebrew "canon" was closed, or the last inspired Book of the Old Testament written, according to Jewish "Tradition," by Ezra, about 444 B. C. (*Ib.* i, 658, 662.) In truth, however, several of the Books of the Old Testament were written much later, and were never heard of by Ezra; and "some found their way in, others not, on grounds of taste—the taste of the period," says Wellhausen. (*Einleitung*, p. 652, 6th Ed.)

The popular idea is that when the "moving" of the above inspired

45

66 sacred writings was ended, the moving Spirit retired from the field of Hebrew, and later of Christian literature, and thus closed the "sacred canon" of the respective Hebrew and Christian Testaments. This will be seen to be a mistake, in the judgment of the True Christian Church, according to which the Jews evidently did not know their own inspired writings, and curiously omitted from their "canon" a number of divinely "moved" books and scraps of books, which the better-instructed Christian Church has adopted as full of inspiration into its own present official Bible, as we shall notice in its place. There is also a much greater number of such books, of both Hebrew and Christian origin, which the inspired Church formerly and for ages regarded as inspired and "canonical," but which it now repudiates as "apocryphal" and acknowledges as forgeries; as we shall also duly note.

There is, indeed, an immense mass of religious writings, the work of Jewish or Christian priests or professional religious persons, or composite productions of both sets of forgers, which are generally known as "apocrypha" or pious forgeries; but which each and all have been held by the Church through many ages of faith as of the highest inspired sanctity and accredited with the full rank of "canonical" truth of God.

The term apocryphal or forged "takes in those compositions which profess to have been written either by Biblical personages or men in intimate relation with them." (*CE*. i, 601.) "Since these [apocryphal] books were *forgeries*, the epithet in common parlance today denotes any story or document which is false or spurious; . . . apocryphal in the disparaging sense of *bearing names to which they have no right;* all come under the definition above, *for each of them has at one time or another been treated as canonical.*" (*EB*. i, 249–250.)

That the above 66 (or 73) Books of the accepted Bible of Christianity come exactly, both as to manner of spurious origin and matter of fictional content, within the above definition of apocrypha or forgery, shall be made exceedingly evident. A brief review of these acknowledged religious forgeries in the name of God and of his inspired biographers, will afford a curious and instructive study of the workings of the fervid, credulous and contorted priestly mind, reck-

46

less of truth, and shed a floodlight of understanding on the origins and incredibility of the so-called "canonical" Books of the Bible, Hebrew and Christian alike.

While speaking here immediately of the Jewish Apocrypha or pious forgeries, it is to be noted and borne in mind that it is the Holy-Ghost-guided True Christian Church which alone has accepted and cherished these spurious productions of Jewish priestcraft— (scornfully repudiated by the Jews), has adulterated and re-forged them to more definite deceptive purposes of Christian propaganda, and has outdone Jewry by adding innumerable like forgeries,—"a whole literature" of fabrications—to its own spurious hagiographa, or sacred writings. There will thus occur some necessary and unavoidable over-lappings of Jewish and Christian forgeries in the course of our treatment.

"It must be confessed," admits the *Catholic Encyclopedia*, "that the early Fathers and the Church, during the first three centuries, were more indulgent towards Jewish pseudographs [*i. e.* forged writings] circulating under venerable Old Testament names. The Book of Henoch [Enoch] and the Assumption of Moses had been cited by the canonical Epistle of Jude. Many Fathers admitted the inspiration of Fourth Esdras. Not to mention the Shepherd of Hermas, the Acts of St. Paul (at least in the Thecla portion) and the Apocalypse of St. Peter were highly revered at this and later periods. . . . In the Middle Ages . . . many pseudographic [*i. e.* forged] writings enjoyed a high degree of favor among both clerics and laity." (*CE.* i, 615.)

A curious and edifying side-light on the chronic clerical flair for forgery is thrown by a sentence from the paragraph above quoted from the *Catholic Encyclopedia*. The earliest papal decree condemning certain of these pious forgeries is itself a Christian forgery! "The so-called '*Decretum de recipiendis et non recipiendis libris*,' which contained a catalogue of some half-hundred works condemned as apocryphal, was attributed to Pope Gelasius (495), but, in reality is a compilation dating from the beginning of the sixth century." (*CE.* i, 615.)

And, be it noted, these Christian forgeries were not at all condemned by the Church *as* forgeries and pious lies, but simply because they contained some dogmatic doctrines which were regarded by the Orthodox as "heresies"; they were condemned "always, however, with a preoccupation against heresy." And again in the same article: "Undoubtedly it was the large use heretical circles, especially the Gnostics, made of this insinuating literature, which first called out the animadversions of the official guardians of doctrinal purity." (*Ib.* p. 615.)

The same authority cautiously and clerically explains, that "ancient literature, especially in the Orient, used methods much more free and elastic than those permitted by our modern and occidental culture. Pseudographic [falsified] composition was in vogue among the Jews in the two centuries before Christ and for some time later. This holds good for the so-called 'Wisdom of Solomon,' written in Greek and belonging to the Church's sacred canon.—[This admits that this book of the Catholic Bible is spurious.] In other cases, where the assumed name did not stand as a symbol of a type of a certain kind of literature, the *intention* was not without a degree of at least literary *dishonesty*." (*Ib.* p. 601.)

Apocryphal religious literature consists of several classes, one of the most important subdivisions being that designated as "apocalyptic," and which consists of "pretended prophecies and revelations of both Jewish and Christian authorship, and dating from about 200 B. C. to about 150 A. D.," the latter being the approximate date of the now "canonical" Books of the New Testament. Their general subject is the problem of the final triumph of what is called the Kingdom of God. Speaking particularly of the apocalypses, the best known of which are the Hebrew Book of Daniel, written about 165 B. C., and the Jewish-Christian Book of Revelation imputed to the Apostle John of Patmos, a recent secular authority (corroborated at all points by clerical authorities) points out that many if not all of the Jewish apocalypses are adulterated with "alterations and interpolations by Christian hands, making the alleged predictions point more definitely to Jesus," which pious tampering "gave certain of these Jewish works a very wide circulation in the early Church. . . . The revelations and predictions *are set forth as though actually received and written or spoken by ancient worthies, as Enoch, Moses, etc.* . . . They were once widely accepted as genuine prophecies, and

48

found a warm reception in Jewish and early Christian circles." (*The New International Encyclopedia*, vol. i, p. 745.) This form of pious fraud is admitted as quite the expected thing: "Naturally basing itself upon the Pentateuch and the Prophets, it clothed itself fictitiously with the authority of a patriarch or prophet who was made to reveal the transcendent future" (*CE.* i, 602),—most usually long *ex post facto.*

The vast and varied extent of Jewish-Christian forgery of religious books is shown by the groupings under which the several kinds of apocrypha forgeries are quite exhaustively considered in the technical works treating of them, such as the *Catholic Encyclopedia* and the *Encyclopedia Biblica*, as well as the more popular *Britannica* and *New International* Encyclopedias, where the subject is fully discussed. "Speaking broadly," says the first, "The Apocrypha of Jewish origin are coextensive with what are styled of the Old Testament, and those of Christian origin with the apocrypha of the New Testament. The subject will be treated ["according to their origin"]—as follows: (I) Apocrypha of Jewish origin; (II) Jewish apocrypha with Christian accretions; (III) apocrypha of Christian origin, comprising (1) apocryphal Gospels; (2) Pilate literature and other apocrypha concerning Christ; (3) apocryphal Acts of Apostles; (4) apocryphal doctrinal works; (5) apocryphal Epistles; (6) apocryphal Apocalypses; (IV) the apocrypha and the Church." (*CE.* i, 601.)

What a catalogue of confessed ecclesiastical forgery and fraud in the name of God, Christ and his Apostles, and the Church of God, for the propaganda of priestly frauds as "our Most Holy Faith"!

What will probably—in view of the foregoing and what is yet to come—be appreciated by many as a peculiarly rare bit of apocrypha (in its secondary sense), is the following, uttered apparently with the due and usual ecclesiastical solemnity, in the celebrated *Dictatus* of Pope Gregory VII (1073–1085), stating the presumptuous pretenses of the Papacy:

"*The Roman Church has never erred, nor will it err to all eternity.* No one may be considered a Catholic Christian who does not agree with the Catholic Church. No book is authoritative unless it has received the papal sanction. . . .

49

"The pope is the only person whose feet are to be kissed by all princes"; "the Pope may depose emperors and absolve subjects from allegiance to an unjust ruler." (Cited by Robinson, *The Ordeal of Civilization*, pp. 126, 128; *Library of Original Sources*, vol. iv, p. 320–321.)

This puts the stamp of canonical inspiration and verity on some dozen Jewish books and parts of books of the Catholic Bible which the Jews and the whole body of otherwise discordant sects of Protestants hesitate not unanimously to pronounce apocryphal and forged. These "apocrypha" are either entire rejected Jewish books, all doubtless with Christian "interpolations," or apocryphal chapters or parts, interpolated probably by the same industry into the equally apocryphal books of the accepted Jewish canon. The names of these books, originals and interpolations, and which are not included in the Hebrew Old Testament,—but are in the True Church Bible,—are: Tobit, Judith, Baruch, with the Epistle of Jeremiah, Wisdom of Solomon, Wisdom of Jesus son of Sirach (or Ecclesiasticus), I and II Maccabees, Prayer of Manasseh, Additions to Esther, and Additions to the Book of Daniel, consisting of the Prayer of Azarias, the Song of the Three Holy Children (in the Fiery Furnace), the History of Susannah, the History of Bel and the Dragon, and sundry such precious fables. (See *CE.* iii, pp. 267, 270; iv, 624, *passim.*) These are all included in the Greek Septuagint and in the Latin Vulgate, were read as Scripture in the early Christian Church, and were declared by the Council of Trent, at its Fourth Session, in 1546,—under the Curse of God on all skeptical doubters,—to be "inspired and canonical"; and they are so held by the Roman, and some of the Greek and Oriental Catholic Churches, but are declared "apocrypha" and forged by Jewry and all the rest of Christendom. To several of these *extra*-revelations of Judaism included in the Christian True Bible, head-notes apologetic for their inclusion are attached, of which that to the celebrated Book of Tobit or Tobias is typical: "Protestants have left it out of their modern Bibles, alleging that it is not in the canon of the Jews. But the Church of Christ, which received the Scriptures not from the Jews, but from the Apostles of Christ,—[who were all Jews, to believe the Christian record]—by traditions from them, has allowed this book a place in the Christian [*sic*] Bible from the beginning." (See Cath.

50

Bible, *Tobit, et passim*). We may admire in synopsis the divine inspiration of

THE INSPIRED FABLE OF TOBIT

This Book of Tobit, or Tobias, scoffed both by Jews and Protestants as a ridiculous fable, but held by all True Believers as a precious revelation of God, to disbelieve which is to be damned, is a veritable treasure-trove of exalted heavenly inspiration, for the preservation of which Jew and Gentile alike may be dubiously grateful to the pious "tradition" of the Apostles of Christ, as above said. This Tobias was a very pious and stubborn Israelite of the Captivity, who, before departing, had câched all his available cash with his kinsman Gabelus, of Rages, a city of the Medes, "taking a note of his hand" for its repayment on demand. While captive in a strange and pagan land, Tobias was visited by a piteous calamity, for "as he was sleeping, hot dung out of a swallow's nest fell upon his eyes, and he was made blind"; which affliction Tobias looked reverently to the Lord as visiting upon him as "revenge for my sins"; as a result Tobias became extremely poor, and his wife took in work. At that time there lived in the city of Rages another pious Israelite by name Raguel, who had a marriageable—or rather muchly married daughter, Sara, who was under grave reproach and even imputation of murder, "Because she had been given to seven husbands, and a devil named Asmodeus had killed them, at their first going in unto her," so that she complained that though sevenfold a widow she remained yet a virgin.

At this juncture Tobias bethought himself of the good money he had left with Gabelus of Rages, and after much palaver decided to send his son, Tobias, Jr., a comely youth, with the note of hand in his pocket, and his dog (name unrevealed), on the long journey to recoup the fortune of ten talents of silver. As Tobias, Jr. started on the journey, a beautiful young man, who was really the Archangel Raphael, met him and introduced himself as Azarias, son of Ananias,—(Ananias must have written the account)—and offered to accompany and guide him upon his journey, which offer was gratefully accepted. As the two journeyed they came to the river Tigris; Tobias waded in to wash his feet, when, lo, "a monstrous fish came up to devour him," whereat Tobias called to his companion for help. The Angel told

51

him to take the monster fish by the gill and haul him out, which Tobias seems to have had no trouble in doing. The Angel then directed Tobias to open the yet live and "panting" fish, "and lay up his heart, his gall, and his liver, for thee; for these are necessary for useful medicines"; this done, they cooked the fish and carried it all along for provisions for the trip. As they journeyed, Tobias asked the Angel what these medicinal scraps were good for; "and the Angel answering said, If thou put a little piece of its heart upon coals, the smoke thereof driveth away all kinds of devils, either from man or from woman, so that they come no more to them. And the gall is good for anointing the eyes, in which there is a white speck, and they shall be cured."

So discoursing pleasantly and instructively, the twain arrived at Rages; and the Angel guided Tobias straight to the house of Raguel and his daughter Sara, his sole heiress, and told Tobias to ask for her in marriage. Tobias said that he was afraid of Sara, for he had heard of what happened to those seven other men; but the Angel reassured him, that he would show him how to overcome the devil Asmodeus; that he should marry Sara and go to bed with her for three nights, but should continently confine his activities "to nothing else but to prayers with her"; and, assured the Angel, on the first night "lay the liver of the fish on the fire, and the devil shall be driven away," other holy marvels happening on the succeeding nights; "and when the third night is past, thou shalt take the virgin with the fear of the Lord, moved rather for love of children than for lust." The affair was arranged according to these prescriptions with Sara and her parents; after the wedding supper, the newlyweds were left alone in their boudoir; Tobias did nothing but pray and put a part of the fish liver in the fire, whereupon "the Angel Raphael took the devil, and bound him in the desert of Upper Egypt"; then both prayed some more, the fervid prayers being repeated verbatim. In the morning, Raguel, out of force of habit, called his servants and ordered them to go into the garden and dig an eighth grave for the reception of Tobias; when the maid-servant went to the room to arrange for the removal of the corpse, she to her great surprise "found them safe and sound, sleeping both together." The empty grave was filled up, a big banquet prepared, and the happy bridal couple spent two weeks with the bride's family, while the Angel took the note of hand, went to Gabelus, collected the money, and paid it over to Tobias; Raguel gave Tobias one-half of all his property, and executed a writing to give him one-half of the remainder upon the death of Raguel and wife. Tobias sent the Angel back to Gabelus, to invite him to his wedding, and the Angel made him come.

To proceed swiftly to the climax of marvel, Tobias and the Angel, leaving the hymeneal cortège to follow as best it could, with such impedimenta of wealth, hastened back to the home of Tobias, Sr., where blind father and the mother were in great grief over the supposed loss of their son and the money with him. But at the behest of the Angel, Tobias, Jr. ran into the house, though "the dog, which had been with them in the way, ran before, and coming as if he had brought the news, showed his joy by his fawning and wagging his tail," an act which has since become habitual with dogs which have enough tail to wag. After kissing his mother and father, as the Angel had suggested, Tobias, Jr. took the remaining fish gall out of his traveling bag, and anointed with it the eyes of his father; "and he stayed about half an hour; and a white skin began to come out of his eyes, like the skin of an egg. And Tobias took hold of it, and drew it from his eyes, and immediately he recovered his sight. And they glorified God," and Tobias, Sr. dutifully said, "I bless thee, Lord God of Israel, because thou hast chastised me, and thou hast saved me: and behold I see Tobias my son." Then, "after seven days Sara his son's wife, and all the family arrived safe, and the cattle, and the camels, and an abundance of money of his wife's, and that money also which he had received of Gabelus"; they all feasted for seven days "and rejoiced with all great joy"; then, when Tobias, Sr. suggested doing something handsome for the "holy man" through whom all their good fortune had come, the Angel introduced himself as really not Azariah, son of Ananias, but "The Angel Raphael, one of the Seven, who stand before the Lord"; and he explained, "I seemed indeed to eat, and to drink with you, but I use an invisible meat and drink, which cannot be seen by men"; thereupon in true angel style he dissipated into thin air and they could see him no more. The whole Tobias family then, "lying prostrate for three hours upon their face, blessed God: and rising up they told all his wonderful works." Thus endeth happily the reading of the lesson, dictated by the Holy Ghost to the pious Ananias who recorded it for the edification of True Believers. Let us pray that it is true.

THE PROOF OF THE PUDDING

Until the Council of Trent, in 1546, there was no infallibly defined sanction of inspiration of these Jewish "apocrypha"; like the "canon" sacred Books of the Hebrew Bible, all alike were more or less eclectically accepted and used in the True Church; but, as said: "The Tridentine decree from which the above list is extracted was the first infallible and effectually promulgated pronouncement on the Canon, addressed to the Church universal. Being dogmatic in its purport, it *implies* that the Apostles bequeathed the same Canon to the Church as a part of the *depositum fidei*. . . . We should search the pages of the New Testament *in vain* for any trace of such action. . . . We affirm that such a status *points to Apostolic sanction*, which in turn *must have* rested on revelation either by Christ *or* the Holy Spirit." (*CE.* iii, 270.)

This is luminous clerical reasoning: a lot of anonymous Jewish fables, derided by Jews and all the rest of the world for want of even common plausibility of fact or truth, and as to which the "inspired" Christian Books said to emanate from Apostles, are silent as the grave, are declared after 1500 years to have the ear-marks of Apostolic sanction, which "must have" been founded on divine revelation to them "either by Christ *or* the Holy Spirit,"—which the Church claims are one and the same Person; and it is curious that the "infallible" Council couldn't say which was which, but vaguely and uncertainly opined it *must have been* one *or* the other. So much for infallible cock-suredness as to "inspiration" of Holy Scriptures. Even the Old Testament itself, says our logician of inspiration, "reveals no formal notion of inspiration," though, again, "the later Jews *must have* possessed the idea." (*Ib.* p. 269.) The cursory notice which we shall take of the Old Testament books will serve to confirm that they reveal no notion at all of inspiration; that the later Jews *must have had the idea* that they were inspired, does not much help the case for them.

In addition to these rejected Jewish books admitted into full canonical fellowship by the inerrant True Church, there are several other

Jewish apocrypha which are only semi-canonical and admitted into a sort of bar-sinister fellowship with the legitimates. They have a place in the Orthodox Bible for the "edification" of the Faithful, but are usually printed in the Appendix as suggestive to the devout that they will not be damned for not fully believing these particular forgeries.

Among these are two very celebrated books forged in the name of the great Restorer of Israel, Ezra, under the titles of *Third* and *Fourth Esdras*, as the name is written in the True Bibles. "Third Esdras," says the *Encyclopedia*, "is one of the three uncanonical books appended to the official edition of the Vulgate. . . . It enjoyed exceptional favor in the early ages of the Church, being *quoted as Scripture with implicit faith* by the leading Greek and Latin Fathers." (*CE*. i, 605.) In like errant faith was regarded its companion forgery, *Fourth Esdras*, of which the same ecclesiastical authority says: "The personage serving as the screen of the author of this book is Esdras (Ezra). . . . Both Greek and Latin Fathers cite it as prophetical. . . . Notwithstanding this widespread reverence for it in early times, it is a *REMARKABLE FACT* that the book never got a foothold in the Canon or liturgy of the Church . . . and even after the Council of Trent, together with Third Esdras, it was placed in the appendix to the official edition of the Vulgate. . . . The dominant critical dating assigns it to a Jew writing in the reign of Domitian, A. D. 81–98,"— the "screen" Ezra being gathered to his fathers since about 444 B. C. (*Ib.* p. 603–604; v, 537–8; *EB*. i, 653, 1393.) It is curious that it is regarded as "remarkable" that the Holy Ghost did not "fall" for this particular forgery, when it did for so many others!

EZRA "RESTORES" THE LAW

A remarkable apocryphal tale relating to the Hebrew Scriptures is enshrined by pseudo-inspiration in chapter 14 of this Fourth of Esdras, regarding the miraculous restoration of Hebrew Holy Writ after its total perishment. In the calamity of the capture and destruction of the Holy City by Nebuchadnezzar, 586 B. C., the Temple of Solomon was destroyed, together with the entire collection of the sacred Rolls of Scriptures, so that not a scratch of inspired pen remained to tell the tale of theocratic Hebrew history and its "revealed" religion. This inconsolable and apparently irreparable loss afflicted the holy People all the time of the Babylonian captivity. But upon their return to the restored City of God, and over a century after their loss, God, we are told in Fourth Esdras, inspired Ezra and commissioned him to reproduce the sacred lost Books, which, judging from the result of his inspired labors, were many more than the supposed twenty and two of the supposed old Hebrew Canon. Accordingly Ezra, employing five scribes, dictated to them (from inspired memory) the textual contents of the lost sacred Books, and in just forty days and nights reproduced a total of 94 sacred books, of which he designated 24 as the sacred canon, the remaining 70 being termed esoteric and reserved for the use of only the wisest. This inspired fable was eagerly accepted for truth by the early Church Fathers, many of whom, from Irenæus on, "admitted its inspiration"; and it was frequently quoted and commented on as canonical by such Church luminaries as Tertullian, St. Ambrose, Clement Alexandrensis, Origen, Eusebius, St. Jerome, *et als.*, and was prevalently accepted as Scripture throughout the scholastic period. (*EB.* i, 654, 1392–94; *CE.* i, 537–8, 601, 615.)

This legend, however, had, through a better understanding of "the powers of ordinary human memory," quite faded out by the time of the Reformation, but only to make way for a more modern and rationalistic one, invented by the Jew Levita, who died in 1549. According to his new fable, Ezra and the Talmudic "Men of the Great Synagogue" simply united into one volume the 24 books which until that time had circulated separately, and divided them into the three great divisions yet recognized, of the Law, the Prophets, and the Hagiographa or holy writings. This fabulous statement of Levita "became the authoritative doctrine of the orthodoxy of the seventeenth and eighteenth centuries." (*EB.* i, 654.) This new legend is cited simply to show how prone is the credulous clerical mind to accept as truth the most baseless fables; and how, when one of their precious bubbles of faith is pricked by tardy exposure or common sense, they eagerly catch at the next which comes floating by.

HEBREW HOLY FORGERIES

THE "FINDING OF THE LAW"

Another ancient priestly fiction, which to this day passes current among the credulous as inspired truth of God, is the fabled "finding of the Law" as recorded in the Word of God. We are all familiar with the notable "finding" by the late lamented Prophet Joseph Smith— thereto led by the Angel Moroni—of the golden plates containing the hieroglyphic text of Book of Mormon, near Palmyra, N. Y. in 1823–1827. (*Book of Mormon*, Introd.) History repeated itself. A like remarkable discovery was made in the year 621 B. C., this time by a priest, with the help of a witch or lady fortune-teller. As related in 2 Kings xxii, corroborated by 2 Chronicles xxxiv, in the eighteenth year of the "good king" Josiah of Judah, while some repair work was being done in the Temple, Hilkiah the priest of a sudden "found the book of the law of Yahveh given by Moses," over 800 years before, and never heard of since. Hilkiah called in Shaphan the scribe, and they took the great "find" to Josiah the King. To verify the veracity of the high-priest, Huldah the lady prophet was consulted; being intimately familiar with the sentiments of God, she at once declared that Yahveh was very angry about it, "because," as the King said, "our fathers have not hearkened unto the words of this book, to do after all that is written in this book"; and the King at once set about to carry into effect the laws prescribed in Deuteronomy,—just then for the first time in the history of Israel ever heard of or acted upon. This "book of the law given to Moses" 800 years before was doubtless the priestly work of Hilkiah, palmed off under the potent name of Moses to force its very reluctant observance and belief on the superstitious Jews. That this is the fact is the consensus of the scholars, as summarized in the *Encyclopedia Biblica*, and any modern work of O. T. criticism. An examination of the Bible texts themselves, as made in my previous work, demonstrates that this holy "Law of Moses" was totally unknown and unobserved through all the history of Israel from its beginnings until Josiah, and was then composed by his priests and enlarged into the present Pentateuch during and after the captivity in Babylon.

FORGERY IN CHRISTIANITY

THE "SEPTUAGINT" TRANSLATION INTO GREEK

As priestly forged tales were fabricated to account for the origin and preservation of the sacred Hebrew Books, so like pious fraud was adopted to account for their very notable translation into Greek, in what is known as the Septuagint Version. After the conquests by Alexander the Great and his establishment of the city of Alexandria in Egypt, immense numbers of Jews were settled in the new city, which quickly became the commercial and intellectual center of the ancient world, with Greek the universal language. The holy Hebrew language had become a dead language to the Jews of the "Dispersion"; their synagogue services could not be conducted in the mother tongue. The Alexandrian Jews were accordingly under necessity to render the "Law" into Greek for their public use; and this was gradually done by such of them as thought themselves able to do such work. But this common-place mode of rendering the sacred Hebrew into a Gentile speech did not satisfy the pious wonder-craving Jewish mind. Accordingly, somewhere about 200 B. C., an anonymous Jew invented a more satisfactory tale, which has had incalculable influence on the Christian faith and dogmas. This pious Israelite had the customary recourse to religious forgery; he forged a letter in the name of one Aristeas, an official of Ptolemy II, Philadelphus, the Greek king of Egypt, 285–247 B. C., purporting to be addressed to his brother, Philocrates, and giving a marvelous history of the Translation.

Here, in substance, is what we read of the first origin of the Version, limited therein to the "Law" of Moses, as first related by Josephus. Ptolemy had recently established a library at Alexandria, which he purposed should contain a copy of every obtainable literary work extant. This Library became the most extensive and celebrated of the ancient world, containing some 700,000 manuscript books at the time it was savagely destroyed, in 391 A. D., by the benighted Christian zeal and fury of Bishop Theophilus of Alexandria and his crazy monks of Nitria, as related in Kingsley's *Hypatia* or any history of the times. (*CE.* xiv, 625.) At the suggestion of Demetrius, his Librarian, fables the pseudo-Aristeas through Josephus, that he should enrich the Library with a copy of the sacred Law of the Jews, Ptolemy wrote to Eleazar the chief priest at Jerusalem, sending the letter and mag-

58

nificent presents "to God" by the hand of a delegation including Aristeas, requesting a copy of the Law and a number of learned Jews competent to translate it into Greek. The embassy was successful; a richly ornamented copy of the holy Law, written in letters of gold, was sent to the King, together with seventy-two Doctors of Israel, deputed to deliver the Book and to carry out the wishes of the King. They were received with great honor, says pseudo-Aristeas, and duly fêted for several days; they were then conducted across the long causeway to the Island of Pharos to the place which was prepared for them, "which was a house that was built near the shore, and was a quiet place, and fit for their *discoursing together about their work.* . . . Accordingly they made an accurate interpretation, with great zeal and great pains," working until the ninth hour each day, and visiting Ptolemy every morning. "Now when the *Law* was transcribed, and the labour of interpretation was over, which came to its conclusion in seventy-two days," the work was read over to the assembled Jews, who rejoiced that "the interpretation was happily finished"; they were enjoined to report any *errors* or omissions which they might discover, to the "Seventy," who would make the necessary *corrections* in their work. (Josephus, *Antiq. Jews*, Bk. XII, chap. 2; *CE.* xiii, 722.) Thus the translation was only of "The Law," the Five Books of Moses; and it was open team-work, all the Seventy-two working together, comparing and discussing as they proceeded, and expressly enjoining the Jews to note and report for correction all errors of omission or commission which they might discover.

Thus the pseudo-Aristeas, as cited by Josephus; though, as a matter of fact, this Septuagint Version, so-called because of the legendary Seventy-(two), was in the grossest manner inaccurate, and imported innumerable errors into the Christian religion which was based upon and propagated for several centuries only through the Septuagint texts. Indeed, "the text of the Septuagint was regarded as so unreliable, because of its freedom in rendering, and of the alterations which had been introduced into it, etc., that, during the second century of our era it was discarded by the Church." (*CE.* iv, 625.) We shall notice the fearful error of Isaiah's "virgin-birth" text; for other well-known instances, it makes out Creation 1195 years earlier than the Hebrew and Vulgate, 4004 B. C., and the venerable Methuselah is made to survive the Flood by fourteen years.

Despite, however, its patently legendary character, the pseudo-Aristeas' account, the forged letter and the story, were eagerly accepted as genuine and authentic by Fathers, Popes and ecclesiastic writers until the sixteenth century, when their spurious character was revealed by the nascent modern criticism. "The authenticity of the letter, called in question first by Louis Vivés (1492–1540), professor at Louvain, is now universally denied." (*CE*. xiii, 722.)

The Fathers, however, could not rest content with this unvarnished original fabrication in the name of Aristeas, of an ordinary human and errant translation of the "Law"; they avidly set about embellishing it in the accepted clerical style, adding fanciful and lying details to emphasize the miraculous and inspired origin of the Version. As this notable instance serves admirably to illustrate the childish and uncritical credulity of the Fathers, their reckless disregard of truth, their chronic zest for any untruth or fable suitable to pander to the glory of God and enhance the pious superstition of the Faithful, let us here watch the growth of this simple human yarn of the Jewish Aristeas-forger into the wonderful and ever more embellished miracle as it passes from Father to Father,—exactly as the Gospel-fables grew from "Mark" to "John." According to Fathers Tertullian, St. Augustine, St. Jerome, *et als.*, the 72 were inspired by God each severally for the entire work; in translating they did not consult with one another; they had been shut up *incomunicados* in separate cells on Pharos, either singly or in pairs, and their several translations, when finished and compared, were found to agree entirely both as to sense and the expressions employed, with the original Hebrew text and with each other (St. Clement of Alexandria, St. Irenæus, Justin Martyr). Finally, the 72 translated not only the Law, but the entire Old Testament,—several of whose Books were not yet at the time written.

Father Justin Martyr adds near-eye-witness verification to the false and already embroidered history, saying that the "Seventy" were, by order of the King, "shut up in as many separate cells, and were obliged by him, each to translate the whole Bible apart, and without any communication with each other, yet all their several translations were found to agree verbatim from the beginning to the end, and were by that means demonstrated to be of divine inspira-

60

tion"; and he adds, for confirmation of faith!—like Paul, protesting he is not lying in anticipation of the accusation: "These things, ye men of Greece, are no fable, nor do we narrate fictions; but we ourselves having been in Alexandria, saw the remains of the little [cells] at the Pharos still preserved." (*Ad Græc.* ch. xiii; *ANF.* i, 278–9.) But in repeating the tale to the Roman Emperor, Father Justin makes the unhappy blunder of saying, that Ptolemy "sent to *Herod*, who was at that time king of the Jews, requesting that the books of the prophets [pseudo-Aristeas said the "Law"] be sent to him; and the king did indeed send them" (I *Apol.* ch. xxxi; *ANF.* i, 173); whereas Herod lived some 300 years after Ptolemy died. This forged fable is time and again repeated as sober truth. Bishop Saint Irenæus emphasizes the miraculous nature of the translation of *all* the Books, saying that when the 72 identical translations were compared, "God was indeed glorified, and the Scriptures were acknowledged as truly divine; . . . even the Gentiles present perceived that the Scriptures had been interpreted by the inspiration of God. And there was nothing astonishing in God having done this. . . . He inspired Esdras the priest (after the return from captivity) to recast all the words of the former prophets, and to re-establish with the people of God the Mosaic legislation." (*Adv. Hær.* III, xxi, 2; *ANF.* i, 451–2.)

In the course of a century or two before the Christian Era, the other Hebrew sacred books were likewise translated into Greek for the use of the Greek-speaking Jews of "the Dispersion," together with numbers of the forged Jewish apocrypha, and all these were added to the rolls of "Scriptures." This final and adulterated form of the Septuagint "was the vehicle which conveyed these additional Scriptures [*i. e.* the apocryphal *Tobias*, etc.] into the Catholic Church." (*CE.* iii, 271.) This vagary of the Holy Ghost in certifying the ill-translated and tampered Septuagint for the foundations of Christian Faith, was very disastrous, as *CE.* points out: "The Church had adopted the Septuagint as its own; this *differed from the Hebrew* not only by *the addition of several books and passages* but also *by innumerable variations of text*, due partly to the ordinary process of *corruption* in the transcription of ancient books, partly to the *culpable temerity*, as Origen called it, *of correctors* who used not a little freedom in *making 'corrections,' additions, and suppressions*, partly to *mistakes in translation*, and finally in great part to the fact that the original Septuagint had been made from a Hebrew text quite different from that fixed at Jamnia as the one standard by the Jewish Rabbis." (*CE.* vii, 316.) So Yahveh only knows what he actually said and did in the 4004 years up to the time his Son came to try to "redeem" his people from some of the tangles of his Holy Law.

Matters grew worse as time progressed: the ex-Pagan Greek Fathers who founded Christianity, propagated the new Faith for several centuries only from the tortuous texts of this falsified Septuagint, which was the only Old Testament "Scriptures" known to and used by them as the source of the "prophecies fulfilled by Jesus Christ" and the holy mysteries of the Jewish-Christian Faith. "Copies of the Septuagint," says *CE.*, "were multiplied, and, *as might be expected, many changes, deliberate* as well as involuntary, crept in." (*CE.* xiii, 723.) Indeed, the itch for Scripture-scribbling was so rife among such ex-Pagan Christians as could write and get hold of a copy, that St. Augustine complains: "It is possible to enumerate those who have translated the Scriptures from Hebrew into Greek, but not those who have translated them into Latin. In sooth, in the early days of the faith whoso possessed a Greek manuscript and thought he had some knowledge of both tongues was daring enough to undertake a translation." (*De Doct. Christ.* II, xi; *CE.* ix, 20.) So the Faith was founded on befuddlement of the Blessed Word of God as any nondescript scribbler palmed it off to be.

We shall more than abundantly see that Holy Church never possessed or used a single book of "Scripture" or other document of importance, to the glory of God and the glorification of the Church, which was not a rank original forgery and bristled besides with "many deliberate changes" or forged interpolations.

THE SEPTUAGINT AND THE "VIRGIN-BIRTH" FRAUD

The most colossal of the blunders of the Septuagint translators, supplemented by the most insidious, persistent and purposeful falsification of text, is instanced in the false translation of the notoriously false pretended "prophecy" of Isaiah vii, 14,—frauds which have had the most disastrous and fatal consequences for Christianity, and to humanity under its blight; the present exposure of which should instanter destroy the false Faith built on these frauds.

The Greek priest who forged the "Gospel according to St. Matthew," having before him the false Septuagint translation of Isaiah, fables the Jewish Mary yielding to the embraces of the Angel Gabriel to engender Jesus, and backs it up by appeal to the Septuagint translation of Isaiah vii, 14:

"Behold, a virgin shall be with child, and shall bring forth a son, and they shall call his name Emmanuel." (Matt. i, 23.)

Isaiah's original Hebrew, with the mistranslated words underscored, reads: "Hinneh *ha-almah harah* ve-yeld*eth* ben ve-kar*ath* shem-o immanuel";—which, falsely translated by the false pen of the pious translators, runs thus in the English: "Behold, *a virgin shall* conceive and bear a son, and *shall* call his name Immanuel" (Isa. vii, 14.) The Hebrew words *ha-almah* mean simply *the young woman*; and *harah* is the Hebrew past or perfect tense, *"conceived,"* which in Hebrew, as in English, represents *past and completed* action. Honestly translated, the verse reads: "Behold, *the young woman has conceived*—[is with child]—and bear*eth* a son and call*eth* his name Immanuel."

Almah means simply a young woman, of marriageable age, whether married or not, or a virgin or not; in a broad general sense exactly like *girl* or *maid* in English, when we say shop-girl, parlor-maid, barmaid, without reference to or vouching for her technical *virginity*, which, in Hebrew, is always expressed by the word *bethulah*. But in the Septuagint translation into Greek, the Hebrew *almah* was erroneously rendered into the Greek *parthénos, virgin*, with the definite article *ha* in Hebrew, and *e* in Greek, (the), rendered into the indefinite "*a*" by later falsifying translators. (See *Is It God's Word?* pp. 277–279; *EB.* ii, 2162; *New Commentary on the Holy Scripture*, Pt. I, p. 439.) And St. Jerome falsely used the Latin word *virgo*.

"As early as the second century B. C.," says the distinguished Hebrew scholar and critic, Salomon Reinach, "the *Jews perceived the error and pointed it out to the Greeks; but the Church knowingly per-*

sisted in the false reading, and for over fifteen centuries she has clung to her error." (*Orpheus,* p, 197.) The truth of this accusation of conscious persistence in known error through the centuries is proved by the confused confession of St. Jerome, who made the celebrated Vulgate translation from the Hebrew into Latin, and intentionally "clung to the error," though Jerome well knew that it was an error and false; and thus he perpetuated through fifteen hundred years the myth of the "prophetic virgin birth" of Jesus called the Christ.

Being criticized by many for this falsification, St. Jerome thus replies to one of his critics, Juvianus: "I know that the Jews are accustomed to meet us with the objection that in Hebrew the word *Almah* does not mean a *virgin,* but a *young woman.* And, to speak truth, a virgin is properly called *Bethulah,* but a young woman, or a girl, is not *Almah,* but *Naarah"!* (Jerome, *Adv. Juvianum,* I, 32; *N&PNF.* vi, 370.) So insistent was the criticism, that he was driven to write a book on the subject, in which he makes a very notable confession of the inherent incredibility of the Holy Ghost paternity-story: "For who at that time *would have believed the Virgin's word* that she had conceived of the Holy Ghost, and that the angel Gabriel had come and announced the purpose of God? and would not *all* have given their opinion against her *as an adulteress,* like Susanna? For at the present day, *now that the whole world has embraced the faith,* the Jews argue that when Isaiah says, 'Behold, a virgin shall conceive and bear a son,' the Hebrew word denotes a young woman, *not a virgin,* that is to say, the word is ALMAH, not BETHULAH"! (Jerome, *The Perpetual Virginity of Blessed Mary, N&PNF.* vi, 336.)

So the Greek Father or priest who forged the false "virgin-birth" interpolation into the manuscript of "Matthew," drags in maybe ignorantly the false Septuagint translation of Isaiah vii, 14, which the Latin Father St. Jerome purposely perpetuated as a pious "lie to the glory of God." The Catholic and King James Versions purposely retain this false translation; the Revised Version keeps it in, but with a gesture of honesty, which is itself a fraud, sticks into the margin in fine type, after the words "a virgin" and "shall conceive," the words, "Or, *the maiden is with child and beareth,*"—which not one in thousands would ever see or understand the significance of. So it is not some indefinite "a virgin" who 750 years in the future "shall conceive" and "shall bear" a son whose name she "shall call" Immanuel, or Jesus; but it was some known and definite young female, married or un-married—but *not* a "virgin"—who had already conceived and was already pregnant, and who bear*eth* a son and call*eth* his name Im-manuel, . . . who should be the "sign" which "my lord" should give to Ahaz of the truth of Isaiah's false prophecy regarding the pending war with Israel and Syria, as related in Isaiah vii, and of which the total falsity is proven in 2 Chronicles xxviii, as all may read.

Although Papal Infallibility has declared that "it will never be lawful to grant . . . that the sacred writers *could have made a mis-take*" (Leo XIII, Encyc. *Provid. Deus; CE.* ii, 543), yet, the fraud being notorious and exposed to the scorn of the world, and being driven by force of modern criticism, *CE.* definitely and positively—though with the usual clerical soft-soaping, confesses this age-long clerical fraud and falsification of Holy Writ, and relegates it to the junk-heap of discredited—but not discarded—dogmatic myth:

"Modern theology does not grant that Isaiah vii, 14, contains *a real prophecy fulfilled* in the virgin birth of Christ; it *must maintain,* there-fore, that St. Matthew *misunderstood* the passage when he said: 'Now all this was done that it might be fulfilled which the Lord spoke by the prophet, saying, Behold, *a virgin shall be* with child, and bring forth a son, etc."! (*CE.* xv, 451.)

Thus is apparent, and confessed, the dishonesty of "Matthew" and of the Church of Christ in perverting this idle, false and falsified text of Isaiah into a "prophecy of the virgin birth of Jesus Christ," and in persisting in retaining this falsity in their dishonest Bibles as the basis of their own bogus theology unto this day of the Twentieth Century. The Church, full knowing its falsity, yet clings to this pre-cious lie of Virgin Birth and all the concatenated consequences. Thus it declares its own condemnation as false. Some other viciously false translations of sacred Scripture will be duly noticed in their place.

As Thomas Jefferson prophetically wrote,—as is being verified:

"The day will come when the mystical generation of Jesus by the Su-preme Being as his father, in the womb of a virgin, will be classed with the fable of the generation of Minerva in the brain of Jupiter"!

The marvels of the canonical apocrypha of the Hebrew sacred Books, or of the whole 94 miraculously "restored" by Ezra, could not slake the thirst of the Jewish intellect for such edifying histories, and their priests were very industrious in supplying the demands of piety and marvel-craving. Making use, as above admitted, of the most "venerable Old Testament names," they forged a voluminous literature of fanciful and fantastic fairy-tales in the guise of sacred history, revelations, oracles or predictions, all solemnly "set forth as though actually received, and written or spoken by ancient worthies, as Enoch, Moses, etc., which were widely accepted as genuine, and found a warm reception in Jewish and early Christian circles." Scarcely is there a Biblical notable of Israel in whose name these pious false writings were not forged, including Adam and Eve, and most of the ante- and post-Diluvian Patriarchs. It is impossible here to much more than mention the names of some of the principal ones of these extra-canonical apocrypha and forgeries of the Jews, as listed in the *Catholic Encyclopedia* and the *Encyclopedia Biblica*, most of them worked over with surcharge of added Christian forgeries, to adapt them to their pious propaganda.

The names of these "intriguing" volumes of forgotten lore, listed somewhat after the order of their distinguished pretended authors and times, are: Life of Adam and Eve; Testament of Adam; The Book of Creation; the Books of Seth (son of Adam); Book of Enoch (grandson of Adam); Secrets of Enoch; Parables of Enoch; Book of Lamech; Book of Noah; Book of Zoroaster (identified with Ham, son of Noah); Apocalypse of Noah; Apocalypse of Abraham; Testament of Abraham; Testament of Isaac; Testament of Jacob; The Testaments of the Twelve Patriarchs; Testament of the Three Patriarchs; Testament of Naphthali; The Prayer of Menasseh; The Prayer of Joseph; The Story of Asenath (wife of Joseph); Prayer of Asenath; The Marriage of Asenath; The Assumption of Moses; The Testament of Moses; Book of Jannes and Mambres (the Egyptian magicians with whom Moses contended); Penitence of Jannes and Mambres; The Magical Books of Moses; The Book of Jubilees, or

Little Genesis; Book of Og the Giant; Treatise of the Giants; Josippon; Book of Jasher; The Liber Antiquitatem Bibliarum, ascribed to Philo; The Chronicles of Jerameel; Testament of Job; Psalm CLI of David, "when he fought with Goliath"; Testament of Solomon; The Contradictio Salomonis (a contest in wisdom between Solomon and Hiram); The Psalms of Solomon; Apocalypse of Elijah; Apocalypse of Baruch; The Rest of the Words of Baruch; History of Daniel; Apocalypse of Daniel; Visions of Daniel; Additions to Daniel, *viz.:* The History of Susanna (Chap. 13), the Song of the Three Children, Story of Bel and the Dragon (Chap. 14); Tobit; Judith; Additions to Esther; The Martyrdom of Isaiah; The Ascension of Isaiah; III and IV Esdras; Apocalypse of Esdras; Story of the Three Pagans, in I Esdras; I, II, III, and IV Maccabees; The Prophecy of Eldad and Medad; Apocalypse of Zephaniah; Stories of Artaphanus; Eupolemus; Story of Aphikia, wife of Jesus Sirach; The Letter of Aristeas to Philocrates; The Sibylline Oracles.

Quite half of the above Jewish false-writings, separately listed under the grouping of "Jewish with Christian Accretions," the *Catholic Encyclopedia* describes with comments such as "recast or freely interpolated by Christians," "many Christian interpolations," etc., "presenting in their ensemble a fairly full Christology" (*CE.* i, 606). If the pious Christians, confessedly, committed so many and so extensive forgeries and frauds to adapt these popular Jewish fairy-tales of their God and holy Worthies to the new Christian Jesus and his Apostles, we need feel no surprise when we discover these same Christians forging outright new wonder-tales of their Christ under the fiction of the most noted Christian names and in the guise of inspired Gospels, Epistles, Acts and Apocalypses.

THE "INSPIRED" HEBREW SCRIPTURES

The processes of the formation of the Hebrew Old Testament Scriptures are, however, interesting and intriguing, if sacred tradition is true. According to priestly lore, the man Moses, "learned in all the wisdom of the Egyptians" (another Christian assurance; Acts vii, 22), sat down in the Wilderness of Sinai and under divine inspiration wrote his Five Books of prehistorical history, codes of post-exilic divine Law, and chronicles of contemporary and future notable events, including four different names of his father-in-law—(*viz.:* Jethro, Ex. iii, 1; Reuel, Ex. ii, 18; Jether, Ex. iv, 18, and Raguel, Num. x, 29, while a fifth name, Hobab, is awarded him in Judges iv, 11), together with a graphic account of his own death and burial, and of the whole month afterwards spent by all Israel mourning his death. He also records the death of his brother Aaron at Mt. Hor (Num. xx, 28; xxxiii, 38), just six months before his own death; though, in amazing contradiction, he elsewhere records Aaron as having died at Mosera, just after leaving Sinai (Deut. x, 6), thirty-nine years previously,—and thus nullifies the entire history of the wonderful career and deeds of Aaron as high priest during the whole 40 years of wandering in the Wilderness, of which the Books of Exodus, Leviticus and Numbers are largely filled; as also many other matters and things occurring for some centuries after his death, and known as "post-Mosaica" to the scholars.

Joshua, the successor of Moses, next wrote the history of his life and times, working in, too, a sketch of his own death and funeral obsequies (Josh. xxiv, 29–30), and quoting the celebrated miracle of the sun standing still, of which he says, "Is it not written in the Book of Jasher?"—which Book of Jasher was not itself written until several hundred years later, at least in or after the time of David; for it is recorded: "And he [David] bade them teach the children of Judah the use of the bow; behold, it is written in the Book of Jasher." (2 Sam. i, 18.)

The Book of Judges was written by nobody knows whom, nor when, except that it was long "post-exilic." It relates that, "Now the children of Judah had fought against Jerusalem, and had taken it" (Jud. i, 18); whereas it was not until David had reigned seven years and six months in Hebron, that "the King and his men went to Jerusalem" and failed to capture it, "nevertheless, David took the stronghold of Zion, and called it the City of David." (2 Sam. v, 5–9.) It is further recorded in Judges that the tribe of Dan made a silver idol of the Hebrew God and hired a grandson of Moses to serve it, and "he and his sons were priests to the tribe of Dan until the captivity of the land" (Jud. xviii, 30)—about a thousand years later.

The gifted Samuel, Prophet of the heathen High Places of Baal-worship, gives his name and inspiration to two books of mythical history written piecemeal until the "return from captivity," as above indicated, and early in his work he records the historic episode of the calling up of his own ghost from the dead by the famous Witch of En-dor. (1 Sam. xviii, 1, 7–19.)

The ex-bandit David, "man after God's own heart"—after murdering a man to get his adulterous wife, and engendering of her his all-wise son and hero, Solomon, wrote the 150 songs of the Hebrew Hymn Book, many of his psalms singing of the long posthumous Babylonian Captivity.

Solomon himself, who was son-in-law to nearly everybody in the heathen nations round about who had eligible daughters, wrote the wisdom of the ages into his Book of Proverbs, though not one of them is by Solomon, and in his lighter (headed or hearted) spells penned his erotic Canticles, which for realistic lubricity quite outdo Boccaccio, and would be really unmailable under the Postal Laws if they weren't in the Holy Bible and clerically captioned "The Church's Love unto Christ." These are indeed but one collection out of the great many pornographic stories of The Holy Ghost's *Decameron*, enshrined in God's Holy Word for delectation of the Puritans of Faith.

Other divinely inspired and anonymous writers, falsely entitling their effusions under the names of this or that Prophet or other wholly fictitious personage, as Job, Esther, Ruth, Daniel, gave forth yet other inspired histories, books of oracles or prophecies, apocalypses or high powered visions into Futurity, and a miscellany of sacred novels, love-stories and nondescript musings or ravings known collectively as the hagiographa or holy writings of the Jews. All these together, now thirty-nine in number, comprise the Hebrew Bible or Old Testament. It being out of question to review each of these here, it may be stated with assurance that not one of them bears the name of its true author; that every one of them is a composite work of many hands "interpolating" the most anachronistic and contradictory matters into the original writings, and often reciting as accomplished facts things which occurred many centuries after the time of the supposed writer, as Psalms, Isaiah, Daniel, and the so-called "historical" books. For scientific detailed demonstration of this the *Encyclopedia Biblica* digests the most competent authorities; my own *Is It God's Word?*

makes the proofs from the sacred texts themselves. See the recent "Religious Book of the Month Club's" notable *Unraveling the Book of Books,* by Trattner. (1929.)

But as the Christian religion depends more vitally on Genesis and Moses than on all the other sacred writings and writers, we may appeal to the admissions of *CE.,* thereto driven by force of modern criticism, for the destruction and abandonment of the Moses Mythus:

"It is true that the Pentateuch, so long attributed to Moses, is now held by the vast majority of non-Catholic, and by an increasing number of Catholic, scholars to be a compilation of four independent sources put together in final shape soon after the Captivity." (*CE.* i, 622.)

This scores strongly for Hebrew-Christian forgery and fraud in attributing this primitive system of Bible "science" and barbarous law to a god as a pretext for priestly domination of the superstitious people. That God-given forged law thus prescribes for priestcraft: "The man that will do presumptuously, and will not hearken unto the priest, . . . even that man shall die." (Deut. xvii, 12.) The whole Five Books of Moses are thus a confessed forgery in the names of Moses and of God; every one of the *Thus saith the Lord* a thousand times repeated, with speeches and laws put into the mouth of the God, are false and forged. Speaking of the "difficulty, in the present condition of Old Testament criticism, of recognizing more than a small portion of the Pentateuch as documentary evidence contemporary with Moses,"—who, if he ever lived, which may be confidently denied, —never wrote a line of it, *CE.* further confesses to the natural evolution—*not* the "divine revelation"—of the Hebrew mythology into a (no less mythological) monotheistic religion: "The Hegelian principle of evolution . . . applied to religion, has powerfully helped to beget a tendency to regard the religion of Israel as *evolved* by processes not transcending nature, from a polytheistic worship of the elements to a spiritual and ethical monotheism." (*CE.* i, 493.) But this finally and very late evolved monotheism is neither a tardy divine revelation to the Jews, nor a novel invention by them; it was a thousand years antedated by Amenhotep IV and Tut-ankh-amen in Egypt,—nor were even they the pioneers. We have seen the admission that the Zoroastrian Mithra religion was "a divinely revealed Monotheism" (*CE.* ii, 156).

70

But the Hebrews were confessed and notorious idolaters and polytheists until after the Captivity; that fact is a thousand times alleged throughout the Scriptures as the sole reason for their troubles and captivity. As above suggested, and as thoroughly demonstrated by the texts in my other book, the Hebrew God Yahveh was but one of the many gods worshipped by the Hebrews; and Yahveh never claimed more than to be a "God above all gods," to be preferred before them all;—as at Sinai he enacted: "Thou shalt have no other gods *before* [in preference to] me,"—thus omitting the other gods.

FORGERY BY CONTRADICTIONS

Contradictions throughout the Bible, Old and New Testaments alike, abound by the many thousands, and in virtually every book of both Testaments,—as every one knows who has read the Bible even casually. See some thousand and more of the most notorious and vital ones are cited in "deadly parallel" in my *Is It God's Word?* as one of the most conclusive proofs of uninspired human origin and of confusion worse confounded of tinkering, "interpolation" and forgery outright, by the pious priests of Israel and Judah, and the Ezra "school" of forgers of the "Law and the Prophets."

OUR "PHONY" CHRISTIAN ERA

"It was a monk of the 6th century, named Dionysius Exiguus (Dennis the Little), who fixed our present Christian era, laying down that Jesus Christ was born on the 25th of December, A. U. C. 753, and commencing the new era from the following year, 754. That date, as we shall see, *cannot be correct* and, instead of being an improvement on, is farther from the truth than the dates assigned by the early Fathers, St. Irenæus and Tertullian, who fixed the date of the Nativity in the 41st year of Augustus, that is to say, 3 years B. C., or A. U. C. 751 . . . All this points to the fact that Herod died in the year 4 B. C., and that our Saviour must have been born before that date . . . Our Saviour was born some time before Herod's death, probably two years or more. So that, if Herod died in the year 4 B. C., we should be taken to 6 or 7 B. C. as the year of the Nativity" (*CE.* 735–6).

This, of course, discredits the date given by the inspiration of

71

Luke, and demonstrates that both he and Matthew merely alleged fictitious dates for what in all human probability was a purely fictitious event. The new Era of Christ was, however, very slow in gaining recognition; the first official secular document dating by it was a charter of Charlemagne, after 800 A. D., and it did not come into general use until about 1000 A. D. I may mention a fiery sermon I once heard, in which the expounder of truth vindicated the glory of God by declaiming that every Jew and Infidel confessed to Jesus Christ every time he dated a letter or mentioned the year of an event. Being simply a hearer of the Word, I could not rise to suggest, that by the same token we confess more to the Pagan gods than to the Christian,—for more than half the months and every day of the week are named for Pagan deities, and we name them much more often than we do the years of grace and salvation of Christ. After this bad start from Gospel error and contradiction, we now turn to further evidences of "Gospel truth" in contradictions and forgery.

Among the most signal of these incessant contradictions and scientific impossibilities of Divine Inspiration, are those relating to the capital matter,—for the credit of the Christian Religion, of the time and manner of Creation of earth and Man, based on Holy Writ and on the "chronology" worked out, with several hundred disparate results, from the inspired pedigrees of the ante-Diluvian Patriarchs. So fatally important is this to Christianity, that the True Church—"which never deceived anyone" and "has never erred,"—speaking through CE., thus admits that Christianity stands or falls with— "the *literal, historical sense of the first three chapters of Genesis* in as far as they bear on *the facts touching the foundations of the Christian religion, e. g.*, the creation of all things by God at the beginning of time, the special creation of man, the formation of the first woman from the first man, the unity of the human race"! (*Papal Biblical Commission*, June 30, 1909; *CE*. vii, 313). Thus: No Adam and Eve, no Garden of Eden and Talking Snake, no "Fall" and Curse—therefore: No Saviour Jesus Christ, no Plan of Salvation, no truth in the Christian Religion! The fatal point is elucidated with inexorable logic and dogmatic truth by the "Reformed" ex-Father Peter Martyr: "So important is it to comprehend the *work of creation* that we see the creed of the Church take this as its starting point. Were this Article taken away, there

72

would be no original sin; the promise of Christ would become void, and all the vital force of our religion would be destroyed"! Father Luther inherited the same faith and bequeathed it to his dissident following: "Moses spoke properly and plainly, and neither allegorically nor figuratively; and therefore the world with all creatures was created in six days." Calvin, in his "Commentary on Genesis," argues that the Genesis account of Creation is literally true, and warns those who dare to believe otherwise, and thus "basely insult the Creator, to expect a Judge who will annihilate them." Again he says: "We know on the authority of Moses, that longer ago than 6000 years the world did not exist." So too, the Westminster Confession of Faith, in full Protestant force and effect today—specially lays it down as "necessary to salvation to believe that all things visible and invisible were created not only out of nothing but exactly in six days." And the Churches have murdered countless thousands to impress this beautiful impossible truth.

Notwithstanding the crushing disproofs of those primitive forged "Fables of Moses," by every fact of astronomy, geology, anthropology, biology, and kindred sciences, known to schoolboys today, Faith clings fatuously to its fetiches: Arkansas ("Now laugh!"), Mississippi, Tennessee, three States of the Twentieth Century United States, have made it crime by Law to teach the sciences which discredit the Genesis Myths, upon which Christian Superstition utterly depends; and like medieval laws are sought to be imposed in all our States. The True Church, like all the others, still founds its "Faith and Morals" upon these old Hebrew forgeries of Genesis and peddles them to its Faithful; but it knows better. Thus the whole True Faith is shipwrecked by these heretical confessions of *CE.*, forced from it by the truths of heretical Modernism, in full face of the fierce inspired fulminations of the Syllabus of Errors: "In an article on Bible chronology it is hardly necessary in these days to discuss the date of the Creation. At least two hundred dates have been suggested, varying from 3483 to 6934 years B. C., all based on the supposition that the Bible enables us to settle the point. But it does nothing of the kind. . . . The literal interpretation has now been entirely abandoned; and the world is admitted to be of immense antiquity"! (*CE.* iii, 731.) Again the "sacred science" of Genesis and of Christianity is further admitted to be false, and the fabulous "Septuagint" Bible on which Christianity was founded before the era of the second century forgeries of Gospels and Epistles, to be a holy fraud, in these further excerpts accrediting the true revelations of modern Science as against those of Moses:

"The church . . . does not attach decisive influence to the chronology of the Vulgate, the official version of the Western Church, since in the Martyrology for Christmas day, the creation of Adam is put down in the year 5199 B. C., which is the reading of the Septuagint. It is, however, certain that we cannot confine the years of man's sojourn on earth to that usually set down. . . . Various explanations have been given of chapter v (Genesis) to explain the short time it seems to allow between the Creation and the Flood. . . . The total number of years in the Hebrew, Samaritan, and Septuagint differs, in the Hebrew it being 1656, in the Samaritan 1307, and in the Septuagint 2242. . . . According to Science the length of this period was much greater than appears from the genealogical table. . . . In any case, whether we follow the traditional or critical view, the numbers obtained from the genealogy of the Patriarchs in chapter xi must be greatly augmented, in order to allow time for such a development of civilization, language, and race type as had been reached by the time of Abraham." (*CE.* iii, 731–3.)

FORGERY BY FALSE TRANSLATIONS

We have noted the capital forgery wrought by the Church in consciously and unconscionably adopting and perpetuating the false translation in the Septuagint, of the *"virgin shall conceive"* pretended prophecy of Isaiah vii, 14. Indisputably the whole forged fabric of supernatural Christianity is based on, and depends upon, this one monumental forgery falsely used to give credit to the Christian forgery of "the Gospel according to Matthew" as to the Divine and miraculous "Virgin birth of Jesus Christ." Out of scores of other notoriously falsified translations of the sacred Old Testament texts, attention is here called only to several of the most signal ones which vitally affect and destroy the validity of the most essential pretensions of truth of the Christian religion. These frauds of translation and others, have been thoroughly examined and supported by numerous texts from the original Hebrew, and falsified verses of the English versions, in my *Is It God's Word?*, to which references must be made for a more complete treatment than is here pertinent. Those now cited in summary are all of them deliberate falsifications and forgeries in translation which go to the vitals of the Hebrao-Christian system of holy imposture.

If the Hebrew originals had been truthfully translated, we should have no such false pretenses for faith as the Hebrew One God anciently revealed to Adam, and to Moses, no Adam, no man "but little lower than the angels" because of his immortal soul, no unique "revelation" of the "Ineffable Name" Jehovah to Moses; all that we would have,—all that the Hebrew texts reveal—is a primitive polytheistic idolatry of the crudest and most superstitious order. Let us see.

(a) The "God" Forgery

The first sentence of the translated Bibles is a falsification and forgery of the highest importance. We read with awed solemnity of faith: "In the beginning God created the heaven and the earth" (Gen. i, 1). The Hebrew word for God is *el;* the plural is *elohim,* gods. The Hebrew text of Genesis i, 1, reads: *"Bereshith bara elohim,"* etc.,— "In-beginning created *gods* the-heavens and-the-earth." And, in the same chapter we read in Hebrew *honestly translated,*—thirty times the word *"elohim," gods*, to whom are attributed all the works of creation in the six peculiar "days" of Genesis. This is plainly evident from the Hebrew texts of Genesis i, which even false intention could not hide in the translation, "And-said *elohim* (gods), Let-*US*-make man (*adam*) *in-image-OUR*, after-likeness-*OUR*" (i, 26). And when "adam" had eaten of the forbidden fruit of the tree of knowledge, "the *Lord God*" said, "Behold, the-man has become like one of *US*, to know good and evil" (iii, 27). And when the Tower of Babel was abuilding, "The *Lord* [Heb. Yahveh] said . . . Come, let *US* go down," etc. And thus, some 2570 times the *plural, elohim, gods*, is used in the Hebrew texts, but is always falsely translated "God" in the false singular, when speaking of the Hebrew deity, Yahveh.

In the three Genesis verses above quoted, we have three different designations of the Hebrew deity or deities: *elohim,* gods, falsely translated "God"; "Lord God" (Heb. *Yahveh-elohim*); and "Lord"

(Heb. *Yahveh*). Yahveh is the proper name of the Hebrew God, in English rendered Jehovah: *Yahveh-elohim* is a Hebrew "construct-form" honestly meaning "Yahveh-of-the-gods." Invariably (with rare exceptions to be noted), these personal names are falsely rendered "Lord" and "Lord God," respectively, for purposes of pious fraud which we shall now expose to the shame of a theology of imposture. We will return to this after noting a pair of others.

(b) The "Adam" Forgery

There was no first man "Adam," according to the Hebrew texts of the story. The word *adam* in Hebrew is a common noun, meaning *man* in a generic sense; in Genesis i, 26, we have read: "And *elohim* (gods) said, Let us make *adam* (man)"; and so "*elohim* created *ha-adam* (the-man); . . . male and female created he them" (i. 27). And in the second story, where man is first made alone: "Yahveh formed *ha-adam* (the-man) out of the dust of *ha-adamah*—the ground" (ii, 7). Man is called in Hebrew *adam* because formed out of *adamah*, the ground; just as in Latin man is called *homo* because formed from *humus*, the ground,—*homo ex humo*, in the epigram of Father Lactantius. (Lact., *Divine Institutes*, ii, 58; *ANF*. vii, 58.) The forging of the common noun *adam* into a mythical proper name Adam, was a post-exilic fraud in the forging of fictitious genealogies from "in the beginning" to Father Abraham.

(c) The "Soul" Forgery

In Genesis i is the account of the creation of *elohim*—gods—on the fifth day, of "*nephesh hayyah*—the moving creature that hath life," and of "*nephesh hayyah*—every living creature"—out of the *waters* (i, 20, 21); and on the sixth day of "*nephesh hayyah*—the living creature" out of the *ground* (i, 24); and he gave to *ha-adam—the-man* dominion over "*kol nephesh hayyah*—everything wherein there is life." (i, 30.) So reads the Hebrew text—all these dumb animal living creatures are by God called "*nephesh hayyah*,"—literally "living soul," as will be found stuck into the margins of the Authorized Version. In chapter ii we have the history of *ha-adam* made from *ha-adamah*; and, in wonderful contrast to these lowly "living creatures"

76

(*nephesh hayyah*), Yahveh-elohim "breathed into his nostrils *nish-math hayyim*—(living breaths), and *ha-adam* became *nephesh hayyah*—a living soul"! (ii, 7.) In Hebrew *nephesh* everywhere and simply means *soul*, and *hayyah* (living) is the feminine singular adjective from *hai*, life. Man, therefore, was created exactly the same as the other animals; all had or were *nephesh hayyah*—living souls, indistinctly. The "false pen of the scribes," who in translation made the dumb animals merely *living creatures*, and "Creation's microcosmical masterpiece, Man," a "living soul," falsely altered these plain words so as to deceive into a belief of a special God-breathed soul in man, far different from the brute animal that perisheth.

(d) The "Mosaic Revelation" Forgery

When Yahveh appeared to Moses in the Burning Bush, and announced himself as "the God of thy fathers," he was a total stranger to Moses; Moses did not at all know him, had never heard of him; so that he asked, "What is thy name?"—so that he could report it to the people back home in Egypt, who had never heard it. After some intermission, the God came directly to the point, and declared—I quote the exact words—one of the most notorious falsities in Holy Writ:

"And *elohim* spake unto Moses, and said unto him, *anoki Yahveh*—I am the *Lord!*

"And I appeared unto Abraham, unto Isaac, and unto Jacob, by the name of el-shaddai, but by my name Yahveh (JEHOVAH) *was I not known to them.*" (Ex. vi, 2, 3.)

Here we have the positive averment of the Hebrew God himself to the effect that here, for the first time since the world began, is "revealed" to mankind the "ineffable name" of Yahveh, here first appearing in the Bible translations, and there printed as JEHOVAH in capital letters for more vivid and awe-inspiring impression. But this is a capital Lie of the Lord, or of his biographer who imputed it to him. In verse 4 of Genesis ii, the *name* YAHVEH first appears; "in the day that *Yahveh-elohim* made the earth and the heavens." Its first recorded use in the mouth of a mythical personage, was when Mother Eve "conceived, and bare Cain, and said, I have gotten a man from *Yahveh*

77

—the Lord." (Gen. iv, 1.) One hundred and fifty-six times the personal *name* YAHVEH occurs in the Book of Genesis alone; and scores of these times in the mouths of Abraham, of Isaac, and of Jacob, as any one may read in Genesis, with the assurance that every single time that the title "the Lord" and "the Lord God" appears, it is a false translation by the priests for the Hebrew personal name YAHVEH. Throughout the Hebrew "Scriptures" the Divine Name thousands of times occurs: "The sacred name occurs in Genesis about 156 times; . . . in round numbers it is found in the Old Testament 6000 times, either alone or in conjunction with another Divine name." (*CE.* viii, 329, 331.) More exactly, "What is called the Tetragrammaton, YHVH, appears in the Old Testament 6823 times as the *proper name* of God as the God of Israel. As such it serves *to distinguish him from the gods of the other nations.*" (*EB.* iii, 3320.) Thus was the Hebrew tribal god YAHVEH distinguished from Bel, and Chemosh, and Dagon, and Shamash, and the scores of "gods of the nations"; just as Bill distinguishes its bearer from Tom, Dick, and Harry. This was precisely the Hebrew usage—to distinguish one heathen god from another. And this the false translators sought to hide, giving names to all the "other gods," but suppressing a *name* for the Hebrew deity, who as "the Lord," or "the Lord God," was high and unique, "a god above all gods,"—the one and only true God.

But yet more malicious and evil-intentioned of deception: 6823 times is the *name* of the Hebrew God concealed by false rendition for the deliberate purpose of forging the whole Hebrew Bible, as translated, into semblance of harmony with the false avowal of Exodus vi, 3, that "by my *name* YAHVEH was I *not known* unto them." Search as one may, outside Exodus vi, 3, the god-name YAHVEH (Jehovah) is never to be found in the translations in a single instance, except in Psalm lxxxiii, 18, and Isaiah xii, 2 and xxvi, 4. The false translations thus "make truth to be a liar," the lie of Exodus vi, 3 to seem the truth; and a barbarous heathen tribal god among a hundred neighbor and competitive gods to be the nameless One Lord God of the Universe. The Hebrew-Christian One God is a patent Forgery and Myth; a mythological Father-god can have no "only begotten Son"; Jesus Christ is a mythus even before he is mythically born in the

78

fancies of the Church Fathers, as we shall soon have ample evidence to prove.

With respect to the mythical Hebrew-Christian God or gods, we may safely say, as says Father Justin Martyr apropos of the other mythic Pagan gods: "And we confess that we are atheists, so far as gods of this sort are concerned." (*First Apology*, ch. vi; *ANF*. i, 169.)

THE ANCIENT IDEA OF "HISTORY"

We may pause a moment to catch a valuable view which will be of great aid to understanding the mental processes of the ancient writers in their portrayal of events, real or fanciful, which they set about to record as "history." These pioneers of historical literature lived in an age of simple-minded credulity, and everything which they saw recorded or heard related, however extravagant and seemingly incredible or impossible, passed all as perfectly good history in their receptive and uncritical minds. Speaking of the legendary, the traditional, the supernatural stories, myths, folk-lore and fables,—"in short, everything which seemed to testify to the past,"—which formed the raw material of the early historians, the *Encyclopedia Biblica* gives a graphic picture of primitive history-writing, not only Hebraic but Gentilic:

"Their sources, like those of the Greek logographers with whom it is natural to compare them, were poems, genealogies, often representing clan-groupings, tribal and local traditions of diverse kinds, such as furnish the materials for most of the Book of Judges; the historical traditions of sanctuaries; the sacred legends of holy places, relating theophanies and other revelations, the erection of the altar or sacred stone, the origin of popular usages—*e. g.* Bethel; laws; myths of foreign or native origin; folk-lore and fable,—in short, everything which seemed to testify of the past.

"To us the greater part of this material is not in any proper sense historical at all; but for the early Israelite as for the early Greek historian it was otherwise; our distinctions between authentic history, legendary history, pure legend, and myth, he made as little as he recognized our distinction of natural and supernatural. It was all history to him; and if one part of it had a better attestation than another, it was certainly the sacred history as it was told at the ancient sanctuaries of the land.

"The early Hebrew historians did not affix their names to their works; they had, indeed, no idea of authorship. The traditions and legends which they collected were common property, and did not cease to be so when they were committed to writing; the written book was in every sense the property of the scribe or the possessor of the roll. Only a part of the great volume of tradition was included in the first books. Transcribers freely added new matter from the same sources on which the original authors had drawn, the traditions of their own locality or sanctuary, variants of historical traditions or legend. Every new copy was thus in some measure a fresh rescension. . . . Scribes compared different copies, and combined their contents according to their own judgment or interests. . . . Of records or monuments there are but a few traces, and these for the most part doubtful." (*EB.* ii, 2075–76.)

To say nothing now of the Old or New Testament "canonical" and "apocryphal" literature, countless examples of this imaginative method of history-writing abound in all the ancient writers, as all who are familiar with such classics as Herodotus, Thucydides, Xenophon, Josephus, Livy, will readily recall. One of the most inveterate forms of imaginative creation on the part of the old historiographers was the invention of sayings and whole speeches which, just as do the fiction-writers of today, they put entire into the mouths of the personages of whom they were writing, which discourses they not only invented whole, but always wrought them in the style and manner of the writer and his epoch, and not in those of their ancient subjects. All are familiar with such instances in Homer, Dante, Shakespeare and Milton, and which we all know are pure inventions of those writers. Naming several of the ancient historians above mentioned, and others, a distinguished philosopher of history thus describes the art:

"Such speeches as we find in Thucydides (for example), of which we can positively assert that they are not *bona-fide* records. . . . Thus Livy puts into the mouths of the old Roman Kings, Consuls, and generals, such orations as would be delivered by an accomplished advocate of the Livian era. . . . In the same way he gives us descriptions of battles, as if he had

80

been an actual spectator; but whose features would serve well enough for battles in any period." (Hegel, *The Philosophy of History,* p. 2.)

Speaking of much later times, and of a different class, but like type, of writers, Hegel again says: "In the Middle Ages, if we except the Bishops, who were placed in the very centre of the political world, the Monks monopolized this category as naïve chroniclers." (*Ib.* p. 3.)

As typical illustration of the principles and practices above described of the best of the ancient writers, but more especially as an example of the kind of "history" written by the most learned and illustrious historian of Jewry, fellow-countryman and contemporary of the supposed Apostolic writers of the New Testament books, it is of the highest significance to cite some of the solemn historical recordations of Josephus, from two of his most famous works; they will make more appreciated at their real value some of the inspired historical recitals of contemporaneous sacred history.

In his *Antiquities of the Jews* Josephus follows closely the subject matter and order of narration of the early Old Testament books, beginning with the Creation, giving the full substance of those histories, and adding quaint comments all his own and expansions and embellishments unknown to or unrecorded by Moses. In Eden, not only the Talking Snake could speak, but all the now dumb animals: "All living creatures had one language, at that time" (I, i, 4). After our parents had eaten of the Fruit of Knowledge and, discovering themselves naked, hid themselves from the Creator, "This behaviour surprised God," who delivers a lengthy speech of reproval not recorded by Moses (*Ib.*); and such orations are plentiful and detailed between God and all the other notables who came into personal contact with him; a gem is his oration to Noah. He relates the wars waged by the wicked posterity of Cain, to the great distress of Adam, who predicted the two-fold destruction of the earth, once by water and again by fire. As the Sethites were good people and intelligent, and had made great discoveries in astronomy, which they wished preserved for such posterity as might survive the yet future Flood, "they made two pillars, the one of brick, the other of stone; they inscribed their discoveries on them both, that in case the pillar of brick should be destroyed by the

Flood, the pillar of stone might remain, and exhibit these discoveries to mankind; and also inform them that there was another pillar of brick erected by them. Now this remains in the land of Siriad to this day." (*Ib.*, I, ii, 2.) He relates with naïve and realistic garnishment the tale of Sodom, and Lot and his daughters, and of Lot's wife turned to a pillar of salt, which is Gospel truth, "for I have seen it, and it remains at this day"! (*Ib.* I, xi, 4.) These historical drolleries might be quoted *ad infinitum* from Jewry's greatest historian.

The name of Solomon was most potent conjure in the Orient through all the succeeding centuries; the spells and charms, amulets and fetiches inscribed with his mystic symbol and pronounced in his name, were the terror of all the devils who so populated the Jewish mind, and the Christian. A noted instance of the potency of this Name, exhibited before the Roman Emperor Vespasian and his court and army, and witnessed by Josephus himself, so circumstantial, so faith-compelling, so artless and childishly fabling, that I am constrained to quote it for the light it sheds on the "historical" methods of the "age of apocryphal literature":

"God also enabled him [Solomon] to learn that skill which expels demons, which is a science useful and sanative to men. He composed such incantations also by which distempers are alleviated. And he left behind him the manner of using exorcisms, by which they drive away demons, so that they never return, and this method of cure is of great force unto this day; for I have seen a certain man of my own country, whose name was Eleazar, relieving people that were demoniacs in the presence of Vespasian, and his sons, and his captains, and the whole multitude of his soldiers. The manner of the cure was this: he put a ring, that had a root of one of the sorts mentioned by Solomon, to the nostrils of the demoniac, after which he drew out the demon through his nostrils; and when the man fell down immediately, he abjured him to return into him no more, making still mention of Solomon, and reciting the incantation which he composed. And when Eleazar would persuade and demonstrate to the spectators that he had such a power, he set a little way off a cup or basin full of water, and commanded the demon, as he went out of the man, to overturn it, and thereby to let the spectators know that he had left the man; and when this was done, the skill and wisdom of Solomon was shown very manifestly; for which reason it is, that all men may know the vastness of Solomon's abilities, and how he was beloved of God, and that the extraordinary virtues of every kind with which this king was endowed, may not be unknown to any people under the sun; for this reason, I say, it is that we have proceeded to speak so largely of these matters." (Josephus, *Antiq. Jews*, Bk. VIII, Ch. ii, 5; Whitson's trans.)

This is followed by the full text of the autograph letters between Solomon and Hiram regarding the building of the Temple.

Whether the same kind of root of Solomon's magical powers just above used by Eleazar, or one of another species of like power, it was very difficult to obtain and the quest was attended with many dangers, which of course enhanced the value and potency of its magic; but here is Josephus's solemn description of the plant and account of the eerie and risky manner of securing this treasure, known locally as Baaras root:

"Its colour is like that of flame, and toward evening it sends out a certain ray like lightning: it is not easily taken by such as would do it, but recedes from their hands, nor will yield itself to be taken quietly, until either the urine of a woman, or blood, be poured upon it; nay, even then it is certain death to those that touch it, unless anyone take and hang the root itself down from his hand, and so carry it away. It may also be taken another way, without danger, which is this: they dig a trench quite round about it, till the hidden part of the root be very small, then they tie a dog to it, and, when the dog tries hard to follow him that tied him, this root is easily plucked up, but the dog dies immediately, as if it were instead of the man that would take the plant away; nor after this need anyone be afraid of taking it into their hands. Yet, after all this pains in getting, it is only valuable on account of one virtue it hath, that if it be only brought to sick persons, it quickly drives away those called demons, which are no other than the spirits of the wicked, that enter into any men that are alive and kill them, unless they can obtain some help against them." (Josephus, *Wars of the Jews*, Book VII, Chap. iv, 3.)

Instead of artful mendacity, some readers, in view of this, may charitably impute artless simplicity of wit to some of the devil-exorcising fable-mongers of the New Testament, the pious Fathers who forged its Books.

If such examples are abounding in the most brilliant of Jewish historians, distinguished for nobility of lineage, for statesmanship and for literary ability, what may be expected from the admittedly "ignorant and unlearned men" such as traditionally wrote those Gospels and Epistles of the Christians? We may now appreciate the

83

full significance of the admission of the *Catholic Encyclopedia,* speaking of the Church Fathers and writers through all the Ages of Faith "before the eighteenth century," of whom it says:

"The early ecclesiastical writers were unconscious of nearly all the problems to which criticism has given rise. . . . Looking at the Divine side, they deemed as of trifling account questions of authorship, date, composition, accepting unreservedly for these points such traditions as the Jewish Church had handed down. . . . The Fathers saw in every sentence of the Scripture a pregnant oracle of God. Apparent contradictions and other difficulties were solved without taking possible human imperfections into view. Except in regard to the preservation of the sacred text there was nothing to elicit a critical view of the Bible in the age of the Fathers, and this applies also to the Scholastic period." (*CE.* iv, 492.)

CHRISTIAN "REVELATIONS" IN JEWISH FORGERIES

Christians no doubt believe in simple faith that the wonderful inspired truths of their New Testament were original pronouncements of Jesus Christ or directly revealed by him to his holy Apostles, who in turn revealed them to the populace for the first time as the "good news" of the new religion for the salvation of sinful man. Even a brief glance at a few of the most notable of the Jewish forgeries of the "age of apochryphal literature" will dispel that pious belief, and show the most characteristic and essential doctrines and dogmas of Christianity to be but refurbished vagaries of the fanciful and fabulous speculations of already existing Jewish apocryphal writings of the times just preceding and within the new Christian era. These writings were put forth falsely as the utterances of long since dead or wholly legendary Old Testament notables, and were neither inspired nor revealed heavenly truth, but simply vain and forged speculations of their fantastic writers. We shall see the cardinal tenets of "revealed" Christianity in a glance at a few of these Jewish pseudographs, and let the Christian apologist explain.

"This literature is of the highest value today because of the light it throws on the growth of eschatological and Messianic doctrines among the Jewish people just previous to the rise of Christianity, especially since these doctrines have, in a purified form, found a permanent place in the Christian system." (*New Int. Encyc.* i, 745.)

HEBREW HOLY FORGERIES

The Book of Enoch, forged in the name of the grandson of Adam, is the fragmentary remains of a whole literature which circulated under the pretended authorship of that mythical Patriarch. In its present form, the work, of 104 chapters, is composed of five Books, with the following titles, of which those of Books 3 and 4 are of particular significance, namely: 1. The Rape of Women by Fallen Angels, and the Giants that were Begotten of Them; 2. The Visions of Enoch begun; 3. The Visions continued, with Views of the Messiah's Kingdom; 4. Man's Destiny revealed in Dreams from the Beginning to the End of the Messianic Kingdom; 5. The Warnings of Enoch to his own Family and to Mankind. This work is a composite of at least five unknown Jewish writers, and was composed during the last two centuries B. C. The forged Book of Enoch is quoted as genuine and inspired in the Christian Epistle of Jude (14, *et seq.*), and as "Scripture" in the near-canonical Epistle of Barnabas; with the early Church Fathers and Apologists, among whom Justin Martyr, Irenæus, Athenagoras, Tertullian, Clement of Alexandria, Anatolius, Origen, St. Augustine, etc., "it had all the weight of a canonical book," but was finally condemned as a forgery by the forged Apostolic Constitutions,—an instance of the very dubious divine guidance of the inspired Church against all error. Father Tertullian devotes an entire chapter "Concerning the Genuineness of the Prophecy of Enoch," in which he gives fantastic patristic reasons as to how the Book survived Noah's Flood, either by the providence of Noah himself or by the Providence of God as in the mythical case of Esdras. In answer to the scoffing objections that the Jews rejected the Book, "I suppose," he seriously argues, "that they do not think that, having been *published before the Deluge*, it could have safely survived that world-wide calamity, the abolisher of all things." But, he urges, "let them recall to their memory that Noah, the survivor of the deluge, was the great-grand-son of Enoch himself," and that Noah probably preserved it at the behest of Methuselah. But, again, "If Noah had not preserved it in this way, there would still be this consideration to warrant our assertion of the genuineness of this Scripture: he could equally have *renewed* it, under the Spirit's inspiration, after it had been destroyed by the violence of the Deluge, as, after the destruction of Jerusalem by the Babylonian storming of it, every document of the Jewish literature is generally agreed to have been restored through Ezra." But the good Father had other and equally cogent clerical reasons for accepting the Book as inspired Scripture: "But since Enoch in the same Scripture has preached likewise concerning the Lord, nothing at all must be rejected *by* us which pertains *to* us; and we read that 'every Scripture suitable for edification is divinely inspired.' . . . To these considerations is added the fact that Enoch possesses a testimony in the Apostle Jude." (*On the Apparel of Women*, II, ii; *ANF*. iv, 15–16.) By this excerpt from the pious Father may be judged the value of the "testimony" of Apostles and Church Fathers as to the inspiration, truth and authenticity of holy "Scriptures,"—which is *nil*.

Of the immense significance of these forged Jewish "sacred writings" in general upon Christian "revelation," and of the fabulous *Book of Enoch* in particular, with its elaborated myth of the Messiah, *CE.* thus confesses: "Jewish Apocalyptic is an attempt to supply the place of prophecy, which had been dead for centuries, and has its roots in the sacred oracles of Israel. . . . Naturally basing itself upon the Pentateuch and the Prophets, it clothed itself *fictitiously* with the authority of a patriarch or prophet who was *made to reveal* the transcendent future. . . . Messianism *of course* plays an important part in apocalyptic eschatology, and the *idea* of the Messias in certain books received a *very high development*. . . . The parables of Henoch, with *their pre-existent Messias*, mark the highest point of *development*—(hence *not* Divine Revelation)—of the Messianic *concept* to be found in the whole range of Hebrew literature." (*CE.* i, 601, 602.) From these uninspired ravings of Jewish forgers came thus the "divine revelation" of the co-eternal "Son of God" worked up instead of the old "revealed" *human* King "of the seed of David."

The forged Book of Enoch, thus vouched for, is notable for being "the earliest appearance of the *Messiah* in non-canonical literature." It is of the greatest importance for its doctrine of the Jewish Messiah, who here appears as wholly an earthly human deliverer and King over Israel forever, and for the origin of the exalted titles applied to the Messiah in the New Testament Books, as well as of a number of supposedly distinctive Christian doctrines, first "revealed" by Jesus the Christ. In this Book we first find the lofty titles: "Christ" or "the Anointed One," "Son of Man," "the Righteous One," "the Elect One,"

—all of which were boldly plagiarized by the later Christians and bestowed on Jesus of Nazareth. The Messiah, just as in the New Testament of later times, exists from the beginning (48, 2); he sits on the throne of God (45, 3); and all judgment is committed unto him (69, 27). The acceptance of Enoch as a Messianic prophet by the Christians led to his rejection by the Jews. Here is the earliest invention of the Christian Hell of fire and brimstone for eternal torture: "The wicked shall go down into the Sheol of darkness and fire and dwell there forever"; this being "one of the earliest mentions of Sheol as a hell of torment" (*CE.* i, 602–3; *EB.* i, 223–5). It is the oldest piece of Jewish literature which teaches the general resurrection of Israel, a doctrine expanded to include Gentiles in later "interpolations" into New Testament books. It abounds in such "Christian" doctrines as the Messianic Kingdom, Hell, the Resurrection, and Demonology, the Seven Heavens, and the Millennium, all of which have here their apocryphal Jewish promulgation, after being plagiarized bodily from the Persian and Babylonian myths and superstitions, as we have seen confessed. There are numerous quotations, phrases, clauses, or thoughts derived from Enoch, or of closest kin with it, in several of the New Testament Gospels and Epistles, which may be readily found and compared as catalogued in the authorities below cited;—Pagan-Jewish myths and doctrines which shared in moulding the analogous New Testament "revelations" or formed the necessary link in the development of doctrines from the Old to the New Testament. The *CE.* says of the Book of Enoch:

"It has left its imprint on the New Testament and the works of the early Fathers. . . . Clement of Alexandria, Tertullian, Origen, and even St. Augustine suppose the work to be *a genuine one of the patriarch.* . . . The work is a compilation, and its component parts were written in Palestine by Jews of the orthodox school . . . in the *latter* part of the second century *before* Christ. (See *CE.* i, 602, *passim; EB.* v, 220–224.)

In Fourth Esdras, as in the Apocalypse of Baruch, we find for the first time, the fatal phrase and doctrine, "all mankind sinned with Adam" (*CE.* i, 604), whence Paul forged his fearful and accursed dogma of original sin and eternal damnation. Fourth Maccabees, erroneously ascribed by Eusebius and others to Josephus, dates from about 4 B. C., just after the death of Herod. It is strongly indoctrinated with the Stoic philosophy, from which the author "derived his four cardinal virtues, Prudence, Justice, Fortitude, Temperance; and it was through Fourth Maccabees that this category was appropriated by early Christian ascetical writers" (*CE.* i, 605–6), and later "canonized" by the Church. (*CE.* xi, 391.)

The Assumption of Moses was forged in the name of that Worthy as its genuine author, about the beginning of or early in the Christian era, with the ostensible purpose of confirming the Mosaic Laws in Deuteronomy. It gives the parting communications of Moses to his successor, Joshua, and unfolds, in a series of pretended predictions, delivered in written form, the course of Israel's history down to Herod's time. Here is found the legend of the dispute between Michael Archangel and Satan over the body of Moses, which the Christian Epistle of Jude (v. 9) cites as God-inspired truth. (*CE.* i, 602–3.) The Book of Jubilees, or little Genesis, is a fabricated embellishment of the Old Testament Genesis, written in the name of Moses somewhere between 135 B. C. and 105 B. C., or 60 A. D., and purports to be a revelation made to Moses by the 'Angel of the Face' of events from Adam to Moses' own day; the Patriarchs are made the exponents of the writer's own Pharisaic views and hopes. It is quoted as good "Scripture" by Greek and Latin Fathers down to the twelfth century, when its forged character was disclosed.

One of the most important of apocryphal apocalyptic forgeries is the Apocalypse of Baruch, "a pseudograph with evident Christian interpolations" (*CE.* i, 604), written by a Jewish Pharisee about 50–90 A. D., who speaks in the first person in the name of Baruch, secretary of the Prophet Jeremiah. The book begins by declaring that the word of the Lord came to him in the *25th year* of King Jeconiah,—who reigned *only three months*, and was carried away captive to Babylon eleven years *before* the fall of Jerusalem, 586 B. C., which event the forgery bewails; it is filled with the Messianic hopes of Jewry at the time of the later fall of Jerusalem in 70 A. D. The book furnishes a setting and background of many distinctive New Testament doctrines and problems, treating of Original Sin, which it traces to the sin of Adam, Forgiveness, Works, Justification, Free Will, etc., and thus enables us to estimate the contributions made in this respect by Jewish

88

forgeries to inspired Christian thought as developed in the so-called Pauline Epistles,—which Paul never wrote. Some notable Fathers, such as Athenagoras, St. Justin Martyr, and St. Irenæus, cite Baruch as a Prophet, and vouch for him as on the same footing as Jeremiah, just as Irenæus vouches for Susanna and Bel and the Dragon as the inspired work of Daniel. (*CE.* i, 604; iii, 271; *EB.* i, 220.)

Father Justin, in several chapters, accuses the Jews of having "removed from Esdras and Jeremiah passages clearly mentioning the Saviour," as also from Psalms; he says: "they have altogether taken away many Scriptures from the translation effected by those Seventy elders who were with Ptolemy, and by which this very man who was crucified is proved to have been set forth expressly as God, and man, and as having been crucified, and as dying." (*Dial. Trypho*, chs. lxxi-lxxiv; *ANF.* i, 234–235.) But these passages, says Middleton, were never in the Hebrew Scriptures; "they were not erased by the Jews, but added [to their copies] by the Christians, or forged by Justin." (*Op. cit.*, pp. 41, 42.)

To what extent these pious Jewish forgeries formed the background and basis of the Christian doctrines and dogmas of pretended direct "revelation," and informed the thought and utterance of Jesus Christ —the raw material and working tools of the Christian propagandist, may be realized from this explicit acknowledgement:

"The most important and valuable of the extant Jewish apocrypha are those which contain the visions and revelations of the unseen world and the Messianic future. Jewish apocryphal literature is a theme which deserves the attention of all interested in the *development* of the religion of Israel, that body of concepts and tendencies in which are fixed the roots of the great *doctrinal principles of Christianity* itself, just as its Divine Founder took his temporal generation from the stock of orthodox Judaism.

"The Jewish *apocryphas* furnish the completing links in the progress of Jewish theology and fill what would otherwise be a gap, though a small one, between the advanced stage marked by the deutero-canonical—[*i. e.* long doubted but finally accepted]—books and its full maturity *so relatively perfect* that Jesus could suppose as existing in the popular consciousness, without teaching *de novo,* the doctrines of Future Retribution, the Resurrection of the body, and the existence, nature and office of angels." (*CE.* i, 601.)

FORGERY IN CHRISTIANITY

All these divine and "revealed" doctrines of Christian faith we have seen to be originally heathen Zoroastrian mythology, taken over first by the Jews, then boldly plagiarized by the ex-Pagan Christians. Dean Milman, of St. Paul's, thus describes the universality of these notions among the heathens and the borrowing by the Jews and Christians of what were originally Pagan superstitions—now become articles of Christian revelation:

"Satan, angels, immortality, resurrection—*all Persian and Zoroastrian doctrines imbibed by the Jews.* . . . During the whole life of Christ, and the early propagation of the religion, it must be borne in mind, that they took place in an age, and among a people, which superstition had made so familiar with what were supposed to be preternatural events, that the wonders awakened no emotion, or were speedily superceded by some new demand on the every-ready belief." (Milman, *History of Christianity*, I, 93.)

Thus, again, the most precious Christian truths, of supposed divine "revelation" through God, Christ and apostles—were plagiarizations from forged Jewish pseudo-Scriptures, taken over into them from long contact with the Zoroastrian Persians. These myths and superstitions Jesus the Son of God found ready at hand "in the popular consciousness" of the ignorant wonder-craving Jewish peasantry; and, Lo, our "revealed" Christian religion! We may begin to suspect the later "inspired" books of the "Apostles" as not beyond the taint of Pagan superstition and of the suspicion of Christian forgery.

CHAPTER III

CHRISTIAN "SCRIPTURE" FORGERIES

"Nothing stands in need of LYING but a LIE."

To such an extent are the origins of the Christian Religion wrapped in obscurity, due to the labyrinthine confusions and contradictions and forgeries of its early records, that it is quite impossible to extricate, with any degree of confidence, a thread of historic truth from the tangle.

The 27 New Testament booklets, attributed to eight individual "Apostolic" writers, and culled from some 200 admitted forgeries called Gospels, Acts, and Epistles, constitute the present "canonical" or acceptedly inspired compendium of the primitive history of Christianity. The only available method to extract from them approximately just judgments as to the rise and progress of the new system of beliefs, must be by a series of tentative assumptions of relative truth of sundry details of the narratives. By relative truth of any tentatively assumed "fact," I mean such "fact" with relation always to its contradictory,—one or the other must necessarily be false—while both may be—and probably are. For, as virtually every alleged "fact" recorded in Gospels, Acts and Epistles is off-set by a contradictory recital, rendering one or the other untrue, neither can be assumed with assurance; the actuality of either, and of all, is thus made doubtful, and is subject to total rejection as our study of the booklets develops.

On such provisional assumption that sundry of the things recorded possibly may have happened as in one manner or the other related, we are able to reach several obvious conclusions as to the order and approximate times of those dubiously-assumed happenings. In view, however, of what we have seen, and shall soon more abundantly see, of the shifty and fraudulent methods of ecclesiastical "history"-writing and propaganda, we may be prepared for some rude upsettings of our inherited traditions of Christian fact and faith.

The central character of the Christian faith, Jesus, to assume him as a historical personage, was a Jew, as were, by tradition, his disciples and entourage. As is, of course, well known: "Christianity took its rise in Judaism; its Founder and His disciples were orthodox Jews, and the latter maintained their Jewish practices, at least for a time, after the day of Pentecost. The Jews themselves looked upon the followers of Christ as a mere Israelitish sect, . . . 'the sect of the Nazarenes' (Acts xxiv, 15),"—the believers in the Promised Messiah. (*CE.* iii, 713.) In this they were grievously deceived and disappointed, as, too, the world knows: "Christ's humble and obscure life, ending in the ignominious death on the cross, was the very opposite of what the Jews expected of their Christ." (*CE.* i, 620.)

Jesus was a native of Galilee, "his own country" (Mt. ii, 23; xiii, 54–55), *or* of Judæa, "his own country" (John iv, 43–44). He was born "in the days of Herod the King" (Mt. ii, 1), about 6 B. C., *or* "when Cyrenius was governor of Syria" (Luke ii, 1–7), about 7 A. D., or some 13 years later. (*CE.* viii, 377; *EB.* i, 307–8.) The destructive contradictions as to his lineage and parentage, and other essential particulars, are reserved for opportune notice. Jesus became a Jewish sectarian religious teacher of the zealot reformer type; so zealous that his own family thought him insane and sent out to apprehend him (Mark iii, 31); many of the people said of him, "He hath a devil, and is mad" (John x, 20); his own disciples, seeing his raid into the Temple after the money-changers, shook their heads and muttered the proverb: "The zeal of thine house hath eaten me up" (John ii, 17).

His ministry, of about one year, according to the first three Gospels, of some three years according to the fourth, was, by his own repeated assertion, limited exclusively to his own Jewish people: "I am not sent but unto the lost sheep of the house of Israel" (Mt. xv, 24; cf. Acts iii, 25–26; xiii, 46; Rom. xv, 8); and he straitly enjoined on his Twelve Apostles: "Go not into the way of the Gentiles, and into any city of the Samaritans enter ye not: But go rather to the lost sheep of the house of Israel" (Mt. x, 5–6); to the woman of Canaan

92

who pleaded with him to have mercy on her daughter, "grievously vexed with a devil," he retorted: "It is not meet to take the children's bread, and cast it to dogs" (Mt. xv, 22–28; vii, 6). His own announcement, and his command to the Twelve, was "Preach, saying, The Kingdom of Heaven is at hand" (Mt. x, 7),—the exclusively Hebraic Kingdom of the Baptist (Mt. iii, 2), as of the Jewish Messianic apocrypha which we have noticed. Jesus lived at the height of the "age of apocryphal literature," and in due time got into it, voluminously.

Before his death, time and again he made and repeated the assurance—the most positive and iterated of all the sayings attributed to him—of the *immediate end of the world* and of his quick triumphant return to establish the Kingdom of God in the new earth and reign on the reëstablished throne of David forever. Time and again he said and repeated: "Verily I say unto you, There be some standing here, which shall not taste of death, till they see the Son of man coming in his Kingdom" (Mt. xvi, 28; Mk. ix, 1; Lk. ix, 27); "this generation shall not pass, till all these things be done" (Mk. xiii, 30).—So quickly would this "second coming" be, that when the Twelve were sent out on their first preaching tour in little Palestine, their Master assured them: "Ye shall not have gone over the cities of Israel till the Son of man be come" (Mt. x, 23). Caiaphas, the high priest before whom Jesus was led after his capture in the Garden, solemnly conjured him "By the living God" for the truth; and Jesus replied: "Nevertheless I say unto *you*, Hereafter *shall ye see* the Son of man . . . coming in the clouds of heaven." (Mt. xxvi, 63, 64; Mk. xiv, 61, 62.) Some people are expecting him yet. Of course, there were, could be, none but Jews in heaven, or in this new Kingdom of Heaven on the new earth: "Salvation is of the Jews." (John iv, 22.) It was 144,000 Jews, the "sealed" saints, who alone constituted the original Jewish "Kingdom of God" (Rev. vii).

With these explicit data we arrive at the first obvious and positive conclusion: With the expectation of a quick and sudden end of the world and of all things human, no books were written on the subject in that generation or, for a little leeway, the next or so, after the death of the expected returning King. The scant number of credulous Jews who accepted this preachment as "Gospel truth" and lived in this

93

expectation, were nourished with neighborhood gossip and oral traditions of the "good news," and needed and had no written books of inspired record of these things. Thus many years passed. Only as the dread consummation was delayed, and the hope deferred sickened the hearts of the expectant Jews and they waned in faith, and as accused by Paul and Barnabas, "put it from you," did the defeated propagandists of the "Faith that failed at the Cross," give the shoulder to the Jews and "turn to the Gentiles" (Acts xiii, 46), and begin to expand the failing new Jewish faith among the superstitious Pagans of the countries round about. But this was still by the spoken word; on all the supposititious "missionary tours" the Word was spread by word of mouth; written gospel books were not yet. When at last, the "coming" being still unrealized—these books began to be written, we can accurately determine something of the order of their writing, and finally, though negatively, the approximate times when they were written, by ascertaining when they were *not yet* written.

We have seen that for a century and more the only "Scriptures" used by the Jewish propagandists of the Christ were the Greek Septuagint translations of the old Hebrew sacred writings, "the Law and the Prophets" (*CE.* v, 702; i, 635); supplemented by sundry Jewish apocrypha and the Pagan Sibylline Oracles; these were the only "authorities" appealed to by the early "Fathers" for the propaganda of the new faith. Indubitably, if the wonderful "histories" of their Christ and the inspired pretended writings of his first Apostles, forming now the New Testament, had then existed, even in scraps of writing, they would have been the most precious and potent documents of propaganda, would have been snatched at and quoted and appealed to with infinite zeal and ardor, as they have been through the centuries since. But, for some 150 years, as we shall see, little or nothing besides Old Testament and Pagan Oracles were known or quoted. As said by the great critic, Salomon Reinach, "With the exception of Papias, who speaks of a narrative by Mark, and a collection of sayings of Jesus, no Christian writer of the first half of the second century (*i. e., up to* 150 A. D.) quotes the Gospels or their reputed authors." (Reinach, *Orpheus*, p. 218.) So, patently, as yet no "Gospels" and but few if any "Epistles" of our "canon" had as yet been written.

94

Again, we read the 23 booklets from and including Acts to Revelation: there is not a solitary reference to, a word of quotation from, any of our four Gospels; scarce a trace of the wonderful career and miracles of Jesus the Christ; not a word of his "gospel" or teachings mentioned or quoted. These Epistles, indeed, "preach Christ crucified" (from oral tradition), as the basis of the propagandists' own "gospel." But the written "Gospel of Jesus Christ" (his life and words and deeds), was unknown: indeed, jealous of the so-called Petrine preaching which "perverts the gospel of Christ" as preached by him, the soi-disant Apostle Paul fulminates: "But though we, or an angel from heaven, preach any other gospel unto you than that which *we* have preached, let him be accursed" (Gal. i, 7, 8);—so early did priestly intolerance and priestly curses on opponents come into holy vogue. Therefore the conclusion is inevitable, that when those 23 Acts and Epistles were written, none of the four "Gospel" biographies of Jesus the Christ had yet seen the light. "Written Gospels are neither mentioned nor implied in the NT epistles, nor in that of Clemens Romanus, nor, probably, in that of Barnabas, nor in the Didaché. Luke (i, 1–4) implies that 'many gospels' were current" (*EB*. ii, 1809), at the time that Gospel was written.

The Acts and Epistles, therefore, with Revelation, were written *before* any of the Gospel biographies. If these Christ-histories had existed, how eagerly would they have been seized upon to garnish and glorify the preachment of the early propagandists of the Faith that failed at the Cross,—and would have perished wholly but for the all-believing Pagan Gentiles, who, when they heard it, "were glad, and glorified the word of the Lord" (Acts xiii, 48), as orally delivered.

"THE AGE OF APOCRYPHAL LITERATURE"

As the long years passed and one generation of disappointed "Messiah" Jews was gathered unto its fathers and was followed by another, the believers in the promised "second coming" for the establishment of the Jewish Kingdom grew restless, and made pertinent complaint, "Saying, Where is the promise of his coming? for since the fathers fell asleep, all things continue as they were from the beginning of the creation" (2 Peter ii, 4),—and as they yet continue.

95

Dubbing these reasonable but disturbing inquirers "scoffers," the crafty Peter tried in typical priestly form to squirm out of the embarrassing situation created by the positive promises of the Christ and the inspired preachments of himself and his apostolic confrères, by the shifty rejoinder: "But, beloved ["*scoffers*"], be not ignorant of this one thing, that one day is with the Lord as a thousand years, and a thousand years as one day" (2 Peter ii, 8)—which doesn't mean anything for an honest answer; and time and again they cajole the impatient credulous: "Ye have need of patience; . . . for yet *a little while*, and he that shall come, will come." (Heb. x, 36, 37; cf. 1 Thess. iv, 16–18; 2 Thess. iii, 5; James v, 7, 8; *et passim.*) But he isn't come yet, these 2000 years.

It was at this critical juncture, to revive and stimulate the jaded hope of the Jewish believers and to spread the propaganda amongst the all-believing Pagans, that the written Christ-tales began to be worked up by the Christian propagandists. Before their admiring eyes they had for models the "whole literature" of Jewish apocryphal or forged writings, plus the Pagan Oracles: with immense zeal and industry they set about to imitate the example before them, and to reforge these Jewish and heathen forgeries to more definite Christian uses, and to forge anew another whole literature of distinctively Christian forgeries and fabulous histories of the Christ. "In this form of propaganda the Christians proved themselves to be apt pupils of the Jews. So common, indeed, had become in early Christian times, the invention of such oracles that Celsus terms Christians *Sibyllistai*, believers in sibyls, or sibyl-mongers" (*EB.* i, 246), that is, peddlers of Christian forgeries in Pagan form (*Ib.* p. 261). How great was this pious fabrication we can only judge from the two hundred, more or less, of false histories, gospels, epistles and revelations which have survived, entire or fragmentary, or by title only, through the long intervening centuries of faith, and of which 27 are yet cherished as of Divine inspiration.

"THE IDEA OF INSPIRATION"

Before sketching the welter of these lying works of Christian hands and childish minds, we may define, by high priestly authority, the status of the problem of divine inspiration, and just how the notion of "canonicity" or official inspiration, came to be, now attributed to, now withdrawn from, this heterogeneous mass or mess of pious scribblings, and finally clung to only 27 of yet asserted sanctity. These admissions are very illuminating.

We have seen that the Hebrew Old Testament itself "reveals no formal notion of inspiration," though, we are assured, "the later Jews *must have* possessed the idea" (*CE.* iii, 269);—thus only an idea or notion somehow acquired, but not through divine illumination, for as we read, of all the mass of Jewish holy forgeries "each of them has at one time or another been treated as canonical" or divinely inspired. (*EB.* i, 250.) Whether the Christian notion or idea as to the divine inspiration of their own new forgeries was of any better quality may now appear.

The New Testament and the inspired Apostles are silent on the subject and left the matter to serious doubts and disputations for many centuries: "There are no indications in the New Testament . . . of a definite new Canon bequeathed by the Apostles to the Church, *or of a strong self-witness* to Divine inspiration," admits the *CE.* (iii, 274); that is, there is nothing in the 27 booklets which would lead to the suspicion of their "inspiration" or truth. There was then no *Church* for them to *bequeath* to, nor was the Canon settled, as we shall see: "It was not until about the middle of the second century— [when we shall see the books were really written]—that under the rubric of *Scripture* the New Testament writings were assimilated to the Old. . . . But it should be remembered that the inspired character of the New Testament is a *Catholic dogma,* and *must* therefore *in some way* have been revealed to, and taught by, Apostles"! (*Ib.* p. 275.) This is a strikingly queer bit of clerical dialectic, and leaves the question of the "some way" of revelation to the Apostles and of their transmission of the "dogma" to posterity, in a nebulously unsatisfying state.

Further, the dubious and disputed status of the sacred writings through centuries, and the ultimate settlement of the controversies by the *ipse dixit* of a numerical majority of the Council of Trent, in 1546,—after the Reformation had forced the issue, is thus admitted: "The idea of a complete and clear-cut canon of the New Testament existing from the beginning, that is, from Apostolic times, *has no foundation in history*. The canon of the New Testament, like that of the Old, is *the result of a development*, of a process at once stimulated by disputes with doubters, both within and without the Church, and retarded by *certain obscurities and natural hesitations*, and which did not reach its final term until the dogmatic definition of the Tridentine Council. . . . And this want of an organized distribution, secondarily to the absence of an early fixation of the Canon, left room for *variations and doubts* which lasted far into the centuries." (*CE.* iii, 274.) The *modus operandi* of the Holy Council in ultimately "canonizing" Jerome's old Vulgate Version, and its motive for doing so, are thus exposed by the keen pen of the author of *The Rise and Fall:*

"When the Council of Trent resolved to pronounce sentence on the Canon of Scripture, the opinion which prevailed, after some debate, was to declare the Latin Vulgate authentic and *almost* infallible; and this sentence, which was guarded by formidable anathemas, secured all the books of the Old and New Testament which composed that ancient version. . . . When the merit of that version was discussed, the majority of the theologians urged, with confidence and success, that it was absolutely necessary to receive the Vulgate as authentic and inspired, unless they wished to abandon the victory to the Lutherans, and the honors of the Church to the Grammarians." (Gibbon, *A Vindication*, v, 2; *Istoria del Consiglio Tridentino,* L. ii, p. 147.) A number of these books were bitterly disputed and their authenticity and inspiration denied by the leading Reformers, Luther, Grotius, Calvin, etc., and excluded from their official lists, until finally the Reformed Church followed the example of the Church hopeless of reform and swallowed the canon whole, as we have it today,—minus, of course, the *Tobit, Judith,* and like inspired buffooneries of the True Bible.

Such books and the vicissitudes of their authenticity are thus described: "Like the Old Testament, the New has its deutero-canonical [*i. e.* doubted] books and portions of books, their canonicity having formerly been a subject of some controversy in the Church. These are, for entire books: the Epistle to the Hebrews, that of James, the Second and Third of John, Jude, and Apocalypse; giving seven in all as the number of the N. T. contested books. The formerly disputed passages are three: the closing section of St. Mark's Gospel, xvi, 9–20, about the apparitions of Christ after the resurrection; the verses in Luke about the bloody sweat of Jesus, xxii, 43, 44; the *Pericope Adulterae*, or narrative of the woman taken in adultery, St. John, vii, 53 to viii, 11. Since the Council of Trent *it is not permitted for a Catholic to question* the inspiration of these passages." (*CE.* iii, 274.) Besides the forgery of the above and other books as a whole, we shall see many other instances of "interpolated" or forged passages in the Christian books.

"THE LYING PEN OF THE SCRIBES"

Speaking of the doubtful historicity of the celebrated Æsop of the famous Fables which go under his name, a critic well states a valid test of historicity: "We may well doubt, however, whether he (Æsop) ever existed; we have the most varied accounts of him, many of which are on their face pure inventions; and the fables which passed under his name were certainly not written until long after the period in which he is supposed to have lived." (*NIE.* i, 191.) We may have occasion to apply this test to the personality of Jesus of Nazareth and sundry apostolic personages; in any event it is peculiarly applicable to the numerous Christian stories and fables treating of them, which on their face are pure inventions, and which were admittedly forged in the names of Jesus himself and of all of his Apostles and of many of the shining lights of the new Christian faith, just as we have seen was done in the Jewish forgeries in the names of the Old Testament notables from Adam on down the catalogue.

Leaving for the moment aside the 27 presently accepted booklets of the N. T., and admitting the many Christian forgeries of Christ-fables, *CE.* thus apologetically explains: "The genuine Gospels are silent about long stretches of the life of our Lord, the Blessed Virgin, and St. Joseph. This reserve of the Evangelists did not satisfy the pardonable curiosity of many Christians eager for details. . . . Enterprising spirits responded to this natural craving *by pretended gospels* full of romantic fables, and fantastic and striking details; their fabrications were eagerly read and *accepted as true* by common folk who were *devoid of any critical faculty* and who *were predisposed to believe* what so luxuriously fed their pious curiosity. Both Catholics and Gnostics were concerned in writing these fictions. The *former* had no motive other than that of a PIOUS FRAUD." (*CE.* i, 606.) The motive above admitted for feeding with pious frauds the "natural craving" of the ignorant and superstitious Christians for marvel-mongering by the Church, is confirmed by a distinguished historian: "A vast and ever-increasing crowd of converts from paganism, who had become such from worldly considerations, and still hankered after wonders like those in which their forefathers had from time immemorial believed, lent a ready ear to assertions which, to more hesitating or better-instructed minds, would have seemed to *carry imposture on their very face*." (Draper, *The Intellectual Development of Europe,* i, 309.)

This being thus frankly confessed, our clerical writer describes the general character of these pious frauds: "The Christian apocryphal writings in general imitate the books of the N. T., and therefore, with a few exceptions, fall under the description of Gospels, Acts, Epistles, and Apocalypses." (*CE.* i, 606.) Further apologizing for these Christian forgeries, and giving a smear of clerical whitewash to the forgers, it is speciously pleaded, that "the term *apocryphal* in connection with special gospels must be understood as bearing no more unfavorable an import than uncanonical." They were *forgeries* pure and simple; and their pious value is urged, that "the apocryphal Gospels help us to understand the religious conditions of the second and third centuries,"—as indeed they do, in a light very damaging to any suspicion of truthfulness, common honesty, or anything above the most mediocre intelligence of the pious Fathers and Faithful who put these gross fabrications into circulation in the name and for the sake of Christ. Their pious plea is: "*Amor Christi est cui satisfecimus.*" (*Ib.* p. 606.) Of these pious frauds it adds: "The quasi-evangelistic compositions concerning Christ . . . are *all* of *Orthodox* origin." (*Ib.* p. 607.)

"CHRISTIAN EVIDENCES"—FORGED

When the new Faith went forth to conquer the Pagan world for Christ, the pious Greek Fathers and priests of the Propaganda soon felt the need of something of more up-to-date effectiveness than Old Testament texts and Sibylline Oracles; they needed something concrete out of the New Dispensation to "show" to the superstitious Pagans to win them to the Christ and his Church: something tangible, visible; compellingly authentic proofs. Like arms of proof for the holy warfare, the invincible weapons of truth—"the whole armour of God"—they forged outright for the conquest of the unbeliever. What more convincing and compelling proofs of Jesus the Christ, his holy Apostles, and their wondrous works of over a century ago, than the following authentic and autograph documents and records, held before doubting eyes:

A "GOSPEL" WRITTEN BY JESUS CHRIST'S OWN HAND;

LETTERS AND PORTRAITS OF JESUS CHRIST AND HIS PERSONAL CORRESPONDENCE;

LETTERS WRITTEN BY HIS VIRGIN MOTHER;

PILATE'S OFFICIAL REPORT TO THE EMPEROR OF THE TRIAL AND CRUCIFICTION OF JESUS, WITH PILATE'S CONFESSION OF FAITH;

THE REPLY OF TIBERIUS, AND THE TRIAL OF PILATE;

OFFICIAL DOCUMENTS OF THE ROMAN SENATE ABOUT JESUS;

GOSPELS, EPISTLES, ACTS, BY EVERY ONE OF THE TWELVE APOSTLES;

OFFICIAL DOCUMENTS OF CHURCH LAW AND GOVERNMENT, WRITTEN IN GREEK, BY THE APOSTLES;

RECORDS OF THE EARLIEST "POPES" AND "APOSTOLIC SUCCESSION;"

SCORES OF OTHER PIOUS FORGED DOCUMENTS TO BE RELATED BELOW.

Armed with lying credentials and "proofs" of the fictitious persons and performances for which credence must be won among the credulous pagans, the priests and Vicars of God propagated their stupendous "LIES to the glory of God" and the exaltation of the Church. We shall catalogue these crude forgeries somewhat more fully, and look into some of the more notorious.

FORGED GOSPELS, ACTS, EPISTLES

Half a hundred of false and forged Apostolic "Gospels of Jesus Christ," together with more numerous other "Scripture" forgeries, was the output, so far as known now, of the lying pens of the pious Christians of the first two centuries of the Christian "Age of Apocryphal Literature"; all going to swell the "very large number of apocryphal writings of distinctly Christian origin which were produced from the second century onward, to satisfy an unhealthy craving for the occult and marvelous or to embellish the stories of the saints." (*NIE.*, i, 746.) These N. T. apocrypha include "numerous works purporting to have been *written by apostles or their associates*, but not able to secure a general or permanent recognition. These may be classified thus: (a) Gospels; (b) Acts of Apostles; (c) Epistles; (d) Apocalypses; (e) Didactic Works; (f) Hymns. (*Ib.* p. 748.) "The name Gospel," says *CE.* (vi, 656), "as indicating a written account of Christ's words and deeds, has been, and still is, applied to *a large number* of narratives of Christ's life, which circulated both before and after the composition of our Third Gospel (cf. Luke i, 1–4). The titles of *some fifty such works* have come down to us. . . . It is only, however, in connection with some twenty of these 'Gospels' that some information has been preserved. . . . Most of them, as far as can be made out, are late productions, the apocryphal character of which is generally admitted by contemporary [*i. e.*, present day] scholars." Naming first as Nos. 1–4 "The Canonical Gospels," now falsely labelled with the names of Matthew, Mark, Luke, and John, the twenty best known ones are listed as follows; *viz:* The Gospels according to the Hebrews; of Peter; According to the Egyptians; of Matthias; of Philip; of Thomas; the *Proto-Evangelium* of James; Gospel of Nicodemus (*Acta Pilati*); of the Twelve Apostles; of Basilides; of Valentius; of Marcion; of Eve; of Judas; the Writing Genna Marias; the Gospel *Teleioseos*. (*CE.* vi, 656.)

Individual Gospels were forged in the names of each of the Twelve Apostles, severally, and a joint fabrication under the name of "The Gospel of the Twelve," was put into the mouths of the twelve Apostles, using the first person to give the ear-marks of authenticity to their forged utterances; and separately, "Almost every one of the Apostles had a Gospel fathered upon him by one early sect or another." (*EB.* i, 259.) Several seem to have been fathered upon Matthew besides the one that wrongly heads the list of the "canonical Four," such as the Gospel of Matthias, Traditions of Matthias, also a supposed and *probably non-existent* writing in Hebrew hypothesized as the basic document of the Four; probably also the so-called *Logia*, a papyrus scrap of one sheet discovered at Oxyrhynchus, Egypt, and containing alleged sayings of Jesus which in part correspond with, in part radically differ from the sayings attributed to him in the Four. He was also made responsible for a so-called Gospel of St. Matthew, dating from the 4th or 5th century, which "purports to have been written by Matthew and translated by St. Jerome." (*CE.* i, 608.)

This authority also lists the famous *Protevangelium Jacobi*, or Infancy Gospel of James, the Arabic Gospel of the Infancy, that of Gamaliel, the Gospel according to the Hebrews, also According to the Egyptians; of the Nazarenes; Gospels of St. Peter, of St. Philip, of St. Thomas, of St. Bartholomew, of St. Andrew, of Barnabas, of Thaddeus, even notable forged Gospels of Judas Iscariot, and of Mother Eve; also the Gospel by Jesus Christ. We have the Gospel of Nicodemus, the History of Joseph the Carpenter, the Descent into Hades, the Descent of Mary, the Ascents of James, the Prophecy of Hystaspes, the Didaché or Teachings of the Apostles; the Gospel of the Nativity of the Virgin Mary, the *Transitum Mariæ* or Evangelium Joannis. This last named pious Christian work, as described by *CE.* (i, 607–8) is forged in the name of St. John the Apostle, and is "prefaced with a spurious Letter of the Bishop of Sardis, Melito"; it records how "the Apostles are preternaturally transported from different quarters of the globe to the Virgin's deathbed, those who have died being resurrected for the purpose"; a Jew who dares touch the sacred body instantly loses both hands, which are restored through the mediation of the Apostles. Christ, accompanied by a band of angels, comes down to receive his mother's soul; "the Apostles bear the body to Gethsemane and deposit it in a tomb, whence it is taken up alive to Heaven"; this being an extraordinary miracle, for the body was dead and the soul carried to heaven from her home and the dead body laid in the grave, where it comes to life again for the Heaventrip. This clumsy fable, says *CE.*, considerably "influenced the Fathers" (*Ib.* i, 608), who were notoriously childish-minded. A very noted and notorious forgery was the Gospel of Paul and Thecla, of which Father Tertullian relates, that this story was fabricated by an Elder of Asia Minor, who, when convicted of the fraud—[this being the only known instance of such action],—confessed that he had perpetrated it "for the love of St. Paul." (Reinach, *Orpheus*, p. 235.) The *Protevangelium Jacobi* was "an Apocryphal work by a fanciful fabulist, unhampered by knowledge of Jewish affairs, composed before the end of the second century with a view to removing the *glaring contradictions* between Matthew and Mark," regarding the birth and life of Jesus Christ. (*EB.* iii, 3343.) An "Epistle on the Martyrdom of the Apostles Peter and Paul was at a later period attributed to St. Linus. . . . It is apocryphal, and of later date than the History of the Martyrdom of the two Apostles, by some attributed to Marcellus, which is also apocryphal." (*CE.* ix, 273; see *Acta Apostolorum, Apocrypha,* xiv.) Other noted Fatherly fabrications were the celebrated Epistles I and II of Clement to the Corinthians, and the Pseudo-Clementine *Recognitions* and *Homilies,* purporting to be written by the very doubtful Bishop of Rome of that name; very voluminous, and written about 140 A. D., not a line of New Testament "scriptures" do they quote, but they quote freely from the O. T. and from various Jewish, Christian and Pagan works. (*EB.* iii, 3486.)

Besides the above complete "Gospel" forgeries, there are several more, and fragments of others, which purport to contain "sayings" attributed to Jesus which are not contained in the Four Gospels; and which are known as *Agrapha,* that is, things *not written.* Among these are the *Logia* of Oxyrhynchus above mentioned; the Fayum gospel-fragment, a papyrus purporting to give words of Christ to Peter at the Last Supper, "in a form which diverges largely by omissions from any in the canonical gospels." (*EB.* i, 258.) These *Agrapha* "do not embrace the lengthy sections ascribed to Jesus in the '*Didiscalia*' and the '*Pistis Sophia*'; these works also contain some brief quotations of alleged words of Jesus; . . . nor the *Sayings* contained in religious romances, such as we find in the apocryphal Gospels, the apocryphal Acts, or the Letter of Christ to Abgar. . . . In patristic citations . . . Justin Martyr, Clement of Alexandria, Origen, make *false quotations,*"—citing instances. (*CE.* i, 225, 226.) In the class of *Agrapha* are also "words in the Gospels not regarded as genuine, as Mt. vi, 13b; xvii, 21; Mk. xvi, 9–20; John vii, 53; viii, 2; also alleged quotations from the Old Testament in the New Testament not found in the Old Testament." (*NIE.* i, 240.)

Of apocryphal Acts of Apostles we are edified by the Acts, or Travels (Greek, *Pereodoi*) of Peter, (and separately) of John, of Thomas, of Andrew, and of Paul; another Acts of Philip, Acts of

Matthew, of Bartholomew, of John, of Judas Thomas. There is a whose collection of *Martyrdoms* of the several Apostles. Of apocryphal Epistles, the most famous is the Correspondence between the *Abgar* of Edessa, and Jesus; between the Roman Philosopher Seneca and Paul; apocryphal Epistles of Paul, to the Laodiceans, to the Alexandrians, the Third Epistle to the Corinthians. Forged Apocalypses abound, of which that of Peter, the Vision of Hermas, the Vision of Paul, the Apocalypse of Paul, the Apocalypse of the Virgin Mary. The didactic Preaching of Peter, the Teaching of the Apostles, or *Didaché*, containing warnings against Judaism and polytheism, and words of Jesus to the Apostles; another set containing a lament of Peter for his denial of Jesus, and various ethical maxims; a Syriac Preaching of Simon Cephas; a collection of Hymns or Odes of Solomon. As if these were not enough for Christian edification, "many heretical or Gnostic works of the same apocryphal kind were changed into orthodox by expurgation of objectionable matter or by rewriting, using the same outlines; thus a series of Catholic Acts was produced, written from an orthodox standpoint." (*NIE.* i, 748.) A very celebrated forgery was the Shepherd of Hermas, forged by Hermas, supposed brother of Pius, Bishop of Rome, about 150 A. D. See the vast catalogue (*CE.* i, 601–615).

A whole literature of Christian forgery grew up and had immense vogue under the designation of *Acta Pilati,* or Acts of Pilate. One of the most popular of these was called the Gospel of Nicodemus, of which *CE.* says: "The alleged Hebrew original is attributed to Nicodemus; the title is of medieval origin. The apocryphon gained wide credit in the Middle Ages. . . . The 'Acta' are of orthodox composition. The book aimed at gratifying the desire for extra-evangelical details concerning our Lord, and at the same time, to strengthen *faith in the Resurrection of Christ,* and at general edification." (i, 3.) The Descent into Hades is an enlargement of the reputed official acts or reports of Pilate to the Roman Emperor. Speaking of the Pilate Literature as a whole, the *Catholic Encyclopedia,* in a paragraph which pointedly admits the falsifying frauds of three luminous liars and forgers of the Faith, Justin Martyr, the great Bishop Eusebius, and Father Tertullian, explains that these *Acta* "dwell upon the part which a representative [Pilate] of the Roman Empire played

105

in the supreme events of our Lord's life, and to shape the testimony of Pontius Pilate, even at the cost of exaggeration and amplification— [hear the soft-pedaling note], into a weapon of apologetic defense, making the official bear witness to the miracles, Crucifixion, and Resurrection of Jesus Christ. . . . It is characterized by exaggerating Pilate's weak defense of Jesus into a strong sympathy and practical belief in his Divinity." (*CE.* i, 609.) Father Tertullian, in his *Apologia* (xxi), relates the Report of Pilate to the Emperor, sketching the miracles and death of Jesus Christ, and says, "All these things Pilate announced to Tiberius Cæsar." Bishop Eusebius thus relates the fable as taken from the *Apologia* of Father Tertullian: "The fame of Our Lord's remarkable resurrection and ascension being now spread abroad, . . . Pontius Pilate transmits to Tiberius an account of the circumstances concerning the resurrection of our Lord from the dead. . . . In this account, he also intimated that he had ascertained other miracles respecting him, and that having now risen from the dead, he *was believed to be a God* by the great mass of the people. Tiberius referred the matter to the Senate, . . . being obviously pleased with the doctrine; but the Senate, as they had not proposed the matter, [rejected it]. But he continued in his opinion, threatening death to the accusers of the Christians; a divine providence infusing this into his mind, that the Gospel having freer scope in its commencement, might spread everywhere over the world." (Eusebius, *HE.* II, 2.) Father Justin Martyr, in his *Apologia*, "appeals confidently as a proof of them to the '*Acta*' or records of Pilate, existing in the imperial archives." Eusebius relates spurious anti-Christian Acts of Pilate composed in the fourth century, the *Acta Pilati* or Gospel of Nicodemus, *Anphora Pilati, Paradoseis;* a still later fabrication is the Latin *Epistola Pilati ad Tiberium.* Also the Letter of Herod to Pilate and Letter of Pilate to Herod; the Narrative of Joseph of Arimathea. The pseudo-Correspondence of Jesus with Abgar, King of Edessa, is found in Eusebius (*Hist. Eccles.*, I, xiii), "*who vouches that he himself translated it from the Syriac documents in the archives of Edessa,* the metropolis of Eastern Syria. . . . 'This,' adds Eusebius, 'happened in the year 340 of the Seleucid era, corresponding to A. D. 28–29.' " (*CE.* i, 609, 610.) More monumental lies to the glory of God than those of the distinguished Church Fathers are not.

CHRISTIAN "SCRIPTURE" FORGERIES

"A collection of apocryphal Acts of the Apostles was formed in the Frankish Church in the sixth century, probably by a monk." (*Ib.* p. 610.) There were also "the works accredited to Dionysius the Areopagite, who was not the author of the works bearing his name." (*Ib.* p. 638.)

Of highest importance because "these Acts are the chief source for details of the martyrdom of the two great Apostles," as admits the *CE.*, special notice is made of the "Catholic" *Acts of Sts. Peter and Paul*, of which many MSS of "the legend" existed, the material import of which is thus not quite honestly summarized: "The Jews have been aroused by the news of Paul's intended visit (to Rome), and induce Nero to forbid it. Nevertheless the Apostle secretly enters Italy; his companion is mistaken for himself at Puteoli and beheaded. In retribution that city is swallowed up by the sea. Peter receives Paul at Rome with joy. The preaching of the Apostles converts multitudes and even the Empress. Simon Magus traduces the Christian teachers, and there is a test of strength in miracles between that magician and the Apostles, which takes place in the presence of Nero. Simon essays a flight to heaven but falls in the Via Sacra and is dashed to pieces. Nevertheless, Nero is bent on the destruction of Peter and Paul. The latter is beheaded on the Ostian Way, and Peter is crucified at his request head downward. Before his death he relates to the people the '*Quo Vadis?*' story. Three men from the East carry off the Apostles' bodies but are overtaken. St. Peter is buried at 'the place called the Vatican,' and Paul on the Ostian Way. *These Acts are the chief source for details of the martyrdom of the two great Apostles.* They are also noteworthy as emphasizing the close concord between the Apostolic founders of the Roman Church." (*CE.* i, 611–12.)

The reader is desired to bear well in mind the foregoing paragraph, and particularly the last two sentences, the former of immense significance when we come to review the falsified fiction of the foundation of the Roman Church by Peter,—the "chief source" of which portentous claim is confessedly founded on the crude and fantastic "legend" of an admittedly forged document. Another admission of forgery by the Fathers, before introducing them formally, may be noted: "Such known works as the Shepherd of Hermas, the Epistle of Barnabas, the *Didaché* or Teaching of the Twelve Apostles, and the Apostolic Canons and Constitutions, though formally apocryphal, really belong to *patristic literature*" (*CE.* i, 601),—that is, they are forged writings of the Fathers.

THE FORGED "APOSTLES' CREED"

The "Apostles' Creed," forged by the Fathers several centuries after the Apostles, must be added to the Patristic list. Of this famous Creed, which every Christian presumably knows by rote and piously recites in numberless services, *CE.* again confesses it spurious: "Throughout the Middle Ages it was generally believed that the Apostles, on the day of Pentecost, while still under the direct inspiration of the Holy Ghost, composed our present Creed, each of the Apostles contributing one of the Twelve articles. This legend dates back to the sixth century, and is foreshadowed still earlier in a sermon attributed to St. Ambrose, which *takes notice* that the Creed was 'pieced out by twelve separate workmen.' " (*CE.* i, 629.) Indeed, "not a few works have been falsely attributed to St. Ambrose." (*CE.* i, 387; cf. p. 406.)

We may smile at the peculiarly clerical way in which *CE.* would "whitewash" the great Bishop of Milan, St. Ambrose (c. 340–397), from the lie direct which admittedly he told in that Sermon,—saying that the Bishop simply "takes notice that the Creed was pieced out," *etc.;* the truth being that Ambrose positively affirmed the fable as truth, and may have invented it. His positive words are: "that the Twelve Apostles, as skilled artificers, assembled together, and made a key by their common advice, that is, the Creed; by which the darkness of the devil is disclosed, that the light of Christ may appear." (Ambrose, *Opera*, tom. iii., *Sermon* 38, p. 265; quoted in *The New Testament Apocrypha*, New York, The Truth Seeker Co.)—a work which I feel impelled to commend to all who wish to know at first hand the 25 remarkable Church "Gospel" forgeries there collected.

THE FORGED ATHANASIAN CREED

In likewise the celebrated Athanasian Creed of the Church, attributed to St. Athanasius and so held by the Church "until the seven-

108

teenth century" (*CE.* ii, 34), with most evil results, is now an admitted forgery. In words of Gibbon: "St. Athanasius is not the author of the creed; it does not appear to have existed within a century after his death; it was composed in Latin, therefore in one of the Western provinces. Gennadius, patriarch of Constantinople, was so much amazed by this extraordinary composition, that he frankly pronounced it to be the work of a drunken man." (*Petav. Dogmat. Theologica,* tom. ii, 1, vii, c. 8, p. 687; Gibbon, p. 598.)

JESUS CHRIST'S FORGED LETTERS

We may look for a moment at several of the most notorious of the forgeries perpetrated for the glory of God and for imposture upon the superstitious Christians to enhance Pagan credulity in the tales of Christ. If the Gospel tales were true, why should God need pious lies to give them credit? Lies and forgeries are only needed to bolster up falsehood: "Nothing stands in need of lying but a lie." But Jesus Christ must needs be propagated by lies upon lies; and what better proof of his actuality than to exhibit letters written by him in his own handwriting? The "Little Liars of the Lord" were equal to the forgery of the signature of their God,—false letters in his name, as above cited from that exhaustless mine of clerical falsities, the *Catholic Encyclopedia,* which again describes them, and proves that they were forged by their great Bishop of Cæsaria: "The historian Eusebius records [*HE.* I, xii], a legend which he himself *firmly believes* [?], concerning a correspondence that took place between Our Lord and the local potentate (Abgar) at Edessa. Three documents relate to this correspondence: (1) the Letter of Abgar to Our Lord; (2) Our Lord's answer; (3) a picture of Our Lord, painted from life. This legend enjoyed a great popularity, both in the East, and in the West, during the Middle Ages. Our Lord's Letter was copied on parchment, marble, and metal, and used as a talisman or an amulet." (*CE.* i, 42.) But it is not true, as we have seen already confessed, that Eusebius innocently believed that these forgeries were genuine— for they were all shamelessly forged by Eusebius himself: "*who vouches that he himself translated it from the Syriac documents in the archives of Edessa.*" (*CE.* i, 610.) Again it is said by *CE.,* that these forged letters, with the portrait, were "accepted by Eusebius without hesitation, and used by Addision in his work on Christian Evidences as genuine" (*Ib.* vi, 217).

It should be mentioned, first, that *Abgar* was not a personal name of a King of Edessa, but was a generic title of all the rulers of that small state: "By this *title* all the toparchs of Edessa were called, just as the Roman Emperors were called Cæsars, the Kings of Egypt Pharaohs or Ptolemies, the Kings of Syria Antiochi." (*ANF.* viii, 651, note.) With this first check on the forging Bishop, here is what he said in his Church History, Book I, chapter the thirteenth. (p. 63 *seq.*) Note the false fervor of the holy Bishop to sugar-coat his circumstantial and commodious lie and fraud: "While the Godhead of our Saviour and Lord Jesus Christ was proclaimed among all men by reason of the astonishing mighty-works which He wrought, and myriads, even from countries remote from the land of Judæa, who were afflicted with sicknesses and diseases of every kind, were coming to Him in the hope of being healed, King Abgar sent Him a letter asking Him to come and heal him of his disease. But our Saviour at the time he asked Him did not comply with his request. Yet He deigned to give him a letter in reply. . . . Thou hast in writing the evidence of these things, which is taken from the Book of Records which was at Edessa: for at that time the Kingdom was still standing. In the documents, then, which were there, in which was contained whatever was done by those of old down to the time of *Abgar*, these things are also found preserved down to the present hour. There is, however, nothing to prevent our hearing the very letters themselves, which have been *taken by us from the archives*, and are in words to this effect, translated from Aramaic into Greek.

"Copy of the letter which was written by King Abgar to Jesus, and sent to Him by the hand of Ananias—[the Bishop was the Ananias in this tale, and aptly named his letter-carrier],—the Tabularius, to Jerusalem:

'Abgar the Black, sovereign of the country, to Jesus, the good Saviour, who has appeared in the country of Jerusalem: Peace. I have heard about Thee, and about the healing which is wrought by Thy hands without drugs and roots. For, as it is reported, Thou makest the blind to see, and the lame to walk; and Thou cleansest the lepers, and Thou castest out unclean spir-

110

its and demons, and Thou healest those who are tormented with lingering diseases, and Thou raisest the dead. And when I heard all these things about Thee, I settled in my mind one of two things: either that Thou art God, who has come down from heaven, and doest these things; or that Thou art the Son of God, and doest these things. On this account, therefore, I have written to beg of Thee that Thou wouldest weary Thyself to come to me, and heal this disease which I have. For I have also heard that the Jews murmur against Thee, and wish to do Thee harm. But I have a city, small and beautiful, which is sufficient for two.'

"Copy of those things which were written by Jesus in reply by the hand of Ananias, the Tabularius, to Abgar, sovereign of the country:—

'Blessed is he that believeth in me, not having seen me. For it is written concerning me, that those who see me will not believe in me, and that those will believe who have not seen me, and will be saved. But touching that which thou hast written to me, that I should come to thee—it is meet that I should finish here all that for the sake of which I have been sent; and, after I have finished it, then I shall be taken up to Him that sent me; and, when I have been taken up, I will send to thee one of my disciples, that he may heal thy disease, and give salvation to thee and to those who are with thee.'

"To these letters, moreover, is appended the following, also in the Aramaic tongue";—here following the official record of the visit of one "Thaddæus the apostle, one of the Seventy," and his wonderful works in Edessa. "These things were done in the year 340. In order, moreover, that these things may not have been translated to no purpose word for word from the Aramaic into Greek, they are placed in their order of time here. Here endeth the first book." (*HE.* i, 13; *ANF.* viii, 651–653.) Bishop Eusebius is thus seen to have been a most circumstantial liar and a well-skilled forger for God. From this episcopal lie sprouted like toadstools a whole literature of "various books concerning Abgar the King and Thaddæus the Apostle," in which are preserved to posterity a series of five letters—very much in the style of modern patent-medicine testimonials—written by Abgar to Tiberius Caesar and to neighboring potentates, endorsing Jesus and his healing powers; with a reply from Tiberius declaring that "Pilate has officially informed us of the miracles of Jesus." With respect to the other letters testimonial, it is recorded: "Abgar had not yet received answers to these letters when he died, having reigned thirty-eight years." (*Ibid.* pp. 657–741, 706.)

These crass episcopal forgeries were welcomed into the Church, and for fifteen centuries have gone unrebuked by Pope or Church. Even since the Reformation so strong was the belief in the Abgar-Jesus forgeries, that notable prelates in England, including Archbishop Cave, have "strenuously contended for their admission into the canon of Scripture. . . . The Reverend Jeremiah Jones observes, that common people in England have this Epistle in their houses, in many places, fixed in a frame, with the picture of Christ before it; and that they generally, with much honesty and devotion, regard it as the word of God, and the genuine Epistle of Christ." (Quoted in editorial note to the Epistles, in *The Lost Books of the Bible*, p. 62.) To such state of superstitious credulity does the Church with its pious impostures prostitute the minds of its ignorant and credulous votaries. The portrait of Jesus, referred to above, is said, in other versions of the Letter, to have been sent by Jesus to the King; this portrait is now displayed at *both* Rome and Genoa. (*NIE.* i, 38.)

OTHER FORGERIES FOR CHRIST'S SAKE

The pious fancy of the Fathers forged another official Letter, in the name of what *CE.* calls "a fictitious person," one Lentulus, pretended predecessor of Pilate as governor of Judæa, to the Roman Senate, giving a description of the personal appearance of Jesus Christ, and closing with the words, "He is the most beautiful of the sons of men." This letter, says *CE.* "was certainly apocryphal"; it was first printed in the *Life of Christ*, by Ludolph the Cartusian; though it is thought to be traceable to the time of Diocletian. (*CE.* ix, 154.) This notion of the personal beauty of Jesus is not shared by the "tradition" of the Fathers; for Jesus Christ is declared by Cyril of Alexandria to have been "the ugliest of the sons of men"; a tradition also declared by Fathers Justin Martyr and Tertullian; to offset which evil notion there was forged "a beautiful Letter, purporting to have been written by Lentulus to the Roman Senate." (*Ib.* vi, 235.) But St. Augustine, says *CE.*, "mentions that in his time there was

112

no authentic portrait of Christ, and that the type of features was still undetermined, so that we have absolutely no knowledge of His appearance." (*De Trinitate, lib.* vii, ch. 4, 5; *CE.* vi, 211, n.)

This, however, is contrary to the venerated Church fable and artistic forgery current under the title of "St. Veronica's Veil," based on the tale in Luke (xxvii, 27) of the woman of Jerusalem who offered to Jesus a linen cloth to wipe his face as he was carrying his cross towards Calvary. On wiping his sweating face, the supposed authentic likeness of the features of the Christ was miraculously impressed upon the cloth. The lucky lady "went to Rome, bringing with her this image of Christ, which was long exposed to public veneration. To her are likewise traced several other relics of the Blessed Virgin venerated in several Churches of the West. To distinguish at Rome the oldest and best known of these images it was called *vera icon* (true image), which ordinary language soon made *veronica* . . . By degrees *popular imagination* mistook this word for the name of a person" (*CE.* xv, 362),—and, Lo! *Saint Veronica* emerges from the canonized Saint-mill of Holy Church. Here we plainly see myth-in-the-making; and may appreciate the moral splendor as well as crafty thriftiness of the Church of God which thus supplies its Faithful ready-made with one of the most cherished female Saints of the Calendar,—a confessed myth and forgery. His Holiness especially displayed and vouched for this fake on March 19, 1930, when he preached his crusade against Russia. But the Church also, in the Roman Martyrology, credits this holy icon to Milan, so as to fool many other Faithful. (*Ib.* p. 363.) This mythical female Saint "has also been confounded with a pious woman who, according to [Bishop] Gregory of Tours, brought to the neighboring town of Bazas some drops of the blood of John the Baptist, at whose beheading she was present," and *CE.* doesn't even wink. (*Ib.*)

JOSEPHUS FORGEDLY TESTIFIES OF JESUS

So many confessed Christian forgeries in Pagan and Christian names having been wrought to testify to Jesus Christ, it was, "one naturally expects," says *CE.*, that a Jewish "writer so well informed as Josephus" must know and tell about Jesus; "one naturally expects, therefore, a notice about Jesus Christ in Josephus." And with pride it pursues: "Antiquities, VIII, iii, 3, *seems* to satisfy this expectation." It proceeds to quote the passage, which differeth only as one translation naturally differs from another, from that in the Whitson translation; so I follow *CE*. In Chapter iii Josephus treats of "Sedition of the Jews against Pontius Pilate"; in section 1 he relates the cause and the suppression of the mutiny, the ensigns of the army displaying the idolatrous Roman Eagle, brought into the Holy City; in section 2 he tells of the action of Pilate in bringing "a current of water to Jerusalem, and did it with the sacred money," thus again arousing a clash with the fanatics; "there were great numbers of them slain by this means." Passing for the moment the notorious section 3, Josephus the Jew begins section 4: "About the same time, also, *another sad calamity* put the Jews in disorder," which he proceeds to relate, ending the long chapter. Note that these section numbers were not put in by Josephus, but are modern editor's devices to facilitate citation, like the chapters and verses in the Bible. And now for the much-debated section, sandwiched, in a whole chapter on "Seditions of the Jews," between the accounts of two massacres of his countrymen and "another sad calamity"; and thus we read—note the *parentheses* of *CE*. (viii, 376):—

"About this time," quotes *CE*., "appeared Jesus, a wise man (if indeed it is right to call Him a man; for He was a worker of astonishing deeds, a teacher of such men as receive the truth with joy), and He drew to Himself many Jews (and many also of the Greeks. This was the Christ). And when Pilate, at the denunciation of those that are foremost among us, had condemned Him to the cross, those who had first loved Him did not abandon Him. (For He appeared to them alive on the third day, the holy prophets having foretold this and countless other marvels about Him.) The tribe of Christians named after Him did not cease to this day." (sec. 3.)

About this time, *also* "another sad calamity [?] put the Jews into disorder," (sec. 4) continues Josephus. *CE*. devotes over three long columns to the task of trying to prove that this section 3, or at least "the portions *not in parentheses*,"—is genuine, and was written, sometime before his death in 94 A. D., by the Jewish Pharisee, Josephus. "A testimony so important," well says *CE*., "could not escape the critics,"—and it has not. We cannot follow the lengthy and labored arguments; the simple reading of the section, in its bizarre context, and a moment's reflection, condemn it as a pious Christian forgery. If the Pharisee Josephus wrote that paragraph, he must have believed that Jesus was the Prophesied Messiah of his people—*"This was the Christ,"* Josephus is made to aver; he must then needs have been of "the tribe of Christians named after Him." But whatever Josephus may have said about Jesus is, indeed, *not* "a testimony so important" —when we remember what he did aver that he saw with his own eyes: the pillar of salt into which Mrs. Lot was turned; and Eleazar the magician drawing the devil by a ring and Solomonic incantations, through the nose of one possessed, before Vespasian and all his army. If Josephus had written that he knew Jesus the Christ personally, and had personally seen him ascend into heaven through the roof of the room in Jerusalem (Mk. xvi, 19, 20), *or* from the open countryside by Bethany (Lk. xxiv, 50, 51), *or* "on the mount called Olivet" (Acts i, 9, 12),—we should remember that pillar of salt and that devil-doctor, and smile.

But, when and how did this famous passage get into *The Antiquities of the Jews?* it is pertinent to ask. The first mention ever made of this passage, and its text, are in the Church History of that "very dishonest writer," Bishop Eusebius, in the fourth century,—he who forged the Letters between Abgar and Jesus, falsely declaring that he had found the original documents in the official archives, whence he had copied and translated them into his Ecclesiastical History. *CE.* admits, and I have the *Contra Celsum* here before me,—that "the above cited passage *was not known to Origen and the earlier patristic writers,*"—though they copied from Josephus the forged tale of the Letter of Aristeas about the translating of the Septuagint; and "its very place in the Josephan text is uncertain, since Eusebius (Hist. Eccl., II, vi) must have *found* it before the notices concerning Pilate, while it now stands *after* them" (*HE.* I, ii, p. 63); and it makes the curious argument, which implies a confession: "But the spuriousness of the disputed Josephan passage does not imply the historian's ignorance of the facts connected with Jesus Christ"! For a wonder, that "a writer so well informed as Josephus" should not, perhaps, know by hearsay, sixty years after Jesus Christ, some of the remarkable things circulated about him in current country-side gossip—(if, indeed, it were then current). But the fact is, that with the exception of this one incongruous forged passage, section 3, the wonder-mongering Josephus makes not the slightest mention of his wonder-working fellow-countryman, Jesus the Christ,—though some score of other Joshuas, or Jesuses, are recorded by him, nor does he mention any of his transcendent wonders. But, as *CE.* and I were saying, none of the Fathers, before Eusebius (about 324), knew or could find a word in the works of Josephus, of this momentous "testimony to Jesus," over a century after Origen. That it *did not exist in the time of Origen* is explicit by his own words; he cites the supposed references by Josephus to John the Baptist and to James, and expressly says that Josephus *ought to have spoken of Jesus* instead of James; though Origen does not correctly describe the reference to James; and the James passage, if not that also about John, has a suspicious savor of interpolation.

For a clear understanding of this, I will quote the passage of Origen in his work against Celsus; it completely refutes the claim that Josephus wrote the disputed and forged section 3. Origen says:

"I would like to say to Celsus, who represents the Jew accepting John somehow as a Baptist, who baptized Jesus, that the existence of John the Baptist, baptizing for the remission of sins, is related by one who lived no great time after John and Jesus. For in the 18th book of his *Antiquities of the Jews,* Josephus bears witness to John as having been a Baptist, and as promising purification to those who underwent the rite. Now this writer, although *not believing in Jesus as the Christ,* in seeking after the cause of the fall of Jerusalem and the destruction of the temple [said that it was 'to avenge James the Just'], whereas he *ought to have said* that the conspiracy against Jesus was the cause of these calamities befalling the people, since they put to death Christ, who was a prophet, says nevertheless—being, although against his will, not far from the truth—that these disasters happened to the Jews as a punishment for the death of James the Just, who was a brother of Jesus (called Christ),—the Jews having put him to death, although he was a man most distinguished for his justice." (Origen, *Contra Celsum,* I, xlvii; *ANF.* iv, 416.)

Josephus is thus quoted as bearing witness to John the Baptist, *not* as the Heaven-sent "forerunner" of the Christ, but simply as a Jewish religious teacher and baptizer on his own account; and not a word by Josephus about the Christ, in whom it is admitted that he did not believe as such, nor even mentions as the most illustrious of those baptized by John, to the wondrous accompaniment of a voice from Heaven and the Holy Ghost in dove-like descent upon his head as he came up from the water. But Origen, in his effort to get some Christian testimony from him, misquotes Josephus and makes him say that John was baptizing "for the remission of sins," whereas Josephus expressly says that the efficacy of John's baptism was *not* for remission of sin but for the purification of the body, as any washing would be. To vindicate Josephus against Origen, the former's words are quoted. Josephus recounts the defeat of Herod by Aretas, king of Arabia Petrea; and goes on to say :—

"Now some of the Jews thought that the destruction of Herod's army came from God, and that very justly, as a punishment of what he did against John, that was called the Baptist; for Herod slew him, who was a good man, and commanded the Jews to exercise virtue, both as to righteousness toward one another, and piety toward God, and so to come to baptism; for that the washing would be acceptable to him, if they made use of it, *not* in order to the putting away of some sins, but for the purification of the body: supposing still that the soul was thoroughly purified beforehand by righteousness. Now, when many others came in crowds about him, for they were greatly moved by hearing his words, Herod, who feared lest the great influence John had over the people might put it into his power and inclination to raise a rebellion, (for they seemed ready to do anything he should advise,) thought it best, by putting him to death, to prevent any mischief he might cause, and not bring himself into difficulties, by sparing a man who might make him repent of it when it should be too late. Accordingly, he was sent a prisoner, out of Herod's suspicious temper, to Macherus, the castle I before mentioned, and was *there* put to death." (Josephus, *Antiq. Jews,* Bk. XVIII, v, 2.)

Beginning in section 4 of the same Book, and at length in various chapters, Josephus goes into details regarding Salome; but never a word of the famous dance-act and of the head of John the Baptist being brought in on a charger to gratify her murderous whim; the historical reason for the murder of John was political, not amorous or jealous, as related by Gospel-truth.

Father Origen again falls into error in citing Josephus, this time in the dubious passage where Josephus, who does not believe in the Christ, yet gives him that title in speaking of the death of James. With typical clerical bent Father Origen imputes the fall of Jerusalem and

117

the destruction of the temple to the sin of the Jews in crucifying the Christ; and says that Josephus, in seeking the cause of the disasters which befell the Holy City and people, attributes them to the killing of the Christ's brother. The Holy City and temple were destroyed in 70 A. D., which was well after the time of the supposititious James, as his demise is recorded in the suspected passage of Josephus. He relates the death of Festus, which was in 62 A. D., the appointment by Nero of Albinus as his successor, and the murder of James at the instigation of the high priest Ananus, before Albinus can arrive. This sentence is to be read in the text of Josephus:

"Festus was now dead, and Albinus was but upon the road; so he (Ananus) assembled the sanhedrin of judges, and brought before them the brother of Jesus, who was called Christ, whose name was James, and some others; and when he had formulated an accusation against them as breakers of the law, he delivered them to be stoned." (Jos., *Antiq. Jews*, Bk. XX, ix, 1.)

Bishop Eusebius cannot pass over this chance to turn another Jewish testimony for his Christ; he says that "The wiser part of the Jews were of the opinion that this—(the killing of James)—was the cause of the immediate siege of Jerusalem . . . Josephus also has not hesitated to superadd his testimony in his works. 'These things,' he says, 'happened to the Jews to avenge James the Just, who was the brother of him that is called Christ, and whom the Jews had slain, notwithstanding his preëminent justice.'" (Euseb. *Hist. Eccles.* Bk. II, ch. 23.)

The reader may judge of the integrity of these pretended Jewish testimonies to the Baptist and to the brother of the Christ, both suspicious *per se*, and both falsely cited by Father Origen, who in all this could not find the famous section 3, first found a century later by Bishop Eusebius; and which Origen makes it positive Josephus had not written and could not have written. Is it a violent suspicion, and uncharitable, to suggest that the holy Bishop who forged the Letter of his Christ, and lied about finding it in the Edessa archives, really "found," in the sense of *invented*, or forged, the Josephus passages first heard of in his Church History?

But Bishop Eusebius, with a sort of "stop thief" forethought, himself imputes forgery to those who would question or discredit his own pious inventions, while with unctuous fervor of pretended truth he appeals to the wonderful "testimonies of Josephus," which he has just fabricated. After quoting and misquoting Josephus with respect to John the Baptist and Jesus Christ, he thus solemnly vouches for their false witness: "When such testimony as this is transmitted to us by an historian who sprung from the Hebrews themselves, both respecting John the Baptist and our Saviour, what subterfuge can be left, to prevent those from being convicted destitute of all shame, who have forged the acts against them?" (Eusebius, *HE*. I, xi.) The Bishop justly pronounces his own condemnation. This, says Gibbon, "is an example of no vulgar forgery." (Chap. xvi.) In view of the convicting circumstances, and of his notoriously bad record, it is not uncharitable to impute this Josephus forgery to Bishop Eusebius.

THE OWL-ANGEL FORGERY

Another story of Pagan superstition related by Josephus, and twisted by the Christian invention of Bishop Eusebius and the sacred writers of *Acts* into inspired "history" and truth of God, is the celebrated angel-owl passage relating to the tragic death of the King, Herod Agrippa. Josephus tells that Herod went to Cæsarea to attend a celebration in honor of Cæsar; that as Herod entered the stadium, clad in a robe of silver tissue, the rays of the sun shone upon it resplendently, making him look like a supernatural being; whereupon the crowd cried out hailing him as more than mortal, as a god; but his mortality was quickly made evident by his sudden illness and death. It may be explained that the word "angel" (Greek, *angelos*) means simply "messenger" or herald. Thus proceeds Josephus:

"But as he [Herod] presently afterward looked up, he saw an *owl* sitting upon a certain rope over his head, and immediately understood that this bird was a messenger [Gr. *angelos*] of ill-tidings." Herod was shortly seized with "severe pains in his belly," and died after five days of suffering." (Jos. *Antiq. Jews*, XIX, viii, 2.)

This was too Paganish and prosaic for the pious Christian fancy of Bishop Eusebius; so while he was forging the "Jesus passage," he proceeded to give Christian embellishment for edification to the "owl" story, with its use of the word "angelos." So he quotes in full the narration of Josephus, under the chapter heading "Herod Agrippa persecuting the Apostles, immediately experienced divine Judgment." He first relates the "martyrdom of James" by Herod, and the imprisonment of Peter, as recorded in Acts, and proceeds: "The consequences, however, of the king's attempts against the apostles, were not long deferred, but the avenging minister of divine justice soon overtook him. . . . As it is also recorded in the book of Acts, he proceeded to Cæsarea, and there on a noted festival, being clad in a splendid and royal dress, he harangued the people. . . . The whole people applauding him for his harangue, as it were the voice of a god, and not of a man, the Scriptures relate, 'that the angel of the Lord immediately smote him, and being consumed by worms, he gave up the ghost.' It is wonderful to observe, likewise, in this singular event, the *coincidence* of the history given by Josephus, with that of the sacred Scriptures. In this he [Josephus] plainly *adds his testimony to the truth,* in the nineteenth book of his Antiquities, where *he relates* the miracles in the following words: [here quoting Josephus in full, until he reaches the owl-story, when he thus falsifies]: —'After a little while, raising himself, he saw *an angel* [*angelos*] hanging over his head upon a rope, and this he knew immediately to be an omen of evil'! Thus far Josephus: in which statement, as in others, I can but admire his agreement with the divine Scriptures"! (Eusebius, *HE.* II, x.) An angel hanging on a rope over one's head might well have been taken by a superstitious person as ominous of something—maybe of a hung angel. This pious story, with the *owl* piously metamorphosed into an *angel,* was apparently cribbed from Josephus also by the writer of Acts, or maybe "interpolated" into it by the fanciful Bishop. There we find this Pagan-Jewish anecdote retold by divine inspiration, thus embellished over Josephus and Eusebius: "And immediately the angel of the Lord [Gr. *angelos Kuriou*] smote him, because he gave not God the glory: and he was eaten of worms and gave up the ghost"! (Acts xii, 20–23.) Note the almost identical words, except for the progressive embellishments: Josephus' owl thus became first an angel of evil omen, then the avenging minister of the wrath of God, aided by devouring worms to give true Christian zest and spite to the simple Pagan superstition. Herod

120

probably died from acute indigestion caused by the excesses of the festivities, or from an attack of peritonitis or appendicitis. Profane history of the event does not chronicle the devouring, avenging worms of God.

The forgery of pious documents of every imaginable character was among the most constant and zealous activities of the holy propagandists of the Christian Faith, from the beginning to the critical era when forgeries were no longer possible or profitable. A fitting close to this review is the following omnibus confession—the Churches cheating each other by forgeries:

"Indeed, in later times, we hear of recovered autographs of Apostolic writings in the controversies about the Apostolic origin of some Churches or about claims for metropolitan dignity. So the autograph of the Gospel of St. Matthew was said to have been found in Cyprus. . . . Eusebius (Hist. Eccles. vii, 19) relates that in his time the seat of St. James was as yet extant in Jerusalem. Of old pictures of Apostles, see Eusebius, ibid, vii, 18. Whether or not even the oldest of these statements are historically true remains still a mooted question. We regard it as useless to record what may be found on these topics in *the vast amount of matter* that makes up the apocryphal Acts of the Apostles and other legendary documents." (*CE.* i, 635.)

Among some of these not already mentioned are found "The Gospel of Our Lord Jesus Christ, The Canons of Pseudo-Hippolytus, The Egyptian Church Ordinance." (*CE.* i, 636.) Also: "In the last years of the fifth century a famous document *attributed* to Popes Gelasius and Hormisdas adds . . . a list of books disapproved, the works of heretics, and *forged Scriptural documents.*" (*CE.* vi, 4.) A glance at the Index-volume of *CE.* reveals the numerous forged works attributed to many of the Fathers of the early Church, listed under the word *Pseudo*, or false, which word is to be understood as prefixed to each of the following names: *Pseudo*-Alquin, Ambrosius, Antoninus, Areopagite, Athanasius, Augustine, Barnabas, Callisthenes, Chrysostom, Clement, Epiphanius, Gelasius, Gregory Nazianzen, Hegesippus, Hippolytus, Ignatius, Isidore, Jonathan, Justin, Matthew, Prochorus, Tertullian, Zacharius. The pious ignorant "Christians, who for the most part are untrained and illiterate persons," as shown in the

121

Octavius of Minucius Felix (v, xi), and the whole Church, were gulled by these frauds for a thousand years.

Before looking into the forgery of the New Testament Books, we shall first draw, from their own words, cameo pen-sketches of those great men of God and of Holy Church, who under the fond name of Fathers, but with the minds and devious ways of little children, forged the sacred documents of the Faith, and by their pious labors of fraud and forgery founded what is credulously called the Church of Christ and the Most Holy Christian Faith.

CHAPTER IV

THE SAINTLY "FATHERS" OF THE FAITH

"The greater Saint, the greater Liar." *Diegesis.*
"The principal historians of the patristic period cannot always be completely trusted." (*CE.* vi, 14.)

EMBRACED WITHIN *CE.'s* confession of patristic untrustworthiness and perversion of truth is every "Father" and Founder of the Church of Christ of the first three centuries of the fabrication of the new Faith,—as by their own words will now be demonstrated. Yet upon these self-same not-to-be-trusted fabulists and forgers do the truth and validity of the Christ and the Christian religion solely and altogether depend. They destroy it.

The Fathers of our country, framers of our Constitution and form of government, were men of personal honor and of public probity; the most of them were Infidels. The "Fathers" and founders of the Christian religion and Church of Christ were, all of them, ex-Pagan charlatans—"we who formerly used magical arts," as Father Justin Martyr admits (I *Apology*, xiv), who took up the new Christian superstition and continued to ply the same old magical arts under a new veneer, upon the ignorant and superstitious pagans and near-pagans, as the ensuing pages will demonstrate. The Fathers will show themselves to be wholly destitute of common sense of opinion and of common honesty of statement, credulous and mendacious to the n-th degree.

It is of capital importance to an intelligent and adequate understanding of the Christian religion, of which these Fathers were the originators and propagandists, to see their work in the making; and to know the mental and moral limitations and obliquities of these fatuous, fabling, forging Fathers of the Church. We shall see them to be grotesquely credulous of every fable, many of which themselves fabricated; reckless of truth to the highest degree; fluent and unscrupulous

123

Liars of the Lord, whose lies, if thereby the "glory of God" were made the more to abound, they, like Paul, counted it no sin (Rom. iii, 7), as we have seen confessed. Like Paul, "being crafty," they made a holy craft of catching the credulous with guile; and like Paul, they boasted of it. (2 Cor. xii, 16.)

For the ampler appreciation of the utter incapacity of these pious ex-Pagan and ex-Magician Fathers to comprehend truth or to tell it, and of their childish and reckless irresponsibility in relating as truth what they knew was not true, we need but look briefly at their records and wonder at their moronic mentality. For this purpose, and to watch the snow-ball-like roll and growth of their Fatherly "traditions" and fabrications into forged Church, Creed, and Dogma, a brief sketch is given, in chronological order—a veritable Roll of Dishonor—of the chiefest of them; citing under each name a few—out of innumerable—of their extravagant, childish-minded and tortuous precepts and practices of Christian propaganda; together with sundry forgeries perpetrated by them or in their sainted names.

An admirable norm and test of trustworthiness is stated by Middleton, one of the keenest critics of the Miracle-mongering of the Fathers: "The authority of a writer who affirms any questionable fact, must depend on the character of his veracity and judgment. In many cases the want of judgment alone has all the same effect, as the want of veracity, too, towards invalidating the testimony of a witness; especially in cases of an extraordinary or miraculous nature, where the weakness of men is more apt to be imposed upon." (*A Free Inquiry*, p. 26.) It will give pause to think, to that yet great and priest-taught class of Believers who, like the Fathers themselves, "think the credibility of a witness sufficient evidence of the certainty of all facts indifferently, whether natural or supernatural, probable or improbable, and knowing no difference between faith and facts, take a facility of believing to be the surest mark of a good Christian." (*Ibid*, Preface, v.) Their faith reasons—if at all—in the terms of Father Tertullian: "It is by all means to be believed, because it is absurd; the fact is certain, because it is impossible." (*De Carne Christi*, ch. v; *ANF*. iii, 525.)

The mental limitations of the Fathers we have seen several times admitted and apologized for by *CE.*; further it confesses of them: "It was natural that in the early days of the Church, the Fathers,

124

writing with *little scientific knowledge,* should have a tendency" to fall into sundry comical and preposterous errors "now entirely abandoned" (iii, 731). This is but another of its many luminous confessions of the ignorance and uncritical credulity of the pious Fathers, extending over fifteen hundred years of Church history, and even yet!

The childlike mental processes of the Fathers, their all-accepting credulity, and the utter worthlessness of their opinions and "traditions" as to things divine and human, is oft-admitted and will be made manifest. We shall soon see that the Four Gospels which Christians, with childlike faith accept as the genuine handiwork of the apostles and immediate companions of Christ, are anonymous forgeries of a century and more after their time, and that the other New Testament booklets, Acts and Epistles of the alleged apostles, are so many other forgeries made long after their times.

The forged New Testament booklets and the foolish writings of the Fathers, are the sole "evidence" we have for the alleged facts and doctrines of our most holy Faith, as is admitted by *CE.:* "Our documentary sources of *knowledge* about the *origins of Christianity* and its earliest *development* are chiefly the New Testament Scriptures and various sub-Apostolic writings, *the authenticity of which we must to a great extent take for granted* here. (*CE.* iii, 712.) The Christian religion and the Church thus confessedly exist upon data and documents the authenticity and verity of which "must be taken for granted,"—but which are well known, and are here easily shown, to be false and fabricated, with deceptive intent.

PATRISTIC "TRADITION"

This word "tradition," of Fathers and Church, we shall frequently meet, such "tradition" being urged as evidence of the reality and verity of these things with easy gesture "taken for granted" by the beneficiaries of the System based upon them. What, then, is "tradition"? Of what value is "tradition," as evidence of things naturally incredible and unverifiable,—of alleged events and miraculous happenings over a century before the "traditions"—invariably contradictory—which first allege them as facts for Faith? For instance: "The famous texts of Irenæus on Apostolic Succession are a testimony to the faith [*i. e.*

125

"traditions"] of the second century, rather than an example of historical narrative." (*CE.* vii, 341.)

Tradition is popular stories and hand-me-down reports or gossip current in the community or passing current among any particular class of people; it is of the same stuff as legend is made of. One pious Father or propagator of the Faith would aver some wonder-tale which would attract credulous interest; the next, in repeating it, invariably embroiders it with new fancies, and so it grows like a snowball of fables. We have seen the example of the garnishments of the Fathers to the forged Aristeas-tale regarding the Septuagint; we shall see the Fatherly "traditions" suddenly crop up a century or two after some alleged event, embroider and expand—and contradict themselves from Father to Father in the telling, with respect to every single instance: Gospel-tales, forged "apocrypha" narratives, false foundations of churches, bishops, popes, apostolic successions. Thus the Fathers inflated their originally fictitious "traditions" of this and that, and on such bases the New Testament and the Church of Christ arose. Of course, the credibility of any "tradition" or alleged fact depends wholly on the credit of the first narrator of it; to all later repeaters it is purely *hearsay*, and gains no further credit from the number of those repeating the original tale. If a thing is a lie when first told, repetition *ad infinitum* cannot make it into a truth.

In a note to one instance of patristic tradition recorded in the bulky collection, the editors of the *ANF.*, to which we are indebted for most of what follows regarding these fatuous Fathers, make this sentential comment: "Hearsay at second-hand, and handed about among many, amounts to *nothing* as evidence." And this is the comment of Father Bishop Eusebius, the first Church historian, on the "traditions" of good Father Bishop Papias, first of the sub-Apostolic Fathers: "These sayings [of Jesus Christ and apostles] consisted of a number of strange parables, and doctrines of our Saviour, which *the authority of so venerable a person*, who had lived with the apostles, *imposed on the Church as genuine.*" (*Hist. Eccles.* Bk. III, ch. 39.) But this is simply another fictitious "tradition," that Papias "lived with the apostles," for he did not, as his own words and *CE.* will disclose when we come to sketch that pious fabulist of a Father. Such are

126

patristic and ecclesiastical "traditions," of which sufficient examples
are yet to be noticed.

THE TWELVE "TRADITIONAL" APOSTLES

There were Twelve Tribes of Israel; and Moses, coming down from
Sinai, appointed twelve young men "according to the twelve tribes of
Israel" to sacrifice at the twelve phallic pillars which he set up to
celebrate the giving of the Law. (Ex. xxiv, 4–5.) So "tradition" has
it that Jesus appointed Twelve Apostles: "The number twelve was
symbolical, corresponding to the twelve tribes of Israel" (*EB.* i, 264);
but the whole story is fictitious, says *EB.* (iii, 2987), with the soundest
Scriptural basis for its conclusion. As this—and many other fictional
features of the Christ-biographies—are fully examined in my *Is It
God's Word?* (Chaps. XIII–XIV), I must refer to it for the confused
"traditions" of the Twelve, for the purpose of showing their wholly
fictitious character.

After the same "symbolical" fashion the legendary "Seventy
Elders of Israel," commanded by Yahveh and chosen by Moses (Num.
xi, 16, 24), had their counterpart in the equally legendary "Seventy
Disciples, whom also the Lord appointed" (Luke x, 1),—and who
furnished so many zealous missionaries and early church-founders, as
their "records" pretend, and so many of which are by *CE.* declared to
be fraudulent and forged. Bear in mind that the "Gospel" records, as
we shall see, are anonymous forgeries of a century and more after the
"traditional" events recorded; and the unreliable nature of "tradition" is further illustrated.

The probability if not assurance will appear the stronger, as we
proceed with the Fathers and with the "sacred writings," that the Holy
Twelve had no existence in the flesh, but their "cue" being taken from
the Old Testament legends, they were mere names—*dramatis personæ*
—masks of the play,—of "tradition," such as Shakespeare and all
playwrights and fiction-writers create for the actors of their plays and
works of admitted fiction.

A very curious and challenging admission is made by *CE.* in speaking of the noted forgeries, long regarded as inspired, of the "Pseudo-

127

Dionysius the Areopagite," who "clave unto Paul" after his Mar's Hill harangue (Acts xvii, 34), and in whose name many precious forgeries—"a series of famous writings" (*CE.* v, 13)—were forged by pious Christians "at the very earliest in the latter half of the fifth century," and which were "of highest and universally acknowledged authority, both in the Western and in the Eastern Church, lasting until the beginning of the fifteenth century," followed by a "period of sharp conflict waged about their authenticity, begun by Laurentius Valla, and closing only within recent years." (*CE.* v, 15.) "Those writings," says *CE.*—with more far-reaching suggestion than intended,—"*with intent to deceive, weave into their narrative certain fictitious personages, such as Peter, James, John, Timothy, Carpus, and others.*" (*CE.* vii, 345.) If these great Apostles and "pillars of the Faith" are "fictitious personages" in the long-revered but now admitted forgeries of Pseudo-Dionysius, by what token may they be any the less *fictitious personages* in the hundreds of other equally forged Christian writings which we shall notice,—as also in the to-be-demonstrated forgeries of Gospels, Acts and Epistles, in which the identical personages, or *dramatis personæ*, play their imaginary and self-contradictory rôles, as we shall promptly see? For fifteen hundred years, and until "only within recent years," were the Dionysian forgeries tenaciously proclaimed as genuine by the Holy-Ghost-guided Church; may it not have been equally mis-guided as to the "authenticity" of its Gospels and other "sacred writings"? If, in the venerated "*pseudo-Areopagite*," the sainted Peter, Paul, John, *et als.*, are admittedly "*fictitious personages*," how do they acquire the flesh and blood of *actual persons* in Gospels and Epistles? We shall see.

I. *The Apostles*

Two of them, the principal, Peter and John, are described to be "*anthropoi agrammatoi kai idiotai*—unlearned and ignorant men" (Acts iv, 13); all Twelve were of the same type and well matched. They were variously picked up from among the humblest and most superstitious of the Galilee peasants, fishermen and laborers, "called" personally, we are told, by the Son of God, the proclaimed King-to-be of the Jews, to be his counsellors and associates in the establishment of his earthly and heavenly Kingdoms—of Jews. As for the King-to-be and his prospective Court, a saddening and repellent portraiture is sketched in the inspired Biographies: though it is true, "The chronology of the birth of Christ and the subsequent Biblical events is most uncertain." (*CE*. vii, 419.) His parents and family regarded him as insane and sought to restrain him by force. (Mark iii, 21; cf. John x, 20.) He and his Apostle-band toured Palestine with a retinue of barefoot and unwashed peasant men and women, shocking polite people by their habits of not washing even their hands to eat when invited as guests, and by the violence of their language. These traits ran in his peasant family and relatives. His cousin, known as John the Baptist, was a desert dervish, unwashed and unshorn, who wore a leather loin-strap for clothes and whose regular diet was wild bumble-bee honey and raw grasshoppers. His own brother James was as unkempt and filthy as any Saint in the calendar; of him Bishop Eusebius records: "James, the brother of the Lord, . . . a razor never came upon his head, he never anointed with oil, and *never used a bath*"! (*HE*. II, 23.) With the Master at their head, the Troupe wandered up and down the little land, proclaiming the immediate end of the world, playing havoc with the legions of devils who infested the peasantry, and preaching Hell and Damnation for all who would not heed their fanatical preachments.

APOSTOLIC GREED AND STRIFE

As for the Twelve, the hope of great reward was the inspiredly recorded motive of these peasants who left their petty crafts for hope of greater gain by following the lowly King-to-be. The zeal and greed for personal aggrandizement of the Chosen Twelve is constantly revealed throughout the inspired record. Hardly had the Holy Twelve gotten organized and into action, when the cunning and crafty Peter, spokesman for the craft, boldly came forward and advanced the itching palm: "Then answered Peter and said unto him, Behold, we have forsaken all, and followed thee; *what shall we have therefore?*" (Matt. xix, 27.) And the Master came back splendidly with the Promise: "And Jesus said unto them, Verily I say unto you, That ye which have followed me, in the regeneration, when the Son of Man shall sit in the throne of his glory, ye also shall sit upon twelve thrones, judging the

129

twelve tribes of Israel" (Matt. xix, 28). But even these brilliant future rewards could not satisfy the greed of the Holy Ones, and led not to gratitude, but to greater greed and strife.

The Mother of James and John, probably inspired by them, and zealous for their greater glory, came secretly with her two sons, to Jesus, "worshipping him, and desiring a certain thing of him" (Matt. xx, 20) ; and when Jesus asked her what it was, "she saith unto him, Grant that these my two sons may sit, the one on thy right hand, and the other on the left, in thy Kingdom." (v. 21.) But Mark contradicts the assurance of Matthew that it was Mrs. Zebedee who came and made the request, and avers that "James and John, the sons of Zebedee, come unto him, saying, Master, we would that thou shouldst do for us whatsoever we shall desire," and stated their own modest demand for preferment. (Mark x, 35–37.) But, in either contradictory event, both agree that "when the ten heard it, they were moved with indignation against the two brethren." (Matt. xxix, 24 ; Mark x, 41.)

Not during the whole one- or three-years of association with their Master, did these holy Apostles abate their greed and strife. Several times are recorded disputes among them as to "who should be greatest among them" (Matt. xviii, 1 ; Mark ix, 33–34 ; Luke ix, 46)—here again the "harmony of the Gospels" assuring the constant inharmony of the Apostles. And even at the Last Supper, when Jesus had announced that one of them would that night betray him to death, "there was also strife among them, which of them should be accounted the greatest." (Luke xxii, 24.) And great was the disgust of the Master at his miserable Apostles, and especially at the craven and crafty Peter. Jesus had spurned him with blasting scorn, "and said unto Peter, Get thee behind me, Satan : thou art an offense to me" (Matt. xvi, 23) ; and again the Gospels are in Harmony (Mt. xvi, 23 ; Mk. viii, 33). Such are the Holy Apostles of Jesus Christ, said to be painted by some of themselves through inspiration. This "Satan" Peter, later constituted "Saint" Peter, shall again deserve our attention.

II. *The Apostolic Fathers*

Under this rubric *CE.* lists, as those who were "converted with the apostles," and, after them, were the first propagandists of the

THE SAINTLY "FATHERS" OF THE FAITH

Truth, the Catholic Saints Clement, Ignatius, Polycarp, Barnabas, and Hermas; they fill up the first half of the second century of the era. The "traditions" preserved of these saintly Fathers of the Church are very scanty and dubious; but from what exists they were all within the apostolic description of Peter and John, "ignorant and unlearned men," and like Bishop Papias, as described by Bishop Eusebius, "men of very small minds, if we may judge from their own words," of which we shall now read for ourselves. It will be noted that all these Fathers, like all the sub-apostolic Fathers for the first two centuries and more, were ex-Pagans, and (with the alleged exception of "Pope" Clement), were Greeks of scattered parts of the Empire, who wrote and taught in Greek, and with the very questionable exception of Clement, had nothing to do with "the Church which sojourns at Rome." Each was the Bishop and head of his own local, and independent, Church; and never once does one of them (except Clement of Rome, in a forged Epistle), speak of or mention the Church of Rome, or more than barely mention Peter (and only as *one* of the Apostles), nor mention or quote a single book of the New Testament,—though they are profuse in quoting the Old Testament books, canonical and apocryphal, the Pagan gods, and the Sibylline oracles, as inspired testimonies of Jesus Christ. The significance of all this will appear.

1. CLEMENT OF ROME (about 30–96 A. D.). He is alleged to be the first, second, third, or fourth, Bishop, or Pope, of Rome (*CE.* iv, 13); and to be the author of two Epistles to the Corinthians, besides other bulky and important forgeries, thus confessed and catalogued by *CE:*

"Many writings have been falsely attributed to Pope St. Clement: (1) The 'Second Clementine Epistle to the Corinthians.' Many critics have believed them genuine [they having been read in the Churches]. . . . But it is now admitted on all hands that they cannot be by the same author as the genuine [?] Epistle to the Corinthians. . . . (2) Two 'Epistles to Virgins.' (3) At the head of the Pseudo-Isidorian Decretals stand five letters attributed to St. Clement. (4) Ascribed to Clement are the 'Apostolic Constitutions,' 'Apostolic Canons,' and the 'Testament of our Lord.' (5) The 'Clementines' or 'Pseudo-Clementines,' including the *Recognitions* and *Homilies,*" hereafter to be noticed. (*CE.* iv, 14–15; cf. 17, 39.)

The second of these alleged Epistles of Clement to the Corinthians is thus admittedly a forgery, together with everything else in his name but the alleged First Epistle. The case for this First Epistle is little if any better; but as it is the very flimsy basis of one of the proudest claims of Holy Church—though suppressed as "proof" of another claim which it disproves,—it is, as it were, plucked as a brand from the burning of all the other Clementine forgeries, and placed at the head of all the writings of the Fathers. Of this I Clement *EB.* says: "The author is *certainly not Clement of Rome,* whatever may be our judgment as to whether or not Clement was a bishop, a martyr, a disciple of the apostles. The martyrdom, set forth in *untrustworthy Acts,* has for its sole foundation the identification of Clement of Rome with Flavius Clement the consul, who was executed by command of Domitian,"—A. D. 81–96. (*EB.* iii, 3486.) This First Epistle is supposed to have been written about the year 96–98, by Clement, friend and co-worker of Paul, according to the late "tradition" first set in motion by Dionysius, A. D. 170. But "This Clement," says *CE.,* after citing the Fathers, "was probably a Philippian." (*CE.* iv, 13.) "Who the Clement was to whom the writings were ascribed, cannot with absolute certainty be determined." (*ANF.* i, 2.)

It is notable that the pretendedly genuine "First Epistle" does not contain or mention the name of any one as its author, nor name Clement; its address is simply: "The Church of God which sojourns at Rome, to the Church of God sojourning at Corinth." There is only one MS. of it in existence, a translation into Latin from the original Greek. This is the celebrated MS. of "Holy Scripture" known as Codex A, which was discovered and presented to Charles I of England by Cyril of Alexandria, in 1628; the Fathers cited both I and II Clement as Scripture. On this MS., at the end of I Clement, is written, "The First Epistle of Clement to the Corinthians": a subscription which proves itself a forgery and that it was not written by Clement, who could not know that a later forger would write a "Second Clement," so as to give him occasion to call his own the First. (*ANF.* viii, 55–56.)

By whomever this "First Epistle" was written, by Father, Bishop, or Pope of Rome, his zeal and his intelligence are demonstrated by his argument, in Chapter xxv, of the truth of the Resurrection; in proof of which he makes this powerful and faith-compelling plea:

132

"Let us consider that wonderful sign [of the resurrection] which takes place in Eastern lands, that is, in Arabia and the countries round about. There is a certain bird which is called a phoenix. This is the only one of its kind, and lives five hundred years. And when the time of its dissolution draws near that it must die, it builds itself a nest of frankincense, and myrrh, and other spices, into which, when the time is fulfilled, it enters and dies. But as the flesh decays a certain kind of worm is produced, which, being nourished by the juices of the dead bird, brings forth feathers. Then, when it has acquired strength, it takes up that nest in which are the bones of its parent, and bearing these it passes from the land of Arabia into Egypt, to the City called Heliopolis. And, in open day, flying in the sight of all men, it places them on the altar of the sun, and having done this, hastens back to its former abode. The priests then inspect the registers of the dates, and find that it has returned exactly as the 500th year was completed." (*ANF.* i, p. 12. Note: "This fable respecting the phoenix is mentioned by Herodotus (ii, 73) and by Pliny (*Nat. Hist.* x, 2), and is used as above by Tertullian (*De Resurr.*, sec. 13), and by others of the Fathers." *CE.* iv, 15.)

The occasion for the pretended writing of this Epistle, and the very high significance of it, will be noticed when we treat of the origin of the Church which sojourns at Rome.

2. IGNATIUS: Saint, Bishop of Antioch (born in Syria, c. 50— died rather latitudinously "between 98 and 117"). "More than one of the early ecclesiastical writers has given credence, though apparently without good reason, to the legend that Ignatius was the child whom the Saviour took up in his arms, as described in Mark, ix, 35." (*CE.* vii, 644.) "*If* we include St. Peter, Ignatius was the third Bishop of Antioch," (*CE.* vii, 644),—thus casting doubt on another and a most monumental but confused Church "tradition." He was the subject of very extensive forgeries; fifteen Epistles bear the name of Ignatius, including one to the Virgin Mary, and her reply; two to the apostle John, others to the Philippians, Tarsians, Antiocheans, Ephesians, Magnesians, Trallians, Romans, Philadelphians, Smyrneans, and to Polycarp, besides a forged *Martyrium*; the clerical forgers were very active with the name of Saint Ignatius. Of these, eight Epistles and the *Martyrium* are confessedly forgeries; "they are by common consent *set aside as forgeries*, which were at various dates and *to serve special purposes*, put forth under the name of the celebrated Bishop of

133

Antioch" (*ANF.* i, 46; *CE.* vii, 645); though, says *CE.*, "*if* the *Martyrium* is genuine, this work has been greatly interpolated." As to the seven supposed by some to be genuine, "even the genuine epistles were *greatly interpolated to lend weight to the personal views* of its author. For this reason they are incapable of bearing witness to the original form" (*CE.* vii, 645); and even the authenticity of the "genuine seven" was warmly disputed for several centuries. The dubious best that *CE.* can say is: "Perhaps the *best evidence* for their authenticity is to be found in the letter of Polycarp to the Philippians, which mentions each of them by name . . . *UNLESS*, indeed, that of Polycarp itself be regarded as interpolated or *FORGED*." (*Ib.* p. 646.)

As good proofs as may be that these "seven genuine" are late forgeries, are: of each one of them, as printed in the *ANF.*, there are "two recensions, a shorter and a longer," printed in parallel columns, thus demonstrating that the longer at least is "greatly interpolated"; the most significant being a reference to Peter and Paul, constituting the "interpolated" part of Chap. vii of the Epistle to the Romans, hereafter noticed. That as a whole they are late forgeries, is further proved by the fact, stated by Cardinal Newman, that "the whole system of Catholic doctrine may be discovered, at least in outline, not to say in parts filled up, in the course of his seven Epistles" (*CE.* vii, 646); this including the impossibilities—for that epoch—of the elaborated hierarchy of the Imperial Church as having been instituted by the humble Nazarene,—who was to "come again" and put an end to all earthly things within the generation; the infallibility of the Church, the supernatural virtue of virginity, and the *primacy of the See of Rome*,—at the supposed time of Ignatius, a little horde of nondescripts burrowing in the Catacombs of imperial Rome! Oh, Church of God: never a scrap of paper even touched by you but was a loathsome forgery to the glory of your fictitious God and Christ! So as Father Saint Ignatius did not write anything authentic, he escapes the self-condemnation of the other Apostolic Fathers. May his martyred remains rest in peace.

3. POLYCARP: (69–155). Saint, Bishop of Smyrna, Martyr. Only one Epistle, addressed to the Philippians, remains of Polycarp, and of it *CE.* discusses the "serious question" of its genuineness, which

134

depends upon that of the Ignatian Epistles, and *vice versa*, above discussed; it says: "If the former were forgeries, the latter, which supports—it might almost be said presupposes—them, *must be a forgery* from the same hand." (*CE*. xii, 219.) Poor Church of God, cannot you produce something of your Saints that isn't a forgery?

But if Saint Polycarp did not write anything genuine, his Church of Smyrna did itself proud in doing honor to his pretended Martyrdom, in A. D. 154–5, or 165–6 (*Ib.*)—so exact is Church "tradition." In one of the earliest Encyclicals—(not issued by a Pope)—the wondrous tale is told. It is addressed: "The Church of God which sojourns at Smyrna, to the Church of God sojourning in Philomelium, and to all the congregations of the Holy and Catholic—[first use of term]—Church in every place"; and proceeds in glowing words to recount the virtues, capture, trial and condemnation to death by fire, of the holy St. Polycarp. Just before his capture, Polycarp dreamed that his pillow was afire; he exclaimed to those around, "prophetically, 'I am to be burned alive.'" The forged and fabling Epistle proceeds: "Now, as Polycarp was entering into the stadium, there came to him a voice from heaven, saying, 'Be strong, and show thyself a man, O Polycarp.' No one saw who it was that spoke to him; but those of our brethren who were present heard the voice" (Ch. ix). Then the details of his trial before the magistrates, and the verbatim report of his prayer when led to his fate (xiv). Then (Chap. xv):

"When he had pronounced this *amen,* and so finished his prayer, those who were appointed for the purpose kindled the fire. And as the flame blazed forth in great fury, we, to whom it was given to witness it, beheld a great miracle, and have been preserved that we might report to others what then took place. For the fire, shaping itself into the form of an arch, like the sail of a ship when filled with the wind, encompassed as by a circle of fire the body of the martyr. And he appeared within not like flesh which is burnt, but as bread that is baked, or as gold and silver glowing in a furnace. Moreover, we perceived such a sweet odor (coming from the pile), as if frankincense or some such precious spices had been smoking there. (Ch. xvi.) At length, when those wicked men perceived that *his body could not be consumed by the fire,* they commanded an executioner to go near and pierce him through with a dagger. And on his doing this, *there came forth a dove,* and a great quantity of blood, so that the fire was extinguished"! (*Letter of the Church at Smyrna, ANF*. i. 39–44; *CE*. xii, 221.)

Even this holy Encyclical, at least as to its appended date, is not without suspicion; for, "The possibility remains that the *subscription was tampered with* by a later hand. But 155 *must be* approximately correct." (*CE.* xii, 221.) Oh, for something saintly above suspicion!

4. BARNABAS: (no dates given) : Saint, a Jew; styled an Apostle, and variously a Bishop, and wholly "traditional." "Though nothing is recorded of Barnabas for some years, he *evidently* acquired a high position in the Church"; for "a rather late tradition recorded by Clement of Alexandria and Eusebius—[over 200 years later]—says he was one of the Seventy Disciples; but Acts (iv, 36–37)" indicates the contrary. "Various traditions represent him as the first Bishop of Milan, as preaching at Alexandria and at Rome, whose fourth Bishop, St. Clement, he is said to have converted, and as having suffered martyrdom in Cyprus. The traditions are all late and *untrustworthy*. He is credited by Tertullian (*probably falsely*) with the authorship of the Epistle to the Hebrews, and the so-called Epistle attributed to him." (*CE.* ii, 300, 301.) Saint Barnabas, or his clerical counterfeiter, had some queer notions of natural history. Expounding the reasons why Moses banned certain animals as "unclean" and unfit for "Kosher" food, the Saintly writer says: that Moses banned the hare, "Because the hare multiplies, year by year, the places of its conception; for as many years as it lives, so many it has"; and the hyena, "Wherefore? Because that animal annually changes its sex, and is at one time male, and at another female"; and the weasel, "For this animal conceives by the mouth." (*Epist. Barnabas*, Ch. x; *ANF.* i, 143.) Perhaps from this, other holy Fathers derived the analogous idea, to save the rather imperiled virginity of "the proliferous but ever Virgin mother of God," Mary, that she "*per aurem concepit*—conceived through her ear"—as sung in the sacred Hymn of the Church:

> "Gaude Virgo, mater Christi,
> Quae per aurem concepisti,
> Gabriele nuntio."
> (Lecky, *Rationalism in Europe,* I, p. 212.)

Thus we have, in *CE.* (*supra*) several Fathers imputed as liars, and a suspicion suggested as to Paul's inspired Epistle to the Hebrews

(which is another forgery), and the admission of a forged Epistle of
Saint Barnabas. Poor Church of Christ!

5. HERMAS: Saint, Martyr, seems to have missed being Bishop,
"first or second century,"—though the Church Saint record is so confused that I cannot vouch whether this one is the reputed author of the
forged Epistle of Barnabas. But "in the lists of the Seventy Apostles
by the *Pseudo*-Doretheus and the *Pseudo*-Hippolytus [two more
forgeries], Hermas figures as Bishop of Philippi. No one any longer
supposes that he was the author of the *Shepherd of Hermas*, the date
of which is about 40 A. D., though from Origen onwards Church-writers
have expressed this view, and accordingly have given that allegorical
work a place among the writings of the apostolic Fathers." (*EB*. ii,
2021; cf. *CE*. vii, 268.) The latter says that this "work had great
authority in ancient times and was ranked with Holy Scripture" and
included as such in the MSS. of Holy Writ; but it is called "apocryphal and false,"—like everything else the Holy Church has ever had
for "Scripture" or for self-aggrandizement. The pious author quotes
the quaint forged *Eldad and Medad* as Scripture, and the Pagan
Sibyls as inspired Oracles of God.

III. *The Sub-Apostolic Fathers*

6. PAPIAS: (about 70–155 A. D.); Bishop of Hieropolis, in
Phrygia, of whose "life nothing is known" (*CE*. xi, 459); who, after
the Apostles and contemporary with the early Presbyters, was the first
of the sub-Apostolic Fathers. He was an ex-Pagan Greek, who flourished as a Christian Father and Bishop during the first half of the
second Christian century; the dates of his birth and death are unknown. He is said to have written five Books entitled "Expositions of
the Oracles of the Lord,"—that is, of the Old Testament "prophecies"; these are now lost, "except a few precious fragments" (*CE*. vi,
5), whether fortunately or otherwise may be judged from the scanty
"precious fragments" preserved in quotations by some of the other Fathers. According to Bishop Eusebius (*HE*. iii, 39), quoted by *CE*. (xi,
549), "Papias was a man of very small mind, if we may judge by his
own words";—though again he calls him "a man well skilled in all manner of learning, and well acquainted with the [O. T.] Scriptures."

(*HE*. iv, 36.) As examples, Eusebius cites "a wild and extraordinary legend about Judas Iscariot attributed to Papias," wherein he says of Judas: "his body having swollen to such extent that he could not pass where a chariot could pass easily, he was crushed by the chariot, so that his bowels gushed out." (*ANF*. i, 153.) This Papian "tradition" of course impeaches both of the other contradictory Scriptural traditions of Judas, towit, that "he went and hanged himself" (Matt. xxvii, 5), and Peter's alleged statement that "falling headlong, he burst asunder in the midst and all his bowels gushed out." (Acts i, 15–18.) Bishop Eusebius says that Bishop Papias states that "those who were raised to life by Christ lived on until the age of Trajan,"—Roman Emperor from 98–117 A. D. Father Papias falls into what would by the Orthodox be regarded as "some" error, in disbelieving and denying the early crucifixion and resurrection of Jesus Christ—evidently not then a belief; for he assures us, on the authority of what "the disciples of the Lord used to say in the old days," that Jesus Christ lived to be an old man; and so evidently died in peace in the bosom of his family, as we shall see explicitly confessed by Bishop Irenæus. Father Papias relates the raising to life of the mother of Manaïmos; also the drinking of poison without harm by Justus Barsabas; which fables he supported by "strange parables of the Saviour and teachings of his, and other *mythical* matters," says Bishop Eusebius (quoted by *CE.*), "which the authority of so venerable a person, who had lived with the Apostles, imposed upon the Church as genuine." (Eusebius, *Hist. Eccles.* Bk. III, ch. 39.) But Father Papias—this is important to remember—is either misunderstood or misrepresented, in his claim to have known the Apostles, or at least the Apostle John; for, says *CE.*, in harmony with *EB.* and other authorities: "It is admitted that he could not have known many Apostles. . . . Irenæus and Eusebius, who had the works of Papias before them, understood the *presbyters* not to be Apostles, but disciples of disciples of the Lord, or even disciples of disciples of the Apostles." (*CE.* xi, 458; see Euseb. *HE.* III, 39.) This fact Papias himself admits, that he got his "apostolic" lore at second and third hand: "If, then, any one who had attended on the elders came, I asked minutely after their sayings,—what Andrew or Peter said, or what was said by Philip, or by Thomas, or by James, or by John, or by Matthew, or by any other of the Lord's disciples:

which things Aristion and the presbyter John, the disciples of the Lord, say. For I imagined that what was to be got from books was not so profitable to me as what came from the living and abiding voice." (Papias, *Frag.* 4; *ANF.* i, 153.)

One of the "wild and mythical matters" which good Father Papias relates of Jesus Christ, which is a first-rate measure of the degree of his claimed intimacy with John the Evangelist, and of the value of his pretended testimony to the "Gospels" of Matthew and Mark, to be later noticed, is the "curious prophecy of the miraculous vintage in the Millennium which he attributes to Jesus Christ," as described and quoted by *CE*. In this, Papias assures us, on the authority of his admirer Bishop Irenæus, that he "had immediately learned from the Evangelist St. John himself," that: "the Lord taught and said, That the days shall come in which vines shall spring up, each having 10,000 branches, and in each branch shall be 10,000 arms, and on each arm of a branch 10,000 tendrils, and on each tendril 10,000 bunches, and on each bunch 10,000 grapes, and each grape, on being pressed, shall yield five and twenty gallons of wine; and when any one of the Saints shall take hold of one of these bunches, another shall cry out, 'I am a better bunch, take me, and bless the Lord by me.'" The same infinitely pious twaddle of multiplication by 10,000 is continued by Father Papias with respect to grains of wheat, apples, fruits, flowers, and animals, precisely like the string of jingles in the nursery tale of *The House that Jack Built;* even Jesus got tired of such his own alleged inanities and concluded by saying: "And those things are *believable by all believers;* but the traitor Judas, not believing, asked him, 'But how shall these things that shall propagate thus be brought to an end by the Lord?' And the Lord answered him and said, 'Those who shall live in those times shall see.'" "This indicates," explains Bishop Irenæus, who devotes a whole chapter to the repetition and elaboration of this Christ-yarn as "proof" of the meaning of Jesus, that he would drink of the fruit of the vine with his disciples in his father's Kingdom,—"this indicates the large size and rich quality of the fruits." (*CE.* xi, 458; Iren. *Adv. Hær.* IV, xxxiii, 4; *ANF.* i, 564.) How far less wild a myth, one may wonder, is this prolific propagation than that fabled by this same John the Evangelist in his supposed "Revelation," wherein he saw in heaven the River of Life proceeding out of the Throne of God and of the Lamb, and "in the midst of the street of it, and on either side of the River, was there the Tree of Life, which bare twelve manner of fruits, and yielded her fruit every month: and the leaves of the Tree were for the healing of the nations." (Rev. xxii, 1, 2.) Verily, "out of the mouth of babes and sucklings thou hast perfected praise"! (Mt. xxi, 16.)

7. JUSTIN MARTYR: (c. 100–165): Saint, Martyr, a foremost Christian Apologist. A Gentile ex-Pagan of Samaria, turned Christian, and supposed to have suffered martyrdom in the reign of Marcus Aurelius, in whose name he forged a very preposterous rescript. His principal works, in Greek, are his two *Apologies,* the first addressed to the Emperor Antoninus Pius, whose reply he also forged; the second to "the sacred Senate" of Rome; his *Dialogue with Trypho the Jew,* and his *Hortatory Address to the Greeks.* He describes himself and fellow Christian Fathers as "we who formerly used magical arts." (*I Apol.* ch. xiv.) The burden of his arguments is Pagan "analogies" of Christianity, the contents of many of his chapters being indicated by their captions, as "The Demons Imitate Christian Doctrine," and "Heathen Analogies to Christian Doctrine," in chapters xiv and xv of his *First Apology,* and elsewhere. His whole faith in Christ and in Christianity, he declares, is confirmed by these heathen precedents and analogies: "Be well assured, then, Trypho, that I am established in the knowledge of and faith in the Scriptures by those counterfeits which he who is called the Devil is said to have performed among the Greeks; just as some were wrought by the Magi in Egypt, and others by the false prophets in Elijah's days. For when they tell that Bacchus, son of Jupiter, was begotten by [Jupiter's] intercourse with Semele, and that he was the discoverer of the vine; and when they relate, that being torn in pieces, and having died, he rose again, and ascended to heaven; and when they introduce wine into his mysteries, do I not perceive that [the devil] has imitated the prophecy announced by the patriarch Jacob, and recorded by Moses? . . . And when he [the devil] brings forward Æsculapius as the raiser of the dead and healer of all diseases, may I not say in this matter likewise he has imitated the prophecies about Christ? . . . And when I hear that Perseus was begotten of a virgin, I understand that the deceiving serpent counterfeited this also." (*Dial, with Trypho,* ch. lxix; *ANF.* i, 233.)

Father Justin accepts the heathen gods as genuine divine beings, but says they are only wicked demons who lead men astray; and he says that these "evil demons, effecting apparitions of themselves, both defiled women and corrupted boys." (*I Apol.* ch. v, ch. liv, *passim.*) The devils "having heard it proclaimed through the prophets that the Christ was to come, . . . they put forward many to be called the sons of Jupiter, under the impression that they would be able to produce in men the idea that the things which were said in regard to Christ were mere marvellous tales, like the things which were said by the poets. . . . The devils, accordingly, when they heard these prophetic words, said that Bacchus was the son of Jupiter, and gave out that he was the discoverer of the vine"; and so through many twaddling chapters, repeating the argument with respect to Bellerophon and his horse Pegasus, of Perseus, of Hercules, of Æsculapius, etc., as "analogies" prophetic of baptism, sacraments, the eucharist, resurrection, etc., etc. The *Pagan myths and miracles are true; therefore* like fables of the Christ are worthy of belief: "And when we say also that the Word, who is the first-born of God, was produced without sexual union, and that He, Jesus Christ, our Teacher, was crucified and rose again, and ascended into heaven, we propound nothing different from what you believe regarding those whom you esteem sons of Jupiter. . . . But as we have said above, wicked devils perpetrated these things. . . . And if we assert that the Word of God was born in a peculiar manner, different from ordinary generation, let this, as said above, be no extraordinary thing to you, who say that Mercury is the angelic word [Logos] of God. . . . And if we even affirm that He was born of a virgin, accept this in common with what you accept of Perseus. And in what we say that he made whole the lame, the paralytic, and those born blind, we seem to say what is very similar to the deeds said to have been done by Æsculapius." (*I Apol.*, chs. xxi, xxii; *ANF.* i, 170; cf. *Add. ad Græc.* ch. lxix; *Ib.* 233.)

Father Justin also retails to the Emperor the old fable of Simon Magus and his magical miracles at Rome, and attributes it all to the work of the devils. For "the evil spirits, not being satisfied with saying, before Christ's appearance, that those who were said to be sons of Jupiter were born of him, but after he appeared, . . . and when they learned how He had been foretold by the prophets, . . . put forward

141

again other men, the Samaritans Simon and Menander, who did many mighty works by magic; . . . and so greatly astonished the sacred Senate and people of the Romans that he was considered a god, and honored with a statue; . . . which statue was erected in the river Tiber, between the two bridges, and bore this inscription in the language of Rome: 'Simoni Deo Sancto—To Simon the holy God" (I *Apol.* chs. xxvi, lvi; *ANF.* i, 171, 182; cf. Iren. *Adv. Hær.* ch. xxiii; *ANF.* i, 347–8; Euseb. *HE.* II, 13.) We have seen this much embroidered "tradition" myth exploded, and the statue discovered and deciphered, it being a simple private pious monument to a Pagan god!

Father Justin in many chapters cites and appeals for Christian proofs to "The Testimony of the Sibyl," of Homer, of Sophocles, of Pythagoras, of Plato. (*Add. ad Græc.* chs. 18–20; *ANF.* i, 279–280.) Of the Sibyl, so often quoted: "And you may in part learn the right religion from the ancient Sibyl, who by some kind of potent inspiration teaches you, through her oracular predictions, truths which seem to be much akin to the teachings of the prophets. . . . Ye men of Greece, . . . do ye henceforth give heed to the words of the Sibyl, . . . predicting, as she does in a clear and patent manner, the advent of our Saviour Jesus Christ," quoting long verses of Christian-forged nonsense. (*Ib.* chs. 37–38; *ANF.* i, 288–289.)

8. IRENÆUS (120–c. 200) Saint, Martyr, Bishop of Lyons; ex-Pagan of Smyrna, who emigrated to Gaul and became Bishop; "information of his life is scarce, and [as usual] in some measure inexact. . . . Nothing is known of the date of his death, which *may* have occurred at the end of the second or beginning of the third century." (*CE.* vii, 130.) How then is it known that he was a Martyr? Of him Photius, ablest early critic in the Church, warns that in some of his works "the purity of truth, with respect to *ecclesiastical traditions,* is adulterated by his *false and spurious readings*" (Phot., *Bibl.* ch. cxx);—though why this invidious distinction of Irenæus among all the clerical corruptors of "tradition" is not clear. The only surviving work of Irenæus in four prolific Books is his notable *Adversus Hæreses,* or, as was its full title, "A Refutation and Subversion of Knowledge falsely so Called,"—though he succeeds in falsely subverting no little real knowledge by his own idle fables. This

work is called "one of the most precious remains of early Christian antiquity." Bishop St. Irenæus quotes one apt sentiment from Homer, the precept of which he seems to approve, but which he and his Church confrères did not much put into practice:

"Hateful to me that man as Hades' gates,
  Who one thing thinks, while he another states."
      (*Iliad,* ix, 312, 313; *Adv. Haer.* III, xxxiii, 3.)

JESUS DIED OF OLD AGE!

Most remarkable of the "heresies" attacked and refuted by Bishop Irenæus, is one which had just gained currency in written form in the newly published "Gospels of Jesus Christ," in the form of the "tradition" that Jesus had been crucified to death early in the thirties of his life, after a preaching career of only about one year, according to three of the new Gospels, of about three years, according to the fourth. This is rankly false and fictitious, on the "tradition" of the real gospel and of all the Apostles, avows Bishop Irenæus, like Bishop Papias earlier in the century; and he boldly combated it as "heresy." It is not true, he asserts, that Jesus Christ died so early in life and after so brief a career. "How is it possible," he demands, "that the Lord preached for one year only?"; and on the quoted authority of John the Apostle himself, of "the true Gospel," and of "all the elders," the saintly Bishop urges the falsity and "heresy" of the Four Gospels on this crucial point. Textually, and with quite fanciful reasonments, he says that Jesus did not die so soon:

"For he came to save all through means of Himself—all, I say, who through Him are born again to God—infants, and children, and boys, and youths, and old men. He therefore passed through every age, becoming an infant for infants, thus sanctifying infants; a child for children, thus sanctifying those who are of this age; a youth for youths, and thus sanctifying them for the Lord. So likewise He was an old man for old men, that He might be a perfect Master for all, not merely as respects the setting forth of the truth, but also as regards age, sanctifying at the same time the aged also, and becoming an example to them likewise. Then, at last, He came on to death itself, that He might be 'the first-born from the dead.'

"They, however, that they may establish their false opinion regarding that which is written, 'to proclaim the acceptable year of the Lord,' main-

143

tain that he preached for one year only, and then suffered in the twelfth month. [In speaking thus], they are forgetful to their own disadvantage, destroying His work and robbing Him of that age which is both more necessary and more honourable than any other; that more advanced age, I mean, during which also, as a teacher, He excelled all others. . . .

"Now, that the first stage of early life embraces thirty years, and that this extends onward to the fortieth year, every one will admit; but from the fortieth and fiftieth year a man begins to decline towards old age, *which our Lord possessed while He still fulfilled the office of a Teacher, even as the Gospel and all the elders testify;* those who were conversant in Asia with John, the disciple of the Lord, (affirming) *that John conveyed to them that information.* AND HE REMAINED AMONG THEM UP TO THE TIMES OF TRAJAN [Roman Emperor, A. D. 98–117]. Some of them, moreover, saw not only John, but the other Apostles also, and heard the very same account from them, and bear testimony as to [the validity of] the statement. *Whom then should we rather believe?"* (Iren. *Adv. Hær.* Bk. II, ch. xxii, secs. 3, 4, 5; *ANF.* I, 391–2.)

The Bishop's closing question is pertinent, and we shall come back to it in due course.

Irenæus also vouches his belief in magic arts, repeating as true the fabulous stories of Simon Magus and his statue in the Tiber and the false recital of the inscription on it; and as a professional heresy-hunter he falls upon Simon as the Father of Heresy: "Now this Simon of Samaria, from whom all heresies derive their origin. . . . The successor of this man was Menander, also a Samaritan by birth; and he, too, was a perfect adept in the practice of magic." (*Adv. Hær.* I, xxiii; *ANF.* i, 348.)

9. TERTULLIAN: Bishop of Carthage, in Africa; ex-Pagan born about 160, died 220. He was "the first of the Latin theological writers; . . . and the first witness to the existence of a Latin Bible . . . Tertullian's canon of the O. T. included the deutero-canonical books —[*i. e.* the forged apocrypha]. . . . He also cites the Book of Henoch [Enoch] as inspired, . . . also recognizes IV Esdras and the Sibyl." (*CE.* xiv, 525.)

He was the most violent diatribist of them all in promoting the Christian religion, but renounced Christianity after 200 and became equally violent in propagating the extravagant heresy of Montanus. In this recantation of faith he gave evidence that he was in error in his former complete acceptance of Christianity as the last word and

144

irrevocable posture in revealed truth,—and revealed his own errant credulity. In attacking the heretics—before he became one, of the most preposterous sect,—he thus formulates the assurance of the finality of Christian Faith: "One has succeeded in finding *definite truth, when he believes. . . . After we have believed, search should cease.*" (*Against Heresies*, ch. xi; *ANF.* iii, 248.) Tertullian is noted for several declamations regarding the assurance of faith which have become famous, as they are fatuous: "*Credo quia incredibilis est*—I believe because it is unbelievable"; and, like Paul's "I am become a fool in glorying," he vaunts thus his own folly: "Other matters for shame I find none which can prove me to be shameless in a good sense, and foolish in a happy one, by my own contempt for shame. The Son of God was crucified; I am not ashamed [to believe it] because men must needs be ashamed of it. And the Son of God died; it is by all means to be believed, because it is absurd. And He was buried and rose again; the fact is certain because it is impossible." (*De Carne Christi*, ch. v; *ANF.* iii, 525.) Reasoning thus,—or quite without reason—Christians yet believe these confessed absurdities and impossibilities.

Tertullian denounces the sin of theatre-going, and in this awful illustration he invokes his God to witness of one of his lies to God's glory: "We have the case of the woman—the Lord Himself is witness—who went to the theatre, and came back possessed. In the outcasting (exorcism), accordingly, when the unclean creature was upbraided with having dared to attack a believer, he firmly replied: 'And in truth I did most righteously, for I found her in my domain.'" (*De Spectaculis*, ch. xxvi; *ANF.* iii, 90.) In one of his sumptuary diatribes on woman's dress—yet a favorite theme of the Vicars of God, though nowadays the complaint is of nether brevity—he warns and assures: "to *us* the Lord has, even by revelations, measured the space for the veil to extend over. For a certain sister of ours was thus addressed by an angel, beating her neck," and telling her that she had as well be "bare down to your loins" as any elsewhere below the neck. (*On the Veiling of Virgins*, ch. xvii; *ANF.* iv, 37.) And he expresses the clerical concept of women, saying that "*females, subjected as they are throughout to men*, bear in their front an honourable mark of their virginity." (*Ib.* ch. x, p. 33.) The celibate Fathers all glorified the suppression of sex: "Marriage replenishes the earth, virginity fills Paradise," says

145

St. Jerome. (*Adv. Jovianum*, I, 17; *N&PNF*. vi, 360.) The Fathers regarded Woman as did St. Chrysostom: "a necessary evil, a natural temptation, a desirable calamity, a domestic peril, a deadly fascination, and a painted ill!" Good Father Tertullian, in his *Exhortation to Chastity*, has chapters captioned: "Second Marriage a Species of Adultery," and "Marriage Itself Impugned as akin to Adultery." (*On Chastity*, chs. ix, x; *ANF*. iv, 55.)

Strongly, and upon what seems good physiological reason, he "denies the virginity of Mary, the mother of Christ, *in partu*, though he affirms it [oddly] *ante partum*." (*CE*. xiv, 523.) Father Tertullian was strong in advocacy of virginity not alone feminine, but of the men, exclaiming, "So many men-virgins, so many voluntary eunuchs" (*Ib.*). He commends with marked approval the fanatical incitation of the Christ to self-mutilation "for the kingdom of heaven's sake" (Mt. xix, 11), and avers that to this same cause was due Paul's much-complained-of "thorn in the flesh," saying: "The Lord Himself opens the kingdoms of heaven to eunuchs, as being Himself a virgin; to whom looking, the apostle [Paul] also—*for this reason*—gives the preference to continence (I Cor. vii, 1, 7, 37, 40). . . . 'Good,' he says, 'it is for a man not to have contact with her, for nothing is contrary to good except evil.'" (*On Monogamy*, ch. iii; *ANF*. iv, 60.) For like reason it was, he assures, that Noah was ordered to take two of each animal into the ark, "for fear that even beasts should be born of adultery. . . . Even unclean birds were not allowed to enter with two females each." (*Ib*. ch. iv; p. 62.) Father Tertullian shares the fantastic notions of natural history stated by Bishop St. Barnabas; in proof of the eternal renovation of all things, Tertullian says: "The serpent crawls into a cave and out of his skin, and uncoils himself in a new youth; with his scales, his years, too, are repudiated. The hyena, if you observe, is of annual sex, alternately masculine and feminine. . . . The stag, feeding on the serpent, languishes—from the effects of the poison—into youth." (*On the Pallium*, ch. iii; *ANF*. iv, 7.) Magic admirably supplements nature and medical remedies as cure for the scorpion's sting, assures Father Tertullian: "Among cures certain substances supplied by nature have very great efficacy; *magic* also puts on some bandages." (*Scorpiace*, ch. i; *ANF*. iii, 633.)

Like all the credulous ex-Pagan Fathers of Christianity, Tertullian is a confirmed Sibyllist, and believes the forged Pagan oracles as inspired truth of God. Citing several of her "prophecies," he assures with confidence: "And the Sibyl is thus proved no liar." (*Pallium*, ch. ii; *ANF*. iv, 6.)

Tertullian admits, in a *tu quoque* argument, that the Christians are sun-worshippers: "You [Pagans] say we worship the sun; so do you." (*CE*. xiv, 525; *Ad. Nationes*, xiii; *ANF*. iii, 123.) He is in common with the Fathers in the belief in magic and astrology, which since Christ, however, are turned into holier channels in token of His divinity: "But Magi and astrologers came from the East (Matt. ii). We know the mutual reliance of magic and astrology. The interpreters of the stars, then, were the first to announce Christ's birth, the first to present gifts. . . . Astrology now-a-days, forsooth, treats of Christ—is the science of the stars of Christ; not of Saturn, or of Mars. But, however, that science has been allowed until the Gospel, in order that after Christ's birth no one should thenceforward interpret anyone's nativity by the heaven." (*On Idolatry*, ch. ix; *ANF*. iii, 65.)

In common with all the Fathers, Tertullian appeals to the Phœnix as proof supreme of the resurrection of the body. It will be noticed, that the modern false translators of our Bibles have slipped in another bit of falsification by suppressing the word "phœnix" in the passage quoted by Tertullian, and have substituted the word "palm-tree" to express the flourishing state of the righteous, as there depicted:

"Then take a most complete and unassailable symbol of our hope [of resurrection], subject alike to life and death. I refer to the bird which is peculiar to the East, famous for its singularity, marvelous from its posthumous life, which renews its life in a voluntary death; its dying day is its birthday, for on it it departs and returns: once more a *phœnix* where just now there was none; once more himself, but just now out of existence; another, yet the same. What can be more express and more significant for our subject; or to what other thing can such a phenomenon bear witness? God even in His own Scripture says: 'The righteous shall flourish like the *phœnix*' [Greek Septuagint: *Dikaios os phœnix anthesei;* Ps. xcii, 12]. Must men die once for all, while birds in Arabia are sure of a resurrection?" (Tert., *On the Resurrection of the Flesh*, ch. xiii; *ANF*. iii, 554.)

Father Tertullian vouches, too, with the other Fathers, for the bogus official Report of Pilate to Caesar, and for Pilate's conversion to Christianity, saying: "All these things Pilate did to Christ; and now in fact a Christian in his own convictions, he sent word of Him to the reigning Cæsar, who was at the time Tiberius. Yes, and even the Cæsars would have believed on Christ, if either the Cæsars had not been necessary for the world, or if Christians could have been Cæsars." (*Apol.* ch. xxi; *ANF.* iii, 35.) Father Tertullian gives full credence to the fable of the Septuagint, and assures the Emperors: "To this day, at the temple of Serapis, the libraries of Ptolemy are to be seen, with the identical Hebrew originals in them." (*Apology, to the Rulers of the Roman Empire*, I, xviii; *ANF.* iii, 32.) And, as all the other Fathers, he gives full faith and credit to the Pagan gods as "effective witnesses for Christ";—"Yes, and we shall prove that your own gods are effective witnesses for Christ. . . . Against the Greeks we urge that Orpheus, at Piera, Musæus at Athens, (etc.) imposed religious rites. . . . Numa Pompilius laid on the Romans a heavy load of costly superstitions. Surely Christ, then, had a right to reveal Deity." (*Apol.* ch. xxi; *ANF.* iii, 36.) Like the other Fathers, Tertullian is also in the ranks of patristic forgers of holy fables, being either the author or the publisher of "The Passion of the Holy Martyrs Perpetua and Felicitas," the fabulous Martyrdom of two of the Church's most celebrated bogus Saints, annexed to his accredited works. (*ANF.* iii, 699–706.)

10. CLEMENT OF ALEXANDRIA: (c. 153–c. 215). Ex-Pagan; head of the catechetical school of Alexandria; tutor of Origen. He wrote an *Exhortatio to the Heathen, the Pædagogus*, or *Instructor*, and eight books called *Stromata*, or *Miscellanies*. From the latter a few random passages are taken which fully accredit him among the simple-minded and credulous Fathers of Christianity.

Clement devotes ample chapters to showing the "Plagiarism by the Greeks of the Miracles related in the Sacred Books of the Hebrews"; he quotes as inspired the forged book "Peter's Preaching," and the heathen Sibyls and Hystaspes; he assures us, with his reason therefor, that "The Apostles, following the Lord, preached the Gospel to those in Hades. For it was requisite, in my opinion, that as here, so also there, the rest of the disciples should be imitators of the Master." Abraham was a great scientist: "As then in astronomy we have Abraham as an instance, so also in arithmetic we have the same

148

Abraham," the latter diploma being founded on the feat that Abraham, "hearing that Lot had been taken captive, *numbered* his own servants, 318"; this mystic number, expressed in Greek letters T I E, used as numerals: "the character representing 300 (T) is the Lord's sign (Cross), and I and E indicate the Saviour's name," *et cetera*, of cabalistic twaddle. (Strom. VI, xi; *ANF*. ii, 499.) Clement believes the heathen gods and the Sibyls, and all the demi-gods and myths of Greece: "We have also demonstrated Moses to be more ancient, not only than those called poets and wise men, but than most of their deities. Not alone he, but the Sibyl, is more ancient than Orpheus. . . . On her arrival at Delphi she sang:

'O Delphians, ministers of far-darting Apollo,
I come to declare the mind of Ægis-bearing Zeus,
Enraged as I am at my own brother Apollo.' " (*Strom*. ii, 325.)

11. ORIGEN: born in Alexandria, Egypt, about 165; a wild fanatic, he made himself "a eunuch for the Kingdom of Heaven's sake"; died at Tyre or Cæsarea about 254; was the first of the Fathers said to be born of Christian parents; he was a pupil and protégé of Clement of Alexandria. Origen was the greatest theologian and biblical scholar of the Church up to his time; he was the author of the famous *Hexapla*, or comparative edition of the Bible in Hebrew, with Greek transliteration and the Greek texts of the Septuagint and other versions in six parallel columns. Origen was badly tainted with the Arian heresy which denied the divinity of Jesus Christ, and was deposed from the priesthood, but his deposition was not generally recognized by all the Churches,—which again proves that they were not then subject to Rome. For sheer credulity and nonsense Father Origen was the peer of any of the Pagan-born Patriarchs of "the new Paganism called Christianity," as is evidenced by the following extracts from his chief works.

Accepting as living realities the heathen gods and their miracles, he argues that the Hebrews must have had genuine miracles because the heathens had many from their gods, which were, however, only devils; that the Hebrews viewed "with contempt all those who were considered as gods by the heathen, as not being gods, but demons, 'For all the gods of the nations are demons' (Ps. xcvi, 5). . . . In

149

the next place, miracles were performed in all countries, or at least in many of them, as Celsus himself admits, instancing the case of Æsculapius, who conferred benefits on many, and who foretold future events to entire cities,"—citing instances. If there had been no miracles among the Hebrews "they would immediately have gone over to the worship of those demons which gave oracles and performed cures." (*Contra Celsum*, III, ch. ii–iii; *ANF*. iv, 466.) The heathen oracles were indeed inspired and true, but were due to a loathsome form of demoniac inspiration, which he thus—(with my own polite omissions)—describes:

"Let it be granted that the responses delivered by the Pythian and other oracles were not the utterances of false men who pretended to a divine inspiration; but let us see if, after all, that they may be traced to wicked demons,—to spirits which are at enmity with the human race. . . . It is said of the Pythian priestess, that when she sat down at the mouth of the Castalian cave, the prophetic spirit of Apollo entered her private parts; and when she was filled with it, she gave utterance to responses which are regarded with awe as divine truths. Judge by this whether that spirit does not show its profane and impure nature." (*Contra Celsum*, VII, iii; *ANF*. iv, 611–612). . . . "It is not, then, because Christians cast insults upon demons that they incur their revenge, but because they drive them away out of the images, and from the bodies and souls of men." (*Ib*. c. xliii, p. 655.)

Father Origen clung to the pagan superstition that comets and new stars portend and herald great world-events, and urges that this undoubted fact gives credibility to the fabled Star of Bethlehem: "It has been observed that, on the occurrence of great events, and of mighty changes in terrestrial things, such stars are wont to appear, indicating either the removal of dynasties or the breaking out of wars, or the happening of such circumstances as may cause commotions upon the earth"—why not then the Star of Bethlehem? (*Contra Celsum*, I, lix; *ANF*. iv, 422.) All the stars and heavenly bodies are living, rational beings, having souls, as he curiously proves by Job and Isaiah, as well as upon clerical reason:

"Let us see what reason itself can discover respecting sun, moon, and stars. . . . To arrive at a clearer understanding on these matters, we ought first to inquire whether it is allowable to suppose that they are living and rational beings; then, whether their souls came into existence at the same time with their bodies, or seem to be anterior to them; and also whether, after the end of the world, we are to understand that they are to be released from their bodies; and whether, as we cease to live, so they also will cease from illuminating the world. . . . We think, then, that they may be designated as living beings, for this reason, that they are said to receive commandments from God, which is ordinarily the case only with rational beings: 'I have given commandments to all the stars' (Isa. xiv, 12), says the Lord." (*De Principiis*, I, vii; *ANF.* iv, 263.)

12. LACTANTIUS: (–?–330). Ex-Pagan, and eminent Christian author and defender of the faith. On account of his great reputation for learning, he was invited by the Emperor Constantine to become the tutor of his son Crispus, about 312–318 A. D. Thus, omitting two entire volumes (V and VI) of the Fathers, we are brought to the beginning of Christianity as the official or state religion—accredited yet by fables and propagated by superstitious myth. The great work of Lactantius, *The Divine Institutes*, dedicated to the Emperor, was thus addressed: "We now commence this work under the auspices of your name, O mighty Emperor Constantine, who were the first of the Roman princes to repudiate errors, and to acknowledge and honour the majesty of the one and only true God." (I, i.) This work, in seven lengthy Books, occupies over 200 double-columns of vol. VII of the Ante-Nicene Fathers.

Written for the purpose of confirming Constantine in his very uncertain "Christian" faith, and to appeal for conversion of the higher classes of the Pagans under the imperial favor, no work of the Fathers is more positive in the recognition of the Pagan gods as divine realities, who are rather demons of very active malignity; and none equalled him in profuse appeals to the Pagan gods and the Sibyls as their prophetesses, as divine "testimonies" to Jesus Christ and virtually every natural and supernatural act attributed to him in the romantic Gospels. In fact, his whole work is a sort of digest of Pagan mythology taken as divinely true and inspired antecedents and evidences of the fictitious "facts" of the new Paganism called Christianity. We have already noticed some of his tributes to the Sibyls as prophecies of Jesus Christ; as it is impossible to cite but a few out of exceeding many, these are selected, demonstrating the origins of the heathen

151

gods as actually demons; the verity of their being, words and deeds, and that they one and all testify of Jesus Christ and the holy mysteries of the Christian faith. In a word, Christianity is founded on and proved by Pagan myths. And first, of the demon-gods, for whom he thus vouches:

"God in his forethought, lest the devil, to whom from the beginning He had given power over the earth, should by his subtility either corrupt or destroy men, . . . sent angels for the protection and improvement of the human race; and inasmuch as He had given these a free will, He enjoined them above all things not to defile themselves. . . . He plainly prohibited them from doing that which He knew that they would do, that they might entertain no hope of pardon. Therefore, while they abode among men, that most deceitful ruler of the earth . . . gradually enticed them to vices, and polluted them by intercourse with women. Then, not being admitted into heaven on account of the sins into which they had plunged themselves, they fell to the earth. Thus from angels the devil makes them to become his satellites and attendants.

"But they who were born from these, because they were neither angels nor men, but bearing a kind of mixed nature, were not admitted into hell as their fathers were not into heaven. Thus there became two kinds of demons; one of heaven, the other of the earth. The latter are the evil spirits, the authors of all the evils which are done, and the same devil is their prince. Whence Trismegistus calls him the ruler of demons. . . . They are called demons, that is, skilled and acquainted with matters; for they think that these are gods.

"They are acquainted, indeed, with many future events, but not all, since it is not permitted to them entirely to know the counsel of God. These contaminated and abandoned spirits, as I say, wander over the whole earth, and contrive a solace for their own perdition by the destruction of men. Therefore they fill every place with snares, frauds and errors; for they cling to individuals, and occupy whole houses from door to door. . . . And these, since spirits are without substance and not to be grasped, insinuate themselves into the bodies of men; and secretly working in their inward parts, they corrupt the health, hasten diseases, terrify their souls with dreams, harass their minds with phrenzies, that by these means they may compel men to have recourse to their aid." (Lact. *Divine Instit.* II, xv; *ANF.* vii, 64.)

He assures us, in chapter headings, and much detail of text: "That Demons have no Power over Those who are Established in the Faith" (Ch. xvi); "That Astrology, Soothsaying, and Similar Arts are the

Inventions of Demons" (Ch. xvii). These demon-gods are the most potent witnesses to the Christian faith, and scores of times he cites and appeals to them. The Hermes Trismegistus so often quoted and vouched for, is the god Mercury "Thrice Greatest," and is the greatest of the Christian witnesses. In many chapters the "divine testimonies" of Trismegistus, Apollo, and the other demon-gods, are confidently appealed to and their proofs recited. He proves the immortality of the soul and the resurrection of the dead by renewed appeals to Hermes, Apollo, and the Sibyl: "Of the Soul, and the Testimonies concerning its Eternity" (Ch. xiii). "And I will now allege the testimony of the prophets. . . . *Hermes*, describing the nature of man, that he might know that he was made by God, introduced this statement. . . . Let us therefore seek greater testimony. A certain Polites asked *Apollo* of Miletus whether the soul remains after death or goes to dissolution; and he replied in these verses [quoting the response]. What do the Sibylline poems say? Do they not declare that this is so, when they say that the time will come when God will judge the living and the dead?—whose authority we will hereafter bring forward. . . . Therefore the Son of the most high and mighty God shall come to judge the quick and the dead, *as the Sibyl testifies* and says [quoting]. . . . '*Dies irae, dies illa, Teste David et Sibylla.*'" (*Ibid*, VII, chs. xiii, xxii; *ANF*. vii, 210, 218.)

Malignantly powerful as these demon-gods are, the simple but potent name of Christ, or the "immortal sign" of the Cross, on the instant renders them impotent and puts them to flight; all the demon-gods may be evoked by magic, only Christ cannot be thus conjured.

As for man—here occurring the famous epigram *Homo ex humo*: "He formed man out of the dust of the ground, from which he was called man, because he was made from the earth. Finally Plato says that the human form was godlike; as does the Sibyl, who says,—'Thou are my image, O man, possessed of right reason.' (*Ib.* II, lviii; p. 58.) Chapter vi is entitled, "Almighty God begat His Son; and the Testimonies of the Sibyls and of Trismegistus concerning Him"; and he urges: "But that there is a Son of the Most High God is shown not only by the unanimous utterances of the prophets, but also by the declaration of Trismegistus and the predictions of the Sibyls [quoting them at length]. The Erythrean Sibyl proclaims

153

the Son of God as the leader and commander of all [quoting]. . . .
And another Sibyl enjoins: 'Know him as your God, who is the Son
of God'; and the Sibyl calls Him 'Counsellor.' " (*Ib.* IV, vi; p. 105.)

THE PAGAN "LOGOS" CHRISTIANIZED

Treating at length of the prolific adoption and adaptation by "that
new Paganism later called Christianity," of the terms, rites and ceremonies of Paganism, *CE.* says: "Always the Church has forcefully
moulded words, and even concepts (as Saviour, Epiphany, Baptism,
Illimination, Mysteries, *Logos,* to suit her own Dogma and its expression. It was thus that John could take the [Pagan] expression 'Logos,'
mould it to his Dogma, cut short all perilous speculation among Christians, and assert once for all that the 'Word was made Flesh' and
was Jesus Christ." (*CE.* xi, 392.) And thus Father Lactantius, appealing to Pagan gods and Sibyls for cogent confirmation, deals with
the ancient Pagan notion of the "Logos," converted now into a "revealed" and most holy Christian Mystery and the Son of God:

"For though He was the Son of God from the beginning, He was born
again a second time according to the flesh: and this two-fold birth of His
has introduced great terror into the minds of men, and overspread with
darkness even those who retained the mysteries of true religion. But we
will show this plainly and clearly. . . . Unless by chance we shall profanely imagine, as *Orpheus* supposed, that God is both male and female.
. . . But *Hermes* also was of the same opinion, when he says that He was
'His own father' and 'His own mother' ['self-father and self-mother']. . . .
John also thus taught: 'In the beginning was the Word, and the Word was
with God, and the Word was God. The same was in the beginning with
God. All things were made by Him, and without Him was not anything
made.'

"But the Greeks speak of Him as the *Logos,* more befittingly than we
do as the word, or speech: for *Logos* signifies both speech and reason, inasmuch as He is both the speech and reason of God. . . . Zeno represents
the *Logos* as the arranger of the established order of things, and the framer
of the universe. . . . For it is the spirit of God which he named the soul
of Jupiter. For *Trismegistus,* who by some means or other searched into
almost all truth, often describes the excellence and majesty of the Word."
(Lact. *Div. Inst.* IV, viii-ix; *ANF.* vii, 106–7.)

154

THE SAINTLY "FATHERS" OF THE FAITH

As there can be no more positive and convincing proof that the Christ was and is a Pagan Myth,—the old Greek "Logos" of Heraclitus and the Philosophers revamped by the Greek priest who wrote the first chapter of the "Gospel according to St. John" and worked up into the "Incarnate Son" of the old Hebrew God for Christian consumption as the most sacred Article of Christian Faith and Theology, I append to the admission of Father Lactantius the culminating evidences of the "Gospel" and the further confession of the Church through the *Catholic Encyclopedia*. The inspired "revelation" of the Holy Ghost concerning the holy Pagan doctrine of the "Creative *Logos*" or "Word of God," made flesh in Jesus Christ, is thus "taken and moulded to his dogma" by the Holy Saint John:

"In the beginning was the *Logos,* and the *Logos* was with God, and the *Logos* was God. The same was in the beginning with God. All things were made by him [*i. e.* by the *Logos*]; and without him was not anything made that was made." (John, i, 1–3.)

The doctrine of the *Logos* was a Pagan speculation or invention of the Greek philosopher Heraclitus, who lived 535–475 Before Christ, and had never heard of Christ. From it the science of Logic takes its name; and on it the first principle of Stoicism and the Christian doctrine of "The Word" are based. If this startling statement out of secular history is questioned, let *CE.* bear its clerical witness to the Pagan origin of the *Logos* and the curious Christian metamorphosis of it wrought by "St. John" and the Church Fathers:

"The word *Logos* (Gr. *Logos;* Lat. *Verbum*) is the term by which Christian theology in the Greek language designates the Word of God, the Second Person of the Blessed Trinity. Before St. John had *consecrated* this term *by adopting it,* the Greeks and the Jews had used it to express religious conceptions which, under divers titles, have exercised a certain influence on Christian theology. . . . It was in Heraclitus that the *theory* of the *Logos appears for the first time,* and it is doubtless for this reason that, first among the Greek philosophers, Heraclitus was regarded by St. Justin (Apol. I, 46) as a Christian before Christ. . . . It *reappears in the writings of the Stoics,* and it is especially *by them* that this *theory is developed.* God, *according to them,* 'did not make the world as an artisan does his work —[though Genesis ii says he did]—but it is by wholly penetrating all matter—[thus a kind of *ether*]—that He is the *Demiurge* of the universe.' He penetrates the world 'as honey does the honeycomb' (Tertullian, Adv. Hermogenem, 44). . . . This Logos is at the same time *a force and a law* —[How, then, a Second *Person* Trinitarian God?]. . . . Conformably to *their* exegetical habit, the Stoics made *of the different gods* personifications of the Logos, *e. g. of Zeus* and above all *of Hermes*. . . . In the [apocryphal] Book of Wisdom this personification is more directly implied, and a parallel is established between Wisdom and the Word. In Palestinian Rabbinism the Word (Memra) is very often mentioned. . . . It is the Memra of Jahveh which lives, speaks, and acts. . . . Philo's problem was of the philosophical order; God and man are infinitely distant from each other; and it is necessary to establish between them the relations of action and of prayer; the Logos is here the intermediary. . . . Throughout so many diverse [Pagan and Jewish] concepts may be recognized a fundamental doctrine: the Logos is an intermediary between God and the world; *through it God created the world* and governs it; through it also men know God and pray to Him. . . . The term Logos is found only in the Johannine writings. . . . This resemblance [to the notion in the Book of Wisdom] suggests *the way by which the doctrine of the Logos entered into Christian theology.*" (*CE.* ix, 328–9.)

Thus confessedly is the Divine Revelation of the "Word made flesh" a Pagan-Jewish Myth, and the very Pagan Demiurge is the Christian Christ—"Very God"—and the "Second Person of the Blessed Trinity"! Here is the evolution of a Pagan speculation into a Christian revelation: Heraclitus first devised "the theory of the Logos"; by the Stoics "this theory is developed" into the Demiurge —"at the same time a force and a law"—which wrought the several works of creation instead of Zeus or Hermes. In the admittedly forged *Book of Wisdom,*—which is nevertheless part of the inspired Canon of the Catholic Bible,—the Pagan Demiurge becomes Divine Wisdom and "paralleled" with "the Word" of the Hebrew God, and "is the Memra of Jahveh which lives, speaks, acts." The Jewish philosopher Philo evolved it into "an intermediary—[Mediator]— between God and the world, through which God created the world." This Pagan notion echoes in: "There is one mediator between God and men, the man Christ Jesus." (1 *Tim.* ii, 5.) Then comes the Christian Greek priest who wrote the first chapter of "the Gospel according to John," and, Lo! "the Logos [Word] was God. . . . All things were made by him"! The Pagan speculation is first philoso-

156

phized, then personified, then Deified into the "Second Person" of a Blessed Trinity which was first dogmatized in 381 A. D.; and the blasphemy laws of England and a number of American States decree imprisonment for ridiculing this Most Holy Mystery of Christian Faith. Yet Christians decry the doctrine of Evolution and pass laws to outlaw teaching it.

Having pursued these incontestable Pagan "proofs" through his seven Books, and so vindicated the truth and divinity of Christianity, the eminent Doctor Lactantius concludes with this strange apostrophe to the near-Pagan Emperor, assuring him of the overthrow now of all error and the triumph of Catholic Truth: "But all *fictions* have now been hushed, Most Holy Emperor, since the time when the great God raised thee up for the restoration of the house of justice, and for the protection of the human race. . . . Since the truth now comes forth from obscurity, and is brought into light"! (*Ib.* VII, xxvi; p. 131.) Father Lactantius then quite correctly, from a clerical viewpoint, defines truth and superstition, but oddly enough confuses and misapplies the terms so far as respects the Christian religion: "Truly religion is the cultivation of the truth, but superstition is that which is false. . . . But because the worshippers of the gods imagine themselves to be religious, though they are superstitious, they are neither able to distinguish religion from superstition, nor to express the meaning of the names." (*Ib.* IV, xxviii; p. 131.)

13. AUGUSTINE (354–430): Bishop of Hippo, in Africa; "Saint, Doctor of the Church; a philosophical and theological genius of the first order, dominating, like a pyramid, antiquity and the succeeding ages. . . . Compared with the great philosophers of past centuries and modern times, he is the equal of them all; among theologians he is undoubtedly the first, and such has been his influence that none of the Fathers, Scholastics, or Reformers has surpassed it." (*CE.* ii, 84.) This fulsome pæan of praise sung by the Church of its greatest Doctor, justifies a sketch of the fiery African Bishop and a look into his monumental work, *De Civitate Dei*—"The City of God," written between the years 413–426 A. D. This will well enough show the quality of mind of the man, a monumentally superstitious and credulous Child of Faith; and throw some light on the psychology of the Church which holds such a mind as its greatest Doctor,

157

towering like a pyramid over the puny thinkers and philosophers of past centuries and of modern times. We may let *CE.* draw the biographical sketch in its own words, simply abbreviated at places to save space. Augustine's father, Patricius, was a Pagan, his mother, Monica, a convert to Christianity; when Augustine was born "she had him signed with the cross and enrolled among the catechumens. Once, when very ill, he asked for baptism, but, *all danger being passed,* he deferred receiving the sacrament, thus yielding to a deplorable *custom of the times.*" When sixteen years old he was sent to Carthage for study to become a lawyer; "Here he formed a sinful liason with the person who bore him a son (372)—[Adeodatus, "the gift of God"]—'the son of his sin'—an entanglement from which he only delivered himself, at Milan, after fifteen years of its thralldom." During this time Augustine became an ardent heretic: "In this same year Augustine fell into the snares of the Manichæans. . . . Once won over to this sect, Augustine devoted himself to it with all the ardor of his character; he read all its books, adopted and defended all its opinions. His furious proselytism drew into error [several others named]. It was during this Manichæan period that Augustine's literary faculties reached their full development." . . .

In 383 Augustine, at the age of twenty-nine, went to Italy, and came to Milan, where he met and fell under the influence of Bishop Ambrose—[he who forged the Apostles' Creed]. "However, before embracing the Faith, Augustine underwent a three years' struggle. . . . But it was only a dream; his passions still enslaved him. Monica, who had joined her son at Milan, prevailed upon him [to abandon his mistress]; and though he dismissed the mother of Adeodatus, her place was soon filled by another. At first he prayed, but without the sincere desire of being heard.—[In his "Confessions" (viii, 17) he addresses God: "Lord, make me pure and chaste—*but not quite yet*"! Finally he resolved to embrace Christianity and *to believe as the Church believed.*]—The grand stroke of grace, at the age of thirty-three, smote him to the ground in the garden at Milan, in 386. . . . From 386 to 395 Augustine gradually became acquainted with the Christian doctrine, and in his mind *the fusion of Platonic philosophy with revealed dogmas* was taking place. . . . So long, therefore, as his philosophy agrees with his religious doctrines,

158

St. Augustine is frankly neo-Platonist; as soon as a contradiction arises, he never hesitates to *subordinate* his philosophy to religion, *reason to faith!* (p. 86) . . . He thought too easily to find Christianity in Plato, or Platonism in the Gospel. Thus he had imagined that in Platonism he had discovered the entire doctrine of the Word and the whole prologue of St. John." Augustine was baptized on Easter of 387. He did not think of entering the priesthood; but being in church one day at prayer, the clamor of the crowd caused him to yield, despite his tears, to the demand, and he was consecrated in 391, and entered actively into the fray. A great controversy arose "over these grave questions: Do the hierarchical powers depend upon the moral worth of the priest? How can the holiness of the Church be compatible with the unworthiness of its ministers?—[The moral situation must have been very acute to necessitate such a debate]. In the dogmatic debate he established the Catholic thesis that the Church, so long as it is upon earth, can, without losing its holiness, tolerate sinners within its pale for the sake of converting them"[?]—or their property.

In the *City of God*, which "is considered his most important work," Augustine "answers the Pagans, who attributed the fall of Rome (410) to the abolition of Pagan worship. In it, considering the problem of Divine Providence with regard to the Roman Empire, in a burst of genius he *creates the philosophy of history*, embracing as he does with a glance the destinies of the world grouped around the Christian religion, the only one which goes back to the beginning and leads humanity to its final term." (*CE.* ii, 84–89.) Let us now admire

AUGUSTINE'S "PHILOSOPHY OF HISTORY"

—whereof, says His present Holiness in a special Encyclical on the great Philosopher: "The teaching of St. Augustine constitutes a precious statement of sublime truths." (*Herald-Tribune*, Apr. 22, 1930.)

The *City of God*, by which he intends the Christianized World-City of Rome, is a ponderous tome, which cost Augustine some thirteen years to write. Like the work of all the Fathers it is an embellished rehash of the myths of the Old Testament, highly spiced with "proofs" from the Pagan gods and their prophetic Sibyls, the same style of exegesis being also used for the Gospels, all of which he accepts as Gospel truth. He begins his philosophizing of history by swallowing the "Sacred Science" of Genesis whole; he entitles a chapter: "Of the Falseness of the History which allots Many Thousand Years to the World's Past"; and thus sneeringly dismisses those who knew better: "They are deceived, too, by those highly mendacious documents which profess to give the history of many thousand years, though reckoning by the sacred writings, we find that not yet 6,000 years have passed. . . . There are some, again, who are of opinion that this is not the only world, but that there are numberless worlds." (*Civ. Dei*, Bk. xii, 10, 11; *N&PNF.* ii, 232, 233.) Such persons are not to be argued with but to be ridiculed: "For as it is not yet 6,000 years since the first man, who is called Adam, are not those to be ridiculed rather than refuted who try to persuade us of anything regarding a space of time so different from, so contrary to, the ascertained truth?" (*Ib.* xviii, 40; p. 384.) To prove that "there were giants in those days," and that the ante-Diluvians were of greater size than men of his times, he vouches: "I myself, along with others, saw on the shore at Utica a man's molar tooth of such a size, that if it were cut down into teeth such as we have, a hundred, I fancy, could have been made out of it. . . . Bones of almost incredible size have been found by exposure of sepulchres." (xv, 9; p. 291.) And he shows how, "according to the Septuagint, Methuselah survived the Flood by fourteen years." (xv, 11; p. 292.) He accepts the earth as flat and inhabited on the upper side only: "As to the fable that there are Antipodes, that is to say, men who are on the opposite side of the earth, where the sun rises when it sets to us, men who walk with their feet opposite ours, is on no ground credible." (xvi, 9; p. 315.)

Augustine is credited with a scientific leaning towards the doctrine of Evolution and as recognizing the origin of species; but some of his species are truly singular, and withal are but variations from the original divine norm of Father Adam, who is father of them all. In all soberness, tinged with a breath of skepticism with respect to some, he thus philosophizes: "It is reported that some monstrous races of men have one eye in the middle of the forehead; some, the feet turned backward from the heel; some, a double sex, the right breast like a man, the left like a woman, and that they alternately beget and bring

160

forth; others are said to have no mouth. . . . They tell of a race who have two feet but only one leg, and are of marvellous swiftness, though they do not bend the knee; they are called Skiopedes, because in the hot weather they lie down on their backs and shade themselves with their feet. Others are said to have no head on their shoulders. . . . What shall we say of the Cynocephali, whose doglike head and barking proclaim them beasts rather than men? But we are not bound to believe all we hear of these monstrosities. . . . But who could enumerate all the human births that have differed widely from their ascertained parents? No one will deny that all these have descended from that one man, . . . that one first father of all. . . . Accordingly, it ought not to seem absurd to us, that as in the individual races there are monstrous births, so in the whole race there are monstrous races; . . . if they are human, they are descended from Adam." (xvi, 8; p. 315.)

It is not alone in the realm of the *genus homo* that oddities exist, in the animal world there are some very notable singularities, for which the Saint vouches with all confidence as out of his personal knowledge and experience. Several times he repeats the marvel of the peacock, "which is so favored by the Almighty that its flesh will not decay," and "which triumphs over that corruption from which even the flesh of Plato is not exempt." He says: "It seems incredible, but a peacock was cooked and served to me in Carthage; and I kept the flesh one year and it was as fresh as ever, only a little drier." (xxi, 4, 5; pp. 455, 458.) The now exploded doctrine of abiogenesis was strong with Augustine; some animals are born without sexual antecedents: "Frogs are produced from the earth, not propagated by male and female parents" (xvi, 7; p. 314); "There are in Cappadocia mares which are impregnated by the wind, and their foals live only three years." (xxi, 5; p. 456.) There was much question as to the efficacy of hell-fire in toasting lost souls through eternity. The master philosopher of all time solves the knotty problem in two chapters, under the titles: "2. Whether it is Possible for Bodies to last Forever in Burning Fire," and, "4. Examples from Nature proving that Bodies may remain Unconsumed and Alive in Fire." In the first place, before the lamentable Fall of Adam, our own bodies were imperishable; in Hell we will again get unconsumable bodies: "Even this human flesh was constituted in one fashion before there was Sin, —was constituted, in fact, so that it could not die." (xxi, 8; p. 459.) But there are other proofs of this than theological say-so, the skeptical may have the proofs with their own eyes in present-day Nature: "There are animals which live in the midst of flames. . . . The salamander is well known, that it lives in fire. Likewise, in springs of water so hot that no one can put his hand in it with impunity, a species of worm is found, which not only lives there, but cannot live elsewhere. . . . These animals live in that blaze of heat without pain, the element of fire being congenial to their nature and causing it to thrive and not to suffer,"—an argument which "does not suit our purpose" on the point of painless existence in fire of these animals, in which particular the wisdom of God has differentiated the souls of the damned, that they may suffer exquisitely forever; in which argument Augustine implies the doctrine, as feelingly expressed by another holy Saint, the "Angelic Doctor" Aquinas: "In order that nothing may be wanting to the felicity of the blessed spirits in heaven, a perfect view is granted to them of the tortures of the damned"; all these holy ones in gleeful praise to God look down at the damned disbelievers "tormented with fire and brimstone in the presence of the holy angels, and in the presence of the Lamb: and the smoke of their torment ascendeth for ever and ever; and they have no rest day nor night." (Rev. xiv, 10, 11.)

In the realm of inorganic nature are many marvels, a long catalogue of which our philosopher makes, and at several places repeats; some of these are by hearsay and current report, for which cautiously he does not vouch the truth; "but *these I know to be true:* the case of that fountain in which burning torches are extinguished, and extinguished torches are lit: and the apples of Sodom, which are ripe to appearance, but are filled with dust"! (xxi, 7; p. 458.) The diamond is the hardest known stone; so hard indeed that it cannot be cut or worked "by anything, except goat's blood." (p. 455.)

The greatest of Christian Doctors, pyramid of philosophers, has abiding faith in the reality of the Pagan gods, who, however, as held by all the Fathers, are really demons or devils; they are very potent as wonder-workers and magicians. Some of them, however, are evidently not of a malicious nature: "The god of Socrates, if he had a

162

god, cannot have belonged to this class of demons." (xiii, 27; p. 165.) Time and again he vouches for and quotes the famous Hermes Trismegistus, who he assures us was the grandson of the "first Mercury." (viii, 23, 24; pp. 159, 161.) And for history he says, that "At this time, indeed, when Moses was born, Atlas is found to have lived, that great astronomer, the brother of Prometheus, and maternal grandson of the elder Mercury, of whom that Mercury Trismegistus was the grandson." (xviii, 39; p. 384.) Also that "Picus, son of Saturn, was the first king of Argos." (xviii, 15; p. 368.) He accepts as historic truth the fabulous founding of Rome by Romulus and Remus, their virgin-birth by the god Mars, and their nursing by the she-wolf, but attributes the last to the provident interference of the Hebrew God. Some of his comments might be applicable to One later Virgin-born. "Rhea, a vestal virgin, who conceived twin sons of Mars, as they will have it, in that way honoring or excusing her adultery, adding as a proof that a she-wolf nursed the infants when exposed. . . . Yet, what wonder is it, if, to rebuke the king who had cruelly ordered them to be thrown into the water, God was pleased, after divinely delivering them from the water, to succor, by means of a wild beast giving milk, these infants by whom so great a City was to be founded?" (xviii, 21; p. 372.)

The great philosopher, at one with Cicero in this respect, distinguishes between the ancient fables of the gods in an age of ignorance and superstition, and those true histories of their later deeds in a time, such as that of the Founding of the City, when intelligence reigned among men. A singular reversion to the mental state of the Homeric ages would seem to have come upon men with the advent of the new Faith. Cicero had related the fables of Homer and contrasted them with the true history of Romulus and his more enlightened times, saying: "Homer had flourished long before Romulus, and there was now so much learning in individuals, and so generally diffused an enlightenment, that scarcely any room was left for fable. For antiquity admitted fables, and sometimes very clumsy ones; but this age of Romulus was sufficiently enlightened to reject whatever had not the air of truth"! On this the great Saint Augustine thus philosophizes,—accounting, indeed, for the age-long persistence of all superstitions, as due to inheritance and early teaching: "But who

163

believed that Romulus was a god except Rome, which was then small and weak? Then afterwards it was necessary that succeeding generations should *preserve the traditions of their ancestors; that, drinking in this superstition with their mother's milk,* their nation should grow great and dominate the world"? (xxii, 6; p. 483.) In likewise it may be queried: Who believed that Jesus was a virgin-born god except superstitious Pagans who already believed such things of Romulus, Apollo, Æsculapius, *et id omne genus?* and the succeeding generations, "drawing in this superstition with their mother's milk," have passed it on through the Dark Ages of Faith even unto our own day. Even the great St. Jerome has said, that no one would have believed the Virgin-birth of Jesus or that his mother was not an adulteress, "until *now, that the whole world has embraced the faith*"—and would therefore believe anything—except the truth!

All who did not believe such things, when related by the ex-Pagan Christians, were heretics instigated by the devil; for "the devil, seeing the temples of the gods deserted, and the human race running to the name of the living Mediator, has moved the heretics under the Christian name to resist the Christian doctrine." (xviii, 51; p. 392.) Whether St. Augustine, in his earlier Pagan years, practiced the arts of magic, as did many of the other ex-Pagan Christian Fathers, he maintained a firm Christian faith in magic and magicians, and explains how the gift is acquired. He gives an account of a remarkable lamp which hung in a temple of Venus in a great candelabra; although exposed to the open air, even the strongest winds could not blow out the flame. But that is nothing strange to the philosophic mind of the Saint: "For to this [unextinguishable lamp] we add a host of marvels wrought by man, or by magic, that is, by man under the influence of devils, or by the devils directly,—*for such marvels we cannot deny without impugning the truth of the sacred Scriptures we believe.* . . . Now, devils are attracted to dwell in certain temples by means of the creatures who present to them the things which suit their various tastes. . . . The devils cunningly seduce men and make of a few of them their disciples, who then instruct others. . . . Hence the origin of magic and magicians." (xxi, 6; p. 457.) A most notable example of magical power is that which transforms men into animals, sometimes effected by the potent word, sometimes through material means, as where sundry inn-keepers used to put a drug into food which would work the transformation of their guests into wild or domestic animals.

The philosopher Saint vouches for such magical metamorphoses as of his own knowledge and on unimpeachable authority. At much length he relates: "A certain man named Præstantius used to tell that it happened to his father in his own house, that he took that poison in a piece of cheese, . . . and that he had been made a sumpter horse, and, along with other beasts of burden, had carried provisions for the Rhœtian Legion. And all this was found to have taken place just as he told. . . . These things have not come to us from persons we might deem unworthy of credit, but from informants we could not suppose to be deceiving us. Therefore, what men say and have committed to writing about the Arcadians being often changed into wolves by the Arcadian gods, or demons rather, and what is told in the song about Circe transforming the companions of Ulysses, if they were really done, may, in my opinion, have been in the way I have said—[that is, by demons through the permission of God]. . . . As for Diomede's birds, . . . that they bring water in their beaks and sprinkle it on the temple of Diomede, and that they fawn on men of Greek race and persecute aliens, is no wonderful thing to be done by the inward influence of demons." (xviii, 18; p. 370.) To the Saint and to all the Fathers, the air was full of devils: "All diseases of Christians are to be ascribed to these demons; chiefly do they torment fresh-baptized Christians, yea, even the guiltless new-born infant." (*De Divinatione Dæmonorum*, ch. iii),—a whole tome devoted to the prophetic works of the Devil, "after the working of Satan with all power and signs and lying wonders," as avouched in Holy Writ (II Thess. ii, 9); for: "The responses of the gods are uttered by impure demons with a strong animus against the Christians." (*De Civ. Dei*, xix, 23; p. 416.) And no wonder, for "by the help of magicians, whom Scripture calls enchanters and sorcerers, the devils could gain such power. . . . The noble poet Vergil describes a very powerful magician in these lines," (quoting; xxi, 6; p. 457).

Again, like all the holy Fathers and Popes down at least to Benedict XIV, elsewhere quoted, the great philosopher and Saint is a devoted Sibyllist, and frequently quotes and approves the utterances

165

of these Pagan Seeresses, inspired by the devil through the permission of the Christian God to reveal the holy mysteries of the Christian Faith. Augustine devotes a chapter, entitled "Of the Erythræan Sibyl, who is known to have sung many things about Christ more plainly than the other Sibyls," to these signal Pagan proofs of the Christ; and he dwells with peculiar zest on the celebrated "Fish Anagram." On this theme he enlarges: "This Sibyl certainly wrote some things concerning Christ which are quite manifest [citing instances]. . . . A certain passage which had the initial letters of the lines so arranged that these words could be read in them: '*Iesous Xristos Theou Uios Soter*'—[quoting the verses at length]. . . . If you join the initial letters in these five Greek words, they will make the word Ixthus, that is, 'fish,' in which word Christ is mystically understood, because he was able to live, that is, to exist, without sin, in the abyss of this mortality as in the depths of water." (xviii, 23; p. 372-3.)

With full faith the great Doctor Augustine accepts the old fable of the miraculous translation of the Septuagint, and to it adds some new trimmings betraying his intimate knowledge of the processes and purposes of God in bringing it about: "It is reported that there was an agreement in their words so wonderful, stupendous, and plainly divine, each one apart (for so it pleased Ptolemy to test their fidelity), they differed from each other in no word, or in the order of the words; but, as if the translators had been one, so what all had translated was one, because in very deed the one Spirit had been in them all. And they received so wonderful a gift of God, in order that these Scriptures might be commended not as human but divine, for the benefit of the nations who should at some time believe, as we now see them doing. . . . If anything is in the Hebrew copies and not in the version of the Seventy, the Spirit of God did not choose to say it through them, but only through the prophets. But whatever is in the Septuagint and not in the Hebrew copies, the same Spirit chose rather to say it through the latter, thus showing that both were prophets." (xviii, 42, 43; pp. 385-387.) If this latter be true, that some divine revelation is found in the Septuagint which is not in the Hebrew, and *vice versa*, how then can it be true, as the Saint has just said, and as all the Fathers say, that there was perfect agreement between the Hebrew original and the Greek translations? If matters in the Hebrew text were omitted in the Greek, then the inspired truth of God was not in those parts of the original, or else what was inspired truth in the Hebrew became now false; and if there was new matter now in the Greek, such portions were not translation but were interpolations or plain forgeries of the translators, yet inspired by God. The divine origin of the Hebrew language, as invented by God for the use of Adam and Eve and their posterity, is thus fabled by the great Doctor: "When the other races were divided by their own peculiar languages [at Babel], Heber's family preserved that language which is not unreasonably believed to have been the common language of the race, and that on this account it was henceforth called Hebrew." (p. 122.) As for the origin of writing, our Saint agrees with St. Chrysostom, St. Jerome, and other erudite Saints, that "God himself showed the model and method of all writing when he delivered the Law written with his own finger to Moses." (White, *Warfare of Science against Theology*, ii, 181.)

This greatest philosopher of all time attacks with profound learning a problem which, he says, he had "previously mentioned, but did not decide," and he proceeds with acutest wisdom to solve the question: "Whether angels, inasmuch as they are spirits, could have bodily intercourse with women?" With all the powers of his mighty philosophico-clerical mind he reasons on the ethereal nature of angels, and reaches the conclusion, fortified by many ancient instances, that they can and do. There are, he points out, "many proven instances, that Sylvans and Fauns, who are commonly called 'Incubi,' had often made wicked assaults upon women, and satisfied their lusts upon them: and that certain devils, called Duses by the Gauls, are constantly attempting and effecting this impurity." (*City of God*, xv, 23; p. 303.) As the greatest Doctor and Theologian of the Church, he discusses weightily what books of Scripture are inspired and canonical, which are fables and apocryphal: "Let us omit, then, the fables of those Scriptures which are called apocryphal. . . . We cannot deny that Enoch, the seventh from Adam, left some divine writings, for this is asserted by the Apostle Jude in his canonical Epistle"! (*Ibid*, p. 305.) Thus the great Doctor vindicates the potentiality of the Holy Ghost, in the guise of the angel Gabriel, to maintain carnal copulation with the "proliferous yet Ever Virgin" Mother of God; and vouches for the divinity of the crude Jewish forgery of the Book of Enoch, which

167

is duly canonized as genuine and authentic work of the mythical Patriarch, by the equally mythical "Apostle" author of the forged Epistle of Jude. So great a Doctor of the Church looks, by now, very much like an extraordinary "quack doctor" peddler of bogus nostrums.

Such are a few picked from numberless ensamples of the quasi-divine wisdom and philosophy of this unparalleled, pyramidal Saint and Doctor of the Church, who "never hesitated to subordinate his reason to Faith." Most luminously and profoundly of all the Fathers and Doctors, Augustine spoke the mind and language of the Church and of its Pagan-born Christianity; more ably than them all he used the same methods of propaganda of the Faith among the superstitious ex-Pagan Christians; with greater authority and effect than all the others, he exploited the same fables, the same falsehoods, the same absurdities, exhibited to the n-th degree the same fathomless fatuity of faith and subjugation of reason to credulity.

A final appeal to the Pagan Sibyls and to the fabulous Phœnix for "proofs" of the Christian mysteries, I add from the famous forged *Constitutions of the Holy Apostles,* falsely through the centuries attributed as the individual and collective inspired work of the mythic Twelve: "If the Gentiles laugh at us, and disbelieve our Scriptures, let at least their own prophetess *Sibylla oblige them to believe,* who says thus in express words: [quoting]. If, therefore, this prophetess confesses the Resurrection . . . it is vain for them to deny our doctrine. They say there is a bird single in its kind which affords a copious demonstration of the Resurrection. . . . They call it a phœnix, and relate [here repeating the old Pagan fable of the self-resurrecting phœnix]. If, therefore, as even themselves say, a resurrection is exhibited by means of an irrational bird, wherefore do they disparage our accounts, when we profess that He who by His power brings that into being which was not in being before, is able to restore this body, and raise it up again after its dissolution?" (*Apost. Const.* V, 1, vii; *ANF.* vii, 440–441.)

CHRISTIAN PAGANISM

The whole of Paganism we have seen taken over bodily into "that new Paganism later called Christianity," by the ex-Pagan Fathers of the Christ's Church, and all its myths and fables urged by them as the credible and *only* "evidence of things not seen" of the new Faith. What does it all signify for proof of Christian Truth? "Nothing stands in need of lying but a Lie"; and by that unholy means we see the holy false new Faith established among the ignorant and superstitious Pagans.

These sainted ex-Pagan Fathers of Christianity, one and all, fully and explicitly accepted and believed in childlike simplicity of faith the reality and potency of their old heathen gods, reducing them only in immortal rank to demons or devils of fantastic origin and powers permitted by the One True God to work true miracles; by their inspired oracles to foretell futurity and the most sacred mysteries of the Christian faith, and maliciously to "imitate"—hundreds of years in advance—its most holy rites and sacraments; to endow their votaries with the gift of magic and the powers of magical practices,—practices to this day performed by their priestly successors under more refined euphemisms of thaumaturgy. To the malignant works of the Devil and the hordes of devils the Fathers imputed, and their now-a-day successors yet impute, the working of mighty lying wonders designed to thwart, and often very effective in "queering" the inscrutable plans and providences of their Almighty God. "When pious Christians," mordently says Middleton, "are arrived at this pitch of Credulity, as to believe that evil spirits or evil men can work real miracles, in defiance and opposition to the authority of the Gospels, their very piety will oblige them to admit as miraculous whatever is wrought in the defense of it, and so of course make them the implicit dupes of their wonder-workers." (*A Free Inquiry*, p. 71.)

This review of the ex-Pagan Fathers of Christ's True Church is made at some length because of its capital, fatal importance to the notion of the "authority," veracity and credibility of these the sole witnesses and vouchers for the pretended truth and validity of the new faith, and the "Gospel" wonders reputed as having occurred a century and more before their times, and for the foundation of the Church and the miraculous fundamentals of the Christian religion. Fabling, false and fatuous in point of every single pretended "proof" which they offer for Christianity, in every respect fatal to their intelligence, their intellectual honesty, their common veracity and general and

169

particular credibility with respect to matters both natural and supernatural—How can they be believed as to the miracles and miraculous and incredible basic "truths" of Christianity? False in one thing, false and discredited in all, must be the verdict of every one concerned to know the truth of the new Faith sponsored and established alone through the mongering of Pagan myths of these fatuous, childishly credulous, unscrupulous ex-Pagan Fathers of Christianity. They knew not fable from fact, and scrupled not to assert fable for fact, recklessly lying to the greater glory of God and glorification of themselves and their Paganized Church, in the name of Divinely revealed Truth of God. But, as we have seen, there can be no "divine revelation" of fanciful "fact" and dogma which for centuries had been, and in the early Christian ages were, the current mythology of credulous Pagandom. Thus the system of veneered Paganism which the ex-Pagan Fathers revamped under the name of Christianity, cannot be true; by a thousand tokens and tests of truth it is not true.

In the words of King Lear is the whole mythical scheme to be appraised and adjudged,—and junked:

> ". . . . . It is a tale
> Told by an idiot, full of sound and fury,
> Signifying nothing!"

BUT—*"What profit has not that fable of Christ brought us!"*

Our review of the fabling forging Fathers of Christianity brings us through the epoch of the establishment of Christianity—the whole of the second and third centuries of the Christ,—the epoch (in the latter half of the second), when the forged "Gospel" biographies of the Demiurge-Christ, and the forged Epistles of the Apostles, were, out of hundreds of like pious Christian forgeries, worked into shape and put into circulation by the growing Churches zealously gathering swarms of illiterate and superstitious ex-Pagan "converts"—or perverts—into the Fold of Christ. With Eusebius and Lactantius, contemporaries and retainers of the "Christian" Constantine, we see the official "triumph" of Christianity in the early fourth century; with the Sainted Augustine, late in the fourth and early in the fifth centuries, we see the new Faith, by dint of Christian persecuting laws and

170

of patristic lying, well established in the Empire,—"the human race running to the name of the living Mediator," but yet, at the instigation of the Devil, disturbed and threatened with extinction by the Christian "heretics," of whom Augustine says there were ninety-three warring sects up to his time; and against whom this great Doctor and Saint produced that fearful text of the Wedding Feast, "Compel them to come in," and that other fatal bloody precept of the Christ: "Those mine enemies, which would not that I should reign over them, bring hither, and slay them before me,"—murderous slogans of the Church Persecutrix which bloodily carried it to final triumph through a thousand years of the Dark Ages of Faith, as we shall soon see.

Others of the noted Fathers of the epochs under review will be noticed as the occasion arises. There are many of them; the four "great Latin Fathers . . . are undoubtedly Sts. Augustine, Jerome, Ambrose, and Gregory the Great"; died 604. (*CE*. vi, 1.) Vast is their output of puerile superstition and pettyfogging dialectic, of which we have seen but some random ensamples. The overwhelming volume of patristic palaver of nonsense is evidenced by the "Migne Collection" of their writings, which comprises 222 ponderous tomes in Latin and 161 in Greek. (*CE*. vi, 16.)

In the next chapter we shall consider the "canonical" Gospels and Epistles, and the palpable convincing and convicting evidences of their forgery by the priests and Fathers—original forgeries themselves with multiplied forged "interpolations" or purpose-serving later additions to each of the original sacred forgeries.

CHAPTER V

THE "GOSPEL" FORGERIES

"Whether a Church which stands convicted of having forged its Creed, would have any scruple of forging its Gospels, is a problem that the reader will solve according to the influence of prejudice or probability on his mind." Taylor, *Diegesis,* p. 10.

LET US NOW take up the holy Evangels and Epistles of Christ-propaganda. After even our cursory examination of the welter of Gospels, Acts, Epistles and other pious frauds of Christian missionary-work, all admittedly forged by holy hands in the early Christian "age of apocryphal literature" in the names of Jesus Christ himself, of the Twelve pseudo-apostles and other Worthies, including Mother Eve, even the most credulous and uncritical Believer must feel the intrusion of some question: How came the four "Gospels according to" Matthew, Mark, Luke, John, to be sometime accepted as genuine and inspired? and, Why are there only Four out of so much greater a number, as we have seen in circulation and acceptance? The questions are pertinent, and shall be given fair answer.

This entire aggregation of forged religious writings, under the guise of genuine Gospels, Acts, Epistles, Apocalypses, falsely attributed to apostolic writers, is known together as "Old Christian Literature," whether now called "canonical" or apocryphal. Of it *EB.* says that this present distinction "does not, in point of fact, rest upon any real difference in the character or origin of the writings concerned, but only upon the assumption of their differing values as sacred or non-sacred books." (*EB.* iii, 3481.) Furthermore, the common characteristic and motive of them all is thus described, or explained: "To compose 'letters' under another name, especially under the name of persons whose living presentment, or real or supposed spiritual equip-

172

ment, it was proposed to set before the reader, was then just as usual as was the other practice of introducing the same persons into narratives and reporting their 'words' in the manner of which we have examples, in the case of Jesus, in the Gospels, and, in the case of Peter, Paul, and other apostles, in the Acts." (*EB.* iii, 3481.)

"The Gospel has come down to us," says Bishop Irenæus (about 185 A. D.), which the apostles did at one time proclaim in public, and, at a later period, by the will of God, handed down to us in the Scriptures, to be the ground and pillar of our faith. . . . For, after our Lord rose from the dead [the apostles] departed to the ends of the earth, preaching the glad tidings of the good things sent from God to us, who indeed do equally and individually possess the Gospel of God." (Iren., *Adv. Hær*, Bk. III, ch. i; *ANF*. i, 414.) Bishop Irenæus and Bishop Papias have both averred that the Christ lived to old age (even as late as 98–117 A. D.), flatly denying thus as "heresy" the Gospel stories as to his crucifixion at about thirty years of age. In any event, the Apostles, according to the record, scattered "to the ends of the earth, preaching," orally, before they wrote anything at all.

But, says *CE.*, although "the New Testament was not written all at once, the books that compose it appeared one after another in the space of fifty years, *i. e:*, in the second half of the *first* century." (*CE.* xiv, 530.) That this last clause is untrue will be fully and readily demonstrated. This statement, too, contradicts Bishops Papias and Irenæus, who are, positively, the only two of the second century Fathers who up to their times at all mention written Gospels or their supposed authors, as we have seen and shall more particularly notice.

And *CE.* says, as *is* true, of the earliest existing manuscripts of any New Testament books: "We have New Testament MSS. written not much *more than 300 years* after the composition of the books"; and it admits (though with much *diminution of truth*, as we shall see) : "And in them we find numerous differences, though but few of them are important." (*CE.* xiv, 526.) In this *CE.* at another place, and speaking much more nearly the truth, contradicts itself, saying: "The existence of *numerous* and, at times, *considerable differences* between the four canonical Gospels is a fact which has long been noticed and which all scholars readily admit. . . . Those evangelical records (SS. Matthew, Mark, Luke) whose mutual resemblances are obvious and strik-

173

ing, and . . . the narrative (that of St. John) whose relation with the other three is that of dissimilarity rather than that of likeness." (*CE.* vi, 658.)

But the so-called "canonical" books of the New Testament, as of the Old, are a mess of contradictions and confusions of text, to the present estimate of 150,000 and more "variant readings," as is well known and admitted. Thus *CE.*: "It is easy to understand how numerous would be the readings of a text transcribed as often as the Bible, and, as *only one reading can represent the original*, it follows that *all the others are necessarily faulty.* Mill estimated the variants of the New Testament at 30,000, and since the discovery of so many MSS. unknown to Mill, this number has greatly increased." (*CE.* iv, 498.) Who, then, is "inspired" to distinguish true from false readings, and thus to know what Jesus Christ and his entourage really said and did, or what some copyist's error or priest's forgery make them say or do, falsely? Of the chaos and juggling of sacred texts in the Great Dioceses of Africa, *CE.* says: "There never existed in early Christian Africa an official Latin text known to all the Churches, or used by the faithful to the exclusion of all others. The African bishops willingly allowed corrections to be made in a copy of the Sacred Scriptures, or even a reference, when necessary, to the Greek text. With some exceptions, it was the Septuagint text that prevailed, for the O. T., until the fourth century. In the case of the New, the MSS. were of the Western type. On this basis there arose a variety of translations and interpretations. . . . Apart from the discrepancies to be found in two quotations from the same text in the works of two different authors, and sometimes of the same author, we now know that of several books of Scripture there were versions wholly independent of each other." (*CE.* i, 193.)

Bishop Victor of Tunnunum, who died about 569 A. D. and whose work, says *CE.*, "is of great historical value," says that in the fifth century, "In the consulship of Messala, at the command of the Emperor Anastasius, the Holy Gospels, as written *Idiotis Evangelistis,* are corrected and amended." (Victor of T., *Chronica,* p. 89–90; cited by Dr. Mills, *Prolegom.* to R. V., p. 98.) This would indicate some very substantial tinkering with Holy Writ; which process was a continuing one, for, says *CE.*, "Under Sixtus V (1585–90) and Clement

VIII (1592–1605) the Latin Vulgate *after years of revision* attained its *present* shape." (*CE.*, xii, 769.) And the Vulgate, which was fiercely denounced as fearfully corrupt, was only given sanction of divinity by the Council of Trent in 1546, under the Curse of God against any who questioned it. Though this amendatory tinkering of their two Holinesses was *after* the Council of Trent had put the final Seal of the Holy Ghost on the Vulgate in 1546!

STILL TINKERING AT IT!

The ancient clerical trick of tampering with the "Word of God" and amending its plenary Divine Inspiration and Inerrancy, goes on apace today, even to the extent of putting a veneer of civilization on the barbarian Hebrew God, and warping his own barbarian words so as to make a semblance of a "God of Mercy" out of the self-styled "Jealous God" of Holy Writ.

In 1902, after the sacred Council of Trent, in 1546, had put the Curse of God on any further tinkering with the Inerrant Bible, His Holiness Leo XIII appointed a Commission of Cardinals, known as the Pontifical Biblical Commission, to further amend Divine Inspiration; in 1907, "the Commission, with the approval of the sovereign pontiff, invited the Benedictine Order to undertake a collection of the *variant readings* of the Latin Vulgate as a remote preparation for a *thoroughly amended edition.*" (*CE.* ii, 557.) This august body has recently laid before His Holiness, after all these years of labor, the revised text of the revelations of Moses in the Book of Genesis; and is now worrying with Exodus and the "Ten Commandments" in chapter XX thereof.

Associated Press dispatches published to the world today, relate that "the Vatican's International Commission on the revision of the Bible [is] taking steps to *correct* one of the most famous Biblical passages, Exodus xx, 5, *now believed* to have been *mistranslated*"*!* (N. Y. *Times*, May 18, 1930.) The actual text, and "what the Vatican Commission *thinks it should read*," are here quoted in the "deadly parallel" columns, so that all may judge of the immense farce and fraud of this capital falsification;—the material tampering being indicated by italics:

FORGERY IN CHRISTIANITY

Exodus xx, 5—as is.	*Ditto—as falsified.*
"For I the Lord thy God am a *Jealous God, visiting the iniquities of the fathers upon the children* unto the third and fourth generation *of them that hate me*"; . . .	"For I, the Lord thy God, am a *God of loving-kindness and mercy, considering the errors of the fathers as mitigating circumstances in judging the children* unto the third and fourth generation"!

Even a fool knows that no set of words, humanly or divinely devisable, could bear such enormity of contrary translation; this is self-evident. The simple Hebrew words of verse 5 do not admit of a word of tampering in translation. Even the present translations into modern languages make apparent the correctness of the familiar rendering. The words of verse 5—"visiting the iniquities . . . of them that hate me," close with a semicolon, followed immediately by their antithesis:—"*And* shewing mercy [Heb. *chesed*] unto thousands of *them that love me*, and keep my commandments." (v. 6; Deut. v, 9, 10.) The "Jealous God" pursues the progeny of those "that hate" him, and "shews mercy . . . to them that love" him. The inspired "correction" of the "mistranslation" leaves verse 6 meaningless and redundant.

But the two simple Hebrew words chiefly involved make this fraudulent "correction" ridiculous and impossible. In Hebrew, Yahveh says from Sinai: "*Anoki yahveh elohe-ka EL QANNA*—I Yahveh thy God [am a] *Jealous God.*" The only false translation in this verse is "*Lord* thy God" for the 6,000-times falsified "*Yahveh* thy God," as elsewhere noted. Always "*qanna*" means "jealous"—and is used of the "*jealous* god," husband, wife, etc. The "joker" in this false "correction" is apparent from the word "*chesed*—mercy," hundreds of times used in Holy Writ. There is *no* Hebrew word meaning "loving-kindness"; this is a fanciful rendering given by the pious translators to the same old word "*chesed*—mercy." Even the Infallible One knows —or can look in a Hebrew dictionary or concordance and see—that "*el qanna* . . . visiting iniquity"—cannot be twisted into "*el chesed* and *chesed* . . . shewing *chesed*—mercy" to only those that love him. And how many thousands of "corrections" of words "now believed mis-

176

translated," would be necessary to whitewash the barbarian Yahveh of Holy Writ into a "whited sepulchre" of civilized deity!

SOME TESTS FOR FORGERY

We have seen the debauchery of forgery out of which the Four Gospels were born. This makes pertinent the critical statement of one of the latest authorities on the subject: "Few genuine texts have come down to us from beyond the Middle Ages—most documents reaching us in the form of later copies made by scribes in monasteries"; and he adds: "The mere fact that documents have been accepted for centuries does not itself protect them from the tests of historical criticism." (Shotwell, *See of Peter*, Gen. Introd. xix, xxii.) It is pertinent to add here a paragraph from *CE.* which states with entire accuracy the elementary principles upon which literary criticism rests; due to the application of just these principles by honest and fearless critics, the Bible has been stripped of every clerical pretense of inspired inerrancy and of even common literary and historical honesty; so that even the inerrant Church has been driven to confess countless errors and forgeries; even, as we have seen, to the frank repudiation of the fables of Creation, the Mosaic authorship of the Pentateuch, and the divine revelation of the Hebrew religion, which is thus shown to be a very human evolution. These critical principles have destroyed the vast mass of Hebrew and Christian apocrypha; and may now be applied to the New Testament booklets which yet make false pretense to divine inspiration of truth. Says *CE.:*

"Some broad principles [of literary criticism] are universally admitted by critical scholars. A fundamental one is that *a literary work always betrays the imprint of the age and environment in which it was produced;* another is that a plurality of authors is proved by well-marked differences of diction and style, at least when they coincide with *distinctions of viewpoint or discrepancies in a double treatment of the same subject.* A third received canon holds to a radical dissimilarity between ancient Semitic and modern Occidental, or Aryan, methods of composition." (*CE.* iv, 492.)

The lines last above in italics point to the most fatal of all proofs —that of "double treatment" or forged "interpolations," than which

nothing is clearer evidence of tampering and later fraudulent alterations of text. The most radical dissimilarity between the ancient Semitic methods of religious composition and our modern Occidental notions of literary honesty—or even of intelligent forgery—is, that the
Hebrew and Greek religious forgers were so ignorant or careless of
the principles of criticism, that they "interpolated" their fraudulent
new matter into old manuscripts without taking care to erase or suppress the previous statements glaringly contradicted by the new
interpolations. Though, as the great masses of the ignorant Faithful
couldn't read, it may have suited the design of the priests to retain both
contradictory matters, either of which might be used according to occasion to impose on their credulous Flocks.

When, therefore, in the same document, two statements of alleged
fact or doctrine are found, one of which is in glaring contradiction of
the other, one or the other is inevitably both false and to a moral certainty the work of a later and different hand. When, furthermore, one
of the statements is consonant with the time and conditions under
which it was supposedly written, or to which it refers, and the contradictory "betrays the imprint of the age and environment in which
it was written," later and different from that of the original, and/or
betrays "distinctions of viewpoint or discrepancies" from the earlier
version, inevitably the latter convicts itself of being forged. With
these established and admitted principles in mind, we may now look a
bit closely at these questioned documents of the Four Gospels.

THE GOSPEL TITLES

These Four are themselves forgeries and apocryphal "in the sinister sense of bearing names to which they have no right," as well as by
their contents being false, with many forged "interpolations" or spurious additions. Even if the Four Gospels were themselves genuine, as
we shall see they are not, yet admittedly their present titles are not
original and given to them by the writers. The present clerical position, seeking to save the works, is that, like the Acts of the Apostles,
"the name was subsequently attached to the book, *just as the headings
of the several Gospels were affixed to them.*" (*CE.* i, 117.) More particularly speaking of the Gospel titles, the same authority says: "The
178

first four historical books of the New Testament are *supplied* with titles (Gospel According to [Gr. *kata*] Matthew, According to Mark, etc.) which, however ancient, *do not go back to the respective authors* of those sacred writings. . . . That, however, *they do not go back to the first century* of the Christian era, or at least that *they are not original*, is a position generally held at the present day. . . . It thus appears that *the titles of the Gospels are not traceable to the Evangelists themselves*." (*CE*. vi, 655, 656.) The very fact that the late second century Gospel-titles are of Gospels "according to" this or that alleged apostle, rather than "The Gospel *of* Mark" etc., is itself confession and plenary proof that "Mark," *et als.*, were not—and were not intended to be represented as—the real authors of those "according to" Gospels. The form of the titles to the Epistles—also later tagged to them,—as "The Epistle *of* St. Paul to the Romans," etc. makes this clear and convincing, that no Apostles wrote the "according to" Gospel-biographies of the Christ.

It is obvious, too, from an attentive reading of the Four Gospels, that they are not arranged in our present collection in their order of composition; "Matthew" certainly is not first in order, and is only put first because it begins with the "Book of the Generation of Jesus Christ." The Gospel "according to Mark" is now well established as the earliest of the first three, the "Synoptics," and "John" is clearly the latest. There has been much dispute on this point: "The ancient lists, versions, and ecclesiastical writings are far from being at one with regard to the order of these (4) sacred records of Christ's words and deeds. In early Christian literature the canonical *Gospels are given in no less than eight orders,* besides the one (Matthew, Mark, Luke, John) with which we are familiar." (*CE*. vi, 657.)

Let us pause a moment to catch the full force of these admissions by *CE*. and note their consequences fatal to the pretense of Apostolic authorship or origin of these Gospels. We shall shortly see amplest proofs that none of the Four existed until well into the last half of the second century after so-called Christ and Apostles; but here we have, by clearest inference, an admission that the Gospels were not written by Apostles or their contemporaries. These titles "do not go back to the respective authors of those sacred writings; . . . do not go back to the first century; . . . are not original; . . . are not

179

traceable to the Evangelists." What an anomaly, in all literature! most especially in apostolic "sacred records of Christ's words and deeds"!

Here we have these wonderful and "only true" inspired writings of the companions of the Christ, eye-witnesses to his mighty career, written for the conversion and salvation of the world, floating around loose and anonymous for a century and a half, without the slightest indication of their divine source and sanction! All the flood of forged and spurious gospels, epistles, acts and revelations—"the apocryphal and pseudo-Biblical writings with which the East especially had been flooded" (*CE.* iii, 272), bore the names of the pretended writers, from the false Books of Adam and Enoch to the forged "Gospel of Jesus Christ" and the "Apocalypse of St. Peter." But the authentic and true Gospels of the genuine Apostles of Christ, are nameless and dateless scraps of papyrus! Imagine the great Fathers and Bishops of the Churches, the inspired and all-wise "Popes" of the Church at Rome, rising in their pulpits before the gaping Faithful; taking up an anonymous roll of manuscript, and announcing: "Our lesson today is from, (ahem!) one of the wonderful Gospels of our Lord and Saviour Jesus Christ; but, (ahem!) I don't really know which one. It is by either Matthew, or Mark, or Luke, or John, I'm sure; but the writer forgot to sign or insert his name. We will, however, worship God by reading it anonymously in faith. No, here is one with a name to it; we will now read from the inspired 'Gospel of Barnabas,' or the sacred 'Shepherd of Hermas.' Let us sing that grand and reassuring old Hymn, 'How firm a foundation, ye Saints of the Lord, Is laid for your faith in His wonderful Word!' Let us pray for more faith; and remember to believe what I have told you. *Ite, missa est*—It's all over, beat it!"

Books, evidently, do not go the rounds of readers nor of inspired Churches for over a century without a title or name. The first mention of the names or titles, as of the "Gospels" to which they were "supplied" was, as we shall see, not until about 185 A. D., when the "Gospels according to" the Four first appear in ecclesiastical literature, and thereupon began their career in the current use of the Churches, and therefore, evidently, then first came into existence. The Four Gospels thus, self-evidently, did not—could not for more than a century exist anonymous, without the Apostolic titles certifying their origin

180

and authenticity. To pretend otherwise is sheer deceit and false pretense.

THE "CANONICITY" OF THE FOUR GOSPELS

The only possible pretext whereby generations of men should be persuaded or cozened or compelled to accept and believe the Gospels (as well as the other N. T. books), even under the genial threat "he that believeth not shall be damned," is that these books were written by immediate companions and apostles of the Christ, faithful eye-witnesses to his work and word, commanded and inspired by Christ, God, or the Holy Ghost (which one is not explicit), to write and publish these wonderful biographies of the Christ. This is explicitly the teaching and dogma of the Church: no real Apostolic author, no true Gospel.

Through pious Christian fraud and forgery, there were fraudulently in vogue some couple of hundred "books current under an Apostle's name in the Early Church, such as the Epistle of Barnabas and the Apocalypse of St. Peter," as *CE.* (iii, 274) admits of these fraudulent "sacred writings"—*with* Apostolic titles. Our Ecclesiastical authority then states the "certain indubitable marks" whereby true Apostolic authenticity, essential to validity and credence, must be known: "For the primitive Church, *evangelical character* was the *test* of Scriptural sacredness. But to *guarantee* this character it was *necessary* that a book should *be known as composed* by the official witnesses and organs of the Evangel; hence to *certify the Apostolic authorship*, or at least *sanction*, of a work *purporting* to contain the Gospel of Christ." (*CE.* iii, 274.) All purported "Gospels" as to which Apostolic authorship or sanction could not be guaranteed and certified were, of course, spurious, as is natural and proper. Yet, for centuries, false and forged "Gospels," etc., as the two just named, bore the Apostolic certificates of authenticity—now confessed to be false.

THE "MARK" FABLE BELIES "CANONICITY"

The impossibility of the pretense that the precious Four Gospels circulated nondescript and anonymous in the Churches for a century and a half, is patently belied by the specific instance of the "Gospel according to Mark," of which Gospel we have the precise "history" recorded three centuries after the alleged notorious event. Bishop Eusebius is our witness, in his celebrated Church History. He relates that Peter preached orally in Rome, Mark being his "disciple" and companion. The people wanted a written record of Peter's preachments, and (probably because Peter couldn't write), they importuned Mark to write down "that history which is called the Gospel according to Mark." Mark having done so, "the Apostle (Peter) having ascertained what was done by revelation of the Spirit, was *delighted* . . . and that history *obtained his authority* for the purpose of being read in the Churches." (*HE*. Bk. II, ch. 15.) Thus Peter was dead at the time, but his ghost got the news and somehow communicated its delight and approval for the document to be a "Gospel" for the Churches. But in a later section the Bishop gives another version: the people who heard Peter "requested Mark, who *remembered well* what he [Peter] had said, to reduce these things to writing. . . . Which, when Peter *understood*, he directly *neither hindered nor encouraged* it." (*HE*. Bk. VI, ch. 14.) Peter, thus, was alive, but wholly indifferent about his alleged Gospel.

The impossibilities of these contradictory fables need not detain us now. But both join in declaring that the "Gospel according to Mark" was publicly given to the Churches, at Rome, just before or after the death of Peter, 64–67 A. D. The moment, then, that this famous manuscript fell from the inspired pen—(but it was *not* inspired: Mark only "*remembered* well"),—the Great Seal of the Holy Ghost was upon it, and it bore before the world the notorious crown of Canonicity,—and this fact was of course known to all the Roman Church. And so, of course, of the other three; every papyrus containing these precious productions of Divine Inspiration must *ipso facto* be "canonized" and notoriously sacred and of Divine sanction from the very day they were written. Every Church, Father, Bishop, and Pope must certainly have known the fact, and have glorified in their precious possession.

But so it was—*not*. Pope Peter evidently did not and could not know it; he was "martyred in Rome" 64–67, the Church tells us; and the earliest date clerically claimed for "Mark" is some years after the fall of Jerusalem in 70 A. D. The great Pope Clement I (died 97

A. D.?), first-to-fourth "successor" to Pope Peter, knew nothing of his great Predecessor's "Gospel according to Mark"; for, admits the *CE*.: "The New Testament he never quotes verbally. Sayings of Christ are now and then given, but not in the words of the Gospels. It cannot be proved, therefore, that he used any one of the Synoptic Gospels." (*CE*. iv, 14.) Of course, he did not, could not; they were not then written. And no other Pope, Bishop or Father (except Papias and until Irenæus), for nearly a century after "Pope Clement," ever mentions or quotes a Gospel, or names Matthew, Mark, Luke or John. So for a century and a half—until the books bobbed up in the hands of Bishop St. Irenæus and were tagged as "Gospels according to" this or that Apostle, there exists not a word of them in all the tiresome tomes of the Fathers. It is humanly and divinely impossible that the "Apostolic authorship" and hence "canonicity" or divine inspiration of these Sacred Four should have remained, for a century and a half, unknown and unsuspected by every Church, Father, Pope and Bishop of Christendom—if existent. Even had they been somewhat earlier in existence, never an inspired hint or human suspicion was there, that they were "Divine" or "Apostolic," or any different from the scores of "apocryphal or pseudo-Biblical writings with which the East especially had been flooded,"—that they were indeed "Holy Scripture." Hear this notable admission: "It was not until about the *middle of the second century* that under the rubric of *Scripture* the New Testament writings were assimilated to the Old"! (*CE*. iii, 275),—that is, became regarded as apostolic, sacred, inspired and canonical,—or "Scriptures."

To argue and prove that the Four *were* regarded as "Apostolic" and hence "canonical" *after* the middle of the second century, argues and proves that until that late date they were *not* so regarded,—which we have seen is impossible if they had been written by Apostles a hundred years and more previously and authorized by them "for the purpose of being read in the Churches," as the very ground and pillar of their foundation and faith.

Follow the proofs and argument of the Church to its own undoing: "From the testimony of St. Irenæus (A. D. 185) alone there can be no reasonable doubt that the Canon of the Gospel was inalterably fixed in the Catholic Church *by the last quarter of the second century* . . .

to the exclusion of any *pretended* Evangels. [Sundry writings mentioned] presuppose the authority enjoyed by the Fourfold Gospel *towards the middle of the second century*. . . . Even Rationalistic scholars like Harnack admit the canonicity of the quadriform Gospel between the years 140–175." (*CE*. iii, 275.) Even *CE*. does not prove or claim that it was any earlier; so here the Church and the Rationalists are in accord on this fatal fact! Certainly Popes Peter and Clement I, not to review the silent others, would have "inalterably fixed" the Divine Canonicity of the Four a century before, if they had known about these precious productions of the Apostles;—if, *in fact*, they had *existed*, the known works of Holy Apostles and apostolic men! But until "towards the middle of the second century" there was no "canon" or notion of divinely inspired Apostolic Gospels—simply for the reason that until just about that period they were not in existence.

The sudden appearance at a certain late date, of a previously unknown document, which is then attributed to an earlier age and long since dead writers, is one of the surest earmarks of forgery. Thus *CE*. speaking of another monumental Church forgery—(the "False Decretals" of Isidore, hereafter noticed)—urges this very fact as one of the most cogent grounds of the detection of that forgery: "These documents *appeared suddenly* in the ninth century and are *nowhere mentioned before that time*. . . . . Then again there are endless anachronisms,"—just as in the Gospels and Epistles. (*CE*. vi, 773.) More ample and compelling proofs of this destroying fact will soon be made.

THE GOSPELS "ACCORDING TO" GREEK PRIESTS

According to the names "supplied" to the Four Gospels, as to the other New Testament books, the "Apostolic" authors were all of them Jews; the same is supposedly true of most of the now confessed apocrypha. All these were forgeries in the names of Jewish pseudo-apostles. But all of the Gospels, the other New Testament Books, and the forged apocrypha, were written in Greek. Self-evidently, these "ignorant and unlearned" peasant Apostles, speaking a vulgar Aramaic-Jewish dialect, could neither speak nor write Greek,—if they

184

could write at all. The Old Testament books were written mostly in Hebrew, which was a "dead language," which only the priests could read; thus in the synagogues of Palestine the rolls were read in Hebrew, and then "expounded" to the hearers in their Aramaic dialect. But these Hebrew "Scriptures" had been translated into Greek, in the famous Septuagint version which we have admired. Here is another significant admission by *CE.*: it speaks of "the supposed wholesale adoption and approval, by the Apostles, of the Greek, and therefore larger Old Testament," that is, the Greek version containing the Jewish apocrypha; and then admits the fact: "The New Testament undoubtedly shows a preference for the Septuagint; out of about 350 texts from the Old Testament [in the New], 300 favor the Greek version rather than the Hebrew." (*CE.* iii, 271.) It was also the Greek Septuagint and Greek forged Oracles, that were exclusively used by the Greek Fathers and priests in all the Gospel-propaganda work of the first three centuries. Obviously, the Gospels and other New Testament booklets, written in Greek and quoting 300 times the Greek Septuagint, and several Greek Pagan authors, as Aratus, and Cleanthes, were written, not by illiterate Jewish peasants, but by Greek-speaking ex-Pagan Fathers and priests far from the Holy Land of the Jews.

There is another proof that the Gospels were not written by Jews. Traditionally, Jesus and all the "Apostles" were Jews; all their associates and the people of their country with whom they came into contact, were Jews. But throughout the Gospels, scores of times, "the Jews" are spoken of, always as a distinct and alien people from the writers, and mostly with a sense of racial hatred and contempt. A few instances only can be given; they all betray that the writers were *not* Jews speaking of their fellow Jews. The Greek writer of "Matthew" says: "this saying is commonly reported among the Jews until this day" (Mt. xxviii, 15),—showing, too, that it was written long afterwards; a Jew must have said "among our people," or some such. It is recorded by "Mark": "For the Pharisees, and all the Jews, except they wash their hands oft, eat not, holding to the tradition of the elders" (Mk. vii, 3); no Jew writing for his fellow-Jews would explain or need to explain this Jewish custom, known to and practiced by "all the Jews." Luke names a Jew and locates geographically his place of residence: "Joseph, of Arimathea, a city of the Jews"; an American writer, speaking of Hoboken, could not say "a city of the Americans"; nor did Jews need to be told by a Jew that Arimathea was a "city of the Jews." The Greek priest who wrote "John" is the most prolific in telling his Pagan readers about Jewish customs and personalities; absurd in a Jew writing for Jews: "After the manner of the purifying of the Jews" (ii, 6); "And the Jews' passover was at hand" (ii, 13); "Then answered the Jews, and said unto Jesus" (iii, 1); "Then there arose a question between some of John's disciples—[all Jews]—and the Jews about purifying" (iii, 25); "And therefore did the Jews persecute Jesus" (v, 16); "Therefore the Jews sought the more to kill him" (v, 18). More: "And the passover, a feast of the Jews, was nigh" vi, 4); no American would say "the Fourth of July, a holiday of the Americans," though a French writer might properly so explain. "After these things Jesus would not walk in Jewry, because the Jews sought to kill him" (vii, 1); "for they feared the Jews: for the Jews had agreed already" (ix, 22); "His disciples said unto him, Master, the Jews of late sought to stone thee with stones" (xi, 8); "As the manner of the Jews is to bury" (xix, 40), which need be explained to no Jew. These and many like passages prove that no Jews wrote the Gospels; that they were written by foreigners for foreigners; these foreigners were Greek-speaking aliens unfamiliar with Jewish customs; the writers were therefore ex-Pagan Greek priests who were zealously *"selling"* the *"glad tidings of great joy"* to the ignorant and superstitious Pagan populace.

THE FOUR GOSPELS—"CHOSEN"

The Four Gospels are thus demonstrated as: not written by Jews; not written by any of the "Twelve Apostles"; not written nor in existence for over a century after the supposed Apostles. When finally the Gospel "according to" Luke came to be written, already, as "Luke" affirms, there were "many" other like pseudo-Apostolic Gospel-biographies of the Christ afloat (Luke, i, 1); he added just another. In his Commentary on Luke, Father Origen confirms this fact as well known: "And not four Gospels, but *very many*, out of which these *we have chosen* and delivered to the churches, we may perceive." (Origen, *In Proem. Luc.*, Hom. 1, vol. 2, p. 210.) How, and why, out of half a hundred of other lying forgeries of Gospels, were these sacred Four finally "chosen" as truly "Apostolic," inspired, and canonical? Nobody knows, as *CE.* confesses.

It is a very strange and fatal confession, in view of the insistent false pretense of the Church for centuries of the patent Divinity of the Four Gospels, and of its own infallible inspiration and Divine guidance against all doubt and error; but it confesses:

"It is indeed impossible, at the present day, to describe the precise manner in which *out of the numerous works ascribed* to some Apostle, or simply bearing the name of *gospel,* only four, two of which are *not* ascribed to Apostles, *came to be considered* as sacred and canonical. It remains true, however, that *all the early testimony* which has a distinct bearing on the number of the canonical Gospels recognizes four such Gospels and none besides. Thus, Eusebius (d. 340) . . . Clement of Alexandria (d. about 220), . . . and Tertullian (d. 220), were familiar with our four Gospels, frequently quoting and commenting on them." (*CE.* vi, 657.)

The statement as to "*all* the early testimony" in favor of these Four only, is not only untrue, but it is contradicted by a true statement on the same page as the last above; it is, too, a further humiliating confession of blind and groping uncertainty with respect to the very foundation stones on which the Infallible Church is built, and makes a bit less confident the forged assurance that the Gates of Hell —to say nothing of human Reason—shall not yet prevail against the ill-founded structure. Here is the destructive admission:

"In the writings of the Apostolic Fathers one does *not*, indeed, meet with unquestionable evidence in favor of *only four* canonical gospels. . . . The canonical Gospels were *regarded* as of Apostolic authority, two of them being ascribed to the Apostles St. Matthew and St. John, respectively, and two to St. Mark and St. Luke, the respective companions of St. Peter and St. Paul. *Many other gospels* indeed *claimed Apostolic authority,* but to none of them was this claim *universally allowed* in the early Church. The only *apocryphal work* which was at all *generally received, and relied upon,* in addition to our four canonical Gospels, is the 'Gospel according to the Hebrews.' It is a well-known fact that St. Jerome regards it as the Hebrew original of our Greek Canonical Gospel according to St. Matthew." (*CE.* vi, 657.)

Thus, admittedly, "numerous works" of pretended and false "gospels," some fifty, were forged and falsely "ascribed to some apostle"

187

by devout Christians; after a century and a half only four "came to be considered" and were finally "chosen"—selected—as of divine utterance and sanction. Why? one may well wonder.

WHY FOUR GOSPELS?

Why Four Gospels, then,—when only one would have been aplenty and much safer, as fewer contradictions—out of the fifty ascribed by pious forging hands to the Holy Twelve? The pious Fathers are ready here, as ever, with fantastic reasons to explain things whereof they are ignorant or are not willing to give honest reasons for. "The saintly Bishop of Lyons," says *CE.* with characteristic clerical solemnity when anyone else would laugh, "Irenæus (died about 202), who had known Polycarp in Asia Minor, not only admits and quotes our four Gospels, [he is the *very first* to mention them!]—but argues that there must be just four, no more and no less. He says: 'It is not possible that the Gospels be either more or fewer than they are. For since there are four zones of the world in which we live, and four principal winds, while the Church is scattered throughout the world, . . . and the pillar and ground of the Church is the Gospel, . . . it is fitting that we should have four pillars, breathing out immortality on every side and vivifying our flesh. . . . The living creatures are quadriform, and the Gospel is quadriform, as is also the course followed by our Lord"! (*CE.* vi, 659.) Thus far *CE.* quoting the good Bishop; but we may follow the Bishop a few lines further in his very innocent ratiocinations from ancient Hebrew mythology, in proof of the divine Four:

"For this reason were four principal covenants given to the human race: One prior to the deluge, under Adam; the second, that after the deluge, under Noah; the third, the giving of the law, under Moses; the fourth, that which renovates man, and sums up all things by means of the Gospel, raising and bearing men upon its wings into the heavenly Kingdom. . . . But that these Gospels alone are true and reliable, and admit neither an increase nor diminution of the aforesaid number, I have proved by so many and such arguments. For, since God made all things in due proportion and adaptation, it was fit also that the outward aspect of the Gospel should be well arranged and harmonized. The opinion of those men, therefore, who handed the Gospel down to us, having been investigated, from their very fountainheads, let us proceed also [to the remaining apostles], and in-

188

quire into their doctrine with regard to God." (Iren. *Adv. Hær.* III, xi, 8, 9; *ANF.* i, 428–29.)

The true reason, however, for four finally "chosen" and accepted Gospels, is that stated by Reinach, after quoting Irenæus and other authorities: "The real reason was *to satisfy each of the four principal Churches each of which possessed its Gospel:* Matthew at Jerusalem, Mark at Rome, or Alexandria, Luke at Antioch, and John at Ephesus." (Reinach, *Orpheus,* p. 217.) This reason for the use of a different Gospel by each of the principal and independent Churches,— for the special uses of each of which the respective Gospels were no doubt worked up by forging Fathers in each Fold,—is confirmed by Bishop Irenæus himself in this same argument. Each of the four principal sects of heretics, he says, makes use in their Churches of one or the other of these Four for its own uses, for instance: Matthew by the Ebionites; Mark by "those who separate Jesus from Christ"; Luke by the Marcionites; and John by the Valentinians; and this heretical use of the Four, argues the Bishop, confirms their like acceptance and use by the True Churches: "So firm is the ground upon which these Gospels rest, that the very heretics bear witness to them, and starting from these documents, each of them endeavors to establish his own peculiar doctrine—[citing the use by each sect of a different Gospel as above named]. Since, then, our opponents do bear testimony to us, and make use of these documents, our proof derived from them is firm and true." (Iren., *op. cit.* sec. 7.) The "canonical Four," verily, as *CE.* confesses, were manufactured precisely for the purpose of meeting and confuting the heretics, as were the gradually developed and defined sacred dogmas of the Orthodox Church, even that of the Trinity. The fabrication of the Four can be seen working out under our very eyes, in the light of the foregoing statement of Irenæus, and of that of *CE.* to be quoted.

In the next section we shall see proven, that no written Gospels existed until shortly before 185 A. D., when Irenæus wrote; they are *first mentioned* in chapter xxii of his Book II; the above quotation is from Book III, when use of them became constant. Evident we see it to be, from what Irenæus has just said, that the sects of heretics named were making use, each of them of one of the just-published

Four as well as of other "spurious gospels"; the Orthodox claimed the Four as their own, and finally established the claim. The "gospel" up to about this time, a century and a half after Jesus Christ, was entirely *oral* and "traditional"; the Gnostics and other heretics evidently were first to reduce some "gospels" to writing; the Orthodox quickly followed suit, in order to combat the heretics by "apostolic" writings. This is clear from the following, that "the spurious gospels of the Gnostics prepared the way for the canon of Scripture,"— meaning, for the now "canonical Scripture"; for, as the "canon" was not dogmatically established until 1546, the Four were not "canonized" when Irenæus wrote in 185,—when the "way was prepared" for them by the earlier heretical "spurious gospels." Thus *CE*. writes:

"The endless controversies with heretics have been indirectly the cause of most important doctrinal developments and definitions formulated by councils to the edification of the body of Christ. Thus the spurious gospels of the Gnostics *prepared the way* for the canon of Scripture: the Patripassian, Sabellian, Arian, and Macedonian heresies drew out a clearer concept of the Trinity; the Nestorian and Eutychian errors led to definite dogmas on the nature and Person of Christ. And so on down to Modernism, which has called forth a solemn assertion of the claims of the supernatural in history." (*CE*. vii, 261.)

Heresy means "Choice"; heretics are those who choose what they will believe, or whether they will believe at all. It was to foreclose all choice on the part of believers, that the divinely-inspired, apostolic fictions of the Four Gospels were drawn up for the first time to combat the "spurious gospels" of the free choosers. Heresy could not exist in the time of Jesus Christ, for *he laid down nothing for belief*, except "He that believeth on *me* shall be saved" against his immediate "second coming" and end of the world. The gospels are thus anti-heretical documents of the second century, after Gnosticism first appeared.

In this connection it may be mentioned, as complained by Augustine, that there were some 93 sects of heretics during the first three centuries of the Christian Faith; all these were Christian sects, believing in the tales of Jesus Christ and him crucified, but each of them as rivals struggling for the profits and power of religion and warring to suppress all others and make itself master in pelf and power. Hence the Fathers thundered against the heretics. The inspired Four Gospels, contradictory at every point, were impossible to believe in all points; they left every one free to disbelieve all, or to believe such as he could.

So incredible, even on their face, were one and all of these canonical Four Gospels, that the fanatic Father Tertullian thus stated the grounds of his holy faith in them: "*Credo quia incredibilis est*—I believe because it is unbelievable"; and St. Augustine, greatest of the Fathers, declared himself in these terms: "*Ego vero Evangelio non crederem, nisi me Catholicæ Ecclesiæ conmoveret Auctoritas. . . . Ego me ad eos teneam, quibus præcipientibus Evangelio credidi*—I would not believe the Gospel true, unless the authority of the Catholic Church constrained me. . . . I hold myself bound to those, through whose teachings I have believed the Gospel." (Augustine, *On the Foundation*, sec. 5, Ed. Vivès, vol. xxv, p. 435; *Orpheus*, p. 223.)

In the work often cited, Bishop Irenæus either falsely quotes the Gospel of Mark, or the sacred text has been seriously altered in our present copies; he says: "Mark commences with a reference to the prophetical spirit, saying, 'The beginning of the Gospel of Jesus Christ, as it is written in Esaias the prophet'" (sec. 8, p. 428), as if Isaiah testified to the Gospel. The Bishop also quotes two long passages, one a written letter of the Apostles "unto those brethren from among the Gentiles who are in Antioch, and Syria, and Silicia, greeting,"—which are not in the Acts of the Apostles or any other New Testament book as we now have them. (Iren., *Adv. Hær.* III, xi, 14; p. 436.) The good Bishop seems either to have fabricated this alleged Epistle and passage, or other pious hands falsified the sacred Scriptures by forging them out of its pages. So it is evident that these inspired booklets, as we now know them, at least differ in very many material respects from the "traditional Gospel" and from the form in which the Four Gospels were first reduced to writing. Many other instances exist, of which some of the most notorious will be shown in the course of the chapter.

INSPIRATION AND PLAGIARISM

In this connection a few words may be said as to the chronological order and manner of composition of the first three or Synoptic Gospels. "Historically Mark is the earliest, and its study the foundation of critical enquiry. But the ordinary Christian is not a historical critic." (*New Commentary*, Pt. III, p. 126; cf. pp. 33, 45.) With the latter statement all will agree; with the first *CE.* is in agreement with the leading critics, though holding to the exploded "tradition" that one Mark wrote "Mark," or, in its words: "*If*, then, a consistent and widespread early *tradition* is to count for anything, St. Mark *wrote a work* based upon St. Peter's Preaching." (*CE.* ix, 676.) The later writers of "Matthew" and "Luke" copied bodily from "Mark," with the utmost literality in many places, but with the greatest freedom of changes, additions and suppressions at others, to suit their own purposes. But one comparison, that between "Mark" and "Matthew," can here be given; the method extends quite as notably to "Luke." Thus *CE.* discloses the process: "Mark is found *complete* in Matthew, with the exception of numerous slight omissions and the following pericopes. . . . In all, 31 verses are omitted"; and so with respect to the "analogies" with the other two. "Parts peculiar to Matthew are numerous, as Matthew has 330 verses that are distinctly his own." (*CE.* x, 60, 61; cf. for thorough examination, *New Comm.* Pt. III, pp. 33, *seq.*) "These 'Matthean additions,' as they are called, . . . *seem* to be authentic when they relate our Lord's words; but, when they relate incidents, they are *extremely questionable*." (*New Comm.* Pt. III, p. 127–128.)

We have just seen the same authority admit the want of authenticity of one set of words imputed by Matthew to his Lord; our next section will demonstrate another famous "Matthean addition" to be a gross and bungling forgery. This bodily copying from Mark, with so many "additions and suppressions," implies, as we have seen, "a very free treatment of the text of Mark in Matthew and Luke (a freedom which reaches a climax in the treatment of Mk. x, 17f. in Mt. xix, 16f.). . . . Just as the latter (Matthew) *tampered* more with the Markan order than St. Luke did." (*New Comm.* Pt. III, 36, 40.) But this textual tampering is well explained, for clerical apologists: "Nor need such freedom surprise us. Mark, at the time when the others used it, *had not attained anything like the status of Scripture*, and an evangelist using it would feel free, or might indeed feel bound, to *bring its*

192

contents into line with the traditions of the particular Church in which he lived and worked"! (Ib. p. 36.)

This perfectly confirms the position taken in the section "Why Four Gospels?" that these Gospels were framed up each in a different Church, to meet its own uses and special purposes, and in answer to the "gospels" of the Heretics. "Mark," being first in order, was probably in the hands of several Churches, some of whose "traditions" did not accord with the "gospel" narratives therein retailed; the local gospel-mongers, therefore, taking "Mark" as good "copy" for a start, took their blue-pencil styluses in hand and "edited" its text by profuse "tampering" until they produced, severally, the "gospels according to" Matthew and Luke, for use in more "orthodox" and approved form according to the local traditions. The "John" gospel-fabrication alone of the Four quite disregarded the "Mark" document, and is in the most complete contradiction with it, and with all the first three. The "Big Four" gradually won their way against and were "chosen" from all the other fifty or more in circulation, which then became "apocrypha," or admitted forgeries.

GOSPELS LATE FORGERIES

We have seen the admissions of *CE.* that the earliest notice of the Four Gospels now known to us was towards the close of the second century, quoting as the *earliest witnesses* the African Bishops, Clement of Alexandria and Tertullian, both of whom died about 220 A. D. It presents, however, one earlier witness to Gospels going in the name of the Four: "Irenæus, in his work *Against Heresies* (A. D. 182–188), testified to the existence of a Tetramorph, or Quadriform Gospel, given by the Word and unified by one Spirit," (*CE.* iii, 275),—of which we have just had occasion to admire his quaint and cogent proofs. This first mention, by Irenæus, of Four Gospels, with the names of their supposed writers, we shall in a moment quote; first we will get the record in honest and correct form by citing an even earlier partial naming of something like Gospels, and their reputed writers.

1. Bishop Papias, about 145 A. D., is the very first namer of some-

thing like written "Gospels" and writers; and this is what he says, quoting his anonymous gossipy old friends, the presbyters:

"And the presbyter said this. MARK having become the interpreter of PETER, wrote down accurately whatsoever he *remembered*. It was not, however, in exact order that he related the sayings or deeds of Christ. For he neither heard the Lord, nor accompanied him. . . . For one thing he took especial care, not to omit anything he had heard, and not to put anything fictitious into the statements. MATTHEW put the Oracles (of the Lord) *in the Hebrew language,* and each one interpreted them as best he could." (Papias, quoted by Eusebius, *Hist. Eccles.* iii, 39; *ANF.* i, 154–5.)

Here, then, over one hundred years after Christ, we have *the first mention* of written gospels and of Mark, and the recital, by hearsay on hearsay, that he wrote down "whatsoever he *remembered*" that Peter had said the Lord had said and done. This is rather a far cry from divine inspiration of inerrant truth in this first hearsay by memory recital of the supposed Gospel-writers. Thus "Mark" is admittedly *not* "inspired," but is hearsay, haphazard "traditions," pieced together a generation and more afterwards by some unknown priestly scribe. But note well, even if Mark may have written some things, alleged as retailed by Peter, yet this is not, and is not an intimation even remotely, that this by-memory record of Mark is the "Gospel according to Mark" which half a century after Papias came to be known. Indeed, such an idea is expressly excluded; Mark's notes were "not in exact order," but here and there, as remembered; while the "Gospel according to Mark" is, or purports to be, very orderly, proceeding from "The beginning of the gospel of Jesus Christ" orderly and consecutively through to his death, resurrection and ascension. It includes the scathing rebuke administered by the Christ to Peter: "Get thee behind me, Satan: for thou savourest not the things that be of God" (Mk. viii, 33); one may be sure that Peter never related these eminently deserved "sayings of Christ" to Mark or to anyone.

Moreover, the present "Gospel according to Mark" relates the crucifixion of Jesus at about thirty years of age, after one year's ministry; which is wholly false, as Jesus died at home in bed of old age, in effect says Bishop Papias, on the "tradition" of these same presbyters. So, every other consideration here aside, Papias is not a witness to "The Gospel according to Mark." As for Matthew, Papias

194

simply reports the elders as saying that Matthew wrote down the "ORACLES" or *words* of the Lord, and in Hebrew; the "Gospel according to Matthew" is much more than mere "words of the Lord"; it is the longest and most palpably fictitious of the "Lives" of the Christ; it was written in Greek, and very obviously by a Greek priest or Father, many years after the reputed time of Jesus Christ. And Bishop Papias, more than a century after Christ, did not have in his important church, and had never seen, these alleged apostolic writings, and only knew of some such by the gossip of the elders at second or third hand. So we must count Papias out as a witness for these two of our written Gospels. None of the present Four Gospels was thus in existence in about A. D. 145. And it is obvious that, even by "tradition," the Gospels in the names of Luke and John did not exist in the time of Papias.

2. Justin Martyr (145–149) quotes sundry "sayings" of Jesus which we find here and there in the present Four,—just as like alleged "sayings" identically are to be found in almost any of the confessedly forged or apocryphal gospels; but he names no names nor Gospels, but only says "memoires of the apostles," or simply "it is said." (See all instances cited, in *EB*. ii, 1819.) So Justin is no witness to our present Four Gospels, which evidently did not exist in his time about 150 years after Jesus Christ,—though he assiduously quotes the Sibyl and the heathen gods as proofs of Jesus Christ, as we have seen.

3. Irenæus (182–188) makes the very first mention of Four Gospels and names the reputed authors. These are textually the interesting, and as we shall see, at least in part, spurious words of Bishop Irenæus:

"Matthew also issued a Gospel—[see it grow—Papias said only "oracles of the Lord"] among the Hebrews in their own dialect, while Peter and Paul were preaching at Rome, and laying the foundations of the Church. After their departure, Mark, the disciple and interpreter of Peter, did also hand down to us in writing what had been preached by Peter. Luke also, the companion of Paul, recorded in a book the Gospel preached by him. Afterwards, John, the disciple of the Lord, who also had leaned upon his breast, did himself publish a Gospel during his residence at Ephesus in Asia." (Iren. *Adv. Hær.* Bk. III, Ch. 1, i; *ANF*. i, 414.)

195

Irenæus, therefore, about the year 185 of our Lord, to use a medium date, or some one hundred and fifty years after his death, is the first of all the zealous Christ-bearers to record the fact that, at the time he wrote, there were in existence four wonderful biographies or histories of the Lord and Savior Jesus Christ, two under the names of holy Apostles, and, he "implies that the Gospels of Mark and Luke were, in effect, apostolic, as being written by companions of Peter and Paul." (*EB.* i, 1830.) If any such apostolic and authentic works had been in existence before the years, we will say, 150–180 A.D., it is beyond comprehension and possibility that the zealous Fathers, who so eagerly quoted, and misquoted, the Old Testament and its apocrypha, the forged New Testament apocrypha, and the heathen Oracles, in proof of their Christ, should have been silent as clams about the apostolic Jesus-histories "according to" Matthew, Mark, Luke and John. Even all the later Fathers, and ecclesiastical writers, and the *CE.*, admittedly are unable to trace their genealogy further back into "the age of apocryphal literature" than about 150 A. D. or later. It is impossible, therefore, to believe or to pretend, that these Four Gospels were written by apostles and their personal disciples, some hundred years and more before they were ever heard of by the zealous and myth-mongering Fathers. A confused medley of alleged words and wonderful deeds of the Christ, handed down by ancient tradition or new-invented for any occasion, existed in oral "tradition," and were worn threadbare by rote repetition ; but never a written word of the Four for a century and a half after the apostles had their say, and had handed down that wonderful and inexhaustible "Deposit of Faith," which, oral and unedited, is yet drawn upon until this day by the inspired Successors of Peter for their every new Dogma.

One may turn the thousands of pages of the *Ante-Nicene Fathers* before Irenæus in vain to find a direct word of quotation from written Gospels, nor (except as above recorded) even bare mention of the names of Matthew, Mark, Luke or John, as writers of Gospels. The above words of Irenæus are registered in his Book III, chapter i; in the first two Books, while, like Justin, he quotes "sayings" which are to be found in our present texts, as in the apocryphas, he does not mention "Gospel" or any of the four reputed evangelists, until chapter xxii of Book II, where he mentions the word "Gospels" and those

196

of John and Luke, and assails their record of the early death of Jesus as "heresy." But beginning with chapter x of Book III, he bristles with the names of and direct quotations from all Four; and so with all the following Fathers. It seems, therefore, a fair inference that Irenæus had just heard of these Four Gospels at the time the last chapters of the second of the two Books were composed; and that they came into existence, or to his knowledge, just before the time he began to compose Book III. And certainly these Four Gospels could not have been in existence and circulation very long before they would come to the eager hands of the active and prolific Bishop of Lyons, who had recently come from the tutelage of his friend Polycarp,—"disciple of the Apostle John"—venerable Bishop of Smyrna, who sent him to Lyons, and who, for his part, shows not a suspicion of knowledge of them. And these Gospels, just now come into existence, were immediately and fiercely attacked by Bishop Irenæus as false and "heresy" in the vital points of the crucifixion and early death of Jesus, who, says the Bishop, lived to very old age, even maybe till the times of Trajan, 98–117, as vouched for by the Apostle John and other apostles and by the [oral] "Gospel." This, too, casts discredit on these Gospels as containing authentic record of the apostolic "traditions," condemned in this vital particular by the only two Bishops, Papias and Irenæus, who—for a century and a half—mention any Gospel-writings at all.

"LUKE" DISCREDITS APOSTOLICITY

Moreover, at the time that the Gospel bearing the name of Luke was published, already many Gospels or purported histories and sayings of Jesus Christ were in active circulation: "Forasmuch as *many* have taken in hand to set forth in order a declaration of those things which are most surely believed among us, Even as they delivered them unto us, which from the beginning were eye-witnesses and ministers of the word; it has seemed to me good *also*, having had a perfect understanding of all things from the very first, to write unto thee, in order, most excellent Theophilus, that thou mightest know the certainty of those things, wherein thou hast been instructed." (Luke, i, 1–4). Now, these "many" Gospels were clearly not by any of the apostles, else Luke would certainly have so stated; they were *not*

197

"inspired" writings, but they were by sundry anonymous "eye-witnesses and ministers of the word"; they are either totally lost to posterity, or are among the fifty admittedly forged and apocryphal Gospels which we have previously noticed. Thus we see two of the "Four," i. e., "Mark," and "Luke" are, on their face, *uninspired*, hear-say, and long *ex post facto*.

That neither apostle nor contemporary of Jesus wrote a line of "gospel" is thus perfectly evidenced by Luke: "According to the prologue of Luke, no eye-witness of the life of Jesus took pen in hand—none at least appear to have produced any writings which Luke would have called a 'narrative.' " (*EB.* ii, 1892.) These conclusions are confirmed by the learned clerical translators and editors of the *ANF*, respectively, as follows:

"Though a few of the Apocryphal Gospels are of comparatively early origin, *there is no evidence that any Gospels purporting to be what our Four Gospels are, existed in the first century*, or that any other than fragmentary literature of this character existed even in the second century." (Ed. note to Apocrypha of the New Testament, *ANF.* viii, 349.)—"There is abundant evidence of the existence of many of these *traditions* in the second century, though it cannot be made out that any of the books were then in existence in their present form." (Translator's Introductory Notice to Apocryphal Gospels. *ANF.* viii, 351.)

Such apocryphal gospels would naturally contain—as they do—many of the same reputed words and deeds of the Christ as those now reported by Luke and the others; many are indeed in large sections in the very same words. Luke does not say or imply that these "many" were false, but, on the contrary, being by alleged "eye-witnesses" they were necessarily more or less the same things which Luke undertook, not to belie or correct, but simply to repeat in good order for the edification of his friend Theophilus. It is very significant, for the date of the authorship of "Luke," to note the fact that the only Theophilus known to early Church history is a certain ex-Pagan by that name, who, after becoming Christian, and very probably before being instructed in the certainty of the faith by "Luke," himself turned Christian instructor and Father, and wrote the Tract, in three Books, under the title *Epistle to Antolychus*, preserved in the Collection of Ante-Nicene Fathers, vol. ii, pp. 89–121. This Theophilus became

198

THE "GOSPEL" FORGERIES

Bishop of Antioch about 169–177 A. D. (*CE.* xiv, 625); and thus illuminates the date of "Luke."

That these Four Gospels, then, are forgeries, falsely ascribed to Apostles and their companions, a century and a half after Christ and the apostles, and were compounded of very conflicting "traditions" and out of the existing 50 or more forgeries circulating in apostolic names—is proven as positively as negative proofs permit, and "beyond a reasonable doubt"—which is proof ample for conviction of capital crime.

Most people, says Bishop Papias, took pleasure in "voluminous falsehoods" in reporting or writing of Jesus Christ and his life and deeds, for which reason, says the Bishop, he was driven to "the living voice of tradition" for his own accounts,—samples of which we have seen. These fanciful and distorted oral traditions, finally reduced into some fifty fantastic written records of "voluminous falsehoods," were later, about the time of Book III of Bishop Irenæus, crystallized into four documents, one each of which was held by one of the principal churches as its authoritative biography of the Christ, or "gospel"; to which, the titles "According to" Matthew, Mark, Luke, John, were tacked for pretended apostolic sanction.

The truth of the late second century origin of the Gospels and Epistles may be garnered from the guarded words of a standard theological textbook on Christian Evidences: "The Christian literature which has survived from the latter part of the first century and the beginning of the second is scanty and fragmentary—[which could not be true if the Gospels and Epistles had then existed]. But when we come into the light of the *last quarter of the second century*, we find the *Gospels of the canon* in undisputed possession of the field." (*The Grounds of Theistic and Christian Belief*, by George Parker Fisher, D.D., LL.D.; 1902.)

Summarizing the results of critical study of the four Gospels, upon *all* the evidences, internal and external, which are there fully reviewed, the conclusions of modern Biblical scholarship are thus recorded by the *Encyclopedia Biblica:*

As to *Matthew:* "The employment of various sources, the characteristic difference of the quotations from the LXX (Septuagint) and the original (Hebrew), the indefiniteness of the determinations of time and place, the

199

incredibleness of the contents, the introduction of later conditions, as also the artificial arrangement, and so forth, have long since led to the conclusion that for the authorship of the first Gospel the apostle Matthew must be given up." (*EB.* ii, 1891.)

As to *Mark:* "According to Papias, the second gospel was written by Mark. . . . In what Papias says the important point is not so much the statement that Mark wrote the gospel as the further statement that Peter supplied the contents orally. . . . The supposition that the gospel is essentially a repetition of oral communications by Peter, will at once fall to the ground. . . . Should Mark have written in Aramaic, then he cannot be held to have been the author of canonical Mark, which is certainly not a translation, nor yet, in view of the LXX quotations which have passed over into all three gospels, can he be held to have been the author of the original Mark." (*EB.* ii, 1891.)

As to *Luke:* "This tradition [that Luke was the author of the third gospel and of Acts] cannot be traced farther back than towards the end of the second century (Irenæus, Tertullian, Clement of Alexandria, and the Muratorian fragment). . . . It has been shown that it is impossible to regard Luke with any certainty as the writer even of the 'we' sections of Acts, not to speak of the whole book of Acts, or of the Third Gospel. . . . If Luke cannot have been the author of Acts, neither can he have been the author of the Third Gospel." (*EB.* ii, 1893, 2831.)

As to *John:* "No mention of the Fourth Gospel which we can recognize as such carries us further than to 140 A. D. As late as 152, Justin, who nevertheless lays so great value upon the 'Memorabilia of the Apostles,' regards John—if indeed he knows it at all—with distrust, and appropriates from it a very few sayings. . . . If on independent grounds some period shortly before 140 A. D. can be set down as the approximate date of the production of the gospel [a certain statement in it is explained]. . . . The Apostolic authorship of the gospel remains impossible, and that not merely from the consideration that it cannot be the son of Zebedee who has introduced himself as writer in so remarkable a fashion, but also from the consideration that it cannot be an eye-witness of the facts of the life of Jesus who has presented, as against the synoptists, an account so much less credible, nor an original apostle who has shown himself so readily accessible to Alexandrian and Gnostic ideas, nor a contemporary of Jesus who survived so late into the second century and yet was capable of composing so profound a work." (*EB.* ii, 2550, 2553.)

None of these Four Gospels, then, being of apostolic authorship or even of the apostolic age, but anonymous productions of over a century after the apostles, all are exactly of like origin and composition as all the other fifty apocryphal Jesus-writings: the Four "do not, in point of fact, rest upon any real difference *in the character or origin* of the writings concerned," from all the other fifty admittedly apocryphal and forged gospels dating about the middle of the second century, at the height of the Christian age of apocryphal literature. They are therefore late Christian forgeries of the Catholic Church.

FORGERIES IN THE FORGED GOSPELS

That the Four Gospels, as we have them, are very late productions, issued in the names of apostles a century and more dead, and are therefore forgeries, is now proven beyond peradventure. That they are not, even in the form that Bishop Irenæus first knew them, each the work of one inspired mind and pen, is as readily and conclusively provable. They are, each and all Four, clumsy compilations framed by different persons and at very different times, as is patent on their face; they are thus concatenations of forgeries within forgeries. This we shall now demonstrate.

The Church claims these Four Gospels to be apostolic and divine works, and together with all the other books of the Trentine Bible, to be throughout divinely inspired, having God himself for their Author. This 1546 Dogma of the Infallible Church has been thus reaffirmed by the Sacred Vatican Council (A. D. 1870):

"These books are sacred and canonical because they contain revelation without error, and because, written by the inspiration of the Holy Ghost, they have God for their Author." (*CE*. ii, 543.)

More recently, Pope Leo XIII, in his Encyclical *Prov. Deus.* (1893), thus reaffirms the plenary inspiration and inerrancy of Holy Writ:

"It will never be lawful to restrict inspiration merely to certain portions of the Holy Scriptures, or to grant that the sacred writers *could have made a mistake*. . . . They render in exact language, with *infallible truth*, all that God commanded, and nothing else"! (*Ib.*)

For the Protestant sects the notion of divine inspiration and inerrant truth of Scripture—excepting always the dozen and more of Old Testament "apocryphal" Books and parts, as *Tobias* and the history of the Assyrian great god *Bel and the Dragon*,—a typical

201

profession is that of the first Article of the Baptist Declaration of Faith: "The Holy Bible was written by men divinely inspired, . . . and is a perfect treasure of heavenly instruction. . . . It has God for its Author, and truth without any admixture of error for its matter."

All this priestly "confidence stuff" must remind one of what Cicero said of the Roman augurs. Even *CE.*, valiant but often perplexed defender of the orthodox Faith, can not give full credit to that inspired canard, which even the infallible authors of it could not have themselves believed. Timorously "reasoning in chains" and minimizing the truth, the orthodox apologist, forced by scholarly criticism, confesses—utterly belying Council and Holiness:

"In *all the Bible,* where the same event is several times narrated by the same writer, or narrated by several writers, there is some slight [*sic*] divergency, as it is natural there should be with those who spoke or wrote *from memory*. Divine inspiration covers the substance of the narration." (*CE.* i, 122.)

Those sacred writers, putting on papyrus rolls from errant and therefore necessarily uninspired "memory," their intimate familiarities with the thoughts and desires, purposes and providences of God, make not "some slight divergencies" from accurate recording of the promptings of the Spirit to them; they committed incessant contradictions of so gross a nature as to impeach and destroy the possibility of truth and credibility of virtually every word they said or wrote "in all the Bible," Old and New Testaments alike. I have so fully exposed some thousands of these glaring and self-destroying contradictions in my previous work, that here I simply notice only those most vital ones which are pertinent and incidental to our present subject of apostolic forgeries.

In a work accompanying the Revised Version of the Bible, in which the Revisers pointed out some 30,000 (now over 150,000) variant readings in the New Testament, the reverend author makes this naïve explanation: "In regard to the New Testament, no miracle has been wrought to preserve the text as it came from the pens of the inspired writers. That would have been a thing altogether out of harmony with God's method of governing the world"! (Dr. Alex. Roberts, *Companion to the Revised Version*, p. 4.) One may wonder at the writer's intimacy with God's governmental methods, as well as at God's indifference to the preservation of his miraculously-revealed Holy Word, so awfully necessary to save us from eternal damnation; when, as we shall see, by special miraculous intervention and providence he has, the Church vouches, preserved wholly "incorrupt" through the Ages of Faith countless whole cadavers and ghastly scraps and miraculous relics galore of the unwashed Saints of Holy Church.

CONTRADICTIONS AND TRUTH

No more compelling proofs of forgery in a document can well be than glaring contradictions between two parts of the text. Remember that in the "age of apocryphal literature" there were no printed books, thus fixing the text, and no "copyright" existed. All books, sacred and profane, were manuscripts, tediously written by hand on rolls of papyrus or sheets of parchment-skin; like the manuscripts of the Gospels, Epistles, etc., they were usually unsigned and undated, and frequently gave no clue to the anonymous writers. When one man came into possession of a manuscript which he desired, he sat down and copied it by hand, or employed slaves or professional copyists to do the labor. There was absolutely no check against errors of copying, or intentional omissions, alterations or insertions into the text, to suit the taste or purpose of the copyist. Religious books were written, and copied, by priests, monks or Fathers; religious notions and doctrines were very diversely held, and developed or were modified incessantly. Traditions of what was said or done by Jesus Christ and the apostles were, we have seen, very variant and conflicting. Very often, as we shall see, conflicting traditions or accounts are found in the same book. As no honest writer of intelligence and care would put into one short work which he is writing, two totally contradictory statements regarding the same fact, the only way in which such contradictions can occur in what purports to be an original or genuine manuscript, is by the intentional insertion by a later copyist of the new and contradictory material, euphoniously called "interpolations" (*CE.* iv, 498, *post*),—without the critical sense to perceive the contradiction, and omit the original statement with which his addition conflicts.

Father Tertullian, in his work *Against Heresies*, denying that Christians do such things—do not need to, he says, because the Scriptures are favorable to the Orthodox,—accuses the Heretics of such practices, and naïvely explains how such interpolations or forgeries of text are done, and why they needs must be:

"All interpolation must be believed to be a later process. . . . One man perverts the Scriptures with his hand, another their meaning by his exposition. . . . Unquestionably, the Divine Scriptures are more fruitful in resources of all kinds for this sort of facility [of introducing interpolations]. Nor do I risk contradiction in saying that the very Scriptures were even arranged by the will of God in such a manner as to furnish materials for heretics, inasmuch as I read that 'there must be heresies' (I Cor. xi, 19), which there cannot be without Scriptures"! (*Praes.* xxxviii–xxxix; *ANF.* iii, 262.) Speaking of instances related to the birth of Jesus Christ, *EB.* makes a remark, which it extends to others, and is generally applicable to the conflicting Gospel narratives:

"From the nature of the case both canonical narratives were accepted by faith and incorporated with each other. *The gospels themselves supply ample justification of a criticism of the gospel narratives. In spite of all the revisions which the gospels received before they became canonically fixed,* they still not unfrequently preserve references to conditions which are irreconcilable with the later additions." (*EB.* iii, 3343, 3344.)

"For Christian orthodoxy," says the same authority, "reconcilability of the two canonical accounts was always a necessary dogma"; and on this point, the orthodox *CE.* makes a quaint but typically clerical argument, in effect that the confessed contradictions of Holy Writ make it all the more credible: "As can readily be seen, variations are naturally to be expected in four distinct, and in many ways independent, accounts of Christ's words and deeds, so that their presence, instead of going against, rather makes for the substantial value of the evangelical narratives"! (*CE.* vi, 659.) Fanciful and disingenuous as this is, and derogatory of the Papal theory that it is *not possible* that "the sacred writers could have made a mistake," the argument loses even its rhetorical force when we find the most monumental contradictions in the inspired words of the same

204

writer in the same inspired little book. We will notice some of the most obvious and fatal forgeries by "interpolations" into the Gospel Christ-tales.

JESUS—MAN OR GOD?

The Jews, in their "canonical," more definitely in their apocryphal or admittedly forged Scriptures, expected a "Messiah," or anointed King of the race and lineage of David, who should deliver them from the rule of their enemies,—at the time of the Gospel tales, the Romans; previously, the Assyrians, Persians, and Greeks, successively. This King, says Isaiah, shall sit and reign "upon the throne of David, and upon his kingdom, to establish it" (Isa. ix, 7); and that this prophecy was in order of fulfillment, Gabriel the Angel announced to Mary the Ever-Virgin Mother of eight sons and daughters: "Thou shalt bring forth a son, and shalt call his name Jesus; and the Lord God shall give unto him the throne of his father David: And he shall reign over the house of Jacob forever." (Lk. i, 32, 33.) There is not a word of "prophecy" anywhere that this King should be divine, a Son of the God of Israel; he was to be a human king of the house of Jacob, of David. There were many false pretenders to the still vacant Messiah-ship, and even Jesus was not the last to proclaim himself the Messiah or Christ: "For many shall come in my name, saying, I am Christ; and shall deceive many." (Mt. xxiv, 4, 23, 24; Mk. xiii, 6, 21, 22.)

That this Messiah Jesus who was come was mere man, but instinct with the spirit of God, is positively avowed by both Peter and Paul. Says Peter in his first sermon at Pentecost: "Ye men of Israel, hear these words: Jesus of Nazareth, *a man* approved of God among you [etc.]. The patriarch David . . . therefore being a prophet, and knowing that God had *sworn with an oath* to him, that *of the fruit of his loins according to the flesh*, he would raise up Christ to sit upon his throne." (Acts, ii, 22, 29, 30.) And Paul: "There is one God, and one mediator between God and men, the *man* Christ Jesus" (1 Tim. ii, 5); and again: "Jesus Christ of the seed of David" (2 Tim. ii, 8). Therefore, in the times when the two cited sacred books were, by whomever, written, Jesus was at that time regarded simply as a man, a "son" or descendant of David. So, when, many years later, the Gos-

205

pels "according to" Matthew and Luke came to be by whomever written, in their original form Jesus Christ was mere man.

Matthew's first chapter begins very humanly and explicitly: "The book of the generation of Jesus Christ, the son of David, the son of Abraham"; and Matthew gives an unbroken line of human begettings, father of son, until "And *Jacob* begat Joseph the husband of Mary, of whom was born Jesus, who is called Christ"! (Matt. i, 1–16.) And Matthew names and catalogues twenty-eight generations between David and Jesus, to-wit: David, *Solomon . . . Jacob*, Joseph,—Jesus, —a purely human ancestry. Also Luke still reflected the belief, held at the time he wrote, that Jesus was of human ancestry; he gives his human genealogy all the way back to Adam, and through many mythical patriarchs who assuredly never existed. This human genealogy by Luke vastly differs, however, from that of Matthew; instead of twenty-eight generations from David, through *Solomon . . . Jacob* and Joseph, our Luke genealogist makes out in detail forty-two generations, to wit: *David, Nathan, . . . Heli*, Joseph, Jesus; and only three of the intermediate names are the same in the two lists. So one or the other of the two inspired genealogies is fictitious, false and forged, necessarily: both are, of course, if Jesus was *not* the son of David, but the immediate "Son of God." The truth is thus stated: "The genealogy could not have been drawn up *after Joseph ceased to be regarded as the real father of Jesus.*" (EB. iii, 2960.)

And *CE.* thus scraps the inspired genealogy of Luke: "*The artificial character of Luke's genealogy* may be seen in the following table [copying Luke's list] . . . The artificial character" is shown by details cited. (*CE.* vi, 411.) It also explodes the seventeenth century clerical pretense,—heard often today—in attempted explanation of these glaring contradictions, that one or the other of these sacred genealogies, preferably that of Luke, was the genealogy, not of Joseph, but of Mary: "It may be safely said that patristic tradition does not regard St. Luke's list as representing the genealogy of the Blessed Virgin." (*CE.* vi, 411.) And, as *CE.* itself points out, Mary is not mentioned as in the line of descent from David in either list. To bring her into the genealogy, in one list or the other, it must have been written: "And Jacob begat *Mary* the wife of Joseph," instead of "And

206

Jacob begat Joseph the husband of Mary": *or* "And Jesus . . . being
. . . the son of *Mary*, which was the *daughter* of Heli," instead of the
recorded "the *son* of Joseph (as was supposed), which was the son of
Heli" (Luke iii, 22–31). Both the genealogies are false and forged
lists of mostly fictitious names, in the original Gospel-forgeries, fabricated to prove Jesus a direct son or descendant of David, and thus
to fulfill the terms of the pretended prophecies that the human Messiah
should be of the race and lineage of David the king.

Moreover, Joseph and Mary *both knew nothing* of the Holy-
Ghostly paternity of their child Jesus. The celebrated Angelic "Annunciation" of this Fable to the "prolific yet ever-virgin Mother of
God," recorded by Dr. Luke (i, 28), is itself a *forgery*, admits *CE.*:
"The words: 'Blessed art thou among women' (v. 28) are *spurious*
and taken from verse 42, the account of the Visitation . . . [Add-
ing] The opinion that Joseph at the time of the Annunciation was an
aged widower and Mary 12 or 15 years of age, is founded only upon
apocryphal documents"—like all the rest of these Fables of Christ.
(*CE.* i, 542.) Simeon came into the temple when Joseph and Mary
had brought the child there "to do for him after the custom of the
law," and indulged in some ecstasies which would have been quite
intelligible if Gabriel had made the revelations attributed to him;
but, hearing them, "*Joseph and his mother marvelled* at those things
which were spoken of him" (Lk. ii, 33). It is false, the original says:
"His *father* and his mother marvelled." etc. Here is another holy
forgery stuck into Luke ii, as is the later verse, "and *Joseph* and
his mother knew not of it" (v. 43). The true original reads "and
his *parents* knew not of it,"—just as in verse 41; "Now his *parents*
went to Jerusalem every year at the feast of the passover"; and as
in verse 48, "thy *father* and I have sought thee sorrowing." In
"John," Jesus is twice expressly called the *son of Joseph*; Philip says
to Nathaniel, "We have found him of whom Moses in the law, and the
prophets, did write, Jesus of Nazareth, *the son of Joseph*" (i, 45);
and again: "Is not this Jesus, *the son of Joseph*, whose *father* and
mother we know?" (vi, 42);—all which "convincingly proves that in
the mind of the narrator Joseph and Mary *were and knew themselves
to be*, in the natural sense of the words, the parents of Jesus." (*EB.*

207

iii, 3344.) The same authority thus sums up the whole of the New Testament evidence prior to the "interpolations" of miraculous birth: "The remark has long ago and often been made that, like Paul, even the Gospels themselves know nothing of the miraculous birth of our Saviour. On the contrary, their knowledge of his natural filial relationship to Joseph the carpenter, and to Mary, his wife, is still explicit." (*Ibid.*) And if Jesus had been a God he could hardly have been crazy; yet his own family thought him so and sent to arrest him as a madman, as above noticed. It is therefore self-evident, that the original Jesus "tradition," down as late as Papias and Irenæus, regarded Jesus simply as a man, and as a very old man when he died a peaceful and natural death. But the zeal to combat and win the Pagans, when, after the failure with the Jews, the Gospel "turned to the Gentiles," and to exalt the man Jesus into a God, as was Perseus or Apollo, grew with the Fathers; by the same token Jesus was now made to be the son of the Hebrew God Yahveh: we have heard the Fathers so argue. So later pious tampering grafted the "Virgin-birth" and "son of God" Pagan myths onto the simple original "traditions" of merely human origin as the "son of David," carelessly letting the primitively forged Davidic genealogies remain to contradict and refute them. These "interpolations" are self-apparent forgeries for Christ's sake, in two of the Gospels.

But if Tertullian spoke truly (if the passage is genuine with him), the other Gospels have been yet further tampered with; for Tertullian explicitly says: "Of the apostles, John and Matthew, and apostolic men, Luke and Mark, these *all start* with the same principles of the faith . . . how that He was *born of the Virgin*, and came to fulfill the law and the prophets." (*Adv. Marcion*, IV, ii; *ANF.* iii, 347.) As these Gospels now stand, Mark and John say not a word of the Virgin-birth, but throughout assume Jesus to have been of human birth, and only "son of God" in a popular religious sense; for "son of God" was in current usage to mean any person near and dear to God. Indeed, the Greek text of the Gospels makes this plain, that no supernatural progeneration and actual God-sonship was intended. In most instances the Greek texts read simply "son of God—*huios Theou*," not "*the* Son—*o huious*": the definite article is a clerical falsification.

208

THE "GOSPEL" FORGERIES

"UPON THIS ROCK I WILL BUILD MY CHURCH"

Of transcendent importance as the sole basis of the Church's most presumptuous False Pretense—its Divine founding by Jesus Christ—this Peter-Rock imposture, the most notorious, and in its evil consequences the most far-reaching and fatal of them all, will now be exposed to its deserved infamy and destruction.

Upon a forged, and forced, Greek Pun put into the mouth of the Jewish Aramaic-speaking Jesus, speaking to Aramaic peasants, the Church of Christ is falsely founded. "The proof that Christ constituted St. Peter the head of His Church is found in the two famous Petrine texts, Matt. xvi, 17–19, and John xxi, 15–19." (*CE.* xii, 261.) The text in John is that about "Feed my Lambs"; but this forgery is not of present interest. The more notorious "proof" is Matthew's forged punning passage: "Thou art *Peter*, and upon this *rock* I will build my church," etc.

It may first be noticed, that "Matthew" is the only one of the three "Synoptic" gospelers to record this "famous Petrine text." And he records this pun as made in *Greek*, by Jesus—*just before his crucifixion*, under very exceptional circumstances, and upon the inspiration of a "special divine revelation" then and there first made by God to Peter, as below to be noted. But in this, "Matthew" is flatly contradicted by "John," who ascribes this as an *Aramaic* pun by Jesus *in the very first remark that he made to Peter, upon his being introduced by his brother Andrew*, on the self-same day of the baptism of Jesus; when "Andrew first findeth his brother Simon . . . and brought him to Jesus"; whereupon, "when Jesus beheld him, he said, Thou art Simon son of Jona: *thou shalt be called Cephas*, which is by interpretation, A stone." (John i, 42.) Thus was Simon Barjona nicknamed "Cephas—Rock" by Jesus on the very first day of the public appearance and mission both of Jesus and of Peter, and *not* a year or more later, towards the close of the career of Jesus! So the famous Petrine Pun, if ever made by Jesus—as it was *not*—was made in the Aramaic speech spoken by these Galilean peasants; the Greek Father who forged the "Gospel according to John" had to attach the translation into Greek of the Aramaic "Cephas," into "Petros, a stone," for the benefit of his Greek readers.

209

After this first explosion of the famous Greek "Rock" pun on which the Church is founded, and as the matter is of highest consequence, let us expose the "Matthew" forgery of the whole "Petrine text" by arraying the three Synoptics in the "deadly parallel," in the order of their composition and evolution from simple to complex fabrication:

Mark (viii, 27–33).

"And Jesus went out, and his disciples, into the towns of Cæsarea Philippi: and by the way he asked his disciples, saying unto them, Whom do men say that I am?

"And they answered, John the Baptist: but some say, Elias; and others, One of the prophets.

"And he saith unto them, But whom say ye that I am? And Peter answereth and saith unto him, Thou art the Christ.

Luke (ix, 18–22).

"And it came to pass, as he was alone praying, his disciples were with him; and he asked them, saying, Whom say the people that I am?

"They answering said, John the Baptist; but some say, Elias; and others say, that one of the old prophets is risen again.

"He said unto them, But whom say ye that I am? Peter answering said, The Christ of God.

Matthew (xvi, 13–22).

"When Jesus came into the coasts of Cæsarea Philippi, he asked his disciples, saying, Whom do men say that I the Son of man am?

"And they said, Some say that thou art John the Baptist: some, Elias; and others, Jeremias, or one of the prophets.

"He saith unto them, But whom say ye that I am? And Simon Peter answered and said, Thou are the Christ, the Son of the living God.

"And Jesus answered and said unto him, Blessed art thou, Simon Barjona: for flesh and blood hath not *revealed* it unto thee, but my Father which is in heaven.

"And I say unto thee, That thou art *Peter,* and upon this *rock* I will build my church; and the gates

Mark. *Luke.* *Matthew.*

of hell shall not prevail against it. [Here about the *Keys*, and "binding and loosing"].

"And he charged them that they should tell no man of him.

"And he straitly charged them, and commanded them to tell no man that thing.

"Then charged he his disciples that they should tell no man that *he was Jesus the Christ*.

"And he began to teach them, that the Son of man must suffer many things, and be rejected of the elders, and of the chief priests, and scribes, and be killed, and after three days rise again.

"Saying, The Son of man must suffer many things, and be rejected of the elders and chief priests and scribes, and be slain, and be raised the third day."

"From that time forth began Jesus to shew unto his disciples, how that he must go unto Jerusalem, and suffer many things of the elders and chief priests and scribes, and be killed, and be raised again the third day.

"And he spake that saying openly. And Peter took him, and began to rebuke him.

"Then Peter took him, and began to rebuke him, saying, Be it far from thee, Lord: this shall not be unto thee.

"But when he had turned about and looked on his disciples, he rebuked Peter, saying, Get thee behind me, Satan: for thou savourest not the things that be of God, but the things that be of men."

"But he turned and said unto Peter, Get thee behind me, Satan: thou art an offence unto me: for thou savourest not the things that be of God, but those that be of men."

Let it be noted, in passing, that all three of the Synoptists expressly aver in the above narration, as elsewhere in their texts, that Jesus positively declared and predicted, that he should be put to death, and after three days rise again: distinctly, his Resurrection

211

from the dead. All three on this important point are liars, if John be believed; for after the crucifixion and burial of Jesus, and the discovery on the third day of his empty grave by the Magdalene, which she immediately reported to Peter and John, they ran doubting to the grave, looked in, and "saw, and believed"; and John positively avers: "For as yet they *knew not* the scripture, that he must *rise again from the dead.*" (John xx, 9.) But this inspired assertion contains a grave anachronism: for "as yet" there was, of course, *no* "scripture" about the death and resurrection at all, nor for well over a century afterwards, as in this chapter is proven.

Let us examine for a moment into the context of this "famous Petrine text" and into its antecedents, in order to get the "stage setting" of this dramatic climacteric Pun of such vast and serious consequences unto this day.

The original simple narrative is told in the earlier writer, "Mark," and copied almost verbatim into "Luke." There Jesus is reported to have put a sort of conundrum to the Twelve, "saying unto them, Whom do men say that I am?" The answer showed a very superstitious belief in reincarnations or "second comings" of dead persons to earth; for "they answered, John the Baptist: but some say, Elias; and others, One of the prophets, or Jeremias," to fuse the somewhat disparate replies. Jesus himself shared this reincarnation superstition, for he had positively asserted that John the Baptist *was* Elijah *redivivus:* "This *is* Elias, which was for to come," (Matt. xi, 14; xvii, 11–13); though John, being questioned about it, "Art thou Elias?" contradicted the Christ, "and he saith, I am *not.*" (John i, 20, 21.)

After hearing the disciples report what others said about him, who he was, Jesus then "saith unto them, But whom say *ye* that I am? And *Peter* answereth and saith unto him, *Thou art the Christ.* And he charged them that they should tell no man of him" (Mk. viii, 27–30; Lk. ix, 18–22). There was certainly nothing novel or unexpected in this alleged reply of Peter; it was exactly the proclaimed mission of Jesus as the "promised Messiah," as the precedent texts of "Mark" verify. On the day of his baptism by John, before all the people, "the heavens opened . . . And there came a voice from heaven, saying, Thou art my beloved Son" (i, 2); what the devils cried out in the

212

synagogue, "I know thee who thou art, the Holy one of God" (i, 24) ; just what all the devils unanimously proclaimed before the disciples and all hearers, "And unclean spirits, when they saw him, . . . cried, saying, Thou art the son of God" (iii, 2) ; just what the possessed man with the legion of devils cried out before all the disciples, "What have I to do with thee, Jesus, thou Son of the most high God" (v, 7) ;—all as recorded by "Mark" prior to the above reply by Peter. So, naturally, Peter's "confession" caused no surprise ; it was the expected thing : so *Jesus made no remark on hearing it*, except the peculiar injunction that "they should tell no man"—what all men and devils already knew by much-repeated hearsay. So Jesus at once proceeded to speak of his coming persecution, death, and resurrection ; "And Peter took him, and began to rebuke him. But when he had turned about and looked on his disciples, he rebuked Peter, saying, Get thee behind me, Satan : for thou savourest not the things that be of God, but the things that be of men" (Mk. viii, 31–33). The identical story in its same simple form, minus the Satan colloquy, is told also in Luke (ix, 18–22). This is the round, unvarnished tale of the first Greek Father "gospel" writers, a century after the reputed conversation, and long before the "primacy of Peter" idea dawned as a "good thing" upon the Fathers of the Church. There is not a word about "church" in the passage, nor in the entire "gospel according to Mark," nor in Luke, nor in even the much later "John."

The later Church Father who wrote up the original of the "gospel according to Matthew," copied Mark's story substantially verbatim, Mark's verses 27–33, being nearly word for word reproduced in Matthew's 13–16, 20–24 of chapter xvi ; the only material verbal difference being in Peter's answer, in verse 16, where Peter's words are expanded : "Thou art the Christ, *the Son of the Living God*,"—obviously padded in by the "interpolator" of verses 17–19, which we now examine.

As the years since "Mark" rolled by, the zeal of the Fathers to exalt Peter increased ; we have seen many admitted forgeries of documents having that purpose in view. So it was, obviously, a new forging Father who took a manuscript of "Matthew," and turning to the above verses copied from "Mark," added in, or made a new manuscript copy containing, the notable forgery of verses 17–19. There, onto the commonplace and unnoticed reply of Peter, "Thou art the Christ," the pious interpolator tacked on:

"the Son of the living God. And Jesus answered and said unto him, Blessed art thou, Simon Barjona: for flesh and blood hath not revealed it unto thee, but my Father which is in heaven. And I say also unto thee, that thou art Peter, and upon this rock I will build my church; and the gates of hell shall not prevail against it. And I will give unto thee the keys of the Kingdom of heaven: and whatsoever thou shalt bind on earth shall be bound in heaven and whatsoever thou shalt loose on earth shall be loosed in heaven." (Matt. xvi, 16b–19.)

It is impossible that the original writer of "Matthew" should have written those remarkable and preposterous verses, in which Jesus is made to take Peter's commonplace announcement, "Thou art the Christ," as a "special revelation from heaven" to Peter and a great secret mystery here first "revealed";—this matter of common notoriety and even devil-gossip throughout Israel, as we have seen from "Mark's" numerous Christ-texts; the same is true in Luke. These avowals that Jesus was the Christ are even more numerous and explicit in "Matthew" up to the interpolation. That Jesus was "Christ" is the identical disclosure and announcement, which had been declared by Gabriel to Mary; by a dream to the suspicious Joseph; by wicked Herod, who "demanded of them where *Christ* should be born" (ii, 4); by the voice from heaven proclaiming to the world, "This is my beloved Son" (iii, 17); that was declared by the Devil in the wilderness, "If thou be the Son of God" (iv, 6); that the Legion of Devils cried aloud, "What have we to do with thee, Jesus, thou son of God" (viii, 29); that Jesus himself avowed of himself time and again, "All things are delivered unto me by *my Father*, Lord of heaven and earth" (xi, 25–27); that all the crew of Peter's fishing-boat acclaimed when they "worshipped him, saying, Of a truth thou art the Son of God" (xiv, 33). Just two chapters earlier in Matthew, is the fable of Jesus and Peter "walking on the water," as "foretold" by the Sibyls; when Peter began to sink, he was rescued and dragged aboard the little fishing boat by Jesus;—"*and they that were in the ship came and worshipped him, saying, Of a truth thou art the son of God.*" (Mt. xiv, 29–33.) So that Peter's wonderful information was no novelty and special divine rev-

214

elation, to himself, but was the common credulity and gossip of the whole crew of fishermen, devils and Palestinian peasantry. And long before, on the very next day after his baptism by John, and before Peter was "called" or even *found,* and when his brother Andrew went and found him to bring him to Jesus, Andrew declared *to Peter:* "We have found the *Messias,* which is, being interpreted, *the Christ"!* (John i, 41.) And, on the next day Nathaniel said to Jesus: "Rabbi, thou art the Son of God; thou art the King of Israel"! (John i, 49.) Peter's wonderful "special revelation" and confession thus lose all originality and are without merit of the great "reward" which *CE.* (xii, 261) says Jesus bestowed upon him for this pretended original and inspired discovery, as we shall in due order notice.

That Jesus Christ never spoke the words of those forged verses, that they are a late Church forgery, is beyond any intelligent or honest denial. The *first mention* of them in "patristic literature," and that only a reference to the "keys," is this scant line of Father Tertullian, in a little tract called *Scorpiace* or "The Scorpion's Sting," written *about 211* A. D., in which he says: "For though you think heaven is still shut, remember that the Lord left to Peter and through him to the Church, the keys of it." (*Scorpiace,* x; *ANF.* iii, 643.) That Jesus did not use the words of those verses, interpolated into a paragraph of Matthew copied bodily and verbatim by the original "Matthew" writer from "Mark," and repeated in their original form by "Luke," is thus conclusive from "internal" evidences; the later and embroidered form is a visible interpolation and forgery. That this is true, is demonstrated, moreover, by the inherent impossibility of the thing itself.

THE "CHURCH" FOUNDED ON THE "ROCK"

First of all, in proof that Jesus Christ never made this Pun, did not establish any Christian Church—nor even a Jewish reformed synagogue,—are his own alleged positive statements to be quoted in refutation of the other forged "missionary" passage in Matthew: "Go ye into all the world, and teach all nations." The avowed mission of Jesus, as we have seen from his reputed words, was exclusively to his fellow Jews: "I am not sent but to the lost sheep of the house of Israel"; and he expressly commanded his disciples not to preach to the

Gentiles, nor even to the near-Jewish Samaritans. He proclaimed the immediate end of the world, and his quick second coming to establish the exclusively Jewish Kingdom of Heaven, even before all the Jews of little Palestine could be warned of the event—that "the Kingdom of Heaven is at hand." It is impossible, therefore, that Jesus could have so flagrantly contradicted the basic principles of his exclusive mission as the Jewish promised Messiah, and could have commanded the institution of a permanent and perpetual religious organization, an "*ecclesia*" or "Church," to preach his exclusively Jewish Messianic doctrines to all nations of the earth, which was to perish within that generation. This is a conclusive proof of the later "interpolation" or forgery of this punning passage.

On this point says *EB.*:

"It would be a great mistake to suppose that Jesus himself founded a new religious community" (c. 3103).—"A further consideration which tells against the genuineness of Mt. xvi, 18b, is the occurrence in it of the word *ecclesia*. It has been seen to be impossible to maintain that Jesus founded any distinct religious community. . . .

"As for the word itself, it occurs elsewhere in the Gospels only in Mt. xviii, 17. There, however, it denotes simply the Jewish local community to which every one belongs; for what is said relates not to the future but to the present, in which a Christian *ecclesia* cannot, of course, be thought of." (c. 3105) . . . "It is impossible to regard as historical the employment of the word *ecclesia* by Jesus as the designation of the Christian community." (*EB.* iii, 3103, 3105, 3117.)

Indeed, as said by a contemporary wit, the truth is that "Jesus Christ did not found the Church—he is its Foundling. His parent, the Jewish church, abandoned the child; the Roman church took it in, adopted it, and gave his mother a certificate of good character." (*The Truth Seeker*, 10/23/26.)

Jesus spoke Aramaic, a dialect of the ancient and "dead" Hebrew. The true name of the fisherman "Prince of the Apostles," just repudiated by Jesus as "Satan," was *Shimeon*, or in its Greek form, Simon, who was later "surnamed Peter." He attained somehow the Aramaic nickname Kepha, or in its Greek form, Cephas, meaning a rock; this evidently furnished to the Greek punster the cue for his play on words: "Thou art *Petros* [Greek, *petros*, a rock; cf. Eng. petrify, petroleum,

216

etc.], and upon this *petros* [rock] I will build my *ecclesia* [church]."
Jesus could not have made this Greek play on words; neither Peter
nor any of the other "ignorant and unlearned" Jewish peasant disciples could have understood it. Much less could Jesus have said, or the
apostles have understood, this other Greek word *"ecclesia,"* even had
it been possible for Jesus, facing the immediate end of the world—proclaimed by himself—to have dreamed of founding any permament religious sect. There was nothing like *ecclesia* known to the Jews; it was
a technical Greek term designating the free political assemblies of the
Greek republics. This is illustrated by one sentence from the Greek
Father Origen, about 245 A. D., when the Church had taken over the
Greek political term *ecclesia* to denote its own religious organization.
Says Origen, using the word in both its old meaning and in its new
Christian adaptation: "For the Church [*ecclesia*] of God, *e. g.*, which
is at Athens; . . . Whereas the assembly [*ecclesia*] of the Athenians," etc. (Origen, *Contra Celsum*, iii, 20; *ANF.* iv, 476.) The
Greek Fathers who, a century later, founded the Church among the
Pagan Greek-speaking Gentiles, adopted the Greek word *ecclesia* for
their organizations because the word was familiar for popular assemblies, and because the translators of the Septuagint had used *ecclesia*
as the nearest Greek term for the translation of the two Hebrew words
qahal and *edah* used in the Old Testament for the "congregation" or
"assembly" of all Israel at the tent of meeting.

These Hebrew words (*qahal, edah*) had also a more general use, as
signifying any sort of gathering or crowd, religious or secular. Thus
"sinners shall not stand in the congregation [Heb. *edah*] of the righteous" (Ps. i, 5); or of a mob of wicked ones: "I have hated the congregation [Heb. *qahal*] of evil doers" (Ps. xxvi, 5); and even of the
great assemblage of the dead: "The man that—[etc.], shall remain
in the congregation [Heb. *qahal*] of the dead" (Prov. xxi, 16); all
these various senses being rendered *"ecclesia"* in the Greek Septuagint
translation.

Thus no established and permanent organization of disciples of
the Christ is implied by the term *ecclesia*, even if Jesus could have used
the Aramaic equivalent of that Greek term; at most it would have
only meant the small group of Jews which might adopt the "Kingdom
of Heaven" watchword and watchfully wait until the speedy end of the

world and the expected quick consummation of the proclaimed King-dom,—not yet come to be, these 2000 years.

This only possible meaning is made indisputable by the one other instance of the use of the Greek word *ecclesia* attributed to Jesus,—and that also by the myth-mongering "Matthew." Here Jesus is made to lay down some rules for settling the incessant discords among his peasant believers in the Kingdom: "Moreover, if thy brother shall trespass against thee . . . tell it to the church [*ecclesia*] but if he neglect to hear the *ecclesia*, let him be unto thee as an heathen man and a publican" (Matt. xviii, 15–17);—that is, kick him like a dog out of your holy company and exclude him from share in the coming Kingdom. There was, of course, no organized Christian "Church" in the lifetime of Jesus; he could only have meant—(if he said it), that disputes were to be referred to the others of the little band of Kingdom-watchers, who should drop the "trespasser" out of their holy group if he proved recalcitrant and insisted upon the right of his opinion or action. But Jesus never said even this; it is a forged later compan-ion-piece to the "Rock and Keys" forgery, as is proven by the follow-ing verse 18—(a *repetition* of xvi, 19)—regarding the "binding and loosing" powers given to itself by the later forging Church when it assumed this preposterous prerogative of domination.

The "On this Rock" forgery of Matt. xvi, says Reinach, "is ob-viously an interpolation, made at a period when a church, separated from the synagogue, already existed. In the parallel passages in Mark (vii, 27, 32) and in Luke (ix, 18–22), there is not a word of the pri-macy of Peter, a detail which Mark, the disciple of Peter, could hardly have omitted if he had known of it. The interpolation is posterior to the compilation of Luke's gospel." (*Orpheus*, pp. 224–225.)

As aptly said by Dr. McCabe; "It [the word *ecclesia*] had no mean-ing whatever as a religious institution until decades after the death of Jesus Christ. In the year 30 A. D. no one on earth would have known what Jesus meant if he had said that he was going to 'found' an *ec-clesia* or church, and that the powers of darkness would not prevail against it, and so on. It would sound like the talk of the Mad Hatter in *Alice in Wonderland*." (*The Story of Religious Controversy*, p. 294.) Indeed, it may be remarked, it is the "powers of darkness" of mind which have so far prevailed to perpetuate this fraud; the powers of the light of reason are hastening to its final overthrow.

"PETER-ROCK-CHURCH" DENIED AB SILENCIO

"Luke" was not present when this moumental pronouncement of the "Rock and Keys" was allegedly made; Peter may have forgotten to tell him of it, or "Luke" may have forgotten that Peter told him. And Peter may have forgotten to tell of it and of his peerless "primacy" to his own "companion" and "interpreter" Mark, or Mark may have forgotten that Peter told him, and thus have failed to record so momentous an event. But John, the "Beloved Disciple" was right there, with Matthew, himself, one of the speakers and hearers in the historic colloquy,—and John totally ignores it. The silence of all three discredits and repudiates it. Moreover, and most significantly, Peter himself, in his two alleged Epistles, has not a word of his tremendous dignity and importance conferred on him by his Master; never once does he describe himself in the pride of priestly humility, "Peter, Servant of the servants of God," or "Prince of Apostles: or even "Bishop of the Church which sojourns at Rome," or any such to distinguish himself from the common herd of peasant apostles. Peter must have been very modest, even more so than his "Successors."

Furthermore, the official "Acts of the Apostles" never once notes this divinely commissioned "primacy" of Peter; and every other book of the New Testament utterly ignores it. Paul is said to have written a sentaceutious "Epistle to the Romans," and to have written two or three Epistles from Rome, where Peter is supposed to have been, enthroned as divine Vicar of God and Head of the Church Universal; and yet never a word of this tremendous fact; Paul did not know it, or ignores it. The "Epistles of Paul," fourteen of them, and the "Acts," are replete with defiances of Paul to Peter,—"I withstood him to his face"; and in all the disputes between them, over matters of the faith and the fortunes of the new "Church," not a single one of the Apostles rises in his place and suggests that Peter is Prince and Primate, and that Peter's view of the matters was *ex-cathedra* the voice of God, and he, having spoken, the matter was settled. Paul, in all his Epistles, never gives a suspicion that he had ever heard, even from Peter, of the latter's superior authority.

Thus the admitted principal, if not only "proof" which the Church urges for its Divine and "Petrine" foundation is found to be—like every other Church muniment and credential, a clerical forgery, a priestly imposture. We shall glance at some other like examples of the Christian art of "Scripture" falsification.

"GO, TEACH ALL NATIONS" FORGERY

Applying Tertullian's test of authenticity, that contradictory passages betray a later "interpolation," the closing verses, 16–20, of the last chapter of Matthew—as of Mark 9–20,—are themselves late interpolations or forged passages.

Matthew previously quotes Jesus as declaring: "I am not sent but unto the lost sheep of the house of Israel" (xv, 24; x, 6); and his command to the Twelve: "Go not into the way of the Gentiles, . . . but go rather to the lost sheep of the house of Israel" (x, 5, 6). Also Matthew (as Mark) has reiterated the assurance of the immediacy of the end of the world and the "second coming" in glory: "Ye shall not have gone over the cities of Israel, till the Son of Man be come." (Mt. x, 23; cf. x, 7; xxvi, 28, 34, *passim.*) So that neither in reason nor in truthful statement could it be possible for Jesus to have met the Eleven a few days after his resurrection, in Galilee, and commanded them in this wonderful language: "Go ye therefore, and *teach all nations*, baptizing them *in the name of the Father, and of the Son, and of the Holy Ghost:* . . . and, lo, I am with you alway, even unto the end of the world"—which he had just, and repeatedly, averred should happen in the life-time of his hearers and before they could preach even to the Jews of little Palestine. (Mt. xxviii, 18, 20; cf. Mk. xvi, 15–16.) This "command" could only have been "interpolated" into the forged ending of Matthew and Mark long after the original form of the tradition of Jesus had been first written, and when the "second coming" in the "Kingdom of God" and the immediate "end of the world" had become impossible of further credit by lapse of long years of time and disappointed expectation. It could also only have been written *after* the gospel of the "Kingdom" for the Jews had failed,

220

and the apostles had "turned to the Gentiles," which was not, even on the face of Scripture, until after the so-called "Council of Jerusalem," when the Jewish apostles, after bitter quarrel with the interloper Paul, had recognized Paul's pretended "revelation" of mission to the Gentiles and had parcelled out the propaganda work, Paul to the uncircumcised Gentiles, all the others, Peter included, to "the circumcision" only; though the entire story of the Council is itself a contradictory fabrication, as demonstrated by *EB*. (i, 916, *et seq.*)

ACTS BELIES THE "GO, TEACH ALL NATIONS" FORGERY

Culminating proof that Jesus Christ never uttered this command, to "Go, teach all nations," of Matthew and Mark, and that it is a forgery long after interpolated into the original forged texts, is found in the positive "history" of the inspiredly forged Acts of the Apostles, in Holy Writ itself. If Jesus Christ, just arisen from the dead, had given that ringing and positive command to Peter and the Eleven, utterly impossible would it have been for the remarkable "history" recorded in Acts to have occurred. Acts, too, disproves the assertion of Mark that, straightway, after the command was given to the Eleven, "they went forth, and preached everywhere" (Mk. xvi, 20),—that is, to all nations thereabouts, the Pagan Gentiles. A further contradiction may be noted: Matthew says that the command was given to the Eleven in Galilee, on "a mountain where Jesus had appointed them" (Mt. xxviii, 16–19),—and some days after the resurrection; whereas Mark records that the command was given to the Eleven "as they sat at meat," evidently in a house in Jerusalem, through the roof of which Jesus immediately afterwards ascended into heaven (Mk. xvi, 14–19); after which they immediately "went forth, and preached everywhere" (verse 20). But they did not, as the silence of the other two Gospels, and the positive evidence of Acts and several of the Epistles, proves; together with the promised disproof of the "Go, teach all nations" command, for preaching the Kingdom to the Gentile Pagans, now to be produced.

Cornelius, the leader of the Italian Band at Cæsarea, a Roman Gentile Pagan, had a "revelation" that he should go to Joppa to find Peter, evidently with a view to "conversion" and admission into the new all-Jewish sect. A companion vision in a trance was awarded to

221

Peter, seemingly to prepare him for the novel notion of community with Gentiles; though "Peter doubted in himself what this vision which he had seen should mean"; but at this juncture the messengers came from Cornelius, and related to Peter the vision of Cornelius, and his request that Peter come to see him. Evidently, *Peter had never heard of the Master's command*, alleged to have been given by Jesus *to Peter himself*, and the others: "Go, teach all nations" of the uncircumcised, for he said to the messengers: "Ye know how it is *an unlawful thing* for a man that is a Jew to keep company, or come unto one *of another nation*"; but recalling the vision from which he had just awaked, he added: "but God hath shewed me" that it was permissible now to deal with "one of another nation." So, Peter went along to Cornelius, and he asked "For what intent ye have sent for me?" Cornelius repeated the vision, and said, "Now we are all here present before God, to hear all things that are commanded thee by God." At this, Peter was evidently greatly surprised, and "opened his mouth, and replied; Of a truth I perceive that God is no respecter of persons: But that in every nation he that feareth him, and worketh righteousness, is accepted with him." Thus clearly *Peter had never heard his Jesus command:* "Go, teach all nations"; it required this new "revelation"—some years later—for him to tardily and finally "perceive" that God accepted even "one of another nation." Clearer yet is this, that up to this time, "salvation is of the Jews" only, by Peter's next words: "The *word which God sent unto the children of Israel* . . . which was published *throughout Judæa*—[*not* to "all nations"], and began in Galilee, after the baptism which John preached—[*not* baptism "in the name" of the Trinity]. . . . And he [Jesus] commanded us to preach unto all the people"—of the children of Israel. And now for proof positive: Peter was now "showed" the new dispensation: a visitation of the Holy Ghost came upon the Pagans present, who thereupon all "spake with tongues," to the great amazement of Peter and his Jewish companions: "They of the circumcision which believed were *astonished*, as many as came with *Peter, because that on the Gentiles* was *also* poured out the gift of the Holy Ghost," which had been promised only to all believing Jews. Ignorant thus of the Christ's pre-ascension command to *him* and the Eleven, to teach all men, but *now* convinced that "one of another nation" was acceptable with God, and should be baptized,

222

Peter yielded, and argued for his companions to consent: "Then answered Peter, Can any man forbid water, that these should *not be baptized*, which have received the Holy Ghost as well as we? And he commanded them to be baptized in the name of the Lord" (Acts x),— *not* in the name of the Trinity, as Matthew alleges that Jesus himself had commanded Peter himself to do. So this bit of Scripture "history" is positive refutation of the "Go, teach all nations, baptizing them in the name of the Father, and of the Son, and of the Holy Ghost" forgery.

And none of the others of the Twelve had ever heard the command. For immediately that they learned of this flagrant "heresy" of Peter, "that the Gentiles have also received the word of God," they were piously outraged and furious against Peter: "And when Peter had come up to Jerusalem, they that were of the circumcision *contended with him*, Saying, Thou wentest in to men uncircumcised, and didst eat with them." Peter put up a long argument in defense, urging the "revelation" to Cornelius and his own trance vision, quoted the gospels of Matthew and John—(*not yet in existence!*),—and wound up: "Forasmuch then as God gave them the like gift as he did unto us, . . . what am I, that I could withstand God?" This line of argument pacified the other apostles; "When they heard these things, they held their peace, and glorified God, saying, *Then* hath God *also to the Gentiles* granted repentance unto life." (Acts xi.) Perfect proof is this, that the alleged "Go, teach all nations" command of the Christ to Peter and the other apostles, is a falsification, a late forgery into Matthew and Mark: for if Jesus had so commanded these same apostles, the special revelations would not have been necessary; Peter's doubt and hesitation, and the row of the others with Peter for baptizing Cornelius and his Band could not have occurred, would have been impossible and absurd; as would have been the apostolic rows of the "Council of Jerusalem," recorded in Acts xv and belied by Paul in Galatians ii, as is made evident in *EB.* (i, 916.)

This incontrovertible fact, that Jesus Christ never uttered that command, "Go, teach all nations," and that the texts so reciting are later forgeries to serve the Gentilic propaganda of the Faith after the Jews had rejected it,—is confessed by *CE.* in these destructive words: "The Kingdom of God had special reference to *Jewish beliefs.* . . .

A *still further expansion* resulted *from the revelation directing* St. Peter *to admit to baptism* Cornelius, a devout Gentile." (*CE.* iii, 747.) If Jesus Christ, preaching the exclusive Jewish Kingdom, had revised and reversed his God-ordained program, and had commanded "Go, *teach all nations, baptizing* them," the "expansion" would have resulted then and there from the command itself,—not from the "revelation" and apostolic row some years later, which would have been unnecessary and supererogatory—as it was unseemly. Thus another pious lie and forgery is exposed and confessed.

Even more plain and comprehensive are the words of this same divine forged command of the Christ, as recorded by Mark: "Go ye into all the world, and preach the gospel to every creature. And he that believeth and is baptized shall be saved; but he that believeth not shall be damned." (Mk. xvi, 15–16.) It should be a relief to many pious Hell-fearing Christians to know that their Christ did not utter these damning words, and that they may disbelieve with entire impunity; that they are priestly forgeries to frighten credulous persons into belief and submission to priestcraft. The proofs of this from the Bible itself we see confirmed by clerical admissions under compulsion from exposure of the fraud.

Thus this whole section, says Reinach, is a "late addition" to Mark, "and is not found in the best manuscripts." (Orpheus, p. 221.) We have seen that *CE.* includes this section among those rejected as spurious up to the time that the Holy Ghost belatedly vouched for it at the Council of Trent in 1546, putting the seal of divine truth upon this lie. Both these parallel but exceedingly contradictory closing sections of Matthew and Mark, are spurious additions made after the "end of the world" and "second coming" predictions had notoriously failed, in order to give pretended divine sanction to the "turning to the Gentiles," after the Jews, to whom alone the Christ was sent and had expressly and repeatedly limited his mission, had rejected his claim to be Messiah.

The Gentile Church of Christ has therefore no divine sanction; was never contemplated nor created by Jesus Christ. The Christian Church is thus founded on a forgery of pretended words of the pretended Christ. This proposition is of such immense significance and importance, that I array here the admissions of the forgery, in addition to

224

the demonstration of its falsity above given. The virtual admissions of *CE.* totally destroy the authenticity of the entire spurious section, Mark xvi, 9–20, together with the correlated passages of the equally spurious "Matthean addition," copied from Mark, with embellishments into Matthew.

THE FORGED GOSPEL ENDINGS

"The conclusion of Mark (xvi, 9–20) is admittedly not genuine. Still less can the shorter conclusion lay claim to genuineness. . . . Almost the entire section is a compilation, partly even from the fourth gospel and Acts." (*EB.* ii, 1880; 1767, n. 3; 1781, and n. 1, on "the evidence of its spuriousness.") "The longer form . . . has against it the testimony of the two oldest Uncial MSS. (Siniatic and Vatican) and one of the two earliest of the Syriac Versions (Siniatic Syriac), all of which close the chapter at verse 8. In addition to this, is the very significant silence of Patristic literature as to anything following verse 8." (*New Standard Bible Dictionary,* p. 551.) The acute and careful critical reasonings and evidences upon which the foregoing conclusions are based, I have omitted from these extracts, to present them in full in the following ample review from *CE.,* which, "reasoning in chains" fettered upon it by the Trentine Decree, yet fully establishes the impeaching facts and substantially confesses the forgery into "Mark," while "saving its face" for the "inspiration" of the forgery by clerical assumption of "some other inspired pen" as the source of the text, which makes it "just as good" as any other, when invested with the sanctity of the sanction of the Council of Trent. Says *CE.:*

"But the great textual problem of the Gospel (Mark) concerns the genuineness of the last twelve verses. Three conclusions of the Gospel are known: the long conclusion, as in our Bibles, containing verses 9–20, the short one ending with verse 8, and an intermediate form [described]. . . . Now this third form may be dismissed at once—[as an admitted Bible *forgery*]. No scholar regards this intermediate conclusion as having any title to acceptance.

"We may pass on, then, to consider how the case stands between the long conclusion and the short, *i. e.* between accepting xvi, 9–20, as a genuine portion of the original Gospel, or making the original end with xvi, 8. Eusebius . . . pointing out that the passage in Mark beginning with verse

9 *is not contained* in all the MSS. of the Gospel. The historian then goes on himself to say that in nearly all the MSS. of Mark, at least *in the accurate ones,* the Gospel ends with xvi, 8. . . . St. Jerome also says in one place that the passage *was wanting* in nearly all Greek MSS. . . . As we know, he incorporated it in the Vulgate. . . . If we add to this that the Gospel ends with xvi, 8, in the *two oldest* Greek MSS.—[Siniatic and Vatican]—[also in the Siniatic Syriac, some Ethiopic, Armenian, and other MSS.] indicate doubt as to whether the true ending is at verse 8 or verse 20. (p. 678.) . . .

"Much has been made of the silence of some of the third and fourth century Fathers, their silence being interpreted to mean that they either did not know the passage or rejected it. Thus Tertullian, SS. Cyprian, Athanasius, Basil the Great, Gregory of Nazianzus, and Cyril of Alexandria.

"When we turn to the internal evidence, the number, and still more the character, of the peculiarities is certainly striking [citing many instances from the Greek text]. . . . But, even when this is said, the cumulative force of the evidence against the Marcan origin of the passage is considerable. (p. 678.) . . . The combination of so many peculiar features, not only of vocabulary, but of matter and construction, leaves room for *doubt* as to the Marcan authorship of the verses. (p. 679.) . . .

"Whatever the fact be, it is not at all certain that Mark did not write the disputed verses. *It may be that he did not; that they are from the pen of some other inspired writer* [!], and were appended to the Gospel in the the first century or the beginning of the second. . . . Catholics are not bound to hold that the verses were written by St. Mark. But they are *canonical* Scripture, *for* the Council of Trent (Sess. IV), in defining that all parts of the Sacred Books are to be received as sacred and canonical, had especially in view *the disputed parts of the Gospels,* of which this conclusion of Mark is one. Hence, whoever wrote the verses, they are *inspired,* and must be received as such by every Catholic." (*CE.* ix, 677, 678, 679.)

The *New Commentary on the Holy Scripture* has a special section entitled "The Ending of St. Mark's Gospel," in which it reviews the evidences in much the same manner as *CE.*, with additional new and able criticism; it thus concludes,—not being fettered by the dogmatic decision of the Council of Trent, which *CE.* so clerically yields to in the letter but evades in the spirit:

"It is practically certain that neither Matthew nor Luke found it in their copies of Mark [from which they copied in making up the gospels under those names: see pp. 33, 45]. . . . The Last Twelve Verses are con-

226

structed as an independent summary with total neglect of the contents of xvi, 1–8. . . . It is as certain as anything can be in the domain of criticism that the Longer Ending did not come from the pen of the evangelist Mark. . . . We conclude that *it is certain that the Longer Ending is no part of the Gospel.*" (*New Commentary,* Pt. III, pp. 122, 123.)

More shaming proofs and confessions of forgery of pretended words of the Christ there could not be, than of this falsified command to preach a forged Gospel to the credulous dupes of Paganism. Gentile Christianity collapses upon its forged foundations.

THE BAPTISMAL FORGERY

The contradictory "baptismal formulas," the simple "in the name of the Lord" of Peter in Acts, and the elaborated forgery of Matthew, "in the name of the Father, and of the Son, and of the Holy Ghost," are sufficiently branded with falsity in the preceding paragraphs, and may be dismissed without further notice. This "Trinitarian Formula" is most palpably a late forgery, never uttered by Jesus Christ; for the Holy "Trinity" was not itself officially invented until the Council of Constantinople, in 381 A. D. Admittedly, "of all revealed truths this is the *most impenetrable to reason"; it* is therefore called a "mystery." (*CE.* xv, 52.) Of this Baptism-formula of Matthew, the ex-priest scholar, McCabe, says: "It was fraudulently added to the gospel when the priesthood was created." (*LBB.* 1121, p. 4.) Bishop Gore's English Divines thus cautiously confess the fraud: "Matthew's witness to the teaching of the risen Lord in these verses is widely rejected on two grounds. . . . The witness of Acts makes it almost certain that baptism at first was into the name of Jesus Christ, and not formally into the name of the Blessed Trinity. . . . It is quite likely that Matthew here expresses our Lord's teaching in language which the Lord Himself did not actually use." (*New Comm.,* Pt. III, p. 204; cf. *EB.* i, 474.) Another blasting priestly fraud of "Scripture" forgery is thus exposed and confessed!

A MEDLEY OF FORGERIES

After the foregoing colossal forgeries within the originally forged Gospels of Jesus Christ, there yet remain many other viciously dishonest falsifications of text. A little trinity of them only will be noted.

FORGERY IN CHRISTIANITY

THE "WOMAN IN ADULTERY" FORGERY

The *CE.* has admitted that the so-called *pericope adulteræ* was regarded as spurious until the Council of Trent, in 1546, declared it divine truth; but Reinach says: "The episode of Jesus and the woman taken in adultery, which was inserted in John's gospel in the fourth century, was originally in the [apocryphal] 'Gospel according to the Hebrews.'" (*Orpheus*, p. 235.)

THE JOHN XXI FORGERY

The entire chapter xxi of John is likewise a surcharge of forgery in that gospel; it may be disposed of with this terse comment of *EB.*: "As xx, 30–31 constitutes a formal and solemn conclusion, xxi is beyond question a later appendix. We may go on to add that it does not come from the same author with the rest of the book." (*EB.* ii, 2543.)

THE "LORD'S PRAYER" FORGERY

As may be seen by mere comparison, the "Doxology" at the end of the Lord's Prayer in Matthew (vi, 13): "For thine is the kingdom, and the power, and the glory, forever. Amen," is an interpolation into the original text, and is omitted as spurious by the Revised Version; it is *not* in the Catholic "True" Version. But, it may be remarked, the whole of the so-called Lord's Prayer is not the Lord's at all; it is a late patch-work of pieces out of the Old Testament, as readily shown by the marginal cross-references,—just as we have seen that the "Apostles Creed" was said to have been patched up by inspired lines from each apostle. The Sermon on the Mount, in which its most used form is found, is a concatenation of supposed *logia* or "sayings" of Jesus, drawn out through three chapters of "Matthew"; it was delivered before "the multitudes" which surrounded the Master and his disciples, and in the middle of the fictitious discourse. This is not true, according to "Luke," who makes it out a private talk in reply to a question by one of the Twelve: "And it came to pass, that, as (Jesus) was praying in a certain place, when he ceased one of his disciples said to him, Lord, teach us to pray, as John also taught his disciples. And he said unto them, When ye pray, say, Our Father," etc. (Luke xi, 1–

2.) Indeed, the entire "Lord's Prayer" in Matthew, copied from Luke and expanded with considerable new material, is as to such new matter a forgery, confesses *CE.*: "Thus it is that the shorter form of the Lord's Prayer in Luke, xi, 2–4, is in almost all Greek manuscripts lengthened out in accordance with Matthew, vi, 9–13. Most *errors of this kind* proceed," etc. (*CE.* iv, 498.) I shall quote now the whole of *CE.'s* paragraph, admitting this and other "deliberate corruptions" of the New Testament texts, with clerical apologetic reasons therefor:

"(b) Errors Wholly or Partly *Intentional.*—Deliberate corruption of the Sacred Text has always been *rather* rare, Marcion's case being exceptional. Hort (Introduction (1896), p. 282) is of the opinion that 'even among the *unquestionably spurious* readings of the New Testament there are no signs of deliberate falsification of the text for dogmatic purposes.' Nevertheless it is true that the scribe *often selects* from various readings that which *favours* either his own individual opinion or *the doctrine that is just then more generally accepted.* It also happens that, in perfectly good faith, he changes passages which seem to him corrupt because he fails to understand them, that he adds a word which he deems necessary for the elucidation of the meaning, that he substitutes a more correct grammatical expression, and that he *harmonizes* parallel passages. Thus it is that the shorter form of the Lord's Prayer in Luke, xi, 2–4, is in almost all Greek manuscripts lengthened out in accordance with Matthew, vi, 9–13. Most errors of this kind proceed from inserting in the text marginal notes which, in the copy to be transcribed, were but variants, explanations, parallel passages, simple remarks, or perhaps the *conjectures* of some studious reader. All readers have observed the predilection of copyists for the most verbose texts and their tendency to complete citations that are too brief; hence it is that an *interpolation* stands a far better chance of being perpetuated than an omission." (*CE.* iv, 498.)

Thus, as to the "Lord's Prayer" in Matthew, its "variants" from Luke are confessed forgeries; every circumstance of the two origins is in contradiction. Like the whole "Sermon on the Mount," the Prayer is a composite of ancient sayings of the Scripture strung together to form it, as the marginal cross-references show throughout.

THE "UNKNOWN GOD" FORGERY

At this point I may call attention to a notable instance in *Acts* of a fraudulent perversion of text; Paul's use of the pretended inscription on the statue on Mars' Hill, "To the Unknown God," on which is based his famous harangue to the Athenians: "Whom therefore ye ignorantly worship, him declare I unto you." This omits the truth, for the whole inscription would have been fatal to his cause. The actual words of the inscription, together with some uncomplimentary comment on "Paul's" manipulation of the truth, are presented by the famous Catholic "Humanist" Erasmus. First he states the chronic clerical propensity to warp even Scripture to their deceptive schemes: "In general it is the public charter of all divines, to mould and bend the sacred oracles till they comply with their own fancy, spreading them (as Heaven by its Creator) like a curtain, closing together, or drawing them back as they please." Then he discloses the dishonest dodge of the great Apostle of Persecution: "Indeed, St. Paul minces and mangles some citations which he makes use of, and seems to wrest them to a different sense from that for which they were first intended, as is confessed by the great linguist St. Jerome. Thus when that apostle saw at Athens the inscription of an altar, he draws from it an argument for the proof of the Christian religion; but leaving out a great part of the sentence, which perhaps if fully recited might have prejudiced his cause, he mentions only the last two words, viz., *To the Unknown God*; and this, too, not without alteration, for the whole inscription runs thus: 'TO THE GODS OF ASIA, EUROPE, AND AFRICA, TO ALL FOREIGN AND UNKNOWN GODS'"! (Erasmus, *The Praise of Folly*, p. 292.) That the original Greek text of *Acts* used the *plural* "gods" is shown by the marginal note to Acts xvii, 23, in the King James Version. From this dreary exposure of "Gospel" forgeries we pass to the forged "Epistles of the Apostles."

THE FORGED EPISTLES, ETC.

There are 21 so-called Epistles or Letters found in the New Testament under the names of five different "apostles" of Jesus Christ. Making a significant reservation which seems to question the plenary inspiration of the Council of Trent, "There are," says *CE.*, "thirteen Epistles of St. Paul, and *perhaps* fourteen, *if*, with the Council of Trent, we consider him the author of the Epistle to the Hebrews." (*CE.* xiv, 530.) If Paul, the "apostle of the Gentiles," didn't write the Letter to the Hebrews, some Church Father must have forged it in his name. This was admitted by the early Fathers: "Tertullian ascribed it to Barnabas, and Origen confessed that the author was not known." (Reinach, *Orpheus*, p. 235; *CE.* xiv, 525; *New Comm.* Pt. III, p. 596.) "The Epistle to the Hebrews," says *EB.*, "had already been excluded from the group [of then supposed Pauline Epistles] by Carlstadt (1520), and among those who followed him in this were Luther, Calvin, Grotius, etc." (*EB.* iii, 3605.) So *CE.*'s cautious clerical reservation is justified, and the forgery of *Hebrews* in the name of Paul may be taken as established, the inspired Council of Trent to the contrary notwithstanding.

But the entire "Pauline group" is in the same forged class with Hebrews, says *EB.* after exhaustive consideration of the proofs, internal and external:

"With respect to the canonical Pauline Epistles, . . . there are *none of them by Paul;* neither fourteen, nor thirteen, nor nine or eight, nor yet even the four so long 'universally' regarded as unassailable. They *are all, without distinction, pseudographia* [false-writings, forgeries];—[it adds, with a typical clerical striving after saving something from the wreckage] this, of course, not implying the least depreciation of their contents. . . . The group . . . bears obvious marks of a certain unity—of having originated *in one circle*, at one time, in one environment; but *not of unity of authorship.*" (*EB.* iii, 3625, 3626.) They are thus all uninspired anonymous church forgeries for Christ's sweet sake!

Besides the so-called Pauline Epistles, another group, *i. e.* those attributed to Peter, John, Jude and James, is known as "Catholic Epistles," so called because addressed to the Church at large; "not one of them is authentic." (Reinach, *Orpheus*, p. 239; cf. *EB.*, under the various titles.) A third small group, Titus and 2 Timothy, are called "Pastoral Epistles" because they are addressed to pastors of churches. These, with Acts and the Book of Revelation, complete the tale of the Old-Christian Literature finally approved, in 1546, by the Council of Trent as divinely inspired, along with the inspired nonsense of Tobias, Judith, Bel and the Dragon, and like late Hebrew pious forgeries. With respect to the Apocalypse *Revelation*, attributed to the Apostle John, this has long been held to be impossible; nor is *Revelation* by the same writer as the Fourth Gospel falsely attributed to John, as we have seen. The results of ancient patristic denials and of modern critical scholarship are thus summed up: "John . . . is not the author of the Fourth Gospel; so, in like manner, in the Apocalypse we may have here and there a passage that may be traced to him, but the book as a whole is not from his pen. Gospel, Epistles, and Apocalypse all come from the same *school*." (*EB.* i, 199.) "The author of Revelation calls himself John the Apostle. As he was *not* John the Apostle, who died perhaps in Palestine about 66, he was a forger." (*Orpheus* p. 240.) The same can truly be said as to all the others.

It is impossible here to review the criticism of the twenty-three booklets individually. The comment of *EB.* on the Epistle to the Philippians, as not written by Paul, is fairly applicable to them all: "What finally puts an end to all doubt is the presence of unmistakable traces of *the conditions of a later period.* . . . More particularly, everything that points to *a considerably advanced stage in the development of doctrine*." (*EB.* iii, 3709.) This principle of criticism will be admitted by anyone; we have read it from *CE.* as "universally admitted," to wit: "A fundamental one is that a literary work *always betrays* the imprint of the age and environment in which it was produced." (*CE.* iv, 492.) Paul and Peter are reputed to have died together in Rome under Nero, in 64 (67) A. D. We have shown the impossibility of the existence of "New Testament" writings, and of a "church" during the first several generations which daily expected the end of the world and the sudden second coming of the Christ to set up the supernatural Kingdom of God, among, of, and for Jews only. More especially impossible is it, that a *Catholic* or "universal" Church among the far-scattered cities and nations of the Gentiles should have existed even in embryo within the scant, say 35 years between the reputed death of Jesus about 30 A. D. and the deaths of Paul and Peter in 64 (67) A. D. Most impossible would it have been for such Gentile Church then to have had the intricate hierarchical organization of Bishops, presbyters, deacons, priests, and "damnable heresies," portrayed as actually existing and in active function, by these apocryphal Epistles. They are self-evidently the product of an elaborately organized church,—just as they are more elaborately laid out and their several jurisdictions and functions defined in the admittedly

232

forged *Apostolic Constitutions* and *Canons*, forged in the names of the apostles in the following centuries. Nothing from ancient times can be or is more positively proven false and forged than every book and text of the New Testament, attributed to apostles. Who can now deny this?

THE "EPISTLE OF PETER" FORGERIES

Owing to the peculiar importance attributed to them by the Church, as among the most unquestionable of its "proofs" of authentic divine foundation and sanction, the so-called Epistles I and II of Peter call for a few words of special refutation. These two Peter books were, in truth, questioned and denied from the early days. Bishop Eusebius, the first Church Historian, (*HE.* III, iii, 25), says of II Peter that it was "controverted and not admitted into the canon"; and, says *EB.*, "The tardy recognition of II Peter in the early church supports the judgment of the critical school as to its unapostolic origin." (*EB.* iii, 3684.)

The critical considerations which lead to the rejection of both Epistles as "not Petrine" and "not of the apostolic age," may be very briefly summarized: That I Peter is addressed to the "sojourners of the Dispersion" in Asia Minor, which was Paul's reserved territory. "There is no trace of the questions mooted in the apostolic age. . . . The historical conditions and circumstances implied in the Epistle indicate, moreover, a time far beyond the probable duration of Peter's life. . . . The history of the spread of Christianity imperatively demands for I Peter a later date than 64 A. D.," the alleged date of Peter's death. The second Epistle, II Peter, is vaguely addressed to Christians in general (i, 1), yet in iii, 1, the writer inconsistently assumes that the First Epistle was addressed to the same readers; and he tells them (i, 6 and iii, 15) that they had already received instructions from him (ostensibly Peter), and also letters from Paul. "The relation of II Peter to I Peter renders a common authorship extremely doubtful. The name and title of the author are different. . . . The style of the two epistles is different. . . . It is late and unapostolic." (*EB. Peter, Epistles of,* iii, 3678–3685; cf. *New Comm.* Pt. III, pp. 639, 653, 654.) "The genuineness of I Peter cannot be maintained.

Most probably it was not written before 112 A. D." (*EB.* 2940.) "The two letters of Peter are Graeco-Egyptian forgeries." (Reinach, *Orpheus,* p. 240.) The Church pretense that I Peter was written at Rome ("Babylon") will be judged in its more appropriate place. In the early list of supposedly apostolic Books drawn up by Tertullian as accepted and read in the several Churches, while he "cites the Book of Enoch as inspired, . . . also recognizes IV Esdras, and the Sibyl, . . . he does not know James and II Peter. . . . He attributes Hebrews to St. Barnabas." (*CE.* xiv, 525.) Bishop Dionysius complains that his own writings "had been falsified by the apostles of the devil; no wonder, he adds, 'that the Scriptures were falsified by such persons.'" (*CE.* v, 10.) The "Peter" Books are other instances.

THE "GOD MANIFEST" FORGERY

In the King James or "Authorized" Version we read: "Great is the mystery of Godliness: God was manifest in the flesh," etc. (1 Tim. iii, 16.) In the "Revised Version" this "God manifest" forged interpolation is shamed out of the text, which there honestly reads: "He who was manifested in the flesh," etc. Thus the great "mystery of godliness," premised in the text, is no longer a mystery; and the fraudulent insertion into the text by some over-zealous Christian forger, seeking to bolster up an "apostolic" pedigree for the later "tradition" of the divinity of the Christ, is confessed. This pious "interpolation" was probably made at the time and by the same holy hands which forged the "Virgin-birth" interpolations into "Matthew" and "Luke." This passage is but one of a whole series of "Spurious Passages in the New Testament," catalogued by Taylor, in the appendix to his *Diegesis,* (p. 421). This pious fraud was first detected and exposed by Sir Isaac Newton.

THE "THREE HEAVENLY WITNESSES" FORGERY

Bishop Clement of Alexandria, writing around 200 A. D., thus quotes a comparatively trivial and inocuous passage from the forged First Epistle of St. John (v, 7),—which, through fraudulent tampering later became one of the "chief stones of the corner" of the Holy Church that the Fathers built: "John says: 'For there are three that

234

bear witness, the spirit, and the water, and the blood: and these three are one.' " (Clem. Alex., *Fragment from Cassiodorus*, ch. iii; *ANF.* iii, 576.) This is self-evidently the original text of this now famous, or infamous, passage. Turning now to the Word of God as found in the "Authorized" Protestant and in the Chaloner-Douay Version of the Catholic Vulgate, we read with wonder:

"7. For there are three that bear record in heaven, the Father, the Word, and the Holy Ghost: and these three are one.
"8. And there are three that bear witness in earth, the spirit, and the water, and the blood: and these three agree in one." (I John, v, 7, 8.)

Let us now turn to the same text, or what is left of it, in the Revised Version. Here we read, with more wonder (if we do not know the story of pious fraud behind it), what seems to be a garbled text:

"8. For there are three who bear witness, the Spirit, and the water, and the blood: and the three agree in one."

Erasmus first detected the fraud and omitted the forged verse in his edition of the Greek Testament in 1516. (*New Comm.* Pt. III, p. 718–19.) This verse 7, bluntly speaking, is a forgery: "It had been wilfully and wickedly interpolated, to sustain the Trinitarian doctrine; it has been entirely omitted by the Revisers of the New Testament." (Roberts, *Companion to the Revised Version*, p. 72.) "This memorable text," says Gibbon, "is condemned by the silence of the Fathers, ancient versions, and authentic manuscripts, of all the manuscripts now extant, above four score in number, some of which are more than 1200 years old." (Ch. xxvii, p. 598.) Speaking of this and another, Reinach says: "One of these forgeries (I John v, 7) was subjected to interpolation of a later date. . . . If these two verses were authentic, they would be an affirmation of the doctrine of the Trinity, at a time when the gospels, and Acts and St. Paul ignore it. It was first pointed out in 1516 that these verses were an interpolation, for they do not appear in the best manuscripts down to the fifteenth century. The Roman Church refused to bow to the evidence. . . The Congregation of the Index, on January 13, 1897, with the approbation of Leo XIII, forbade any question of the authenticity of the text relating to the 'Three Heavenly Witnesses.' It showed in this instance a wilful ignorance to which St. Gregory's rebuke is specially applicable: 'God does not need our lies.' " (*Orpheus*, p. 239.) But His Church does; for without them it would not be; and without the forged "Three Heavenly Witnesses," and the forged "Baptism Formula" of Matthew (xxviii, 19), there would be not a word in the entire New Testament hinting the existence of the Three-in-One God of Christianity. The Holy Trinity is an unholy Forgery!

Lest it be thought by some pious but uninformed persons that the foregoing imputation may be either false or malicious, we shall let *CE.* make the confession of shame, with the usual clerical evasions to "save the face" of Holy Church confronted with this proven forgery and fraud. From a lengthy and detailed review, under separate headings, of all the ancient MSS., Greek, Syriac, Ethiopic, Armenian, Old Latin, and of the Fathers, the following is condensed, but in the exact words of the text:

"The famous passage of the Three Witnesses [quoting I John, v, 7]. Throughout the past three hundred years, effort has been made to expunge from our Clementine Vulgate edition of the canonical Scriptures the words that are bracketed. Let us examine the facts of the case. [Here follows the thorough review of the MSS, closed in each instance by such words as: "The disputed part is found in none"; "no trace"; "no knowledge until the twelfth century," etc. etc.] The silence of the great and voluminous St. Augustine, [etc.] are admitted facts that militate against the canonicity of the Three Witnesses. St. Jerome does not seem to know the text,—[Jerome made the Vulgate Official Version].

"Trent's is the first certain œcumenical decree, whereby the Church established the Canon of Scripture. We cannot say that the Decree of Trent necessarily included the Three Witnesses"—[for reasons elaborately stated, and upon two conditions discussed, saying]: "Neither condition has yet been verified with certainty; quite the contrary, textual criticism seems to indicate that the *Comma Johanninum* was not at all times and everywhere wont to be read in the Catholic Church, and it is *not contained* in the Old Latin Vulgate. However, the Catholic theologian must take into account more than textual criticism"! (*CE.* viii, 436.)

A confessed forgery of Holy Writ consciously kept in the "canonical" text as a fraudulent voucher for a false Trinity—such is "The Three Heavenly Witnesses"—to the shame and ignominy of the Holy

236

Church of Christ, which "has never deceived any one," and which "has never made an error, and never shall err to all eternity"! This is not an error, however; it is but one more deliberate clerical "lie to the glory of God."

CHAPTER VI

THE CHURCH FORGERY MILL

"Nevertheless, the *forging* of papal letters *was even more frequent* in the Middle Ages than *in the early Church.*" (*CE.* ix, 203.)

LYINGLY FOUNDED ON forgery upon forgery, as has been made manifest by manifold admissions and proofs, the Church of Christ perpetuated itself and consolidated its vast usurped powers, and amassed amazing wealth, by a series of further and more secular forgeries and frauds unprecedented in human history—faintly approximated only by its initial forgeries of the fundamental gospels and epistles of the "New Testament of our Lord and Saviour Jesus Christ," and of the countless other forged religious documents which we have so far reviewed. These first relate to the infancy of the Church—constitute its false certificates of Heavenly birth and of Divine civil status. They are, as it were, the livery of heaven with which Holy Church clothed its moral nakedness until it attained maturer strength and became adept to commit the most stupendous forgeries for its own self-aggrandizement and for the completer domination of mind and soul of its ignorant and superstitious subjects.

The record which we shall now expose is the most sordid in human annals,—of frauds and forgeries perpetrated for the base purposes of greed for worldly riches and power, and designed so to paralyze and stultify the minds and reason of men that they should suffer themselves to be exploited without caring or daring to question or complain, and be helpless to resist the crimes committed against them. Into this chapter we shall compress in as summary manner as possible the revolting record of Christian fraud by means of forged title deeds to vast territories, forged documents of ecclesiastical power spiritual and temporal, forged and false Saints, Martyrs, Miracles and Relics

238

—surpassing the power of imagination or accomplishment by any other than a divinely inspired Church which "has never deceived anyone," and which "never has erred"—in its profound, cynical knowledge and exploitation of the degraded depths of ignorance and superstition to which it had sunk its victims, and of their mental and moral incapacity to detect the holy frauds worked upon them. This was the glorious Age of Faith—the Dark Ages of human benightedness and priestly thralldom—when Holy Church was the Divinely-illumined and unique Teacher of Christendom, and when the Christian world was too ignorant to be unbelieving or heretic,—for "unbelief is no sin that ignorance was ever capable of being guilty of."

In those "Dark Ages, as the period of Catholic ascendency is justly called" (Lecky, *History of European Morals*, ii, 14), "men were credulous and ignorant," says Buckle; "they therefore produced a religion which required great belief and little knowledge." Again he says: "The only remedy for superstition is knowledge. . . . Nothing else can wipe out that plague-spot of the human mind." It was, indeed, agrees *CE.*—(from 432 to 1461)—"an age of terrible corruption and social decadence" (xiv, 318); and of its mental state it says: "To such an extent had certain imaginary concepts become the common property of the people, that they repeated themselves as auto-suggestions and dreams." (*CE.* ix, 130.) But exactly this period—the "Dark Ages of Catholic ascendency,"—with centuries before and since, was the heyday of Holy Faith and Holy Church: it may well be wondered who was responsible for such conditions, when only Holy Church existed, in plentitude of power, the inspired Teacher of Christendom? During all these centuries, "the overwhelming importance attached to *theology* diverted to it all those intellects which in another condition of society would have been employed in the investigations of science." (Lecky, *History of Rationalism in Europe*, i, 275; cf. Bacon, *Novum Organum*, I, 89.) What else could be expected, was possible, when "a boundless intolerance of all divergencies of opinion was united with an equally boundless toleration of all falsehood and deliberate fraud that could favor received opinions?" (Lecky, *History of European Morals*, ii, 15.) Indeed, "few people realize the degree in which these superstitions were encouraged by the Church which claims infallibility." (Lecky, *Hist. Rationalism*, i, 79, n.) It is confessed:

239

THE FORGED APOSTOLIC CONSTITUTIONS

For more than a thousand years, until their fraud was exposed by modern historical criticism, these voluminous and most commodious forgeries formed the groundwork and foundation of some of the most extravagant pretensions of the Church and its most potent instrument of establishment and dominion of its monarchical government *The Apostolic Constitutions,* which we have admitted for naïveté of invention with respect to the Apostolic Prince Peter and Simon Magus in their magic contests in Rome, is in fact "a fourth-century pseudo-Apostolic collection. . . . It purports to be the work of the Apostles, whose instructions, whether given by them individually or as a body, are supposed to be gathered and handed down by the pretended compiler, [Pope] St. Clement of Rome, the authority of whose name gave fictitious weight to more than one such piece of early Christian literature. . . . The Apostolic Constitutions were held generally in high esteem and served as the basis for much ecclesiastical legislation. . . . As late as 1563 . . . despite the glaring archaisms and incongruities of the collection it was contended that it was the genuine work of the Apostles . . . could yet *pretend, in an uncritical age,* to Apostolic origin." (*CE.* i, 636.)

The *Constitutions,* pretending to be written by the apostles, laid down in minute detail all the intricacies of organization of several centuries later; there being elaborate chapters "concerning bishops," presbyters, deacons, all kinds of clergy, liturgies, and Church proceedings and services, undreamed of by "apostles," or in the "apostolic age." The prescriptions regarding the selection of bishops are quite democratic, and vastly different from present papal practices; the Churches, too, are distinctly episcopal and independent. The nature of these provisions, as well as the *grossly false and fraudulent* character of the whole, a vast arsenal of papal aggression, may be seen by the following passage in the apostolic first person: "Wherefore we, the twelve apostles of the Lord, who are now together, give you in charge those divine constitutions *concerning every ecclesiasti-*
240

cal form, there being present with us Paul, the chosen vessel, our fellow apostle, and James the bishop, and the rest of the presbyters, and the seven deacons. In the first place, therefore, *I Peter say*, that a bishop to be ordained is to be, as we have already, all of us, appointed, . . . chosen by the whole people, who, when he is named and approved, let the people assemble, with the presbyters and bishops that are present, on the Lord's day, and let them give their consent. . . . And if they give their consent," etc. (*Apost. Const.* VIII, 2, iv; *ANF.* vii, 481–482.)

THE FORGED "APOSTOLIC CANONS"

From the same pious forging hand, says *CE.* (i, 637), comes the related *Apostolic Canons* (composed about 400), "a collection of ancient ecclesiastical decrees concerning the government and discipline of the Church; . . . in a word, they are a handy summary of the statutory legislation of the primitive Church. . . . They claim to be the very legislation of the Apostles themselves, at least as promulgated by their great disciple Clement. Nevertheless, their claim to genuine Apostolic origin is quite *false* and untenable. . . . The text passed into Pseudo-Isidore, and eventually Gratian included (about 1140) some excerpts of these canons in his 'Decretum,' *whereby a universal recognition and use were gained for them in the law schools.* At a much earlier date, Justinian (in his sixth Novel) had recognized them as the work of the Apostles, and confirmed them as eccclesiastical law." (*CE.* iii, 279, 280.) Here the pious priests of God palmed off these self-serving forgeries on the great but superstitious Emperor and fraudulently secured their enactment into imperial law. In the same article is a description of "a larger number of forged documents appearing about the middle of the ninth century," among which "the Capitula of Benedict Levita, Capitula Angilrammi, Canons of Isaac of Langres,—above all the collection of Pseudo-Isidore" (*Ib.* 285), which arch-forgery we shall describe in its turn.

THE FORGED LIBER PONTIFICALIS

This famous, or infamous, official fabrication, "The Book of the Popes," is notorious for its spurious accounts of the early and mythical "successors of St. Peter." The *Liber Pontificalis* purports to be "a history of the popes, beginning with St. Peter and continued down to the fifteenth century, in the form of biographies" of their respective Holinesses of Rome. (*CE.* ix, 224.) It is an official papal work, written and kept in the papal archives, and preserves for posterity the holy lives and wonderful doings of the heads of the Church universal. "Historical criticism," says *CE.*, "has for a long time dealt with this ancient text in an exhaustive way . . . especially in recent decades." The *Liber* starts off in a typically fraudulent clerical manner: "In most of its manuscript copies there is found at the beginning a *spurious correspondence* between Pope Damasus and St. Jerome. These letters *were considered genuine* in the Middle Ages. . . . Duchesne has proved exhaustively and convincingly that the first series of biographies, *from St. Peter to Felix III* (IV, died 530) were compiled at the latest under Felix's successor, Boniface II (530–532). . . . The compiler of the Liber Pontificalis utilized also *some* historical writings, a number of *apocryphal* fragments (e.g. the *Pseudo-*Clementine Recognitions), the Constitutum Sylvestri, the *spurious* Acts of the alleged Synod of the 275 Bishops under Sylvester, etc., and the fifth century Roman Acts of Martyrs. Finally, the compiler distributed arbitrarily along his list of popes a number of papal decrees taken from unauthentic sources; he likewise attributed to earlier popes liturgical and disciplinary regulations of the sixth century. . . . The authors were Roman ecclesiastics, and some were attached to the Roman Court." (*CE.* ix, 225.) The general falsity of the *Liber* is again shown and the fraudulent use made of it by the later Church forgers, thus indicated: For instances, "in the 'Liber' it is recorded that such a pope issued a decree that has been lost, or mislaid, or *perhaps never existed at all.* Isidore seized the opportunity to *supply* a pontifical letter suitable for the occasion, attributing it to the pope whose name was mentioned in the 'Liber.' " (*CE.* v. 774.) Thus confessed forgery and fraud taint to the core this basic record for some five centuries of the official "histories" and Acts of Their Holinesses of the primitive and adolescent years of the Holy Church. Pope Peter and his "Successors" for a century or more are thus again proven pious fictions and frauds.

THE CHURCH FORGERY MILL
THE "CONVERSION OF CONSTANTINE" FRAUD

As several of the most monumental of these holy Church forgeries are associated with the first "Christian" Emperor, Constantine, and His contemporary Holiness, Pope Sylvester I (314–335), we may first notice the pious forged miracles which brought Constantine to Christ—rather to the Christians, and thus blightingly changed the history of the world. Constantine, Augustus of Rome, was the bastard son of the Imperator Constantius Chlorus and a Bythnian barmaid who became his mistress, and, later, by virtue of opulent gifts to the Church, was raised to Heaven as St. Helena. Constantine was a picturesque "barbarian" Pagan, with a very bloody record of family—and other—murders to his credit, mostly made to further his political ambitions. He was rival of the four Cæsars who shared the divided government, against whom he was engaged in titanic struggle, to win the sole crown of empire. The Christians were now become rather numerous in East and West, some two and a half or three millions out of the hundred millions of the Empire, sufficient to make their adherence and support important to the contestant who could gain control of them. To curry their favor and support Constantine adopted the tactics of his sportive father, Constantius, and made show of friendly disposition to them and even of possible adoption of the new faith.

The occasion and the purely selfish and superstitious motive for the alliance of Constantine with the Christians and their God, are described by the three noted Church historians of the period,—all writing after his death,—Eusebius, Socrates and Sozomen, all of whom give substantially the following account, here abbreviated from Eusebius, "Father of Church History," and an intimate of the Emperor, in his ludicrously laudatory *Life of Constantine:*

"Being convinced that he needed some more powerful aid than his military forces could afford him, on account of the wicked and *magical enchantments* which were so diligently practiced by the tyrant Maxentius, he sought divine assistance. . . . He considered, therefore, *on what God he might rely for protection and assistance.* While engaged in this enquiry, the thought occurred to him, that, of the

243

many emperors who had preceded him, who had rested their hopes on a multitude of gods, . . . none had *profited* at all by the pagan deities, whom they sought to propitiate . . . all had at last met with an unhappy end, . . . while the God of his father had given to him, on the other hand, manifestations of his power. . . . Reviewing, I may say, all these considerations, he judged it to be folly indeed to join in the idle worship of those who were no gods, . . . and *therefore* felt it incumbent on him to honor his father's God alone." (Eusebius, *Life of Constantine*, I, 27; *N&PNF*. I, 489; cf. Socrates, *Eccles. Hist.* I, 2; *Ib.* II, 1–2; Sozomen, *Eccles. Hist.* I, 3; *Ib.* p. 241.) So, Constantine chose the Christian's God to offset the "magical enchantments" of the Pagan gods in favor of his rival, Maxentius. The Christians flocked to his court and armies, and proud prelates of the Church hung around him and flattered his hopes. After several military successes aided by the Christians, the rival armies faced for decisive contest near the historic Milvian Bridge, in the environs of Rome, in the year 312. All are familiar with the fabulous priestly story of the miraculous Fiery Cross said to have been hung out in heaven just before the battle in the sight of Constantine and all his army, blazing with the famous device "*In Hoc Signo Vinces*—By this Sign Conquer"— though it was in Greek and read "*En Touto Nika,*"—and by virtue of which Constantine was himself conquered for Christ—or for His Church.

Here we may again see the "god in the machine"—a pious Christian fraud in the making, and watch its growth from nothing in proportion of wonder from lying Father to Father as it is handed on. Very remarkable it is, that Father Bishop Eusebius wholly omits this portentous event, though he devotes a large part of Book IX and all of Book X of his *History of the Church* (written in 324), to Constantine, and enthusiastically describes the Battle of the Milvian Bridge. Although he lugs divine intervention by the Christian God into every phase of the campaign, he is content with this colorful, naïve, account: "But the emperor (Constantine), stimulated by the divine assistance, proceeded against the tyrant, and defeating him in the first, second, and third engagements, he advanced through the greatest part of Italy, and came almost to the very gates of Rome. Then God himself drew the tyrant [Maxentius], as if bound in fetters, to a considerable

244

distance from the gates [*i.e.* to the Milvian Bridge] ; and here He confirmed those miraculous events performed of old against the wicked, and which have been discredited by so many, as if belonging to fiction and fable, but which have been established in the sacred volume, as *credible to the believer*. He confirmed them, I say, as true, by an immediate interposition of his power, addressed alike I may say to the eyes of believers and unbelievers. As, therefore, anciently in the days of Moses, the chariots of Pharaoh and his forces were cast into the Red Sea, thus also Maxentius, and his combatants and guards about him, sunk into the depths like a stone, when he fled before the power of God which was with Constantine." And, in commemoration of such signal divine aid, Constantine "immediately commanded a trophy of the Saviour's passion [a Cross] to be placed in the hand of his own statue" in Rome. (Eusebius, *HE.* IX, ix, p. 397–9.) And with all this miraculous embellishment, not a word of the Fiery Cross in Heaven, nor of the "miraculous conversion" of Constantine.

The pious fable, whether by him invented or not, is first recorded by Father Lactantius, tutor to Constantine's son Crispus before the pious father murdered his son ; he tells it—after Constantine's death—in its primitive and more modest form—a simple dream by night, in which Jesus the Christ appeared to Constantine, and was seen or heard—or was fabled—to tell Constantine to decorate the shields of his soldiers with the holy "sign of the Cross" before they went into the fight ; this he did and won the battle—*post hoc, ergo propter hoc:* Constantine may perhaps quite naturally have had such a dream—dreams have many vagaries, and the priests were ever at his ear. But the "heavenly sign," the Labarum or Monogram of Christ, which Constantine was by divine revelation or priestly suggestion directed to place on the shields of his soldiers, was no novel thing requiring a divine revelation, even in a dream, to suggest to the Christian priests of a Pagan emperor; "for it had been a familiar Christian symbol prior to his conversion." (*CE.* viii, 718.) By a similar divine revelation or priest-prompting, the Persian Cambyses had tied cats to the shields of his soldiers in their campaign in 525 B. c. against the cat-worshipping Egyptians, who thus dared not strike with their swords; the Christians worshipped the Cross of which the Pagans were superstitiously afraid, as we have seen from Father Lactantius. The result was at least the same, as related by Father Lactantius:

"And now a civil war broke out between Constantine and Maxentius. . . . At length Constantine . . . led his whole forces to the neighborhood of Rome, and encamped them opposite to the Milvian Bridge. . . . Constantine was *directed in a dream* to cause the *heavenly sign* to be delineated on the shields of his soldiers, and to proceed to battle. He did as he had been commanded, and he marked on their shields the letter X, with a perpendicular line drawn through it and turned round thus at the top, being the cipher of Christ. . . . The bridge in the rear (of Maxentius) was broken down. The *hand of the Lord prevailed*, and the forces of Maxentius were routed." (Lact., *On the Death of the Persecutors*, ch. xliv; *ANF*. vii, 318.)

These Christ-monogram crosses were probably, to the mind's eye of Lactantius, simple wooden or painted miniatures like the more life-sized one which a modern Holiness specially exorcised and sent along as an amulet or pious fetich of success on a recent disastrous Polar Expedition. But by the time Bishop Eusebius came on to embellish the tale, the model at least was a thing truly of beauty and wonder. In his *Life of Constantine*, the holy Bishop, who was on the Emperor's payroll, thus in substance relates:

"Constantine, having resolved to liberate Rome from the tyranny of Maxentius, and having meditated on the unhappiness of those who worshipped a multitude of idols, as contrasted with the good fortune of his own father Constantius, who had favoured Christianity, resolved to worship the One True God; and while he was in prayer to God that He would reveal Himself to him, and stretch forth His right hand to succor him, he had a vision after midday, when the sun was declining, in a luminous form over the sun, and an inscription annexed to it, 'Touto Nika'—(*by this conquer*), and at the sight of it he and all his forces were astounded, who *were spectators of the miracle*. . . . The following night, when Constantine was asleep, Christ appeared to him with that sign, which had been displayed to him in the heavens, and commanded him to make a standard according to the pattern of what he had seen, and to use it as a defense against his enemies; and as soon as it was day Constantine called together the workers in gold and precious stones, and ordered them to fashion it accordingly"—

246

(it being, by his description, certainly rich, if not gaudy). And Bishop Eusebius states that Constantine, "a long time after the event, *affirmed with an oath the truth* of what the Bishop had recorded" of this wonderful unhistorical fact. (Eusebius, *Life of Constantine*, I, 26–31; *N&PNF.* i, 489–491; *CE.* viii, 717–8; Wordsworth, *op. cit.* i, 358–9.) In a note to the last reference, the acute Protestant clerical mind, in eager defense of even the most absurd Catholic fables, is seen at play: "It has been objected (by Dean Milman and others) that it is incredible that a warlike motto on the Cross, converted into a military standard, should be suggested by Him who is Prince of Peace. But He Who is Prince of Peace is also Lord of Hosts; and Christ is revealed not only in the Psalms, but also in the Apocalypse, as a Mighty Warrior going forth conquering and to conquer." Clerical persons are really Funny-mentalists!

The pious Bishop Eusebius, exemplar of Christian historical unveracity to the glory of God and Church, begins his *Life of Constantine* with this rhapsody over Constantine dead: "When I raise my thoughts even to the arch of heaven, and there contemplate his thrice-blessed soul in communion with God himself, freed from every mortal and earthly vesture, and shining in a refulgent robe of light, honoured with an ever-blooming crown, and an immortality of endless and blessed existence, I stand as it were without power of speech or thought and unable to utter a single phrase, but condemning my own weakness, and imposing silence on myself, I resign the task of speaking his praises worthily to the immortal God, who alone has power to confirm his own sayings." (Eusebius, *Life*, I, 2; *N&PNF.* i, 481–2.)

Here is the thrice-blessed Holy Emperor's record before he was "freed from every mortal and earthly vesture," and before his blood-stained earthly vestments were exchanged for that refulgent robe of light in which he communed with God himself; this record is of the one item only of family murderings: Maximian, his wife's father, 310; Bassianus, his sister Anastasia's husband, 314; Licinianus, his nephew, son of his sister Constantina, 319; Fausta, his wife, in a bath of boiling water, 320; Sopater, Pagan philosopher and his former intimate Counsellor, 321; Licinius, his colleague Cæsar and his sister Constantina's husband, 325; with this last, and the beheading of his own son Crispus, 326, he fitly inaugurated and consecrated the celebrated Council of Nicæa, which he invoked to settle the famous puzzle, whether Jesus Christ, the Son, being born of the Father, were not consequently less ancient than his Sire, so that there was a time when the Begotten Son did not exist, and whether they were "of the same substance," or different. It may be noticed, that the devout "Christian" Emperor regarded this as a trifling matter of dispute not justifying the terrible row which it kicked up among the clericals, splitting the subjects of the Empire into throat-cutting factions for four centuries. In his opening Address to the Council which he called to establish peace among the priests, he turned to Alexander, Bishop of Alexandria, and to Arius, his presbyter, and their respective howling factions, and declared: "I understand, then, that the origin of this controversy is this—[the question stated by Alexander on this point, and the negative reply of Arius]. Let therefore both the unguarded question and the inconsiderate answer receive your mutual forgiveness. . . . For as long as you continue to contend about *these small and insignificant questions*, it is not fitting that so large a portion of God's people should be under the direction of your judgment, since you are thus divided among yourselves"! (Eusebius, *Life of Constantine*, II, 69–71; *N&PNF*. i, 516–7.)

With respect to the Christian Emperor's murderings, the good Bishop Lardner, with truly Christian modern moderation, admits that the murderous atrocities of Constantine above listed "seem to cast a reflection upon him"! But the holy Emperor was truly conscientious and scrupulously concerned for his soul's salvation on account of them; for it is recorded by the Church historian Sozomen, that Constantine is said to have sought first Pagan, then Christian, absolution from these murders, first from Sopater, then from the Christian bishops. He relates the anxious solicitations of the murderer thus: "It is reported by the Pagans that Constantine, after slaying some of his nearest relations, and particularly after assenting to the murder of his own son Crispus, repented of the evil deeds, and inquired of Sopater, the philosopher, concerning the means of purification from guilt. The philosopher, so the story goes, replied that such moral defilement could admit of no purification. The Emperor was grieved at this repulse; but happening to meet some bishops who told him that he would be cleansed from sin, on repentance and on baptism, he was delighted with their representations, and admired their doctrines, and became a Christian, and *led his subjects to the same faith*. It appears to me that this story was the invention of persons who desired to vilify the Christian religion. . . . It cannot be imagined the philosopher was ignorant that *Hercules* obtained purification at Athens by the celebration of the mysteries of Ceres after the murder of his children, and of Iphitus, his guest and friend. That the Greeks held that purification from guilt of this nature could be obtained, is obvious from the instance I have just alleged, and he is a false calumniator who represents that Sopater taught the contrary, . . . for he was at that period esteemed the most learned man in Greece." (Sozomen, i, 5; ii, 242–3.) It is said that the rebuff of Sopater denying Pagan absolution was the motive of his murder by the Christian Emperor. Howbeit, Constantine cautiously denied himself the saving Christian rite of baptism until he was on his deathbed, in Nicomedia, in the year of his forgiving Lord 337. (Euseb., *Life*, iv, 62; Soc., i, 39; Soz., ii, 34; *CE*. i, 709.) But none can deny the superiority of Christianity over Paganism in this point of saving grace. The Christian historian, however, clearly avers that some of the divinest sacraments of Christian Revelation, forgiveness of sin by God and absolution per priests, were ancient features of the Pagan "Mysteries," of which even sinful Pagan demigods might be the beneficiaries.

But "the mighty and victorious Constantine, adorned with every virtue of religion, with his most pious son, Crispus Cæsar, resembling in everything his father,"—as his doxology is sung—before the murder of Crispus—by good Bishop Eusebius (*HE*. ix, p. 443),—was rather dubiously a "practicing" Christian; he remained until death Pontifex Maximus, or Sovereign Pontiff of the Pagan religion, a title which the Christian Bishops could not erogate until the Christian Emperors abandoned it; he ordered the auspices or divination by inspection of the entrails of birds, and on his death, amply baptized with blood and by the deathbed heretic Christian rite, he was apotheosized according to Pagan custom and raised as a god to heaven—to rank along with his Christian Sainted Mother, St. Helena, of whom more anon.

In this ecstatic vision of the celestial beatitude of Constantine, the good Bishop Eusebius was, from the orthodox or "right-thinking" viewpoint sadly mistaken. Constantine went unshriven to Hell and everlasting torment; not indeed for his crimes but for his errant creed, as a disbeliever in the Divinity of Jesus Christ and in the Holy Trinity —which, indeed, had not been yet invented. The majority of the Council of Nicæa had by force and terrorism decreed that Jesus Christ was of the "same substance" as his father God, co-eternal and co-equal, *ergo* also God. But Constantine heretically disbelieved this inspired dogma; he banished Athanasius and other "Trinitarian" prelates; even "the death of Arius did not stay the plague. Constantine now favored none but Arians; he was baptized in his last moments by the shifty [Arian] prelate of Nicomedia; and he bequeathed to his three sons [themselves either Pagans or Arian heretics] an empire torn by dissensions which his *weakness and ignorance* had aggravated." (*CE.* i, 709.) To such a "weak and ignorant" Emperor is due, however, the salvation of Christianity from oblivion, and upon him is lavished the adulations of the now "indefectible Church" which his favor alone made possible. As for the pious Bishop Eusebius, he was himself an Arian heretic, and from his point of view he may have thought that he visioned Constantine glorious in Heaven. So much for divergent religious standpoints, which at the first Church Council "proved a beginning of strife, . . . bequeathed an empire torn with dissensions, . . . [until] the Catholic bishops, the monks, the *sword* of Clovis, and *the action of the Papacy*, made an end of it before the eighth century" (*CE.* i, 710),—thus nearly four hundred years of throat-cutting and persecutions before Constantine was finally proved a villainous heretic, the fatal effects of his "weakness and ignorance" overcome, and "Catholic Truth" began to assume its full sway undisputed through the long intellectual night of the Christian Dark Ages of Faith.

CHRISTIAN FORGERIES FOR POWER AND PELF

The "league with Death and covenant with Hell" whereby the new Paganism called Christianity became the official State religion being now signed and sealed, and soon enforced by laws of bloody persecution, we shall now admire the most monumental of the holy forgeries by which the Church consolidated its vast and nefast

250

dominion over the minds and bodies of the quickly degraded populations under its sway.

THE "CONSTANTINE" FORGERIES

A series of Church forgeries of the greatest magnitude and most far-reaching evil consequences grew up around the name of Constantine, forged in his name or falsely associated with it in the nefarious work of almost limitless larceny of territorial possessions and of papal sovereignty. A bit of historical background is necessary to properly appreciate the underground workings of Providence in disposing the success of these designs,—whereby, as said by Dr. McCabe, "Pope Adrian I induced Charlemagne to found the papal states by producing two of the most notorious and most shameless forgeries ever perpetrated: 'The Acts of St. Sylvester,' and 'The Donation of Constantine,' documents which mendaciously represented the emperor Constantine as giving most of Italy to the papacy, and which were fabricated in Rome in the eighth century and were used by the popes to maintain this gigantic fraud."

The intricate intriguing and conspiracies of the embryo papacy under their Holinesses Zacharias, Stephen II, Adrian I, Leo III, and of the semi-barbarian aspirants for the Frankish monarchy, Clovis, Charles Martel, Pepin, Charlemagne, cannot be here recounted. According to the picturesque account of Bishop St. Gregory of Tours— whose History is a thesaurus of the revolting social and moral degradation of the times, Clovis was converted as the result of his vow to the God of his Christian wife Clotilda, that if victory were granted to him in a great battle against the Alemanni, in which he was hard pressed, he would become a Christian. Miracles at once attested the Divine favor: "St. Martin showed him a ford over the Vienne by means of a hind; St. Hilary preceded his armies in a column of fire." (Von Ranke, i, 12.) It will be remembered that all the barbarian nations of the time were "heretic" Christians of the hated Arian sect, who denied the divinity of Christ and derided the Holy Trinity; the Franks thus became the only "orthodox" Christians and the defenders of the True Faith on behalf of the Popes. Winning the fight, Clovis and 3000 of his army were baptized on Christmas day by Bishop St. Remigius of

251

Rheims. When this good Bishop came to perform the baptismal ceremony on the king in the cathedral of Rheims, "the chrism for the baptismal ceremony was missing, and *was brought from heaven* in a vase (ampulla) borne by a dove. This is what is known as the Sainte Ampoule of Rheims, preserved in the treasury of the Cathedral of that City, and used for the coronation of the kings of France from Philip Augustus down to Charles X"! (*CE.* v, 71.)

FORGED DEEDS OF EMPIRE

The Merovingian kings of the Franks had become mere puppets in the hands of their "Mayors of the Palace," in league with the bishops of Rome. At last "Pepin addressed to the pope the suggestive question: 'In regard to the Kings of the Franks who no longer possess the royal power, is this state of things proper?' . . . Pope Zacharias replied that such a state of things was not proper—[that "he should be king who possessed the royal power"]. *After this decision the place Pepin desired was declared vacant.* . . . Still this external coöperation of the pope in the transfer of the Kingdom would necessarily *enhance the importance of the Church.* Pepin was also obliged to acknowledge the increased power of the Church by calling on it for moral [?] support." (*CE.* xi, 663.) In pay or reward for this "moral support" given by the Church, Pepin, it is said, gave to the Church some considerable territories around Rome, which at the incitation of the Pope he had wrested by arms from the neighboring Lombards.

THE FORGED LETTER OF ST. PETER

To this alleged gift Pepin was induced not alone by the sentiment of guilty gratitude to Zacharias and Stephen, the latter of whom crowned him King of the Franks in 751; for further persuasion His Holiness Stephen II procured from the Vatican Forgery Mill the identical autograph letter of St. Peter himself, prophetically addressed "To the King of the Franks," and so mystically worded that: "When Stephen II performed the ceremony of anointing Pepin and his son at St. Denis, it was St. Peter who was regarded as the mystical giver of the secular power"! (*CE.* xi, 663.) This cunning Papal

forgery and fraud is thus described by a high authority: "The pontiff
. . . dictated his letter in the name of the apostle Peter, closely
imitating his epistles, and speaking in a language which implied that
he was possessed of an authority to anoint or dethrone kings, and to
perform the offices, not of a messenger, of a teacher sent from God,
which is the highest characteristic of an apostle, but of a delegated
minister of His power and justice." (*Historians' History of the
World*, vol. viii, p. 557.)

Also: "The Frankish king received the title of the former representative of the Byzantine Empire in Italy, *i. e.* 'Patricius,' and was also
assigned the *duty of protecting the privileges* of the Holy See. . . .
After the acknowledgment of his territorial claims the pope was in
reality a ruling sovereign, but he had placed himself under the protection of the Frankish ruler, and had sworn that he and his people would
be true to the king" (*CE.* xi, 663),—the divine birthright thus swapped
for a mess of political potage: for over a thousand years since it has
been a mess indeed. Thus by conspiracy, fraud, and unrighteous conquest was laid the foundation of the sacred "Patrimony of Peter,"
and the unholy league between the papacy and the French kings, which
reached full fruition in the holy massacres of the Albigenses, of the
Vendée, and of St. Bartholomew.

A HOLY CONSPIRATION

The next step in the progress "conquering and to conquer" of
Christ's prostituted Church was on a broader stage and with yet
vaster consequences. Pepin died in 768, dividing his realms between his
two sons, Carloman and Charles, later "by the Grace of God" and
great villainy known to fame as Charles the Great or Charlemagne;
Charles receiving the German part, Carloman the French. On the
death of Carloman, in 771, Charles seized the Frankish kingdom. The
widow and young heirs of Carloman fled for protection and aid to
Desiderius, king of the Lombards, part of whose stolen territory the
pope held for God and Church. Desiderius was also father of the repudiated first wife of Charles; the holy matrimonial mess is thus
defined: "Charles was already, *in foro conscientiæ,* if not in Frankish
law, wedded to Himiltrude. In defiance of the pope's protest, Charles

married Desiderata, daughter of Desiderius (770); three years later he repudiated her and married Hildegarde, the beautiful Swabian. Naturally, Desiderius was furious at this insult, and the dominions of the Holy See bore the first brunt of his wrath." (*CE.* iii, 612.) Charles thereupon "had to protect Rome against the Lombard"; finally the Lombards were "put to utter rout"; Charles proceeded to Rome; and "history records with vivid eloquence the first visit of Charles to the Eternal City. . . . Charles himself forgot pagan Rome and prostrated himself to kiss the threshold of the Apostles, and then spent seven days in conference with the successor of Peter. It was then that he undoubtedly *formed many great designs for the glory of God and the exaltation of Holy Church*, which, in spite of human weaknesses, and, still more, *ignorance*, he did his best to realize." (*Ib.* 612.) The principal fruit of this weakness and ignorance of Charles seems to be that he could so easily let himself be duped by His Holiness through the enormous forgeries for Christ's sake that were now imposed upon him. In 774 Charles finally defeated Desiderius and "assumed the crown of Lombardy, and renewed to Adrian [now Holiness of Rome] the donation of territory made by Pepin." The "genuineness of this donation," as well as of "the original gift of Pepin," have been much questioned, says *CE.*, but are "now generally admitted,"—which is none too assuring; but another document, this time favorable to Charles, is just the other way: "The so-called 'Privilegium Hadriani pro Carolo' granting him full right to nominate the pope and to invest all bishops, is a *forgery*." (*CE.* xi, 612). Here is precisely the reason and only effective use of this forged "Donation of Constantine"—it was the basis for the inducement to Charlemagne to win the Lombard territories for the Church and to reinstate it in the "Patrimony of 'Peter," largely swollen by the pretended new gifts of the ambitious king, who, in the seven days' conference with His Holiness, had, undoubtedly, formed together "some great designs for the glory of God and the exaltation of Holy Church," now begun to be realized.

The quarter of a century passed, and much history was made. The Roman emperors ruled from Constantinople; Roman popes and kings were legitimately their liegemen; "the Emperor of Constantinople, legitimate heir of the imperial title," now becomes the victim of papal and kingly conspiration, thus brought to its climax: "On Christmas Day, 800, took place the principal event of the life of Charles. During the Pontifical Mass celebrated before the high altar beneath which lay the bodies of Sts. Peter and Paul, the pope (Leo III) approached him, placed upon his head the imperial crown, did him formal reverence after the ancient manner, saluted him as Emperor and Augustus and anointed him," while the Roman rabble shouted its approval. Thus, again by collusion and usurpation, began that Holy Roman Empire, of nefast history, which Bryce qualifies as "neither holy, nor Roman, nor empire"; but the Vicars of God were now well started on their way to worldly grandeur and moral degradation. Now for their forgeries.

THE POPE SYLVESTER FORGERIES

The monumental forgeries which were boldly used by their Holinesses to dupe Charlemagne and Christendom into recognizing the papal claim of right of ownership and sovereignty over a great part of Italy are a series of spurious documents harking in pretended date and origin back to the "first Christian emperor" Constantine and to His Holiness Pope St. Sylvester (314–335). About the name of Sylvester arose "the Sylvester Legend later surrounded with *that network of myth,* that gave rise to the *forged document* known as the Donation of Constantine." (*CE.* xiv, 257.) This fable, says Prof. Shotwell, "made its way, gathering volume as it went, reënforced eventually by a forged Donation, until it had imposed upon all Europe the conception of Sylvester as the potent influence behind Constantine's most striking measures and of Constantine himself as the dutiful servant of the See of Peter." (*See of Peter,* xxvi.) The extensive variety but common general nature of these Sylvester forgeries is thus indicated:

"At an early date legend brings Pope St. Sylvester into close relationship with the first Christian emperor, but in a way that is contrary to historical fact. These legends were introduced especially into the 'Vita beati Sylvestri,' and in the 'Constitutum Sylvestri'—an apocryphal account of an alleged Roman council which belongs to the Symmachian forgeries and appeared between 501 and 508, and also in the 'Donatio Constantini.' The accounts given in all these writings concerning the persecution of Sylvester, the healing and baptism of Constantine, the emperor's gift to the pope, the rights granted to the latter, and the council of 275 bishops at Rome, are entirely legendary" (*CE.* xiv, 370–371).

THE FORGED "DONATION OF CONSTANTINE"

"Ah, Constantine! to how much ill gave birth,
Not thy conversion, but that plenteous dower,
Which the first wealthy Father gained from thee!"
Dante, *Inferno*, xix, 115.

The *Catholic Encyclopedia*, artless revealer of the frauds of the Church for which it is an authorized spokesman, gives this account of the famous *Donatio Constantini*, which is describes as "*a forged document* of Emperor Constantine the Great, by which large privileges and rich possessions were conferred on the pope and the Roman Church. . . . It is addressed by Constantine to Pope Sylvester I (314–35), and consists of two parts. . . . Constantine is made to confer on Sylvester and his successors the following privileges and possessions: the pope, as successor of St. Peter, has the primacy over the four Patriarchs of Antioch, Alexandria, Constantinople, and Jerusalem, also over all the bishops in the world. . . . The document goes on to say that for himself the Emperor has established in the East a new capital which bears his name, and thither he removes his capital, since it is inconvenient that a secular emperor have power where God has established the residence of the head of the Christian religion. The document concludes with maledictions against all who violate these donations and with the *assurance that the emperor has signed them with his own hand and placed them on the tomb of St. Peter*. This document is without doubt a *forgery*, fabricated somewhere between the years 750 and 850. As early as the 15th century *its falsity was known and demonstrated*. . . . Its genuinity was yet occasionally defended, and the *document still further used as authentic*, until Baronius in his Annales Ecclesiastici admitted that the 'Donatio' was a forgery, whereafter it was soon universally admitted to be such. It is so clearly a fabrication that there is no reason to wonder that, with the *revival of historical criticism* in the 15th century, the true character of the document was at once recognized. . . . The document obtained wider circulation by its incorporation with the 'False Decretals' (840–850)." (*CE.* v, 118, 119, 120.)

By Lord Bryce a graphic sketch of this notorious fraud is given, with comments as to the mental and moral qualities of the priestcraft which it reflects. It is, he says, the—"most stupendous of medieval forgeries, which under the name of Donation of Constantine commanded for seven centuries the unquestioning belief of mankind. Itself a portentous falsehood, it is the most unimpeachable evidence of the thoughts and beliefs of the priesthood which framed it, sometime between the middle of the eighth and the middle of the tenth century. It tells how Constantine the Great, cured of his leprosy by the prayers of Sylvester, resolved, on the fourth day of his baptism, to forsake the ancient seat for a new capital on the Bosphorus, lest the continuance of the secular government should cramp the freedom of the spiritual, and how he bestowed therewith upon the Pope and his successors the sovereignty over Italy and the countries of the West." (Bryce, *Holy Roman Empire*, Ch. vii, p. 97; Latin text, extracts, p. 98.) In addition to these extraordinary investitures, all forms of imperial pomp, privileges and dignities were spuriously granted to the Pope and his clerics, "all of them enjoyed by the Emperor and his senate, all of them showing the same desire to make the pontifical a copy of the imperial office. The Pope is to inhabit the Lateran palace, to wear the diadem, the collar, the purple cloak, to carry the scepter, and to be attended by a body of chamberlains. Similarly his clergy are to ride on white horses and receive the honors and immunities of the senate and patricians," including "the practice of kissing the pope's foot, adopted in imitation of the old imperial court." (*Ib.* pp. 97–98.)

The grossness and absurdity of these stupendous forgeries, with their pious recitals of Constantine's leprosy cured by Sylvester's prayers, the consequent conversion and baptism of the Emperor in the Lateran font, and the abandonment of Rome by Constantine in order to leave it free for God's Vicar, just up from the catacombs, to ape imperial pomp, is made manifest by a moment's notice of dates, and recollection of contemporary history. Sylvester's Holiness dates from 314, he died in 335; Constantine in 337. Constantine's "conversion" by the "In Hoc Signo" miracle, was in 312, before Sylvester became pope; at no time did Constantine have leprosy, other than moral, therefore no physical cure was wrought by Sylvester's prayers, and certainly no moral cleansing worthy of note; Constantine was not baptized by Sylvester in Rome, but heretically received that rite long after Sylvester's death, and just before his own, in Nicomedia of Asia Minor. (*CE.* i, 709.) But Christians were too sodden in ignorance to know these things, and it was only with the "revival of historical criticism" which marked the beginning of the end of the Ages of Faith, that the truth was disclosed, or could have been perceived. In words that blast and sear with infamy the perpetrators and the conscious beneficiaries of this monumental fraud and forgery, Gibbon says:

"Fraud is the resource of weakness and cunning; and the strong, though ignorant barbarian, was often entangled in the net of sacerdotal policy. . . . The Decretal and the Donation of Constantine, the two magical pillars of the spiritual and temporal monarchy of the popes. This memorable donation was first introduced to the world by an epistle of Adrian the first, who exhorts Charlemagne to imitate the liberality, and revive the name, of the great Constantine. . . . So deep was the ignorance and credulity of the times, that the most absurd of fables was received, with equal reverence, in Greece and in France, and is still enrolled among the decrees of the canon law. The emperors, and the Romans, were incapable of discerning a forgery, that subverted their rights and freedom. . . . The popes themselves have indulged a smile at the credulity of the vulgar; *but a false and obsolete title still sanctifies* their reign; and, by the same fortune which has attended the decretals and the Sibylline Oracles, *the edifice has subsisted after the foundations have been undermined.*" (Gibbon, *Rise and Fall of the Roman Empire*, ch. xiv, pp. 740, 741, 742.)

The falsity of the *Donation* was first alleged and proved, in 1440, by the acute Humanist critic Lorenzo Valla, who has the exposure of more than one Church forgery to his credit, and who narrowly escaped the Holy Inquisition; and yet the document *"was still used as authentic"* by Holy Church until the great Churchman critic Baronius forced the confession of the fraud, but the Church still for centuries clung to the fruits of its fraud, and would not give them up, with their revenues

258

and rotten "sovereignty." The ancient forgery of "Donation" was finally canceled by Italian patriot bayonets in 1870, and the stolen territories of "Peter's Patrimony" restored to United Italy. That these Papal territories were not of "divine" right, nor of even forged muniments which can be plausibly urged, is thus confessed: "All of this, of course, is based upon painstaking *deductions* since no document has come down to us either from the time of Charlemagne or from that of Pepin." (*CE.* xiv, 261.) This is confirmed, and the precarious nature of the usurped tenure thus stated: "Nominally, Adrian I (772–775) was now monarch of about two-thirds of the Italian peninsula, but his sway was little more than nominal. . . . It was in no slight degree owing to Adrian's political sagacity, vigilance, and activity, that *the temporal power of the Papacy did not remain a fiction of the imagination.* . . . The temporal power of the popes, of which Adrian I must be considered the real founder." (*CE.* i, 155–156.)

In a paragraph which gives a word of credit to Valla for his exposure of the forgeries of the "Donation" and the immense and remarkable "Pseudo-Areopagite" Forgeries, previously mentioned, the vast extent of the output of the Vatican Forgery-Mill—and the evil persistence of the Church in clinging to them after exposure, is thus admitted: "Lorenzo Valla, 1440, counselled Eugenius IV not to rely on the Donation of Constantine, which he *proved to be spurious.* . . . It was Valla who first denied the authenticity of those writings which for centuries had been going about as the treatises composed by Dionysius the Areopagite. *Three centuries later* the Benedictines of St. Maur and the Bollandists *were still engaged in sifting out the true from the false in patristic literature,* in hagiology, in the story of the foundation of local churches" (*CE.* xii, 768),—such Liars of the Lord were the pious parasites of Holy Church.

THE "SYMMACHIAN FORGERIES"

Among the sheaf of forged documents above confessed by *CE.* are the so-called "Symmachian Forgeries," forged by or in behoof of His Holiness Pope St. Symmachus (498–514), products of the Church Forgery Mill operated by the Pope to further papal pretentions of the independence of the Bishops of Rome from the just criticisms and judgment of ecclesiastical tribunals, and putting them above law clerical and secular. Whenever there was need for false precedents, a simple turn of the crank of the wheel of the papal forgery-mill produced them just to order. Thus, in this instance: "During the dispute between Pope St. Symmachus and the anti-pope Laurentius, the adherents of Symmachus drew up four apocryphal writings called the 'Symmachian Forgeries'. . . . The object of these forgeries was to produce alleged instances from earlier times to support the whole procedure of the adherents of Symmachus, and, in particular, the position that the Roman bishop could not be judged by any court composed of other bishops." (*CE.* xiv, 378.) Our Confessor is careful twice to impute these confessed forgeries to the "adherents" of His Holiness; but they were forged for him, used, of course with his knowledge and consent, to further his cause in the dispute; they are thus distinctly forgeries by His Holiness.

THE "FALSE DECRETALS" FORGERIES

A "record of forgery in the interest of the Church which resembles nothing else in history," in the words of Dr. McCabe, has so far been presented; the climax and capstone is now to be seen in what Voltaire terms "the boldest and most magnificent forgery which has deceived the world for centuries," the so-called "False Decretals of Isidore." While it is true, as said by Reinach, that "never yet has the papacy acknowledged that for 1000 years it made use of forged documents for its own benefit," yet we have seen a thousand confessions of the *fact* of forgery, and either the admission or the inevitable inference, that they were used by the Church in the fraudulent obtention of viciously illicit ends. The following brief paragraph of further confession from *CE.*, is pregnant with suggestion of the moral depravity of popes and priests, the whole Church, the sodden ignorance of the votaries of Holy Church, cleric and lay, the darkness of the life of mind and spirit till at the "Renaissance" men were reborn indeed, and after slow and painful growth of learning and of freeing from fear, began to expose the Church in its forgeries, frauds, and vices. The tone of *CE.* is quite apologetical for this particular monument of Church fraud; it seeks palliation in the conditions of ignorance of the Middle Ages; but it forgets that Holy Church purposely produced this ignorance, and that Popes and Church are illumined by the Holy Ghost of their God against all ignorance and error so that its "Church never has erred and never shall": but maybe this statement is itself an error. *CE.* now speaks for this gigantic fraud of Holy Church, the False Isidorian Decretals:

"Isidorian Decretals is the name given to certain apocryphal letters contained in a collection of canon laws composed about the middle of the ninth century. . . . Nowadays every one agrees that these *so-called papal letters are forgeries*. These documents, *about 100 in number*, appeared suddenly in the ninth century and are nowhere mentioned before that time. . . . The pseudo-Isidore makes use of documents written long after the times of the popes to whom he attributed them. The popes of the first three centuries are made to quote documents that did not appear until the fourth or fifth century, etc. Then again there are endless anachronisms. The *Middle Ages were deceived by this huge forgery*, but during the *Renaissance men of learning* and the canonists generally *began to recognize the fraud*. . . . Nevertheless the *official edition* of the 'Corpus Juris,' in 1580, upheld the genuineness of the false decretals." (*CE.* vi, 773.) But the God-guided Vicars of God knew they were forgeries.

"Upon these spurious decretals," says Hallam, "was built the great fabric of papal supremacy over the different national churches; a fabric which has stood after its foundations crumbled beneath it; for no one has pretended to deny, for the last two centuries, that the imposture is too palpable for any but *the most ignorant ages* to credit." (*History of the Middle Ages*, Bk. VII, ch. ii, 99.) Though on their face affecting only matters spiritual and causes ecclesiastical, they soon had all Europe strangled as in the tentacles of a giant octopus, by a process thus described by Lord Bryce: "By the invention and adoption of the False Decretals it (the Church) had provided itself with a legal system suited to any emergency, and which gave it unlimited authority through the Christian world in causes spiritual and over persons ecclesiastical. Canonical ingenuity found it easy in one way or another to make this include all causes and persons whatsoever; for crime is always and wrong is often sin, nor can aught be done anywhere which may not affect the clergy." (*Holy*

Roman Empire, ch. x, 152.) "The Forgery," says Dr. Draper, "produced an immense extension of papal power, it displaced the old Church government, divesting it of the republican attributes it had possessed, and transforming it into an absolute monarchy. It brought the bishops into subjection to Rome, and made the pontiff the supreme judge of the whole Christian world. It prepared the way for the great attempt, subsequently made by Hildebrand, to convert the states of Europe into a theocratic priest-kingdom, with the pope at its head." (*Conflict between Religion and Science*, ch. x, 271.)

The false pretense back of the huge forgery was that the documents included were genuine papal letters and decretals of the earliest popes, thus carrying back the Church's late pretensions to the very first of the Church and to the pretended and fictitious associates and "successors" of Peter. These spurious documents are taken up seriatim by the critical Father Dupin, as outlined in *ANF.*, viii, and each in its turn pronounced a forgery. From the "Introductory Notice to the Decretals," I think it pertinent to quote the following paragraph:

"These frauds, which, pretending to be a series of 'papal edicts' from Clement and his successors during the *ante-Nicene ages*, are, in fact, the manufactured product of the *ninth century*,—the most stupendous imposture of the world's history, the most successful and the most stubborn in its hold upon enlightened nations. Like the mason's framework of lath and scantlings, on which he turns an arch of massive stone, the Decretals served their purpose, enabling Nicholas I to found the Papacy by their insignificant aid. That swelling arch of vanity once reared, the framework might be knocked out; but the fabric stood, and has borne up every weight imposed upon it for ages. Its strong abutments have been *ignorance and despotism.* Nicholas produced his *flimsy framework of imposture,* and amazed the whole Church by the audacity of the claims he founded upon it. The age, however, was unlearned and uncritical; and, in spite of remonstrances from France under lead of Hincmar, bishop of Rheims, the West patiently submitted to the overthrow of the ancient Canons and the Nicene Constitutions, and bowed to the yoke of a new canon law, of which these frauds were not only made an integral, but the essential, part. The East never accepted them for a moment. . . . The Papacy created the Western schism, and contrived to call it 'the schism of the Greeks.' The Decretals had created the Papacy, and they enabled the first Pope to assume that communion with himself was the test of Catholic communion: hence his excommunication of the Easterns, which, after brief intervals of relaxation, settled into the chronic schism of the Papacy, and produced the awful history of the medieval Church in Western Europe." (*ANF*. viii, 601.)

THE FORGED DECRETUM OF GRATIAN

Great and pernicious as were the influences of the forged Isidorian Decretals, there yet remained a step to bring the Forger Church to the height of its age-old ambitious scheme to completely imitate the olden Roman Empire and dominate the world. "The School of Bologna had just revived the study of Roman law; Gratian sought to inaugurate a similar study of canon law. But while compilations of texts and official collections were available for Roman law, or 'Corpus juris civilis,' Gratian had no such assistance. He therefore adopted the plan of inserting the texts in the body of his general treatise; from the disordered mass of canons, collected from the earliest days, he selected the law actually in force. . . . The *science of canon law* was at length established." (*CE*. ix, 57.) But this disordered mass out of which Gratian selected was very largely the old forged reliances of the Church; thus in making his selections "Gratian alleges *forged* decretals" (*CE*. iv, 1),—including the Constantine Donation, the Isidore forgeries, *etc*. Yet, withal, "the 'Decretum' of Gratian was considered in the middle of the twelfth century as a *corpus juris canonici, i. e.* a code of ecclesiastic laws then in force." (*CE*. iv, 671.) It clinched the rivets in the forged fetters of the Church upon the neck of Christendom, and sanctioned the principles which in the next century were invoked to found and justify the Holy Inquisition. Of this celebrated document, the beginning of the "science" of Church legistic sophistry, Draper says: "The most potent instrument of the new papal system was Gratian's Decretum, which was issued about the middle of the Twelfth Century. It was a mass of fabrications. It made the whole Christian world, through the papacy, the domain of the Italian clergy. It inculcated that it is *lawful to constrain men to goodness, to torture and execute heretics, and to confiscate their property; that to kill an excommunicated person is not murder;* that the pope, in *his unlimited superiority to all law, stands on an equality with the Son of God."* (*Conflict between Science and Religion,* ch. x, p. 273.)

THE FULL FRUITION OF FORGERY

As said by Dr. McCabe: "There was no need of further forgeries. Now securely established on its basis of forged donations of temporal power and territory, forged decretals stating its spiritual powers, and forged lives of saints and martyrs, the papacy was so strong and prosperous that the popes actually dreamed of forming a sort of United States of Europe with themselves as virtual presidents. Nearly every country was in some ingenious way made out to be a fief of the Papacy and bound to recognize the Pope as its feudal monarch." (*LBB.* 1130, 44–5.)

Founding thus its religion, that newer form of Paganism called Christianity, on falsehood and forged "Scripture" documents; its pretensions to superiority and "primacy" on gross "interpolations" into the forged Scriptures; its spurious claims to territorial possessions and temporal sovereignty upon forged title-deeds and Donations; its "spiritual" and legal domination upon forged Church law and constitutions,—thus was the visible Church of Christ brought to the perfection of its power and degradation. For fifteen hundred years every document under which it claimed, it forged; it forged until it had no longer need of forgery, for nothing was left to forge; forged so long as it could forge with impunity, for with the Renaissance its old forgeries began to be discovered and exposed, and it could commit undetected no further documentary forgeries.

Such is the objective side, as it were, of the Christian religion and its Church. Its subjective side, the subjugation of its victims by imposed ignorance and superstition, through limitless forgeries of miracles, martyrs, saints and relics, remains to be briefly noticed as a sort of by-product of the Holy Church Forgery Mill.

THE FRUSTRATED EMS REVOLT

Not to mention the revolt known as the "Reformation," the discovery of the unholy and criminal practices of the Church in the matter of its claims of primacy and jurisdiction, as defined in the Isidorian False Decretals, led to one tardy and half-way ecclesiastical effort of revolt within the Roman Church, which might have developed into something worth while to humanity as a whole, but that "political considerations" intervened to bring it to naught. It is cited simply by way of historical reminder, and as suggestive of what may yet be effectively accomplished to the full extent of popular repudiation.

The Congress of Ems, in 1786, was a gathering of the representatives of a number of German Archbishops and other clergy, "for the purpose of protesting against papal interference in the exercise of episcopal powers and fixing the future relations between these archbishops and the Roman pontiff. . . . On 25 August, 1786, these archiepiscopal representatives signed the notorious 'Punctation of Ems,' consisting of twenty-three articles, which aimed at making the German archbishops practically independent of Rome. *Assuming that Christ gave unlimited power of binding and loosing to the Apostles and their successors,* the bishops, the 'Punctation' maintains that all prerogatives and reservations which were not actually connected with the primacy during the first three centuries *owe their origin to the Pseudo-Isidorian decretals, universally acknowledged as false,* and, hence, that the bishops must look upon all interference of the Roman Curia with the exercise of their episcopal functions in their own dioceses as encroachments on their rights. . . . It may easily be seen that the articles of the 'Punctation' lower the papal primacy to a merely honorary one and advocate an independence of the archbishops in regard to the pope which is entirely incompatible with *the Unity and Catholicity of the Church of Christ*,"—such are the unctuous objections made by Christ's Church. However, the Punctations were "ratified by the Archbishops, and sent to Emperor Joseph II for his support. The Emperor was pleased with the articles, and would have pledged his unqualified support *if* his councillors had not *for political reasons* advised him otherwise." (*CE.* v, 409–10.) Rejecting the "assumption," now known to be false and forged, that Christ had anything at all to do with Peter and the Rock-and-Keys forgery, all may now feel free to discard these primitive "Scripture" frauds just as all the others of the Church which have been exposed as false and abandoned.

FORGERY IN CHRISTIANITY

FORGED SAINTS,
MARTYRS AND MIRACLES

"Throughout Church History there are miracles so well authenticated that their truth cannot be denied." (*CE.* x, 345.)

" . . . after the working of Satan with all power and signs and lying wonders." (2 Thess. ii, 9.)

Look we for a moment on this picture and on that, the counterfeit presentment, to slightly adapt *Hamlet,* of two modern Miracles, published to the world in the Metropolitan press,—a sort of study in what may be called Comparative Credulity. The first, although they "read it in the paper," no Christian or no Infidel will hesitate to laugh at or commiserate as a ridiculous superstition, taken advantage of by greedy priests to exploit their credulous dupes. Only benighted heathen Buddhists religiously believe the following:

"Peasant says Buddha Arose and Cured Him.
"Chinese Tale of a 'Miracle' by Stone Image Causes Religious
"Revival at Peking

"Peking, Sept. 7. A tremendous revival of religious superstition is being experienced by the Buddhists of Peking and vicinity, because an aged peasant vows that he was cured (last week) of a long-standing ailment when one of the stone images of the sitting Buddha at Palichwang Pagoda rose to its feet, stepped forward, and then raised its arm in sign of benediction.

"The old peasant, named Chang Chi-kuang, is a farmer, living near Palichwang Pagoda [a short distance from the Peking gate of the Great Wall]. Chang Chi-kuang, who, his neighbors say, has long suffered from lung trouble [passing by with a load of garden-truck which he was carrying afoot into the city], became exhausted, and stopped for rest and for refuge from the heat in the shade of an old tree near the Pagoda, which is thirteen stories high and was built 500 years ago, and in the days of the Ming emperors.

"Chang Chi-kuang, as he lay resting in the shade, found his gaze focused on the figure of the sitting Buddha, in the third story of the Pagoda. . . . The figure rose, Chang says, took two steps, and raised its arms with a gesture of blessing. At this point, according to Chang, he nearly swooned. He then fell to his knees in devout worship, and when he raised his head after a long prayer the Buddha had gone back to the place and position of the last few hundred years.

"The story of this miracle has spread rapidly. Every day now thousands

266

of pilgrims go to Palichwang from Peking and from the villages and farms in this part of the province.

"Both sides of the road from the Peking gate to the Pagoda are now lined with booths where incense *is sold,* and hundreds of Lama priests, with their begging bowls, now *reap a rich gathering from the pious pilgrims.* . . . And old Chang swears that he is now in better health than he has enjoyed since he was a boy." (Special Correspondence of the *New York Times,* October 14, 1928.)

The foregoing religious news item is found archived in the "Morgue" of the Great "Religious" Daily under the discrediting caption "Superstitions"; it will be noticed that the word "Miracle" in the headline is printed in quotes. No such skeptical note is to be found in its next—Christian—report.

Hundreds of millions of pious priest-ridden Christians do believe the following, testified under oath in a military court,—other hundreds of millions will regard it as they do the Buddhist tale above related,—and the Christian one below:

"Soldier's Story of a Miracle Saves Him at Court-Martial.

"Croatian newspapers tell how a miracle figured as a determining factor in a court-martial trial. During the Austrian invasion of Upper Italy a Croatian soldier was suspected of having stolen a pearl necklace from a statue of the Holy Virgin in a pilgrims' church and was brought to trial. He admitted having taken the necklace, but insisted that it was a gift to him.

"He said that he had gone into the church to pray, and had lamented before the statue of the Virgin the sad lot of his family, whom he had been compelled to leave destitute. Thereupon, he said, the Holy Virgin bowed her head, and took the pearls from her neck and handed them to him.

"The Court could not venture to reject this story offhand, as there was general belief in the miracle-working power of the statue. So it referred the matter to two Bishops, asking them whether such a miracle was within the domain of possibility.

"The Bishops were perplexed. If they answered 'Yes,' they might be protecting a rascal. But if they said 'No,' they would destroy the repute of that church for miraculous power and phenomena. Finally they answered that such a miracle was within the range of possibility; and in consequence the soldier was acquitted.

"But the Colonel of the regiment to which the soldier belonged was either skeptical or of a most prudent turn of mind, for after the verdict of the court had been announced he issued his order: 'In future no soldier under my command is permitted, under heavy penalty, to accept a gift from anybody.' " (*New York Times*, Oct. 10, 1926.)

It is not reported whether this episcopal pair of men of God were unfrocked for perjury and the perversion of justice, or even gently chided by His Holiness.

The "lying wonders" of saints, martyrs and miracles are so intimately related, and so inextricably interwoven the one form of pious fraud with the others, that they must needs be bunched together in this summary treatment of but few out of countless thousands, millions perhaps, of them recorded for faith and edification in the innumerable "Acts" and "Lives" and wonderworks of the Holy Church of God. Those which are here mentioned are picked at random from a turning of the pages of the fifteen ponderous tomes of *CE.*, where they may be verified under the respective names of the Saints. With scarcely an exception they are soberly recounted as actual verities of the past and living realities of the present.

The degraded state of mind of the Faithful, and the moral depravity of the Church which for nearly two millennia, and yet into the twentieth century, peddles these childish fables as articles of Christian faith, may be known by the mere fact of the existence in limitless numbers of these precious myths. Founded by Jean Bolland, of Belgium, in the early years of the 1600's, an important Church Society, known as the Bollandists, yet exists and industriously carries on its labors. "This monumental work, the *Acta Sanctorum* of the Bollandists, has become the foundation of all investigation in hagiography and legend." (*CE.* ix, 129.) For some three centuries its task has been and yet is, to edit and publish in official *Acta Sanctorum* the Lives and "Acts"—authenticated records—of every Saint in the Holy Roman Calendar. Arranged in order of dates of their "feast days," so numerous is this heavenly mill-made host that up to the month of October over 25,000 officially authenticated Saints are recorded; the Saint-library of the Society has over 150,000 saintly volumes. As it costs about $50,000 to turn out one Saint by canonization, and "not less than $20,000" for beatification or the bestowal of the title of Blessed (*CE.* ii, 369),—the Church revenue from this single source is seen to have been considerable.

268

THE CHURCH FORGERY MILL

Holy Church is very careful and conscientious in its processes of certifying Saints; at least two allegedly genuine and fully authenticated miracles must be *proven* to have been performed by the candidate alive or worked by his relics after death, before final payment is required and the name certified as a Saint to the Calendar. A fairly modern instance showing this clerical scrupulosity may be cited, that of the Venerable Mary de Sales, who died in 1875:—"Wishing to save the world over again, Jesus Our Lord had to use means till then unknown," that is, "The Way" invented by Mary; but no miracles were satisfactorily proved to justify making her a Saint; however, her sanctity was proved, and she was decreed Venerable; some miracles must later have been proved up in her behalf, or the requisite $20,000 paid,—for in 1897 her Beatification was decreed. (*CE.* ix, 754.)

However, even Infallibility may be fooled sometimes, even if not all the time. The most notorious instance is that of the holy Saint Josaphat, under which name and due to an odd slip of inerrant inspiration, the great Lord Buddha, "The Light of Asia," was duly certified a Saint in the Roman Martyrology (27 Nov.; *CE.* iii, 297). More modernly, in 1802, an old grave was found containing a cadaver and a bottle "supposed to contain the blood of a martyr"; the relics were enshrined in an altar, and the erstwhile owner of the remains was duly and solemnly canonized as Saint Philomena; but this was "by mistake"; and thus were fooled two infallible Holinesses, Gregory XVI and Leo III. (*CE.* xii, 25.)

"SPECULA STULTORUM"

Before thumbing the wonder-filled pages of *CE.* to pick out from thousands, sundry examples of the inspired and truthful histories of Saints and Martyrs, recorded for the moral edification and mental stultification of the Faithful of the Twentieth Century,—when only the miracles of Science in benefit of humanity are recognized by many as real,—we may note the comment of that Exponent of "Catholic Truth" conscientiously questioning a case or two of the certified Saint-records. With respect to one of the notable female Saints, St. Catherine of Alexandria, it is candidly explained: "Unfortunately these Acts have been transformed and distorted by fantastic and diffuse descriptions which are entirely due to the imagination of the

narrators—[a notable one of whom was the great Bossuet of France],
—who cared less to state authentic *facts* than to charm their readers
by recitals of the marvellous." (*CE.* iii, 445.) Speaking of another
case, St. Emmeram: "The improbability of the tale, the fantastic
details of the Saint's martyrdom, and the fantastic account of the
prodigies attending his death, show that the writer, *infected by the
pious mania of his time*, simply added to the facts *imaginary details*
supposed to redound to the glory of the martyr." (v, 406.) How often
have we heard from this same exponent of "Catholic Truth" this same
exculpation of priestly pious mendacity in wondermongering!

Questioning a few such instances, implicitly carries with it the moral
assurance that all the others, related as unquestioned fact, are free
from such taint of fraud,—are, indeed, among those "miracles so
well authenticated that their truth cannot be denied." Indeed, the reality and authenticity of very many, for example, the bubbling blood of
the sixteen-hundred-year-old martyred St. Januarius, and its frequent
efficacy in stopping eruptions of the Volcano Mt. Vesuvius, are explicitly affirmed by the *Catholic Encyclopedia*, which is now to be quoted.
It may be suspected, however, that even these certified Saint-tales,
like so many others, are fakes and "belong to the common foundation
of all legends of saints" (*CE.* i, 40), the fraud of which is confessed.

Very portentous is this St. Januarius, "martyred" about 305:
"His holy blood is kept unto this day in a phial of glass, which being set
near his head, bubbles up as though it were fresh," in the church of
St. Januarius at Naples; a long article is replete with plenary proofs
of this and other miracles of the Saint. He was thrown into a fiery
furnace, but the flames would not touch him and his companions; his
executioner was struck blind, but the Saint cured him. His holy remains were brought to Naples, and are famous on account of many
miracles, as recorded in the official papal "present Roman Martyrology," a longer account being given in the Breviary, as quoted in
these words of assurance: "Among these miracles is remarkable the
stopping of eruptions of Mount Vesuvius, whereby both that neighborhood and places afar off have been like to be destroyed. It is *also well
known and is the plain fact*, seen even unto this day, that when the
blood of St. Januarius, kept dried up in a small glass phial, is put in
sight of the head of the same martyr, it is wont to melt and bubble up
270

in a very strange way, as though it had but freshly been shed. . . . For more than four hundred years this liquefaction has taken place at frequent intervals"; elaborate tests, the last reported in 1902 and 1904, have been unable to account for the phenomenon except as due to miracle. "It has had much to do with many conversations to Catholicism. Unfortunately, however, allegations have often been made as to the favourable verdict expressed by scientific men of note, which are not always verifiable. The supposed testimony of the great chemist, Sir Humphrey Davy, who is declared to have expressed his belief in the genuineness of the miracle, is a case in point." (*CE*. viii, 295–7.)

This Holy Bottle of blood might well be borrowed to stop the present eruption of Mt. Ætna in Sicily, which (as this is written), is destroying several populous towns and "the most intensively cultivated land in Sicily," by a torrent of lava a mile in width, against which the local Patron seems impotent: "The lava struck Mascali, a town of 10,000 inhabitants last night, just after the townsfolk had finished celebrating the feast of their patron, St. Leonardo, whose statue was carried on the shoulders of four old men." (*N. Y. Herald-Tribune*, Nov. 8, 1928.) But such pious thaumaturgies do not seem to be overly potent this year. In this unguarded *a priori* surmise I find myself mistaken, and apologize to the gentle reader and to Holy Church. There is no need to borrow the Vesuvius-stopping Blood of St. Januarius; Sicily has its own local Ætna-stopper, the Holy Veil of St. Agatha, "which, according to tradition, has arrested the flow of lava toward Catania in the past." This sacred and potent relic, a bit tardily, after several large towns have been wiped out, has now "been exposed in the cathedral by order of the Archbishop Cardinal Nava, who also issued an appeal for prayers by all in the diocese. He exhorted the population to remain calm and *maintain their faith*. On previous occasions prayers to St. Agatha were said when an eruption occurred, and the lava stopped short before Nicolosi and Linguaglossa, twenty-five miles north of Catania." (*N. Y. Sun*, Nov. 13, 1928.) This tardy exposition of the Relics and order for prayers,—after scientific examinations and airplane explorations had shown that the fiery forces were about spent and "the lava showing signs of solidification and emissions from the smoking mountain lessening,"—is somewhat posthumous, or humorous; the devastation was already wrought. If

271

ignorant Christendom, and legends were fabricated by the thousands to authenticate the spurious bits of bone." (*LBB.* 1130, p. 40.) "Such," says *CE.*, "are the 'Martyrium S. Polycarpi,' admitting, though it does, much that may be due to the pious fancy of the eye-witness"; also "the 'Acta SS. Perpetuæ et Felicitas.' "

The Saint-mill of Holy Church began operations very early, or reached for grist far back into antiquity for the beginnings of its Calendar of Saints. The first Saint who greets us among the countless hordes of canonized Holy Ones is no less a primitive personage than St. Abel, the younger son and second heir of our mythical Father Adam, of Eden, who was canonized by Jesus Christ himself, we are told, "as the first of a long line of prophets martyred for justice's sake," as is the clerical interpretation of Matt. xxiii, 34–35, "That upon you may come all the righteous blood shed upon the earth, from the blood of Abel unto the blood of Zacharias,"—a bloody invocation in later centuries peculiarly appropriate to the Church of Jesus Christ. This is a genuine surprise, for no miracles wrought by St. Abel are recorded, and no generous canonization fees seem to have been paid for his account into the Treasury of the Lord in Rome.

OLD PAGAN STUFF

Many of the Pagan gods were converted into Christian Saints, and seem to have brought over with them the special curative or prophylactic attributes for which they were invoked as specifics. Indeed, the whole system was purely Pagan: "Cures, apparitions, prophecies, visions, transfigurations, stigmata, pleasant odour, incorruption,— all these phenomena were also known to antiquity. Ancient Greece exhibits stone monuments and inscriptions which bear witness to cures and apparitions in ancient mythology. History tells of Aristeas of Proconnessus, Hermotimus of Claxomenæ, Epimenides of Crete, that they were *ascetics and thereby became ecstatic*, even to the degree of the soul leaving the body, remaining far removed from it, and being able to appear in other places." (*CE.* ix, 129.) The pious plan of temporal salvation in the Ages of Faith is thus historically vouched: "The whole social life of the Catholic world before the Reformation was animated with the idea of protection from the citizens of heaven.

There were patrons or protectors in various forms of illness, as for instance: St. Agatha, diseases of the breast; Apollonia, toothache; Blaise, sore throat; Clare and Lucy, eyes; Benedict, against poison; Hubert, against bites of dogs." (*CE.* xi, 566.) "Catania honours St. Agatha as her patron saint, and throughout the region around Mt. Ætna she is invoked against the eruptions of the volcano, as elsewhere against fire and lightning." (i, 204.)

To the infamous sanctified fable of St. Hugh are imputed sundry unholy accusations and persecutions against the Jews,—(here only repeated because they are falsely affirmed in the inspired Bull of Canonization. A Christian child was lyingly alleged to have been crucified by the Jews; the earth refused to receive its body, and it was thrown into a well, where it was found with the marks of crucifixion upon it; nineteen Jews were infamously put to death for the fabulous crime, and ninety others were condemned to death but released, for the sake of greed, upon payment of large fines; "Copin, the leader, stated that it was a Jewish custom to crucify a boy once a year"! (*CE.* vii, 515); similar infamies of falsehood are related in connection with St. William of Norwich. (*CE.* xv, 635.)

Here is a monumental miracle with every assurance of verity. "St. Winefride was a maiden of great personal charm and endowed with rare gifts of intellect. The fame of her beauty and accomplishments reached the ears of Caradoc, son of the neighboring Prince Alen." She refused all his advances; frightened by his threats she fled towards the church where her uncle St. Beuno was celebrating Mass. "Maddened by a disappointed passion, Caradoc pursued her and, overtaking her on the slope above the site of the present well, he drew his sword and at one blow severed her head from the body. The head rolled down the incline and, where it rested, there gushed forth a spring." St. Beuno, hearing of the tragedy, left the altar, and accompanied by the parents came to the spot where the head lay beside the spring. "Taking up the maiden's head he carried it to where the body lay, covered both with his cloak, and then re-entered the church to finish the Holy Sacrifice. When Mass was ended he knelt beside the Saint's body, offered up a fervent prayer to God, and ordered the cloak which covered it to be removed. Thereupon Winefride, as if awakening from a deep slumber, rose up with no sign of the severing of the head except

274

a thin white circle round her neck. Seeing the murderer leaning on his sword with an insolent and defiant air, St. Beuno invoked the chastisement of heaven, and Caradoc fell dead on the spot, the popular belief being that the earth opened and swallowed him. Miraculously restored to life, Winefride seems to have lived in almost perpetual ecstacy and to have had familiar converse with God." The place where this signal miracle occurred was at the time called "Dry Hollow," but with its miraculous spring its name was changed to Holywell, and it stands there in Wales to this day, a bubblingly vocal witness to the verity of this holy yarn. Born in 600, beheaded and reheaded at sweet sixteen, she died Nov. 3, 660; "her death was foreshown to her in a vision by Christ Himself." (*CE.* xv, 656–657.) "For more than a thousand years this Miraculous Well has attracted numerous pilgrims; documents preserved in the British Museum give us its history, with the earliest record of the miraculous cures effected by its waters. These ancient cures included cases of dropsy, paralysis, gout, melancholia, sciatica, cancer, alienation of mind, blood spitting, etc. etc., also deliverance from evil spirits." (*CE.* repeats the history of St. Winefride, or Gwenfrewi, in vii, 438.)

St. Wolfgang, by a unique miracle, "forced the devil to help him build a church."—*Et id omne genus—ad nauseam.* Such is a handful of the holy chaff of faith, purveyed by Holy Church to all Believers to this day. Scores of like saint-lies are here omitted to save space.

These gross and degrading impostures by forged miracles not only went unrebuked and unchecked by the Vicars of God; many of the vice-Gods were among the most prolific miracle-mongers of the ages of Faith. One of the most notorious wonder-workers and wonder-forgers of Holy Church was no less a personage than His Holiness Pope St. Gregory the Great (590–604). He has the doubtful distinction of being the author of four celebrated volumes of *Dialogi,* which are a veritable thesaurus of holy wonders. From this treasury of nature-fakery we have seen the old Pagan example, affirmed as Christian fact by Gregory, as quoted by *CE.,* of the man carried off by mistake by the Angel of Death, but restored to life when the oversight was discovered. He also relates a great flood of the Tiber which threatened to destroy Rome, until a copy of His Holiness's "Dialogi" was thrown into the swollen waters, which immediately subsided, and the Holy City was thus saved. His Holiness solemnly records the case of an awful bellyache suffered by a holy nun, which he avers was caused by her having swallowed a devil along with a piece of lettuce which she was eating without having taken the due precaution of making the sign of the cross over it to scare away any lurking imps of Satan; and this devil, when commanded by a holy monk to come out of the nun, derisively replied: "How am I to blame? I was sitting on the lettuce, and this woman, not having made the sign of the cross, ate me along with it!" (*Dial.* lib. i, c. 4.) When elected Pope in 590 the city of Rome was afflicted by a dreadful pestilence; the angels of the angry God of all mercies were relentlessly flinging fiery darts among the devout Christian populace. To conjure away the pestilence —due perhaps primarily to the filth of the Holy City and its inhabitants—His Holiness headed a monkish parade through the stricken city, when of a sudden he saw the Archangel Michael hovering over the great Pagan mausoleum of Hadrian, just in the act of sheathing his flaming sword, while three angels with him chanted the original verses of the *Regina Cœli;* the great Pope made the Sign of the Cross and broke into Hallelujahs—(that is, "Praise to Yahveh," the old Hebrew war-god). In commemoration of the wondrous event, the pious Pope built a Christian chapel, dedicated to St. Michael, atop the Pagan monument, and over it erected the colossal statue of the Archangel in the sword-sheathing act, which stands there in Rome to this day—the Castel Sant' Angelo, in enduring proof of the miracle and of the veracity of papal narratives. (*CE.* vi, 782.) The authorship of this monkish Hymn to the Queen of Heaven being unknown, pious invention supplied its true history: "that St. Gregory the Great heard the first three lines chanted by angels on a certain Easter morning in Rome while he walked barefoot in a great religious procession, and that the Saint thereupon added the fourth line." (*CE.* xii, 719.) Such is ecclesiastical "history."

The literary attainments of His Holiness Gregory were tempered, if not corrupted, by his holy zeal, for "in his commentary on Job, Gregory I warns the reader that he need not be surprised to find mistakes of Latin Grammar, since in dealing with so holy a work as the Bible a writer should not stop to make sure whether his cases and tenses are right." (Robinson, *The Ordeal of Civilization*, p. 62.) However, his zeal for more material things was not thus hampered: "Pope Gregory I contrived to make his real belief in the approaching end of the world yield the papacy about 1800 square miles of land and a revenue of about $2,000,000. He used bribes, threats and all kinds of stratagems to attain his ends." (McCabe, *LLB.* 1130, p. 40.)

His Holiness Gregory I was himself one of the greatest thaumaturgists of the Ages of Faith: "the miracles attributed to Gregory are very many." (*CE.* vi, 786.) When Mohammed was forging his inspired Book of Koran, the illuminating spirit, in the guise of a dove, would perch on his shoulder and whisper the divine revelations into his ear,—a miracle which none but quite devout Mohammedans believe. But Peter the Deacon, in his *Vita* of His wonder-working Holiness, records that when St. Gregory was dictating his *Homilies on Ezekiel:* "A veil was drawn between his secretary and himself. As, however, the pope remained silent for long periods at a time, the servant made a hole in the curtain and, looking through, beheld a dove seated on Gregory's head with his beak between his lips. When the dove withdrew its beak the holy pontiff spoke and the secretary took down his words; but when he became silent the secretary again applied his eye to the hole and saw that the dove had replaced its beak between his lips." (*CE.* vi, 786.) No good Christian can doubt, after this proof, that their Holinesses are constantly and directly inspired and guided by the Holy Ghost, as Holy Church assures. Wonderful as this bit of Gregory's history is, to recommend him to lasting remembrance, "his great claim to remembrance lies in the fact that he is the real father of the medieval papacy." (*Ibid.*) These qualities of the Holy Father which we have noticed may to an extent explain some of the eccentricities of the Medieval Papacy.

FORGED AND FAKED RELICS

"Making every allowance for the errors of the most extreme fallibility, the history of Catholicism would on this hypothesis represent an amount of imposture probably unequalled in the annals of the human race."
Lecky, *History of Rationalism*, i, 164.

As loathsome an example as is to be found in the annals of Christian apologetics for fraud and imposture is this from *CE.*, following a long and revolting exposition of the Christian frauds with respect to holy Relics of the Church:

"Still, it would be presumptuous in such cases to blame the action of the ecclesiastical authority in permitting the continuance of a cult which extends back into remote antiquity. [*i. e.* into Paganism.] . . .

"Supposing the relic to be spurious, NO DISHONOR IS DONE TO GOD by the continuance of an error handed down in perfect good faith for many centuries"! (*CE.* xii, 337.)

It may well be that the holy God of the Christians is immune to dishonor by worship through lying Christian frauds; but one may question the dishonor to the human mind wrought by the impostures of God's Vicars and his Church, cozening men into holy faith in lies; to say nothing of the shaming dishonor of Church and priest, who with utter want of good faith and common honesty created and fostered all these degrading Churchly cheats.

Before viewing some of these priestly impostures, never once rebuked or prevented by pope or priest, but, rather, industriously stimulated by them for purposes of perpetuating ignorance and superstition, and of feeding their own insatiate avarice, *CE.* will be invoked to give a graphic, though clerically casuistic and apologetic review of the debauchery of morals and mind which made possible these scandalous unholy practices of Holy Church.

"Naturally it was impossible for popular enthusiasm to be roused to so high a pitch in a matter which easily lent itself to error, fraud, and greed for gain, without at least the occasional occurrence of many grave abuses. . . . In the Theodosian Code the sale of relics is forbidden (vii, ix, 17), but numerous stories, of which it would be easy to collect a long series, beginning with the writings of Pope St. Gregory the Great and St. Gregory of Tours, prove to us that many unprincipled persons found a means of enriching themselves by a sort of trade in these objects of devotion, *the majority of which no doubt were fraudulent.* At the beginning of the ninth century the exportation of the bodies of martyrs from Rome had assumed the proportions of a regular commerce, and a certain deacon, Deusdona, acquired an unenviable notoriety in these transactions. What was in the long run hardly less disastrous than fraud or avarice, was the keen rivalry between religious centers, and the *eager credulity fostered* by the desire to be known as the possessor of some unusually startling relic. In such an atmosphere of lawlessness doubtful relics came to abound. There was always disposition to regard any human remains accidentally discovered near a church or in the catacombs as the body of a martyr . . . the custom of making facsimiles and imitations, a custom which persists to our own day in the replicas of the Vatican statue of St. Peter—[itself a fraud]—or of the Grotto of Lourdes—all these are causes adequate to account for *the multitude of unquestionably spurious relics* with which the treasuries of great medieval churches were crowded. . . . Join to this the large license given to the occasional unscrupulous rogue IN AN AGE NOT ONLY UTTERLY UNCRITICAL but often curiously morbid in its realism, and it becomes easy to understand the multiplicity and extravagance of the entries in the relics inventories of Rome and other countries.

"Such tests [to secure the Faithful against deception] were applied as the historical and antiquarian science of that day were capable of devising. Very often, however, this *test* took the form of *an appeal to some miraculous sanction,* as in the well known story repeated by St. Ambrose, according to which, when doubt arose which of the three crosses discovered by St. Helena was that of Christ, the healing of a sick man by one of them dispelled all further hesitation. Nevertheless it remains true that many of the more important ancient relics *duly exhibited* for veneration in the great sanctuaries of Christendom or even at Rome itself must now be pronounced to be either certainly spurious or open to grave suspicion. To take one example of the latter class, the boards of the crib (Præsæpe)— a name which for more than a thousand years has been associated, as now, with the basilica of Santa Maria Maggiore—can only be considered to be of doubtful authenticity. . . . Strangely enough, an inscription in Greek uncials of the eighth century is found on one of the boards, the inscription having nothing to do with the Crib but being apparently concerned with some commercial transaction. It is hard to explain its presence on the supposition that the relic is authentic. Similar difficulties might be urged against the supposed 'Column of the Flagellation' venerated at Rome in the church of Santa Prassede, and against many other famous relics. . . . Neither has the church ever pronounced that any particular relic, not even that commonly venerated as the wood of the Cross, is authentic; but she *approves* of honour being paid to those relics which with reasonable probability are believed to be genuine, and which are invested with due ecclesiastical sanctions." (*CE.* xii, 737.) Such sophistry!

The pettifogging sophistry of the foregoing argumentation, as of that which follows from the same clerical source, needs no comment. The Church of God, headed by his own Vicar General on earth, divinely guided against all error in matters of faith and morals, and which can detect the faintest taint of heresy of belief further than the most gifted bird of rapine can scent a carcass, can make no apology for permitting these degrading superstitions, which it not only tolerates but actively propagates and encourages, for the rich revenues they bring in. What a catalogue of its most sacred mummeries is branded with the infamy of fraudulent in the following:

"The worship of *imaginary* saints or relics, devotion based upon *false* revelations, apparitions, *supposed* miracles, or *false notions* generally, is usually *excusable in the Worshipper on the ground of ignorance* and good faith; but there is no excuse for those who use similar means to exploit popular credulity for their own pecuniary profit. The originators of such falsehoods are liars, deceivers, and not rarely thieves; but a milder judgment should be pronounced on those who, after discovering the imposture tolerate the improper cultus [!] . . . The Catholic devotions which are connected with holy places, holy shrines, holy wells, famous relics, etc., are commonly *treated as superstitions* by non-Catholics. . . . It must be admitted that these *hallowed* spots and things have occasioned many legends; that popular credulity was in some cases the principal cause of their celebrity; that here or there *instances of fraud can be adduced;* yet, for all that, the principles which guide the worshipper, and his good intentions, are not impaired by an undercurrent of error as to facts. [!] Moreover . . . *the Church is tolerant of 'pious beliefs' which have helped to further Christianity* [!] Thus, alleged saints and relics are suppressed as soon as discovered, but belief in the *private revelations* to which the feast of *Corpus Christi, The Rosary, the Sacred Heart,* and many other devotions owe their origin is neither com-

280

manded nor prohibited; here each man is his own judge. . . . *The apparent success which so often attends a superstition can mostly be accounted for by natural causes.* . . . When the object is to ascertain, or to effect in a general way, one of two possible events, the law of probabilities gives an equal chance to success and failure, and success does more to support than failure would do to destroy superstition." (*CE.* xiv, 340, 341.) All these holy cults are thus confessed frauds and superstitions fostered by ecclesiastic greed.

Let us remember that no True Church in Christendom can be built and consecrated without a box of dead man's bones or other fetid human scraps and relics deposited under the holy altar of God. The decree of the second council of Nice, A. D. 787, reaffirmed by the Council of Trent in 1546, forbade the consecration of any Church without a supply of relics. (*CE.* xii, 737.) Thus the ancient superstition is sanctioned and its observance made mandatory; an unceasing demand is created, and the market supply is more than equal to the pious demand. Hence the great and valuable, and fraudulent, traffic above confessed and clerically palliated.

THE "INVENTION OF THE CROSS," ET AL

"The Legend as to the discovering of the Cross of Christ" (*CE.* vii, 203). The Holy City, Jerusalem, was twice destroyed by the Romans, in 70 A. D. by Titus, and again as the result of the rebellion of Bar-Cochba, 132–135 A. D. The work was peculiarly thorough; not one stone was left upon another; the site was plowed over as a mark of infamy, and the ground is said to have been sown with salt so that nothing might ever grow there again: though pious myths soon flourished exuberantly. Later a pagan city was established on the site, named Ælia Capitolina, and a great Temple of Venus was erected on a suitable spot. Over two centuries later, about 326 A. D., a great and venerated Catholic lady Saint made a pious pilgrimage to the Holy City, namely, St. Helena, sainted mother of the new "Christian" Emperor Constantine. This is the St. Helena who got her start as a Pagan barmaid in a wild country village; she fell into the graces of the Roman Imperator Constantius as he marched through the country, became his mistress by "*concubinatus,*" and bore unto him and the Church him who was afterwards the godly Emperor Constantine. (*CE.* iv, 300.) Upon the pilgrimage of the pious Dowager-mother to Jerusalem, great pomp and ceremony attended her visit, under the auspices of the good Bishop Macarius. By order of the Bishop and in honor of the Christian Saint, the Temple of Venus was torn down; it was found to have been built over an empty rock grave— therefore identically the authentic sepulchre of Jesus Christ. Is it true, that this destroyed Temple of Venus and the inclosed Holy Sepulchre were inside the walls of the City, while the Gospels inspiredly aver that the grave was outside the walls: a trifling discrepancy for Faith.

Rummaging the ruins, a vaulted underground room or cellar was found: its wonderful contents make to pale into triviality the lately discovered tomb-treasures of Tut-ankh-Amen. There propped against the cellar-wall was the whole apparatus of the Cruci-fiction: the three identical Crosses whereon had hung the Christ and the two thieves; the very Nails wherewith they had been fastened; the autograph trilingual Inscription set by Pilate over the head of the Christ; the precise Spear which had pierced his side; the cruel Crown of Thorns which tore his brow; the holy Seamless Coat which he had worn and for which the Roman soldiers gambled in the hour of death (it's curious that the winner should have left it behind); the sacred Shroud in which the dead God was buried. The Pilatic Inscription was not *in situ;* it had evidently been knocked off and lay apart, a "separate piece of wood, on which were inscribed in white letters in Hebrew, Greek and Latin, the following words: 'Jesus of Nazareth, the King of the Jews,'" as recorded by Sozomen, the Church historian. (*Eccles. Hist.* ii, 1; *N&PNF.* II, p. 258.)

Due to its unfortunate separation from its original position, it was for the moment impossible to distinguish the True Cross of Christ from those of the thieves. A miracle was vouchsafed, however, to identify the real Cross of the Christ: the True Cross bowed itself down before the Saintly Empress; or, a sick woman—or a sick man—was cured upon touching the True Cross after having tried the other two in vain—according to which priestly version is the more truthful. Sozomen (*supra*) says that it was "a certain lady of rank in Jerusalem who was inflicted with a most grievous and incurable disease," whose miraculous curing attested the True Cross; "a dead person was also restored to life" by its thaumaturgic touch:—"all as predicted by the prophets and by the Sibyl." Some tinge of dubiety may be thrown upon the report of Bishop Macarius, who made the wondrous discoveries, first recorded by the Church historians Socrates, about 439 A. D. (*Eccles. Hist.* I, xvii), and Sozomen, who wrote a little later (*Eccles. Hist.* II, i), by the fact that the earliest Church Historian, the very informative and fabling Bishop Eusebius (d. 340), in his *Life of Constantine* (III, iii, and III, xxviii), gives a very circumstantial account of the visit of the ex-Empress St. Helena to Jerusalem, and of the erection of a Christian Church over the Holy Sepulchre, but he is silent as the grave about the discovery of any Cross of Christ or any of the other holy marvels. The notable event is known, in Church parlance, as "The Invention of the Cross"—which exactly it was.

The subsequent "history" of the Cross of Christ is a tangle of typically clerical contradictions and impossibilities. "Very soon after the discovery of the True Cross, its wood was cut up into small relics and scattered throughout Christendom." (*CE.* iv, 524.)

"We learn from St. Cyril of Jerusalem (*before 350*) that the wood of the Cross, discovered about 318, [it was in 326] *was already distributed throughout the world.*" (*CE.* xii, 736.) But these assurances of St. Cyril and of *CE.* seem out of harmony with the accredited history of the capture and asportation of the reputed integral True Cross by Chosroes (Khosru) II, King of Persia, who took Jerusalem in 614, massacring 90,000 good Christians, captured the Cross of Christ among his booty, and carried it off *whole* in triumph to Persia! (*CE.* iii, 105),—with results very disastrous to the Faith: "The shock which religious men received through this dreadful event can hardly now be realized. The imposture of Constantine bore bitter fruit; the sacred wood which had filled the world with its miracles was detected to be a helpless counterfeit, borne off in triumph by deriding blasphemers. All confidence in the apostolic powers of the Asiatic bishops was lost; not one of them could work a wonder for his own salvation in the dire extremity." (Draper, *The Intellectual Development of Europe*, i, 328; Gibbon, p. 451.) The truly miraculous nature of this True Cross is thus described by Draper: "The wood of the Cross displayed a property of growth, and hence furnished an abundant supply for the de-

283

mands of pilgrims and an unfailing source of pecuniary profit to its possessors. In the course of subsequent years there was accumulated in the various churches of Europe, from this particular relic, a sufficiency to have constructed many hundred crosses." (*Op. cit.* i, 309.) On a great porphyry column before the Church of St. Sophia at Constantinople, stood a statue of the Pagan god Apollo; the face was altered into the features of the Emperor Constantine, and the Nails of the True Cross, set around like rays, were used to garnish the crown upon his head. Another of these holy Nails has for centuries adorned and consecreated the crown of the emperors of the Holy Roman Empire. The horses of a regiment of cavalry could probably be shod with the copious supply of these Holy Nails now venerated as sacred relics.

"It is remarkable," says *CE.*, "that St. Jerome, who expatiates upon the Cross, the Title, and the Nails, discovered by St. Helena, says nothing either of the Lance or of the Crown of Thorns, and the silence of Andreas of Crete in the eighth century is still more surprising." But in due time this oversight was piously repaired. Bishop Gregory of Tours, among other faithful Church chroniclers, produces the Crown of Thorns, and, as an eyewitness to it, "avers that the thorns in the Crown still looked green, a freshness which was miraculously renewed every day"; which episcopal assurance, skeptically remarks *CE.*, "does not much strengthen the historical testimony for the authenticity of the relic." But, "in any case, Justinian, who died in 565, is stated to have given a thorn to St. Germanus, which was long preserved at Saint-Germain-des-Près, while the Empress Irene sent Charlemagne several thorns which were deposited by him at Aachen. . . . In 1238 Baldwin II, the Latin Emperor of Constantinople, anxious to obtain support for his tottering empire, offered the Crown of Thorns to St. Louis, King of France. It was then actually [in pawn] in the hands of the Venetians as *security for a heavy loan*, but it was redeemed and conveyed to Paris, where St. Louis built the Sainte Chapelle for its reception." The further history of the holy spurious relic is traced in detail; as late as 1896 "a magnificent new reliquary of rock crystal was made for it"; but by that time the holy relic, like a fighting-cock with his tail-feathers clawed out, was a sorry sight: "The Crown, thus preserved, consists only of a circlet of rushes, without any trace of thorns." A ray of light on Church fakery is thrown

284

by the closing comment: "That all the reputed holy thorns of which notice has survived cannot by any possibility be authentic will be disputed by no one; more than 700 such relics have been enumerated"! (*CE.* iv, 540, 541.)

As for the Holy Lance, which pierced the side of the dying God, also resurrected by pious diligence of "invention," its devious and dubious history is thus traced by our modern ecclesiastical mummery-monger: "A spear believed to be identical with that which pierced our Saviour's body, was venerated at Jerusalem at the close of the sixth century. The sacred relics of the Passion fell into the hands of the pagans. Many centuries afterwards (*i. e.* in 1241), the point of the Lance was presented by Baldwin to St. Louis, and it was enshrined with the Crown of Thorns in the Sainte Chapelle. Another part of the Lance is preserved under the dome of St. Peter's in Rome. . . . Rival lances are known to be preserved at Nuremberg, Paris, etc. Another lance claiming to be that which produced the wound in Christ's side is now preserved among the imperial insignia at Vienna; another is preserved at Cracow. Legend assigns the name of Longinus to the soldier who thrust the Lance into our Saviour's side; according to the same tradition, he was healed of ophthalmia and converted by a drop of the precious blood spurting from the wound." (viii, 773–4.)

There was also timely discovered, by some notable chance or miracle, the very stairway, "consisting of twenty-eight white marble steps, . . . the stairway leading once to the Prætorium of Pilate, hence sanctified by the footsteps of Our Lord during his Passion," as we are assured by *CE.* (viii, 505.) This famous relic, the "Holy Stairs," which somehow escaped the two destructions of Jerusalem and the ravages of time for nearly three centuries, was "brought from Jerusalem to Rome about 326 by St. Helena, mother of Constantine the Great. . . . It is now before the Sancta Sanctorum (Holy of Holies) of the Lateran Palace. The Sancta Sanctorum receiving its name from the many precious relics preserved there, also contains the celebrated image of Christ, 'not made with hands,' which on certain occasions used to be carried through Rome in procession. . . . The Holy Stairs may only be ascended on the knees. . . . Finally Pius X, on 26 February, 1908, granted a plenary indulgence—[*i. e.* a permanent escape from Purgatory]—to be gained as often as the Stairs are devoutedly ascended after confession and communion." (*CE.* viii, 505.) It is related that Father Luther was performing this holy penitential climb of the "Scala Sancta," when suddenly the vast sham and fraud of his religion burst upon his consciousness: the Reformation was a consequence. In passing this famous "Mother of Churches," St. John Lateran, we may admire the wonderful portrait of Jesus Christ which adorns its sacred walls; the painting of it was begun by Dr. St. Luke himself, but being left incomplete, it was finished by an angel.

ANCIENT FAKES YET ACCREDITED

Think not that these ancient frauds of the Church have been discarded in shame by the Church now that their fraudulent origin and purpose are exposed to public obloquy and ridicule. In full blaze of world attention and publicity of the Twentieth Century, God's own Vicar vouches before the world for these tawdry impostures, brought forth before the world to lend climax of superstitious solemnity to his crazy Crusade of prayer and incited pious hatred against the brave efforts of the Russians to undo the fell work of the Church in that unhappy land. Associated Press dispatches from Vatican City announce: "To lend emphasis to the protest here, celebrated relics kept at St. Peter's—a portion of the true cross; St. Veronica's Veil, with which Christ is said to have wiped His face on His way to Calvary, and the centurion's lance which pierced His Side—will be displayed." (*N. Y. Herald-Tribune*, March 19, 1930.) "After the ceremony those present will receive benediction with the sacred relics." (*N. Y. Sun*, Mch. 13, 1930.) Nearby, "the stones of the pavement on which the Apostles [Peter and Paul] knelt in prayer and which are said to contain the impression of their knees, are now in the wall of the Church of Santa Francesca Romana." (*CE.* xiii, 797.) Such lying vouchers are fit setting for the crusade of unholy lies and hate against a people which for centuries has been kept in grossest ignorance and superstition by greedy priestcraft, now repudiated by its victims.

The foregoing solemn vouching for antique fakeries provoked a deal of skeptical ridicule throughout the world, even among some of the Faithful: so it must needs be emphasized by repetition, with some notable other Fake Relics added for "assurance doubly sure." So,

when the Pagan Festival of Easter dawned on the Pagan "Day of the
Venerable Sun," His Royal-Holiness came forth in the full splendor
of the Pagan Pontifex Maximus to celebrate the Event, and by his
Infallible presence to vouch again for the genuineness of these holy
spurious Relics. Probably he wore and ostentated in the joy of its
recovery, the celebrated "so-called Episcopal Ring of St. Peter, rich
with sapphires and diamonds," stolen from the Vatican treasury in
1925, and recently recaptured with the thief. (*Herald-Tribune*, Dec.
3, 1929.) It is possible that he sat in state in the very Throne or "Chair
of St. Peter," which the Fisherman Pope used, as dubiously vouched
by *CE*. under that caption. In any event, whatever throne he used was
planted immediately above the *grave* where lies the headless cadaver of
St. Peter himself, for "the skulls of Sts. Peter and Paul" were later
viewed at the Lateran, and there "shown for the adoration of the
Faithful." As announced in several Press dispatches, an inventory of
the holy Relics and ceremonials is here recorded. In preparation for
the Sacred Event in the Twentieth Century: "The major basilicas will
all have on display their most precious relics. . . . The *purported*
Cradle of Bethlehem [made out of an eighth century packing case]
will be brought forth. Those attending mass at the Lateran will be
able to view the skulls of Sts. Peter and Paul, and a bit of what *is
believed* [by whom, not stated] to be the True Cross—[carried off
entire in 614 by the Persians] ; . . . the *reputed* Lance of the Roman
centurion who speared the side of Christ, and the 'Holy Veil' or napkin
offered to Christ by St. Veronica,"—who is a myth forged from "vera
icon." (*A.P.* dispatch, Apl. 19, 1930.) Also: "A fragment of the Cross
and two Thorns from the crown of the Saviour. . . . The Sancta
Scala (Holy Stairs), . . . drew the usual Good Friday throngs of
the Faithful today. . . . Processions were held inside the ancient edifices to *honor* the relics, [including] what, *according to tradition*, are
the heads of the apostles St. Peter and St. Paul . . . shown for the
adoration of the Faithful." (*Herald-Tribune*, Apl. 19, 1930.) Then
came the consummation and solemn Infallible accrediting of these
"most precious relics" :—"Pope Celebrates Easter Mass. . . . Relics
of the Passion [surrounded him],—a *reputed* fragment of the Cross, a
piece of the Spear which pierced [reputedly] the side of the Saviour,
and the Veil of St. Veronica, . . . were displayed from the balcony

above the Papal Altar." (*Ibid*, Apl. 21, 1930.) Now at last, in Twentieth Century, "*Roma locuta est—causa finita est*"—and these originally bogus frauds are genuine and authentic Relics—for the Faithful who may believe it.

Samples of the "seed of the Serpent" of Eden, the scales that fell from the eyes of Elijah's servant, the original wicked flea, the two dwarf mummies of Bildad the Shu-hite and Ne-hi-miah, the 200 Philistine trophies brought in by David as his marriage dot (1 Sam. xviii, 25–27), the horn of salvation, and the instruments of Cornelius's Italian Band, are about the only honest-to-goodness authentic Biblical relics which seem not to be preserved among the countless holy fake treasures of Holy Church. The famous juvenile pocket-inventories of Tom Sawyer and Huckelberry Finn, and the monstrous fakeries of the late lamented Phineas Barnum, are paltry trivialities beside the countless and priceless Relic-treasures of Holy Church, religiously guarded for "veneration" by True Believers blessed by the privilege of paying—"the more you pay the more you merit" is the maxim— to gaze in rapt awe at, and to kiss and fondle, these ghastly and ghoulish, false and forged, bloody scraps and baubles of perverted piosity. The foreskin of the Child Christ miraculously preserved exists to this day; enough of his diapers and swaddling-cloths, as of the sanitary draperies of his Ever-Virgin Mother, are of record to stock a modern department store. During the era of the unholy Crusades the soldiers of Christ brought from the Holy Land countless numbers of duly certified bottles of the Milk of the Virgin Mother of God, and drove a thrifty business selling them to churches and superstitious dupes through Europe.

Yet in existence are several portraits of the Mother of God, "said to have been painted by St. Luke; they belong to the sixth century." (*CE*. xv, 471.) "There is still preserved at Messina a letter attributed to the Blessed Virgin, which, it is claimed, was written by her to the Messenians when Our Lady heard of their conversion by St. Paul." (x, 217; cf. list of several: i, 613.) "The Shroud of the Blessed Virgin is preserved in the Church of Gethsemane." (xiv, 775.) The Holy Winding Sheet or shroud of the Christ was formerly "exposed for veneration" at Troyes; but the Bishop "declared after due inquiry that the relic was nothing but a painting and opposed its exposition.

Clement VI, by four Bulls (1390), approved the exposition as lawful."
After being stolen and hawked about, this sacred relic "is now exposed and honoured at Turin." (xv, 67–68.) There must be something
wrong about this, for "The Diocese of Perigueux has a remarkable
relic: The Holy Shroud of Christ, brought back after the first crusade. An official investigation in 1444 asserted the authenticity of the
relic." (xi, 668.) The Minster treasury of the Cathedral of Aix-la-
Chapelle, or Aachen, where Charlemagne enshrined the Holy Thorns,
"includes a large number of relics, vessels, and vestments, the most
important being those known as the four 'Great Relics,' namely,
the cloak of the Blessed Virgin, the swaddling-clothes of the infant
Jesus, the loin-cloth worn by Our Lord on the Cross, and the cloth
on which lay the head of John the Baptist after his beheading. They
are exposed every seven years, and venerated by thousands of Pilgrims (139,628 in 1874, and 158,968 in 1881") ! (i, 92.)

Without comment we let *CE.* record for the faith of its readers,
several of the very notable and most remunerative Relics treasured
by Holy Church. That they are all impossible, are all bogus, all crude
forgeries and fakes only possible of credit by the most credulous
child-minds, needs no comment. The sordid debasement of the human
mind to the degree of credulity here displayed, the crass dishonesty
of the false pretenses which give credit to these things for purposes
of extortion from silly dupes of religion, the vastness of the grand
larceny thus perpetrated in the name of God,—are beyond orderly
comment.

"The possession of the seamless garment of Christ is claimed by
the Cathedral of Trier *and* by the parish church of Argenteuil; the
former claims that the relic was sent by the Empress St. Helena,
basing their claim on a document sent by Pope Sylvester to the Church
of Trier, but this cannot be considered genuine. . . . The relic itself
offers no reason to doubt its genuineness. Plenary indulgences were
granted to all pilgrims who should visit the cathedral of Trier at the
time of the exposition of the Holy Coat, which was to take place
every seven years." (vii, 400–1.) "The Church venerates the Holy
Innocents, or Martyrs, the children massacred by Herod, estimated
in various Liturgies as 14,000, 64,000, 144,000 boys. The Church of
Paul's Outside the Walls is believed to possess the bodies of several

of the Holy Innocents. A portion of these relics was transferred by Sixtus V to Santa Maria Maggiore. The Church of St. Justina at Padua, the cathedrals of Lisbon and Milan, and other Churches also preserve bodies which they claim to be those of some of the Holy Innocents. It is impossible to determine the day or the year of the death of the Holy Innocents, since the chronology of the birth of Christ and the subsequent Biblical events is most uncertain"! (*CE.* vii, 419.)

In the cathedral of Cologne are preserved the skulls of the Three Wise Men who followed the Star of Bethlehem. In the neighboring Church of St. Gereon are distributed over the walls the bones from a whole cemetery, dug up and displayed as those of that mythical Saint and his Theban Band of 10,000 Martyrs; in fitting competition are the spoils of the neighboring graveyard, yielding the bones of St. Ursula and her 11,000 Virgin Martyrs. The miraculous bones of Santa Rosalia in Palermo are the bones of a deceased goat!

"The city of Tarascon has for its patron, St. Martha, who, according to the legend, delivered the country from a monster called 'Tarasque.' The Church of 'Saintes Marias de la Mer' contains three venerated tombs; according to a tradition which is attached to the legends concerning the emigration of St. Lazarus, St. Martha, St. Mary Magdalen, and St. Maximus, these tombs contain the bodies of the three Marys of the Gospels." (*CE.* i, 238.)

The Abbot Martin obtained for his monastery in Alsace the following inestimable articles: A spot of the blood of our Saviour; a piece of the True Cross; the arm of the Apostle James; part of the skeleton of John the Baptist; a bottle of the Milk of the Mother of God. (Draper, *The Intellectual Development of Europe,* ii, 57.) But perhaps none of these impostures surpassed in audacity that offered by a monastery in Jerusalem, which presented to the beholder ONE OF THE FINGERS OF THE HOLY GHOST! (Draper, *Conflict between Science and Religion,* p. 270.) Also there were displayed sundry choice collections of the *wing and tail feathers* of the said Holy Ghost, from time to time shed off or pulled out when, in the disguise of a Dove, It (or He or She) came down and perched on people. In England at the time of Henry VIII (1501), Our Lady's girdle was shown in not less than eleven places, and Our Lady's milk, in a condensed form, in eight places. One of these girdles the good Queen-mother procured for Catherine of Aragon, on her marriage with Henry, to present to her when the expected time should come. During the plague of 1531, Henry VIII, for a goodly price, bought some precious relic waters to avert the plague from himself: a tear which Our Lord shed over Lazarus, preserved by an angel who gave it in a phial to Mary Magdalene; and a phial of the sweat of St. Michael when he contended with Satan, as recorded in the Book of Enoch and vouched for in the sacred Book of Jude. (Hackett, *Henry VIII*, pp. 11, 234.) The Cathedral of Arras, in France, possesses some highly venerated and remarkable relics, to wit, some of the Holy Manna which fell from Heaven in the year 371 during a severe famine; and the identical Holy Candle, a wax taper, which was presented by the Blessed Virgin to Bishop Lambert, in 1105, to stop an epidemic. (*CE*. i, 752.) This same waxen Holy Candle has burned continuously from 1105 to at least 1713 without being to the slightest degree diminished, as his view of it was then reported by Anthony Collins, in his *Discourse of Free Thinking*; he expresses the doubt whether the attendant clergy would permit a careful scrutiny to be made of the phenomenon.

A final job lot of these holy fetiches as recorded by Dr. McCabe with some pertinent comments, may be admired: "At Laon the chief treasures shown to the public were some milk and hair of the Virgin Mary. This was Laon's set-off to the rival attraction at Soissons, a neighboring town, which had secured one of the milk-teeth shed by the infant Jesus. There seems to have been enough of the milk of the Virgin—some of it was still exhibited in Spanish churches in the nineteenth century—preserved in Europe to feed a few calves. There was hair enough to make a mattress. There were sufficient pieces of 'the true cross' to make a boat. There were teeth of Christ enough to outfit a dentist (one monastery, at Charroux, had the complete set). There were so many sets of baby-linen of the infant Jesus, in Italy, France and Spain, that one could have opened a shop with them. One of the greatest churches in Rome had Christ's manger-cradle. Seven churches had his authentic umbilical cord, and a number of churches had his foreskin (removed at circumcision and kept as a souvenir by Mary). One church had the miraculous imprint of his little bottom on a stone on which he had sat. Mary herself had left enough wedding rings, shoes, stockings, shirts, girdles, *etc.* to fill a museum; one of her shifts is still in the Chartres cathedral. One church had Aaron's rod. Six churches had the six heads cut off John the Baptist. . . . Every one of these things was, remember, in its origin, a cynical blasphemous swindle. Each of these objects was at first launched upon the world with deliberate mendacity. . . . One is almost disposed to ask for an application to the clergy of the law about obtaining money under false pretenses." (McCabe, *The Story of Religious Controversy,* p. 353.)

HOLY OILS, WATERS, AND FETICHES

These sacred and sanctified wonder-working objects are too numerous to more than mention a few of the most celebrated. Miraculous "waters" were in great profusion distilled or in some weird way extracted from numbers of dead Saints, "blessed" for a variety of purposes, and vended under the names of the productive Saints; as "The Water of St. Ignatius," of Sts. Adelhaid, Vincent Ferrer, Willibrord, etc. That of St. Hubert was notably a specific for the bite of mad dogs. The formulæ for these holy extracts or emulsions, with their properties and miraculous effects, are set forth in the official "Rituale Romanum." (*CE.* xv, 564.) The widely celebrated "Oil of Saints" was in immense vogue and possessed wonderful properties, as vouched by *CE.* under that title. This holy unction was "an oily substance which is said to have flowed, or still flows, from the relics or burial places of certain saints, and water which has in some way come in contact with their relics. These oils are or have been used by the faithful, with the belief that they will cure bodily and spiritual ailments . . . the custom prevailed of pouring oil over the relics or reliquaries of martyrs and then gathering it in vases, sponges or pieces of cloth. This oil, *oleum martyris,* was distributed among the faithful as a remedy against sickness. . . . At present the most famous of the oils of saints is the oil of St. Walburga (*Walburgis oleum*). It flows from the stone slab and the surrounding metal plate on which rest the relics of St. Walburga in her church in Eichstadt in Bavaria. The fluid is caught in a silver cup and is distributed to the faithful for use against diseases of the body and soul. Similarly of the Oil of St. Menas, of which thousands of little flasks have recently been discovered, found at many places in Europe and Africa; there is also a like Oil of St. Nicholas of Myra, which emanates from his relics at Bari in Italy, whither they were brought in 1087. A certain substance like flour, is recorded by St. Gregory of Tours, to emanate from the sepulchre of St. John the Evangelist; also that from the sepulchre of the Apostle St. Andrew emanated manna in the form of flour and fragrant oil." A list half a column long is given of other saints from whose relics or sepulchres oil is said to have flowed. (*CE.* xi, 228–9.)

THE AGNUS DEI

"These are discs of wax impressed with the figure of a lamb and blessed at stated seasons by the Pope. The rule still followed is that the great consecration of the Agnus Dei takes place only in the first year of each pontificate and every seventh year afterwards. It seems probable that they had their beginning in some *pagan* usage of charms or amulets, from which the ruder populace were weaned by the employment of this Christian substitute [charm or amulet] blessed by prayer. The early history of Catholic ceremonial affords numerous parallels for this Christianizing of pagan rites. . . . So the purpose of these consecrated medallions is to protect those who wear or possess them from all malign influences. In the prayers of blessing, special mention is made of the perils from storm and pestilence, from fire and flood, and also of the dangers to which women are exposed in childbirth. Miraculous effects have been believed to follow the use of these objects of piety. Fires are said to have been extinguished, and floods stayed. They were much subject to counterfeit, the making of which has been strictly prohibited by various papal bulls,"—(this proving the obtaining of money by false pretenses in the papal monopoly of peddling them to the moron Faithful). "There are also Agnus Deis made from wax mingled with the dust which is believed to be that of the bones of martyrs; these are called Paste de' SS. Martiri, or Martyrs' Paste." (*CE.* i, 220.) The peddling of these frauds has not yet been forbidden by the criminal code, nor by the Vicars of God who gain by them. Three pages of a separate article are devoted to the potent prayers in Liturgies, several in doggerel

Latin verse, on pages 221–223. One of these inspired Papal invocations over the sacred amulets is quoted by Dr. White:

"O God, . . . we humbly beseech thee that thou wilt bless these waxen forms, figured with the image of an innocent lamb, . . . that, at the touch and sight of them, the faithful shall break forth into praises, and that the crash of hailstorms, the blast of hurricanes, the violence of tempests, the fury of winds, and the malice of thunderbolts may be tempered, and evil spirits flee and tremble before the standard of the holy cross, which is graven upon them." (White, *Warfare between Science and Religion*, i, 343.)

The recurrence in modern times of the above recited catastrophes raised by imps of the devil, not unseldom doing damage even to the Faithful and to their sacred edifices, must be due to the punible neglect to have a supply of these thaumaturgic crackers on hand at the time and place of the flagellations of the Evil One.

THE TRAGEDY OF THE "MYSTICAL MARRIAGE"

What to a Rationalist may seem a very inhuman superstition—though often attenuated by the clerical formula "With all my worldly goods I thee endow," pronounced to his earthly vicar by the happy "Bride of Jesus Christ," is the unctuously so-called Mystical Marriage, the nuptial ceremony whereby a deluded female enters into the joys of her Lord without actually sharing them. This holy mummery is thus described by the oft-cited Exponent of Catholic Truth:

"Christian virginity has been considered from the earliest centuries as a special offering made by the soul to its spouse, Christ. . . . In many of the lives of the Saints, the mystical marriage consists of a vision in which Christ tells a soul that He takes it for His bride, presenting it with the customary ring, and the apparition is accompanied by a ceremony; the Blessed Virgin Mary, saints and angels are present. . . . Moreover, as a wife should share in the life of her husband, and as Christ suffered for the redemption of mankind, the mystical bride enters into a more intimate participation of His sufferings,—[*casus omissus* being the sharing of the nuptial joys also involved in the notion of marriage]. Accordingly, in three cases out of four, the mystical marriage has been granted to stigmatics. History [priest-written, of course] has recorded seventy-seven mystical marriages, in connection with female saints, blesseds and venerables";— a number of whom are named, including, appropriately, St. Mary Magdalen *dei Pazzi*—"of the Crazy Ones"—as were they all. (*CE.* ix, 703.)

CHAPTER VII

THE "TRIUMPH" OF CHRISTIANITY

> "Destruction to the Triumphant Beast!"
> Giordano Bruno.
> *"Ecrasez l'Infame!"*
> Voltaire.

EVEN MORE INDUCIVE than its own sweet reasonableness and persuasive truth, as accredited by the records and vouchers we have examined, were several very effective forcible aids to the propagation of the new Faith in the hearts and minds—and upon the bodies —of the Pagan populations. The strange phenomenon of the persistence of Christianity into the XXth Century can be understood only by consideration of the means employed for, and the medium of unculture permitting, the propagation of this forged faith through the centuries of the Dark Ages of Faith, with its medieval "hangover" into the present scientific era.

PRIESTLY TERRORISM
GOD-ORDAINED MURDER FOR UNBELIEF

The Jewish forgers of the near-sacred Books of Enoch, Esdras, etc.; had pilfered from the Sacred Books and System of Zoroaster of Persia, their superstitions of angels and devils and hell-fire, and had invented the infernal doctrines of Original Sin and eternal damnation therefor,—all which counterfeit passed to and became current among the religious zealots of the debased Judaism then in vogue. Attributing their "revelation" or invention to Jesus Christ himself, the second-century forging Fathers of the new Faith bodily plagiarized these ready-made Pagan-Jewish superstitions, and by the potent "Sign of the Cross" metamorphosed them into holy "revelations" and inspired truths, the which to doubt was to be damned.

295

FORGERY IN CHRISTIANITY

The fanatic Hebrew religion and its derivative Christianity are the only religions ever known on earth based on and maintained by systematic persecution and murder. God-given laws of murder for disbelief were decreed at Sinai. A holy monopoly of priests was founded, and the divine ukase ordained: "They shall keep their priesthood, and the stranger that cometh nigh shall be put to death." (Num. iii, 10.) Murder was God-decreed: "The man that will do presumptuously, and will not hearken unto the priest, . . . even that man shall die." (Deut. xvii, 12.) Again the Jealous God decrees: "He that sacrificeth to any other god—[thus admitting the other gods]— save unto Yahveh alone, he shall be utterly destroyed." (Ex. xxii, 20; Deut. xvii, 2–5.) The *ne plus ultra* of inspired atrocity of Divine legislation is this infamy devised by priests and attributed to their mythic God: "If thy brother, the son of thy mother, or thy daughter, or *the wife of thy bosom*, or thy friend, which is as thine own soul, entice thee secretly, saying, Let us go serve other [more civilized] gods, . . . Thou shalt not consent unto him, nor hearken unto him; neither shalt thine eye pity him, neither shalt thou spare, neither shalt thou conceal him: But *thou shalt surely kill him:* thine hand shall be the first upon him *to put him to death*, and afterwards the hand of all the people. And *thou shalt stone him with stones, that he die"!* (Deut. xiii, 6, 8–10; xvii, 2–7.) Old Elijah murdered by his God's help two companies of soldiers and their captains by calling down fire from heaven, and 450 priests of Baal and 400 priests of the phallic Asherahs, to prove by these 1000 murders "if I be a man of the gods." (2 Kings, i, 12.) His old side-partner Elisha stood by and watched God-sent bears which he had invoked tear and eat forty small children who ill-manneredly thumbed their noses at his old bald pate; and throughout the blessed Old Testament of God some hundreds of thousands of people were murdered by God outright and by his holy priestly agents, simply for differences of opinion or of conduct with respect—or disrespect—to the holy Hebrew God and religion. Only, fortunately, probably little of it is true.

The Son of the Hebrew God came in course of time to Jewry ostensibly to make amends for some of his Father's damning vengeances. He came "to fulfill the law"; not only that, he overdid it and added to it sundry fiery climaxes of cursing and damnation, religious bigotry and intolerance unique to the "Gospel of Love" and of redemptive salvation. For sanctions *ad terrorem* of the new preachments of Christ who "came to bring the sword," Jesus himself kindled the fires of Hell and decreed eternal damnation for unbelief: "He that believeth not shall be damned"; "Depart from me, ye cursed, into everlasting fire"; "Except ye repent, ye shall all likewise perish"; "He that believeth not the Son, the wrath of God abideth on him"! These genial persuasions to belief in the priests were added to by Paul the Persecutor; harking back to his God's Law of Sinai: "He that despised Moses' law died without mercy; . . . Of how much sorer punishment . . . shall he be thought worthy who hath trodden under foot the Son of God?"—"The same shall drink of the wine of the wrath of God, and shall be tormented with fire and brimstone in the presence of the holy angels and of the Lamb: And the smoke of their torment ascendeth forever and ever: and they shall have no rest day or night" from "the fierceness of the wrath of Almighty God"! All this is for the happy Hereafter; but the pious deviltry begins by Hell-on-earth, as the gentle Jesus himself prescribed: "Those mine enemies, which would not that I reign over them, bring hither, and slay them before me." (Luke, xix, 27.) The whole body of Apostles appealed for Divine permit, that "we command fire to come down from heaven, and consume them" (Luke ix, 54), who sought to imitate their pious devil-enchantments. Peter, Prince of Apostles, takes up the bloody cue: "Every soul which will not hear that prophet shall be destroyed" (Acts, iii, 23); and Bigot Paul enjoins proscription, boycott and murder for the dissentient: "For there are many *unruly* and vain *talkers . . . whose mouths must be stopped*" (Titus, i, 10, 11): and "He that troubleth you . . . I would they were even *cut off*" (Gal. v, 10, 12). The Church Persecutrix is thus amply warranted of its God in its holy task of "preserving the purity of the Faith" by fire and sword. Right quickly it began to "deal damnation 'round the land on all they deemed the foe" of the Faith and its priests. The rule of death to heretics was proclaimed by the "Prince" and executed by sword and stake by his holy "Successors" so long as they were let: "There shall be false teachers among you, who privily shall bring in damnable heresies, . . . and bring upon themselves swift destruction" (2 Peter, ii, 1); and his arch-coadjutor Paul continued to go up and

297

down the land "breathing out threatenings and slaughter" against all who despised his holy preachments.

As we shall hear confessed: "Toleration came in only when Faith went out; lenient measures were resorted to only where power to apply more severe measures was wanting"! (*CE.* vii, 262.) The infernal fact that Intolerance is the "natural accompaniment" of Religion, and that obsessed religionists are no different from a man-burning mob of lynchers, is thus again confessed: "A kind of iron law would seem *to dispose mankind to religious intolerance.* (p. 35.) ... When Christianity became the religion of the Empire, and still more when the peoples of Northern Europe became Christian nations, the close alliance of Church and State, ... heresy, *in consequence,* was a crime which secular rulers *were bound in duty* to punish. ... The heretic, in a word, was simply *an outlaw* whose offense, in the popular mind, deserved and sometimes received a punishment as summary as that which is often dealt out in our day by an infuriated populace to the authors of justly detested crimes. That such intolerance was not peculiar to Catholicism, but was the NATURAL ACCOMPANIMENT OF DEEP RELIGIOUS CONVICTION in those, also, who abandoned the Church, is evident from the measures taken by some of the Reformers—[ex-children of True Church, who were there schooled and drilled in the infamies]—against those *who differed from them in matters of belief.* ... Moreover, ... the spirit of intolerance prevalent in many of the American colonies during the seventeenth and eighteenth centuries may be cited in proof thereof." (*CE.* viii, 35, 36.) The only way to kill the pernicious flower of Faith is to uproot and destroy the noxious weed!

THE GOSPEL OF FEAR AND TREMBLING

Such as this, repeated *ad infinitum* for terror, coupled with the threats of the quick "Second Coming," when the Unbelievers should receive reward "unto the resurrection of damnation" (John v, 29), effectively seared the Gospel of fear and trembling into the superstitious Pagan dupes of Christianity.

Hear for a moment the zealous Father Tertullian throw the fear of Hell into the trembling Pagan patrons of the theatre and the circus. As quoted by Gibbon from the *De Spectaculis* (Ch. 30), they are introduced with some pertinent words descriptive of the spirit of bigoted Christianity: "These rigid sentiments, which had been unknown to the ancient world, appear to have infused a spirit of bitterness into a system of love and harmony. The ties of blood and friendship were frequently torn asunder by the difference of religious faith; and the Christians, who, in this world, found themselves oppressed by the power of the Pagans, were sometimes seduced by resentment and spiritual pride to delight in the prospect of their future triumph. 'You are fond of spectacles,' exclaims the stern Tertullian; 'expect the greatest of all spectacles, the last and eternal judgment of the universe. How shall I admire, how laugh, how rejoice, how exult, when I behold so many proud monarchs, and fancied gods, groaning in the lowest abyss of darkness; so many magistrates, who persecuted the name of the Lord, liquefying in fiercer fires than they ever kindled against Christians; so many sage philosophers blushing in red-hot flames with their deluded scholars; so many celebrated poets trembling before the tribunal, not of Minos, but of Christ; so many tragedians, more tuneful in the expression of their own sufferings; so many dancers——.' But the humanity of the reader will permit me to draw a veil over the rest of this infernal description, which the zealous African pursues in a long variety of affected and unfeeling witticisms." (Gibbon, Ch. xv, p. 146–7.)

UNBORN BABES TO BURN FOREVER

The damnable doctrine of Infant Damnation was one of the most terrifying and effective impostures of the Church to drive helpless victims into the fold of Christ. Infamous enough was the earlier doctrine of exclusive salvation, that the unbaptized adult, the individual outside the Church was the heir to eternal damnation. But soon the terror was extended to the just-born infant, to even the fœtus in its mother's womb. St. Augustine affirmed this atrocity with all his vehemence; all the Fathers without exception dinned it eternally,—as yet today. A treatise of the greatest authority, *De Fide*, long attributed to Augustine, but now known to be the work of Bishop St. Fulgentius (*CE.* vi, 317) thus states the horrid doctrine: "Be assured, and doubt not, that not only men who have attained the use of their reason, but also little children who have begun to live in their mothers' womb and have there died, or who, having been just born, have passed away from the world without the sacrament of holy baptism, administered in the name of the Father, Son and Holy Ghost, must be punished by the eternal torture of undying fire; for although they have committed no sin by their own will, they have nevertheless drawn with them the condemnation of original sin, by their carnal conception and nativity." (sec. 70.) Lecky, who quotes the passage, thus comments the effects as witnessed in practice throughout the Middle Ages: "Nothing indeed can be more curious, nothing more deeply pathetic, than the record of the many ways by which the terror-stricken mothers attempted to evade the awful sentence of their Church. Sometimes the baptismal water was sprinkled upon the womb; sometimes the still-born child was baptised, in hopes that the Almighty would antedate the ceremony; sometimes the mother invoked the Holy Spirit to purify by His immediate power the infant that was to be born; sometimes she received the Host or obtained absolution, and applied them to the benefit of her child. For the doctrine of the Church had wrung the mother's heart with an agony that was too poignant for even that submissive age to bear." (*Rationalism in Europe,* i, 362–364.) And all this on account of an apple eaten four thousand years before they were born; willed by the Deity who had foreordained their birth and premature death, before His Holy Church could come at the Baptismal fees!

A CONTRAST IN TOLERANCE

With the miraculous "conversion of Constantine"—to at least the practical advantages of Christianity as providing numerous partizans to his ambitious cause and great numbers of recruits to his armies, the Church of Christ emerged from obscurity and catacombs; by dint of servile flatteries, bold impostures, and shameless forgeries, of which we have seen examples, it quickly insinuated itself into imperial favor and popular regard, and soon dominated the superstitious court and populace. This was a signal triumph for Faith, which now became popular and the means to preferment; the truth of the Christ did now

300

more rapidly spread and abound. That such considerations, much more of this material world worldly than of the other-world of the spiritual, best further the cause of Christ and are its most powerful propaganda, is thus delicately confessed: "When a Government, for instance, reserves its favors and functions for the adherents of the State religion, the army of civil servants becomes a more powerful body of missionaries than the ordained ministers"! (*CE.* vii, 259.) Thus began that funest League with Death and Covenant with Hell between State and Church, persistent yet to this day!

THE EDICT OF MILAN (*313*)

But until the Christian priests poisoned his mind with their arrogant pretensions, Constantine was truly liberal in his policy of "religious indifferentism" or toleration. His broad-minded and statesman-like grasp of the principles of liberty of belief in any and all forms of religious superstition, or in none at all, rose to heights never since attained until Thomas Jefferson's Virginia Statute for Religious Freedom, reflected in Art. VI and Amendment I of the Federal Constitution. Constantine's Edict of Milan, of 313, was the first charter of religious freedom and toleration, securing equality and liberty of worship to the Christians,—and very quickly repudiated by them as against all others; it is preserved and thus quoted by Lactantius:

"Not many days after the victory, Licinius . . . on the ides of June (13th), while he and Constantine were consuls for the third time, he commanded the following edict for the restoration of the Church, directed to the president of the province, to be promulgated:—

"When we, Constantine and Licinius, emperors, had an interview at Milan, and conferred together with respect to the good and security of the commonweal, it seemed to us that, amongst those things that are profitable to mankind in general, the reverence paid to the Divinity merited our first and chief attention, and that it was proper that the Christians and all others should have *liberty to follow that mode of religion which to each of them appeared best;* so that God, who is seated in heaven, might be benign and propitious to us, and to everyone under our government. And therefore we judged it a salutary measure, and one highly consonant to right reason, that no man should be denied leave of attaching himself to the rites of the Christians, or to whatever other religion his mind directed him, that thus the supreme Divinity, to whose worship we freely devote ourselves, might continue to devote His favour and beneficence to us. . . . For it befits the

301

well-ordered State and the tranquillity of our times that each individual be allowed, according to his own choice, to worship the Divinity; and we mean not to derogate aught from the honour due to any religion or its votaries." (Lact., *Of the Manner in Which the Persecutors Died,* ch. xlviii; *ANF.* VII, 320; Eusebius, *HE.* viii, 17.)

CHRISTIAN INTOLERANCE

But no sooner had the priests of the new Superstition foisted themselves securely into power, and by their threats of hell-fire dominated the superstitious minds of the ex-Pagan Constantine and his sons and successors, than the old decrees of persecution under which the Christians had themselves suffered, were revamped and with fiendish ferocity turned by them into engines of fearful torture and destruction of Pagans, Jews, and "heretic" Christians alike; and religious intolerance became the corner-stone of the Church Persecutrix. In the famous Code of Theodosius, about 384, it was at priestly instigation enacted:

"We desire that all the people under our clemency should live by that religion which divine Peter the apostle is said to have given the Romans. . . . We desire that heretics and schismatists be subjected to various fines. . . . We decree also that we shall cease making sacrifices to the gods. And if anyone has committed such a *crime, let him be stricken with the avenging sword.*" (*Cod. Theod.* xvi, 1, 2; v, 1; x, 4.)

What a shaming Christian contrast to the Pagan Edict of Milan, granting religious liberty and tolerance to all! In these laws of the now "Christian" empire priestly intolerance is made the law of the land; the accursed words "Inquisition of the Faith" and "Inquisitors" first appear in this Christian Code. "Theodosius I was called the Great because he was the first Emperor to act against heathenism, and also because he contributed to the victory over the Arians." (*CE.* iii, 101.)

Even the "Infidel" Moslem, in his crude Koran, teaches a doctrine of tolerance to shame the Bible and the Christians: "Those who follow the Jewish religion, the Christians, the Sabeans, and whatever others believe in God and practice doing good, all these shall receive their recompense from the Lord. . . . Virtue does not consist in turning the face towards the East nor towards the West to pray, but in being tolerant." (*Quran*, ix, 59, 76;—from Spanish text.)

FAITH ENFORCED BY LAWS OF MURDER

Holy Fraud and Forgery having achieved their initial triumph for the Faith, the "Truth of Christ" must now be maintained and enforced upon humanity by a millennial series of bloody brutal Clerical Laws of pains and penalties, confiscations, civil disabilities, torture and death by rack, fire and sword, which constitute the foulest chapter of the Book of human history—the History of the Church!

When the Christians were weak and powerless and subjected to occasional persecutions as "enemies of the human race," they were vocal and insistent advocates of liberty of conscience and freedom to worship whatever God one chose: the Christian "Apologies" to the Emperors abound in eloquent pleas for religious tolerance; and this was granted to them and to all by the Edict of Milan and other imperial Decrees. But when by the favor of Constantine they got into the saddle of the State, they at once grasped the sword and began to murder and despoil all who would not pretend to believe as the Catholic priest commanded them to believe. When today the Church screams "Persecution!" and "Bigotry!" at every criticism and every attempt to restrict it in some of its presumptuous usurpations, let it recall a few of the laws of intolerance, plunder and death which it procured and enforced from the moment it got the prostituted power, so long as that power lasted.

Beginning with Constantine, and under succeeding "Christian" emperors, there is a series of scores of laws which the Christians procured to be enacted for the suppression and persecution to death of Pagans, heretics and Jews. These laws and edicts are to be found in the Codes of Theodosius and of Justinian, the two famous codifications of Roman Law. To exhibit the progressive and persistent system of proscription to which all but themselves were persecutingly subjected by the "Orthodox" Christians, I shall simply quote the titles of some of these laws, with indication of the names of the Emperors issuing

303

them, the dates and number of the laws, and the Code or other source in which it is preserved.

LAWS OF CONSTANTINE

The earliest laws of Constantine were those granting religious toleration, as the Edict of Milan (313) already quoted, and laws for the redress of injuries done to Christians; such as release of prisoners and those in servitude, and the restoration of property; chapter 36 declares that "The Church is the heir of those who leave no kindred; and free gifts to it are confirmed"; chapter 41: "Those who have purchased property belonging to the Church or received it as a gift, are to restore it." (Eusebius, *Vita Constantini, N&PNF*. Bk. II, chs. xxiv–xliii.)

"Edict to the People of the Provinces Concerning the Error of Polytheism." (*Ib*. chs. xlviii–xlix.)

"Granting Money to the Churches." (*Ib*. Bk, x, ch. vi.)

"Catholic Clergy exempt from Certain Civic Duties." (*Code Theod.* xvi, 2, 1; 313.) "The Catholic Church freed from Tribute." (*Id.* xi, 1, 1; 315.) "Clergymen freed from Financial Burdens." (*Id.* xvi, 2, 2; 319.) "The Church allowed to Receive Bequests." (*Id.* xvi, 2, 4; 321.)

"Bishop's Powers as Judges and Witnesses": "Whatever may be settled by a sentence of bishops shall ever be held as sacred and venerable. . . . All testimony given, even by a single bishop, shall be accepted without hesitation, by every judge, neither shall the testimony of any other witness be heard, when the testimony of a bishop is brought forward by either party"! (*Const. Sirm.* i; 333.)

"The *Day of the Sun* a Time of Rest." "All judges, and city folk and all craftsmen shall rest on the *venerated day of the Sun*." (*Cod. Just.* iii, 12, 2; 321.)

"As it has seemed most unworthy that the Day of the Sun, famous by its venerable character, . . . Therefore on the festive day." (*Cod. Theod.* ii, 8, 1; 321.)

A number of laws follow in favor of the Pagans, and while prohibiting "private divination and soothsaying," and "Malevolent Magic Prohibited, but Beneficial Magic Encouraged"; also exempting Pagan Flamens, priests and magistrates from sundry restrictions and disabilities. No law of Constantine seems to be preserved which prescribes active persecution; he seems to have sought to hold an even

304

balance of toleration to Pagans and Christians. But that he did enact such laws seems to be proved by recital in the first of the laws of his sons, Constantius and Constans, who were Arian heretics.

LAWS OF CONSTANTIUS AND CONSTANS

"Sacrifice Prohibited.": "Let superstition cease and the folly of sacrifices be abolished. Whoever has dared in the face of *the law of the divine prince, our father* [Constantine] . . . to make sacrifices, shall have appropriate penalty, and immediate sentence dealt to him." (*Cod. Theod.* xvi, 10, 2; 341.)

"All Temples Closed and Sacrifices Forbidden." . . . "but if any one commit any offense of this sort, *let him fall by the avenging sword,*" *and his property forfeited;* judges neglecting to "mete out penalties for these offenses, they shall be similarly punished." (*Cod. Theod.* xvi, 10, 4; 346.)

"Sacrificing and Idolatry Punishable by Death." "We order that all found guilty of attending sacrifices or of worshipping idols shall *suffer capital punishment.*" (*Id.* xvi, 10, 6; 356.)

LAWS OF GRATIAN AND THEODOSIUS

"Wills of Apostate Christians to be Set Aside": "The right of making a will shall be taken from Christians who become pagans; and if such persons make wills, they shall be set aside without regard to circumstances." (*Cod. Theod.* xvi, 7, 1; 381: cf. *Cod. Justin.* i, 7, 2; 382.)

"The Right to Bequeath or Inherit Property Denied Apostates": "We deny to Christians and the faithful who have adopted pagan rites and religion all power of making a will in favor of any person whatsoever, in order *that they may be without the Roman law* [outlaws]; . . . even of enjoying a will with the power of acquiring an inheritance." (*Cod. Theod.* xvi, 7, 2; 383.) "The Right of Making a Will Denied Christians Who enter Temples." (*Id.* xvi, 7, 3; 383.)

LAWS OF THEODOSIUS AND VALENTINIAN

"Testamentary Disqualification for Christian Apostates," and Outlawry as Witnesses.—"Those who betray the sacred faith and profane holy baptism are *shut off from association of all* and *from giving testimony.* . . . They may not exercise the right of making a will, nor enter upon any inheritance; *they may not be made anyone's heir.*" (*Id.* xvi, 7, 4; 391.)

"Sacrificing and Visiting Shrines Prohibited." (*Id.* xvi, 10, 10; 391.) —"Sacrifices Forbidden and Temples Closed." (*Id.* xvi, 10, 11; 391.)

"PAGANISM OUTLAWED."—"If any one dares [to sacrifice, etc.],

St. Agatha's anti-volcano Veil had been gotten out of storage and waved or hung up on the first signs of eruption, some of this history, one way or another, would have been different. But if the Saint can stop volcanoes after the evil deed is done,— Well, one miracle of prevention is better than a larger number of miracles of cure,—which are ineffective to repair the havoc in such cases. Like miracles of liquefaction of Holy Blood yet occur abundantly, as in the noted cases of "Saints John the Baptist, Stephen, Pantaleone, Patricia, Nicholas, Aloysius," *et id omne genus;* so with the bottled "Milk of our Lady" and the canned "fat of St. Thomas Aquinas," on their respective Saint-days! (*CE.* viii, 297.)

The sacred Council of Trent, in 1546, decreed: "That the saints who reign with Christ offer to God their prayers for men; that it is good and useful to invoke them by supplication and to have recourse to their aid and assistance in order to obtain from God His benefits through His Son and Our Saviour Jesus Christ, who alone is our Saviour and Redeemer." (Session xxv.) But the sacred Council, in its preoccupation of combating the nascent outraged revolt and protest of Protestantism, which was filching its most plausible counterfeits for circulation in a hostile camp,—seems to have overlooked this scrap of forged Scripture: "For there is one God, and *one* Mediator between God and men, the *man* Christ Jesus." (I Tim. ii, 5.) The effect, however, of this multiplication of saintly mediators is picturesque; it is finely exemplified in the great painting "The Intercession of the Saints," in the Royal Gallery at Naples: In the background is the plague-stricken city; in the foreground the people are praying to the city authorities to avert the plague; the city authorities are praying to the Carthusian monks; the monks are praying to the Blessed Virgin; the Virgin prays to Christ; and Christ prays to his Father Almighty. The Holy Ghost, who "itself maketh intercession for us with groanings which cannot be uttered," is quite left out of the picture. Just how good and useful it is to invoke the Saints directly, saving Doctor's bills and other inconveniences, will be noticed in the catalogue of Saints below inscribed.

It was in the fifth century, says Dr. McCabe, that "Rome began on a large scale the forgery of lives of martyrs. Relics of martyrs were now being 'discovered' in great numbers to meet the pious demand of let any man be free to accuse him and let him receive, as one *guilty of lese majesté,* . . . for it is sufficiently a *crime.*" (*Id.* xvi, 10. 12; 392.)

LAWS OF HONORIUS AND ARCADIUS

"Pagan Holidays Abolished." (*Cod. Theod.* ii, 8, 22; 395.)—"Privileges of Pagan Priests Abolished." (*Id.* xvi, 10, 14; 396.)—"Rural Temples to be Destroyed." (*Id.* xvi, 10, 16; 339.)—"Temples to be Appropriated by the Churches." (*Id.* xvi, 5, 43; 408.)—"Temples to be Appropriated by the Churches. Temple Buildings and their Revenues to be Confiscated and Idols and Shrines to be Destroyed." (*Id.* xvi, 5, 43; xvi, 10, 19; 407.)

"Only Catholics to Serve as Palace Guards." (*Cod. Theod.* xvi. 5, 42; 408.)

"Laws Against the Pagans to be Enforced": "The Donatists and other vain heretics and those others *who cannot be converted to the worship of the Catholic communion,* Jews and Gentiles who are vulgarly known as pagans; . . . Let all judges understand, and not fail to carry out all decrees against such persons." (*Id.* xvi. 5, 46; 409.)

"Pagans Barred from Civil and Military Offices." (*Id.* xvi, 10, 21; 416.)
"Existing Laws against Pagans to be Enforced." (*Id.* xvi, 10, 22; 423.)
—"Pagans Who Sacrifice Shall *Lose their Property and be Exiled.*" (*Id.* xvi, 10, 23; 423.)

"Pagan Superstition to be Rooted Out": "We are extirpating all heresies and all falsehoods, all schisms and all superstitions of the pagans and all errors that are *inimicable to the Catholic religion.* . . . And since all attempt at supplication is denied forever, they will be punished with the severity befitting *crimes.*" (*Id.* xvi, 5, 63; 423.)

"Pagans Barred from Pleading a Case or Serving as Soldiers": ". . . and *every sect unfriendly with the Catholics should be driven out of every city in order that they may not be sullied by the contagious presence of criminals. We deny to Jews or pagans the right of pleading a case in court or of serving as soldiers.*" (*Const. Sirm.* No. 6; 425.)

LATER LAWS AGAINST PAGANISM

"Pagan Rites Forbidden and Bequests for Pagan Cults Prohibited." (*Cod. Just.* i, 11, 9; 472.)

"Baptized Persons who follow Pagan Practices to Suffer Death. Provisions for the Conversion of the Unbaptized. *Pagans Forbidden to Give Instruction.*" (*Cod. Just.* 1, 11, 10; no date given.)

"Pagans Barred from Office and their Real Property Confiscated." "The Emperors Justin and Justinian. . . . It is our intention to restore the existing laws which affect the rest of the heretics of whatever name they are, (and we label as heretic whoever is not a member of the Catholic Church and of our orthodox and holy faith); likewise the pagans who attempt to

introduce the worship of many gods, and the Jews and the Samaritans.
. . . We forbid any of the above-mentioned persons to aspire to any dignity or to acquire civil or military office or to attain to any rank." (*Id.* i,
5, 12; 527.)

Thus was Pagan Superstition proscribed and destroyed by Christian law and sword; and the identical Pagan Superstitions under the
veneer of the name of Christian established and enthroned. The subject is thoroughly examined by Prof. Maude A. Huttmann, in *The
Establishment of Christianity Through the Proscription of Paganism;*
(Columbia University Press, 1914).

BLOODY RECORD BOASTED

A graphic sketch of the origin, the universal scope, and the crushing effect of the early imperial laws, supplemented and expanded by
those of medieval and more modern times, is given by *CE.*, related with
all the sinister and cynical insolence, sophistry and hypocrisy of
intolerant bigotry. To its Christ it imputes the horrid justification of
the sword and the infernal principles of butchery whereby the Church
Murderess has "made a hell of earth to merit heaven." This recital is
not alone of ancient sacred history; *CE.* admits: "These primitive
views on heresy have been faithfully transmitted and acted on by the
Church in subsequent ages; there is no break in the tradition from St.
Peter to Pious X." (vii, 259.) The principles are yet alive and
cherished, their practical application has only for the time being
"fallen into abeyance," only, for the reason that in these modern
skeptical times "the power to apply more severe measures is wanting."
Here is the admitted ecclesiastical record of repression and murder
to maintain its forged and fraudulent faith:

"When Constantine had taken upon himself the office of lay bishop
(*episcopus externus*) and *put the secular arm at the service of the
Church*, the laws against heretics became more and more rigorous.
Under the purely ecclesiastical discipline no temporal punishment
could be inflicted on the obstinate heretic, except the damage which
might arise to his personal dignity through being *deprived of all intercourse with his former brethren. But under the Christian emperors
rigorous measures were enforced* against the goods and persons of here-

tics. From the time of Constantine to Theodosius and Valentinian III (313–424) various penal laws were enacted against heretics as being guilty of *crime against the State*. In both the Theodosian and Justinian codes they were styled infamous persons; all intercourse was forbidden to be held with them; they were deprived of all offices of profit and dignity in the civil administration, while all burdensome offices, both of the camp and of the curia, were imposed upon them; they were disqualified from disposing of their own estates by will, or of accepting estates bequeathed to them by others; they were denied the right of giving or receiving donations, of contracting, buying, and selling; pecuniary fines were imposed upon them; they were often proscribed and banished, and in many cases scourged before being sent into exile. In some particularly aggravated cases sentence of death was pronounced upon heretics, though seldom executed in the time of the Christian emperors of Rome. Theodosius is said to be the first who pronounced heresy a capital crime; this law was passed in 382 against [several named sects of heretics]. Heretical teachers were forbidden to propagate their doctrines, publicly or privately; to hold public disputations; to ordain bishops, presbyters, or other clergy; to hold religious meetings; to build conventicles or to avail themselves of money bequeathed to them for that purpose. Slaves were allowed to inform against their heretical masters and to purchase their freedom by coming over to the Church. The children of heretical parents were denied their patrimony and inheritance unless they returned to the Catholic Church. The books of heretics were ordered to be burned. (*Vide Codex Theodosianus*, lib. XVI, tit. 5, "*De Hæreticis.*")

"This legislation remained in force and with even greater severity in the Kingdoms formed by the victorious barbarian invaders on the ruins of the Roman Empire in the West. The *burning of heretics* was first decreed in the eleventh century. The Synod of Verona (1184) imposed on bishops the *duty to search out heretics* in their dioceses and hand them over to the secular power. Other Synods, and the Fourth Lateran Council (1215) under Pope Innocent III, repeated and enforced this decree, especially the Synod of Toulouse (1229), which established inquisitors in every parish (one priest and two laymen). *Everyone was bound to denounce heretics, the names of the witnesses were kept secret;* after 1243, when Innocent III sanctioned the laws of Emperor Frederick II and of Louis IX against heretics, *torture was applied in trials;* the *guilty persons* were delivered up to the civil authorities and actually *burnt at the stake.*

"Paul III (1542) established, and Sixtus V organized, the Roman Congregation of the Inquisition, or Holy Office, a regular court of justice [!] dealing with heresy and heretics. (See Roman Congregations.) The Congregation of the Index, instituted by St. Pius V, has for its province the care of faith and morals in literature; it proceeds against printed matter very much as the Holy Office proceeds against persons (see *Index of Prohibited Books*). The present pope, Pius X (1909), has decreed the establishment in every diocese of a board of censors and of a vigilance committee whose functions are to find out and report on writings and persons tainted with the *heresy of Modernism* (Encycl. 'Pascendi,' 8 Sept. 1907). —[At another place the pious clerical reason for this flagrant attempt against the mind and its liberty of inquiry is thus with unctuous priestly speciousness stated: "for it is notorious that clever sophistry coated with seductive language may render even gross errors of faith palatable to a *guileless and innocent heart*"! (*CE.* xiv, 766).]—The present-day legislation against heresy has lost nothing of its ancient severity; but the penalties on heretics are now only of the spiritual order; all the punishments which require the intervention of the secular arm have *fallen into abeyance.* . . .

"The Church's legislation on heresy and heretics is often reproached with cruelty and intolerance. Intolerant it is; in fact its *raison d'être* is intolerance of doctrines subversive of the Faith. Cruelty only comes when the punishment exceeds the *requirements* of the case. . . . It suffices to remark that the inquisitors only pronounced on the guilt of the accused and then handed him over to the secular power to be dealt with according to the laws framed by emperors and kings—[at the instigation of the Church!].

"*Toleration came in only when faith went out;* lenient measures were resorted to ONLY WHERE POWER TO APPLY MORE SEVERE MEASURES WAS WANTING. . . . Christ says: '*Do not think that I am come to send peace upon earth: I came not to send peace, but a sword.*' The history of heresy *verifies this prediction*"! (*CE.* vii, 256–262, *passim.*)

The Church Persecutrix, under this forged Christ-Lie, has shed oceans more of blood than of its boasted "light" upon religion-cursed Christendom. The only "light" it has diffused has been from the flames of "heretic" cities, and the lurid fires of myriads of *Autos-da-Fe*, kindled by hypocrite priests, burning in agony the bodies of countless heroic men and women who scorned to prostitute their minds to the sinister lies of priestcraft, and who have dared defy with their lives the blighting "rule and ruin" dominion of the power-lusting Church.

With a shudder of undying loathing for the cruel cynical Hypocrite, we may admire the sweet charity of tender mercy displayed by the Holy Church of the Christ, exampled in the sanctimonious *Formula of Judgment* whereby its Holy Inquisition handed over the racked and broken errant Child of Faith to the prostituted Secular Arm for the final Act of Murder—the blessed *Auto-da-Fe*, with a prayer for the hated heretics: "*Ut quam clementissime et sine sanguinis effusionem puniretur—should be punished as mildly as possible and without the shedding of blood*"! The while Their Holinesses kept a standing Decree of Indulgences from the pangs of Purgatory for all the hoodlum Faithful who would please and glorify God by attending the sacred ceremonials of Burning, and especially to those who would aid God and the priests by fetching fagots for the consecrated fires, and throw water on the wood so that the priest-set flames would be slower in their purifying work and allow the writhing "Obstinate" longer time to make Peace with God and Holy Church by meet Repentance; in which event, the "reconciled" Child of Faith would be dragged from the flames only partly cremated, and returned to prison cell there to agonize out the remainder of his life in rapt contemplation of the beauties and sweetness of the blessed Christian Religion, crooning "Praise God from whom all blessings flow!"

The foregoing loathsome boasted record of the Church, sinister and infamous as it is, may be complemented by the following cynical and sophistical recital of the mental and moral debauch of ignorance imposed by the Church, concluding with the formal admission that "the theocratic State was *called upon* [by its prostituted mistress the Church] to *avenge with the pyre*" defiance of the lying fraudulent pretensions of the Church:

"During the Middle Ages the Church guarded the *purity and genuineness of her Apostolic doctrine* [!] through the institution of the

310

ecclesiastical (and State) Inquisition. . . . Following the example of the Apostles, the Church today watches zealously over the purity and integrity of her doctrine, *since on this rests her whole system of faith and morals, the whole edifice of Catholic thought, ideals, and life.* For this purpose the Church instituted the Index of Prohibited Books, which is intended to deter Catholics from the unauthorized reading of books dangerous to faith or morals, for it is notorious that clever sophistry coated with seductive language may render even gross errors of faith palatable to a guileless and innocent heart. (p. 766.) . . . Now, formal heresy was likewise strongly condemned by the Catholic Middle Ages; and so the argument ran: Apostacy and heresy are, as criminal offenses against God, far more serious crimes than high treason, murder, or adultery. . . . But, *according to Romans xiii, 11, seq.,* the secular authorities have the right to punish, especially grave crimes, with death; *consequently, 'heretics may be not only excommunicated, but also justly (juste) put to death'* (St. Thomas, II–II, Q; xi, a, 3). . . . The earliest example of the execution of a heretic was the beheading of the ring leader of the Priscillianists by the usurper Maximus at Trier (385). Even St. Augustine, towards the end of his life, favoured State reprisals against the Donatists. . . . Influenced by the Roman code, which was rescued from oblivion, Frederick II introduced the penalty of burning for heretics by imperial law of 1224. The *popes,* especially Gregory IX, *favoured the execution of this imperial law,* in which they saw an effective means for the preservation of the Faith. . . . Unfortunately, neither the secular nor the ecclesiastical authorities drew the slightest distinction between dangerous and harmless heretics, seeing forthwith in every (formal) heresy a *'contumelia Creatoris,'* which the theocratic State *was called upon* to avenge with the pyre." (*CE.* xiv, 766, 768.)

"THE SECULAR ARM"

"Hypocrites! Ye compass land and sea to make one proselyte, and when he is made, ye make him twofold more the child of hell than yourselves!" *Jesus.* (Matt. xxiii, 15.)

"The barbarous penal forms of the Middle Ages are to be credited, *not to the Church, but to the State"!* (*CE.* xiv, 768.) It is a monstrous hypocritical perversion of truth to pretend, as the Church ever does, that these inhuman and devastating legal enactments and deeds of fire and blood, which *ad horrendum* we have just read in faint outline from secular and ecclesiastical history, and which brought several "Most Christian" nations to utter ruin, moral and economic, were the voluntary and spontaneous expressions of the social policy of secular rulers, enacted and wrought against their subjects in order to preserve the peace and safety of the State and to regulate the civil and political conduct of their peoples. The Church, by fraud and fear, brought the secular rulers under her ignominious domination, and forced them by her threats, as we have seen proved and admitted, to make and enforce these infernal enactments and destructions. "This is the stale pretense of the Clergy in all countries, after they have *solicited the government* to make penal laws against those they call heretics or schismatics, and *prompted the magistrates* to a vigorous execution, then to lay all the odium on the civil power; for whom they have no excuse to allege, but that such men suffered, not for religion, but for disobedience to the laws." (*Somers Tracts*, vol. xii, p. 534; cited by Buckle, *Hist. of Civilization in England*, i, p. 246.)

But the Church waited not for the secular rulers to obey her murderous behests to "avenge with the pyre" the crime of disbelieving and deriding the Faith, nor did she lose time while watching the execution of her commands of murder by the secular arm. The Church was itself a secular ruler over then vast territories, the stolen "Patrimony of Peter" or States of the Church; and for those territories their Royal-Holinesses set the example of murder and burning of their own heretics. His Holiness Pope Gregory IX (1227–41) was, we are told, "very severe towards heretics, who in those times were universally looked upon as traitors and punished accordingly. . . . When in 1224 Frederick II ordered that heretics in Lombardy should be burnt at the stake, Gregory IX, then Papal Legate, approved and published the imperial law. In 1231 *the Pope enacted a law for Rome* that heretics condemned by an ecclesiastical court should be delivered to the secular power to receive their 'due punishment.' This 'due punishment' was *death by fire* for the obstinate and *imprisonment for life for the penitent.* In pursuance of this law a number were arrested in Rome,

312

burnt at the stake, and imprisoned." (*CE.* vi, 797.) And it was in Rome, by law and command of His Royal-Holiness Clement VIII, that the defier of the "Triumphant Beast," Giordano Bruno, was burned alive in Rome in 1600.

The hypocritical lie is repeated—and in the same breath belied. "Officially it was *not the Church* that sentenced unrepenting heretics to death, more particularly to the stake . . . Gregory IX . . . admitted the opinion, then prevalent among legists, that *heresy should be punished with death,* seeing that *it was confessedly no less serious an offense than high treason.* . . . [The succeeding popes went from opinions to acts.] In the Bull '*Ad Extirpanda*' (1252) Innocent IV says: 'When those adjudged guilty of heresy have been given up to the civil power by the bishop or his representative, or the Inquisition, the podestà or chief magistrate of the city *shall take them* at once, *and shall,* within five days at the most, *execute the laws made against them.*' Moreover, *he directs* that this Bull and the corresponding regulations of Frederick II [for burning heretics] be entered in every city among the municipal statutes *under pain of excommunication,* which was also visited on those who failed to execute both the papal and the imperial decrees. . . . The passages [of the imperial decrees] which ordered the burning of impenitent heretics *were inserted in the papal decretals.* . . . The aforesaid Bull 'Ad Extirpanda' remained thenceforth a fundamental document of the Inquisition, renewed or reinforced by several popes, Alexander IV (1254–61), Clement IV (1265–68), Nicholas IV (1288–92), Boniface VIII (1294–1303), and others. *The civil authorities, therefore, were enjoined by the popes, under pain of excommunication to execute the legal sentences that condemned impenitent heretics to the stake.* It is to be noted that excommunication itself was no trifle, for, if the person excommunicated did not free himself from excommunication within a year, he was held by the (papal) legislation of that period to be a heretic, and incurred all the penalties that affected heresy." (*CE.* viii, 34.)

Here it may be remarked, that prescription or statute of limitations runs not against the murderer. Thus Holy Church, who has murdered and procured the murder of millions, can never escape the just verdict and fatal sentence for her crimes before the bar of Civilization. Impotent now, senile, but venomous still in intention, she reeks

313

yet with the blood of her slain; their ghosts, like Banquo's, will never down. They cry yet to Humanity: *Ecrasez l'Infame!*

We have just read from *CE.* the confession that "the theocratic State *was called upon* to *avenge with the pyre*" all forms of heresy—or hate for the Church—as a *"contumelia Creatoris."* Again it says— again contradicting its false pretense that the State is alone to be "credited" with these pious infamies: "After the Christianized Roman Empire had *developed* into a theocratic (religious) State, it *was compelled*—[by whom but by the Church with its terrorizing threats to the superstitious rulers]—to stamp *crimes against faith* (apostasy, heresy, schism) as offenses against the State. (cf. Cod. Justin., I, 5, *de Haer.*: 'Quod in religionem divinam committitur, in omnium fertur injuriam.') *Catholic and citizen of the State became identical terms. Consequently crimes against faith* were high treason, and as such were punishable with death." (*CE.* xiv, p. 768.) A truer statement of the direful consequences of this enforced prostitution of the "secular arm" of the State to the criminal purposes of the Church in coercing its false and accursed religion upon humanity, cannot be made than this confession, in specious and unctuous words: "The rôle of heresy in history is that of evil generally. Its roots are in corrupted human nature. *It has come* over the Church *as predicted by her Divine Founder; it has rent asunder the bonds of charity in families, provinces, states, and nations; the sword has been drawn and pyres erected both for its defense and its repression; misery and ruin have followed in its track"!* (*CE.* vii, 261.) The confessed accursed record of Christianity!

The utter dependence of the Church for the beginnings and for the persistence of its bloody dominance, upon the extorted favors and support of the prostituted "Secular Arm" of the State to do its dirty work of subjection, is confessed and illustrated by two instances, one with respect to the overthrow of Paganism, the other accounting for the ultimate suppression of the early heretical sects. Of the former, it is "credited" to the Emperor Gratian: "In the same year, 375, he abolished all the privileges of the pagan pontiffs and the grants for the support of the pagan worship. *Deprived of the assistance of the State,* paganism rapidly lost influence. . . . He made apostasy a crime punishable by the State." (*CE.* vi, 729.) With a clerical slur at the "fanciful speculations of the Eastern sects so dear to the Eastern mind," oblivious of the equally fanciful "Oriental *speculations*" which are the only source of the holy dogmas of Western Christianism, it is cynically recorded: . . . "but, *lacking the support of the temporal power*, they sank—[just as "orthodox" Christianity would have sunk to oblivion]—under the anathema of the guardians of the *depositum fidei*"—holding the sword. (*CE.* vii, 259.)

As elsewhere suggested, it is pertinent to remark, that history would quickly repeat itself in this highly-to-be-desired respect, with the withdrawal of "the support of the temporal power," through the immense and illegal support yet given to the Beggar Church through deadhead tax exemption on its thousands of millions of dollars of ill-gotten, idle and hoarded properties.

"St. Augustine seems to have originated the application of the words 'Compel them to enter in,' to religious persecution. Religious liberty he emphatically cursed: '*Quid est enim pejor, mors animæ quam libertas erroris?*—For which is worse, the death of the soul than the liberty of error?' (*Epistle* clxvi.) Boniface III decreed excommunication of any magistrate who either altered the sentence of the Inquisition, or delayed more than six days in carrying it into execution. In the beginning of the thirteenth century, Innocent III instituted the Inquisition, and issued the first *appeal to princes to employ their power* for the suppression of heresy. In 1209, De Montfort (at Innocent's instigation), began the massacre of the Albigenses. In 1215, the Fourth Council of the Lateran *enjoined all rulers*, 'as they desired to be esteemed faithful, to *swear a public oath* that they would labor earnestly, and *to the full extent of their power, to exterminate from their dominions all those who were branded as heretics by the Church.*' The Council of Avignon, in 1209, enjoined all bishops to *call upon the civil power to exterminate heretics*. The Bull of Innocent III threatened any prince who failed to extirpate heretics from his realm with excommunication, and *with the loss of his realm.*" (Lecky, *History of the Rise and Progress of Rationalism in Europe,* vol. II, chap. iv, *passim.*)

As confessedly "tolerance came in only when faith went out," eternal gratitude and glory are the due meed of RATIONALISM, which has struck the sword and the stake from the armory of Faith, and left it a jaded sycophant begging "tolerance" of and for its bloody self.

England was rather distant from Rome and the English spirit did not yield so debasedly as some others did to the orders and dominion of priestcraft; but so early as Alfred the Great, so vaunted by the Church for his piety and learning, we have this picture of prostitution of State to Church; and the effects on both: "In the joint code of laws published by Alfred and Guthrum, *apostasy was declared a crime*, the payment of Peter's Pence was commanded, and the practice of heathen rites was forbidden. . . . But the clergy, . . . discharging in each district the functions of local state officials, seem never to have quite regained the religious spirit." (*CE.* i, 507.)

Out of scores of instances of legal enactments made by superstitious rulers under the terrors of papal threats, I cite here but one, in the quaint words of a militant philosopher: "Consequent to this claim of the Pope to be the Vicar Generall of Christ in the present Church . . . is the doctrine of the fourth Counsell of Lateran, held under Pope Innocent the third (Chap. 3, *de Hæreticis*), That if a King at the Popes admonition, doe not purge his Kingdom of Hæresies, and being excommunicate for the same, doe not give satisfaction within a year, his Subjects are absolved of the bond of their obedience. Where, by Hæresies are understood all opinions which the Church of Rome hath forbidden to be maintained." (Hobbes, *Leviathan*, Pt. iv, ch. 44, p. 333; 1651.) The infallible but presumptuous claim of the Vicars of God may be stated in the terms of the famous Bull of the "Two Swords":

"Under the *control* of the Church are two swords, that is, two powers. . . . Both swords are in the power of the Church, the spiritual and the temporal; the spiritual is wielded *in* the Church by the hand of the clergy; the secular *is to be employed for the Church* by the hand of the civil authority, but *under the direction* of the spiritual power. The one sword must be subordinate to the other; the earthly power must submit to the spiritual authority, as this has precedence of the secular on account of its greatness and sublimity; for the spiritual power has the right to establish and guide the secular power, and also to judge it when it does not act rightly. . . . This authority, although granted to man, and exercised by man, is not a human authority, but rather a Divine one granted to Peter by Divine commission and confirmed in him and his successors. Consequently, whoever opposes this power ordained of God opposes the law of God." (Bull *Unam Sanctam*, Boniface VIII, Nov. 18, 1302; *CE.* xv, 126.)

THE "TRIUMPH" OF CHRISTIANITY

Our review of the Forgery Founded Church having demonstrated the monstrous falsity of every divine premise of this "Bull," the hollow sham of these sonorous braggart phrases is ghastlily apparent. They are priestly lies!

COMPULSORY AND WHOLESALE CONVERSION

"And the Lord said unto his servant, Go into the highway and hedges, and *compel them to come in,* that my house may be filled." *Jesus.* (Luke xiv, 23.)

Disparaging the commands of its Lord to force them in, his Vicarate apologizes: "Instances of compulsory conversions such as *have occurred* at different periods of the Church's history must be ascribed to the *misplaced zeal of autocratic individuals.*" (*CE.* xi, 703.) The facts of history, as cited by *CE.* itself, belie this apologetic clerical passing of the odium for such felonious duress to autocratic individuals uninfluenced by the "moral" constraint of the Church-beneficiary and unswayed by its anathemas and threats of formal excommunication. A criminal who resorts to murder to prevent the escape of the victims who support him, would readily threaten murder to add greatly to the number of his supporting victims. It was St. Augustine himself, greatest pillar and authority of the Church Persecutrix, who first invoked the Christ's fatal fanatic command, "Compel them to come in," as complementary to the bloody edicts of the earlier "Christian" emperors and of his own fatuous fulminations against the "liberty of error," as above noticed. The first temptation to come to Christ was by bribes, as when Constantine offered a gold coin and a clean baptismal robe to all who would undergo that process; and the example of the Emperor in favoring Christianity drew great numbers of servile subjects to the feast of the Lord. We have read the cynical confession: that when governments favor a religious sect by giving its adherents all the offices and honors of the State and excluding all opponents, "the army of civil servants becomes a more powerful body of missionaries than the ordained ministers." When Clovis came to Christ he tolled 3000 of his retainers into the baptismal font with him at one time. Pepin "had been filled with this lofty conception, consequently extraordinary success attended the missionary labours of the Church.

. . . The conversion of the Avars had been attempted by the Bavarian Duke; after their *subjugation,* they were placed under the jurisdiction" of high prelates of the Church. (*CE.* v, 611.) "When the conversion of their prince was publicly known, the (people) of his kingdom are said to have flocked in crowds to receive the Christian faith." (*CE.* i, 669.)

When Charlemagne spent those seven days in Rome with His Holiness, who tricked him into believing that "his imperial dignity was an act of God, made known, *of course,* through the agency of the Vicar of Christ" (*CE.* iii, 615), and they together formed those "many great designs for the glory of God and the exaltation of the Church," due execution of the command of the Christ, "Compel them to come in," was one of the great designs conspired with His Vicar: "True to his own and his father's understanding with the pope, he invariably insisted on baptism as the sign of submission, punishing with appalling barbarity any resistance, as when, in cold blood, he beheaded in one day 4500 persons at Verdun, in A. D. 782. Under such circumstances it is not wonderful that clerical influence extended so fast. Always bearing in mind his engagement with the papacy, that Roman Christianity should be enforced upon Europe wherever his influence could reach, he remorselessly carried into execution the penalty of death that he had awarded to the *crimes* of: 1. refusing baptism; 2. false pretense of baptism; 3. relapse to idolatry; 4. the murder of a bishop or priest; 5. human sacrifice; 6. eating meat in Lent. To the pagan German his sword was a grim, but convincing missionary." (Draper, *The Intellectual Development of Europe,* i, 374.) This secular authority is confirmed by this clerical admission; that under the Carlovingian Empire, "*in war conversion went hand in hand with victory; in peace Charles ruled through bishops. . . . The Teutonic Order began the great conflict which *after more than half a century of bloodshed dealt the death-blow to paganism* in Prussia." (*CE.* iii, 700, 705.) Conversion by force and arms continued through the Ages of Faith and brought entire nations to Christ: "More lasting success followed the attempts, patterned on the Crusades, to carry on *wars of conversion* and *conquest* in those territories of north-eastern Europe peopled by tribes that had *lapsed from the Faith* or that were still heathen; among such pagans were the Obotrites, Pomeranians, Wiltzi, Serbs, Letts, Livonians,

Finns, and Prussians. The preliminary work was done in the twelfth century by missionaries. They were *aided with armed forces* [by several kings and rulers]. From the beginning of the thirteenth century *Crusades* were undertaken against Livonia, Courland, Esthonia, and Prussia. In Lithuania Christianity *did not win* until 1368." (*CE.* v, 612.) In Hungary, during the tenth and eleventh centuries, "the new *religion was spread by the sword.* . . . With these *laws* King St. Stephen brought over almost all his people to the Catholic Faith. . . . He [a later King] took strong measures against those who had fallen away from the Faith." (*CE.* vii, 548–9.)

Thus it was that by war and bloody imposition rather than by washing in the Blood of the Lamb, "vast tribes of savages who had always been idolaters, who were perfectly incapable, from their low state of civilization, of forming any but anthropomorphic conceptions of the Deity, or of concentrating their attention steadily on any visible object, and who for the most part were converted, not by individual persuasion, but *by the commands of their chiefs*, embraced Christianity in such multitudes that their habits soon became the dominating habits of the Church. From this time the tendency to idolatry was irresistible. The old images were worshipped under new names." (Lecky, *Rationalism in Europe*, i, 218.) The brand of conversion was marked by the outfit of missionaries and military auxiliaries who first caught the barbarians; and if the wrong kind got them first, it made all the difference in the world in point of whether the result was the intelligent working of the Holy Ghost or sheer ignorance. The great Bishop "Ulphilas (311–388) taught the Goths the Arian theology; Arian kingdoms arose in Spain, Africa, Italy. The Gepidae, Heruli, Vandals, Alans, and Lombards received a system which they were as little capable of understanding as they were of defending, and the Catholic bishops, the monks, *the sword* of Clovis, the action of the papacy, made an end of it before the eighth century." (*CE.* i, 707.) Arianism was very simple; it held that there was but a One-Person God, and denied the Blessed Trinity of Three-in-One. Thus Arianism was "an attempt to rationalize the Creed by stripping it of *mystery* so far as the relation of Christ to God was concerned" (*Ib.*). But this simple and de-mystified theology, the non-Catholic barbarians were too ignorant to understand; whereas, the other barbarians whose

319

minds were enlightened by the Holy Ghost at the point of the Catholic sword, were perfectly intelligent to comprehend the Mystery of the Holy Trinity,—which would have stumped Aristotle. The Arians had only to follow the ordinary Multiplication Table—"One times One is One"; whereas the Orthodox had to multiply curiously,—"Three times One is One!" The true formula is—Three times Naught is Nothing!

CONVERSION SKIN DEEP

In truth, however, "these nations were only Christianized upon the surface, their conversion being indicated by little more than their making the sign of the cross." (Draper, *Op. cit.*, i, 365.) True, indeed, it is, as is scores of times confessed: "Paganism had not been renewed in Christ." (*CE.* iii, 700.) "Christians who considered themselves faithful, held in a measure to the worship of the sun. Leo the Great in his day says that it was the custom of many Christians to stand on the steps of the Church of St. Peter and pay homage to the Sun by obeisance and prayers." (*CE.* iv, 297; cf, iii, 724–727.) And generally was it true: "The *pagani* retained the worship of the old gods even after they were all Christianized." (*CE.* vi, 12.) Among the Germans, and it is exactly as with all others, "the acceptance of the Christian name and ideas was at first a purely mechanical one." (*CE.* vi, 485.)

As the result of the superficial veneer, in the early days when persecution occasionally broke out, and offering incense to the statue of Dea Roma or the Emperor was the test of Pagan patriotism, great numbers of laity and even of clergy "flocked at once to the altars of the heathen idols to offer sacrifice." (*CE.* ix, 2.) "The apostates and the timid who had bought a certificate of apostasy, *became so numerous* as to fancy that they could lay down the law to the Church, . . . a state of affairs which gave rise to controversies and deplorable troubles. A bishop, followed by his whole community, was to be seen sacrificing to the gods." (*CE.* i, 191.) At first the Church "imposed perpetual penance and excommunication without hope of pardon" on the backsliders; "however, the great number of *Lapsi* and *Libellatici* . . . led to a relaxation of the rigour of ecclesiastical discipline, leaving the forgiveness of the sin to God alone" (*CE.* i, 624), while their easy return to the decimated fold of Holy Church immensely increased its sacred revenues and extended its sway. However, "when the Roman Empire became Christian, apostates were punished by deprivation of all civil rights. They could not give evidence in a court of law, and could neither bequeath nor inherit property. To induce anyone to apostatize was an offense punishable with death, under the Theodosian Code, XVI, 7, De Apostasis." (*CE.* i, 625.)

Thus by centuries of fraud, fear and force was the "house of God" filled from the highways and the hedges, the forests and the wattle villages, with Pagans "nominally converted to Christianity." Heathen superstitions veneered with the Pagan superstitions called Christianity, blended together for the further bestialization of the Faithful of Holy Church of the Christ, and the pall of the Dark Ages of Faith settled down over benighted, Church-ruled Christendom,—that "civilization thoroughly saturated with Christianity," and "fully absorbed in the supernatural." Two holy characteristics of the Age of Faith, the grovelling fear of guilt and devout concern for the devil, are thus commented: "Superstition is abject and crouching, it is full of thoughts of guilt; it distrusts God and dreads the power of evil" (*CE.* i, 555); and, with the pious Christians, "as among all savages, disease and death were commonly ascribed to evil spirits or witchcraft." (*CE.* xiv, 26.) So through the Ages of Faith!

Holy Church and Divine Christanity being now in full power and possession over mind and body of Christendom, it had free scope to bring forth fruits unto perfection of "Christian Civilization."

THE "FRUITS" OF CHRISTIANITY

"Wherefore, by their fruits ye shall know them." *Jesus.*

What Christianity did for [to] Civilization

The first effects of a new, and particularly an official State Religion, are upon mind and morals,—the state of culture or prevailing civilizing conditions; essentially, on the system of moral and intellectual education of the peoples subject to it. This is recognized by the Church: "As in many other respects, so for the work of education, the advent of Christianity is the most important epoch in the history of mankind." (*CE.* v, 299.) Alas, this is disastrously true, as the Church's own history demonstrates. Jesus Christ, says *CE.*, was the "Perfect

321

Teacher"; "to His Apostles He gave the command, 'Going, therefore, teach ye all nations.' These words are the charter of the Christian Church as a teaching institution" (*ib.*). Here it got its Divine License to teach, and it taught.

How effective was the Church as the Divinely instituted Pedagogue of Christendom, can be justly appreciated only through a knowledge of what kind of education, moral and mental, previously and at the time existed, and what educational system the Church inherited from the "heathens" when it assumed its sacred monopoly of teaching, and by a comparison between the pre-Christian and the Christian systems and results. By what the Church destroyed of existing systems, and by what is produced through its own,—by these fruits of its zeal for Christian teaching must the success of its execution of its Divine Commission be known and judged.

Christianity arose and finally prevailed in the Græco-Roman world, and there is exercised its Divine License as exclusive teacher of faith and morals and of secular education. Before the advent of Christianity, the nations of the Pagan Empire were—we are told—"such as sit in darkness and the shadow of death"; the "Perfect Teacher" came "to give light to them that sat in darkness and in the shadow of death" (Luke, i, 79; cf. Matt. iv, 16). A dismal picture is thus presented, and for centuries was touched up with the darkest colors by Christian preachments, of the moral depravity if not intellectual benightedness of the poor heathens before the "Light of the World" was shed upon them from the Cross on Calvary. The Greeks and Romans knew naught of Moses and the Prophets, had never conned the Ten Commandments, and had never murdered any one "who hearkeneth not unto the priest," as commanded in Deut. xvii, 12. Deplorable indeed must have been their state before the Divine Teacher undertook their enlightenment. The picture of their actual moral and intellectual plight we will scan as drawn by Christian scholars. Here is faintly a sketch of—

"THE GLORY THAT WAS GREECE"

"The education of the Greeks exhibits a progressive development. . . . The ideal of Athenian education was the completely developed man. Beauty of mind and body, the cultivation of every inborn faculty and energy, harmony between thought and life, decorum, temperance, and regularity—such were the results aimed at in the home and in the school, in social intercourse, and in civic relations. 'We are lovers of the beautiful,' said Pericles, 'yet simple in our tastes,' and we cultivate the mind without loss of manliness' (Thucydides, II, 40). . . .

"The Greeks indeed laid stress on courage, temperance, and obedience to law; and if their theoretical disquisitions —[or those of the Christians, for that matter]—could be taken as fair accounts of their actual practice, it would be difficult to find, among the products of human thinking, *a more exalted ideal*. The essential weakness of their moral education was the failure to provide any adequate sanction—[*e. g.*, the fear of Hell and damnation]—for the principles they formulated and the counsels they gave their youth. . . . The practice of religion, whether in public services or in household worship, exercised but little influence upon the formation of character. . . . As to the future life, the Greeks believed in the immortality of the soul; but this belief had little or no practical significance—[as to them, virtue was its own reward]. . . .

"Thus the motive for virtuous action was found, *not in respect* for *Divine law nor in the hope of eternal reward,* but simply in the desire to temper in due proportion the elements of human nature. Virtue is not self-possession for the sake of duty, but, as Plato says, 'a kind of health and good habit of the soul,' while vice is 'a disease and deformity and sickness of it.' The just man 'will so regulate his own character as to be *on good terms with himself,* and to set those three principles (reason, passion, and desire) in tune together, as if they were verily three chords of a harmony, a higher, a lower, and a middle, and whatever may lie between these; and after he has bound all three together and reduced the many elements of his nature to a real unity as a temperate and duly harmonized man, he will then at length proceed to do whatever he has to do' (Republic, IV, 443). This conception of virtue as a self-balancing was closely bound up with that idea of personal worth which has already been mentioned as the central element in Greek life and education. . . . The aim of education, therefore, is to *develop knowledge of the GOOD*." (*CE*. v, 296–7.)

. Saving their depraved want of respect for "Divine law"—(proclaimed by priests), and their woful neglect to provide "adequate sanction"—of "bribe of Heaven and threat of Hell" (priest-devised), for inducement to their Nature-harmonized character, the godless Greeks did fairly well in "developing the knowledge of the good" and attaining the most "exalted ideal"—outside of Jewish-Christian revelation—to be found among mankind, of personal and civic virtue, due alone to their high "idea of personal worth," rather than to the revealed concept of humanity pre-damned, "conceived in sin and born in iniquity," crawling through this Vale of Tears as "vile worms of the dust," of Christian self-confession. But then, God in his inscrutable Wisdom had withheld his precious revelation of Total Depravity from the Greeks,—knowing, probably, that they did not need it, and had bestowed it only on the obscure tribe of barbarian polygamous Hebrews, who eminently fitted the revelation. So it was not the Greeks' fault that they were no worse off, without the revelation, than were the Jews with it. We will come to the Christians anon.

Though, thus, the "Sun of Righteousness" did not illumine the revelationless skies of Greek Culture, the most splendrous stars of intellect and soul which ever—(before the Star of Bethlehem arose)—shone down the vistas of Time, blazed in its zenith. The name of every star in that Pagan Greek galaxy is known to every intelligent person throughout Christendom today; the light from these or those of them illuminates every page and every phase of Art, Literature and Science known today to the inestimable glory of man and boon of humanity. The living germ of some, the unsurpassed perfection of others, is the product of the intellect and the soul of the poor Pagan Greeks who had no Divine Revelation and were bereft of the priceless "benefit of Clergy" as a teaching institution.

Let us gaze for a moment as through the telescope of Time and scan the brilliant luminaries of the heavens of Pagan Greek genius, un-dimmed then by the Light of the Cross. Beginning with those who were about contemporary in their appearance with post-exilic Hebrew revelation, say about 600 B. C., we will name only those immortally known to every highschool student, skipping among the galaxies down to the time, about 400 A. D., when they were for a thousand years eclipsed by the Light of the Cross shining in the "Dark Ages" of Christian Faith.

The Pagan Greeks, unfamiliar with the Hebrew revelation of the Divine Right of Kings—(anointed by priests)—to rule mankind, in-vented Democracy, the right of the people to rule themselves,—a heresy recognized in the Declaration as a self-evident proposition, that all just powers of government are derived from the consent of the

324

governed. News about Moses and his Divine laws not having penetrated into Pagan Greece, a scheme of purely human codes for human conduct was devised by the heathen Lawgivers, Draco, Solon, Lycurgus. The revealed Mosaic History of the Hebrews not being available as a model, the poor Pagan Greeks had to make shift with Herodotus, "Father of History," Thucydides, Xenophon, Strabo, Plutarch, Pausanius, Polybius, Claudius Ptolemy, Dion Cassius. The God-drafted plans of the Tabernacle in the Wilderness and of Solomon's Temple not being at hand to imitate, uninspired Greeks planned and built the Parthenon, the Erechtheum, the Prophylæa, the Temple of Diana of Ephesus, the Temple of Apollo at Corinth, the Serapion and the Museum, "Home of all the Muses," at Alexandria. The summit of human art in sculpture was reached in Pagan Greece, the Apollo Belvidere, the Venus de Milo, the Wingèd Victory, the Laocoön, the friezes of the Parthenon; consummate masters of the "Old Masters" were the Pagans Phidias, Praxiteles, Callimachus, Scopas, Polyclitus, with the chisel; Apelles, Zeuxis, Polygnotus, Parrhasius, Pausias, with the brush. Statesmen and military leaders unknown to Hebrew History, yet whose names are immortal, led the Pagan Greeks to greatness and glory: Themistocles, Pericles, Aristides the Just, Lycurgus, Miltiades, Leonidas, Alexander the Great, who conquered the God-led Jews. Poor heathen orators, who never heard Jehovah speak from Sinai, nor the Christ on the Mount,—their supreme eloquence has echoed down the ages: Demosthenes, Democrates, Æschines, Lysias, Isocrates.

Literature and the Theatre were born in Pagan Greece; the "Classics" of Pagan thought and dramatic majesty came from the minds and pens of uninspired heathen who knew no line of the inspired "Law and Prophets" of the Hebrews, made semi-intelligible and sonorous only by the very free treatment of skilled translators into Elizabethan English; they are the immortal and inimitable standards of literary form, style, culture, in every university, high school, playhouse, and cultured home in Christendom today. For poetry: Homer, Hesiod, Pindar, Anacreon, Theocritus, the burning Sappho; for drama: Æschylus, Sophocles, Euripides, Aristophanes, besides the historians and orators named, the delightful old Æsop, the philosophers and scholars yet to name. The drama, tragedy, comedy, the chorus, melodrama; the epic, the ode, the lyric, the elegy, poetic form and measure, the very words for all these things, pure Pagan Greek. Philosophy—the love of Wisdom—the highest reach of the uninspired human intellect into the mysteries, not of faith and godliness, but of mind and soul, in search of the first principles of being,—the "*ousia* of the *on*," and for the Supreme Good, the noblest rules of human conduct and happiness: Thales, Anaximander, Anaxagoras, Empedocles, Heraclitus, Xenophanes, Leucippus, Democritus, Protagoras, Socrates, Plato of the Academy, Aristotle of the Lyceum, Epicurus, Pythagoras, Zeno the Stoic, Antisthenes the Cynic, whose lofty moral systems have exalted mankind ever since, and whose words and works have dominated civilization and made their names immortal, though none of them knew of Moses, the Christ, or the Apostles,—although Heraclitus invented the "Logos" which St. John worked up into the creative "Word of God" for Christian consumption.

Science, supremest handmaid of civilization, the true "God of this world," its splendid dawn was in Pagan Greece, unshackled by Genesis and Divine Mosaic revelation. Here Greek thought, undeterred by priestly ban and unafrighted by Popish Inquisition, sought to fathom the secrets of Creation and of Nature, to explain the Riddle of the Universe, to make the forces of Nature the obedient servitors of Man. Astronomy was born with Thales [640–546 B. C.], the first of the Seven Sages of Greece. Utterly ignorant of the Divine handiwork of the Six Days, and of universal creation out of universal Nothing, and not having travelled enough to verify the four corners of the flat earth, guarded by the Four Angels of the Corners, guardians of the Four Winds, he sought for the First Principle, the *arché*, of Creation, attributing all matter to changes in atoms; not knowing the revelation that the sun was set in a solid "firmament" arched over the flat earth, and somehow trundled across it daily to light Adam and his progeny, and had been stopped still for Joshua and turned backward ten degrees for Hezekiah, but fancying that it was governed by fixed natural law, by unaided power of mind he calculated and predicted the eclipse of 565 B. C., and discovered the Solstices and Equinoxes; he calculated so nearly the solar revolutions, that he corrected the calendar and divided the year into 365 days, which it still has; he taught the Egyptians to measure the height of the Pyramids by triangulation from the shadow

326

of a rod he set up near them, and invented several of the theorems adopted by Euclid. Anaximander (610–546 B. C.), like his master ignorant of Mosaic astronomy, discovered and taught the obliquity of the ecliptic, due to the erratic behavior of the equator of the earth in swinging round the sun; he approximated the sizes and distances of the planets—not all set on the same solid plane; he discovered the phases of the moon, and constructed the first astronomical globes; he was the first to discard oral teaching, and commit the principles of natural science to writing.

Pythagoras of Samos (c. 584 B. C.), was a universal genius; he coined the word "philosopher," according to Cicero; made discoveries in music, which he conceived as a science based on mathematical principles, and fancied the "music of the spheres." As he hadn't read Genesis, he defiantly (through such ignorance) proclaimed that the earth was a globe revolving around the sun or central fire, and had inhabitable Antipodes,—heathen notions which got several Christian gentlemen into more or less trouble some 2000 years later when they revived the idea. He speculated on eclipses as natural phenomena rather than special dispensations of Providence; he disputed Moses on Geology by claiming that the earth-surface hadn't always been just so, but that the sea had once been land, the land sea; that islands had once formed parts of continents; that mountains were forever being washed down by rivers and new mountains thus formed; that volcanoes were outlets for subterranean fires, rather than public entrances into Hell; that fossils were the buried remains of ancient plants and animals turned into stone, rather than theological proofs of Noah's Flood embedded for confutation of Infidels in the Rock of Faith.

Democritus (c. 460 B. C.), the "Laughing Philosopher," the most learned thinker of his day and renowned for all the moral virtues; he wrote some 72 books on physics, mathematics, ethics, grammar; totally unlearned in Bible science, he scouted the idea of Design in Nature, declaring it lapped in universal law; he upheld belief in secondary or physical causes, but not in a primary immaterial First Cause, declaring that by natural law could all the phenomena of the universe be accounted for; that there was no need of, no room for, supernatural interference or Divine Providence. He left immortal mark on the world of knowledge by his elaborated theory of atoms, or constituents of matter too small to be cut or divided; boldly and logically he applied this theory to the gods themselves, holding that they were mere aggregates of material atoms—(seemingly verified by the fact of eating the body of deity in wafers)—only mightier and more powerful than men,—and seemingly, to walk and talk, hate and kill, there must be something material about them. Modern chemistry, the most universal and useful of the sciences, is founded on modifications of the atomic theory of Democritus.

Hippocrates (c. 460–c. 377 B. C.) is known as the "Father of Medicine." He was the first physician to differentiate diseases, and to ascribe them to different causes, on the basis of accurate observation and common sense. His great axiom was: "To know is one thing; merely to believe one knows is another. To know is science, but merely to believe one knows is ignorance." In his days all sickness and ailments were considered as inflicted directly by the gods; the later revelation that it was all due to devils in the inner works of man was not then known. But the result was the same: all curing was the monopoly of the priests, the friends and favorites of the gods and possessors of all godly lore. As the only physicians, the priests had great revenues and a fine livelihood from the offerings made by patients who flocked for relief to the temples of Æsculapius, which filled the ancient world. Hippocrates sought to separate medicine from religion, thus incurring the venomous attacks of the priests and pious quacks. Never having heard of "fig leaf poultices," or spittle to oust devils, "He laid down certain principles of science upon which modern medicine is built: 1. There is no authority except facts; 2. Facts are obtained by accurate observation; 3. Deductions are to be made only from facts." Not knowing the Christian art of casting out devils, the heathen "Hippocrates introduced a new system of treatment; he began by making a careful study of the patient's body, and having diagnosed the complaint, set about curing it by giving directions to the sufferer as to his diet and the routine of his daily life, leaving Nature largely to heal herself." As about ninety percent of all ills are such as would heal themselves if let alone, or if treated with simple hygienic means, and many cures are greatly aided by "faith" even in Pagan gods, the element of the miraculous is greatly discounted in the successes of the priests of Æsculapius, and possibly in those of Loreto and Lourdes.

328

He had no real successor until Vesalius, the first real surgeon; the Inquisition nearly got him because his anatomical researches disclosed that man had the same number of ribs as woman, not one less to represent that taken for Eve; and he disproved the Church's sacred science of the "Resurrection Bone."

Aristotle (384–322 B. C.) the Stagarite, friend and tutor of Alexander the Great, besides being one of the greatest philosophers, was the foremost man of science of his day, and in his encyclopedic works laid the foundation of Natural science or physics, Natural History, meteorology or the phenomena of the heavens, animal anatomy, to all which he applied the processes of closest research and experiment and the principles of inductive reasoning. By reason of the limitations of his process, and over-dogmatism rather than experiment in some lines, he made many curious mistakes, which ham-strung the human mind for ages. One was the assertion that two objects of different weight, dropped from the same height to the earth, would strike the earth at different intervals of time, the heavier first; when Galileo denied this theory and offered to disprove it by experiment, the pious Christians of Pisa scouted and scorned him; when he ascended the Leaning Tower and dropped two iron balls, one of one pound weight, the other of one hundred, and both struck the ground at the same instant, they refused to accept the demonstration, and drove him out of the city; so strong was the hold of even the errors of Pagan Aristotle on Christian credulity.

Aristotle had not read the cosmic revelations of Moses, and was ignorant of the true history of Creation as revealed through him. He discovered sea shells and the fossil remains of marine animals on the tops of the mountains of Greece, and embedded far down from the surface in the sides of the mountain gorges; he noted that the rocks lay in great layers or strata one above another, with different kinds of fossils in the several strata. In his Pagan imagination Aristotle commented on this: that if seashells were on the tops of mountains far from the sea, why, to get there the tops of the mountains must once have been in the bottom of the sea, the rocks formed under the sea, and the shells and other animal remains embedded in them must once have lived and died in the sea and there have been deposited in the mud of the bottom before it hardened into rock. If Aristotle had climbed Pike's

329

Peak he would have found great beds of ocean coral in the rocks there; sea shell-fish and sponges—(which Aristotle himself first discovered to be animals)—in the rocky walls of the Grand Canyon of the Colorado.

Theophrastus (c. 373–287 B. C.), disciple and successor of Aristotle as head of the Peripatetic School of philosophy; his chief renown was as the first of the botanists, on which study he left some sixteen books; for 1800 years after his death the science lay dormant; not a single new discovery in that subject was made until after the close of the millennium of the Christian Ages of Faith.

Aristarchus (c. 220–143 B. C.) was a celebrated astronomer of the new school at Alexandria. From his predecessors he knew that the earth revolved around the sun, and how the plane of the ecliptic was designed; he calculated the inclination of earth's axis to the pole as the angle of 23½ degrees, and thus verified the obliquity of the ecliptic, and explained the succession of the seasons. Aristarchus had not read Moses on the solid firmament and flat earth; he clearly maintained that day and night were due to the spinning of the earth on its own axis every twenty-four hours; his only extant work is "On the Sizes and Distances of the Sun and Moon," wherein by rigorous and elegant geometry and reasoning he reached results inaccurate only because of the imperfect state of knowledge in his time. By exquisite calculations he added 1/1623 of a day to Callipsus' estimate of 365½ days for the length of the solar year; and is said to have invented a hemispherical sundial.

Hipparchus (c. 150 B. C.) made the first catalogue of stars, to the number of over 1,000; but his master achievement was the discovery and calculation of the "precession of the equinoxes" about 130 B. C. Without telescope or instruments, and with no Mosaic Manual on Astronomy to muddle his thought, by the powers of mathematical reasoning from observation he detected the complex movements of the earth, first in rapid rotation on its own axis, and a much slower circular and irregular movement around the region of the poles, which causes the equator to cut the plane of the ecliptic at a slightly different point each year; this he estimated at not more than fifty seconds of a degree each year, and that the forward revolution in "pre-

330

cession" was completed in about 26,000 years. Such are the powers of the human mind untrammeled by revelation.

Archimedes (287–212 B. C.), one of the most distinguished men of science who ever lived. He discovered the law of specific gravity, in connection with the fraudulent alloys put into Hiero's crown; so excited was he when the thought struck him that, crying "Eureka" he jumped from his bath and ran home naked to proclaim the discovery. He discovered the laws governing the lever, and the principles of the pulley, and the famous endless water-screw used to this day in Egypt to raise water from the Nile for irrigation; he was the first to determine the ratio of the diameter to the circumference of a circle, calculating "π" to be smaller than 3–1/7 and greater than 3–10/71, which is pretty close for a heathen not having the "Book of Numbers" before him. He made other discoveries and inventions too numerous to relate; he disregarded his mechanical contrivances as beneath the dignity of pure science.

Euclid (c. 300 B. C.) is too well known for his "Principles of Geometry" to need more than mention. Erastosthenes (c. 276–194 B. C.) was the Librarian of the great Library of Ptolemy II Philadelphus, at Alexandria, containing some 700,000 volumes. He invented the imaginary lines, parallels of longitude and latitude, which adorn all our globes and maps to this day. Not knowing the revelation that the earth is flat, he measured its circumference. Noticing that a pillar set up at Alexandria cast a certain shadow at noon on the summer solstice, while a similar pillar at Syene cast no shadow at that time, and was thus on the tropic; he measured the distance between the two places, as 5,000 stadia, about 574 miles; described a circle with a radius equal to the height of the pillar at Alexandria, found the length of the small arc formed on it by the shadow, which was 1/50 of the circle, and represented the arc of the earth's circle between Alexandria and Syene; multiplying the distance by 50 he obtained 28,700 miles as the circumference of the earth; a figure excessive due to mismeasurement, but a magnificent intellectual accomplishment. Erastosthenes was also the founder of scientific chronology, calculating the dates of the chief political and literary events back to the supposed time of the fall of Troy; a date quite as uncertain as that of the later birth of

331

Jesus Christ from which the monk Dennis the Little essayed to fix the subsequent chronology of Christian history.

Hero of Alexandria (c. 130 B. C.) discovered the principle of the working-power of steam and devised the first steam-engines. In his *Pneumatica* he describes the æolipyle, which may be called a primitive steam reaction turbine; he also mentions another device which may be described as the prototype of the pressure engine. (*Encyc. Brit.* xxi, 351–2.)

Strabo (c. 63 B. C.–19 A. D.), the most famous early geographer and a noted historian; he left a Geography of the world, as then known, in seventeen books, and made a map of the world; travelled over much of it, and described what he saw. From a comparison of the shape of Vesuvius, not then a "burning mountain," with the active Ætna, he forecast that it might some day become active, as it did in 79 A. D. to the destruction of Pompeii and Herculaneum, described by the Roman philosopher and natural historian, Pliny, who overlooked the Star of Bethlehem, and the earthquake and eclipse of Calvary. Strabo was ignorant of the cosmogony of Moses and the Flood of Noah; so he declared that the fossil shells which he discovered in rocks far inland from the sea proved that those rocks had been formed under the sea by silt brought down by rivers, in which living shell animals had become embedded. If Moses had revealed this interesting fact, much human persecution and suffering would have been avoided.

The principles of Evolution were discovered and taught by most of the ancient Greek philosophers above named and many others, all of whom were profoundly ignorant of the cosmogony of Genesis, and who "endeavored to substitute a natural explanation of the cosmos for the old myths." Anaximander (588–524 B. C.), though he had not read Genesis, anticipated to the very word "slime" used in the True Bible as the material of animal and human creation; "he introduced the idea of primordial terrestrial slime, a mixture of earth and water, from which, under the influence of the sun's heat, plants, animals, and human beings were directly produced." Empedocles of Agrigentum (495–435 B. C.) "may justly be called the father of the evolution idea. . . . All organisms arose through the fortuitous play of the two great forces of Nature upon the four elements." Anaxagoras (500–428) "was the first to trace the origin of animals and plants to pre-existing germs in the air and ether." Aristotle (384–322 B. C.), the first great naturalist, shows "in his four essays upon the parts, locomotion, generation, and vital principles of animals, that he fully understood adaptation in its modern sense; . . . he rightly conceived of life as the function of the organism, not as a separate principle; . . . he develops the idea of purposive progresses in the development of bodily parts and functions." The doctrine is very substantially developed by the Roman Lucretius, 99–55 B. C. (H. F. Osborn, *From the Greeks to Darwin*, pp. 50, *et seq.*)

The vital germs of virtually every modern science had thus their origin and some notable development in the fertile minds of the Greek thinkers and in their great schools of thought, in the centuries which preceded the Advent of the "Perfect Teacher" and his divinely instituted successors in schoolcraft. If these profound researches into Nature had been included in the Curriculum of the Church, rather than fire and sword employed to extirpate them and all who ventured to pursue them, Holy Church would not have had the "Dark Ages of Faith" to record and apologize for. To what perfection of Civilization and Knowledge might Humanity have arrived in these 2000 years wasted on the Supernatural, and the "Sacred Science of Christianity"!

THE POWER THAT WAS ROME

The Greeks with their brilliant culture and educational system lay for the most part remote from the Holy See of God's Teacher-Church at Rome; so it may be that the environment of the Teacher was really in a region which lay in darkness and the shadow of death, and thus its divine efforts were thwarted and rendered desultory. Thus it becomes important to know the degree of intellectual darkness and incapacity which whelmed the Empire of the West. The tale may best be told in the words of its Inspired Tutor.

"In striking contrast with the Greek character, that of the Romans was practical, utilitarian, grave, austere. Their religion was serious, and it permeated their whole life, hallowing all its relations. The family, especially, was far more sacred than in Sparta or Athens, and the position of woman as wife and mother more exalted and influential. . . .

"The ideal at which the Roman aimed was neither harmony nor happiness, but the performance of duty and the maintenance of his rights. Yet this ideal was to be realized through service to the State. Deep as was the family feeling, it was always subordinate to devotion to the public weal. 'Parents are dear,' said Cicero, 'and children and kindred, but all loves are bound up in the love of our common country' (De Officiis, I, 17). . . .

"Thus *the moral element predominated,* and virtues of a practical sort were inculcated: first of all *pietas,* obedience to parents and to the gods; then prudence, fair dealing, courage, reverence, firmness, and earnestness. These qualities were to be developed, not by abstract or philosophical reasoning, but through *the imitation of worthy models* and, as far as possible of living concrete examples. *'Vitae discimus,* We learn for life,' said Seneca; and this sentence sums up the whole purpose of Roman education—[in contrast to "We learn for heaven," as we shall see the Christian Ideal of education].

"In the course of time, elementary schools (*ludi*) were opened, but they were conducted by private teachers and were supplementary to the home instruction. About the middle of the third century B. C. foreign influences began to make themselves felt. The works of the Greeks were translated into Latin, Greek teachers were introduced, and schools established in which the educational characteristics of the Greeks reappeared. Under the direction of the *literatus* and the *grammaticus* education took on a literary character, while in the school of the *rhetor* the art of oratory was carefully cultivated." (*CE.* v, 298; see p. 358–9.)

PAGAN CULTURAL RESULTS

"Pagan education, as a whole, with its ideals, successes, and failures, has a profound significance. It was the *product of the highest human wisdom,* speculative and practical, *that the world has known*—[thus confessedly, as the highest, higher than the Christian]. It pursued in turn the ideals that appeal most strongly to the human mind. It engaged the thought of the greatest philosophers and the action of the wisest legislators. Art, science, and literature were placed at its service, and the mighty influence of the State was exerted in its behalf. In itself, therefore, and in its results, it shows *how much* and how little *human reason can accomplish* when it seeks no guidance higher than itself and strives for no purposes other than those which find, or might find, *their realization in the present phase of existence.*" (*CE.* v, 298.)

The splendors of the intellect and culture of Pagan Greece, its whole harmonious system of education, mental, moral and physical, which were the glory that was Greece, were transported thus to Rome and kindled anew there the torch of Reason which illumined and made splendid the power that was Rome. With clerical disparagement that all this intellectual and moral grandeur was accomplished by human reason alone with "no guidance higher than itself," that is, without the heaven-endowed tutorship of priestcraft, *CE.* yet confesses, that "Pagan education . . . was the product of the highest human wisdom . . . that the world has ever known," pursuing "the ideals that appeal most strongly to the human mind." It was in literature and in law, in history, in government, and in the practical arts and sciences, rather than in pure science, that the Roman genius rose to its highest reaches. The undimmed lustre of the Roman mind yet casts its splendors over the world of thought; Roman law, "the action of the wisest legislators," yet governs the actions of men and nations throughout the civilized world. A few illustrious names of universal renown must suffice to put into high relief the culture of Rome from the dawn of the Christian era till the pall of the Christian Ages of Faith fell over the Roman world. Augustus Cæsar (not to mention Julius), Cicero, Cato, Seneca, the Plinys, Tacitus, Livy, Horace, Vergil, Lucretius, the Scipios, Gaius, Paulus, Papinian, Tribonius, Antoninius Pius, Marcus Aurelius; the roster may be mightily extended and every glorious name be known to every schoolboy.

Thus was the Pagan Roman world intellectually and morally illumined when there befell—

THE CHRISTIAN AGE OF FAITH

under the tutelage of the vicars of the Perfect Teacher. The story again may be told by the accredited apologists who thus explain "The Aim of Christian Education," in response to the Divine Command. All education for practical objects of this life, for all "purposes which might find their realization in the present phase of existence," was piously and disdainfully rejected. For over a millennium, as will be soon admitted, Christian "education" was virtually limited to candidates for the priesthood and to the vain mummeries of monks; with few and straggling exceptions no one but a churchman was taught a word: the simple proof is, that scarce one person in a thousand of the population of Christendom except priests, could read or write his

335

name. The "education" of the Clergy will be known by its fruits, of which we shall have some tastes. Thus *CE.* discloses

"THE AIM OF CHRISTIAN EDUCATION"

"To these Apostles He gave the command, 'Going therefore, teach ye all nations' (Matt. xxviii, 19)—[a forged Mandate, as we have seen]. These [forged] words are the charter of the Christian Church as a teaching institution. While they refer directly to the doctrine of salvation, and therefore to the imparting of religious truth, they nevertheless, or rather by the very nature of that truth and its consequences for life, carry with them the obligation of *insisting on certain characteristics* which have a decisive bearing on *all* educational problems (p. 299–300). . . .

"*The Educational Work of the Church.* Apart from the preaching of the Apostles, the earliest form of Christian instruction was that given to the catechumens in preparation for baptism. Its object was twofold: to impart a knowledge of Christian truth, and to train the candidate in the practice of religion. . . . Until the third century this mode of instruction was an important adjunct to the Apostolate; but in the fifth and sixth centuries it was gradually replaced by private instruction of the *converts,* and by the training given in other schools to those who had been *baptized* in infancy. The catechumenal schools, however, gave expression to *the spirit which was to animate all subsequent Christian education:* they were open to every one who *accepted the Faith,* and they united religious instruction with moral discipline. The 'catechetical' schools, also under the bishop's supervision, *prepared young clerics for the priesthood.* The courses of study included philosophy and theology, and naturally took on an apologetic character *in defense of Christian truth against the attacks of pagan learning.* . . .

"Philosophy and literature were factors which had to be counted with as well as *the educational system,* which *was still largely under pagan control.* . . . *Fear of the corrupting influence of pagan literature had more and more alienated Christians from such studies.* . . .

"[In the Middle Ages] education was *provided for the clergy* in the cathedral schools under the direct control of the bishop and for the laity in parochial schools to which all had access—[but few availed thereof]. In the curriculum *religion held the first place;* other subjects were *few and elementary,* comprising at best the *trivium* and the *quadrivium.* . . . [I cannot forbear to add this]—The history of education records no greater undertaking; for the task was not that of improving or perfecting, [the brilliant system of pagan education], but of creating [the dull schools of religious instruction]; and had not the Church gone vigorously about her business, *modern civilization would have been retarded for centuries* [!]

336

"The monasteries were the sole schools for teaching; they offered the only professional training; they were the only universities of research; they alone served as publishing houses for the multiplication of books; they were the only libraries for the preservation of learning; they produced the only scholars; they were the sole educational institutions of this period. . . .

"Two other movements form the climax of the Church's activity during the Middle Ages. The development of Scholasticism meant the revival of Greek philosophy, and in particular that of Aristotle; but it also meant that *philosophy was now to serve the cause of Christian truth*. . . . Having used the subtleties of Greek thought to sharpen the student's mind, the Church thereupon presented to him *her dogmas without the least fear of contradiction*. . . .

"The same synthetic spirit took concrete form in the universities. . . . In university teaching all the then known branches of science were represented. . . . The university was thus, in the educational sphere, the highest expression of that *completeness* which had all along characterized the teaching of the Church." (*CE.* v, 299–303, *passim.*)

All these "universities were devoted for the most part to the development of theology." (*CE.* vii, 368; i, 264.) The "greatest" of these Christian universities was that of Paris, which originated about 1211; "legends of foundation of universities by Alfred, Charlemagne, and Theodosius II, are myths. The students were not boys, but mature men, *many clergy.* . . . Barbarous Latin of the universities and the wretched translations of Aristotle used in commentaries and lectures: the Scholastic method of teaching with its endless hair-splitting and disputations; much time was spent in gaining very little knowledge of hardly any value," were the charges made by the new school of Humanists, headed by Erasmus, "Prince of Humanists," which destroyed the old Christian ideals of education. (*CE.* xv, 194.)

The wonderful Middle Ages universities, so scorned by the Humanists of the Renaissance, and so fondly cherished by the Church, are not to be confounded in thought with such modernistic institutions as Oxford, Cambridge, Columbia or Harvard—(which all started on a purely "Christian" standard). A revealing pen-sketch of them all, based on that of Paris, is drawn by Prof. James Harvey Robinson: "There were no university buildings, and in Paris the lectures were given in the Latin Quarter, in Straw Street, so called from the straw strewn on the floors of the hired rooms where the lecturer explained the text-book [a handwritten manuscript], with the students squatting on the floor before him. There were no laboratories, for there was no experimentation. All that was required was a copy of the text-book. This the lecturer explained sentence by sentence, and the students listened and sometimes took notes.

"The most striking peculiarity of the instruction of the medieval university was the supreme deference paid to Aristotle. . . . Aristotle was, of course, a pagan. He was uncertain whether the soul existed after death; he had never heard of the Bible and knew nothing of the salvation of man through Christ. One would suppose that he would have been rejected with horror by the ardent Christian believers of the Middle Ages. But the teachers of the thirteenth century were fascinated by his logic and astonished at his learning. . . . He was called 'The Philosopher'; and so fully were scholars convinced that it had pleased God to permit Aristotle to say the last word upon each and every branch of knowledge that they humbly accepted him, along with the Bible, the Church Fathers, and the canon and Roman law, as one of the unquestionable authorities which together formed a complete and final guide for humanity in conduct and in every branch of science. . . . No attention was given to the great subject of history in the medieval universities, nor was Greek taught." (Robinson, *The Ordeal of Civilization*, pp. 207–208.)

The school of Erasmus and the other great Humanists who preceded and followed him brought the Renaissance to its fullness of glory in emancipating the mind from the fetters of the Dark Ages of Faith, and destroyed the rotten fruits of a millennium of "Christian education." Thereupon, says *CE.*, painfully confessing the truth, with reservations, "once the schools were secularized, they fell rapidly under influences which *transformed ideals, systems and methods*. Philosophy *detached from theology*, formulated new theories of life and its values, that moved, at first slowly and then more rapidly, away from the positive teachings of Christianity. Science in turn cast off its allegiance to philosophy and finally proclaimed itself the only sort of knowledge worth seeking. . . .

"During three centuries past, the main endeavor *outside the Catholic Church* has been to establish education on a purely naturalistic basis, whether this be æsthetic culture or scientific knowledge, individual perfection or social service. . . . The Catholic Church has been

338

obliged to carry on . . . the struggle in behalf of those truths on which Christianity is founded; and *her educational* work during the modern period may be described in general terms as *the steadfast maintenance of the union between the natural and the supernatural.* . . . It is specially the parochial school that has served in recent times as an essential factor in the work of religion. . . . Sound moral instruction is impossible apart from religious education. . . . Catholic parents are bound in conscience to provide for the education of their children, either at home or in schools *of the right sort*." (*CE.* v, 295–304, *passim.*) "*Parochial schools . . . aimed at fostering vocations to the priesthood.*" (*CE.* xiii, 555.)

The high Christian educational ideal of fettering Reason with Faith, and the underlying objective of all Church teaching, is again strongly insisted upon by our spokesman for Christian education:

"The Christian Church, by virtue of her Divine charter, 'Going, teach ye all nations,' is essentially a teaching organization. . . . Truths which are not of their nature spiritual, truths of science, or history, matters of culture, in a word, profane learning—these *do not belong* intrinsically to the progamme of the Church's teaching. Nevertheless, they enter into her work by force of circumstances, when, namely, the Christian youth cannot attain a knowledge of them without incurring a grave danger to faith or morals. . . . She *assumes*—[therefore, not divinely ordained to her, but self-erogated]—the task of teaching the secular branches *in such a way that religion is the centralizing,* unifying, and vitalizing force in the educational process." (*CE.* xiii, 555.)

A. THE MORAL "FRUITS" OF CHRISTIANITY

THE CHRISTIAN "MORALITY LIE"

"Apart from Religion the observance of the Moral Law is impossible." (*CE.* x, 559.)

"The wonderful efficacy displayed by the religion of Christ in purifying the morals of Europe has no parallel." (*CE.* iii, 34.)

"Her holiness appears in the fruits which she brings forth." (*CE.* iii, 759.)

The above gems of pious self-gratulation are culled from the plethoric treasure-chest of like paste jewels of ecclesiastical false pretense, and are set in high relief as tribute to the presumptuous genius of Pharisaism. A few more out of many may be displayed as a foil

339

to what follows: "Sound moral instruction is impossible apart from religious education" (*CE.* v, 304),—though this seems to be discounted by this formal admission of the entire efficacy of purely secular ethic of Plato and the Pagans: "All moral conduct may be summed up in the rule: Avoid evil and do good" (*CE.* v, 28); and by this self-evident truth: "Material prosperity and a high degree of civilization may be found where the Church does not exist." (*CE.* iii, 760.) Whether either of these highly beneficent conditions have been found where the Church in plenitude of power and pride did exist, will soon be disclosed. However, these disproofs to the contrary, "The Church has ever affirmed that the beliefs of Theism and morality are essentially connected, and that apart from religion the observance of the moral law is impossible." (*CE.* x, 559.)

Yet we have just read from the teeming pages of *CE.* the glowing tributes to the morally "exalted ideals" of the Pagan Greeks, and that with the Pagan Romans "the moral element predominated"; that "Pagan education, as a whole, was the product of the highest human wisdom that the world has ever known,"—and withal without the Light of the Cross to illumine the Pagan mind and conscience. Indeed, in the next sentences after the last above, *CE.*, waxing philosophical, belies fully its "Morality Lie" thesis, that "apart from religion the observance of the moral law is impossible," by this explicit admission of the *natural* source and origin of Morality: "The Church admits that *the moral law is knowable to reason*: for the due regulation of our free actions, in which morality consists, is simply their right ordering with a view to the perfecting of our rational nature. . . . The Greeks of classical times were in moral questions influenced rather by non-religious conceptions such as that of natural shame than the fear of the gods; while one great religious system, namely Buddhism, explicitly taught the entire independence of the moral code from any belief in God." (*CE.* x, 559.) We shall wonder, as we read the Christian record, how far the "beliefs of Theism" make for morality in higher or more wholesome degree than "the entire independence of the moral code from any belief in God." Morals is from *mores*, "custom"; it is social, not supernatural in origin; humanly conventional, not of divine imposition and sanction. The "morals," customs, of an age or a people depend always on what is then regarded as socially

340

convenient, on the character of education and example given by their preceptors and their environment.

The foregoing clerical admissions of the purely natural origin and sanctions of morals, of the Moral Law, are perfectly valid and convincing; a more formal and incontrovertible statement of the fact and the principle, taken from a special study of the subject, under the title *"Ethics"* in *CE.*, by a Jesuit Professor of Moral Philosophy, is added for the complete refutation of the Christian "Morality Lie":

"Morality, or sum of prescriptions which govern moral conduct. . . . Ethics takes its origin from the empirical fact that certain general principles and concepts of the moral order *are common to all peoples at all times*. . . . It is a *universally recognized principle* that we should not do to others what we would not wish them to do to us. . . . The *general* practical judgments and principles: 'Do good and avoid evil,' 'Lead a life according to reason,' etc., *from which all the Commandments of the Decalogue are derived,* are the basis of the natural law, of which St. Paul (Rom. ii, 14) says, it is written in the hearts of all men, . . . *made known to all men by nature herself."* (*CE.* v, 557, 562.)

It is because only of the nauseating persistence of the dingdonging of this pestilent "Christian Morality Lie," by priest, parson and press, that the loathsome record of the unparalleled moral corruption of the Church and of Christendom under the Church, is here in very summary and imperfect manner displayed in refutation of this immense False Pretense. It rings false from every pulpit and Christian apologist today as it has through all the centuries of Creed and Crime of the Church. Here in thumbnail sketch is the summary of Christian results after a millennium of undisputed moral sway: "The Church was the guide of the Western nations from the close of the seventh century to the beginning of the sixteenth" (*CE.* vii, 370); and for result: "At the beginning of the Reformation, the condition of the clergy, and consequently of the people, was a very sad one. . . . The unfortunate state of the clergy, their corrupt morals." (*CE.* vii, 387.) "The Lateran was spoken of as a *brothel,* and the moral corruption of Rome became the subject of general odium." (*CE.* viii, 426.) That there may be no mistake about the insistent pretense of the Church to teach and impose morality, "The Roman Pontiffs have always, as their office demands, guarded the Christian faith and morals," as admitted by the Apostolic Letter of His Holiness Pius IX, dated June 29, 1868, by which he summoned the celebrated Vatican Council which decreed Papal Infallibility in all matters of faith and morals. (*CE.* i, 176.) Therefore it was, that "the Church of the Middle Ages, having now attained to power, continued through her priests to propagate the Gospel. . . . In the wake of religion *follows her inseparable companion, morality.*" (*CE.* xii, 418.) We shall now see the Church at work for morality and the moral "fruits" of Christianity through the Dark Ages of Faith. "Those were indeed golden days for the ecclesiastical profession, since the credulity of men reached a height which seemed to insure to the clergy a long and universal dominion,—until the prospects of the Church were suddenly darkened, and human reason began to rebel . . . with the rise of that secular and skeptical spirit to which European civilization owes its origin," as Buckle says and demonstrates and I will briefly sketch, after first letting *CE.* reveal facts which are the harvest-fruits of Christian Morality.

How, then, are we surprised to read the official confession, that these same Middle Ages were, of all human epochs, "an age of terrible corruption and social decadence"? (*CE.* i, 318.) Surely the good cleric who penned these shaming words was a moral dyspeptic or must have developed a pessimistic in-growing conscience. We turn the pages of this ponderous Apology for the Faith to find the records of Church history giving the lie to this scandalous and disgraceful confession. There are fifteen great quarto tomes of *CE.*, of over 700 double-column pages each; and surely if this confession is mistaken or untrue, the glorious facts of Church morality, its ever-radiant and redolent "sweetness and light," which cannot be hid, will be made manifest for the confusion of those who might mock over this confession. The following paragraphs are the gleanings from just one, the first, of these fifteen volumes, recording the sacred history of the Church, in which "her holiness appears in the fruits which she brings forth," as therein preserved, and unparalleled "in purifying the morals of Europe" for fifteen centuries and more under her undisputed moral sway. In this one sample volume is the true assay of the "fruits" conserved in them all; a typical cross-section of Church history. Multiply by fifteen the product of these revelations of the "fruits which she

342

brings forth," and even the most unregenerate critic of Christianity must agree with *CE*, that "the wonderful efficacy of the religion of Christ in purifying the morals of Europe has no parallel" in any religion or history known to mankind. The following passages are word for word from Volume I—(unless otherwise indicated),—of the *Catholic Encyclopedia*, arranged roughly in chronological order, through part only of one letter of the Alphabet. They give thus a sort of segmentary cross-cut and bird's-eye-view of the moral and social conditions of Christendom through the centuries, with quite imperfect glimpses of that sweet charity one to another which distinguishes those who love their enemies—in the fashion of King Richard to his brother: "For I do love my brother Clarence so, That I would see his sweet soul In the bosom of good old Abraham!"

Countless instances of Christian "morality" we have already seen in the myriad holy forgeries of the Church throughout fifteen centuries; again are confessed "the many apocryphal [forged] writings in the first five centuries of the Christian era." (*CE*. i, 132.) Whoever would forge for Christ's sake or his own profit would as readily commit any other crime for the same ends, as we shall see to the limit of abhorrence. But the predilect perversity of the Christians clerical and lay, was the "lusts of the flesh," that distinctive "crime" so proscribed and so practiced by the expounders of "Christian virtue," and the "inseparable companion" of the most religious. That "sex-scandals" were rampant in the earliest days of the several infant Churches is manifest in quite all of the second-century Epistles of the New Testament, as any one may read unto edification. The *Agape*, or Christian "love feast" was all its name implies; it was "a form of ancient Pagan funeral feast. From the fourth century onward . . . the *agape* gave rise to flagrant and intolerable abuses" (i, 202). From the first century, "the *Agapetæ* were virgins who consecrated themselves to God with a vow of chastity and associated with laymen, who like themselves had taken a vow of chastity. . . . It resulted in abuses and scandals. . . . . St. Jerome [about 400] asked indignantly, 'Why was this pest of *Agapetæ* introduced into the Church?' St. Cyprian shows that abuses of this kind developed in Africa and the East. The Council of Ancyra, in 314, forbade virgins consecrated to God to thus live with men as sisters. This did not correct the practice entirely, for St. Jerome arraigns Syrian monks for living in cities with Christian virgins. These *Agapetæ* are sometimes confounded with the *Subintroductæ*, or women who lived with clerics without marriage." (202.)

St. Cyprian, *On the State of the Church*, just before the Decian persecution (c. 250), admits: "There was no true devotion in the priests. . . . That the simple were deluded, and the brethren circumvented by craft and fraud. That great numbers of the bishops . . . were eager only to heap up money, to seize people's lands by treachery and fraud, and to increase their stock by exhorbitant usury." (Quoted by Middleton, *Free Inquiry*, Int. Disc. lxvii–ix.)

"Solicitation, in canon law, is the crime of making use of the Sacrament of Penance for the purpose of drawing others into sins of lust. Numerous popes have denounced this crime vehemently, and decreed punishments for its commission . . . in connection with the Confessional, during or before" (xiv, 134). "The crime of abduction was, doubtless, extremely rare among the early Christians. In the fourth century, when men grew bolder, the number of wife-captors became exceedingly numerous. To check this"—a long line of Church enactments listed, down to the Council of Trent (1500's) was futile. (*CE.* i, 33.) While some of the following descriptions are applied to particular time and place, yet as is evident from the content and ensemble, like conditions existed "always and everywhere" through the Middle Ages, that delectable "civilization thoroughly saturated with Christianity." Thus "even in the fourth century, St. John Chrysostom testifies to the decline of fervor in the Christian family, and contends that it is no longer possible for children to obtain proper religious and moral training in their own homes" (555), already so debased was Christianity.

Loving Christian differences of opinion, enhanced by corporal methods of seeking each to force the other to the same opinion, were so ubiquitous and universal that birth was given to a special and deadly new species of human hatred and a distinctive name coined for it: *Odium Theologicum*—Theological Hatred, and the maxim: "Hell hath no fury like an offended Saint." The Father of Church History, Bishop Eusebius, has scathing passages, and he refuses "to record the dissensions and follies which they exercised against each other before the (Diocletian) persecution." (*Hist. Eccles.* Bk. VIII, chap. 2.)

344

And in Chapter 12, entitled "The Prelates of the Church," Eusebius wordily and in figured speech thus in substance describes them: "the different heads of the churches, who from being shepherds of the reasonable flocks of Christ, . . . were condemned by divine justice as unworthy of such a charge; . . . moreover, the ambitious aspirings of many to office, and the injudicious and unlawful ordinations that took place, the divisions among the confessors themselves, the great schisms and difficulties industriously fomented by the factious, . . . heaping up affliction upon affliction: all this I have resolved to pass by," as too shameful to be preserved in detail. Speaking of the Church historian Socrates, who died about 400: "Living as he did in an age of bitter polemics, he strove to avoid the animosities and hatreds engendered by theological differences." (*CE.* xiv, 119.)

We recall the embittered and bloody strifes which waged from the early days of the fourth century between the partizans of Arius, who denied the Divinity of Jesus Christ and consequently the existence of the Blessed Trinity or Three-in-One Godhead, and the "orthodox" or "right-thinking" faction which vociferated that Father and Son were of the same eternal age and "*homoöusion*" or "of the same substance,"—of which puzzle it is assured: "It is manifest that a dogma so mysterious presupposes a divine revelation." (*CE.* ix, 309.) But that "divine revelation" was let into the clerical mind through the efficacious grace of clubs, stones and knives, by force of fraud and deviltry, as thus witnessed: "The great definition of the Homoöusion, promulgated at Nicæa in 325, so far from putting an end to further discussion, became rather the occasion of keener *debate* and for still more distressing *confusion* of statement in the formulation of *theories* on the relationship of Our Lord to His Father. [Other angry Councils with the Holy Ghost were held on the "theory"] at Ariminum for the West, and at Seleucia for the East, in 359. At both Councils, *as the result of dishonest intrigue and an unscrupulous use of intimidation, . . . the Homoöusion was given up* and the Son was declared to be merely similar to—no longer identical in substance with—the Father. St. Jerome's characterization of the issue still affords the best commentary: 'The whole world groaned in wonderment to find itself Arian.' " (*CE.* i, 79.) Thus are divine revelations made manifest! The Christian trait of love for enemies is exemplified: "The sudden death of Arius [attributed to poison] was looked upon by contemporary Catholics *as an answer to the prayers* of the good bishop." (*CE.* i, 285.) All the "new nations" except the Franks, converted under Clovis, were "Arian heretics"; and for some four centuries maybe a million throats were cut in the name of One God or Three, before the "divine revelation" of Three-in-One won out.

"The accession of Constantine found the African Church rent by controversies and heresies: Catholics and Donatists contended not only in a wordy warfare, but also in a violent and sanguinary way. . . . Attempts at reconciliation, at the suggestion of the Emperor Constantius, only widened the breach, and led to armed repression, an ever-growing discontent, and an enmity that became more and more embittered. . . . One act of violence followed another and begot new conflicts. . . . Even in such condition of peril—[the bitter reprisals of the Arian Vandals which filled the fifth century], the Christians of Africa were far from showing those virtues which might be looked for in a time of persecution. . . . Crimes of all kinds made Africa one of the most wretched provinces in the world. Nor had the Vandals escaped the effects of this moral corruption, which slowly destroyed their power and eventually effected their ruin. . . . While one part of the episcopate wasted its time and energies in fruitless theological discussions, others failed of their duty. The last forty years of the seventh century witnessed the gradual fall of the fragments of Byzantine Africa into the hands of the Arabs. . . . In this overwhelming disaster the African Church was blotted out." (*CE.* i, 191–2.) God failed to protect his Holy own!

If prelates and priests, the shepherds of the flocks, wallowed in moral defilement, judge of the state of the witless sheep of the heavenly fold. "Valence, the central see of the Kingdom, had been scandalized by the dissolute Bishop Maximus, and the see in consequence had been vacant for fifty years," till 486. (616.) "Pope St. Agapetus I (535–536) was the son of a Roman priest slain during the riots in the days of Pope Symmachus. His first official act was to burn in the presence of the assembled clergy the anathema which Boniface II had propounded against the latter's rival Dioscurus" (202). St. Angilbert, Abbott, "at this period [about 790] was leading a very worldly life. . . . Angilbert undoubtedly had an intrigue with Charlemagne's un-

346

married daughter Bertha, and became by her the father of two children" (490). "On the death of Pope Formosus (896) there began for the papacy *a time of the deepest humiliation,* such as it has never experienced before or since. After the successor of Formosus, Boniface VI, had ruled only fifteen days, Stephen VI (properly, VII), was raised to the Papal Chair. In his blind rage, Stephen not only abused the memory of Formosus but also treated his body with indignity. Stephen was strangled in prison in the summer of 897, and the six following popes (to 904) owed their elevation to the struggles of the political parties. Christophorus, the last of them, was overthrown by Sergius III (904–911)." (ii, 147.) Pope Agapetus II (946–956), "for ten years, during what has been termed *the period of deepest humiliation* for the papacy. . . . He laboured incessantly to restore the decadent discipline in churches and cloisters; and in quieting disturbances in the metropolitan see of Rheims; and at putting an end to anarchy in Italy" (i, 203). Such periods of "deepest humiliation to the papacy" were quite recurrent: "The Popes Benedict from the fourth to the ninth inclusive belong to *the darkest period of papal history* (900–1048) . . . Benedict VI was thrown into prison by the antipope Boniface VII, and strangled by his orders, in 974. Benedict VII was a layman and became pope by force, and drove out Boniface VII; died 983. . . . Pope Benedict IX had long caused scandal to the Church by his disorderly life. His immediate successor, Pope Gregory VI (1044–46) had persuaded Benedict IX to resign the Chair of Peter, and to do so bestowed valuable possessions on him" (31).

"There can be no doubt that at this period (800's) the law of celibacy was ill observed by priests" (507). St. Arialdo was 'martyred at Milan in 1065, for his attempt to reform the simoniacal and immoral clergy of that city. . . . For inveighing against abuses he was excommunicated by the bishop" (707). Pope Alexander II (1061–73) was a leader in "that great agitation against simony and clerical incontinence. . . . A faction elected Honorius II as pope—public opinion clamoring for reform. Alexander was omnipresent, through his legates, punishing simoniacal bishops and incontinent clergy" (286). "The Church at that time (1072) was torn by the schisms of anti-popes" (541).—"The desperate moral barbarism of the age." (vii, 229.) Pope Anacletus II (1130–38) had before his election supported the popes in their fifty years' war for reform. If we can believe his enemies, he disgraced his office by gross immorality and by his greed in the accumulation of lucre. There can be no doubt that he determined to buy or force his way into the Papal Chair. . . . On the death of Honorius, two popes, Anacletus II and Innocent II were elected and consecrated on the same day, by the factions in the Sacred College. . . . When Anacletus died, another anti-pope, Victor IV, was elected by one faction" (447).

The "glorious thirteenth century," which the Faithful for some unfathomable reason exalt proudly above all the others of the Dark Ages of Faith, was ushered in with the murderous Holy Inquisition and the unholy crusade against the Albigenses, tens of thousands of whom were butchered and the fairest half of France laid desolate. The motive for this unprecedented butchery and devastation is naïvely confessed to be "their *wealth* . . . their contempt for the Catholic clergy, caused by the ignorance and the worldly, too frequently scandalous lives of the latter" (268). "With the zeal of an apostle St. Anthony [d. 1231] undertook to reform the morality of his time; . . . enormous scandals were repaired" (557). "The barons of the Campagna fought with each other and with the Pope and, issuing from their castles, raided the country in every direction, and even robbed the pilgrims on their way to the tombs of the Apostles. . . . William I took captive many wealthy Greeks, the greater number of whom he sold into slavery" (157). "A period of decline followed after the middle of the thirteenth century, when war and rapine did much injury . . . suffered again in the fifteenth and sixteenth centuries from the prevailing social disturbances" (145). "Pope Alexander IV (1254–61) was easily led away by the whisperings of flatterers, and inclined to listen to the wicked suggestions of avaricious persons. . . . He continued Innocent IV's policy of a war of extermination against the progeny of Frederick II. . . . The pecuniary assistance these measures brought him was dearly bought by the embitterment of the English clergy and people against the Holy See. . . . The unity of Christendom was a thing of the past" (288). About 1300, "all looked forward to the time when the religious orders, whose laxity. had been occasioned in great measure by *the general looseness of the times,* would be restored to their former discipline" (484).

348

THE "TRIUMPH" OF CHRISTIANITY

Under Pope Alexander V (1409–1410) "The Great Schism (1378–1417) rent the Church. As cardinal he had sanctioned the agreement of the rival Colleges of Cardinals to join in a common effort for unity. He thus incurred the displeasure of Gregory XII [who deposed him]. At the Council of Pisa (1409) he preached the opening sermon, a scathing condemnation of the rival popes, and presided at the deliberations of the theologians who declared those popes heretics and schismatics . . . in the riven Catholic world. . . . His legitimacy was soon questioned, and the world was chagrined to find that instead of two popes it now had three. . . . Whether or not Alexander was a true pope is a question still discussed" (288–9).

Speaking of "moral" conditions in the Holy City and prevailing in the age, *CE.* thus summarizes the "sweetness and light" of Christendom in the time of His Holiness Sixtus IV (died 1484): "His dominating passion was nepotism, heaping riches and favors on his unworthy relatives. His nephew, the Cardinal Rafael Riario, plotted to overthrow the Medici; the pope was cognizant of the plot, though probably not of the intention to assassinate, and even laid Florence under an interdict because it rose in fury against the conspirators and brutal murderers of Giuliano dei Medici. Henceforth, until the Reformation, the secular interests of the papacy were of paramount importance. The attitude of Sixtus towards the conspiracy of the Pazzi, his wars and treachery, his promotion to the highest offices in the Church of such men as . . . are blots upon his career. Nevertheless, there is a praiseworthy side to his pontificate. He took measures to suppress abuses in the Inquisition, vigorously opposed the Waldenses, and annulled the decrees of the Council of Constance . . . Under him *Rome became once more habitable*, and he did much to improve the sanitary conditions of the city." (*CE.* xiv, 32, 33.)

Pope Alexander VI (1492–1503) was so notoriously infamous and his history is so large and so well known, with his six bastards, including Cesare and Lucrezia Borgia, and his numerous Vatican mistresses and dissolute Papal Court, under whose régime again "the Vatican was a brothel," that he is simply mentioned in his order. When one of his bastard sons "was fished out of the Tiber with his throat cut . . . that it was a warning from Heaven to repent, no one felt more keenly than the Pope himself. He spoke of resigning; and proclaimed his determination to set about *that reform of the Church 'in Head and members' for which the world had so long been clamoring"*; but his grief was assuaged by the attentions of his lady loves, notably pretty Guilia Farnese, niece of the Cardinal, and whose picture as an angel now adorns one of the great frescos of the Vatican. "Long ago Leo the Great (440–461) declared, 'the dignity of Peter suffers no diminution even in an unworthy successor.'" (289, 294, *passim*.) Maybe so; but *the question simply is, "the unparalleled purification of morals" produced by the religion of Christ!*

About this juncture, and after a thousand years of such conditions in the Church and the Heads of the Church, popes, prelates, priests, and monks, and rife among the degraded people, the protests of Christendom swelling steadily for several centuries broke into the Protestant Reformation by force and arms. A thumbnail sketch of the culmination and the causes leading up to it throughout the Middle Age "civilization thoroughly saturated with Christianity," is drawn by *CE.* in two paragraphs here quoted:

"At the time of Gregory VII's elevation to the papacy (1073–85), *the Christian world was in a deplorable condition.* During the desolating period of transition—the terrible period of warfare and rapine, violence, and corruption in high places, which followed immediately upon the dissolution of the Carlovingian Empire [in the 800's], a period when society in Europe seemed doomed to destruction and ruin —the Church had not been able to escape from *the general debasement* [to which it had so signally contributed, if not caused]. The tenth century, the saddest perhaps, in Christian annals, is characterized by the vivid remark of [Cardinal] Baronius that Christ was as asleep in the vessel of the Church. At the time of Leo IX's election in 1049, according to the testimony of St. Bruno, Bishop of Segni, 'the whole world lay in wickedness, holiness had disappeared, justice had perished, and truth had been buried; Simon Magus was lording it over the Church, whose bishops were given to luxury and fornication.' St. Peter Damien, the fiercest censor of his age, unrolls a frightful picture of the decay of clerical morality in the lurid pages of his 'Book of Gomorrah.' . . . Writing in 1075, Gregory himself laments the unhappy state of the Church. 'The Eastern Church has fallen away from the Faith and is now assailed on every side by infidels. Wherever I

350

turn my eyes—to the west, to the north, to the south,—I find everywhere bishops who have obtained their office in an irregular way, whose lives and conversations are strangely at variance with their sacred calling; who go through their duties not for the love of Christ but from motives of worldly gain. And those among whom I live are worse than Jews or Pagans.' . . . Gregory made every effort to stamp out of the Church the two consuming evils of the age, simony and clerical incontinency. . . . Gregory began his great work of purifying the Church by a reformation of the clergy. In 1074 he enacted the following decrees [a series aimed at the two universal vices named]. But they met with vigorous resistance, . . . called forth a most violent storm of opposition throughout Italy, Germany, and France. And the reason for this opposition on the part of the vast throng of immoral and simoniacal clerics is not far to seek." (*CE.* vi, 793–4.) Still, nearly five centuries later:

"Churchmen in high places were constantly unmindful of truth, justice, purity, self-denial; many had lost all sense of Christian ideals; not a few were deeply stained by Pagan [?] vices. . . . The earlier years of Æneas Sylvius [Pope Pius II, 1458–64], the whole career of Rodrigo Borgia (Alexander VI), the life of Farnese, afterwards Paul III, until he was compelled to reform himself as well as the Curia, . . . all with disregard for the most elementary virtues. Julius II fought and intrigued like a mere secular prince; Leo X, although certainly not an unbeliever—[it was His Holiness who framed the famous "witty epigram: 'What profit has not that Fable of Christ brought us' "; *Encyc. Brit.*, 14th Ed. xix, 217]—was frivolous in the extreme; Clement VII drew on himself the contempt as well as hatred of all who had dealings with him, by his crooked ways and cowardly subterfuges which led to the taking and pillage of Rome. Now, it is not unfair to trace in these popes, as in their advisers, a certain common type, the pattern of which was Cesare Borgia, sometime cardinal, but always in mind and action a condottiere [bandit], while its philosopher was Machiavelli. We may express it in the words of Villari as a 'prodigious intellectual activity accompanied by moral decay.' . . . Not only did they fall away from monastic severities, they lost all manly and decent self-control. . . . Worse things than Savonarola had seen were to happen. And a catastrophe was inevitable. Erasmus laughed

351

to scorn the Ciceronian pedantries [of sundry Cardinals named]; he quotes with disgust the paganizing terms in which some Roman preachers travestied the persons and scenes of the Gospels, . . . outcry against cancerous vices which were sapping the life of Italy. . . . [Some] demanded reform according to Catholic principles [!]; . . . [Others] taught education in principle and practice on orthodox lines. . . . The Sorbonne objected, however, to any publication of Scripture without approved Catholic notes; and this in a day which might be justly termed one of rebuke and blasphemy. . . . Poggio, the mocking adversary of the clergy, was for half a century in the service of the popes. Filelfo, a pagan unabashed and foul, was rewarded by Nicholas V for his abominable satires. Pius II had the faults of a smart society journalist, and took neither himself nor his age seriously. Platina, with whom Paul II quarreled on political grounds, wrote a vindicative slanderous book, 'The Lives of the Roman Pontiffs,' which, however, was in some degree justified by the project of reformation 'in Head and members' *constantly put forth and never fulfilled* until Christendom had been rent in twain." (*CE.* xii, 767–768.)

Speaking again of prevailing conditions at the end of a thousand years of inspired care of the Christian morals, by their Holinesses, the following sentences culled from one article are a little cluster of the "fruits" of Christianity: "The scientific and ascetic training of the clergy left much to be desired, the moral standard of many being very low, and the practice of celibacy not everywhere observed. Not less serious was the condition of many monasteries of men, and even of women. . . . The members of the clergy were in many places regarded with scorn. . . . As to the Christian people itself, in numerous districts ignorance, superstition, religious indifference, and immorality were rife. . . . Worldly ideas, luxury and immorality rapidly gained ground at the centre of ecclesiastical life. When ecclesiastical authority grew weak at the fountain head, it necessarily decayed elsewhere. . . . In proportion as the papal authority lost the respect of many, resentment grew against both the Curia and the Papacy. . . . This vast ecclesiastical wealth, . . . such riches in the hands of the clergy. . . . Higher intellectual culture was confined in a great measure to the higher clergy. . . . The parochial clergy were to a

352

great extent ignorant and indifferent." (*CE*. xii, 700–703, *passim*.)

The Church leaped to arms to prevent any reform of these degrading conditions to which her holy guidance had brought Christendom, and for over a century, until the Religious Peace of 1648, with fire and sword made Europe a slaughter-pen in the desperate effort to suppress the revolt and force its forged faith and its creed of love and morals, which we have just seen exemplified, down the throats of revolted and disgusted humanity. The Dominican "Dogs of the Lord" were let loose in all the bloody fiery fury of the Holy Inquisition; Alva, Tilly and Wallenstein ravaged and destroyed Europe, culminating in the glories of Magdeburg and St. Bartholomew for which His Holiness and his Church sang *Te Deums*. "Soon the Counter-Reformation, called into life by the Council of Trent (1545–63) to prevent the loss of the whole of middle Europe, appeared; its success was assured by the aid of the Society of Jesus." (*CE*. v, 612.) Abetted by the crafty and cruel Society of Jesus, under its renowned leader this miracle is said to have been wrought: "St. Ignatius, alive to *the causes which had provoked so many nations to revolt from the clergy* . . . did the most astonishing feat recorded in modern history. He *reformed the Church* by means of the *papacy when sunk to its lowest ebb;* and he took the heathen classics from neo-pagans to make them the instruments of Catholic education. . . . In May, 1527, Rome was laid waste, its churches profaned, its libraries pillaged, by a rabble of miscreants. 'But,' said the Cardinal Cajetan, 'it was a just judgment on the Romans.' . . . It was a change so marked that Scaliger termed the Italians generally hypocrites. . . . The papacy aimed henceforth at becoming an 'ideal government under spiritual and converted men.' Urban VIII (1623–44) was the last who could be deemed a Renaissance pontiff." (*CE*. xii, 769.) This was over one hundred years after the boasted "reformation in Head and members."

So here the Augean stables were at length cleansed; the papacy—for the fourth time in Volume I recorded as "sunk to its lowest ebb," was now to be "an ideal government under spiritual and converted men," and the chronic millennial infamies of Holy Church washed out by a baptism of Faith and "good works meet unto repentance." But was it so?

Adrian VI was Holiness of Rome in 1522–1523: "Appalling tasks

353

lay before him in this [again] *darkest hour of the Papacy*. To extirpate inveterate abuses ; to reform a court which thrived on corruption, and detested the very name of reform ; to hold in leash the young and warlike princes, ready to bound at each other's throats,—these were herculean labours. . . . His nuncio to Germany, Chierigati, [made the exaggerated] acknowledgment, that the Roman Court had been the fountain-head of all the corruptions in the Church. Cardinal Adrian of Castello (in 1517) was implicated in a charge of conspiring with Cardinal Petrucci to poison the pope Leo X, and confessed" (i, 160). "Under the direct orders of the pope, Clement VII, Archbishop B. [in 1538] caused many [Protestants in Scotland] to . . . be put to death. Modern humanity condemns the cruel manner of their execution ; but such severities were the *result of the spirit of the age*" (ii, 374),—which quite as thoroughly inspired the same Protestants and was as villainously practiced by them when they had the chance. The sixteenth century was "a scandalous age." (*CE*. ii, 375.) About 1600 a special Papal representative "was commissioned to reform a convent at Naples, which by the laxity of its discipline had become a source of great scandal. Certain wicked men were accustomed to have clandestine meetings with the nuns" (i, 472). Pope Alexander VII (1655–1667) was "elected after a struggle of eighty days ; at a time when churchmen were being forced to realize the deplorable consequences, moral and financial, of nepotism ; . . . nepotic abuses came to weigh as heavily *as ever* upon the papacy . . . endeavours to enrich their families" (294). Pope Alexander VIII (1689–1691) "bestowed on his relations the riches they were eager to accumulate ; in their behalf, and to the discredit of his pontificate, he revived sinecure offices. Out of compassion for the poor of well-nigh impoverished Italy, he sought to succor them by reducing the taxes" (295).

"The eighteenth century was not an age remarkable for depth of spiritual life" (334). "Here [in the bishopric of St. Agatha, near Naples, in 1762] with 30,000 uninstructed people, 400 mostly indifferent and sometimes scandalous secular clergy, and 17 more or less relaxed religious houses . . . a field so overgrown with weeds that they seemed the only crop" (337). In 1799 "*people were already rejoicing that the Papacy and the Church had come to an end. But the priest, Count Antonio Rosmini . . . published his ideas in 1848 in*

354

the treatise 'Of the Five Plagues of the Church,' in which he also particularly recommended the *reform of the Church. . . . The demand for reform in the States of the Church was in fact* not unjustified." (*CE.* xiv, 264, 265.) Much later like data could be added.

Thus in our search for its sweetness and light, we have as it were scratched the surface of the history of Holy Church, for a thousand five hundred years, as recorded by itself; thus in one volume out of fifteen have we verified the priestly boast: "Her holiness appears in the fruits which she brings forth." The most lurid features, as under long lines of Holinesses, for example, Benedicts, Eugenes, and Johns, fall outside our limited alphabetical scope; we have made no note of the interminable political wars and throat-cuttings joyously promoted by fifteen hundred years of Popes; nor of the infinite bloodlust and greed of the execrated Holy Inquisition and of interminable successions of Popes, papal Curias and blood-sodden prelates. The choice of every Pope is guided by the Holy Ghost itself, aided indirectly but effectively in a hundred instances by bribery and the dagger. Even this trinity of Holy Electors of the Vicars of God has not always kept the "Succession of Peter" in a straight line; a goodly number of times the Spirit has descended upon numerous doublets and triplets of Holinesses at one and the same time: "At various times in the history of the Church illegal pretenders to the Papal Chair have arisen, and frequently exercised pontifical functions in defiance of the true occupant. According to Hergenröther, there are 29 [doublet and triplet sets] in the following order,"—naming them, beginning about 200 A. D. and extending down to 1449. (*CE.* i, 582.) The turmoils and scandals leading to and resulting from these, the priestly anathemas spit at each other, the blood and terror, and the unspeakably debased social conditions which made it all possible—in the name of Christ, can be but faintly imagined. This is but a fractional and imperfect inventory of the crops of "the fruits which she has brought forth" since her first budding out of the graft of Forgery and Fraud upon the iron stock of Force.

What price Religion! Paganism—and Christianity! Which—upon the record—has been the more shameless and debauched, and wrought the worst for morality and civilization? If, but for the glorious "civilizing effects" of Christianity, "civilization would have been retarded

355

for a thousand years"—What would not Civilization be today but for the "sweetness and light" of the Church and its Dark Ages of Faith?

B. THE INTELLECTUAL "FRUITS" OF CHRISTIANITY

THE CHRISTIAN "EDUCATION LIE"

"Of course, the beginnings of all profane knowledge can be traced back to the time when 'priest' and 'scholar' meant one and the same thing." (*CE.* vi, 447.)

"There is nothing more despicable than an ignorant priest." *Cardinal Farnese.* (*CE.* v, 788-9.)

A panoramic view, sketched by pious clerical pens, has passed before us, depicting in high light the outlines of moral and intellectual culture of two civilizations: the one Pagan, secular, brilliant, of pre-Christian Greece and Rome; the other "a civilization thoroughly saturated with Christianity," with Christian morality and culture;—this section, added from *CE.*, must determine its intellectual achievements. So insistent and ever-proclaimed are the clerical claims for the education of Christendom, and its "Christian civilization," which, without its glorious and heroic activities, "would have been retarded for a thousand years," that it is but just and fair to let the Church repeat several times what it claims to have done; then let it tell in its own words what it did.

Here are a few of the exalted cultural claims of the Church: "The Church, although officially the teacher of revealed truth only, has always been interested in the cultivation of every branch of human knowledge. But *the truth unfolded by reason cannot contradict the truth revealed by God!* The Encyclical next shows, by extracts from many Fathers of the Church, what reason helped by revelation can do for [to] the progress of human knowledge"! (Encyc. *Æterni-Patris*, Leo XIII, 1879; *CE.* i, 177.) "The Christian Church during this era—a fact of the greatest importance—was the guardian of the remains of classical literature." (*CE.* vi, 485.) "The preservation of the fragments of Greek and Roman classics now extant is largely due to the monasteries, which for twelve centuries after the fall of the Western Empire were the custodians of manuscripts of the ancient

356

Greek philosophy and the Latin rhetoricians." (*CE.* i, 696.) "In addition to their prescribed studies, *the monks were constantly occupied in* copying the classic texts." (*CE.* v, 303.)

THE MONKS "PRESERVED THE CLASSICS"

In the sweet-sounding music of this clerical chorus, a rudely jarring discord is struck by these dissonant notes: "The *revival* of the classics, *lost for a thousand years in Western Christendom.* . . . The *loss of* Greek authors and the *decline* of Church Latin *into barbarism* were misfortunes *in a universal ruin.*" (*CE.* xii, 277.) An attempt by Charlemagne to establish even rudimentary education was abortive, and "the accumulated wisdom of the past . . . was in danger of perishing," but "When the permanent *renaissance of learning came several centuries later, the light began* again to pierce through the storm-clouds of feudal strife and anarchy." (*CE.* i, 277.) We shall see that every scrap of Greek and Latin learning which, after twelve centuries, slowly filtered into Christendom, came from the hated Arabs through the more hated Jews, after Christian first contact with civilization through the Crusades: "Indeed, whatever influence came from the Mosque passed through the Synagogue before it reached the Church." (*CE.* i, 676.)

In one singular and unintentional way, however, is it true that "the preservation of *fragments* of Greek and Roman classics is due to the monasteries, which were the custodians of manuscripts of the ancient Greek philosophy," science, and literature. Such manuscripts existed in great numbers in the age of Greek and Roman culture; they were written on enduring parchment. When the Light of the Cross dimmed Pagan culture, and its learning became abhorrent to the pious Christian, the monks needed papyrus for their literary efforts, so they gathered in the manuscripts wherever found;—and thus they "preserved" them: "Due to cost of vellum, old books were *scraped* and used again"—(that is the meaning of "Palimpsest")—for the scribbling of the precious monkish chronicles and theological folderol soon to be noticed. "In the West much use was made of old manuscripts from the seventh to the ninth century, when, in consequence of the disturbed state of the country, there was some scarcity of material, and the old

357

volumes of *neglected* authors were used for more *popular* works. . . .
The practice continued down to the sixteenth century. Many
Latin and most Greek manuscripts are on reused vellum. A manuscript in the Vatican contained part of the 91st Book of Livy's
'Roman History.' The famous Sinai Bible discovered by Tischendorff
was written over by lives of female saints. Parts of the Iliad and the
'Elements' of Euclid were covered by monkish treatises. The 'De Re-
publica' of Cicero was discovered under the Commentary of Augustine
on Psalms, and several of his Orations under the Acts of the Council
of Chalcedon." Other such monkish palimpsests were discovered to
contain the Institutes of Gaius; eight orations of the Roman senator
Symmachus, the Comedies of Plautus, parts of Euripides, epistles of
Antoninus Pius, Lucius Verus, Marcus Aurelius, and others, the 'Fasti
Consolaris' of 486, the Codex Theodosianus, are among the precious
remains of Greek and Roman erudition which were "preserved" in this
monkish fashion in the erudite monasteries. (*NIE.* xvii, 762–3.) As for
"monks constantly occupied in copying the classic texts," for the
preservation and diffusion of Pagan culture, it is a joke! They couldn't
read Greek nor good Latin, and nobody else could read at all;—also,
Holy Church and Churchmen loathed Pagan culture and literature.

The Church, however, got an early and fair start on its wonderful
career as the organizer and creator of civilization. In 529 [by priest-
prompted edict of Justinian] "the schools of philosophy were closed.
From that date Christianity had no rival." (*CE.* ii, 43.) We have read
the Imperial Law of Justinian with the fatal title: "Pagans Forbidden
to give Instruction"; consequently "the State schools of the Empire
had fallen into decay." (*CE.* xiii, 555.) Thenceforth the Church, inspired by its Holy Ghost, was the sole Mentor and Instructor of Christendom. Before the dazzling Light diffused by the Church blinds us to
the view, let us take a farewell look at the Pagan civilization of the
Roman world, as recorded under the Antonine Emperors and their
successors, such conditions prevailing quite up to the era of Justinian
and the Church;—it will be a millennium and a half before we see a
spark of such like:

"The internal peace and prosperity were no less remarkable than
the absence of war. Trade and commence flourished; new routes were
opened, and new roads built throughout the Empire, so that all parts

of it were in close touch with the capital. The remarkable municipal life of the period, when new and flourishing cities covered the Roman world, is revealed by the numerous inscriptions that record the generosity of wealthy patrons or the activity of free burghers. . . . Guilds and organizations of all conceivable kinds, *mainly for philanthropic purposes*, came into existence everywhere. By means of these associations the poorer classes were in a sense insured against poverty. . . . The activity of the Emperor was not confined to merely official acts; private movements *for the succour of the poor and of orphans* received his unstinted support. The scope of the alimentary institutions of former reigns was broadened, and the establishment *of charitable foundations* such as that of the 'Puellae Faustinianae' is a sure indication of a general softening of manners and a truer sense of humanity. The period was also one of considerable literary and scientific activity. . . . The most lasting influence of the life and reign of Antoninus was that which he exercised in the sphere of law. Five great Stoic jurisconsults [named] were the constant advisers of the Emperor, and under his protection they infused a spirit of leniency and mildness into Roman legislation which effectually safeguarded the weak and unprotected, slaves, wards, and orphans, against aggressions of the powerful. . . . An impulse was given in this direction which produced the later golden period of Roman jurisprudence under Septimus Severus, Caracalla, and Alexander Severus." (*CE*. i, 587.)

For vivid contrast, we may here recall the "vivid remark" of Bishop St. Bruno, in the year 1049, that "justice had perished" (*CE*. vi, 793); and the confession, relating to the beginning of the Reformation five hundred years later: "Churchmen in high places were constantly unmindful of justice." (*CE*. xii, 767.) The "golden period of Roman jurisprudence" had been replaced by Christian "superstitions in the administration of justice during many centuries of the Middle Ages, and known as ordeals or 'judgments of God.' . . . These 'judgments of God' gave rise to new superstitions. Whether guilty or not, persons subjected to the trials would often put more confidence in charms, magic formulas, and ointments than in the Providence of God." (*CE*. xiv, 341.) Up to as late as 1538 "the legal lore had hitherto been presented in a very barbarous form." (*CE*. i, 273.) As for benevolence, charity, the care of the poor, the protection of the weak against the strong, the cursory Pagan record just quoted must suffice; their continuance in the Christian Dark Ages is sufficiently belied by the shocking social conditions to be cursorily noticed in the general cultural sketch to follow. As for widows and orphans, one of the proudest brags of the clerics, the Church by sword and rack and stake, has made an infinity more of widows and orphans that she ever scantily cared for in her monkish lazzarettos and pestilential lying-in shambles. With respect to slavery, which the Church boasts to have suppressed, this pious lie is nailed by the fact of the gradual shifting of technical slavery into universal serfdom throughout Europe for centuries, and its persistence in "Christian" England, America and Brazil until almost the present generation, and the existence today of millions of slaves in very Christian Abyssinia; and the world knows the part which the Christian soulsavers took in the United States in upholding slavery as a God-ordained institution of the Blessed Bible. But the Church not only aided and abetted slavery; it owned slaves, and it actively engaged in the most revolting forms of slave-trade: "Clement V (1309) *decreed* that resisting Venetians should be sold into slavery, and Gregory XI and Sixtus IV [of blessed memory] *decreed* the same for the Florentines, and Julius II for both Florence and Bologna. The *Bull* by which Nicholas V (1442) *encouraged* Portugal to what became the organized trade in negro slaves. . . . In 1538 Paul III *decreed slavery* against all *Englishmen* who should dare to support Henry VIII against the pope"! (*Encyc. Brit.*, 14th ed. xix, 35.)

The Church mightily prides itself on its suppression of the bloody sports of the arena, the gladiatorial combats, because the monk Telemachus, after 400 A. D., jumped into the arena (with two Pagan companions) and protested against them, which act incited the *Pagan* throng in the Ampitheatre to urge their abolition. But for four hundred years nor Church nor Christian had raised a voice of protest; and during as much of this period as it had the power, the Church was merrily murdering Pagans and heretics; and the cruelties of free combat in the arena were speedily replaced by the infamous torturings and slow burnings of countless human beings for Christ's sweet sake: while bull-fights adorn every holiday and holy day of the "Most Christian" countries today. Fie for Christian "reforms"!

360

THE "TRIUMPH" OF CHRISTIANITY

Following upon the Pagan cultural civilization depicted by *CE.* existing in the closing epoch of the Roman Empire, we have a lengthy account by the same clerical scholars of the Christian culture of the ensuing Age of Faith: "The learning and opinions of the first [Christian] few hundred years were comprehensively set forth in the tremendous work of Isidore of Seville (d. 636). During the *next few centuries*, which were comparatively *barren of literary achievements*, the *only men* to achieve any celebrity were [five named up to 1003]." . . . Others are named up to 1280,—"For all these Albertus Magnus had opened the door to the rich treasure-house of Greek and Arabian learning." (*CE.* vi, 449, 450.) The principal product of Christian erudition up to these times was ludicrous lying legends and saint and martyr tales: "Needless to say that they do not embody any real historical information, and their chief utility is to afford an example of *the pious popular credulity of the times*" (*CE.* i, 131). The state of Christian historical lore through these ages may be appreciated by the following summary:

"The historical literature of the Middle Ages may be classed under three general heads: chronicles, annals, and lives of saints. . . . As a matter of fact, profane history, as dealt with by Pagan historians, no longer appealed to Christian writers. History, as viewed from the Christian standpoint, took into account *only* the Kingdom of God, and to the new generation [of Christians] the centre of such history was the narration of the misfortunes undergone by the Jewish nation, a subject ignored by the Roman historians. Christians had need of a new general history in sympathy with their ideal. . . . Under Charlemagne . . . the great internal misfortunes and dissensions of the kingdom are carefully ignored, so as not to cast discredit on the reigning princes. . . . The majority of these local chronicles reproduce the traditions, popular or local, of the monastery which they concern and confine themselves to recording gossip and various kinds of information, . . . without asking themselves whether the version of these sources had been tainted with legends, and they did not take the trouble to examine the origin and value of their information. . . . The authors were bounded by a limited horizon, often equipped with merely a rudimentary training. Such chronicles, moreover, were often written with the same purpose as the lives of the saints. Those, having

361

a general tendency to enhance as much as possible the glory of their hero, were nothing more than panegyric. Monastic chronicles and annals were not free from this tendency, and often begin with an account of the life of the saint who founded the abbey, concerning themselves more with asceticism than with historical facts and events, which would be of much value to us today. In conclusion, the first part of these chronicles, written for the most part since the eleventh century, almost always recount legends, often based on oral tradition, but sometimes invented for the purpose of embellishing the early history of the monastery, and of *thus increasing the devotion of the faithful.* . . . Chronology especially was often treated carelessly." (*CE.* i, 531–536, *passim.*)

With respect to literature and history we have thus a millennial blank of Christian achievement: but the Church's *forte* was Science, for "the Church fosters and promotes the sciences in many ways,"— so long as they do not contradict the "sacred science of Christianity." This we may see exemplified in the following clerical summarization:

"Speculations concerning the rotundity of the earth and the possible existence of human beings 'with their feet turned towards ours,' were of interest to the Fathers of the early Church *only in so far as they seemed to encroach upon the fundamental Christian dogma* of the unity of the human race, and the consequent universality of *original sin and redemption.* This is clearly seen from the following passage of St. Augustine (*De Civitate Dei*, xvi, 9) : '. . . For Scripture, which confirms the truth of its historical statements by the accomplishment of its prophecies, teaches no falsehood; and it is too absurd to say . . . there is a race of human beings not descended from that one first man.' This opinion of St. Augustine was commonly held *until the progress of science* . . . dissipated the scruples arising from a defective knowledge of geography. A *singular exception* occurs to us in the middle of the eighth century. From a letter of Pope St. Zachary (1 May, 748), addressed to St. Boniface, we learn that the great Apostle of Germany had invoked the papal censure upon Vergilius. Among other alleged misdeeds and errors was numbered that of holding 'that beneath the earth there was another world and other men, another sun and moon.' In reply, the Pope directs St. Boniface to convoke a council and, 'if it be made clear' that Vergilius adheres to this 'perverse teaching, contrary to the Lord and to his own soul,' to 'expel him from the Church, deprived of his priestly dignity'! This is the only information that we possess regarding an incident which is made to figure largely in the *imaginary warfare* between theology and science. . . . The case of the Irish monk who suffered the penalty of *being several centuries ahead of his age* remains on the page of history, like the parallel case of Galileo, as a solemn admonition against a hasty resort to ecclesiastical censure," as *CE.* naïvely remarks. (*CE.* i, 581–2.)

Summing up the vivifying cultural achievements of over a thousand years down to the beginning of the end of the regimen of Church embrutishment of men, this ludicrous composite of confession of debasement and self-laudation greets us: "The Middle Ages did not bequeath to Rome any institutions that could be called scientific or literary academies. As a rule, there was slight inclination for such institutions. . . . A special reason why literature did not get a stronger foothold at Rome is to be found in *the constant politico-religious* disturbances of the Middle Ages. . . . Medieval Rome was certainly no place for learned academies. . . . From the earliest days of the Renaissance *the Church was the highest type of such an academy,* that is, *of the broadest kind of culture"! (CE.* i, 83, 84.) Yet despite this highest type of academy as was the Church, the broadest kind of culture which it personified and radiated, the full splendor of the Renaissance had been reacting upon and illuming the Church for two or three centuries, when we discover this amazing lack of clerical learning and intelligence confessed by the Church. The Protestant heresy was at its zenith; in 1559–74 the Protestants published an Ecclesiastical History called "Centuriators," in thirteen volumes, "showing century by century, how far the Catholic Church had departed from primitive teaching and practices," as *CE.* describes it. This heretic work caused "keen distress and dismay in Catholic circles; and provided the Reformers with a formidable weapon of attack on the Catholic Church. It did much harm. The feasability of a counter-attack appealed to Catholic scholars, but nothing adequate was provided, *for the science of history was still a thing of the future.* Its founder was as yet but 21 years of age"—Baronius, later Cardinal. He studied hard, and later produced his *Annales,* 12 volumes, "which he had foreseen in a vision would be the term of his work," and by which the "Centuries were eclipsed,"—but in which he ruthlessly destroyed by sane and fearless criticism so many thousands of Church saint-and-martyr myths, that "the Annals were condemned by the Spanish Inquisition" (*CE.* ii, 305, 306).

Such was the net—and *gross* result of fifteen hundred years of the much-boasted zeal for learning and teaching of the Divinely-appointed sole Teacher of Christendom, in the broad fields of historical knowledge, literature, and general intellectual culture. In the grand realm of the Sciences, which the Church has ever cherished and encouraged, may we hope for bigger and better results?

CHRISTIAN "SCIENCE"

"The Church, far from hindering the pursuit of the sciences, fosters and promotes them in many ways." (*CE.* xiii, 609.)

"When a *dogma contradicts a scientific assertion, the latter has to be revised*"! (*CE.* xiii, 607.)

The Middle Ages, as generally understood, "is a term used to designate that period of European history between the Fall of the Roman Empire and about the middle of the fifteenth century," (*CE.* x, 235), —the era of the discovery of printing,—a full thousand years. The highly significant and evidently unstudied explanation is made: "The Middle Ages have become *an interlude, clearly bounded on both extremities by a more civilized or humane idea of life*, which men are endeavouring to realize in politics, education, manners, literature, and religion." (*CE.* xii, 765.) Those two clearly bounded extremities are the Pagan civilization of the dying Roman Empire and the secular, skeptical, rationalistic "Renaissance of Knowledge," which *CE.* clerically complains embodied "the ideas and spirit of classic paganism." (i, 34.) We have just seen that during this Millennium "thoroughly saturated with Christianity" there was, in Christendom, no literature, other than theological treatises, monkish chronicles and Saint-tales, and no science of whatever category,—except "sacred science" or theology: "Theology is the very science of faith itself" (*CE.* xiii, 598) ; and we have seen to what intellectual status that sacred science led the human mind. The zeal with which the Church pursued its propagation of the Faith as the central feature of its educational system,

364

with all other branches of human knowledge as an indifferent "side line," we have noted, in the language of the ecclesiastical scientists. The Church maintains that it "fosters and promotes sciences *in many ways*," and inferentially always has encouraged and protected science in all its manifold forms of utilitarian humanism. But Holy Church has some naïve notions of science and of the ecclesiastical limitations imposed upon it. While thus fostering and promoting the sciences, "Yet," says *CE.*, "while acknowledging the freedom due to them, she tries *to preserve them from falling into errors contrary to Divine doctrine*, and from overstepping their boundaries and *throwing into confusion matters that belong to the domain* of faith"! (*Vatican Decrees*, Sess. III, De Fide, ch. 4; *CE.* xiii, 609.)

The priestly principle of the subordination of scientific fact to dogmatic faith is thus naïvely posed:

"Science is limited by truth, which belongs to its very essence. Should science ever have to choose between truth and freedom (a choice not at all imaginary), it must under all circumstances decide for truth, under the penalty of self-extermination. . . . Ethics is more important for mankind than science. Those who believe in revelation, know that the Commandments are the criteria by which men will be judged. (Matt. xxv, 35–46.) . . .

"The demand for unlimited freedom in science is unreasonable and unjust, because it leads to license and rebellion. . . . To submit one's understanding to a doctrine *supposed*—[is that all?]—to be Divine and *guaranteed to be infallible* is undoubtedly more consistent than to accept prevailing postulates of science. . . .

"*When a clearly defined dogma contradicts a scientific assertion*, THE LATTER HAS TO BE REVISED"! (*CE.* xiii, 598–607, *passim.*)

Than this last sentence, a more palpable and ridiculous untruth has never been uttered by the clerical Liars of the Lord. No single scientific fact ever discovered and proclaimed, in all the struggling history of Science in defiance of Church, has ever been "revised," altered or withdrawn in deference to religious Dogma. Every fact of science has proudly and triumphantly defied and refuted Dogma and Church, and made them both cheap and ridiculous. Faith hates facts; they are forever divorced on grounds of congenital incompatibility. The Church, True Church, and Protestant, has screamed and reviled at every truth of Science which was ever discovered; with high priestly anathema, the curse of God, with prison, rack, and stake, it has sought to suppress and kill every thought of the human mind, every bold thinker, whose truths for the benefit of mankind have contradicted and ridiculed it and its holy dogmas. Every single one; I challenge the production of a solitary instance of exception. The catalogue is too vast to even summarize here; for details and proofs the monumental works of Dr. Andrew D. White, *The Warfare between Science and Theology*, and Dr. John W. Draper's *Conflict between Science and Religion*,—(the latter on the Church's *Index of Prohibited Books*), may be profitably consulted and are cheerfully recommended in refutation of this example of priestly mendacity. We have read what happened to that "singular exception," the Irish monk Bishop Vergilius.

But let the false pretense be exposed by a few examples given by the American apologist for "the Holy See, deservedly known as the nursing mother of schools and universities," such as we have above admired. Until these "universities" began, about the year 1211 (*CE.* xii, 766) of the Christian epoch, no one had dared to think; Christendom was too steeped in ignorance and credulity to think. These Middle Ages, says *CE.* (xii, 38), were "a civilization thoroughly saturated with Christianity," and therefore incapable of scientific thought or feeling. "All Greek learning [had been] lost for a thousand years in Western Christendom. . . . The loss of Greek authors and the decline of Church Latin [as well as the Latin Church] into *barbarism* were misfortunes *in a universal ruin.*" (*CE.* xii, 765.) But men's minds could not forever be kept in the chains of priestly dominance; Gulliver began to wake and rouse and to struggle against the multiplied strands of theological cobwebs with which the Lilliputs of Faith had fast bound him while in his millennial sleep of the Christian Dark Ages of Faith. "Under these circumstances," admits *CE.*, "a revival of learning so soon as the West was *capable of it,* might have been foreseen." (*CE.* xxi, 765.) The Church was keen and hostile, and did forsee what was coming. The first University was founded in 1211; in identically that time the Holy Inquisition was established by His Holiness Innocent III to guard against heretics and "other innovators." "The taking of Constantinople in 1204, the introduction of Arabian, Jewish, and Greek works into the Christian schools, the rise of the universities—

these are the events which led to the extraordinary intellectual activity of the thirteenth century. . . . Even in the Christian schools there were declared Pantheists . . . who bade fair to prejudice the cause of Aristotelianism. These developments *were suppressed by the most stringent disciplinary measures* during the first few decades of the thirteenth century. . . . Roger Bacon demonstrated by his *unsuccessful attempts to develop the natural sciences* the possibilities of another kind which were latent in Aristotelianism." (*CE.* xiii, 548, 549.)

Roger Bacon (1214–1294), the "Doctor Mirabilis," whose "attempts to develop the natural sciences" were so drastically suppressed, was the genius of the dawning "Revival of Learning"—the Renaissance. He wrote over eighty books, a number of the most important in a secret cryptogram for fear of the ecclesiastical consequences—which he finally suffered. "It is in these treatises that Bacon speaks of the reflection of light, mirages, burning-mirrors, of the diameters of the celestial bodies and their distances from one another, of their conjunction and eclipses; that he explains the laws of ebb and flow, proves the Julian calendar to be wrong; he explains the composition and effects of gunpowder, discusses and affirms the possibility of steam-vessels and äerostats, of microscopes and telescopes, and some other inventions made many centuries later. . . . 'Pope Nicholas IV, on the advice of many brethren condemned and rejected the doctrine of the English brother Roger Bacon, Doctor of Divinity, which contains many *suspect innovations,* by reason of which Roger was imprisoned' 12 or 14 years" (*CE.* xiii, 112), until death released him from the strangling clutches of the "nursing-mother of schools and Universities,"—which always "encourages Science"!

Roger's great German contemporary "Blessed Albertus Magnus" (c. 1206–1280), was "accused of magic and of neglecting the sacred sciences. . . . Albert respected authority and traditions, was *prudent* in proposing the results of his investigations. . . . sometimes he hesitates and *does not express* his own opinion, probably *because he feared* that his theories, which were '*advanced*' *for those times*—[when Church was "far from hindering the pursuit of the sciences"],— would excite surprise and occasion unfavorable comment." Among the products of his "magic," Blessed Albert "gives an elaborate demonstration of the sphericity of the earth. . . . *More important* than Albert's development of the physical sciences was his influence on the study of philosophy and *theology*. . . . 'All *inferior (i. e.* natural) *sciences should be servants* (ancellae) *of Theology, which is superior and the mistress'* (Aquinas)." (*CE.* i, 265–6.) Thus the Church thwarted and prevented what would have been the much earlier "triumph of scientific discovery, with which, as a rule, . . . the seats of academic authority had too little sympathy." (*CE.* xiii, 549.)

The criminal ignorance and bigotry of the Church are nowhere more convictingly evident than in its repression of medical science through the ages when pestilence and plague swept unchecked through Christendom, while holy priests and monks chanted litanies and scared devils as the sole means of staying the ravages of Disease and Death. Listen to the same old story: "Modern medical science rests upon a Greek foundation. . . . The secret of the immortality of Hippocrates rests on the fact that he pointed out the means whereby medicine became a science. . . . Hippocratic medical science celebrated its renascence in the eighteenth century. . . . Arabian medical science forms an important chapter in the history of the development of medicine, [largely] because it preserved Greek medical science. . . . With the decline of Arabian rule—[and Christian rise, in Spain]— began the decay of medicine. . . . In 1085 Toledo was taken from the Moors, and Spain became the transmitter of Arabian medicine." Here comes in the first medical scientist to defy the Church and escape its Holy Inquisition. Vesalius (born 1511), became physician to the Emperor Charles V; "his eagerness to learn went so far that he stole corpses from the gallows to work on at night in his room. . . . The supreme service of Vesalius is that he *for the first time* [in 1500 years of Church cherishing of Science], with information derived from the direct study of the dead body, attacked with keen criticism the hitherto unassailable Galen, and thus brought about its overthrow. Vesalius is the *founder* of scientific anatomy and of the technique of modern dissection. Unfortunately, he himself *destroyed a part of his manuscripts* on learning that his enemies intended to *submit his work to ecclesiastical censure"!* (*CE.* x, 123–130, *passim.*) Indeed, "at that era a scholar . . . who generally struck out so many new ideas in opposition to the commonly held opinion, could easily be accused of *heresy.*

368

So many of his relations with Protestant scholars appeared suspicious. . . . Personally *he avoided expressing his opinion, in order not to fall under suspicion of heresy"! (CE. xv, 379.)* In defiance of the ban of the Holy Ghost on dissection and anatomy, Vesalius dissected the stolen corpses: his work disproved the Luz, or "Resurrection Bone," the nucleus of the heavenly restoration of the human body, and disclosed that Adam's missing rib, lost since Eve was carved from it some 4500 years previously, was still there. These impious refutations of the Church's sacred science so enraged the clerical savants that it required all the efforts of the Emperor to save his great physician from the Dogs of the Lord and the Holy Inquisition.

A word only may be added on the highly significant question of hospitals and asylums in the Ages of Faith. "The idealism of medieval theological beliefs led to the founding of orphan asylums and hospitals. But the impracticability and 'other-worldliness' of the Middle Ages prevented effective treatment of the diseases of the inmates. Such hospitals were merely dark, crowded, and unsanitary places of refuge for the needy and sick, who received no rational medical attention. . . . The Middle Ages, which some profess to admire, were in reality times of low civilization." For a shocking account of the hospitals, lying-in dens and insane pens of medieval Christian idealism, reference must be made to Dr. Henry W. Haggard's *Devils, Drugs and Doctors;* (cf. *CE.* vii, 492; x, 125). Such as these miserable lazzaretti were, they were for the superstitious Faithful only: "The bigoted Pius V actually directed that no medical assistance should be given to any person who declined spiritual attendance"! (Macauley, *Const. Essays; Church and State*, p. 136.)

But for the benighted theological repression of thought and of discovery of the secrets and powers of Nature, here barely hinted, the germs of modern science and invention which lay latent and struggling in the fertile minds of these great pioneers, would have quickly developed and would have recreated civilization and enriched humanity centuries before they did, when Holy Church got too feeble and discredited longer to enchain the minds of men. But, as it was, the "sacred science of Christianity" must be protected by force and proscription against the facts and knowledge of Nature and the quickening minds of men. To guard its precious Bible "revelations," the Church upheld

369

the Bible and forced all men to close their minds when they opened its sacred pages. At last, Galileo fitted two bits of glass into an old Church organ-pipe, poked it at the "firmament of heaven" which had cost Jehovah a whole day's work, and, Lo! the whole of the "sacred science" of the Church collapsed into universal ruin! The truth of God's revelation became an exploded myth, and its inspired Bible a book of Fable. The holy Church screeched in terror its unholy anathemas. "What, more than all," confesses the *CE.*, "raised alarm [over the discoveries of Copernicus and Galileo], was *anxiety for the credit of Holy Scripture, the letter of which was then universally believed to be the supreme authority in matters of SCIENCE, as in all others.*" (*CE.* vi, 344.) The Church made monstrous efforts to murder the new thought: "we know from the calendar of saints and other sources *how much had been done to check the wild license of thought and speech* in the Peninsula. Giordano Bruno, *renegade* and pantheist, was *burnt* in 1600; Campanella spent [27] long years in prison. The different measures meted out to Copernicus by Clement VII and to Galileo by Paul V *need no comment* [its shame chokes the Church]! The papacy aimed henceforth at becoming an 'ideal government under spiritual and converted men.'" (*CE.* xii, 768.) The Church missed this aim; but with the unholy aid of its Holy Inquisition, which in 1542 it declared to be "the supreme tribunal for the whole world" (*CE.* xiii, 137), and its sacred "Index of Prohibited Books," instituted in 1557, it murdered men and thought for yet several centuries. The up-to-date edition of 1929 closes the minds of the "Faithful" to over 5,000 books of the highest intellectual merit,—as partially catalogued in the news dispatches. (*N. Y. Herald-Tribune*, Nov. 11, and Dec. 1, 1930). This precious Proscription for preserving the "*purity and genuineness of her Apostolic doctrine*" intact for the "*guileless and innocent hearts*" of the Babes of Faith, and to prevent them from learning anything which might put them "on inquiry" as to the "purity and genuineness" of these holy "Apostolic" myths, includes the immortal works of Gibbon, Sterne, Dumas, Victor Hugo, our own Dr. Draper, Anatole France, La Fontaine, Lamartine, Balzac, Rousseau, Steele, Addison, Talleyrand, Henry Hallam, Voltaire, Zola, Maeterlinck,—(this my Book will probably be added by special Decree);—in a word every book by—(mine excluded)—the brilliant and fearless

370

thinkers of the world who have scorned Holy Church, and have been laureated by winning inclusion in this Holy Index of Inspired Ignorance. It is a vain and foolish gesture of Bigotry, defeating its own malicious purpose: "Prohibited Books illuminate the world; words suppressed or condemned are repeated from one end of the world to the other," as Emerson admirably has expressed. But no wonder that "a [Faithful] Christian child knows more of the important truths [of a certain brand] than did Kant, Herbert Spencer, or Huxley," as is the "sour grapes" sneer of *CE.* (xiii, 607) at those whose minds are free to seek and find the truths of Nature and work from them true Miracles of Science for the boundless benefit of Man.

This enlightened *Index*, established at the behest of the Holy Ghost for keeping men ignorant, dates from the foundation of the Faith; it deserves a word of admiration, which may be spoken by its learned apologist: "Before the art of printing was discovered, it sufficed to *burn* a few manuscript copies *to prevent the spreading of a doctrine.* So it was done at Ephesus in the presence of St. Paul (Acts xix, 19). It is known that the other Apostles, the Fathers of the Church, and the Council of Nice (325) exercised the same authority; [citing] the various censures, prohibitions, and indexes issued by cities, universities, bishops, provincial councils, and popes, through the Christian centuries." (*CE.* xiii, 607.) Who wonders that they were "The Dark Ages"?

With the final childish, senile sneer of the Church we will dismiss this phase of examination of the paralyzing efficiency of Faith. Says our guardian of the archaic fossils embedded in the Rock of Faith: "It is true, the *believer is less free* in his knowledge than the unbeliever, but only *because he* [which one?] *knows more.* Hence it is, that a well-instructed *Christian child knows more* of the important truths than did Kant, Herbert Spencer, or Huxley. Believing scientists—[a self-stultification] do not wish to be free-thinkers *just as respectable people do not wish to be vagabonds*"! (*CE.* xiii, 607.)

So be it! But the vagabonds of *Free Thought* are those who, at infinite cost of torture and blood, through all the centuries of Creed and Crime of the Church, and in heroic scorn of the Church and her "sacred science," have made our dearly-earned civilization what even it is to-day. Step by step, from contest to ultimate conquest, in every single

371

conflict of Fact with Faith, the Church has been defeated and has retreated—put to shaming rout. It has been a slow and tortuous progress,—

"For faith, fanatic faith, once wedded fast
To some dear falsehood, hugs it to the last"!

But fantastic Faith has wondrous powers of "accommodation" and specious tenacity of false pretense of being forever inspiredly right. The process of adjustment has throughout a thousand instances been the same: Faith is confronted with a discrediting Fact; it curses it and denies it. When the fact is crammed down its throat and it is forced to recognize it, it lyingly denies that it had ever denied it. Then when all mankind has united in joyful acceptance of the new fact, the arch hypocrite declares that it is entirely in accord with its "sacred science," and tries to steal all credit for it as one of its very own grand contributions to "Christian civilization," and sanctimoniously wheezes, "How much grander a concept it gives of the infinite knowledge and glory of Gawd in His wonderful process of Nature"! Oh, Hypocrisy! Thou art the Church of God! "*Semper eadem*"—lying and shameless!

A thrilling retrospect, and inspirational look into the Future, are thus expressed: "It is to scientific devotion more than to any other cause that man owes his present position on a new earth and under new heavens. Nothing else has so immeasurably enlarged his conception. Everywhere his experiments have opened up stretches of infinity . . . Personified Science might indeed be proud to have begun so humbly and to have achieved so much. By the use of her method men have weighed the planets as in scales, they have read the secrets of the animal and vegetable world. They have discovered 'what is in man,' not wholly, but in some large and wonderful degree. Instead of the burnt-out lamp of dogmatism Science has given to humanity 'the light that shineth more and more unto the perfect day.' In an effort to minimize drudgery and misery her great discoveries have attained to concrete availability in useful arts that have remade the world and increased immeasurably the comfort of men and their joy. . . . Scientific devotion has broadened the horizon of man at every step. In the course of time humanity must leave the shrines of its cherished idols behind

372

and push steadily on! Sensing the poetic nature of this truth, James
Russell Lowell spoke in verse to those of his fellow men who could
understand:

> 'New times demand new measures and new men;
> The world advances, and in time outgrows
> The laws which in our father's times were best;
> And, doubtless, after us, some purer scheme
> Will be shaped out by wiser men then we,
> Made wiser by the steady growth of truth.' " . . .

(Dr. Ernest R. Trattner: *The Autobiography of God*, pp. 289 *et seq.*,
passim. Scribner's; 1930. Cf. *Science Remaking the World:* Cald-
well and Slosson; Doubleday, Page; 1924; *Two Thousand Years of
Science:* Harvey-Gibson; Macmillan; 1929).

In glorious contrast to the murderous principles and practices of
Faith—

> "Reason did never sentence or condemn
> Faith to the torture. Freedom all she claims
> For larger understanding of her aims;
> Hers no evasion, sleight, or stratagem,
> But only fearless quest our ignorance to stem."

THE REBIRTH OF CIVILIZATION

Gulliver Awakes

"The RENAISSANCE—the achievements of the modern spirit in opposition
to the spirit which prevailed during the Middle Ages"! (*CE.* xii. 765.)

During the Dark Ages of Faith men were born into the world with
the same capacities and potentialities of intellect as were the Sages of
Greece and the Jurisconsults and Statesmen of Rome. The poles are
not farther apart, however, day and night not more different in volume
of light, than the pre-Christian and Christian eras in point of intellectual product. Why so vast a difference? Simply—that the pre-
Christian mind was free, and explored unfettered and unafraid the
boundless zones of Nature, in search of the Supreme Good and the
practical benefits to be wrung from the world in which Pagan man
lived for the benefit of himself and of his kind: while the Christian mind

373

was bound by what it regarded as revealed Truth and shackled by theology and priestcraft, which closed every highway and bypath of approach to Nature with the warning sign: "No Thoroughfare. Moses." "When one has once believed, search should cease," as Father Tertullian said. The ban of Eden— "Of the fruit of the Tree of Knowledge thou shalt not eat," was enforced by the Priest by ecclesiastical censorship and burning of books, by the Inquisition of Faith, the Index, the rack, the stake. The ingrained aim and end of Man was Heaven; for that other-worldly destiny alone was he taught and trained; that was the whole Christian scheme of education and outlook on life; the things of this world were contemned and ignored.

Through these Ages of Faith two careers only were open to men— priestcraft and military. With rarest exception only clerical persons could read or write; the great masses of the peoples were utterly illiterate, ignorant, superstitious, devout slaves of priestcraft; their civil status serfs; they lived in filth and squalor unbelievable, wearing their coarse fabric or leathern garments until they rotted off their unwashed bodies, the victims of disease, plagues and famines which often killed off near half the population, and aided by wars and rapine incessant, greatly incited and waged by the political Church to further its corrupt greed and ambition, keep the squalid population of Europe at a standstill, so that it took a century to double the miserable masses, fed on black rye bread and slops, and on lying saint-tales, martyr-myths and forged relics for increase of stupid and credulous devotion to its faithless Faith and Priests, the while they were brutalized and kept savage by the almost daily free spectacles furnished by Holy Church of public torturings and burnings by slow priest-set fires of countless heroic men and women who were unafraid to despise and defy the priests. Faith thus flourished on ignorance and credulity, which the Church diligently fostered and exploited for its unholy purposes of wealth and power, of rule by ruin. As none but priests could read and write, while kings and public men were mere soldiers and illiterates, and public business must be carried on through written documents, the public offices of State, from the King's chancellor and ambassadors to the lowliest clerks, were priests, and thus Priestcraft and Church increased their sinister power and dominance and wealth. These facts explain the sinister motive of the priestly monopoly of literacy, and

374

fully account for the crass ignorance of Christendom which the vaunted Teaching Mission of the Church entailed.

"BENEFIT OF CLERGY"

For a long dark span of centuries Holy Church, as sole and unique, Divinely inspired and guided Teacher of Christendom, plied the gentle art of Pedagogy for the Faithful. The net result of the intellectual efforts of the Inspired Teacher may be summed up and made luminous by a couple of descriptions of the wonderful "benefit of clergy" as a Teaching Institution. Says first Dr. James Harvey Robinson: "For six or seven centuries after the overthrow of the Roman government in the West [476], very few outside of the clergy ever dreamed of studying, or even of learning to read and write. Even in the Thirteenth Century an offender who wished to prove that he belonged to the clergy in order that he might be tried by a church court, had only to show that he could read a single line; for it was assumed by the judges that no one unconnected with the church could read at all. It was therefore inevitable that all the teachers were clergymen, that almost all the books were written by priests and monks, and that the clergy was the ruling power in all intellectual, artistic, and literary matters—the chief guardians and promoters of civilization. Moreover, the civil government was forced to rely upon churchmen to write out the public documents and proclamations. The priests and monks held the pen for the king. Representatives of the clergy sat in the king's councils and acted as his ministers; in fact, the conduct of government largely devolved upon them." (Robinson, *The Ordeal of Civilization*, pp. 157–8.) This "benefit of clergy," in the legal sense in which it is above used, and the degraded state of ignorance which gave occasion for it and the presumptions of the clergy enforcing it, are defined and explained by the clergy: "Benefit of Clergy.—The exemption from the jurisdiction of the secular courts, which . . . was accorded to clergymen. . . . When a clerk was brought before a court, he proved his claim to benefit of clergy by reading, and he was turned over to the ecclesiastical court, *as only the clergy were generally able to read.* This gave rise to the extension of the benefit of clergy to all who could read. [It is added, for historical interest]: The privilege of benefit of

375

clergy was entirely abolished in England in 1827. In the Colonies it had been recognized, but by Act of Congress of 30 April, 1790, it was taken away in the Federal courts of the United States. Traces of it are found in some courts of different States, but it has been practically outlawed by statutes or by adjudication." (*CE.* ii, 446–7.) All this serves to confirm the truth of the statement, that the Church and the clergy imposed and perpetuated Ignorance as the basis of their sordid greed for power and control over the Ignorant.

THE CRIMINAL CRUSADES STARTED THE REVOLT

But—for a wonder under such conditions, and after a thousand years, a slow but portentous change began to manifest itself in sodden Christendom. Note this pregnant statement: "Up to this time (1250) *almost wholly absorbed in the supernatural,* [men now] took more interest in worldly things. Unconditional renunciation of the world came to an end, and men grew more matter-of-fact and practical." (*CE.* vi, 493.) As the result of this "extraordinary change . . . *education found its way among laymen,* and it developed trade." (*Ib.*) This confirms the fact that only priests could read and write or had any sort of "education," in all those Church-taught ages when "scholar and priest meant one and the same thing." Indeed, it is stated: "Only the clergy were generally able to read." (*CE.* ii, 446.) About that time it was that the feeling of nationality first began to stir in minds of civil rulers and of people able to realize the imperial schemes of Holy Church for one great Empire under the rule of the Vicar of God.

To forestall and check this dangerous restlessness of peoples, Kings, and nascent nationality, the Church devised that since time-honored scheme of joining restless factions in war on some common enemy, thus to avert domestic difficulties: here was born the gigantic folly and crime of the Crusades, for the pretended rescue of the empty and apocryphal "Sepulchre of Christ from the Infidel." This titanic scheme and its purposes are naïvely thus confessed: "The idea of the Crusades corresponds to a *political* conception which was realized in Christendom only from the eleventh to the fifteenth century: this supposes *a union of all peoples and sovereigns under the direction of the popes.* . . . The history of the Crusades is therefore intimately connected with that of the popes and the Church. These Holy Wars were essentially a papal enterprise. The idea of quelling all dissensions among Christians, of uniting them under the same standard and sending them forth against the Mohammedans was conceived in the eleventh century, at a time when there were as yet no organized states in Europe." (*CE.* iv, 543, 556.) A more gigantic crime and overwhelming failure of ambitious design was probably never recorded in history. But far different and more transcendent results for civilization were brought about. Indeed, the Crusades were the beginning of European civilization. Says *CE.:* "The Crusades brought about results of which the popes had never dreamed, and which were perhaps the most important of all. They reëstablished traffic between the East and West which, after having been suspended for several centuries, was then resumed with even greater energy; they were the means of bringing from the depths of their respective provinces and introducing into *the most civilized Asiatic countries* Western knights, to whom *a new world was thus revealed, and who returned to their native land filled with novel ideas.* . . . Moreover, as early as the end of the twelfth century, *the development of general culture was the direct result* of these Holy Wars. . . . If, indeed, the Christian civilization of Europe has become universal culture, in the highest sense, *the glory redounds, in no small measure, to the Crusades*"! (*CE.* iv, 556.) "The original aim of the Crusades, it is true, was not attained. But the civilization of Western Europe gained from the Orient the best the East had to give and thus was greatly aided in its development" (*CE.* v, 612). The yet quasi-barbarian rulers and rabbles of Christendom were thus brought into direct contact with a real civilization; had their first glimpse of Arabian culture and civilized refinements of life, saw the men with whom they were in deadly conflict who were vastly their superiors in every ideal and practical accomplishment, and infinitely more humane. One instance will illustrate the difference between Christian brutality and Moslem humanity. When the Christian Crusaders of Christ captured Jerusalem in 1099 and rushed in to rescue the tomb of their dead God from the Infidel, the streets of the Holy City ran with human blood up to the horses' bridles; "the Christians entered Jerusalem from all sides [July 15, 1099] and *slew its inhabitants regardless of age or sex*"! (*CE.* iv, 547.) When nearly a century later (September 17, 1187), Saladin and his "Infidel hosts" recaptured the City and overthrew the Christian Kingdom of Jerusalem, not a murder nor act of violence or outrage was committed on the inhabitants, and the murderous hordes of Christ were allowed to depart in peace. The Christians began to learn what civilization was. Thus "the Crusades—those magnificent expeditions which, inspired and supported by the Church, brought huge masses of people into contact with the Orient. . . . They were the means of spreading . . . the theories and methods of *Arabian scholarship, at that time quite advanced,* and thereby placing the researches of Western scholars *on entirely new bases,* and *putting before them new aims and objects.*" (*CE.* vi, 448.) An immense confession of Christian failure!

THE "INFIDEL" REDEEMS CHRISTENDOM

As very pertinent to an understanding of the Rebirth of Learning, a paragraph will be devoted to a summary notice of Arabian culture and its saving influence on Christian ignorance; for it was the Arabs who brought learning, literature and science to benighted Christendom and created the Renaissance which ended the Dark Ages of Faith.

"When the Arabs came in contact with other civilizations (in the eighth century), notably with that of Persia, their speculative and scientific activities were stimulated into action. About A. D. 750 the Abassides, an enlightened line of Caliphs, came to the throne, who encouraged learning, and patronized the representatives of foreign culture. . . . They made ample use of Greek philosophy, and in their free inquiries into the secrets of nature, in which they soon outstripped the Greeks themselves, *they paid little attention to the precepts of the Koran.* . . . The Arabians translated [the works of Plato, Galen, and Aristotle]. . . . The Arabians developed Greek philosophy in its relation to *medicine, and in this regard they exerted the most far-reaching influence in Europe.* . . . The Arabian philosophy, as is well known, exercised a profound influence on the Scholastic philosophy of the twelfth and succeeding centuries." (*CE.* i, 675–6.) "The Arabian conquerors had learned from the Syrians the arts and sciences

378

of the Greek world. They became especially proficient in medicine, mathematics, and philosophy, for the study of which they erected in every part of their domain schools and libraries. In the *twelfth* century —[the first Christians ones were in the *thirteenth*]—Moorish Spain had nineteen colleges, and their renown attracted hundreds of Christian scholars from every part of Europe. *Herein lay a grave menace to Christian orthodoxy.*

"The BIBLE had been set up *as an infallible source of knowledge* not only in matters of religion, but of *history, chronology, and physical science. The result was a reaction against the very essentials of Christianity.* . . . Biblical chronology, as then [*19th* century] understood, and the literal historic interpretation of the Book of Genesis were *thrown into confusion by the advancing sciences*—astronomy, with its grand nebular hypothesis; biology, with its even more fruitful theory of evolution; geology, and pre-historic archaeology. . . . But able apologists were forthcoming to assay a *conciliation of science and religion*"! (*CE.* i, 621, 622.) Be it noted, that it was not until late nineteenth century, when natural Science had made the "sacred science" of the Bible ridiculous, that the "conciliators" came forth with the Big False Pretense that "the Holy Bible was never intended as a Book of Science, but only of moral and religious edification"! Why then, one wonders, does Holy Bible teach "Science"—abound in what is—though false and ridiculous—essentially teachings of "science": *e. g.* the origin and form of the earth, and its fixity in space at the center of the universe as the "footstool of God"; the position and movements of sun and stars in the phony "firmament of heaven"; the origin and "Fall of Man" and the "special creation" of animals; the geographical absurdities of the Garden of Eden and its Four Rivers, the Flood and the Divine original and purpose of the Rainbow; the differentiation of languages at Babel; the cause of disease as the reactions to malignant devils in the inner works of men, and the Divine prescriptions for cure of the "Great Physician," the "Lord who healeth thee," by spit-salve, prayers of faith, ointment, holy water, and devil-exorcism by ignorant priests? If the Holy Ghost of God wrote or inspired the Bible, funny it is that It talked such foolishness, which was exactly what ignorant priests would have written out of the ignorance and superstitions of their times, without any inspiration of God

379

to confirm them in the nonsense. If the All-Wise God who dictated the Blessed Bible and its foolish "science falsely so called," had just spoken the facts of his own divine Creation, truthfully,—had just once said that the earth is round instead of flat, and revolves on its axis and around the sun instead of standing still while the sun went around it; that disease is caused by dirt and germs instead of by devils; and had given sensible precepts of prophylaxis and of cure; in a word, had "revealed" out of his supposed Infinite Wisdom some of the things which are just now, after some thousands of years of Bible-worship and bloody Church-repression, being painfully and dearly worked out by heroic human effort,—Who would not gladly and proudly hail the "Holy Bible, Book Divine," and for a certainty know that it was truly the intellectual work of a God? But! The priests and the parsons pretend yet that it is Divine; men of science and the coming generation know that it is ignorant priestly Imposture.

But to return to the Arabs, who "in their free inquiries into the secrets of Nature paid little attention to the precepts of the Koran," and were destined to "throw into confusion" the "sacred science" of the Blessed Bible. "It cannot be exactly said when the first translations of Arabic writings began to be received by the Christians of the West: probably about 1000. In the beginning of the twelfth century the contributions of Mohammedan science and philosophy to Latin Christendom became more and more frequent and important. . . . About 1134 John of Luna translated Al-Fergani's treatise 'Astronomy,' which was an abridgement of Ptolemy's 'Almagest,' thereby introducing Christians to the Ptolemaic system,"—followed by a page of other Arabian works translated for the Christians. (*CE.* xii, 49; cf. *ib.* xv, 184.) Thus Christendom got even its grand fable of the earth as the center of the universe from the Greek Ptolemy through the Arabs,— and damned Copernicus and martyred Galileo for daring to disprove it. "In 1085 Toledo was taken from the Moors, and Spain became the transmitter of Arabian medicine." (*CE.* x, 130.) Gerard of Cremona (died 1187), "a twelfth century student of Arabic science and translator from Arabic into Latin, went to Toledo, and soon acquired a great proficiency in Arabic; he translated not only the 'Almagest,' but also the entire works of Avicenna, into Latin; he translated 76 books from Arabic into Latin. His activities, and that of a group of

380

men who formed a regular college of translators at Toledo, *brought the world of Arabian learning within reach of the scholars of Latin Christendom,* and prepared the way for that conflict of ideas out of which sprang the Scholasticism of the thirteenth century." (*CE.* vi, 468.) At this late period of Christian intellectual awakening, now for the first time "Aristotle's philosophy was finding its way through Moorish and Jewish channels into the Christian schools of Europe." (*CE.* vi, 555.) Even "the compass was invented in the East and brought to Europe by the Arabs." (*CE.* i, 379.) And so of scores of inventions and branches of learning which were known to and cultivated by the Infidel Arabs, which through them became elements of the slow civilizing of quasi-barbarian Christendom so long under the divine tutelage of Holy Church and the priests.

Thus Christendom had wallowed through a thousand years of Christian ignorance until it was awakened by the shock of contact with Arabic civilization and learning through the Crusades. Then, slowly and dangerously, "as might have been foreseen, a revival of learning, *so soon as the West was capable of it,*" occurred. (*CE.* xii, 765.) One can only wonder why the Christian West, instructed by God's own Teacher, was not sooner *capable* of learning anything but monkish lore or religious lies. The Church apologizes, that "the Middle Ages occupy those tumultuous years when barbarians turned Christians were learning slowly to be civilized, from 476 [the end of the Roman Empire] to 1400." (*CE.* xii, 765.) But, the Eastern Empire, dominated by the original "Orthodox" Eastern Catholic Church, was never "overthrown by the barbarians," but remained in quiet and undisputed possession of its Faith and "Christian Civilization"; but its whole history is almost as foul and besotted, blood-reddened and Christian-barbarous as the Western Empire. And, since the closing of the Pagan schools in 529 at Christian behest, "the Church had no rival" as sole and inspired civilizer and instructor of Christendom. The poor Arabs were at that time disunited and ever-warring tribes of idolatrous barbarians, steeped in ignorance and "sin." Mohammed fled from their fury in the Great Hegira in 622; he died ten years later, in 632. Yet, in exactly 100 years, even before they were checked by the Christian Charles Martel at the battle of Tours in the heart of France, in the year 732, the Mohammedan Arabs became and remained the most highly civilized people in the world, the masters of an illustrious Empire of far greater extent than Christendom,—and which embraced the greater part of Christendom; and millions of good Christians quickly dropped God and Christ and became worshippers of Allah and his Prophet Mohammed. A strange Providence of the Christian God! This leads to a moment's disposal of one of the most pretentious and specious clerical claims, that the "divinity" of the Christian religion is proved by its "miraculous spread and preservation."

THE "MIRACULOUS ATTESTATIONS" OF CHRISTIANITY

One of the Church's most precious platitudes is its oft-used plea of "the demonstration of the truth of Christianity based on the wonderful propagation of His religion." (*CE*. i, 621.) Starting with a handful of Galilean peasants, in three centuries, up to the time of Constantine, it claims to have been "*preached to every creature which is under heaven*" (Gal. i, 23), and to have won maybe a million or two out of the hundred millions of the Roman Empire. We have seen the mode and manner of "conversion" of very many of these comers to the Christ; as well as of the most dubious Christian efficacy of the hordes of "barbarians" later won by the missionary sword. This "rapid spread" and propagation of the Faith is a "triumphant proof of the divinity and truth of Christianity"! It is also a familiar and threadbare "proof," the "miraculous" persistence and preservation of the Christian religion through some nineteen centuries. If this be a proof, many "false" religions are even more divine and true; for the religions of Brahma, Buddha, Confucius, Zoroaster, have existed and persisted, all for many centuries, some for a millennium, before Christianity, and ever since until now, and they embrace together countless millions more of devout worshippers than does Christianity. And we have seen the conditions of ignorance in which Christianity flourished and the terror by which it was preserved during the ages of Faith; and all world knows what the Church has become, and is faster becoming, with the advent and advance of the Age of Reason.

But if the slow and tortuous spread of Christianity by force and arms is proof of its "miraculous" character, what shall we say of

THE "TRIUMPH" OF CHRISTIANITY

Mohammedanism? "Its uninterrupted spread, from the seventh century to the present time, among all the races of the continent, is *one of the most remarkable facts of history*. Today a Mussulman may travel from Monrovia to Mecca, and thence to Batavia without once setting foot on 'infidel' soil. Three phases in this movement of expansion may be distinguished. In the first (638–1050) the Arabs, in a *rapid advance*, propagated Islam along the whole Mediterranean coast, from Egypt to Morocco, a conquest greatly aided by *the exploitation of the country* by Byzantine [Christian] governors, the divisions among the Christians, and political disorganization. The second period (1050–1750)—all Africa except Ethiopia. . . . The last period of the Mohammedan expansion extends to the present time. . . . Daily, one may say, *Islam spreads*." (*CE.* i, 187.) Christianity retrogresses. Aye, worse than that, for the vaunted miraculous nature and preservation of Christianity: "The one dangerous rival with which Christianity had to contend in the Middle Ages was the Mohammedan religion. Within a century of its birth, *it had torn from Christendom some of its fairest lands*, and extended like a huge crescent from Spain over Northern Africa, Egypt, PALESTINE, Arabia, Persia, and Syria, to the eastern part of Asia Minor. The danger which this *fanatic* religion offered to Christian faith, in countries where the two religions came in contact, was not to be lightly treated." (*CE.* i, 620–1.) Thus at the first onrush of the champions of Mohammed the Impostor, of a notoriously false Faith, the "Infidels" wrested from the devotees of the True Faith their holiest shrines, the empty Sepulchre of their dead God, the sites of his birth, crucifixion and resurrection; and they hold them unto this day. During three hundred years of bloody and fanatic "Holy Wars" united Christendom lost millions of lives and treasure in efforts to "rescue" this empty grave of its Christ from the impudent impostors; but for three hundred years the armies of the Cross were beaten and driven away from their sacred goal. "This immense fact," says Ingersoll, "sowed the seeds of distrust throughout Christendom, and millions began to lose confidence in a God who had been vanquished by Mohammed. . . . At that time the world believed in trial by battle —that God would take the side of the right—and there had been a trial by battle between the Cross and the Crescent, and Mohammed had been victorious." In their Westward course of conquest, "the

383

Moslems even crossed the Pyrennees, threatening to stable their horses in St. Peter's at Rome, but were at last defeated by Charles Martel at Tours, in 732, just one hundred years from the death of Mohammed. This defeat arrested their western conquests and saved Europe. . . . They were finally conquered by the Mongols and Turks, in the thirteenth century, but the new conquerors adopted Mohammed's religion, and in the fifteenth century, overthrew the tottering Byzantine Empire (1453). From that stronghold (Constantinople) they even threatened the German Empire, but were successfully defeated at the gates of Vienna, and driven back across the Danube, in 1683." (*CE.* x, 425.) The Christian God had failed to protect and save the vast majority of his own people. As Dr. Harry Elmer Barnes aptly says: "If the test of the validity of a religion is to be its growth, spread and proselyting capacity, then Mohammedanism can make a more impressive appeal than Christianity. Christianity had the advantage of being launched six and a half centuries before Mohammedanism. Yet today the Mohammedans far outnumber the Christians, and the Mohammedans have, moreover, reconquered the very areas in which Christianity arose and established its first strongholds." (Barnes, *The Twilight of Christianity*, p. 416.) This may close with a quaint specimen of medieval Christian historical learning, from that great literary light of the Church, Monk Matthew Paris (died 1259), who, says *CE.*, "as an historian holds the first place among English chroniclers." In "his great work, 'Chronica Majora,' from the Creation until the year of his death," the erudite Monk explains the unworthy motives why Mohammed quit the True Church and became an impious Infidel: "It is well known that Mohammed was once a cardinal, and became heretic because he failed to be elected pope. Also having drunk to excess, he fell by the roadside, and in this condition was killed by swine. And for that reason, his followers abhor pork even unto this day"! This notable occurrence was probably later than the time when Buddha was canonized a Catholic Saint.

"THE MARKS OF THE BEAST"

"And the Beast was taken . . . which deceived them that had received the Mark of the Beast . . . and both were cast alive into a lake of fire burning with brimstone." (Rev. xix, 20.)

THE "TRIUMPH" OF CHRISTIANITY

The Apocalyptic Marks of the Beast are translated by ecclesiastical sophism into the pretended "Four Marks of the Church": Apostolicity, *Sanctity*, Unity, Catholicity, as branded upon the "Visible Body of Christ" by the Formula of the Council of Constantinople in 381 A. D. (*CE.* iii, 450–758). The first two of these Marks we have seen totally obliterated by the processes of the review of the Record which we have made, and by the seas of blood and clouds of smoke of burning human bodies which have stained them beyond recognition; and the third is simply a frayed figure of clerical speech. Probably no one will envy The Church the fourth and only remaining of its holy Marks. As for "Unity," it is a very relative term; as long as even two units cohere there is unity—of those two. Christendom was once coextensive with the Roman Empire, and was then by force and arms further extended over all the north of Europe; we have seen the process. Then came the Arab incursion, and within one century the Church lost its most splendid fields and Churches, the vast Christian territories of Asia and Africa, and Spain. The "Great Schism" between East and West tore the immense Eastern Empire from the "Unity" of the True "Catholic" Church. The Turks, turned Mohammedan, in turn wrested the lost Eastern Empire from Christianity and it became Infidel, as mostly it remains today. Then came the "so-called Reformation" revolt of Luther: "The effect of the Reformation was to separate from the Church all the Scandinavian, most of the Teutonic, and a few of the Latin-speaking populations of Europe." (*CE.* iii, 704.) To these must be added England, Scotland, Wales, a good part of "Ever Faithful" Ireland; much of the Americas followed in the train of disaster. The age-long causes of this last destruction are well known; they have cried out on nearly every page of this book. Succinctly: "Since the twelfth century, the Church was losing much of its influence on the thoughts of men. . . . The faults and wealth of the clergy must have contributed something. . . . The growth of national divisions, the increased secularism of everyday life, the diminished influence of the Church and the papacy, all these interdependent influences had broken up the spiritual unity of Christendom *at least two centuries before* the Reformation. . . . At the beginning of the seventeenth century, *Christendom was weary of religious war and persecution.* . . . Religious divisions were too deep-seated to permit

385

the reconstruction of a Christian polity." (*CE.* iii, 704.) The final note of despair of the Church,—of rejoicing for all freed from it,— is the conclusion of its review of Christendom: "The word *Christian* has come in recent times to express our common civilization *rather than a religion which so many Europeans now no longer profess*"! (*Ib.*) Let us be rid of the hateful Word!

In a word, men had long since come painfully to realize the incontrovertible truth stated by the historian of Civilization in England: "The prosperity of nations depends upon principles to which the clergy, as a body, are invariably opposed." (Buckle, Vol. II, Pt. 1, p. 42.) What of the divine mark of "unity" is thus left in the Church is the fast disappearing coherence of decaying particles in face of the general débâcle attendant upon the Articles of Death.

WHY—AND WHAT PRICE—RELIGION?

"Leave thy gift upon the Altar, and go thy way." *Jesus.*
"They which minister about holy things, live of the things of the Temple; and they which wait at the Altar are partakers of the things of the Altar." *Paul.*
"The Lord loveth a cheerful giver." *Anon.*

All ancient religions we have seen are admittedly false, all **Pagan** priestcrafts fraudulent. The Pagan priestcraft held the lavished wealth of millions of superstitious dupes, and ruled the minds and destinies of men and nations. The motive and *raison d'être* of priestcraft, confessedly, was greed and graft, wealth and power and privilege. When Paganism later was called Christianity,—No man can deny history by alleging any difference: we have seen too many analogies and identities. At the advent of Christianity, scores of religions flourished throughout the Roman Empire; the Roman world was thick covered with sumptuous Temples and swarmed with plutocratic Priestcraft. So rich were the "pickings" from the superstitious masses and rulers and so alluring the "Get-rich-quick" possibilities of religion, that new creeds and cults were ever in the making. Christianity came along, born in poverty and "made as the filth of the world, and the offscouring of all things" (1 Cor. iv, 13); but even then petty faction leadership had its meed: the believers in the quick end of the world and

386

the Second Coming in the Kingdom, pooled their poor belongings "and laid them down at the apostles' feet"; and these holy ones operated this first pool. But "the Lord added to the Church daily such as should be saved," and it gradually increased in strength if not in grace. As the numbers grew and prestige and contributions increased, many "false teachers" arose among the "Sheep" and brought "damnable heresies" into the Fold. Scores of the "right-thinking" Fathers filled parchments with dreary diatribes "Against all Heresies," of which over ninety flourished in the first three centuries, which *CE.* catalogues and describes the hair-splitting differences of doctrine which gave excuse to splitting the Fold and dividing the spoil, and for cutting throats and beating out brains until the end of the seventh century. All these factious sects of "Christians" waxed more or less powerful and wealthy; the Arian anti-Trinity "heretics," the Donatists, Montanists, Manichæans, Monophysites, and innumerable others divided Europe and the contributions of the credulous for centuries, until suppressed by law and sword of the Orthodox. It is the latter, the True Church, which "gathered gear by every wile (*un*)-justified by honor." An authoritative summary, gleaned at random from *CE.*, of the grafting results is instructive.

"When peace was given to the Church by Constantine, at the beginning of the fourth century, an era of temporal prosperity for the Church set in. As Europe gradually became Christian, the donations for religious purposes increased by leaps and bounds. Gifts of land and money for ecclesiastical purposes were now legally recognized, and though some of the later Roman emperors *placed restrictions* upon the donations of the faithful, yet the wealth of the Church rapidly increased. Whatever losses were suffered in the [incursions of the barbarians], were made up for later, when the conquering barbarians in their turn were converted to Christianity. . . . The wealth of the Church at this period [the "so-called Reformation"] has sometimes been made a matter of reproach to her, . . . admitting that abuses were indeed at times unquestionable." (*CE.* iii, 762.) Such "abuses" and the ghoulish clerical greed were exactly why some of the later Roman emperors "placed restrictions" on grafting the Faithful. Lecky gives a graphic picture of the priests with the itching palm: "Rich widows were surrounded by swarms of clerical sycophants, who addressed them in tender diminutives, studied and consulted their every foible, and, under the guise of piety, lay in wait for their gifts or bequests. The evil attained such a point that a law was made under Valentinian depriving the Christian priests and monks of that power of receiving legacies which was possessed by every other class of the community." (*History of European Morals*, ii, 151.) These shaming facts are confirmed by many of the contemporary Fathers. From the Latin text of St. Jerome I turn into English his mournful admission that the deprivation was justified: "The priests of the idols might receive inheritances; only the clergy and monks were prohibited by this law, and prohibited not by persecutors, but by Christian princes . . . I grieve that we should merit this law." (*Epist.* lii.) We remember that already the Christian emperors, by "persecuting laws," had prohibited Pagans from making wills and from receiving bequests, and the law which declared all wills void which were not made before a priest,— who was there to get his share. The priestly profits rolled up through the Ages of Faith. Out of hundreds of like generalizations and specific instances cited, I make these limited selections, which show the universal process of clerical greed.

"The early Christians were lavish in their support of religion, and frequently turned their possessions over to the Church. . . . Towards the end of Charlemagne's reign the regenerated peoples contributed generously to the support of ecclesiastical institutions." (v, 421.) Indeed, so great had its volume then become, that "Church property excited the cupidity of the various factions, upon the death of Charlemagne." (v, 774.) Even a hundred years previously the Church estates could make a prince's rewards: "Charles Martel is charged with secularizing many ecclesiastical estates, which he took from the churches and abbeys and gave in fief to his warriors as a recompense for their services. This land actually remained the property of the ecclesiastical establishments in question." (vi, 241.) The Church grabbed all and shirked all; as a result, "Naturally there was a desire on the part of the king and princes to force the Church to take her share in the national burdens and duties." (vi, 63.) "To this age belongs the famous grant to the Church of one-tenth of his land by Ethelburt, father of Alfred the Great" (i, 507). "On the authority of the Doomsday Book [of William the Conqueror], the possessions of the Church represented

25% of the assessment in the country [England] in 1066, and 26½% of its cultivated area in 1086." (v, 103.) "In 1127 Stephen gave to these monks his forest in Furness. This grant was most munificent, for it included large possessions in woods, pastures, fisheries, and mills, with a large share in the salt works and mines of the district." (vi, 324.) "The see of Exeter was one of the largest and richest in England. The diocese was originally very wealthy." (v, 708-9.) "The English people at large complained of the enormous revenue which the pope and the Italians drew from their country, . . . the financial demands of the Curia." (vii, 38.) "Bitterness existed for a considerable time between the monks and the people of F., who complained of the abbey's imposts and exactions." (vi, 20.) "Vast sum of money extorted from the English clergy in 1531." (iv, 26.)

In France the clergy formed "a wealthy body of men, gradually extending their possessions throughout the kingdom" during the Middle Ages. (i, 795.) "In 1384 . . . almost a third of the land in the kingdom of Bohemia belonged to the Church." (ii, 613.) In Germany, twelfth century, "the difficulty of administering the vast landed possessions caused the abbots to grant certain sections in fief." (vi, 314.) "The gifts of German princes, nobles, and private individuals increased the landed possessions of the abbey so rapidly that they soon extended over distant parts of Germany,"—long list of provinces. (vi, 313.) "In parts of Germany [in 1770] the number and wealth of the religious houses, in some instances their uselessness, and occasionally their disorders, tempted the princes to lay violent and rapacious hands on them." (iv, 38.) "The luxury of bishops and the worldly possessions of monks" led to violent rebellion in Italy, in twelfth century. (i, 748.) At this and most times, the "prelates were the most powerful and the wealthiest subjects of the State." (ii, 186.) "The steady growth of power and wealth of the Church, since the beginning of the twelfth century, introduced an ever-increasing spirit of worldliness." (vii, 129.) "The liberality of the faithful was a constant incitement to depart from the rule of poverty. This liberality showed itself mainly in gifts of real property, for example, in *endowments for prayers for the dead, which were then usually founded with real estate*. In the fourteenth century began the *land wars* and feuds (*e. g.* the Hundred Years' War in France), which relaxed every bond of discipline and good order." (vi, 284.) To all this and these, "the faults and wealth of the clergy must have contributed something. The spiritual ruler seemed almost merged in the *sovereign of Rome* and the feudal lord of Sicily. Money was needed, and in order to obtain it funds had to be raised . . . and by means which aroused much discontent and affected the credit of Rome. . . . Even in the twelfth century complaints of venality were frequent and bitter." (iii, 703.) "Simony, the most abominable of crimes . . . was the evil so prevalent during the Middle Ages." (xiv, 1, 2.) Hundreds of instances are recited in *CE.* of the teeming wealth wrung by the Church and clergy from the fears of the Faithful; of the inordinate riches of popes and prelates, abbots and monks, Churches and their plethoric treasuries. The Church existed for riches and it got, rather ill-got them in inestimable enormity of amount. From the cradle to the grave of every Faithful who had anything to get, the Church wheedled, extorted or coerced it. Fear was ever the foundation of the Faith and of the "liberality" of contributions to it.

Among the greatest and greediest mints of ecclesiastical finance, were Simony, several times above mentioned,—the sale of every kind of hierarchical office and dignity, from the popedom to the jobs of the meanest servitors of the Servants of God; and the sale of Indulgences, or remissions of the pains of Purgatory. This non-existent place of expiation of "Sin," acquired or "Original," to fit the befouled soul for Heaven, was first charted if not invented by His Holiness Gregory the Great, about 600 A. D. "An indulgence offers the penitent sinner the means of discharging this debt [to God] during the life on earth" (*CE.* vii, 783),—provided that "debt" is adequately liquidated by cash into the coffers of God's Vicars on earth. These indulgences are of various kinds, efficacy and price: "The most important distinction, however, is that between plenary indulgences and partial. By a plenary indulgence is meant the remission of the entire temporal punishment due to sin so that *no further expiation is required in Purgatory.* A partial indulgence commutes only a certain portion of the penalty. . . . Some indulgences are granted in behalf of the living only, while others may be applied in behalf of the souls of the departed" (*Ib.* 783–4). Leo X, he who perpetrated the celebrated aphorism—"What profit has not that Fable of Christ brought us," rose in defense of the

390

revenues, and in his Bull "Exurge Domine," 1520, "condemned Luther's assertions that 'Indulgences are pious frauds of the faithful'; . . . the Council of Trent, 1563, pronounces anathema against those who either declare that indulgences are useless or deny that the Church has power to grant them" (*Ib.*). The flimsy basis of the traffic is thus referred to the forged "famous Petrine text" which we have seen is itself a huge fraud: "*Once it is admitted* that Christ left the Church the power to forgive sins, the power of granting indulgences is logically *inferred*" (p. 785); but logically perfect inferences can readily be made from false premises; the premises must be true to yield valid and truthful "inference" or conclusion. Not only were genuine but false indulgences hawked throughout Christendom, resulting in immense revenues—and abuses, for "one of the worst abuses was that of inventing or falsifying grants of indulgence. Previous to the Reformation, such practices abounded" (p. 787). The Council of Trent sought to stop outside profits from this traffic, declaring it to be "a grievous abuse among Christian people, and of other disorders arising from *superstition*, (*etc.*) . . . on account of the widespread corruption" (*Ib.*); though it seems that now "with the decline in the *financial possibilities* of the system, . . . there is no danger of the recurrence of the old abuses" (p. 788). But still they sell well and net fine revenues; the writer has invested in them several times in Mexico, for souvenirs, —there being no Purgatory for unbelievers in that fiery near-Hell.

A graphic picture is drawn by the great historian of the Middle Ages, which shows Avarice as the cornerstone and effective motive of the Church. Hallam, Von Ranke, and many historians, give revolting examples in the concrete through many ages; here is their summary:

"Covetousness, especially, became almost a characteristic vice. . . . Many of the peculiar and prominent characteristics in the faith and discipline of those ages appear to have been either introduced or sedulously promoted for the purposes of sordid fraud. To these purposes conspired the veneration for relics, the worship of images, the idolatry of saints and martyrs, the religious inviolability of sanctuaries, the consecration of cemeteries, but, above all, the doctrine of purgatory and masses for the relief of the dead. A creed thus contrived, operating upon the minds of barbarians, lavish though rapacious, and devout though dissolute, naturally caused a torrent of opulence to flow in upon the Church. . . . Even those legacies to charitable purposes, . . . were frequently applied to their own benefit. They failed not, above all, to inculcate upon the wealthy sinner that no atonement could be so acceptable to Heaven as liberal presents to its earthly delegates. To die without allotting of worldly wealth to pious uses was accounted almost like suicide, or a refusal of the last sacraments; and hence intestacy passed for a sort of fraud upon the Church, which she punished by taking the administration of the deceased's effects into her own hands. . . . And, as if all these means of accumulating what they could not legitimately enjoy were insufficient, the monks prostituted their knowledge of writing to the purpose of forging charters in their own favor, which might easily impose upon an ignorant age, since it has required a peculiar science to detect them in modern times. Such rapacity might seem incredible in men cut off from the pursuits of life and the hopes of posterity, if we did not behold every day the unreasonableness of avarice and the fervor of professional attachments." (Hallam, *History of the Middle Ages*, Vol. I, Bk. vii, *passim*.)

"STOP! THIEF!"

Ambitious and avaricious Christians who had been unable to get their hands into the "orthodox" Treasury of the Lord, were incited by the vision of the seas of easy money which flowed into it and by the ostentatious opulence of the partakers of the Lord's Altar, to emulate the zeal for riches displayed by the truly Faithful. A lengthy article under the title *Impostors*—[or is it "*Stop! Thief!*"?]—is devoted by *CE.* to the long line of hypocrites with itching palms who broke away from the True Fold the better to fleece the Faithful by their impostures. The period of the Great Schism of the West, particularly, "was also an epoch when many fanatical or designing persons *reaped a rich harvest* out of the *credulity of the populace*." (*CE.* vii, 699.) Many thousands left the True Church and flocked after religious Pretenders of every sort, pouring treasures into their uncanonical coffers, to the great pecuniary deprivation of Holy Church. Dozens of these perverters of the Sacred Revenue through the succeeding centuries are catalogued, coming down to our own near-secular times. Invidiously included under the opprobrious designation of "Impostors" are the inspired Prophet of the Mormons, Joseph Smith, and the inspired Prophetess, Mother Mary Baker-Glover-Patterson-Eddy,—the immense financial success of whose respective religions may well excite envy, and bring them within the terminology of Orthodox *Odium Theologicum*—a "BITTER ENEMY, THE HEAD OF THE RIVAL RELIGION," as is the approved form, to credit *CE.* (vii, 620), in speaking of one's religious rivals. The point of the moral is, that according to Orthodox criteria all these Harvesters in the Vineyard of the Lord are unscrupulous Impostors for revenue only, and batten only by preying on "the *credulity* of the populace,"—which is the by-product of Religion, as we have seen it exemplified. When Ignorance is ended Credulity ceases, and Ecclesiastical Pelf and Power languishing die. If, as profanely jibed, "Without Hell Christianity isn't worth a damn," *a fortiori*—without Revenue, is not Religion without Reason to be?

Made wise by the history of the past, in modern times most constitutions and governments, all in which the Church is not still powerful, have put just restrictions on the rapacity of the Church and have forbidden direct subsidies of support to it and its ministers. Indeed, "In most European countries the civil authority restricts in three ways the right of the Church to receive donations: by imposing forms and conditions; by reserving the right to say what institutions may receive donations, and by requiring the approval of the civil authority." (*CE.* v, 117.) In this country, Federal and State constitutions ordain separation of State and Church, forbid the establishment of any religion, and prohibit grants of money in support of it. But withal, so inveterate is the force of grafting habit, so prone yet the politicians to cater to "The Church" upon the specious pretext that the Church and religion are of some utility for "moral" purposes and as "the Big Policeman" for the restriction of vice and crime—the politicians not being familiar with the "moral record" of the Church, that the Church evades the principle and often the letter of the law, and is yet largely supported and kept alive by the people through the secular State. Some nine billions of dollars of deadhand and deadhead property thus escapes taxation in the United States, and the idle and

393

vicious priestcraft and its system are supported by the State its constitution and laws notwithstanding. For every dollar of tax-exempt property, the taxpayer pays double. The vast majority of the people supports thus a small but vocal minority, which but for such public favors would soon perish off the land, for its own membership could not and would not keep it going if it had to pay the taxes, the burden of which it now shifts to the unbelieving or indifferent majority. The system is unjust and undemocratic, is immoral. In his Annual Message to Congress in 1875, President Grant pointed out that the tax-free property of Churches was at the time about one billion dollars; that "by 1900, without check, it is safe to say this property will reach a sum exceeding three billions of dollars"; and he added:

"So vast a sum, receiving all the protection and benefits of Government without bearing its proportion of the burdens and expenses of the same, will not be looked upon acquiescently by those who have to pay the taxes. In a growing country, where real estate enhances so rapidly with time, as in the United States, there is scarcely a limit to the wealth that may be acquired by corporations, religious or otherwise, if allowed to retain real estate without taxation. The contemplation of so vast a property as here alluded to, without taxation, may lead to sequestration without constitutional authority and through blood. I would suggest the taxation of all property equally, whether church or corporation." (*Messages and Papers of the Presidents,* vol. vii, p. 334–5.)

Sequestration and blood have been required to put a curb on Church greed in many modern and "Christian" countries, even in Italy, Spain and France, the "most favored nations" of Holy Church. Russia and Mexico have followed suit; they had been ground into desperation by the luxurious exactions of their respective Churches, and the debased ignorance and poverty which were thus imposed on their peoples. Every country of Europe, even the "Most Christian," where the Society of Jesus has grasped wealth and power, has been forced to expel the parasites; and to "padlock" the vast establishments of religious orders. If one would take a census of illiteracy and poverty, just in those countries where the Church has had or yet has most power and wealth, the people are most ignorant and impoverished. It may be a "coincidence," but it is a very suspicious matter of fact. All these things are of the "fruits," moral and educational, of Christianity.

394

THE "TRIUMPH" OF CHRISTIANITY

Until now the "damning things of the Church" arrayed in these pages, have been known only as the result of laborious research by a limited number: I broadcast them now so that they may be known to all. Even the "Man of God" may plead ignorance heretofore of the frauds of his Church and the falsity of his religion. Here it is demonstrated to him. To beg money now on the plea that the giver "lendeth to the Lord," that money paid for prayers for the dead relieves the souls in Purgatory,—both these coin-cajoling pleas are now known to be false; obtaining money by these false pretenses, now, is Larceny. This is timely and serious warning, which it may be salutary to heed.

AN APPEAL TO REASON

"If any man is ignorant, let him be ignorant." *Paul.*

"Where we can understand, it is a moral crime to cherish the un-understood." *Shotwell.*

These two quotations represent the difference between the viewpoints of the cleric and the scholar. "A mere recital of facts is of little avail unless certain fundamental principles be kept in view," says our oft-quoted Defender of the Faith,—a truth which I would now drive home to the reader—but in a very different sense than is expressed in the clerical conclusion of the sentence,—"*and* unless the fact of Christian revelation be given its due importance." The False Pretense of "Christian revelation" has been exposed and exploded by the real revelations of falsity and fraud in every pretended one of them, by this same Apologist for Christian imposture. Contrasting the wondrous results of "Christian" training—such as we have seen exemplified—with those suffered by the poor Pagan without any revelation, the same Apologist makes this deprecatory comment: "That he should *learn to think for himself* was of course out of the question. With such a training, the *development of free personality* was of course out of the question." (*CE.* v, 296.) Such a disparaging verdict much rather condemns the Christian system and its aims and results, which obviously are, that its devotees, or victims should be "able to believe automatically a number of things which—[in reason]—they know are not true," and which they must therefore accept "of faith," subjecting their reason to the priest-instilled Faith. It is to the awaken-

395

ing of Reason, in the light of the facts herein presented, that I appeal against the pre-occupations or prejudices of Faith,—those "superstitions drunk in with their mother's milk," and never since questioned with open mind.

The ex-Pagan Fathers of Christianity now turned Defenders of the new Faith, and propagandists of it among their fellow Pagans, were very fervid and eloquent in their appeals to the reason of the Pagans as against their mother-inherited superstitions. In his First Apology to the Emperor Antoninus Pius, Father Justin Martyr makes a fine appeal for the use of reason in defiance of tradition and authority,—a fine gesture to the Pagan,—but a principle seldom applied by a Christian in point of his own imposed creeds: "Reason directs those who are truly pious and philosophical to honor and love only what is true, declining to follow the opinions of the ancients, if these be worthless." (Chap. ii; *ANF.* i, 63.) As the preceding review has shown the opinions of the ancient Fathers to be worthless with respect to the "facts" of the Christian religion, and that that religion is quite worthless either as divine truth or effective police, it should therefore be discarded, except for such good moral precepts as are to be found in it as in all religions and all moral systems.

In those times the Christian Church was small and feeble, and had not yet snatched the cynical power whereby, ever since, it *"requires the acceptance and practice not of the religion one may choose, but of that which God prescribes . . .* to be the only true one," as asserted by His Holiness Leo XIII, in the Encyclical *Immortale Dei,* of November 1, 1885. (*CE.* xiv, 764.) Whereupon, the "choosers" of their religion became "heretics," and were quite *"justly burned,"* as that same Pope admits. But before the successors of Constantine gave the Church the sword and the stake for persuasions unto faith, it was necessary that the Christian Apologists should appeal to reason with the intelligent classes of Pagans. Father Lactantius uses argument in his great Apology addressed to Constantine and intended for the learned Pagans of the imperial entourage, which I would earnestly address now to those who yet hesitate in their inherited Christianity:

"It is therefore right, especially in a matter on which the whole plan of life turns, that every one should place confidence in himself, and use his own judgment and individual capacity for the investigation and weighing

396

of the truth, rather than through confidence in others to be deceived by their errors, as though he himself were without understanding. God has given wisdom to all alike, that they might be able both to investigate things which they have not heard, and to weigh things which they have heard. Nor, because they (our ancestors) preceded us in time, did they also outstrip us in wisdom; for if this is given equally to all, we can not be anticipated in it by those who precede us." (Lact., *Divine Institutes,* II, viii; *ANF.* VII, 51.)

If no one, upon reason, or even by caprice, ever changed his opinion, belief, status, we would all be savages still. In matter of religion, the ancestors of every one of us were once Pagans, and those who became Christians were dubbed "atheists" by those remaining faithful to the old gods,—until they too changed to the new. Then these ex-Pagan ancestors of ours were Catholics, of the "orthodox" or one of the ninety-odd "heretic" brands which finally perished or conformed by Grace of God and the Orthodox sword. Others many of our good Catholic ancestors just a few hundred years ago became "heretics" of the Protestant brands, and so continued or until lately continued,— and then threw off the old tradition of faith, and became Rationalists. Every gradation of change was due to one pregnant cause: increasing intelligence of the individual. Each advance sloughed off sundry inherited articles of faith, which then became discarded superstitions. Dean Milman spoke truly of the reason for the decadence of the Pagan religions; his reasons apply as aptly to the Christian: "The progress of knowledge was fatal to the religions of Greece and Rome. . . . Poetry had been religion; religion was becoming mere poetry." (*Hist. of Christianity,* I, 33.)

Father Lactantius has a Chapter entitled "Cicero and Other Men of Learning Erred in not Turning Away the People from Error." It is a moral crime, as Dr. Shotwell says, to cling to error when we can come to understand it as error. Not only that, urges Lactantius, it is wrong for those who know a vital truth to refrain from striving to turn men away from harmful error. His argument was much applauded by the Church, and is the argument of every missionary to the "heathen" today. Lactantius thus justly chides:

"Cicero was well aware that the deities which men worshipped were false. For when he had spoken many things which tended to the overthrow

397

of religious ceremonies, he said nevertheless that these matters ought not to be discussed *by the vulgar,* lest such discussion should extinguish the system of religion which was publicly received. . . . Nay, rather, if you have any virtue, Cicero, *endeavor to make the people wise:* that is a befitting subject, on which you may expend all the powers of your eloquence . . . in the *dispersion of the errors of mankind, and the recalling of the minds of men to a healthy state."* (Lactantius, *Divine Institutes,* II, iii; *ANF.* VII, 43.)

To this ideal of the use of Reason, which Lactantius and the earlier Fathers of the weakling Church held before the intelligent Pagans to incite them to discard the errors and superstitions of Paganism, this book is devoted in the earnest hope and purpose to evoke the use of Reason to the discard of the identical errors and superstitions of "that newer Paganism later called Christianity," which yet persist among the priest-taught masses of Christendom.

That Christian Appeal to Reason was not with the intelligent classes of Pagandom very effective; more persuasive methods must, therefore, be divised to bring the Pagans to the Altar and Treasury of the Lord. We have read the succession of laws of the now "Christian Emperors," which at the behest of the Priests proscribed Paganism upon pain of death and confiscation, made outlaws of all who refused to take the name of Christian, or continued to offer incense to the old gods, or became "heretics" to the official Faith; all who were guilty of these "crimes—let them be stricken by the avenging sword." As the newer "barbarian" nations came upon the Christian scene, "the Catholic Faith was spread by the sword" among and upon them, and all who hesitated or backslid were murdered by Christian law and sword. Crass ignorance, credulity and superstition were then imposed and enforced upon Christendom in order to "preserve the purity of the faith" in the unthinking minds of unknowing dupes of the Church and the Priests who waxed in wealth and in dominion over witless Christendom. When after a millennium during which men were too ignorant to be heretic, the light of thought and reason began to dawn upon the horizon of the Dark Ages of Faith, the Inquisition and the Index, the tortures of the rack and the stake, were providentially provided for the further preservation of Faith by augment of Ignorance and Terror. In all these holy Ages of Faith, in this "civilization thoroughly saturated with Christianity," the Siamese Twins of Creed and Crime, Faith and Filth, popular Poverty and Ecclesiastical Opulence, stalked hand in hand—"the inseparable companions of Religion." The Renaissance and the Reformation came to enfranchise men from Authority and blind Obedience, and the way was blazed for Rationalism and the Age of Reason. The unquestionable record of all this we have read in the amazing and unblushing confessions of Holy Church itself.

At the time of the Reformation admitted conditions existed which today are infinitely more active and more thoroughgoing: "The Christian religious ideal—[never a matter of practice]—was to a great extent lost sight of; higher intellectual culture, previously confined in great measure to the clergy, but now common among the laity, assumed a secular character. . . . Only a faint interest in the supernatural life survived." (*CE.* xii, 703.) Education is now becoming universal; the hateful history of the Church and of Religion is becoming general knowledge; the Church, forced by ever-growing Secularism and Rationalism, has lost the power of compulsion and all but that of persuasion to belief in its forged and fatuous creeds, with all but the unthinking minority, and is itself almost secularized, held together as a sort of social center for the masses without other social contacts, and as matter of "good form" for the pretentiously pious, were infantile hymns are vocalized to an empty Heaven, and the *unco gude* chorus their petitions to the unhearing and unheeding Throne of Grace, "beseeching the Lord upon the universal prayer-theme of '*Gimme!*'" Universally, too, as old John Duffy poetizes it, "The rich they pray for pounds, and the poor they pray for pence."

The utter futility of prayer in objective sense for the obtaining of the subject-matter of the supplication, even of the "Give us this day our daily bread,"—which many do get and many and more others miserably go without, is confessed by *CE.*, which frankly attributes all these things to the operation of the Law of Chance: "The *apparent success which so often attends superstition can mostly be accounted for by natural causes,* although [it piously adds] it would be rash to deny all supernatural intervention (*e. g.* in the phenomena of Spiritism). When the object is to ascertain, or to effect in a general way, *one of two possible events, the law of probabilities gives an equal*

399

chance to success and failure; and success does more to support than failure would do to destroy superstition, for, on its side, there are arrayed the *religious instinct,* sympathy and apathy, confidence and distrust, encouragement and discouragement, and,—perhaps *strongest of all—the healing power of nature.*" (*CE.* xiv, 341.) There, in a nutshell, is the profound psychology of the priest-instilled "religious instinct," and of the hit-or-miss "efficacy of prayer" for the cajoling of "heavenly gifts" of earthly benefits and of the eversion of the heaven-sent or devil-inflicted evils whereof suffering humanity is the sport and prey,—to the utter indifference of their Celestial Pater!

The last sentence of the clerical admission above—"the healing power of nature," bears destructively upon one of the most insistent of religious superstitions, the efficiency of prayers, and saints, and relics, and shrines, and pious mummeries, to which millions of the afflicted and deluded of God's children resort for the relief of their torments and the cure of their diseases,—which their loving Father God inflicts or prevents. From the earliest times of priestcraft until this very year of grace, the priests and parsons and charlatans of every stripe preach and encourage this ancient heathen superstition, —and reap rich rewards through the imposture. The perfectly natural cause and explanation of numerous occasional instances of success at the game, which incites to further superstition and greater abuses, is curiously but truly confessed: "There are *few religions* in which recourse is not had to *supernatural aid for miraculous cures.* The testimony of reliable witnesses and the numerous ex-votos that have come down to us from antiquity leave no doubt as to the reality of these cures. It was natural that they should have been *viewed as miraculous in an age* when *the remarkable power of suggestion to effect cures* was not understood. Modern science recognizes that strong mental impressions can powerfully influence the nervous system and through it the bodily organs, leading in some instances to sudden illness or death, in others to remarkable cures. Such is the so-called mind cure or cure by suggestion. *It explains naturally many extraordinary cures recorded in the annals of many religions.* Still it has its *recognized limits. It cannot restore of a sudden a half-decayed organ, or heal instantly a gaping wound caused by a cancer.*" (*CE.* xii, 743.)

This thus confesses the huge false pretense of "miracle of God" in

400

such cases of relief or cure of nervous or mental maladies as are claimed for the impostures of Lourdes, St. Anne's, Malden, the Calvary Baptist Holy Rollers and all such shrines of religious imposture and superstition. In antiquity, the fictitious Pagan gods did not exist,—the cures attributed to them and paid for to the priests were entirely due to nature, and the claims of the priests were frauds. The Christians now confess the "recognized limits" of their God to do more than Nature did under the Pagan gods: the pretense of "miracle," of "supernatural intervention" is seen to be as fraudulent in modern times as it is admitted to have been in ancient. The Pagans believed, and prayed, and paid the priests, and some by auto-suggestion found relief or were cured, many others believed, and prayed, and paid—and their natural sufferings were enhanced by their disappointment. But did they cease therefore to believe and pray and pay? Probably then the pious apologetics of defeatism were the same as now. If the thing prayed for cometh to pass—"the gods have—God has—answered our prayers; blessed be their—His—holy name!" and the fortunate results are noised abroad. If by equal chance the prayed-for benefit is unattained, then "God knows better than we what is best for us," and the less said about the failure the better for childlike Faith. When exposed to danger or death we escape, it is "the wonderful Providence of God,"— nothing being thought or said about those so curiously designated "Acts of God" which permitted or inflicted the disaster; whereas, if we die or continue in suffering, why, "God's ways are not our ways"; "the ways of God are beyond our finite understanding," *et cetera* of pious apologies for the silence and failure of God to help his suffering and neglected children.

It would seem that every fossil of credulity embedded in the ancient Rock of Faith has in the course of this review been picked out and the Rock itself drilled through and through for the easy task of final demolition. For nigh two thousand years it has cast its baleful shadow upon civilization, stunting and dwarfing the minds and faculties of men clouded by its worthless bulk. Though vastly undermined and hacked and tottering, the blighting effects of Church and religious superstition are yet in many odious respects persistent; humanity and civilization yet suffer under the lingering disease of priest-imposed delusions and the hateful miasma of religious intolerance in every land cursed yet by priestcraft, parsonate, and the odium of theology.

"When the Devil was sick, the Devil a Saint would be!" The Church is dying now; has been forced despite itself and its enginery of torture and murder, to desist from the worst of its deviltry, to appear a bit civilized; some of its partizans and dupes think it "reformed," pure-minded and clean-handed. It is only measurably so perforce, and reluctantly. Even today the Law of God, conserved in the latest Edition of the holy Canon Law, commands murder for unbelief; these infamous "principles are in their own nature irreformable; . . . owing to *changed conditions* [forced upon it by secular civilization] are to all practical intents and purposes obsolete . . . *The custom of burning heretics is really not a question of justice, but a* question of civilization"! (*CE.* xiv, 769.) Thus the Church confesses itself uncivilized; it retains and insists upon the God-ordained *justice* of burning and murder; but is forced by heretic civilization, acquired in bloody despite of the Church, to conform to the decrees of Civilization. But as—however—Holy Church is impotent, dying, and will soon be dead—then only *De mortuis nil nisi bonum!*—Speed its hastening Death!

Founded in fraud by avarice and ambition, propagated by sword and fire, perpetuated by ignorance and fear; by increase of knowledge and free expression of thought rendered now all but impotent except in will and malice, priestcraft yet grasps for power and dominion over mind and spirit of men. In present default of rack and stake, it struggles yet to impose itself through such unholy means as it can still partially command,—fines and imprisonment under ridiculous medieval laws for the absurd priestly "crimes" of blasphemy and sacrilege, "desecration of the Lord's Day" by innocent diversions instead of attending dull preachings and paying the priests by the gift upon the Altar or in the contribution plate. Odious laws for the repression of human liberty; for the outlawing of honest men who refuse the superstitious forms of Religious Oath imposed in courts and legal proceedings, of which several shocking instances have recently occurred, depriving men of liberty and property, and potentially of life through refusal of their testimony in court. Religious Intolerance flames through the land, as notorious instances have lately made evident. Good Christians yet cordially dislike and distrust all others of differ-

402

ing brands of Faith, which sentiments Christians and Jews religiously reciprocate in holy hatred and intolerance of each other, while all unite in utter abhorrence and damnation of the Liberal and the Unbeliever, condemned alike by private Christian spite and public obloquy, of a vocal and intolerant minority; by political disqualifications for public office wherever this or that Sect is yet in a majority and can enforce its intolerance by law. "A careful study of the history of religious toleration," says the historian of Civilization, "will prove, that in every Christian country where it has been adopted, it has been forced upon the clergy by the authority of the secular classes. At the present day it is still unknown to those nations among whom the ecclesiastical power is stronger than the temporal power." In quite half the countries of Latin America and several of Europe—the most backward and poverty-stricken and priest-ridden of them—yet today public office and honors can be attained only by the votaries of the Sect in power, and the free and public practice of any other than the official cult is prohibited by law. I have the codes of these "Christian" countries.

Even in our own "tolerant" country today, religious fanaticism succeeds in its attacks, to impose by law the "sacred science of Genesis" in the universities and schools to the outlawry of the teachings of the truths of Nature. Preachers and teachers who dare express honest opinions of liberalism or unbelief are by pious religionists discharged and their families deprived of bread and support. Religious Pharisees seek to seize the public schools to disseminate their obsolete superstitions in the minds of youth—the hope of the future, and the last chance of the Church. Individual peace and friendliness, public peace and good understanding are often jeopardized and destroyed by Religion. Corrupt and insulting ecclesiastical government is rampant in many of our large cities and in a number of entire States. In a word, and despite all, the Twentieth Century is still under the hang-over spell of medieval theology and all the holy spites and intolerances of rancorous Religiosity.

The fatal work of Church and Priest through the Christian Era—as herein revealed, has wrought ignorance, superstition and vice: it has been and remains a supreme failure. Faith is become obsolete before Facts. Christianity is proved to be a fraudulent Bankrupt; this is its final adjudication before the bar of Civilization.

FORGERY IN CHRISTIANITY

The Christian Religion—shown to be a congeries of revamped Pagan Superstitions and of Priestly Lies—*is not respectable* for belief: every honest and self-respecting mind must repudiate it in disgust. We can all "Do good, for good is good to do"!

Faith—fondly called "the most precious heritage of the race," is not a thing whereof to be proud; it is not intelligent or of Reason. Not a flicker of intelligence is required to believe: millions of the most illiterate and ignorant of earth's teeming populations are the firmest in their "faith" in every form of religious superstition known to the priests of the world, the most devout believers of this or that imposture,—"most assured of what they are most ignorant" withal. Indeed, as aptly quoted: "Unbelief is no crime that Ignorance was ever capable of being guilty of." Buckle truly says, that to the secular and skeptical spirit European civilization owes its origin: that "it is evident, that until doubt began, progress was impossible" (Ch. vii, 242); and *CE.* has confessed, as is also self-evident,—"Toleration only came in when Faith went out." What a boon then to humanity to hasten and complete its going!

Disbelief, doubt, inquiry of truth, rejection of superstition, is distinctly an act of Intelligence; it often requires heroic virtue of bravery and independence of mind to disbelieve, to revolt against and reject the creeds and credulities of the ignorant community,—as evidenced by the whole holy bloody history of religious rancor and intolerance which has so inadequately but shockingly been reviewed. It is the bravest men and the finest minds, with high courage to dare and defy Holy Church, whom that unholy Hoodlum has murdered, but who have saved and recreated Civilization, as even yet inadequately it has been achieved.

Think to what Civilization might have attained by this Twentieth Century. For nigh two thousand years Christianity has held sway and thrall over the most dominant part of the world and portion of the human race. In each generation for most of the two thousand years there have been hundreds of thousands of men and women—priests, monks, nuns, and "religious" nondescripts, devoted through life to the unrealities of "Other-worldliness" to the utter neglect of the world in which they lived, resolved, all too oft, "to make of earth a hell that they might merit heaven." In the pursuit of such impracticalities, and to force all others to believe, doubtless millions of books and sermons of

404

sophistry have been their output, not to mention ignorance, wars, famines, plagues and bestialities innumerable that they have brought about to the destruction of civilization. Thus, in aggregate, millions of human beings—many of them of very high mental capacity, have devoted some millions of years of labor or of sloth to Theology and Religion,—lives, years and labor wasted! If these years and labors had but been devoted to pure and applied Science, to the discovery and conquest of the powers of Nature, to Knowledge of the Worth While—medicine, surgery, anesthetics, antiseptics, sanitation—the catalogue is endless; to the outlawry of War and the establishment of universal Peace; the abolition of Crime, Poverty, and Disease—in a word, to the Social Sciences and Service, to Humanism and the Humanities, instead of to Theism and Theology—to what glorious heights would not Civilization and Humanity have scaled!

The timorous Religionist—affrighted at the threatened loss of the "consolations of Religion,"—at facing the realities of life without the "opiate" and "crutches" of Faith, often asks: "What are you going to give us in its place?" *A cure!*—so that you will not need these artificial aids. When the surgeon excises a dangerous tumor, or the physician heals a mental or physical disease,—he restores to health of body or mind,—does not inflict some other form of disease in place of the one cured. So with the fictitious mental disorder of Religion,—for that it is a mental disorder of most malignant kind is proved by the inveterate hates and crimes it has caused the sufferers from it to be guilty of through all the Ages of Faith, as disclosed in this review. The sufferer goes through life, actually—or what is the same thing, under the delusion of disability,—hobbling on crutches, or with frequent injections of "dope" to allay real or imagined pain. Either by material means or by "mind cure" he is healed of the real or imaginary ailment: he throws away his crutches, discards his daily narcotic; health and strength come to his members and his whole body; the faculties of the mind are freed from the inhibitions of disease and disability. The grandest cure ever wrought in the man and in humanity is to free the mind from Superstition, to release all the energies of mind and body for the glorious work for Mankind. The noblest and most blest worker for Humanity is the Humanist.

Religious Toleration and freedom of thought and of beneficent research, came in only as religious Faith went out; Civilization began only as the Dark Ages of Faith came to an end. The Church has had its long Night—those Dark Ages of Faith. Therein it shed its boasted refulgence of "sweetness and light"—in the Dark. The Church is very like the fire-fly—the homely Lightning Bug,—it needs darkness in which to shine. But the Day is come; the supernatural Light of the Cross is faded and paled before the luminous truths of Nature discovered now and exploited by free men for the good of mankind.

It remains yet to complete the good work for civilization and humanity by destroying the last lingering works and delusions of decadent and decayed priestcraft; through the universal triumph of Rationalism to fully and finally *Ecraser l'Infame*. Truly and prophetically spoke Zolà: "Civilization will not attain to its perfection, until the last stone from the last church falls on the last priest!"

A new and free Civilization rises from the ruins of the Ages of Faith; with heart aglow and high purpose set on the attainment of the ancient "Supreme Good," it hails the glorious possibilities of the scientific Age of Reason, which will redeem humanity from the blight of the centuries of Unreason. Men may now know and freely and unafraid make known the truth: and the Truth shall make mankind Free.

In the fine imagery of Dr. Trattner, his autobiographic God looks into the now not so distant Future, and thus communes: "Before Me is the Scroll of Destiny. See! Man has already scaled the foot-hills. Not one man alone, or two, or three, but all the nations. Everywhere men and women together are now leading their children forward consecrated to the Ideal. . . . I am satisfied. It is the day—the day of complete Emancipation!"

FINIS—FIDEI

INDEX

(Letter "s" after page-number, signifies *et seq.*)

Aaron, death, 68.

Abduction, 344.

Abel, Christian Saint, 273.

Abgar-Jesus forged correspondence, 106, 109s.

Abraham, great scientist, 148-149.

Absurd, Christianity, therefore believed, 124, 145.

Acta Pilati, forgeries, 105s.

Acts, forged, list of, 104s.

Acts of St. Sylvester, forgery, 251.

Adam: Augustine on monstrous descendants of, 160s; name is false translation, 76; books forged in name of, 66; Sin of, in apocrypha, 87.

Adultery: of animals in Ark, 146; marriage akin to, 145-146; forgery of "Woman taken in," 228.

Æsculapius, miracle cures of, 140-141.

Æsop, historicity compared with Jesus, 99.

African gods and priestcraft, 7.

Agape, Christian scandals, 343.

Agapetæ, Christian scandals, 343-344.

Agatha, St., Volcano-stopper, 271.

Age of Apocryphal Literature, 48, 95s.

Age of Faith, uncritical, 279.

Angus Dei, Christian fetich, 293-294.

Agrapha, Christian forgeries, 104.

Ahriman, Devil of Mithraism, 21-24.

Ahura Mazda, Mithraic God, 21-25.

Albertus Magnus, suppressed scientist, 367.

Albigenses, murder of, 348.

Alexander the Great: virgin birth of, 8; introduced Mithraism, 20, 21; conquered armies of Jehovah, 325.

Almah: does not mean "virgin,"— Virgin Birth fraud, 63-64.

Ambrose, St.: forgery of Apostles' Creed, 108; fables about Cross, 279.

Amending the Bible, 174-176.

Anagram: "Ixthus—fish," forgery, 35s, 166.

Angel-Owl forgery, 119-120.

Angels: Pagan myths, 23s; names of, Babylonian, 24; taken into Jewish apocrypha, 19-20; have sexual intercourse with humans, 167.

Angutkok, American priests, 6.

INDEX

Animals: in Eden talked, 81; in Ark, adultery, 146; freakish notions of "Fathers," 136, 146, 161-162; offended Saints like wild, vi, ix.

Annunciation, to Virgin Mary, forgery, 207.

Anonymous Gospels, impossibility, 181-182.

Anro Mainyus. See *Ahriman*.

Anthon, quoted, 40.

Antichrist, epithet, 3.

Antipodes, Augustine on, 160; the Pope and St. Vergilius, 362s.

Anti-popes, doublet and triplet sets, 355.

Apocalyptic forgeries, Jewish, influence on Christian, 86s.

Apocrypha—forgeries: defined, 46; Age of apocryphal literature, 48, 95s; flood of, 180; classification of, 100s; Church regarded as inspired, 46; apostles vouched for that in Catholic Bible, 50, 54; Christian, "fraudulent intent," 99-100; Jewish, as source of Christian doctrines, 84s; Christian interpolations in Jewish, 67; vogue of Jewish, in Church, 48; came through Septuagint, 61; vouched for by Jesus and Fathers, 89; list of Jewish apocrypha, 66-67; *Esdras*, etc. as Scripture, 55; Original Sin derived from, 87; catalogue of principal Christian apocrypha, 100-107.

Apollo, testifies of Christ, etc., 38.

Apollonius of Tyana, Pagan Christ, 13s.

Apostles: sketch of Twelve, 127-130; fictitious *dramatis personæ*, 127-128; vouched for Jewish forgeries in Vulgate, 50.

Apostles' Creed, forgery, 108.

Apostolic Canons, forgery, 241.

Apostolic Constitutions, forgery, 240-241.

Apostolic Fathers, account of, 130s.

Apostates, numbers and influence of, 320.

Appeal to Reason, 395s.

Aquinas, St. Thomas: vouches for Sibyls, 40; on viewing torments of hell, 162.

Arabs: civilization and learning of; effects on Christendom, 378s; preserved medical science, 368; origins and spread of power, 381s.

Aramaic, language of Jesus and apostles, 216-217.

Archangels, from Mithraism, 24.

Arianism: Constantine on trifling point, 248; rent Empire, 250; conflicts over, 346; Multiplication Table of, 319-320.

Aristeas: forged Letter about Septuagint, 58-59.

Aristotle: sketch of, 329; Articles of Faith due to, 33; influence on Scholasticism, 337-338.

Articles of Faith; due to Aristotle, 33; for Fools, xv.

Asmodeus: a Mithraic devil, 26; a Christian devil in Tobit, 51, 52.

Assumption of Moses (Jewish forgery): Christian doctrines from, 88; inspiration vouched for by Fathers, 47.

Athanasian Creed: forgery, 108-109; exclusive salvation in, 3.

Atheists: St. Justin admits being,

ii

79; outlawed as witnesses, xxix, seq.

Augustine, St.: sketch of, 157s; subjects reason to faith, xv, 158-159; Gospels incredible, xv, 191; on Antipodes, 160, 362; on Creation and giants, 160; vouches for *Enoch*, 87, 167; books on Lying, xxiv; on Liberty of Error, 315; on "Compel them to come in," 171, 315; on Magic, 164-165; on men turned into animals, 165; on monstrous, headless races, *Skiopodes*, 160-161; Sermon to headless race, xxiv; on immortality of peacocks, 161; on truth of fable of Romulus and Remus, 163-164; on salamander and hell, 161-162; on freakish natural History, 161-162; on Septuagint, 60, 166-167; on sexual intercourse of devils and angels, 167; on superstition drunk in with mother's milk, xi, 164; on Sibyls, 36, 165-166.

Authorities, ecclesiastical, for this Book, xxviii.

Avesta, chief Christian doctrines from, 21s.

Avarice and wealth, of Church and clergy, 386s.

Baaras root, for devil-exorcism, 87.

Bacon, Roger, suppressed scientist, 367.

Bankruptcy of Christianity, 403s.

Barbarians, did not overthrow Eastern Empire, 381.

Barnes, Harry Elmer, quoted, 384.

Baronius, Cardinal, "Annals," 363-364.

Baruch (Jewish forgery): Original Sin from, 87; many Christian doctrines from, 88; inspiration of, Fathers on, 89.

Baptism: Pagan ceremony, 29; of Pagan gods into Christian saints, 41; for purification of body, not of soul, 117; formula, in name of Trinity, forgery, 225-227.

Barnabas, Epistle of: Christian forgery, 136; Church regarded as scripture, 181.

Battle, trial by, between Christ and Mohammed, 383.

Beasts, offended Saints like wild, vi, ix.

Bel and Dragon, forgery, inspired, 89.

Believe, because unbelievable, 145.

Benedict XIV, Pope: on inspiration of Sibyls, 40.

Benefit of Clergy, 375-376.

Benevolence: in Buddhism, 28; in Mithraism, 20; in Pagan Rome, 359-360.

Bible: Infallible Truth, God its Author, 201-202; full of errors and contradictions, 202; every Book a forgery, Chaps. II and V; forgeries in O. T., 67s; held by Church as book of Science, 370, 379-380; science in Bible is false, 379-380.

Biblical Commission, Papal: tinkering with Bible texts, 175; on Creation-myths as basis of Christian Religion, 72.

Birth, New: Pagan doctrine, 29.

Blasphemy Laws, in U. S., xxxi.

Blood: lake of in Hell, vi; Holy, liquifying, 270, 272.

Blue Laws, xxxi, *seq.*

Bollandists, and the Saint-mill, 268.

Book of Dead, Egyptian, 17.

Book of Popes, forgery, 241-242.

Books: condemned not for forgery but for heresy, 47; burning of, to keep Faithful from learning the truth, 371; Index of Prohibited, 370-371.

Bootlegging Religion into Public Schools, xiv.

Brothel, Papal Lateran as, 341.

Bryce, Lord, on Donation of Constantine, 257.

Buckle: on clergy opposed to civilization, 386; on toleration forced on clergy, 408; on civilization due to skepticism, 404.

Buddha and Buddhism: sketch of, 27s; identities with Christianity, 28; sayings like those of Jesus, 28; "Life" of Buddha vehicle for Christian truth, 28; canonized as St. Josaphat, 269; miracle by idol of Buddha, 266; Buddha enjoins truth, xxvii.

Burbank, Luther, quoted, v.

Burning: of books, to keep Faithful, ignorant, 371; of heretics, just, 402; approved by Leo XIII, 396.

Cadman, as Mohammedan, if born that way, xii, *seq.*

Cambyses, and sacred cats, 245.

Cardinal: Baronius, on bogus saints, 364; Newman, on Christian doctrines from Paganism, 29; of New York City, on bootlegging religion into schools, xiv.

Canon, of Scriptures: Hebrew canon, when closed, 45; Christian, first fixed by Council of Trent, 54; no suggestion of in N. T., 97; result of denials and disputes, 98; idea of original canon not historical, 97-98.

Canonical, definition of, 45.

Canonicity: defined as apostolic authorship or authority, 181s; Gospels not canonical until late 2nd century, 183-184.

Canon Law: "science of" due to forged Decretum of Gratian, 263; yet enjoins burning and murder of heretics, 402.

Canons, Apostolic, forgery, 241.

Catholic Bible: apocrypha in, 50; forged "Wisdom of Solomon" in, 48.

Catholic Church (see Church): has never erred and never shall err, 49; losses of, 383-385.

Catholic Encyclopedia: admissions of, destroy Christian religion, xxix; examples throughout this book.

Catholics, number of, and 14 sects, in U. S., vii.

Cato, on priests laughing on meeting, xxvii.

Cats, Cambyses' use of sacred, 245.

Censuses in Wilderness, padded like Church statistics, vi.

Centuriators and Catholic historians, 363s.

Cesset Superstitio, in Law prohibiting Paganism, 31, 305.

INDEX

Charlemagne: relations with the popes, 253s; crowned Emperor, 255; alleged gifts to Church doubted, 254, 259.

Cherubim, from Babylonian and Zoroastrian religions, 24.

Children: victims of religion, xi; Faithful know more than philosophers and scientists, 371.

Chinese miracle, 266.

Chosen, Four Gospels, out of many, 186.

Chrism, fables of, 252.

Christian: "word has lost its meaning," 386; religion not respectable, 404; Scripture forgeries, Chap. III, p. 91s.; Era, false, 71-72.

Christianity: origins obscure, 91s, 125s; "miraculous attestations" of, 382s; "triumph" of, Chap. VII, p. 295s; a compound of Jewish and Pagan myths and superstitions: Christian doctrines from Jewish apocrypha, 84-90; from Paganism: 2s, 10s, 17s, 21s, 23s, 29, 90.

Christians: as Sibyllists, 34; as Sun-worshippers, 147.

Christmas: Pagan holiday of Mithraism, 22, 31.

Christology: derived fully from Jewish forgeries, 67.

Christs, Pagan: 13s.

Chronology, Biblical, false, 73-74; Christian Era, false, 71-72.

Church—"Ecclesia": use of word in Matthew, forgery, 213, 217-218; Catholic, never erred, and never shall err, 49; not founded by Jesus, 215-219; founded "on this rock," forgery, 215-219; enchains reason, and enslaves children, xiv-xv; "highest type of culture," 363; claims glory for Science, 372; moral corruption of, 341s; Forgery Mill, Chap. VI, p. 238s; is not civilized, 402; Divine Teaching Mission, 321s; tolerates and encourages superstition, 240, 280; asserted inspiration of Jewish forgeries, 47; is in Politics, xxxiii; beginnings of illicit consortium of Church and State, 251s; statistics of, vi, seq.; is on Toboggan, vii; mental calibre of membership, vii; percentage of members to population, vi; percentage of increase, viii; deserves defeat, ix; losing ground since 12th century, 385s; immense losses of, 383-385; dying, and seems saintly, 402.

Cicero, on Pythian Oracles, x.

City of God, Augustine; account of, 157, 159; extracts from, 159-167.

Civilization: "universal ruin" under Christianity, 357; rebirth of, 373s; due to skepticism, 404; what it would be but for Christianity, 404s; Zolà on its perfection, 406.

Classics, "preserved by Monks," 356s.

Clement of Alexandria: sketch of, 148s; on inspiration of Sibyls, 36, 149; on inspiration of Septuagint, 60; on inspiration of Enoch, 87; makes false quotations, 104.

Clement of Rome, Pope (?): sketch of, 131s; didn't know of Gospels, 182-183; forgeries in his name, 131s; on phœnix as proof of resurrection, 132-133.

Clergy: only ones who could read and write, 374-375; reasons why, *Ib.;* corruption of, 341s, 346s; wealth and greed of, 386s; opposed to civilization, 386; "benefit of clergy," 375-376.

Clovis, "conversion" of, 251.

Codes: of Hammurabi and Moses, 9; of Justinian, laws, 304s; of Theodosius, 31, 304s.

"Compel them to come in," 171, 315, 317.

Constantine: sketch of, 243s; amalgamated all religions, "One State, one Church," 29s; favors Christians, why? 243s; "Conversion of," 243s; Donation of, 251, 256-257; Forgeries regarding, 251s; Edict of Milan, 301; Laws on Magic, 13; religious laws of, 304s; Murders by, 247; seeks Pagan and Christian absolution, 248-249; at Council of Nicæa, 248; Arian until death-bed, 31, 249; baptized Arian, 247; Apotheosized, 249; Eusebius on in Heaven, 247.

Constantine II, Pagan, 31; laws of, 304s.

Constantius Chlorus: favors Christians, why? 244; St. Helena, his mistress, 243.

Constantinople, dedication of, 30.

Constitutions, Apostolic: forgery, 240.

Contradictions: as evidence of forgery, 71s; and Truth, 203s; Bible full of, 202, 204.

Conversion: of Constantine, reasons for, 243s; compulsory and wholesale, 317s; but skin deep, 320s.

Copernicus, 370.

Copying: Gospel of "Mark" into others, 192.

Cornelius, conversion of, and Peter, 221-223.

Council of Trent: first fixed Canon, including apocrypha, 50, 54.

Counterfeit, of Church, taken by Protestants, xviii.

Counter-Reformation, 353.

Court-Martial, and fake Miracle, 267.

Covetousness of Church and clergy, 391-392.

Cradle-Age: best for religion, xii, *seq.;* determines Creed, xi-xiv.

Creation: Genesis account basis of Christianity, 72; but truth of denied by *CE.,* 73, 74; by gods, 75; various dates of, 59; myths of imposed by law, xxx, 73; Augustine on, 160.

Credibility: of Fathers, 124, 168s; of Gospels: Augustine on, 191; Tertullian on, 191.

Creed: determined by Cradle, xi-xiv; is superior to morality (*CE.*) xxvii; Apostles', forgery, 108; Athanasian, forgery, 108-109; exclusive salvation in, 3.

Credulity: popular, 44; of Christians, 99-100; encouraged by Church, 240, 280; source of clerical graft, 392.

INDEX

Crib, Holy, fake relic, 279; vouched for by Pope, 286-287.

Crishna, Pagan Saviour, 27s.

Criticism, literary: principles of, 177; Fathers ignorant of, 99.

Cross, fake relic: "Invention" or Finding of, 281s; subsequent history of, 283; "Fiery," 244s.

Crown of Thorns, fake relic, "invention" of, 284s; 700 thorns, 285.

Crusades: causes and effects of, 376s; against Albigenses, 348; for conversion of Pagans, 317s.

Culture: of Pagan Greece, 322s, 334s; of Pagan Roman Empire, 333s, 358s; of Christian Dark Ages, 335s.

Cure, for religious disease, x, 405.

Cures, "miracle," Pagan and Christian, explained, 400s.

Daeva: Zoroastrian Devil, 25; origin of *Deus* and *Zeus,* 24; of Asmodeus, 26.

Dante, on Donation of Constantine, 256.

Dark Ages: 239, 335s; "saturated with Christianity," 366; a "universal ruin," 357.

Damnation, Infant, 299.

Dawn Man and Shaman, 4s.

Decalogue: fraud, 9; a natural moral code, 341.

Decameron of Holy Ghost, 69.

December 25th, Mithraic holy day, 22.

Decretals, False, of Isidore, forgery, 260s.

Decretum, of rejected books, forgery, 47.

Decretum of Gratian, forgery, 263.

Demiurge, Pagan-Christian, 156.

Demonology: Jewish - Christian, from Mithraism, 24s; in Jewish apocrypha, 87.

Devil: Pagan superstition from Mithraism, 23-25s; Christians, created by God, responsible for, 25; conjuring devils, Josephus on, 82, 83.

Devils: Pagan gods are, 41; origin and activities, 152-153; imitate Christian rites, 31s, 140s; have sexual relations with women, 167; exorcism, Pagan and Christian, 7.

Deus, and *Zeus,* derived from *Daeva,* 24.

Dialogi, of Gregory the Great, 43, 275.

Dictatus, of Gregory VII, 49-50.

Diomede Islanders, superstitions, 6.

Dionysius the Areopagite: forgeries, 128; apostles fictitious, 128.

Disbelief: rising tide of, vi-x; act of Intelligence, 404.

Dishonesty: of preachers, xi; of Patristic literature, 48.

Divine Institutes, of Lactantius; on Sibyls, 37s, 151s.

Doctors of Divinity: cause religious disease, v; dosed, xxxiii.

Donation of Constantine: a huge forgery, 255s; disproofs of, 257-258; for deception of Charlemagne, 254; Bryce on, 257; Dante on, 256; Gibbon on, 258.

Doomsday Book, wealth of clergy, 388-389.

Dreams, origin of notion of the supernatural, 4.
Dualism, Zoroastrian, 23.

Easter, Pagan origin of, 18.
Ecclesia, meaning and use of, 216-217; a forgery, 217s.
Edict of Milan, 301.
Education: in Pagan Greece, 322s; in Pagan Rome, 333; Christian, aims and results of, 335s; "Christian Education" Lie, 356s.
Ems Revolt against Church, 264s.
End of World: Mithraic superstition, 26; taken into Jewish apocrypha, 84s; oft proclaimed by Jesus, 93, 220.
Endings of Gospels of "Matthew" and "Mark," forgeries, 225-227.
Enemy: is rival religionist, 392; Christian love of, vi, 343.
Enoch, Book of: account of, 85-87; inspiration of, 85; preserved by Noah, 85; doctrine of Messiah, etc., from, 86s; genuine and prophetical, 47, 167.
Epistles: forgeries, 104s; list of forgeries, 230-237; none by Paul, 230s; none by Peter, 233s; forgeries in, 234-237.
Era, Christian, account of; is erroneous, 71-72.
Erasmus, "Prince of Humanists": exposed "Unknown God" forgery, 230; on Paul as forger, 230.
Error: Church "never erred, and never shall err," 49.
Errors, in N. T., admitted by *CE.* 173-174, 229.

Esdras, Books, III & IV: forgeries, regarded by Church as Scripture, 55; doctrine of Original Sin from, 87.
Ethics: see Morals.
Eucharist: Mithraic superstition, 23; general Pagan practice, 17.
Eunuch: Paul was, 146; Jesus enjoins making, 146; Origen was, 149.
Eusebius, Bishop of Cæsarea: dishonesty of, xxi; was Arian heretic, xxi; lie about martyrs alive after eaten, xxi; admitted liar by *CE.,* 105-106; lies about Fiery Cross, 244, 246-247; on Conversion of Constantine, 244-247; eulogy on Constantine in Heaven, 247; on Church prelates, 345; on Sibyls, 36; forged Abgar-Jesus Letters, 106, 109s; forged account of Jesus in Josephus, 115, 118; angel-owl forgery, 119-120; fables about Gospel of "Mark," 181-182.
Eve: forge *Life* of, 66; forged Gospel of, 172.
Evidences, of Christianity: 100s; "taken for granted," 125.
Evil, created by God, 23, 25.
Evolution: in Greek philosophy, 332; of Hebrew religion admitted by *CE.,* 70; of human civilization, etc., 74; teaching of banned by law, xxx.
Exorcism: African and Christian, 7.
Ezra: and Hebrew canon, 45; "restores" law, 55s; Fathers vouch for, 56.

INDEX

Fable, of Christ, Leo X, 351.

Failure of Christianity, x, 403.

Faith: not knowledge, xviii; always defeated by facts, 372; fanatic, 372; apologies for failures, 400s; not intelligent, 404; What in place of? Cure! 405.

False Decretals of Isidore, forgery, 260s.

False Translations: evidence of forgery, 76; Adam, 76; *elohim,* etc., 75; Yahveh-Jehovah, 77s; Lord and Lord God, 75-76; phoenix, 147; soul, 76; "virgin," in Isaiah and Matthew, 63s.

"Fathers" of the Faith: character sketches, Chap. IV, p. 123s; all ex-Magicians, 123; in Mithraism, 22; mental and moral obliquity, 24-25, 169-170; all liars, xxii; admitted liars, xxi, *seq.,* 15; approve lying, xxi, *seq.;* opinions worthless, 41; make false quotations, 104; uncritical, 84; vouch importance of Creation myths, 72-73; for *Enoch,* 47, 167; for *Esdras,* 55; for Ezra and the Law, 56; for Jewish apocrypha, 47; for Pagan gods and miracles, 33, *passim;* on "Devilish Imitations," 31s, *passim;* for inspiration of Sibyls, 35s, *passim;* make no mention of Gospels until Papias and Irenæus, 196; immense output of Patristic works, 171.

Fear: origin of religion, 7s; Lucretius on Fear, 8.

Fish: Anagram, 35s, 166; Christian symbol, 36.

Firmament, destroyed by Galileo, 370. Church boasts suppression of Galileo, 370.

Finding: of Book of Mormon, 57; of Law of Moses, 57; of Cross, etc., 281s.

Fiery Cross of Constantine, fables of, 244s.

Forgery: defined by *CE.,* xix-xx; tests for forgery, 177-178; late appearance of document, 184; universality of Christian forgeries, xxv-xxvi, *seq.,* 264; all Christian documents and evidences forged, xvii, 62, 100s; Gospels and Epistles forged, 101s; condemned by Church only when heretical, 48; Christian forgeries in Pagan Oracles, 34s; in Jewish apocrypha, 67; forgeries in names of Fathers, 121; forgery by false translations, 74s; Church founded on forgery, 264.

Forgery Mill of Church: Chap. VI, p. 238s.

Foundling, Jesus Christ is of Church, 216.

Franks, Defenders of the Church, 251, 253.

Fraud: hateful to victims, xxxiii; Pagan frauds, 11, 42; taken into Christianity, 41s; in Christian apocrypha, 100; resource of cunning, 258.

"Fruits," of Christianity: 321s; Moral fruits, 339s; intellectual fruits, 356s.

Freethinkers: Church sneer at as "vagabonds," 371; but have saved Civilization, 404.

Galileo: discoveries of, ruined the Firmanent, 370s; treatment by Church, 370.

Genesis: Christian religion depends on, 72; but discredited by *CE.*, 73-74.

Genesis, Little, forgery, regarded as Scripture, 88.

Genus Shamanensis, 7.

Giants, Augustine on, 160.

"Gimme!", universal prayer theme, 399.

Giordano Bruno, burned, 370.

Gladiatorial combats, stopped by Church? 360.

"Go, teach all nations": forgery, 220-224, 236s, 239; text in forged endings of Gospels, 225-227; discredited by *CE.*, 223-224; false claims of Church, 322, 336, 339.

God, Gods: Pagan gods all devils, 32, 140s, 162s; "other gods" admitted, 71; created evil, 23, 25; African notions of, 29; forgery of One God myth, 75; Hebrew, had no Son, 78.

"God Manifest" forgery, 234.

Gospels: All Forgeries, Chap. V, p. 172; all late compilations, 201s; anonymous, 178-180; impossibility of being anonymous, 181-182; Titles of not apostolic, 178s; Endings of, forgeries, 225-227; oral for century, 94, 173; forged apocryphal, 101s; "many gospels" existed, 186-187; one by Jesus, 101, 103; list of over fifty, 102; no difference between apocryphal and canonical, 200-201; not men-

tioned in Epistles, 95; not written by Jews, but by Greeks, 184-186; not known to "Pope" Clement I, 182-183; not written in first century, 93s, 173s, 199; not known to Papias, 195; first mentioned by Irenæus, 185 A. D., 180, 189, 195s; earliest written by heretics, 189, 190, 193; Christian written to combat heretics, 189-190; Why Four Gospels?, *CE.* doesn't know, 187s; Irenæus explains, 188; real reason, 189-190; one for each principal Church, 189, 192-193; the "Four" Chosen, 186s; order of, 179-180; "canonicity" of, 181s; not regarded as Scripture until late second century, 183-184; contradictions in, 204; Augustine would not believe, unless forced, xv, 191.

Graft and greed of Church and clergy, 386s.

Grant, President, on Church tax-dodging, 394.

Gratian, forged *Decretum*, 263.

Greed and graft, of apostles, 127-130; of Church and clergy, 386s.

Greece: education and morals in, 322s; culture and science in, 324s.

Gregory I, the Great: on lying, xxv; lying *Dialogi*, 43; miracles and miracle tales of, 275s; Holy Ghost, dove-like, dictates to, 277; invented Purgatory, 390.

Gregory VII, braggart *Dictatus*, 49-50.

Guardian Angels, as Mithraic superstitions, 24.

Gulliver awakes, 373s.

Hammurabi, Code, pious fraud of, 9.

Hallam: on *False Decretals*, 261; on Church greed, 391-392.

Heaven: Mithraic myth, 26.

Hebrews: no word for "religion," 9; Holy Forgeries of Chap. III, p. 45s; religion of, not revealed, but natural development, 70, 89.

Hebrews, Book of, forgery, attributed to Barnabas, 234.

Hegel: on evolution of religion, 70; on methods of ancient history, 80-81.

Helena, St.: Pagan barmaid, mistress of Constantius, 243; "discovers" Cross and other fake relics, 281s.

Hell: Mithraic myth, 22s, 26s; taken over into Jewish apocrypha, 87; fire of, first kindled in forged *Book of Enoch*, 87; Augustine on, 161-162; Tertullian on, 298; Christianity without Hell, not worth a Damn, 393.

Heresy: means "Choice," 190; Gospels written to combat, 189-190; Christian laws against, 307s; fearful rôle and results of, 314; all heresies started for revenue, 190, 392s.

Heretics: 93 sects, 190; for revenue only, 190, 392s; justly burned, 396, 402.

Hermas, sketch of, 137; *Shepherd of Hermas.*

Hermes Trismegistus: account of, testimonies for Christ, 38, 153.

Herod Antipas, death, 119-120.

Hippocrates: sketch of, 328; father of Medical Science, 368.

History: ecclesiastical, all vices of clergy, xxviii; ancient notions of, 79s; Hegel on, 80-81; Josephus as example, 81s; Patristic historians, unreliable, 123, *passim.*

Hobbes: on the "Secular Arm," 316.

Holy Ghost: dictates to Pope Gregory, 277; finger and tail-feathers, fake relics, 290.

Holy Innocents, fake relics of, 289.

Holy Spirit: Mithraic myth, 25.

Holy Stairs: fake relic, 258s; Pope vouches for, 286-287; Luther and, 286.

Homoöusion: small, trifling question, 248; throat-cutting over, 345-346.

Humanism: defeating Christianity, ix; triumph of, 405.

Hystaspes, Pagan prophet of Christ, 36.

Ichthus—Fish Anagram, 35s, 166.

Identities: Pagan and Christian "properties," 22s; Buddhist and Christian, 28.

Idolatry, or Saint-worship, 41-42; idols made Christian Saints, 41s, 273.

Ignatius, St. Father, sketch, forged letters of, 133s.

Ignatius Loyola, Jesuit, reforms papacy, 353.

Ignorance: Paul enjoins, 395; Church encourages, 239-240, 280; incapable of unbelief, 404.

Illiteracy, in Christian countries, 394.

INDEX

Imitations, Devilish: of Christian rites and doctrines, 31s, 140s.

Immortality: origin of idea, 4s; Pagan ideas, 90.

Impossible, therefore certain, 124; for Gospels to be anonymous, 181-182.

Impostors: all but True Church, 3, 392.

Incarnation: of Buddha, 27s; Pagan doctrine, 29.

Index of Prohibited Books, 370; 1929 edition, 370.

Indictment: against the Church and Christianity, xvi-xvii.

Indulgences: defined, 390; sale of, 390s; abuses of, 391.

Infant Damnation, 299.

Ingersoll: on inherited beliefs, xii; on robbing the cradle, xiv; on fraud, xxxiii; on effects of Mohammedan conquests, 383.

In hoc signo forgery, 244.

Innocents, Holy, fake relics, 289.

Inquisition: In Theodosian Code, 31; decrees for delivery to Secular Power, 310; for terror and ignorance, 366.

Inspiration: O. T. does not reveal any, 54; of N. T. is only a Catholic dogma (*CE.*), 97; what is inspiration, 96s; Tertullian on, 45; of Gospels not recognized till late second century, 183-184; Inspiration and Plagiarism, 191-192.

Intercession of Saints, Naples Gallery, 272.

Interpolations: proof of forgery, 178, 204.

Intolerance: Christian laws of, 302s; inherent in religion, 298; inseparable from religion, 309; yet rampant, 402s.

Invention, or forgery of the Cross, etc., 281s.

Irenæus: sketch of, 142s; makes false quotations, 141; on Septuagint as inspired, 60-61; on Jesus died an old man, 143-144; on Why Four Gospels, 188, 193; is first to mention Gospels and writers, 195; on Gospels of Christians and heretics, 189.

Isaiah: Virgin Birth fraud, 63s; "sign" false prophecy, 65.

Isidore, *False Decretals*, 260s.

Ite, missa est! 180.

Ixthus—Fish Anagram: 35s, 166.

James, brother of Jesus: death of, 118; never had a bath, 129.

Januarius, St., lying miracles of, stops volcano, 270-271.

Jealous God, whitewash of, 175-176.

Jefferson, on Virgin Birth myth, 65.

Jeremiads, of Church, vi, *seq.*

Jerome, St.: on lying Fathers, xxii; his own lies, xxiii, *seq.;* on St. Paul as liar and forger, xxii; made Vulgate, 64; admits Virgin Birth a fraud, 64.

Jewish Apocrypha, see *Apocrypha.*

Jews, did not write Gospels, etc., 184-186.

Jesus, the Christ: family sketch, 129; considered crazy, 92; as magician, 14; mission to Jews only, 92, 220; preached Jewish

INDEX

Kingdom of God, and end of world, 93; took doctrines from forged Jewish apocrypha, 89-90; vouches for forged apocrypha, 89; his Titles from apocrypha, 86-87; forged Gospel by, 101, 103; laid down nothing for belief, 190; Man or God?—at first only man, 205s; genealogies, false, 206-207; mythical Son of mythical God, 78; personal appearance, 112-113; picture, St. Veronica's Veil, fake, 113; words and deeds like Buddha, 23; correspondence with Abgar, forged, 106, 109s; forged passage on, in Josephus, 113s; date of birth error, 71; died an old man, 138, 143-144, 208; came to bring sword, 309; fearful results, 314.

John, the Baptist: Origen on, 116; Josephus on, 117.

John, Gospel of: forgery, not by "John," 200; chapter xxi, forgery, 223.

Josaphat, St., Buddha canonized as, 23.

Josephus: wild fables in writings, 81s; on conjuring devils, 82s; on Septuagint, 58-59; forged passage on Jesus, 113s; on John the Baptist, 117; owl-angel forgery, 119-120.

Jude, Book of: vouches for Jewish apocrypha, 47; cites Enoch and Assumption of Moses, as genuine, 88.

Judgment, Final: Pagan myth, 17; Mithraic myth, 26.

Jurgen, on Lake of Blood in Hell, v.

Justice: debased by Christians, 359s: was dead, 351.

Justin Martyr, St.: sketch of, 140s; makes false quotations, 104; admitted liar, 105, 106; Pagan gods and myths true, and prove Christ, 141; on inspiration of Septuagint, 60-61; on "restoration" by Ezra, 61; on divinity of Sibyls, 39, 142; on "Devilish imitations," 32, 140s; accuses Jews of forgery, 89; on Simon Magus' statue, 15s; didn't know Gospels, 195; Appeal to Reason, 396.

"Keys of Heaven and Hell," forgery, 214-215.

Kingdom of God, Jewish apocrypha, 86, 223-224.

Kings and Priests, combine to rule, 8s.

Knowledge: banned, v; fatal to religion, x, xi, 397.

Koran: on tolerance, 302-303; disregarded, in quest for truth, 378.

Labarum, Christian symbol, 245.

Lactantius: sketch of, 151s; Pagan gods and devils testify of Christ, 151; as do the Sibyls, 37s, 151s; epigram, homo ex humo, 153; on the Cross, 246; appeal to reason, 396-397.

Lance: fake relic, 284-285; rival lances, 285.

Land-grabbing by Church, 388s.

Larceny: in Church frauds for money-grubbing, 292, 395.

Law: of Moses, post-exilic, 57; "finding" by Josiah, 57; "restored" by Ezra, 55s; vouched for by Fathers, 56; Christian laws of murder, 302s.

Lear, quoted, 170.

Lentulus, Letter to Senate, forgery, 112.

Letters: of Lentulus, forgery, 112; of Jesus-Abgar, forgeries, 106, 109s; forged Letter of St. Peter, 252-253.

Liber Pontificalis, forgery, 241-242.

Library of Alexandria, 58.

Lies: regular system, to promote religion, xvi-xxvii; Church encourages.

Lightning-bug, Church like, 405-406.

Literature: ancient, character of, 48; medieval, 316s; age of apocryphal, 48-49; apocryphal, classified, 48-49; principles of literary criticism, 177; "Old Christian Literature," all forged, 172.

Logia, forged sayings of Jesus, 104.

Logos; Pagan-Jewish-Christian Myth, 154s; in Mithraism, 25; in Greek philosophy, 29; Pagan, Justin on, 33; god Mercury as, 141.

"Lord," "Lord God," false translations, 75-76.

Lord's Prayer, forgery, 228-229.

Lowell, James Russell, quoted, 373.

Lucifer, Mithraic myth, 24.

Lucretius: on Fear as making gods, 8; on Religion, 10.

Luke: "many Gospels," 197-198; date of "Luke," 197-198; Gospel not by Luke, 200. See *Gospels.*

Luther: on killing Church by stopping pay, xxxiv; on Holy Stairs, 286.

Luz, or "Resurrection Bone," 368.

Lying: see Lies.

Madonna and Child, Pagan idol, 17.

Magic: Fathers practiced, 124; Augustine on, 164-165; laws of Constantine, 304.

Man: "religious animal," v; epigram of Lactantius, 153.

Manna: fake relic of, 291; manna of saints, 293.

Mark, Gospel of: not by Mark, 200; first Gospel, copied by others, 192; tampered with, 191; not "scripture" when used by others, 192-193; Eusebius on, 181s; present, not known to Papias, 194-195; forged ending of, 225-227. See *Gospels.*

Marks of the Beast, 385s.

Marriage, Fathers on, 145-146.

Martyrs: alive after eaten by beasts, xxi; forged tales of, 266s.

Matthew, Gospel of: Not by Matthew, 199-200; present, not known by Papias, 194-195; "Virgin Birth" forgery in, 63-65; forged ending of, 225-227. See *Gospels.*

Matthew Paris, on Mohammed, as Cardinal, 384.

Mediator: Mithraic myth, 22, 23.

Medical Science: aid denied to unbelievers, 369; Arabs preserved, 368; Hippocrates, 328, 368;

Vesalius, first reviver of, 368-369.

Membership of Churches, vi, *seq.;* mental calibre of members, vii.

Mercury, as *Logos,* 141.

Mercury Trismegistus, Augustine on, 163; Lactantius on, 38, 153.

Messiah: doctrine of, and Messianic Kingdom, from Jewish apocrypha, 86-89; special "revelation" to Peter, forgery, 209-215.

Methuselah, survived Flood, in Septuagint, 59-60; helped save Book of *Enoch,* 85.

Milan, Edict of, text, 301.

Middle Ages: term defined, 364; "civilization saturated with Christianity," 366; "universal ruin," 357; state of civilization in, 366s.

Milk of Virgin Mary, fake relic, 272, 290-291.

Millennium, in *Enoch* and apocrypha, 87.

Miracles: Pagan frauds, 12; taken into Christianity, 42-43; vouched for by Fathers, 33, 141; forged Christian miracles, 266s; Buddhist and Christian, 266-267; credulity in, 42-43; cures, Pagan and Christian, due to natural causes, 399s.

Miscreant, term, xvi.

Missionaries, selling "Faith" to heathen, x.

Mistakes: Church never made, 49; Bible writers could not make, 201; Bible full of, 202.

Mithraism: "Divinely revealed Monotheism," sketch of, 20s;

rival of Christianity, 18; success and defeat of, 21; relations to Christianity, absorbed, 21s; Mithras, Mediator, Saviour, 22; Emperors favored, 29; Constantine amalgamated, 29s.

Mohammedanism: x; Rev. Cadman as Mohammedan, xiii; rapid spread of, overthrowing Christianity, 383s; Mohammed a Catholic Cardinal, 384.

Monks: in Buddhism, 28; "preserved the classics"? 356-357.

Monotheism: in Mithraism, 20, 70; in Egypt, 70; a development, not revelation, in Israel, 70.

Morals: Christian "Morality Lie," 339s; are purely natural law, 340-341; morality in Pagan Greece, 322s; in Pagan Rome, 333-334; in Buddhism, 28; in Mithraism, "divinely revealed moral code," 20s; moral "fruits" of Christianity, 339s.

Mormon, Book of, "finding," 57.

Moses, Books of, forged, 68-70; Decalogue, natural law, 341.

Mother-of-God, Pagan myth, 17.

Murder: divine precepts of; for unbelief, 171, 295-297; Christianity founded on, 295; murders by Constantine, 247.

Mystical Marriage, cruel Christian fraud, 294.

Mythology, is Theology of dead gods and religions, 43.

Name of Hebrew God, revelation of, false, 77s; false translations of, 75-76.

Natural causes: of success of super-stition, 281; explain prayer and miracle cures, 399s; explain moral code, 340-341.

Natural History, freakish: Augus-tine, 161-162; of Barnabas, 136; of Tertullian, 146.

Nativity, of Jesus: erroneous date, 71; purely human, 205-209.

Newman, Cardinal: on Patristic lying, xxii; on Paganism in Chris-tianity, 29.

New Testament: no evidences of in-spiration, 97; is Catholic dogma, 97; no errors in, 227; admittedly full of, 173-174; "doubtful" books and passages, 98-99; cata-logue of N. T. apocrypha, 101s; forged passages in, 234-237. See *Epistles, Gospels.*

Niebuhr, Reinold, on dishonesty of preachers, xi.

Novelty: Christianity non-patent-able for want of, 19.

Nun: in Buddhism, 28; swallowed devil, 275.

Oaths: religious, in N. C., etc., xxix.

Odium Theologicum: of priests, v, 95, 344, 385s; rival religionists, enemies, 393.

Oils, Holy, fakes, 292s.

Old Testament: reveals no inspira-tion, 54. See Chapter II, p. 45s.

"On this Rock" Pun, forgery, 209-219.

Oracles: Cicero on, x; Anthon on, 40; Sibylline, 34, 36s, *passim.* See *Sibyls.*

Origen, Father: sketch of, 149s; on Gospels "chosen," 186; on *Enoch,* 87; on Pagan inspiration, 150; on stars having souls, 150; on John the Baptist and James, 117; makes false quotations, 104.

Origin, obscure, of Christianity, 91s.

Original Sin: doctrine from Jewish apocrypha, 87.

Ormuzd: See *Ahura Mazda.*

Ordeal: trial by, 359; between Christ and Mohammed, 383.

Outlawry: by law in U. S., xxix *seq.;* early Christian laws, 304s, 307s.

Owl-Angel forgery, 119-120.

Pagan Culture: in Greece, 322s, 334s; in Roman Empire, 333s, 358s.

Pagan Frauds: Chapter I, p. 3s; some instances, 11, 42; adopted by Christians, 41, *passim.*

Pagan Gods: are devils, 32, 41; made into Christian saints, 41s, 273; testify for Jesus Christ, 38s, 40, 148. See *Sibyls.*

Pagan Miracles: held true by Fathers, 33, 141; taken up by Christians, 42; cures, 140, 400s.

Paganism: amalgamated with Chris-tianity, by Constantine, 29; proscribed by successors of Con-stantine, 11, 21, 31, 304s; in Christianity, 4, 10s, 17s, 89-90, 154s, 168s, 273s.

"Paganization" of U. S., vi, ix.

Palimpsests, 357s.

Papacy: corruption of, 347s; lowest ebbs of, 353-354.

INDEX

Papias: sketch of, 137s; fabulous yarns, 138-139; on Gospels, 193-195; on "voluminous lies" for Christ, 199.

Parasites. social, 5-6.

Patent, none for "Christian Revelation," 19.

Pater Patratus, pope of Mithraism, 22.

Patrimony of Peter: origins, 251s; dubious muniments, 254, 259. See *Donation of Constantine.*

Patristic literary dishonesty, 48; traditions, 125-126.

Paul, St.: crafty and liar, 124; eunuch, 146; enjoins ignorance, 395; forger: St. Jerome on, xxii; Erasmus on, 230; as Simon Magus, 16-17; magical contests with Simon, 15-16, 107; no Epistles by, 230s.

Paulus, first Hermit: Jerome's yarns about, xxiii.

Peacock, Augustine on immortality of, 161.

Pentateuch, not by Moses, 70.

Pepin: becomes King, 252; alleged gifts dubious, 254, 259.

Persecution: by Christian law, 31, 302s; world weary of, 385.

Peter, St.: ignorant, 128; name, Simon, Cephas, 216; "Thou art Peter," forgery, 209-215; forged *apocalypse* of, 181; forged Letter to King of Franks, 252-253; Epistles of, forgeries, 233-234; "special revelation" to, forgery, 209-215; no "primacy" of, 219-220, 131; approved "Mark," 181, —did not, 182.

Petrine texts, forgeries, 209-219.

Philanthropy: Buddhist, 28; Pagan, 359s.

Philosophy of History: Hegel on, 80-81; Augustine on, 159s.

Phoenix: proof of resurrection, 133, 147, 168; false translation, 147.

Pilate: forged Report to Tiberius, 105, 106, 147-148.

Pillars, set up by Sethites, 81.

Plagiarism, in Gospels, 192.

Plato, Gospel agrees with, 33.

Platonism, and Christianity, 32, 159.

Plural: *elohim*—gods, 75.

Police, Religion as, 9s.

Politics, Church in, xxxiii.

Polycarp: sketch of, 134-135; martyrdom of, 135.

Popes, Book of, forgery, 241-242.

Popes: in Paganism, 18; in Mithraism, 22.

Poverty, greatest in Christian countries, 394.

Prayer: futility of confessed, 399s; *"Gimme!"* 399.

Prejudices, Christian, ix. See *Odium Theologicum.*

Priestcraft—Priests: origins of, 5s; in Africa, 7; and Kings, 8; opposed to knowledge, v, x; wealth of, Pagan, 8; of Christian, 386s; Pagan Priests all liars, 43.

"Prince of Peace": blood shed for, vi; as Lord of Hosts, 247; came to bring sword, 309.

Probabilities, Law of, explains success of Superstition, 399s.

Profits of Religion, 386s; in "Fable of Christ," 351.

xvii

Prophecies, of Pagan Sibyls, 40s.

Protestants, pass stolen counterfeit, xviii.

Pseudographic writings, vogue of, 48.

Pun, "Upon this Rock," forgery, 209-215.

Purgatory: invented by Gregory the Great, 390; larcenous, 395.

Rationalism: saviour of Civilization, xxxii, 404.

Reason: enchained by Faith, Augustine subordinates to Faith, xv, 158-159; never tortured Faith, 373; Appeal to, 395s.

Reform, "in head and members," never realized, 352, 355.

Reformation, effects on Church, 385-386.

Regina Cœli, fable of, 276.

Reinach, definition of religion, 8; quoted, *passim.*

Relics: forged and faked, 277s; *Cath. Encyc.* on, 278s; frauds of Church, 280; catalogue of, 288s; Pope vouches for, 286-287.

Religion: a disease, v; cure for, knowledge, x, 405; failure of, vi, *seq.;* no good at home, x; due to cradle, xi, *seq.;* origins of, 4s; founded on Fear, 7s; Terrorism, 295s; Reinach's definition, 8; as Big Policeman, 9s; enforced by Ignorance and Terror, 398; Laws of persecution, xxix, *seq.;* 402s; all Pagan religions frauds, 3; of Empire amalgamated by Constantine, 29s; Mithraism, 20s; Buddhism, 27s; Christian,

depends on Genesis fables, 72-73; profits of, 386s; What Price? 386s; True Brand prescribed, 396; and Superstition, Lactantius on, 157; Bankruptcy of, 403s.

Resurrection, of Body: Mithraic myth, 26; in Paganism, 90; taken into Jewish apocrypha, 84, 87-90; proved by Phœnix, *q. v.;* of Jesus, taught by him, 211; but not so, 212.

Resurrection Bone, 396.

Retribution, Future: Mithraic myth, 26; taken into Jewish apocrypha, 89.

Revelation: defined, 18-19; in Mithraism, 26; Pagan notions as, 90; no Christian Patent for, 19; old Pagan stuff, 17, 19, 27; Jewish apocrypha as, 54s; cannot be controlled by Reason, 356; of name of Jehovah, false, 77s; special to Peter, forgery, 209, 212-214.

Revisions of Holy Writ, 174-176.

Revival of Learning, suppressed, 366s.

Revolt, Congress of Ems, 264s.

Rib of Adam, missing until Vesalius, 369.

Rock and Church, forgery, 215-219; Rock and Keys, forgery, 209-219.

Rome: Augustine on foundation, 163-164; education and morals in 333, 358s.

Russia: victim of Church, ix; G. B. S. on religion in, xv; Pope's prayer-crusade against, 286-287.

INDEX

Sabbath, Babylonian origin, 22.

Sacraments, all Pagan, 29.

Sainte Ampule, fraud, 252.

Saints: Pagan gods made into, 41s, 273; Buddha canonized, 269; number and cost of, 268; Christian forgeries of, 266s; care in making, but some slips, 269; Intercession of, picture, 272; prophylactic qualities, 274.

Sant' Angelo, Castel, fable of, 276.

Salamander, evidence for Hell-fire, 161-162.

Salvation, exclusive, 3.

Satan: Mithraic myth, 26s, 90.

Saviour: Mithras as, 22, 23, 26; Crishna as, 27s.

Schools: bootlegging religion in, xiv; public damned by Encyclical, xiv; Pagan schools closed, 358; law closing, 306.

Science, in Greece, 326s.

Science: must not contradict Dogma, 364-365; limited by Theology, 365; because throws Bible into confusion, 380; always victorious, 365; Bible as Book of, 370, 377-380; is *forte* of Church, 362s; Church boasts about, 364s; killed by Church, 365s; Personified, by Trattner, 372-373.

Scripture, Jewish, forgeries, Chap. III, p. 91s; Christian "revelations" in Jewish apocryphal, 84-90.

Second Coming: constantly proclaimed, 93, 220; yet tardy, 95-96.

Secular Arm: compelled to do Christian murders, 310-315; in-famous decree of Inquisition, 310.

Septuagint: sketch of, 58s; Josephus on, 58-59; Fathers fable and vouch for it, 60-61; Augustine on, 166-167; Tertullian on, 148; used by Fathers to propagate Christianity, 62; adopted by Church, 61-62; used until fourth century, 174; gross errors of, 59, 61-62; quoted 300 times in N. T., 185; brought Jewish apocrypha into True Bible, 61; Virgin Birth fraud in, 62s.

Sethites, pillars set up by, 81.

Shamans, origin, 4s.

Shipley, Maynard, book commended, xxxiii.

Sibyls, Oracles: sketch of, 34s; forged by Christians, 35; inspiration of, 36, 39; proofs of Jesus and Christianity, 37s; Fathers vouch for, 36, 37, 39, 40, 142, 151s, 165-166, 168-169.

Sibyllists, Christians were, 34s, 96.

Simon Magus: vouched for by *Acts*, 14s; statue of, 14-15, 141-142, 144; as Paul, 16-17; magic contests with Paul, 15-16, 107.

Simony, source of Church wealth, 390s.

Sin: Pagan forgiveness of, 249; Original, apocryphal, 87.

Skepticism, civilization due to, 404.

Skiopedes, Augustine on, 160-161.

Slavery, Church attitude on, 360s.

Social conditions: in Roman Empire, 358s; in Middle Ages, 347s.

Son of God: Mithraic myth, 25; Jewish usage, 208.

Soul: origin of notion, 4s; false Bible translation, 76; stars have, 150s.

Specula Stultorum, 269s.

Stars: rational and have souls, 150s; of Bethlehem, 150.

State and Church, origins of illicit cohabitation, 8s, 29s, 251.

Statue of Simon Magus; see *Simon Magus*.

Statistics, of Church, vi, *seq.*

"Stop! Thief!"—religious graft, 392s.

Suggestion, explains "miracle cures," 400.

Sun: *"Sol Deus Invictus,"* Supreme God, 30; Christians worshipped, 30, 147.

Sunday: Day of the Unconquered Sun, 30; Mithraic holy-day, 22, 31; made Pagan holiday by Constantine, xxxi, 31, 304; Sunday Laws, xxxi, *seq.*

Supernaturalism: ideal of Christian education, xiv, 399; frauds in, 7; waste of lives for, 404.

Superstition: *CE.'s* definition, 321; Lactantius on, 157; among Romans, 12s; drunk in with mother's milk, xi, 164; of Pagans as Christian revelations, 17s; encouraged by Church, 239-240; success of due to natural causes, 281, 399s; knowledge only remedy for, 239.

Sword: Jesus Christ brought, 309; Bull of Two Swords, 316.

Sylvester, Pope, forgeries, 255.

Symmachian forgeries, 259-260.

Taboos, as religion, 8.

Tax Exemption: of Christians by Constantine, 31, 304s; President Grant on, 393-394.

"Teach all Nations," forgery, 220-224; Church false pretenses, 322, 336, 339.

Temporal Power, 251s, 259.

Temptation by Devil: Mithraic myth, 26.

Terrorism, priestly, 295s.

Tertullian: sketch of, 144s; grounds of faith, 145; believe because impossible, 124; because unbelievable, 191; on result of belief, 374; on devilish imitations, 32; on *Enoch* and its preservation, 85, 86, 87; admitted liar, 106; false report of Pilate, 148; on Hell, 298; on interpolations, 204; on phœnix, 147; on Septuagint, 148; on Sibyls, 147; on women and virginity, 145.

Tests for forgery, 177-178.

Texts of Scripture: no official, 174; tinkering with, 174-176.

Theodosius, "Great" because first Church murderer, 302.

Theology: overshadows all else, 239; central Christian ideal, 364s.

Theophilus, as dating "Luke," 198-199.

Thirteenth Century: Church boasts, 348; intellectual activities suppressed, 367.

Thorns, Crown of: fake relic, history, 284s; 700 thorns from, 285.

INDEX

Three Heavenly Witnesses, forgery, 234-237.

Three Steps, in Mithraism, 26.

Titles: of Gospels, not original, 178s; of Jesus from apocrypha, 86-87.

Tinkering, with Holy Writ, 174-176.

Tobias (*Tobit*), inspired fable of, 51s.

Toboggan, Church on, vi, *seq.*

Toleration: in Empire, 30; Edict of Milan, 301; only when Faith failed, 298; forced by secularism, 403.

Tradition, Patristic: defined, worthless, 125-126.

Translations, False: as evidence of forgery, 74s; of O. T., Augustine on, 62. See *False Translations;* of Septuagint, see *Septuagint.*

Trattner, Dr. Ernest R.: cited, 70; on Science, 372-373; on Day of Emancipation, 406.

Trent, Council of: see *Council of Trent.*

Trinity: Mithraic myth, 25; Pagan superstition, 29; baptism in name of, forgery, 225-227; "Three Heavenly Witnesses," forgery, 235-237.

Trismegistus, Hermes: Lactantius on, 153.

Triumph of Christianity: Chap. VII, p. 295s.

Unbelief: rising tide of, vi, *seq.;* due to increased knowledge, x.

Uncritical, Fathers, 99.

Unknown God, forgery, 229-230.

Unity, Catholic, 385s.

Universities: medieval Christian, 337s.

Valla, Lorenzo, exposed *Donatio,* etc., 258.

Vergilius, on Antipodes, 362.

Veronica, St., fraud, 113s.

Vesalius: revived Medical Science, 368-369.

Vices, clerical, xxviii, *passim.*

Virgin Birth: admitted fraud, 62-65; due to false translation, 63-65; disproved, 205-208; of Romulus and Remus, Augustine on, 163-164; as Pagan commonplace, 17s, 33, 140, 208; Jefferson on, 65.

Virgin Mary: "prolific yet ever-virgin," as adulteress, Jerome, 64; *conceived per ear,* 136; Tertullian on, 146.

Vivès, Louis, exposed Aristeas forgery, etc., 59.

Volcanoes, stopped by Saints, 270s.

Vulgate: by St. Jerome, and Virgin Birth fraud, 64; official Catholic Bible, 74; still tinkering with texts, 174-176.

Waste, on theology and religion, 404.

Wealth and greed of clergy, 386s.

Wisdom of Solomon, admitted forgery in True Bible, 48.

Witnesses, Three Heavenly, forgery, 234-237.

INDEX

Woman, taken in Adultery, forgery, 228.

Women: loss of to Church, vi-viii; Chrysostom on, 146.

Writing: Augustine on origin of, 172.

Yahveh: "God of gods," 32; false translation of name, 75-77.

Zend Avesta, 21s.

Zeus, and *Deus,* from Mithraic *Daeva*—Devil, 24.

Zolà, on perfection of civilization, 406.

Zoroaster: prophet of God, 26; religion of, rival of Christianity, 18; taken into Christianity, 90. See *Mithraism; Paganism.*